Tracks & Sign of Insects & Other Invertebrates

A Guide to North American Species

Charley Eiseman & Noah Charney
With John Carlson

STACKPOLE
BOOKS

To the creatures we accidentally harmed in the making of this book:
Our intention was never to harm you,
but to better understand you,
to share your stories with our readers,
and thereby win you respect.
We hope this changes the way we humans interact with you,
and ultimately benefits your lineages.

Copyright © 2010 by Stackpole Books

Published by
STACKPOLE BOOKS
5067 Ritter Road
Mechanicsburg, PA 17055
www.stackpolebooks.com

Printed in United States of America

First edition

Cover design by Caroline Stover

Cover photos: Darkling beetle and trail, chrysalis of a Milbert's tortoiseshell butterfly, cocoon of a spongillafly (photo by Charles Lewallen), galleries made by emerald ash borer larvae.

Photos by the authors unless otherwise noted.

Information in chapter 4 provided by John Carlson.

Library of Congress Cataloging-in-Publication Data

Eiseman, Charley.
    Tracks & sign of insects & other invertebrates: a guide to North American
  species/Charley Eiseman & Noah Charney, with John Carlson.
       p.   cm.
    Includes bibliographical references and index.
    ISBN-13: 978-0-8117-3624-4
    ISBN-10: 0-8117-3624-5
    1. Insects—North America—Identification.   2. Invertebrates—North America—Identification.   3. Animal Tracks—North America—Identification.   I. Charney, Noah, 1979–   II. Carlson, John, 1976–   III. Title.   IV. Title: Tracks and sign of insects and other invertebrates.
QL473.E37   2010
595.7097—dc22
                                                                    2009030704

Editor's Note: Abbreviations for the states in which the photographs were taken follow the captions.

CONTENTS

Introduction iv

1 Eggs and Egg Cases 1

2 Pupae and Exuviae 81

3 Parasitism, Predation, and Other Causes of Death 105

4 Sign on Vertebrates 129

5 Droppings, Secretions, and Protective
Coverings without Foreign Materials 149

6 Webs and Other Silken Constructions 179

7 Cocoons 217

8 Coverings, Cases, Retreats, and
Nests Made from Foreign Materials 239

9 Sign on Algae, Fungi, and Plants 291

10 Leaf Mines 331

11 Leaf Shelters 363

12 Galls 377

13 Sign on Twigs, Stems, and Stemlike Structures 405

14 Sign on and in Wood 423

15 Sign on Rocks and Shells 439

16 Burrows and Mounds 443

17 Molelike Excavations and Simple Surface Trails 487

18 Tracks and Trails 499

Appendix A: Plants Mentioned in this Book 525

Glossary 533

References 536

Acknowledgments 550

Index 555

About the Authors 582

Introduction

We were on a tight schedule: 15,000 miles in forty days. We had just driven the first 1,600 miles from our starting point in New England—with stops including the Delaware Water Gap, Virginia's Great Dismal Swamp, coastal North Carolina, and the Great Smoky Mountains—and were hoping to make the most of our short time in a new ecoregion, the Inner Plateau of Tennessee, where Noah grew up. In the morning, we packed up our cameras and headed outside, bound to fully explore the surrounding wilderness. Five hours later, Noah's mom poked her head out the front door. "Why are you two still standing around in the driveway?"

The work of invertebrates is all around us. Pausing to examine the miniature worlds we habitually overlook reveals a remarkable diversity of stunningly complex patterns. Perhaps you have already pondered the intricate scratch marks in the algae on your picnic table, wondered what creature is responsible for the papery red discs you find stuck to logs in your woodpile, or wanted to know who has been cutting those clean circular holes out of the leaves in your rosebush. While working on this book, we sought out sign of invertebrates in the depths of pristine wildernesses from all the major ecotypes in North America. Yet the phenomena we found most compelling were the ubiquitous ones that probably can be found right around your house, if not in your house, such as green lacewing eggs, slug tooth marks, leafcutter bee sign, and pirate spider egg sacs. Indeed, when we set out on walks to search for invertebrate sign, we usually found it difficult even to make it to the end of the driveway. There were too many subjects to photograph on the leaves of every shrub and tree we encountered.

When you encounter one of these mystery signs, it's hard to know where to begin in identifying it. Although you may stumble by chance on the answers to some such riddles in the fine print of a conventional field guide, this book is devoted entirely to them. We have brought a large amount of

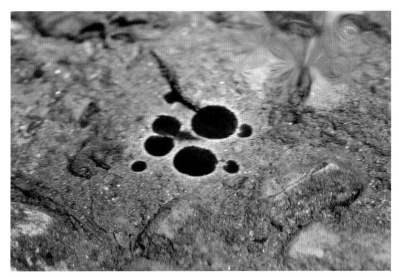

A distinctive but ephemeral insect sign: the shadow of a water strider (Gerridae) on the bed of a stream. (MA)

widely scattered, and sometimes obscure, information together in one place in an effort to make these answers more accessible.

We have attempted to organize this book by what we see, not what we know. Our goal is to provide a tool for when you have no clue what something is, but you can describe what it looks like. You will not find a section describing all the things beetles do. Instead, the life of a beetle is spread across the chapters on eggs, pupae, droppings, and so on. In this way, many of our chapters loosely correspond to the major ethological classes used by ichnologists.

What Is Covered in This Book?

The title of this book, *Tracks and Sign of Insects and Other Invertebrates*, probably requires some explanation. *Tracking*, at its most basic level, is learning to identify animals by the evidence they leave behind. *Tracks* are the animals' actual footprints; everything else is considered *sign*: droppings, feeding traces, nests, remains, burrows, and so on.

Typically, tracking is thought of in terms of studying vertebrates, in particular mammals. But vertebrates—animals with backbones—represent just one phylum out of more than thirty that make up the animal kingdom. In fact, they—or rather, *we*—don't even get a whole phylum, but must share Chordata with the sea squirts. *Invertebrates* are all the members of the animal kingdom that are not vertebrates; that is, everything except mammals, birds, reptiles, amphibians, and fishes. Take a look at the cladogram ("family tree") on the inside of the covers, and you will see that this means much more than just insects. The groups depicted in this tree are only those that are mentioned in this book, and they represent fewer than half of the animal phyla.

Broadening the idea of tracking to include invertebrates introduces a number of interesting types of sign that are not produced by vertebrates. These include webs, cocoons, galls (plant deformities), and evidence of parasitism. Also included in this book are eggs and pupae, which arguably are not true sign but are cryptic life stages of the animals themselves, although certainly hatched eggs and empty pupal skins fall into this category. Regardless of where you draw the line, eggs and pupae are largely neglected in field guides, so they fall within our general mission of shedding light on invertebrate-related mystery objects.

Invertebrates present a formidable challenge in their numbers; there are more species of North American invertebrates than there are words in this book. In order to be as thorough as possible, we provide descriptions that generalize across groups of related species, and then note the most common species representative of these groups and the species with particularly distinctive sign.

As with any field guide, this book aims to help you identify discrete things, and in so doing, it separates its subjects from their natural context. We have tried to include enough about the life histories of the animals involved to give some meaning to the sign we describe. Nevertheless, this book is largely focused on minutiae, and it is easy to lose sight of the major role invertebrates play in the world. With a size-biased perspective, the earth seems to be dominated by vertebrate animals and vascular plants.

A broad interpretation of invertebrate sign includes phenomena that span many spatial and temporal scales, as illustrated by the images scattered through this introductory chapter. At one extreme is the fleeting shadow of a water strider on the bottom of a stream. A much more persistent sign is the forked trunk of a white pine where white pine weevil larvae killed the terminal leader decades ago. At a larger

A more persistent insect sign: forked trunks on white pines are often the result of white pine weevils (Curculionidae: *Pissodes strobi*) killing the terminal leader many years before. (MA)

spatial scale, a whole stand of pines may be decimated by a dense population of bark beetles. You may also consider the feeding activities of vertebrate predators as conspicuous evidence of the presence of insects. A series
of deep holes in a pine made by a feeding pileated woodpecker is a sure
sign that the tree is inhabited by a colony of carpenter ants. For the most
part, this book adopts a more conservative interpretation of invertebrate
sign, focusing on the moderately persistent marks that invertebrates
directly produce.

What Is Not Included?

Images of the actual animals responsible for the sign are conspicuously
absent from this book, except incidentally. More than two thousand species
are mentioned, and there is not room for pictures of them all. Another
desirable but missing feature is range maps. This is partly for the same
reason, but also because the ranges of most species are incompletely
known, and those of many are continually expanding or shifting as a result
of accidental or intentional transportation by humans, as well as climate
change. Many insects are linked to particular plant species, however, and
their ranges can be inferred by the ranges of their host plants. Addition-
ally, in many cases we discuss sign not in terms of individual species, but
of larger groups that are distributed across much of North America. Where
possible, for those insects that have more limited ranges, these have been
indicated parenthetically, sometimes with abbreviations of states and
provinces, but more often by general regions, using somewhere near
Nebraska as the center point of reference. For instance, "NE" indicates the
northeastern United States and eastern Canada; "SW" indicates the southwestern United States and adjacent Mexico.

This book does not include sign of members of other kingdoms, such as
bacteria and protozoa. These are not animals and therefore are not catego-
rized as invertebrates, even though they lack vertebrae. We do, however,
discuss sign of some fungi, viruses, and bacteria that are pathogens of
invertebrates.

Taxonomy and Terminology

A guide to insects and other invertebrates cannot avoid using scientific
names. This is partly to be clear about what animal is being referred to
and partly because many simply do not have common names. We have
included common names wherever possible, although we have omitted
some that are misleading and in most cases are not likely to be recognized anyway. An example is the maple leafminer. To use this name
implies that it is the only insect that mines maple leaves, when in fact
many do so, and it is completely arbitrary to designate one species as *the*
maple leafminer.

Insect sign on a landscape scale: pines killed by extensive tunneling of the mountain pine beetle (Curculionidae: *Dendroctonus ponderosae*). (MT)

Whether or not a common name is used, we have included the Latin binomial name (genus and species) and the family to which the species belongs. For example, the grape flea beetle is *Altica chalybea* (Chrysomelidae). *Altica* is the genus, which includes more than fifty other North American species. When several species in the same genus are mentioned in the same paragraph, the genus is abbreviated; for example, the elm flea beetle, *Altica carinata*, may appear as *A. carinata*.

The Linnaean classification system has seven basic ranks: kingdom, phylum, class, order, family, genus, and species. The leaf beetles (Chrysomelidae) are one family within Coleoptera, the beetles, which is one order within Insecta, the insects, which is one class within the phylum Arthropoda, the arthropods. Within these ranks are many subdivisions. For instance, the genus *Altica* is one of many genera that form the tribe *Alticini*, the flea beetles, which in turn is one of several tribes in the subfamily Galerucinae, the skeletonizing leaf beetles. The names in these divisions all have consistent endings: tribes end in "-ini," subfamilies in "-inae," families in "-idae," and superfamilies in "-oidea." Instead of using common names, one may refer to the groups by modifying these endings to form nouns or adjectives: the galerucines are the skeletonizing leaf beetles; chrysomelid beetles are the leaf beetles.

It's a great system, in theory. The problem is that names are constantly changing, for a variety of reasons. It may be found that two names have been used to describe the same species, so the newer one is discontinued, or what was thought to be one species may actually be two or more species, all but one of which then get new names. Although changes of this sort are clearly necessary, others may seem more arbitrary, such as when one genus is split into several genera or several genera are lumped into one. Ranks also may be changed, such as suborders promoted to orders or families demoted to subfamilies. These changes are ongoing, even at the kingdom level. As a result of all this, common names often turn out to be more stable than the scientific names, to the extent that they may be your only way of knowing what species older literature is referring to if you don't have access to databases of scientific names and their synonyms.

In this book, every effort has been made to use the currently accepted names for all groups, from species on up to phylum. This means that the names used may often differ from those in many, or even most, other books. One would hope that names are beginning to stabilize after more than three hundred years of sorting them out, but it's likely that some will already be out of date by the time this is printed.

Ichnology as a Discipline of Geology

Geologists will recognize this book as an exercise in ichnology, the study of tracks and traces. More specifically, this book focuses on *neo*ichnology, the study of modern traces made during the Holocene (present) era. Geolo-

gists have long been fascinated by *paleo*-ichnology, the study of fossilized tracks and sign. Beyond dinosaur footprints, remarkably abundant invertebrate tracks and sign have been preserved in sedimentary rocks: 30-million-year-old spider webs, 50-million-year-old dung beetle nests, 80-million-year-old leaf mines, 150-million-year-old caddisfly cases, 250-million-year-old scorpion tracks, and 300-million-year-old galls.

For geologists, identifying the trace makers not only tells about the history of the organisms but also provides insight into the ancient environment. If you know the habitat preferences of a suite of fauna and find the tracks of these animals in a plane of sedimentary rock, then you can infer the presence of that habitat when the original sediments were deposited.

Insect sign by association: the feeding sign of vertebrate predators is sometimes the most conspicuous evidence of an insect's presence. In this case, a pileated woodpecker has been hunting carpenter ants (Formicidae: *Camponotus*). (MA)

To describe trace fossils, ichnologists have developed classification systems akin to the Linnaean system used to name biological species. The names describe the traces themselves, not the organisms that created them. The *ethological* system describes traces based on what the animal was doing (ethology is the study of animal behavior). For example, Repichnia is the class of traces that are formed when organisms walk across surfaces (what we think of as classic tracks). In the 1920s, a geologist found a type of Repichnia fossilized in sandstone and described it using the ichnotaxonomic system, with the ichnogenus name *Paleohelcura* and the ichnospecies name *tridactyla*. In the 1940s, another geologist experimenting with live invertebrates hypothesized that *Paleohelcura tridactyla* could have been made by a walking scorpion. But scorpions can make other types of traces, and other types of organisms could potentially make *Paleohelcura tridactyla* tracks. Matching a biological species to an ichnospecies is extremely difficult and rarely achieved. Including the ichnological classifications of the traces we present is beyond the scope of this book, though we hope our efforts are nonetheless helpful to paleoichnologists.

Tip of the Iceberg

Each of the following eighteen chapters could and should be expanded to a whole book of its own. Some of these books already exist, but much more is waiting to be discovered and written about. The choice of which invertebrate sign to represent by images in this book was determined largely by which sign we happened to encounter. We felt it a reasonable assumption that two trained naturalists versed in minutiae examining the natural world over the course of two years would find the most common invertebrate sign. To the extent that this holds true, we have provided representative photographs of the things you are likely to find while wandering the landscape. We no doubt missed many things and probably misidentified a few. This is a book that begs for someone to write another volume. We invite you to visit our websites, www.charleyeiseman.com, www.noahcharney .org, and www.NorthernNaturalists.com, to offer your photos, comments, and corrections. Go out and explore the world and see what you find.

Eggs and Egg Cases

Given that there are almost as many kinds of invertebrate eggs as there are invertebrates, it might seem hopeless to try to identify them. In fact, though, there is a tremendous amount of variation in egg morphology, and species within a given taxonomic group tend to produce eggs that share distinctive features. So although identification to species level may not be possible, determining the order or family often is straightforward. As with all track and sign interpretation, knowing the natural history of the animals involved is key to identifying a list of possible suspects and then whittling it down.

A number of things may be confused with eggs or egg cases, including scale insects, whitefly pupae, small cocoons, and galls. Masses of round fruiting bodies of slime molds, which may be bright pink or other colors, could be mistaken for insect eggs, but they are on short stalks and bear no resemblance to the few kinds of insect eggs that have stalks.

Eggs Absent or Carried or Guarded by Parents

First, it should be noted that you will never see eggs for some species. Scorpions, for instance, all give birth to live young, as do giant cockroaches (Blaberidae). Several types of parasitic insects give birth to live larvae, including the twisted-winged parasites (Strepsiptera), louse flies (Hippoboscidae, which in some cases even give birth to pupae), bot flies (Oestridae) in the subfamily Oestrinae, many tachinid flies, and some blow flies (Calliphoridae) and flesh flies (Sarcophagidae). This is also the case with some parasitic mites.

Aphids give birth to live young throughout the growing season, although they lay eggs that overwinter. Certain other Sternorrhyncha, such as the California red scale (Diaspididae: *Aonidiella aurantii*) and some mealybug species, either give birth to live young or lay fully incubated eggs that hatch almost immediately. Some thrips species also give birth to live young.

Parents in some invertebrate groups lay eggs but carry them until they hatch, so you would not normally find these eggs unattended. This is true of virtually all crustaceans, including crayfish, shrimp, amphipods, copepods, crabs, and isopods (including woodlice). Freshwater bivalves hold their eggs in their gills until the eggs develop into young larvae, with the sole exception of the introduced zebra mussel (Dreissenidae: *Dreissena polymorpha*), whose eggs develop quickly into larvae on being released into the water. Water scavenger beetles (Hydrophilidae) in the subfamily Sphaeridiinae carry their eggs attached to their hind legs, and *Helochares maculicollis* carries her eggs under her abdomen, as do beetles in the related family Epimetopidae. By far the most conspicuous of the egg carriers are giant water bugs of the genera *Abedus* and *Belostoma*, in which the males carry large clusters of the pale, brown, elongated eggs cemented on their backs.

Several other terrestrial arthropods in addition to woodlice carry their eggs. Female two-pronged bristletails (Diplura) in the family Japygidae carry their eggs beneath them until after they hatch. Eggs of whipscorpions (Uropygi) and tailless whipscorpions (Amblypygi) are carried in a transparent sac under the female's abdomen, and a female short-tailed whipscorpion (Schizomida) waits underground with her eggs attached to her abdomen in a spherical mass. A female pseudoscorpion carries her eggs in a raspberry-shaped mass surrounding a sac that is attached to her abdomen. Several types of spiders carry their egg sacs.

Other invertebrates guard their eggs until they hatch, often protecting their hatchlings for some time as well. In many cases, you would not come across these without flipping over logs or looking in other hidden places. Female earwigs excavate cup-shaped cavities in the soil under rocks, boards, or debris, where they stay with their clusters of 2-mm-long, white, cylindrical eggs. Webspinners (Embiidina) guard small clusters of curved, elongated eggs with sloping "lids" in their silk-lined tunnels, and zorapterans guard eggs in their small colonies under logs. Female scolopendromorph centipedes coil around their eggs in excavated chambers under rocks or in rotting wood. Some female geophilomorph centipedes guard their eggs as well, as do male platydesmid millipedes. Mole crickets (Gryllotalpidae) guard eggs in special chambers in their underground tunnels. Bess beetles (Passalidae) live in family groups in decaying logs, where they not only guard their eggs and young, but also help them construct their pupal cells. At least some toad bugs (Gelastocoridae) and acanthosomatid shield bugs guard their eggs until they hatch, as do many treehoppers (Membracidae) and the horse fly *Goniops chrysocoma* (Tabanidae). Termites, ants, and social bees and wasps all protect their eggs and young in their nests.

Eggs Inserted in Terrestrial Vegetation

Many insects have specialized ovipositors that they use to insert eggs into plant tissue. In some cases, no visible trace remains to indicate that they have done so, but in others, you can see obvious marks or bulges. In woody plants, oviposition scars may be evident for years afterward; these are discussed in chapter 13, along with the more conspicuous wounds in herbaceous stems. Some examples of oviposition wounds in other plant tissue are discussed in chapter 9. Gall-making wasps and flies insert their eggs, and the galls that develop are soon more conspicuous than any oviposition mark that might have been there. Within a given insect species, the oviposition sites may be more or less evident, depending on where the eggs are inserted. The eggs tend to be white or sometimes pale yellow or green.

Katydids (Tettigoniidae) have distinctive, flattened, oval eggs, which can be up to about 5 mm long. Some species attach them to the surface of vegetation, but others insert them into various plant tissues. Scudder's bush katydids (*Scudderia*) insert their eggs in the edges of leaves, from which the tips of the eggs may be seen jutting out. The narrow-beaked katydid (*Turpilia rostrata*; FL) neatly inserts its eggs in the edges of palm leaves, giving the leaves a studded appearance.

Sawflies get their name from the sawlike ovipositor that females of most species use to cut a slit into plant tissue before laying each egg. Their eggs may be oval, oblong, or kidney-shaped, and up to about 2 mm long. They absorb plant moisture and increase in size after they are laid, so they can produce conspicuous bulges in leaves and stems. They are often inserted end to end in rows along major leaf veins, or at regular intervals along the edge of a leaf. The larch sawfly (Tenthredinidae: *Pristiphora erichsonii*) inserts its translucent eggs in closely packed slits under the bark of terminal larch twigs, causing the twigs to curl slightly. In some cases, such as with diprionid eggs in conifer needles, the plant tissue may burst open and expose the eggs.

As far as is known, all leafhoppers (Cicadellidae) insert their elongate eggs (generally 0.5 to 1.5 mm long) in plant tissues. They are usually laid singly or a few at a time. When many eggs are inserted parallel to one another under the epidermis of a leaf (e.g., by *Cuerna* species), the epidermis may become separated, appearing as a whitened area. On close inspection, the eggs are clearly visible. Other leafhopper eggs may be visible only as tiny punctures in stems, petioles, or larger leaf veins, sometimes in rows. When in leaves, they are usually inserted in the undersides.

Plant bugs (Miridae) insert their eggs into plant tissue, generally the petioles or stems. The eggs of many have two filaments at one end, which project from the tissue in which they are laid. At least some eggs are described as being tiny, pale green, elongate, and slightly curved. The four-lined plant bug (*Poecilocapsus lineatus*) cuts lengthwise slits in stems, each containing six or more eggs inserted perpendicularly.

Many leaf-mining insects insert their eggs in leaves. In addition to sawflies, this is typical of agromyzid flies. The leaf-mining weevils lay oval, flattened eggs singly in holes chewed in leaves. They swell like sawfly eggs, often causing conspicuous discoloration in the leaf. A few leaf-mining moths have ovipositors equipped to insert eggs into leaves. *Dyseriocrania auricyanea* (Eriocraniidae) inserts its eggs singly near the edges of opening oak and chestnut leaves. They are capsule-shaped and also swell substantially. The maple leafcutter (Incurvariidae: *Paraclemensia acerifoliella*) inserts many tiny, elliptical eggs in the underside of a single maple leaf, often in chainlike rows of six or more. The scars are obvious on the leaf underside and appear as yellow stippling on the upper side.

Trigonalid wasps insert tiny eggs in slits near the margins of leaves. You probably never will see these, but we couldn't resist mentioning the bizarre strategy of these wasps. The eggs do not hatch until swallowed by a caterpillar (or sawfly larva) feeding on the leaf. The trigonalid larvae then need an ichneumon wasp or tachinid fly to parasitize the caterpillar, so they can parasitize the parasitoid. Alternatively, a vespid wasp may abduct the caterpillar and feed it to one of its own larvae, which then becomes the host.

Various other terrestrial insects insert eggs into plant tissues, including thrips (Thysanoptera), fruit flies (Tephritidae; at least some of their eggs have fine, reticulated patterns), spittlebugs (Cercopidae), planthoppers (Fulgoroidea), and seed bugs (Lygaeidae). Harvestmen (Opiliones) also sometimes insert their tiny, spherical white eggs into plant stems or under tree bark.

Pine needle weevils (Curculionidae: *Pachyrhinus*; W) do not exactly insert their eggs but fit in with the general theme of concealing them with vegetation. The female *P. californicus* creates an egg chamber by gluing together three adjacent needles of Monterey or bishop pine, with many oval, white eggs laid along the inside of the chamber. Oviposition holes chewed by other weevils in stems and fruits are discussed in later chapters.

Eggs Inserted in Aquatic Vegetation

A number of aquatic insects also insert their eggs in vegetation. Whereas many of the terrestrial species with this habit are plant feeders that oviposit exclusively in living tissues of their host plants, most of the aquatic species are predators, and the plants are simply secure places for them to deposit their eggs. Therefore, they will oviposit in whatever plants happen to be around and may sometimes use dead plants or rotting wood.

The inserted aquatic eggs you are most likely to notice are those of damselflies (Zygoptera), provided they are inserted in thin plant tissue. We once watched an aurora damsel (Coenagrionidae: *Chromagrion conditum*) insert a series of eggs in the stem of an aquatic plant and were unable to detect any sign of them on close inspection after she was done. A few minutes later, however, we saw another female of the same species inserting eggs in a fern frond, and the location of each egg was revealed by a dark

A fern, just below the water surface, with markings (1.5 mm long) showing where eggs were inserted by an aurora damsel (Coenagrionidae: *Chromagrion conditum*). (MA)

bruise, 1.5 mm long, in the shape of the elongate egg. Damselflies may lay eggs above the waterline, especially spreadwings (Lestidae) that breed in temporary pools; in these species, the eggs are dormant for several months until the water returns. Typically, though, damselflies use floating or submerged leaves and stems. Sometimes a female simply curves her abdomen into the water to oviposit, but often she will completely submerge, backing down a stem and pausing frequently to insert another egg. Although most dragonflies (Anisoptera) deposit their eggs directly in water, darners (Aeshnidae) generally insert elongate eggs in plant tissues just as damselflies do.

The inserted eggs of waterscorpions (Nepidae) have filaments that project from the plant tissue, reminiscent of those in plant bug eggs. These may be seen sticking out of the tops of waterlilies and other floating leaves. *Ranatra* eggs, which are about three times as long as wide, have just two filaments, longer than the body of the egg. *Nepa apiculata* eggs each have a whorl of seven filaments. The number ranges from twelve to seventeen on *Curicta* eggs, which are usually deposited in mud.

Eggs of water treaders (Mesoveliidae) are shaped something like a bottle with a curved neck. A flat surface at the end of the neck is the only portion that is exposed when the egg is inserted in plant tissue. Eggs of backswimmers (Notonectidae) in the genus *Buenoa* are similarly embedded in stems with one surface exposed. It is a smooth, oval area that contrasts with the texture of the inserted portion.

Some predaceous diving beetles (Dytiscidae) lay eggs in underwater stems and leaves, either by first biting a hole or with a piercing ovipositor. *Haliplus* crawling water beetles (Haliplidae) have been observed to bite holes in filaments of *Nitella* algae and insert their white eggs into the empty cells. Some water mites (Hydrachnidae: *Hydrachna*) insert their tiny, reddish eggs in plant tissue.

Egg Cases and Coverings

Many invertebrates cover their eggs with various materials to protect them from desiccation and predation. Those that use excrement are discussed in chapter 5, and those that use mud in chapter 8. The egg cases and coverings described here are those that are made of silk, wax, and other nonexcrement products of the mother's body. In many scale insects, the female's body itself (with or without a waxy covering) becomes the egg covering; see the section on scale insects in chapter 5 for more about these. All spiders encase their eggs in more or less substantial silken sacs; these are discussed in a separate section following this one.

Gelatinous Egg Coverings (Fresh Water)

Many aquatic invertebrates lay eggs in a mass or string with a transparent, gelatinous covering, like a miniature version of the egg masses of some frogs and salamanders. Only eggs that are suspended in a clearly visible

matrix are included here. Eggs of certain true bugs have indistinct coatings, noted in the section on that order (page 53).

Caddisflies

Caddisfly eggs are spherical or nearly so, and they are opaque and often bright green or yellow-orange. They are enclosed in clear, gelatinous masses, usually attached to submerged objects, but some limnephilids attach their masses to objects above

Left: Egg mass of a limnephilid caddisfly on a cattail leaf. (MA) *Bottom left:* A 6-mm caddisfly egg mass, tethered to a submerged plant by a gelatinous string. (MA) *Bottom right:* A 4-mm caddisfly egg mass, attached to the case of a caddisfly larva (removed from the water to take the photo). (CA)

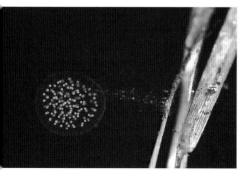

the water or deposit them in dry vernal pools. Eggs of others may be found stuck to structures such as flagpoles and gas pumps, because the artificial lights cause confusion in the adults. When first laid, the masses are relatively small and compact, but they swell considerably as they absorb water. The gelatin is still intact when the larvae hatch and emerge.

Egg masses of many species are oval or spherical blobs. *Phryganea* species (Phryganeidae) lay their eggs in donut-shaped masses, which may hang from a branch just below the water level or be attached to the upper side of a lily pad. A few species deposit eggs in long strings or flat spirals. The number of eggs in a mass ranges from just a few up to several hundred; *Grammotaulius bettenii* (Limnephilidae) deposits its eggs singly.

Snails

Freshwater snails (e.g., Physidae and Lymnaeidae) attach stiff, oval or elongate gelatinous egg masses to various objects in the water. They can appear similar to those of some caddisflies, but the individual eggs tend to be oval rather than spherical and are clear, with the embryo taking up only a small portion. One snail may deposit several masses, each containing a few dozen eggs. Freshwater limpets

Below: **Physid snail egg masses (5 to 9 mm) on a submerged stem. (MA)** *Right:* **Freshwater snail egg masses (1 cm) on the underside of a floating leaf. (TN)** *Bottom:* **Detail of eggs (1 mm each, in a mass 1.3 inches [3.3 cm] long) of a freshwater snail (Lymnaeidae:** *Lymnaea***). (MA)**

(Planorbidae: *Ferrissia*) lay their eggs on the undersides of waterlilies and other aquatic plants. The gelatinous masses are shaped like a pie cut into as many as nine wedges, each slice with one egg in it. The whole flattened mass is enveloped by a thin, firm membrane above and below. The similarly shaped, flattened egg masses of other planorbid snails, with more numerous eggs, are sometimes found in abundance on dead leaves at the bottoms of ponds.

Midges

Chironomid midges also lay eggs in gelatinous strings or masses. The eggs are distinctly elongate, easily distinguishing them from those of caddisflies and snails. The masses often float (or sink) freely rather than being attached to objects. *Glyptotendipes meridionalis* suspends its small egg mass from a disc of silk that floats on the water surface. Egg strings are in

the form of long, skinny tubes, with the eggs aligned more or less lengthwise. Several such strings may be twisted together, or coiled around inside a larger gelatinous tube. Tubular masses of this sort may measure up to 25 mm long by 5 mm wide, containing 1,000 or so eggs. At least one species attaches flattened oval masses, about 1 cm across, to rocks and logs in streams; a string of white eggs broadly meanders back and forth across the width of each mass.

Top: Egg mass (11 mm) of a midge (Chironomidae). (MA) *Bottom:* Egg mass (2 mm) of a biting midge (Ceratopogonidae), close to hatching, in a shallow dish of rainwater. The larger ones are mosquito eggs. (MA)

Eggs of other midges (Culicomorpha) are also regularly arranged in gelatinous masses. Those of *Chaoborus* phantom midges (Chaoboridae) are deposited on the water surface and sink to the bottom. *Mochlonyx cinctipes* deposits its eggs among debris at the edges of pools. The gelatinous egg masses of *Dixa* dixid midges are attached to a solid substrate rather than left floating in the water. Many species of biting midges (Ceratopogonidae) likewise lay their eggs in a small, gelatinous clump or string in the water or at its edge.

Dragonflies

Some dragonflies lay eggs in ropy, gelatinous strings that are draped over aquatic vegetation; others lay theirs in loose, gelatinous masses. The matrix may be colorless or milky white, and at least in some cases, it dissolves within a few days. The eggs are elliptical, about 0.5 mm long, and are at first whitish, becoming brown. In a large mass, they may number over 100,000.

Beetles

Water penny beetles (Psephenidae) deposit bright yellow eggs in compact, jelly-covered, single-layered patches of 400 to 600, about 6 mm across, on submerged stones and vegetation. They live in fast-flowing streams.

A loose, gelatinous string (1.4 inches [3.5 cm] long) of dragonfly eggs, caught on aquatic vegetation. (MA)

Some *Donacia* leaf beetles (Chrysomelidae) deposit eggs on the undersides of waterlily leaves by sticking their abdomens through holes they have chewed. The eggs are laid in concentric arcs and covered with a gelatinous material. They are white or yellow and about 1 mm long.

Other Gelatinous Masses

Horsehair worms (Nematomorpha: Gordioidea) lay their eggs in long, gelatinous strings or broken cords that wrap around aquatic plants. The eggs are said to number in the millions.

Most water mites (Hydrachnidae: *Hydrachna*) have red eggs. Females deposit them in groups of 20 to 400 on various submerged objects, with a jellylike covering over individual eggs or groups of eggs.

Although they are not eggs, freshwater bryozoans (Phylactolaemata) deserve mention here, because they could easily be mistaken for them. These sedentary little animals live in colonies on submerged objects such as twigs and logs, exuding a protective jelly and forming a slimy but firm, gelatinous blob anywhere from just a few centimeters to more than 2 feet across. The individual animals (zooids) are only around 1 mm long. Some colonies give the impression of a disembodied brain.

Gelatinous Egg Coverings (Marine)

Eggs with gelatinous coverings can also be found in marine habitats. Some of these belong to snails, as in fresh water, but others are produced by squids, polychaete worms, and sea slugs.

Snails

Marine snails in several different families produce gelatinous egg masses. Chink shell snails (Littorinidae: *Lacuna*) deposit 5-mm donut-shaped masses on eelgrass. They are pale blue or green at first, eventually turning yellow. Striped barrel snails (Acteonidae: *Rictaxis punctocaelatus*; W) attach white egg masses in the shape of thick coils, about 2 cm long, to the sediment by a thread. Salt marsh snails (Ellobiidae: *Melampus bidentatus*) deposit gelatinous masses of about 850 yolky eggs near the high-tide level. They rely on high spring tides to wash debris over the eggs and keep them

A dried "sand collar" (2.6 inches [6.5 cm]) of a moon snail (Naticidae).

moist until the next tide, when they hatch and are carried away.

The elegant, funnel-shaped structures known as "sand collars" are the eggs of a moon snail (Naticidae) sandwiched between two thin layers of sand, cemented together with mucus. The collar can be up to 3.5 inches (9 cm) in diameter, its form being determined by the size and shape of the female's shell. It is still flexible and rubbery when it shows up on the beach, becoming hard and fragile when it dries.

Squids

In shallow waters of the North Atlantic, longfin inshore squids (Loliginidae: *Loligo pealeii*) communally deposit large numbers of clear, banana-shaped, gelatinous egg masses about 2 inches (5 cm) long. Each mass contains up to 200 eggs.

Polychaete Worms

Polychaete eggs are also surrounded with masses of jelly. Lugworms (Arenicolidae: *Arenicola*), for example, make brownish, translucent, flattened, teardrop-shaped masses, which are several inches long and attached to the sediment by a string at one end. A *Clymenella* bamboo worm (Maldanidae) produces a 1.2-inch (3-cm) oval, transparent, gelatinous egg case, said to resemble a small jellyfish stuck to the top end of the worm's sandy tube.

Sea Slugs

Nudibranch sea slugs generally produce long, thin strings of eggs that are tightly coiled into ribbonlike masses. They are often brightly colored. The red sponge doris (Rostangidae: *Rostanga pulchra*) lays reddish orange eggs on a similarly colored sponge. Sea whip slug (Tritoniidae: *Tritonia wellsi*) eggs are yellow. Rainbow slug (Goniodorididae: *Okenia sapelona*) eggs are white. *Doridella steinbergae* (Corambidae) lays its eggs in a little, crescent-shaped lump of jelly on a bryozoan.

The albatross aglaja (Aglajidae: *Melanochlamys diomedea*), a sea slug but not a nudibranch, attaches oval, gelatinous egg masses to sediment by a short stalk.

Egg Masses Coated with a Resinlike Substance

Insects in a few unrelated groups cover their eggs with a translucent secretion that hardens when it dries. Assassin bugs and tortricid moths deposit their compact egg masses on foliage and bark. Those of tent caterpillar moths surround twigs. Grasshopper eggs are less likely to be seen, since they are laid in soil or in crevices near the ground.

Left: Egg masses of the eastern tent caterpillar moth (Lasiocampidae: *Malacosoma americana*) surrounding black cherry twigs. The mass at left contains viable overwintering eggs; the eggs in the mass at right hatched the previous spring, and their varnish has mostly weathered away. (MA) *Right:* Egg mass of a forest tent caterpillar moth (*Malacosoma disstria*) surrounding a sugar maple twig. (VT)

Tent Caterpillar Moths

Tent caterpillar moths (Lasiocampidae: *Malacosoma*) encircle small twigs with single-layer masses of 200 to 400 eggs. These are covered with a foamy, brown substance that hardens to form a shiny, varnishlike covering.

Assassin Bugs

Some assassin bugs (Reduviidae) cover their masses of upright, bottle-shaped eggs with a firm but sticky secretion. Wheel bug (*Arilus cristatus*) egg masses can be particularly large, around 2 cm across, with a brown resinous matrix that fills the spaces between the whitish caps of the eggs. *Zelus* egg masses are smaller, and the eggs lean into one another so that there is no space between the white caps. The translucent secretion is evident around the edge of the mass. The spined assassin bug (*Sinea diadema*) is said to lay white eggs (those of

Egg mass (2 cm) of a wheel bug (Reduviidae: *Arilus cristatus*). (MD) Photo by Arlene Ripley.

Egg mass (5 mm) of an assassin bug (Reduviidae), probably *Zelus*. (OK) Photo by Sam Houston.

Arilus and *Zelus* are brown except for the caps) in small groups, covered with a reddish yellow secretion.

Tortricid Moths

The rose leafroller (Tortricidae: *Archips rosana*) deposits on smooth bark an imbricate mass of up to 100 or more flattened eggs. Coated with a shiny, translucent, protective substance, the mass is up to 7 mm across. The eggs start out greenish and turn brownish gray. The fruit tree leafroller (*A. argyrospila*) and uglynest caterpillar (*A. cerasivorana*) make similar overwintering egg masses, as do many other tortricids.

Grasshoppers

Most short-horned grasshoppers (Acrididae) lay their elongate (up to about 6 mm) eggs underground, or sometimes on the ground surface, in a "pod" containing from 2 to more than 100 eggs. The female makes a hole by extending her abdomen into the soil, then secretes from the tip of her abdomen a frothy substance in which

Egg mass (9 mm long) of a tortricid moth on a saguaro. (AZ)

her eggs are suspended. The material fills the hole and hardens to form a plug. The resulting pod is said to be distinctive for each species, but generally it is an elongate cylinder, an inch or so long, and more or less curved. Buried masses are coated in soil, but if broken open, the dried substance is typically a translucent yellowish brown. The dried secretion often makes up a very small portion of the volume of the mass; BugGuide.net contributor David Ferguson describes an egg pod as "sort of like a tubular glob of dirty rice." The eggs are whitish when first laid, generally turning brown as they age. The sprinkled broad-winged grasshopper (*Chloealtis conspersa*) usually deposits its eggs in soft wood on the ground through a round hole about 3 mm in diameter. The inch-long pod is parallel with the grain of the wood. Other species may oviposit in animal droppings or between rocks.

If you happen to come across a grasshopper egg pod, you may see signs of parasitism or predation. Some checkered beetle (Cleridae) and blister beetle (Meloidae) larvae develop exclusively in grasshopper egg pods, feeding on the eggs. A single larva of the blow fly *Stomorhina lunata* (Calliphoridae) generally consumes all of the eggs in a pod. Some bombyliid (bee fly) and anthomyiid fly larvae also prey on grasshopper eggs. *Scelio* platygastrid wasps dig into soil to deposit eggs in freshly laid grasshopper egg pods, and their larvae develop within individual eggs.

Eggs with Opaque, Solid, or Frothy Coverings (Terrestrial)

The egg coverings described in this section vary considerably in form and consistency. Cockroaches and earthworms produce smooth, tough, brown egg cases. Dobsonflies and beech splendor beetles apply a smooth, white or whitish coating to flat egg masses. Eggs of mantises and some robber flies and tussock moths are completely concealed in a frothy material, whereas ambush bug eggs are easily seen through the bubbly substance that surrounds them. Certain treehoppers produce sticky white egg coverings, and certain leafhoppers add a white, waxy powder after inserting their eggs in vegetation.

Cockroaches

Cockroaches (Blattaria) enclose their eggs in distinctive hard, purselike cases, called *oothecae*. Depending on the species, they may be pale tan or dark reddish brown and range from about 4 to 12 mm long. Along the serrated crest of the ootheca is a series of little air ducts, with a pair of these connecting each of the 12 to 48 eggs to the outside air. The ootheca is formed inside the female's body, and she may carry it around attached to the tip of her abdomen for some time before depositing it in a sheltered place. The German cockroach (*Blattella germanica*) carries her 7-mm ootheca until the young hatch, as do a few other wood cockroaches (Blattellidae). Most cockroaches, however, deposit their oothecae, often gluing them to a substrate with secretions. Many conceal them with bits of debris or excrement.

When cockroach nymphs hatch, they swallow air, causing the case to split open along the crest as they force their way out together. The case

Left: A tiny cockroach (Dictyoptera: Blattaria) ootheca (4 mm) attached to a pine needle. (NC) Photo by Lynette Schimming. *Right:* A cockroach ootheca like the one on page 14, cleaned to show its structure; visible is the exit hole of a parasitoid wasp. (FL)

The ootheca (12 mm) of a cockroach stuck to the side of a palm tree, covered with debris by the female. (FL)

then snaps shut behind them. Round holes in the side of an ootheca are the emergence holes of parasitoid wasps. If a parasitized ootheca has a single pupal skin inside, it probably is from an ensign wasp (Evaniidae; this family is specific to cockroach eggs, with just one wasp developing per ootheca). Multiple pupal skins indicate chalcid parasitoids such as *Aprostocetus hagenowii* (Eulophidae) or *Systellogaster ovivora* (Pteromalidae).

Mantises

Mantises (Mantodea) also deposit their eggs in oothecae, but theirs contain up to several hundred eggs and are made of a light, frothy substance, which the female shapes as she deposits it (not internally, as is the case with cockroaches). These are attached to vegetation and other surfaces, where they overwinter. A mantis ootheca is more or less oval, and down the center is a series of overlapping scales concealing tiny corridors that lead to a central chamber. The young emerge through these corridors all at once in the spring, and because of the scales, the external change to the ootheca after emergence can be very subtle. A small tassel of white silk may dangle from the central strip, made up of threads from which the nymphs hung when they first emerged. An ootheca with obvious small, round holes indicates emergence of *Podagrion* torymids or other chalcids (e.g., Eupelmidae: *Anastatus mantis* or *Eupelmus neococcidis*). *Thaumaglossa* dermestid beetles (AZ, TX) develop exclusively in mantid oothecae; *Orphinus fulvipes* (FL) sometimes does as well.

A mantis (Mantidae: *Stagmomantis*) ootheca (22 mm) with exit holes of chalcid wasps. (AZ)

Mantis oothecae come in various shades of brown. Those of the four common eastern species can be distinguished by their

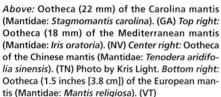

Above: Ootheca (22 mm) of the Carolina mantis (Mantidae: *Stagmomantis carolina*). (GA) *Top right:* Ootheca (18 mm) of the Mediterranean mantis (Mantidae: *Iris oratoria*). (NV) *Center right:* Ootheca of the Chinese mantis (Mantidae: *Tenodera aridifolia sinensis*). (TN) Photo by Kris Light. *Bottom right:* Ootheca (1.5 inches [3.8 cm]) of the European mantis (Mantidae: *Mantis religiosa*). (VT)

shapes. The ootheca of the Chinese mantis (*Tenodera aridifolia sinensis*) is squat and rounded, about 25 mm long and 20 mm wide. That of the European mantis (*Mantis religiosa*) is broadly rounded but more elongate, about 1.6 inches (4 cm) long. The Carolina mantis's (*Stagmomantis carolina*) ootheca is also elongate, but closer to 2 cm long and somewhat flattened on the sides and face. That of the narrow-winged mantis (*T. angustipennis*) is more than three times as long as wide. The ootheca of the Mediterranean mantis (*Iris oratoria*), introduced in California, is very narrow with somewhat concave sides. The one pictured measures 18 mm long, 7 mm high, and 5 mm thick.

Dobsonflies

Dobsonflies (Corydalidae: *Corydalus*) deposit their eggs in conspicuous masses, covered with a white, waxy secretion, on various objects overhanging large streams. The individual eggs are gray and cylindrical, about 1.5 mm long and 0.5 mm wide. A female lays up to 1,000 or more eggs, arranged in one to five layers, in a flat, round mass

about 2 cm across. She covers them with a clear fluid that turns white as it dries. The ring of white material that extends beyond the eggs often remains long after they have hatched.

Ambush Bugs

The eggs of ambush bugs (Reduviidae: Phymatinae) look like shiny black barrels with flat, whitish tops that are etched with bull's-eyes. They are deposited standing upright in a small, loose cluster, glued to the underside of a leaf with a bubbly secretion. This light froth does not quite cover the tops of the eggs, and it is not thick enough to conceal them, but it is still conspicuous after it dries.

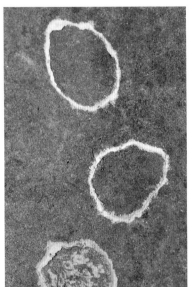

Tussock Moths

Some tussock moths (Lymantriidae) cover their masses of spherical eggs with a white, frothy substance that hardens. The satin moth (*Leucoma salicis*) deposits 50 to 200 eggs in such masses on twigs and other objects. The female white-marked tussock moth (*Orgyia leucostigma*) is wingless and deposits her 400 or so eggs onto her cocoon, covering them with a similar substance.

Robber Flies

A few robber flies (Asilidae) are known to deposit egg masses on twigs and stems, covered with a white froth. The masses can have a ribbed appearance, from being

The froth-covered egg mass of a white-marked tussock moth (Lymantriidae: *Orgyia leucostigma*), deposited on the female's cocoon. The dark speck toward the bottom is an encyrtid wasp egg parasitoid. (NY)

Egg mass (about 15 to 20 mm) of *Mallophora leschenaulti* (Asilidae), a large robber fly. (TX) Photo courtesy of larvalbug.com.

applied in a spiralling motion, but this is more or less obscured by irregular lumps. The air bubbles in the covering are smaller and more regular than in a mantis ootheca, giving it a much smoother appearance, like very fine Styrofoam. *Mallophora leschenaulti*, a large "bee killer" found in Texas and Mexico, makes a mass 15 to 20 mm long. *Megaphorus minutus* (SE) makes smaller masses, about 1 cm or somewhat less. Other robber flies in these genera occur throughout the southern United States and may produce similar egg masses.

Treehoppers

Still smaller white egg coverings are made by *Enchenopa* treehoppers (Membracidae). Like other treehoppers, they insert their eggs in slits in woody twigs. The female then covers each slit with a white, sticky, marshmallowy substance in a mass about 4 mm long. The covering has a more or less corrugated look because it is applied in layers. There are usually several masses close together on a twig. *E. binotata* oviposits in bittersweet; *E. brevis* in leatherwood; and other, as yet unnamed species lay eggs in hoptree, viburnum, redbud, tuliptree, black locust, and walnut. Other treehoppers in the tribe Membracini, mainly with unknown hosts, produce similar egg masses.

Leafhoppers

Certain leafhoppers (Cicadellidae) in the tribe Proconiini (e.g., *Oncometopia*, *Homalodisca*, and some *Cuerna* species) apply a dusting of white, waxy powder to the egg slits they make in plant tissues. The covering consists of tiny secreted proteinaceous

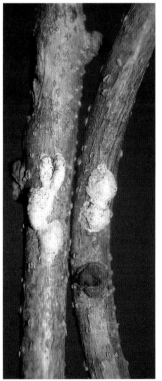

Marshmallowy egg masses (about 4 mm each) of the two-spotted treehopper (Membracidae: *Enchenopa binotata*) on bittersweet vines. (MA)

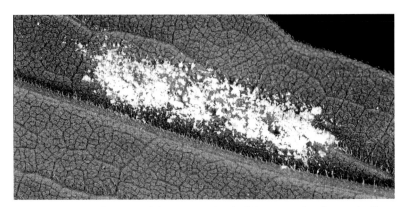

Brochosome-covered egg nest (about 12 mm long) of *Oncometopia orbona*, a leafhopper (Cicadellidae), on the underside of a goldenrod leaf. (IL) Photo by Roman Rakitov.

particles called *brochosomes*, which females store in conspicuous white patches on their forewings. After inserting her eggs, the female uses her hind legs to scrape brochosomes off of her forewings and onto the oviposition site.

Metallic Wood-boring Beetles

The beech splendor beetle (Buprestidae: *Agrilus viridis*) deposits small, round, flat egg masses on beech bark. They are covered with a substance that is whitish with a brownish tinge.

Earthworms

Earthworm (Lumbricidae) eggs are contained in smooth, round, brownish cases, which are deposited in the soil. The covering originates at the swollen band possessed by adult earthworms, called the *clitellum* (Latin for "saddle"). After a worm mates, it produces a sheet of mucus that covers its body from the clitellum forward. Next, the clitellum produces a leathery, proteinaceous sleeve, which the worm then works forward. As the sleeve moves along the worm's body, it collects first the worm's eggs and then the sperm its mate has deposited, finally sliding off the worm's "nose." As it does so, the open ends of the sleeve contract and seal, resulting in an oval case up to a few millimeters long, with a point at either end (size and shape vary among species). The eggs are fertilized by the sperm inside the case.

Egg cases (4 mm each) of the "red wiggler" compost worm (Lumbricidae: *Eisenia foetida*). (MA)

Freshwater Egg Cases

In fresh water, relatively few types of eggs have coverings other than the transparent gelatinous ones described previously. Those that do come in firm cases belong to aquatic earthworms, leeches, flatworms, and water scavenger beetles. The silken larval cases of some microcaddisflies could be mistaken for egg cases (see chapter 8).

Annelids

Aquatic earthworms and other oligochaete worms form egg cases similar to those of terrestrial earthworms, but not as tough and leathery. They are deposited among benthic debris or on various objects in the water. Egg cases of leeches (Hirudinea) are soft, flexible, and formed similarly to those of oligochaetes but tend to be flattened because of the shape of the leech's body. Some leeches carry their egg cases until the eggs hatch, but most deposit them in mud or on objects along the shoreline. A few attach them to their host animals.

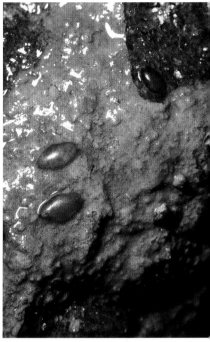

Leech (Hirudinea) egg cases (4 mm each). (ND)

Flatworms

Flatworms (Platyhelminthes) lay their eggs in spherical or oval capsules, up to a few millimeters wide, which may be attached by stalks to the underside of a stone or leaf. Each capsule contains one to several eggs.

Water Scavenger Beetles

Water scavenger beetles (Hydrophilidae) are found in calm waters. Most species enclose their eggs, which may be in a mass of 100 or more, in a case of hardened silk that is secreted from abdominal glands. The case may be attached to vegetation or other objects or left floating free. Some cases have a hornlike respiratory tube that protrudes above the water. These include the cases of *Hydrochara* and *Hydrophilus*, which are brownish, 22 to 24 mm long, and 15 mm tall. Other cases have a long ribbon that extends down into the water. *Cymbiodyta* and *Paracymus* embed their eggs in a loose web. The female *Helochares* carries her egg mass beneath her abdomen in a nearly transparent, bag-shaped case, as do the related hydrophiloids *Epimetopus* (Epimetopidae) and *Spercheus* (Spercheidae).

Marine Egg Cases

A variety of invertebrate egg cases commonly wash up on beaches. The vast majority of these belong to various kinds of snails. Note that the black,

Fragment of a "mermaid's necklace" (1 inch [2.5 cm]) wide), the egg case string of a channeled whelk (Melongenidae: *Busycotypus canaliculatus*). (MA)

four-pronged pouches known as "mermaids' purses" are the egg cases of skates, which are vertebrates.

Whelks

Whelks (Melongenidae) produce tough, parchmentlike egg cases. Those of *Busycon* and *Busycotypus* species are flattened, disc-shaped pouches that are stacked and connected in a long, yellowish string. Although they are initially planted out in the ocean bottom, they often break loose and drift ashore. A whole string (sometimes called a "mermaid's necklace") may be 3 feet long, and each capsule along the string may be 1.4 inches (3.5 cm) across and contain 25 to 50 baby whelks like seeds in a pod. The shape of the individual capsules can be used to identify the species. For instance, a knobbed whelk (*Busycon carica*) capsule is circular with squared edges, like a thick coin. A channeled whelk (*Busycotypus canaliculatus*) capsule is more clamshaped, with a concave bottom, a convex top, and ridges on top radiating from the middle to the thinly sharpened edge.

In waved whelk eggs (Buccinidae: *Buccinum undatum*), the capsules form a ball-shaped mass, which when scrubbed with water produces lather like soap, hence the name "sailor's wash ball." The individual translucent egg capsules of tulip and horse conchs (Fasciolariidae) look something like flattened ice cream cones, about 2 cm or longer.

Tritons

The Oregon hairy triton (Ranellidae: *Fusitriton oregonensis*; NW) produces big sheets of translucent egg capsules packed in a spiral.

Nassa Mud Snails and Rock Snails

Spiky, irregular, 3-mm egg cases sometimes completely coating sticks, rocks, seaweed, and other submerged objects belong to eastern mud snails (Nassariidae: *Nassarius obsoletus*). They are native to the Atlantic but introduced on the Pacific coast. If you peer closely into the transluscent cases, you

Eastern mud snail (Nassariidae: *Nassarius obsoletus*) egg cases (3 mm each) on sea lettuce. (MA)

can make out the tiny, white dots of individual eggs inside. Egg capsules of the three-lined basketsnail (*N. trivittatus*) are similar but somewhat smaller and on short stalks.

Rock snails (Muricidae), including the dogwinkles (*Nucella*) and oyster drills (*Urosalpinx*), deposit their eggs in leathery, yellow, stalked, vase-shaped capsules. These are glued in clusters to rocks, shells, and other substrates. They can be quite abundant in the spring and summer. The bruised nassa (Nassariidae: *Nassarius vibex*) has similar-looking stalked capsules, but they are less than 2 mm long, whereas rock snail capsules are 6 to 8 mm.

A cluster of frilled dogwinkle (Muricidae: *Nucella lamellosa*) egg capsules (each 6 mm long). (WA)

Periwinkles

Some periwinkles (Littorinidae) deposit free-floating, lens-shaped egg capsules, each containing just one or a few eggs. These may be up to a centimeter or so in diameter.

Octopuses

The greater argonaut (Argonautidae: *Argonauta argo*) belongs to a family of octopuses that are sometimes called "paper nautiluses" because their egg cases, up to a foot (30 cm) across, are laterally compressed spirals that look something like nautilus shells. These can occasionally be found washed up on beaches as far north as Cape Cod. Although the female wears it like a shell, she secretes this ridged, white, parchmentlike structure just for the purpose of holding her eggs.

Egg Masses Covered with Hairs

Some moths cover their eggs with hairs from their abdomen, and many others leave incidental small tufts of hairs on or near the eggs. Some, on emerging from their cocoons, use their anal tufts to pick up urticating hairs (hairs that cause irritation when contacted by other animals) from their larval skins and deposit these on their eggs.

Tussock Moths

Female tussock moths (Lymantriidae) often deposit their eggs in masses and usually cover them with hairs from the tips of their abdomens. Gypsy moth (*Lymantria dispar*) females are poor fliers and often deposit their overwintering mass of 100 to 600 eggs just a few centimeters from their pupal skin, generally on tree trunks or man-made structures. The roughly spherical eggs are completely covered with the female's buff-colored hairs. Egg masses of the browntail moth (*Euproctis chrysorrhoea*; now virtually extirpated from North America) are similar, but are deposited on the

Egg mass (1 inch [2.5 cm]) of a gypsy moth (Lymantriidae: *Lymantria dispar*), covered with hairs from the female's abdomen. (MN)

undersides of leaves and hatch in late summer. The flightless female Douglas-fir tussock moth (*Orgyia pseudotsugata*) lays her white eggs on top of her own cocoon and adds a covering of woolly, gray hairs, not thick enough to conceal them. The western tussock moth (*O. vetusta*) does the same.

Tiger Moths

Tiger moths (Arctiidae) also often cover their eggs with body hairs. The eggs of the milkweed tussock moth (*Euchaetes egle*) are well concealed beneath a buff-colored, woolly mass on the underside of a leaf of the host plant. Fall webworm (*Hyphantria cunea*) eggs are deposited in a tight, single-layered mass on the underside of a leaf, with a thin, flat covering of white hairs.

Owlet Moths

Armyworms (Noctuidae: *Spodoptera*) deposit their eggs on the undersides of leaves in irregular heaps, which are more or less thickly covered with white hairs. The cattail borer moth (*Bellura obliqua*) deposits her eggs within 15 inches (38 cm) of the tip of a cattail leaf and covers them with a thick layer of froth and hairs. The oval mass is dirty yellowish white, up to 15 mm long by 10 mm wide, and 3 to 4 mm thick.

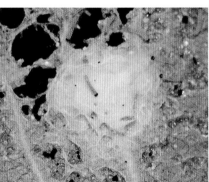

Milkweed tussock moth (Arctiidae: *Euchaetes egle*) egg mass (12 mm across) and hatchlings. (TN)

Tortricid Moths

Oak leafrollers (Tortricidae: *Archips semiferana*) thoroughly cover their small, oval egg masses with whitish hairs. An egg mass is usually located near the crotch of an oak twig, where it overwinters. The eggs hidden beneath are unlike other tortricid eggs; they are barrel-shaped and placed standing upright, side by side.

Woolly Wax Coverings

Some scales and mealybugs (Coccoidea) produce white, fluffy sacs for their eggs. These may appear to be made of silk, but under magnification,

Top right: Egg sac (5 mm) of a felt scale (Eriococcidae). (VT) *Center right:* Egg sac (3.5 mm) of the cottony maple scale (Coccidae: *Pulvinaria innumerabilis*), with the female's scale still attached. (TN) *Bottom right:* Cottony cushion scales (Margarodidae: *Icerya purchasi*) with egg sacs (7 mm each). (CA)

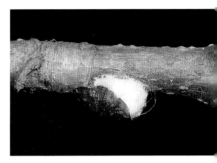

they are revealed to have thick coils of waxy filaments. Two whitefly species (Aleyrodidae) deposit white, waxy material on top of their eggs.

Scale Insects

Felt scales (Eriococcidae) get their name from the white, feltlike egg sacs the females produce. These sacs are oval and at a glance look something like the silken cocoons of some braconid wasps, but they are very soft and have an opening at one end. At least in some species, the eggs inside are bright red.

Cottony scale insects (Coccidae: *Pulvinaria*) produce cottony, white egg sacs, up to about a centimeter long, to which the female's round, brown body often remains attached at one end, propped up at an angle. The egg sac may be a featureless mass, a bit longer than wide, as in the cottony maple scale (*P. innumerabilis*), or long and narrow with a few longitudinal ridges, as in the cottony camellia scale (*P. floccifera*). Each sac has a few thousand eggs inside.

The cottony cushion scale (Margarodidae: *Icerya purchasi*), introduced from the tropics, also has a white egg sac, about a centimeter long, but it is distinctly fluted with about a dozen longitudinal ridges. It contains 600 to 1,000 bright red eggs. (The fluted egg sac of *Crypticerya genistae*, a similar species that arrived in Florida very recently, is up to 2 cm long and often stands erect from the host plant.) The vedalia (Coccinellidae: *Rodolia cardinalis*) is a ladybug that lays oval, red eggs singly or in small clusters on the cottony cushion scale's egg sac. Each larva spends its entire life beneath a single scale.

Mealybugs

Females of many mealybug species (Pseudococcidae) create elongate, cottony egg sacs, substantially larger than their bodies, each of which may contain several hundred oval, lemon yellow eggs. The egg sac of some species, such as the grape mealybug (*Pseudococcus maritimus*), is a loose cottony mass. Other species, such as the apple mealybug (*Phenacoccus aceris*), make a well-defined cottony cylinder. The egg sac of this species is 4 to 9 mm long and 1 to 3 mm wide. Egg sacs are deposited on vegetation or in leaf litter, sometimes with several clustered together. Often the dead female can be found at one end of the sac. The mealybug destroyer (Coccinellidae: *Cryptolaemus montrouzieri*), another introduced ladybug, lays oval, yellow eggs singly in the egg sacs of mealybugs.

Whiteflies

The spiralling whitefly (*Aleurodicus dispersus*) and giant whitefly (*A. dugesii*) deposit their tiny eggs on the undersides of leaves in distinctive spirals, covering them with a white, fluffy wax secretion.

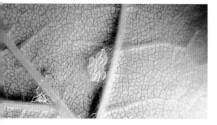

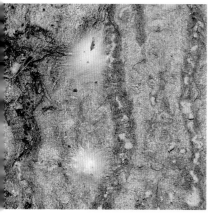

Silk Coverings

In addition to spiders, a few types of insects use silk to cover their eggs. In most cases, these are sparse coverings that conceal the eggs little if at all. The eggs of these insects are elongate, easily distinguishing them from those of spiders, which are spherical.

Barklice

Barklice (Psocoptera) deposit their eggs in small clusters on leaves and bark, covering them in a mesh of silk threads spun from the female's mouth. *Graphopsocus cruciatus* (Stenopsocidae) is a common introduced species that lays clusters of about a dozen eggs on the undersides of leaves. The eggs are white, about twice as long as wide, and the whole cluster is only about 2 mm across. The silken mesh overlaying the eggs is very fine. We have found eggs of an unknown species, on tree bark, that were brown but otherwise similar.

Top left: Freshly laid eggs (2-mm cluster) of the barklouse *Graphopsocus cruciatus* (Stenopsocidae) on the underside of a leaf, covered with fine webbing. (TN) *Center left:* Silk-covered eggs (4-mm cluster) of an unknown barklouse (Psocoptera). (MA) *Bottom left:* Silken egg coverings (3 mm each) of *Aaroniella* (Philotarsidae), a barklouse. (MA)

Aaroniella (Philotarsidae), which we have found several times covering the bark of highbush blueberry with loose, conspicuous webbing, covers its eggs with enough silk to completely conceal them. The coverings appear as white patches, about 3 mm across, with no definite shape, the edges dissipating into finer and less visible crisscrossing threads.

Spongillaflies

Spongillaflies (Sisyridae) lay their eggs on objects overhanging water; as with dobsonflies, the larvae are aquatic and must drop into water when they hatch. The eggs are usually deposited in crevices or depressions, such as the crotches of veins on the undersides of leaves. Eggs are about 0.3 mm long and half as wide. Like those of other neuropterans (and unlike those of barklice), the egg has a small knob at one end. Eggs are glistening white when first laid, becoming yellowish after a few days. They are laid singly or in clusters of up to 20 or so and are covered with a flat, white sheet composed of crosshatching silk threads applied in a zigzag pattern.

Beetles

The terrestrial hydrophilid beetles *Cercyon* and *Sphaeridium* lay their eggs in damp or wet places, embedded in loose webs. The singly laid eggs of minute moss beetles (Hydraenidae) are often also covered with silk and may be in or out of water. *Hydraena* eggs have a blanketlike covering of closely applied silk. Those of *Limnebius* and *Ochthebius* have loosely applied silk or sometimes none at all.

Spider Egg Sacs

Spider eggs are always covered with silk, although in some cases this covering is scant and the eggs inside are clearly visible. The eggs are spherical and typically about 1 mm wide, plus or minus 0.5 mm or so. The tiniest spiders may deposit only one or a few eggs in a sac; a few dozen to a few hundred is more typical, and an egg sac of a large orbweaver may contain more than 2,500 eggs. When first laid, spider eggs are generally surrounded by a clear, viscous liquid, which soon dries, cementing the eggs together. In some egg sacs we have opened, however, the eggs were loose, rolling around freely.

Egg sacs are often spherical or lenticular, resembling little balls, biscuits, or discs. Though many are whitish, some are yellow, red, green, or other colors. Each species makes a characteristic egg sac, and it is often as easy to recognize the species by looking at this as by studying the spider itself. Some generalizations can be made about the egg sacs of various taxonomic groups, but different types may be made by members of the same family of spiders.

A number of types of spiders carry their egg sacs until they hatch, or shortly before. These egg sacs are described in more detail below, as some of them may be found dissociated from their mothers after the spiderlings have emerged, but we will summarize them here, because knowing this natural history information is useful in identifying the spiders. Cellar spiders (Pholcidae) carry their egg sacs in front of them in their chelicerae (though a female may temporarily hang it in her web to catch an insect, clean herself, or mate), as do *Microhexura* funnel-web mygalomorphs (Dipluridae). Nursery web and fishing spiders (Pisauridae) carry their egg sacs under their bodies, held in their jaws and secured from behind by threads from their spinnerets. Spitting spiders (Scytodidae) and huntsman spiders (Sparassidae: *Heteropoda venatoria*) do the same. Wolf spiders (Lycosidae) carry their egg sacs behind them, attached to their spinnerets, as do *Nesticus* cave spiders (Nesticidae).

Many spiders suspend their egg sacs in their webs, and the web characteristics can help in narrowing down the identification. This is the case with many theridiids. Note, however, that pirate spiders (Mimetidae) and kleptoparasitic cobweb spiders (Theridiidae: Argyrodinae) may deposit their egg sacs in the webs of other spiders.

A typical basic spider egg sac consists of a basal plate and a cover plate, each being a thin layer of tightly woven threads molded into a disc. The basal plate is the first sheet of silk spun; the spider lays eggs on this and then spins the cover plate over them, or in some cases she simply wraps the basal plate around the egg mass. She may then pick up the sac and finish it by turning it around with her legs while her spinnerets cover it with more silk. Some spiders add a padding of downy silk, which is often yellow or brown, before finishing the egg sac. The outer covering of silk may be thin and meshy or tough and papery. Generally, spiders that guard their eggs, hide them in a burrow, or hang them protected in a web do not make their sacs as tough as those that abandon them to the elements.

Hidden in a Burrow or Retreat

The egg sacs of burrowing mygalomorphs are hidden within the female's burrow. Those of tarantulas (Theraphosidae) in the Southwest are large, flabby bags, often 2 or 3 inches (5 to 7.5 cm) in diameter. The female occasionally brings it to the burrow entrance to warm it in the sunlight. Among the folding-door spiders (Antrodiaetidae), *Antrodiaetus* species create a lens-shaped egg sac that is broadly attached to the burrow wall, between two-fifths and four-fifths of the distance down the burrow. The *Aliatypus* egg sac, on the other hand, is a pendulous bag, as long as or longer than wide, attached to the wall in the bottom part of the burrow by many fine silk lines on all sides. The top of this egg sac is a concave lid of silk spanning the width of the burrow. The trapdoor spiders (Ctenizidae) make loose, delicate silken bags that often hang from the side of the burrow.

Several families of hunting spiders make flattened, tubelike retreats of white silk, which they use as a shelter during the day, a molting and mating chamber, and a place to deposit their eggs. Some construct these under stones or among debris; others make them in shelters they create by bending or folding leaves. Within the retreat, the eggs are usually enclosed in a flat, circular sac, and the mother often stays in the sac until she dies or the

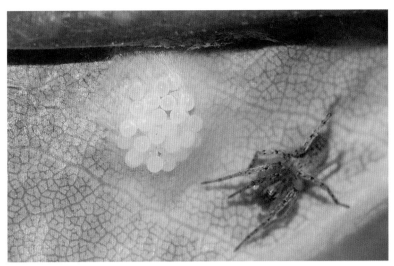

A ghost spider (Anyphaenidae) and her egg sac, found inside a curled leaf. The clearly visible mass of eggs is 7 mm across. (OR)

spiderlings disperse. Female sac spiders (Clubionidae and others) guard their egg sacs (or sometimes uncovered masses of yellow eggs) inside thick, white, closed cells. The long-legged sac spider *Cheiracanthium inclusum* (Miturgidae) female makes a tube of white silk in which she stays with her eggs, which are covered with a very thin sheet of silk. Ghost spiders (Anyphaenidae) stand guard over thin, flattened, white egg sacs within a silk cell, which in turn is often within a folded leaf. The ground spiders *Drassodes saccatus* and *D. neglectus* (Gnaphosidae) fashion large, transparent bags of silk under stones, in which the female makes her egg sac and stays until the spiderlings emerge. *Micaria* females also deposit egg sacs within baglike retreats but usually do not stay with the eggs. A single retreat may contain as many as three egg sacs, which are stiff and resemble rimmed pots. The tiny *Oonops* (Oonopidae) lays a pair of pink eggs that are visible through the white silk of her egg sac, which is constructed inside her cell. The woodlouse hunter (Dysderidae: *Dysdera crocata*) lays about 60 yellow eggs inside her retreat, which is an oval cell of closely woven silk, and gives them a light wrapping of additional silk.

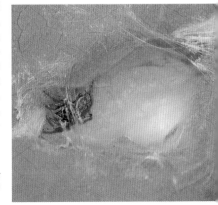

A hammerjawed jumper (Salticidae: *Zygoballus rufipes*) and her 6-mm egg sac, found inside a folded leaf. (PA)

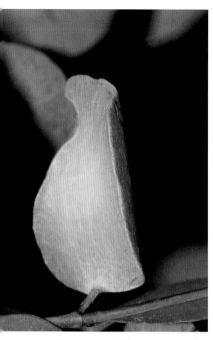

The screen of silk surrounding this leaf conceals the egg sac (2 cm) of an orbweaver (Araneidae). (MT)

Most female jumping spiders (Salticidae) construct distinctive saclike nests, composed of several envelopes, usually with two openings. The eggs are laid within these nests and enclosed in a delicate, lens-shaped sac, which is either affixed to the substrate or suspended from the walls of the nest. There is usually just one egg sac; one exception is *Marpissa*, which stacks 2 to 5 flat egg sacs inside her open silk chamber. In some species (e.g., *Lyssomanes*), the nest is reduced to sparse, light webbing. Females generally guard the eggs until the spiderlings disperse.

Some orbweavers (Araneidae) deposit their egg sacs beneath a covering of silk that the mother does not actually use as a retreat. This is the case with the gray cross spider (*Larinioides sclopetarius*), which commonly attaches its large, round, white egg sacs in sheltered places on the walls of houses and covers them with a sheet of silk.

Tube web spiders (Segestriidae) make no egg sac, depositing spherical masses of 15 or so relatively large eggs inside their tubular retreats. A female southern house spider (Filistatidae: *Kukulcania hibernalis*) lays about 200 eggs and loosely swathes them in a silken ball, about 15 mm across, which she keeps with her in her retreat. A purseweb spider (Atypidae) hangs an elongate egg sac inside her tube-shaped web. Some hacklemesh weavers (Amaurobiidae) create disc-shaped egg sacs within their tubular retreats.

A female desertshrub spider (Diguetidae; SW) spins a series of flattened disc-shaped egg sacs, overlaid on one another like shingles, and along one side of this series she spins a silken retreat for herself. The series of egg sacs may be more than 3 inches (7.5 cm) long, and it is covered with leaves and other debris. The whole affair is suspended within a maze of threads and is attached above to a strong thread. The labyrinth spider and other *Metepeira* species (Araneidae) construct a similar stack of disc-shaped egg sacs in their retreats, which may incorporate only a few bits of debris or resemble a diguetid retreat.

Many spiders hide their eggs in retreats made by folding leaves. See chapter 11 for some examples.

Scant or No Covering, Eggs Clearly Visible

The silk in some spider egg sacs is scant or loose enough that the eggs within are clearly visible. The extreme example is the cellar spiders, which carry their eggs glued together in a spherical ball with just a few threads surrounding them. The egg sac is invisible except on close examination, until the spiderlings hatch and the thin silk case can be seen. Spitting spider egg sacs are globular, just under 4 mm across, pale cream in color, and thin enough that the individual eggs are visible. When the eggs are ready to hatch, the female hangs the sac in a network of threads, loosening the threads of the sac to help the spiderlings emerge.

Flattened/Lenticular, Attached to Substrate

Many spiders make round, flat egg sacs that they attach firmly to rocks, bark, leaves, or other substrates. Some are tough and thin-walled, whereas others have a looser mesh of silk. Flattened egg sacs are made by virtually all of the Dionycha—the group of hunting (non–snare-building) spiders that includes the sac spiders, ground spiders, jumping spiders, and crab spiders—as well as certain members of other groups.

Antmimic Spiders

Some shiny, tough, flattened, disc-shaped egg sacs, usually found attached to the undersides of stones, are made by antmimic spiders (Corinnidae). Those of *Phrurotimpus* range from brown to bright red. *Castianeira* egg sacs often have a metallic luster and can be found attached to the surfaces of stones in pastures. Usually the eggs are visible as round bulges in the surfaces of these smooth sacs.

Left: A *Phrurotimpus* antmimic spider (Corinnidae) egg sac (7 mm), attached to the underside of a rock. (MA) *Right:* The shiny metallic egg sac of a *Castianeira* antmimic spider (Corinnidae). (MA)

Ground Spiders

Egg sacs of ground spiders (Gnaphosidae) may be shiny, pink or white, papery, lens-shaped discs attached tightly to the undersides of stones. Some species spin irregular retreats or sacs in which they live and make their egg sacs. *Zelotes* species make tough, white, pinkish, or brown nipple-shaped egg sacs, either covered with debris or lacquered with saliva and excrement to form a smooth, hard covering that deters predators. *Callilepis* egg sacs resemble those of *Zelotes* but are always white; those of *C. pluto* are deposited within the female's small, irregular web. *Drassyllus rufulus* makes a typical flat gnaphosid egg sac, consisting of two circular sheets of silk with the eggs in between, attached to the underside of a stone; the outer sheet is often covered with dirt or mud for camouflage.

Other gnaphosids make egg sacs that are not so tightly attached to the substrate. *Cesonia bilineata* makes a snowy white egg sac, which she loosely fastens to the lower side of a stone. *Gnaphosa muscorum* makes a snowy white, flat, round egg sac, 12 mm or so in diameter. The female is often found resting on it with some of her legs wrapped around it, in a shallow hole partly lined with silk. The parson spider (*Herpyllus ecclesiasticus*) makes an egg sac similar to this, but within a silk retreat. *Scotophaeus blackwalli* deposits 100 or so eggs in a thick, white egg sac, enclosed in a spacious silken chamber shared with the female.

Sheetweb Spiders

Many of the smaller sheetweb spiders (Linyphiidae) produce small, flat egg sacs, attached to stones or the bark of trees, away from the web. Those of dwarf spiders (Erigoninae) are often papery, containing just a few unusually large eggs, and found on the undersides of stones. The egg sacs of a British species of *Erigone* are nipple-shaped and covered with a waterproof papery layer of silk that may be pinkish or yellow-tinged, resembling the egg sacs of *Zelotes* but much smaller. One female may plaster four or five of these to the underside of a stone close to her web.

A meshweb weaver (Dictynidae) with her 2- to 3-mm egg sacs on the underside of a leaf. (MA)

Meshweb Weavers

Meshweb weavers (Dictynidae; e.g., *Dictyna* and *Emblyna*) make snowy white, relatively thick, lens-shaped egg sacs, usually in or near the web. A single female produces several of these, placing them side by side in an overlapping series.

Zorids

Female zorids (*Zora*) guard their egg sacs without any kind of silken retreat. *Z. pumila* lays about 24 yellow eggs in a loose bundle, surrounds them with a small amount of loose silk, and then covers them with a white sheet through which the eggs can still be seen indistinctly. This sheet extends well beyond the bundle of eggs, giving the egg sac a particularly flattened appearance. The sac may be on the underside of a rock or on vegetation, and depending on the substrate, it may be irregular in shape or a neat oval with smooth edges.

Crab Spiders and Others

Probably the largest of the flat, disc-shaped egg sacs are made by the selenopid crab spiders. They are white, smooth, very flat (without bumps indicating the positions of individual eggs), about 1.2 inches (3 cm) across, and concealed in crevices, where they are tightly sealed to the substrate and left unattended.

Egg sacs of philodromid crab spiders are very flat like those of selenopids but smaller, ranging from a few millimeters to about 2 cm across. Many are guarded by the mother. In some, the individual threads are visible; others are densely woven and stretched taut so that they are smooth and almost look like some sort of fungus. Some of this latter type are often made in the forks of twigs; others are made on leaves or stones.

Some *Xysticus* crab spiders (Thomisidae) make smooth, white, dome-shaped egg sacs, about 2 cm across, with the margins tightly fused to the substrate. *Oxyopes* lynx spiders make similar ones, but closer to 1 cm across (or smaller), and sometimes with a covering of looser, straight threads that extends well beyond the margins. Egg sacs of some thomisid crab spiders are also about 1 cm, with a similar covering, but the sac itself has a more cottony texture. Recluse spiders (Sicariidae) make soft, white, disc-shaped egg sacs among their characteristic webbing, with a diameter longer than the spider's body. A brown recluse (*Loxosceles reclusa*) egg sac is about an inch across. A grass spider (Agelenidae: *Agelenopsis*) deposits a small, disc-shaped egg sac and covers it with a planoconvex (sometimes elliptical) mass of white silk, 8 to 25 mm

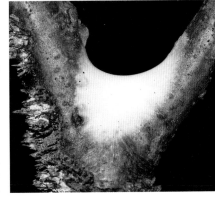

Egg sac (7 mm) of *Philodromus*, a philodromid crab spider. (MA)

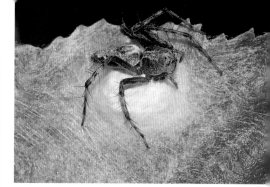

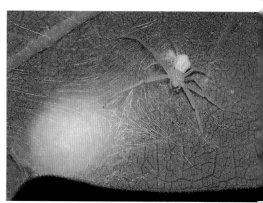

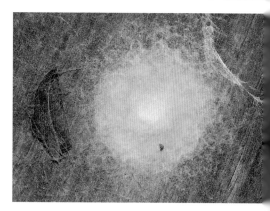

Above: Oxyopes tridens (Oxyopidae), a lynx spider, with her 1-cm egg sac. (AZ) *Top right:* A western lynx spider (Oxyopidae: *Oxyopes scalaris*) with her 7-mm egg sac. (ID) *Second to top right:* A thomisid crab spider with her 1-cm egg sac. (MA) *Third to top right:* Egg sac (1 inch [2.5 cm]) of a brown recluse (Sicariidae: *Loxosceles reclusa*). (TN) *Bottom right:* A funnel-web spider (Agelenidae) guarding her 1.2-inch (3-cm) egg sac. (MA)

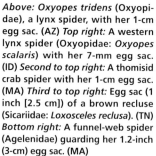

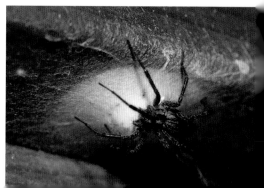

in diameter, and often the female dies still clinging to it. It may be attached to vegetation, or in a protected place such as under loose bark, and it may be partly covered with bits of rotten wood or other debris. Several sacs may be made close together.

Triangle Spider

The egg sac of a triangle spider (Uloboridae: *Hyptiotes*) is flat, more or less elongated, and closely applied to a twig. It is about 6 mm long, covered with a somewhat larger sheet of dirty gray or olive green parchmentlike silk, and always has several pimply bumps.

Dwarf Sheet Spiders

At least some dwarf sheet spiders (Hahniidae: Hahniinae) produce small, lens-shaped egg sacs that are attached to a surface rather than suspended in a web. Those that have been described had fewer than 10, relatively large eggs.

Fluffy, without a Papery Covering

Members of several spider familes make more or less spherical, fluffy egg sacs without a papery outer covering. Some are suspended by silk threads, in a web or otherwise; others are loosely or broadly attached directly to a substrate.

Pirate Spiders

Pirate spiders (Mimetidae) suspend fuzzy egg sacs from rocks, twigs, and other objects, or sometimes from the web or retreat of another spider they have preyed on. *Ero* makes a somewhat pear-shaped, pale brown bag, about 3.5 mm in diameter, covered with an irregular, loose network of coarse, curly, reddish brown silk. This loose covering is twisted together at the top to form a 5- to 25-mm pedicel from which the sac is hung in a cavity, such as beneath a stone or under boards. The egg sacs of *Mimetus hesperus* and *M. puritanus* are of similar construction but larger and bright orange. Those of the latter are oblong, tapering equally at both ends. The egg sac of *M. notius* is about 6 mm across and similar to others in its genus, but the dense central section is white, and the 1 mm thick, curly outer layer is brown. The distinctive feature of this egg sac is a thin, subspherical to elliptical net of silk, 20 to 25 mm across, that completely surrounds it. The sole member of the remaining North American pirate

Egg sac (4 mm wide) of a pirate spider, *Ero* (Mimetidae). (MA)

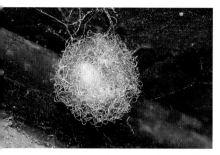

Egg sac of another pirate spider, *Mimetus* (Mimetidae). (MA)

spider genus, *Reo eutypus*, makes loosely woven egg sacs that are pale yellowish white.

Cobweb Spiders

Many cobweb spiders (Theridiidae) make soft, white or tan, fluffy, spherical egg sacs, generally slightly larger than the body length of the spider, which are often suspended in the web. *Theridion frondeum*, a common species in eastern fields and forests, makes a dense, opaque, pure white sac, 4 mm across, and the female may be found with it in a partly folded leaf. The triangulate cobweb spider (*Steatoda triangulosa*), commonly found in basements, creates several loosely woven, spherical, white egg sacs, about 6 mm across, which may be suspended in the web or attached to the ceiling. The eggs inside are plainly visible when present.

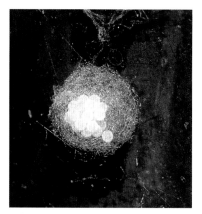

Left: Egg sac (6 mm) of the triangulate cobweb spider (Theridiidae: *Steatoda triangulosa*). (MA) *Right:* An example of a denser cobweb spider (Theridiidae) egg sac (6 mm). (MA)

Orbweavers

Many orbweavers (Araneidae) enclose their eggs in fluffy masses of silk with no definite outline. Since their webs are usually temporary, the egg sacs are generally attached to vegetation or other surfaces. The delicate egg sac of the shamrock orbweaver (*Araneus trifolium*) is whitish, about an inch in diameter, and contains several hundred eggs, which can be seen through the silk. *A. miniatus* guards 2 or 3 white, woolly, spherical egg sacs in folded leaf retreats enveloped in strands of silk. *Araniella displicata* similarly makes a fluffy, entangled mass of yellow silken threads, about 8 mm across, within a rolled-up leaf. The spinybacked orbweaver (*Gasteracantha*

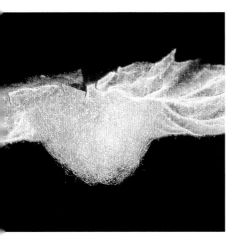
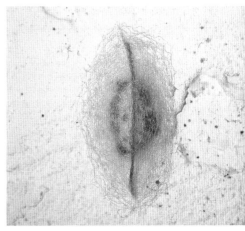

Left: The yellow, fluffy egg sac of an orbweaver (Araneidae). (MA) *Right:* Greenish egg sac of the spinybacked orbweaver (Araneidae: *Gasteracantha cancriformis*). (FL) Photo by Jeff Hollenbeck.

cancriformis) makes loose, fluffy egg sacs with distinctive green silk. The starbellied orbweaver (*Acanthepeira stellata*) deposits its eggs on a leaf and encloses them in a mass of loose, brown silk.

Long-jawed Orbweavers

Long-jawed orbweavers (Tetragnathidae) also generally make soft, fluffy egg sacs. *Tetragnatha* egg sacs have characteristic tufts of silk, which in at least some species are a distinctly different color from the rest of the sac, giving the appearance of a coating of foreign matter. They are attached to twigs and other objects. The oval to elongate, planoconvex, closely fused egg sacs of *T. elongata* are sparsely covered with threads of beadlike, greenish silk. The egg sac of the orchard spider (*Leucauge venusta*) is loose and fluffy, made of orange-white silk, 8 to 9 mm in diameter, and contains several hundred eggs. *Meta ovalis* suspends large, loosely textured, snowy white, oval sacs by several short threads—or sometimes one long string—from the walls of caves. The sac is translucent and the ball of eggs can be seen within.

Egg sacs of *Tetragnatha elongata* (Tetragnathidae), a long-jawed orbweaver. The egg sac of a ray spider (Theridiosomatidae: *Theridiosoma gemmosum*) is visible in the background. (PA)

Sheetweb Spiders

At least some of the larger sheetweb spiders (Linyphiidae: Linyphiinae) make white, fluffy egg sacs. The filmy dome spider (*Neriene radiata*) makes loosely woven masses of white silk surrounding 80 or so nonagglutinated yellow eggs. These egg sacs are about 7 mm across and 4 mm high and are hidden in leaf litter. Egg sacs of a hammock spider (*Pityohyphantes costatus*) have been found toward the tips of spruce twigs, between the bases of the needles, protected externally by a loose network of threads. The egg sac itself is white and globular, about 6 mm in diameter, and composed of crinkled flocculent silk. As with the filmy dome spider, the pale whitish eggs within roll about freely.

Hacklemesh Weavers

The egg sac of the hacklemesh weaver *Callobius bennetti* (Amaurobiidae) is a flat and loosely woven bag, attached near the web to a stone or other object, and covered with an irregular mesh of threads. Arachnologist Darrell Ubick describes *Callobius* egg sacs from the Sierras as being quite fluffy, covered with and surrounded by cribellate silk (see chapter 6), and located inside the female's retreat.

A wolf spider (Lycosidae) carrying her spherical egg sac (5 mm), attached to her spinnerets. (AR)

Relatively Firm, Spherical or Flattened, Free (Not Associated with Web)

In certain spiders, the female spins a single, tightly woven egg sac in the form of a ball or pouch, which she then either carries around with her or loosely attaches to a substrate and guards. With the exception of those of nursery web spiders, none of these egg sacs is ever associated with a web.

Wolf Spiders

Wolf spiders (Lycosidae) make more or less spherical egg sacs, which the female carries attached to her back end. They are composed of two halves, usually joined by a suture of more delicate tissue, which the female tears open to let the spiderlings emerge. This seam is sometimes obvious but often not. Depending on the species, the sac ranges from a few to 10 mm across and may be white, gray, or tan. *Pirata* and *Schizocosa* egg sacs are spherical and white, with little or no seam visible. The egg sac of *Geolycosa missouriensis* is bluish;

in *Pardosa*, it is somewhat flattened and usually yellowish or greenish, sometimes a deep blue, but becoming a dirty gray as it ages.

Cave Spiders

Cave spiders (Nesticidae) carry spherical white or pale yellow egg sacs around with them in the same way wolf spiders do.

Nursery Web Spiders

Nursery web spiders (Pisauridae) construct more or less spherical egg sacs that the female carries beneath her, held by her jaws, until hanging in a nursery web shortly before the spiderlings emerge. In contrast to a wolf spider's egg sac, it is composed of a single piece. Those of *Pisaurina* are bright white, a bit more than 1 cm across, and may be very smooth or somewhat rough in texture. The egg sacs of fishing spiders (*Dolomedes*) are about 2 cm across. They tend to be coarse in texture and more grayish or brownish, sometimes becoming mottled with brown as the outer layer stretches shortly before the spiderlings emerge. Pisaurid egg sacs lose their shape when they are torn open as the spiderlings emerge.

Giant Crab Spiders

The huntsman spider (Sparassidae: *Heteropoda venatoria*) is a tropical species that has been introduced into southern California, Texas, and Florida. Its egg sac is a large (about 15 to 20 mm across and 6 mm thick), slightly pink-tinged, flattened, disc-shaped, cushionlike bag, containing more than 200 eggs, carried beneath the female's body. Spiderlings emerge through a slit made in the margin of the egg sac. Species of *Olios*, the native giant crab spiders, make large, white, cushion-shaped egg sacs similar to the huntsman spider's. Some guard their egg sacs in place, whereas others, such as the golden huntsman spider (*O. fasciculatus*), carry them as *Heteropoda* does. *Trechalea gertschi* (Trechaleidae; Mexico, small portions of NM and AZ) females carry flattened, bivalved egg sacs with their spinnerets.

Thomisid Crab Spiders

Egg sacs of many thomisid crab spiders are white and lens-shaped, formed of two equal valves joined at their edges. They may be a fairly regular, round, cushion shape, free or barely attached to the substrate, or they may be attached along one straight edge. The diameter of the sac may

Egg sac (6 mm) of a thomisid crab spider with the female hiding beneath. (AZ)

be 6 to 10 mm or more; it is greater than the body length of the female, which generally guards the sac in some hidden place (such as inside a folded leaf or under a log) until she dies. Some *Oxyopes* lynx spider egg sacs may be similar, but they are usually more firmly attached to the substrate and in an exposed location on a leaf or twig.

Papery, Suspended Bag

Other spiders make egg sacs with a closely woven exterior as with the ones described above but do not carry them around or fasten them directly to a substrate. They instead suspend their egg sacs either in a web (as is ultimately done by nursery web spiders) or by a strong silken cord (as with the loosely woven sacs of pirate spiders). Egg sacs in this category may be simple spheres or bags but also come in a variety of distinctive shapes.

Garden Spiders

The garden spiders (Araneidae: *Argiope*) make very large, tan, papery egg sacs that are suspended from vegetation by meshworks of tough threads. The black and yellow garden spider's (*A. aurantia*) is roughly spherical, narrowed at the top, and up to 1 inch (2.5 cm) long. Inside the firm, brown covering (which is whitish or yellowish when first made) is a thick layer of fluffy silk, and inside this is a silken cup containing the eggs. The banded garden spider (*A. trifasciata*) makes a hemispherical or kettledrum-shaped egg sac with a distinctly flattened top. The egg sac of the silver garden spider (*A. argentata*) is somewhat flattened from side to side and drawn out to several points along its edges. The silk may have a greenish tinge.

Left: Egg sac of the black and yellow garden spider (Araneidae: *Argiope aurantia*). (FL) Photo by David Almquist. *Above:* Egg sac of the silver garden spider (Araneidae: *Argiope argentata*). (FL) Photo by Jeff Hollenbeck.

Egg sacs of a bolas spider (Araneidae: *Mastophora*). (GA) Photo by Carmen Champagne.

Bolas Spiders

The bolas spiders (Araneidae: *Mastophora* spp.) make globular egg sacs, about 15 mm wide, that each hang from a thick rope as long as or longer than the main body of the sac. The rope is broadly attached to the silk lines or vegetation from which it hangs. The egg sac of *M. bisaccata* is uniformly brown, with several pointed appendages in a ring around the base. Others may lack these projections and may be mottled light and dark. A single female may hang as many as a dozen egg sacs in close proximity.

Ray Spiders

Ray spiders (Theridiosomatidae: *Theridiosoma*) make distinctive, golden brown, somewhat pear-shaped bags, 3 mm long, each of which is suspended by a single thread, up to 1.6 inches (4 cm) long, that is often forked at the top. The top of the sac is a separable cap, which is partly pushed off when the spiderlings emerge. The egg sacs of *T. gemmosum* are especially common in damp areas, and there are often many in close proximity.

Cobweb Spiders

Other tan, papery-textured egg sacs are likely the work of cobweb spiders (Theridiidae). Theirs are usually rounded and lack any sign of a seam, because they are rotated while the outer layer of silk is spun, and they are often suspended in the web. Most often seen are those of the common house spider (*Parasteatoda tepidariorum*). They are pear-shaped, ovoid, or roughly spherical, generally a bit lumpy and irregular, measuring 6 to 9 mm. One female often makes many egg sacs. *Achaearanea globosa* egg sacs are cream-colored and diamond-shaped, pointed at both ends. Those of the

Egg sac (3 mm long) of a ray spider (Theridiosomatidae: *Theridiosoma gemmosum*). (PA)

Left: The common house spider (Theridiidae: *Parasteatoda tepidariorum*) with two egg sacs (each about 8 mm long). (NY) *Right:* A southern black widow spider (Theridiidae: *Latrodectus mactans*) and her egg sacs (each about 1 cm). (TN)

three black widow species (*Latrodectus*) are large (10 to 12 mm in diameter), very smooth, and nearly spherical or somewhat pear-shaped (up to about 14 mm long); they are whitish to light brown, and may have a grayish tinge. Southern black widow (*L. mactans*) egg sacs are usually nearly spherical and generally have a conspicuous nipple at the top; those of northern black widows (*L. variolus*) tend to be more pear-shaped and spread at the top. The red widow (*L. bishopi*), found in dry habitats in Florida, makes a similar smooth, globular egg sac that is whitish. Many smaller cobweb spiders make egg sacs that look more or less like miniature versions of those made by house spiders and black widows.

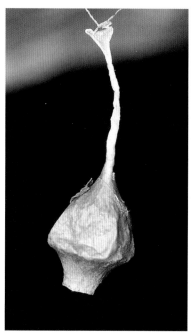

Acanthepeira orbweavers (Araneidae) make papery brown egg sacs that are nearly spherical like those of black widows, but somewhat crinkly like those of the common house spider. They are about 6 mm long.

The kleptoparasitic cobweb spiders (Theridiidae: Argyrodinae) make a distinc-

Egg sac (5 mm) of *Neospintharus trigonum*, a kleptoparasitic cobweb spider (Theridiidae: Argyrodinae). (MA)

tive smooth, lantern-shaped egg sac suspended by a thick cord. The one made by *Neospintharus trigonum* is 6 mm long, with a conical top portion and a lower part contracted into a narrow neck. It is white when first made, later turning brown, and the cord from which it is suspended is about twice as long as the sac. Other species of *Neospintharus*, *Argyrodes*, and *Faiditus* produce variations on this shape, with or without a thick cord. *Rhomphaea fictilium*'s egg sac is yellowish and shaped like a slender vase, about the same size as the spider (6 to 12 mm).

Lampshade Weavers and Barn Funnel Weaver

Each female lampshade weaver (Hypochilidae: *Hypochilus*) spins several small, roughly spherical egg sacs, which are suspended in messy-looking clusters on silk threads near her web under a rock ledge. Those of *H. bonneti*, at least, are covered with bits of detritus. The barn funnel weaver (Agelenidae: *Tegenaria domestica*) hangs messy-looking dirty-white egg sacs from ceilings of man-made structures using a few strands of silk.

Hackled Orbweavers

The hackled orbweaver *Zosis geniculata* (Uloboridae; S) makes a pale pinkish brown sac, about 6 mm in diameter, that is flattened with a starlike outline and suspended in the web. The egg sac of *Uloborus diversus* is similar. *Gea heptagon*, an araneid orbweaver, makes a similarly shaped egg sac that is about 13 mm across and white with streaks of dark silk. It is flattened with a bulging center and drawn out in several straight-edged, pointed lobes, suspended in a sparse tangle web (away from the orb web) by silk strands emanating from the corners.

Uloborus glomosus places a few light brown, elongate sacs, somewhat larger than her body and decorated with irregular bumps or spikes, in a line along a radius of her web and aligns her long body with

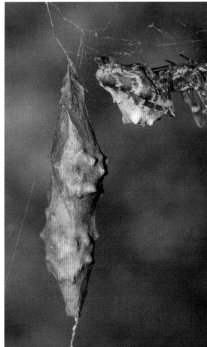

Above: Egg sac of *Zosis geniculata* (Uloboridae), a hackled orbweaver. (FL) Photo by Jeff Hollenbeck. *Right: Philoponella oweni* (Uloboridae) and her 12-mm egg sac. (AZ)

them. *Philoponella oweni* (SW) constructs brown egg sacs covered with similar spikes; the sacs, 5 to 6 mm long and 3 to 5 mm wide, are more or less flat on one side and domed on the other, something like a tiny green lynx spider egg sac. Two may be combined into one elongate sac about 12 mm long. The egg sac is hung under a rock or log near the web, and like the green lynx, the female stays with the egg sac until the young emerge. *P. arizonica* (SW) females make pale, whitish, spindle-shaped egg sacs, usually smooth but occasionally decorated with spikes, each 5 to 9 mm long and about 3 mm wide. The first is suspended from the center of the web, and a new one is added every few days, until a long, slender stick of up to 8 sacs has been formed—something like what *U. glomosus* does, except oriented perpendicularly.

Orbweavers with Egg Sac Chains

Like the uloborids mentioned above, several different araneid orbweavers also have the habit of arranging several egg sacs in a string or chain. The trashline orbweavers (*Cyclosa*) add series of egg sacs to the "trashline" sta-

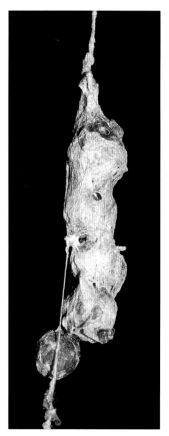

bilimenta in their webs (see chapter 6). The egg sac chains of *Allocyclosa bifurca*, containing up to 8 or so elliptical, somewhat bumpy sacs, may persist long after the web is gone; Comstock (1940) described them hanging from the ceiling of a Florida cottage's veranda "by the hundred." A female *Metepeira* (such as the labyrinth spider, *M. labyrinthea*) makes a string of lenticular egg sacs near the entrance to her retreat in the labyrinth. The basilica spider (*Mecynogea lemniscata*) suspends a chain of 2 to 6 egg sacs from a strong, horizontal cord above her web. They are spherical and brown, covered with a thin layer of white silk. The string of egg sacs can often be found still held in place the following spring, long after the web is gone.

A Mystery

A very common egg sac in the northeastern United States (and perhaps elsewhere) hangs from a horizontal "clothesline" as does the egg sac chain of the basilica spider. It is a single, rounded bag, about 8 mm long, with upper edges that taper out to the

A 23-mm-long string of old basilica spider (Araneidae: *Mecynogea lemniscata*) egg sacs. (NC)

horizontal thread, forming two points. If it has ever been described before, it has been ignored by all of the literature on spiders we have scoured for clues. Based on the spiderlings that emerged from one we collected, we are convinced it is made by a long-jawed orbweaver (Tetragnathidae) of some sort.

Tough and Brown with Distinct Tufts

The brown widow (*Latrodectus geometricus*) makes tough, perfectly spherical egg sacs, about 1 cm in diameter, covered with regularly spaced tufts of silk. These are often found on or near buildings. The

A mysterious and very common egg sac (8 mm), almost certainly of a long-jawed orbweaver (Tetragnathidae). (MA)

green lynx spider (Oxyopidae: *Peucetia viridans*) makes a tough, brown egg sac that is more or less hemispherical, 12 to 25 mm across, with many small, projecting tufts or bumps (these may be on only the more rounded portion or the whole surface). She anchors it firmly to low vegetation with a maze of threads and guards it tenaciously until the spiderlings emerge. The much smaller *Hamataliwa* lynx spiders make a miniature version of this, 4 mm or so across, and suspend it from a branch by several threads.

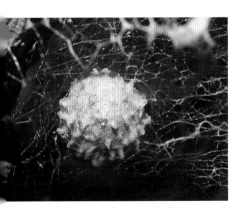
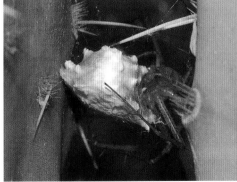

Left: Egg sac (about 1 cm) of a brown widow spider, *Latrodectus geometricus* (Therididae). (GA) *Right:* A female green lynx spider (Oxyopidae: *Peucetia viridans*) guarding her egg sac (about 15 mm) between two prickly pear pads. (AZ)

Debris-Covered

Some spider egg sacs are plastered with layers of mud or decorated with bits of wood, leaves, stones, or other debris, which provide camouflage and further protection from predation and parasitism. This has been noted above in the descriptions of *Zelotes*, *Drassyllus rufulus*, *Agelenopsis*, and

Above: Debris-covered egg sac of *Tegenaria*, a funnel-web spider (Agelenidae), opened to reveal the eggs and internal structure. The unopened 1-inch (2.5-cm) sac was hemispherical with a uniform outer covering of silk. (MI) *Right:* Fluffy egg sac of *Coras* (Amaurobiidae), concealed with bits of debris. (MA)

Hypochilus. Cicurina species (Dictynidae) enclose their eggs in little white sacs, which are covered with bits of earth. The disc-shaped egg sac of the hobo spider (Agelenidae: *Tegenaria agrestis*) is surrounded by a thick layer of small stones and sand or mineral soil, depending on the habitat, and has a thin outer layer of white silk. The finished product is globular, and the egg sac is entirely concealed. Various other funnel-web spiders cover their egg sacs with some amount of debris. We found a *Coras* female (Amaurobiidae) in a woodpile guarding a fluffy, white egg sac that was heavily decorated with bits of debris. *Calymmaria* (Hahniidae) egg sacs are suspended from the underside of the web and are "flattened, angular to somewhat rounded, and covered with a stiff coating of earth" (Ubick et al. 2005). The tiny, obscure leptonetids (S, W) cover their egg sacs with debris and either suspend them from the web or attach them to a substrate.

McCook (1884) described a globular egg sac "about the size of a grape," completely coated in mud, and often found attached by a slender cord of silk to the undersides of boards and other objects on the ground. The spiderlings emerge through the point at the top where the cord is embedded in the mud, and a hole in the side indicates parasitism by an ichneumon wasp. He identified the makers as ground spiders (Gnaphosidae), which he provisionally named *Micaria limnicunae*, while suggesting that they might better be placed in the genus *Herpyllus*. The spider he described has not been linked to a currently valid scientific name. He noted that some egg sacs, apparently made by the same species, had the external case com-

A mud-covered spider egg sac (5 mm wide) evidently belonging to the enigmatic ground spider "*Micaria limnicunae*" (Gnaphosidae). (PA)

posed of bits of old wood, bark, leaves, flowers, insect parts, and only a thin veneer of soil.

Hatching

Spider eggs generally hatch shortly after they are laid, but the spiderlings may stay in the sac long afterward; for instance, in many northern species, the spiderlings hatch in the fall but do not emerge until the spring. In weaker egg sacs, they create a large tear when they emerge, whereas in tough sacs, a few of the spiderlings cut a small, neat, round hole at some point in the sac, and they all emerge one by one through this opening. In a few cases, such as wolf and spitting spiders, the female tears or loosens the sac to help them emerge.

Spiderlings of almost every species molt once before emerging; therefore, opening an egg sac and looking for their tiny exoskeletons under magnification is a good way to confirm that it is in fact a spider egg sac. Cellar spiders and spitting spiders emerge before molting, but in both cases, the spiderlings hang motionless in nearby webbing for several days immediately after hatching until they molt.

Spider Egg Predators and Parasitoids

Spider egg parasitoids include certain frit flies (Chloropidae), such as *Oscinisoma alienum*, *Siphonella oscinina*, and *Pseudogaurax*. A female lays eggs in a partially completed egg sac, and the larvae hatch and feed on the spider eggs after it is finished. Upon emerging from their puparia, the larvae escape the egg sac through an exit hole made by spiderlings that hatch from the eggs they have spared.

Parasitoid wasps, with their long ovipositors, can lay eggs inside the sac after it is finished. Because they have chewing mouthparts, they do not need the help of spiderlings to emerge, and they tend to consume most or

Egg sac of the jumping spider *Phidippus clarus* (Salticidae), opened to reveal the puparia of parasitoid frit flies (Chloropidae: *Pseudogaurax*). (FL) Photo by Jeff Hollenbeck.

all of the eggs. *Arachnopteromalus dasys* (Pteromalidae) larvae develop in the eggs of various uloborids, leaving the egg sacs full of empty spider eggshells and their own pupal skins. Other chalcid and platygastrid wasps leave similar evidence. The solitary larva of many *Gelis* species (Ichneumonidae) develops inside a spider egg sac; transforms in a stiff, white, elongate cocoon; and then chews a hole in the egg sac about 1 mm in diameter through which it emerges. Some other ichneumon wasps have similar habits.

Several mantidfly species (Mantispidae) also develop in spider egg sacs, sucking the eggs dry and making whitish, subspherical cocoons inside. Mantidfly females do not lay their eggs among spider eggs, so the tiny young larvae must actively seek out and bore into egg sacs.

Pirate spiders have been observed eating the egg sacs of their prey spiders.

Egg sac of a nursery web spider (Pisauridae: *Pisaurina mira*), opened to reveal the cocoon of a mantidfly, *Dicromantispa* (Mantispidae). (FL) Photo by Jeff Hollenbeck.

Naked Eggs

At last we come to the plain, unadorned eggs, which are neither inserted in vegetation nor provided with some kind of case or covering. Almost all of the ones you are likely to notice belong to insects. Given how many thousands of species fall into this category, the best we can do here is to give an overview of the characteristics of the eggs of each major group, with a few examples to give a sense of the variation. Most conspicuous eggs will be straightforward to identify to insect order; often it will be possible to determine the family. Pinning down the genus or species is usually not a realistic expectation, although there are exceptions.

First, some general notes on egg location. The context in which you find an egg is an extremely important clue to its identity. Eggs laid on the side of a building are likely from nocturnal insects attracted to the lights at night. They will usually be moth eggs, but you may find eggs of lacewings or certain true bugs in this context; bright lights near a river can also induce stoneflies, mayflies, and caddisflies to attach eggs to flagpoles, gas pumps, and similar lit structures. Eggs laid on leaves may be from either insects with leaf-feeding immature forms, such as butterflies, moths, and leaf beetles, or predators such as lacewings, ladybugs, and syrphid flies. If the former, the plant species can help identify the insect, since most are fairly specific about what plants they eat, and they lay eggs where their young will be able to start feeding as soon as they hatch. If the latter, the plant species is usually of little significance, and the eggs may be just as likely to be laid on bark or some nonliving object. This is not to say that predators always lay their eggs at random; eggs laid among groups of aphids, for instance, are likely to belong to an insect with aphid-eating larvae.

Most conspicuous eggs attached to underwater objects belong to aquatic true bugs, or possibly beetles. The Megaloptera and certain flies deposit their eggs on leaves and other objects over water; dragonflies, mayflies, and stoneflies generally drop or deposit their eggs directly into the water and let them disperse. Eggs of the latter are unlikely to be noticed, except where dragonflies deposit large numbers of eggs that come to rest on vegetation just below the surface.

The eggs most commonly noticed under logs and in similar places are those of slugs and snails, because they tend to be in clusters and are substantially larger than most insect eggs. Many beetles also lay their eggs on or in soil and rotting wood. Dung, carrion, fungus, and rotting fruit are typical places for many flies and certain beetles to lay their eggs. In short, knowing what an insect does as a nymph or larva will usually tell you where its eggs will be found.

Egg size and arrangement can also be important clues to consider. Most insect eggs are in the vicinity of 1 mm long, or perhaps smaller. Nonsnail eggs that approach or exceed 3 mm are likely to be from giant silkmoths, Orthoptera, very large beetles or true bugs, or, if you're lucky, walking-sticks. Laying elongate eggs end to end in a line is a habit peculiar to certain sawflies, leaf-footed bugs, and whirligig beetles. Some true flies, psyllids, and water striders characteristically deposit eggs lying side by side. Certain whiteflies and green lacewings lay their eggs in spirals.

Lacewings, Dobsonflies, Snakeflies, and Relatives (Neuropterida)

Eggs of the Neuropterida are all basically similar: smooth, oblong, and in most cases white or whitish, except for alderfly eggs, which are dark brown. Others may darken before they hatch. Some have stalks or other accessories, but those without can be recognized by the distinctive white knob at one end. This knob marks the location of the *micropyle*, the opening through which sperm reach the actual egg cell within the egg.

Stalked Eggs (Lacewings and Mantidflies)

While working on this book, as we traveled the continent with an eye to tiny details, we encountered the eggs of green lacewings (Chrysopidae) more frequently than any other type of egg, in every region that we visited.

Left: The egg of *Chrysopa oculata*, a green lacewing (Chrysopidae). The egg is about 1.5 mm long, and the stalk about 5 mm. (MA) *Right:* A tight cluster of green lacewing eggs, with the 13-mm stalks twisted together. (MA)

If you're looking for a fun road trip game, every time you get out of the car, see who can find the lacewing eggs first!

Each egg is deposited at the end of a thin, 5- to 13-mm stalk, which the female creates by depositing a drop of fluid on the substrate from the tip of her abdomen, then quickly lifting her abdomen to stretch this drop into a thread. It is often said that the eggs are laid among aphid colonies, but of the dozens of eggs we have found, we saw only one clear instance of this. They may be on plants or just about any other object, and may be single or in clusters. The stalks are said to dissuade ants, and perhaps the other lacewing larvae, from preying on the eggs. *Ceraeochrysa smithi* egg stalks have beadlike droplets of an oily fluid along their length, which the newly

hatched larvae consume as they climb down the stalks. The fluid contains irritants that further deter ants from approaching the egg. The stalks of *Leucochrysa floridana* eggs have similar droplets, but they have a pasty consistency rather than oily, and the larvae do not eat them. *L. floridana* eggs are laid in irregular clusters, whereas *C. smithi* eggs are arranged in a neat spiral. Some

Short-stalked eggs (0.5 mm) of *Climaciella brunnea*, a mantidfly (Mantispidae). (LA) Photo by Mark S. Fox.

other species lay multiple eggs at the end of a single stalk or a number of fused stalks.

The relatively rare beaded lacewings (Berothidae: *Lomamyia*) similarly lay their eggs on stalks, at least sometimes with a cluster of several at the end of a single stalk as is the case with some green lacewings. Beaded lacewing larvae are predators of termites, and the eggs accordingly are laid on rotting wood rather than on foliage. Within twenty-four hours, the eggs develop dark, horizontal stripes from the banded larvae developing inside. Mantidflies (Mantispidae) also lay stalked eggs, but the stalks are much shorter (0.5 to 2 mm or so), and they are deposited in large clusters, often of several hundred.

Owlflies

Owlflies (Ascalaphidae) lay their eggs along twigs, standing upright. Those of *Ululodes* are in two rows on the underside of the twig and are white or light gray, turning slate gray before hatching. They are easily recognized by the series of reddish brown stalks that the female places around the stem a little farther down the twig from the eggs. The stalks, called *repagula*, are actually abortive eggs, and again they function as a physical barrier against ants and are coated with an ant-repellent substance. *Ascaloptynx appendiculatus* lays yellow eggs, turning brown, in a dense clump completely surrounding the twig. Its repagula are contiguous with the viable eggs and look like smaller versions of them. In both genera, the larva hatches by pushing open a neat cap at the top of the egg.

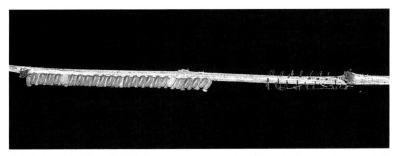

Owlfly (Ascalaphidae: *Ululodes*) eggs and repagula (ant barrier). The egg rows are 1.02 inches (2.6 cm) long. (AZ)

Alderflies and Fishflies

Of the unembellished neuropterid eggs, the most conspicuous are those of the Megaloptera, which are laid on objects overhanging the water bodies where the larvae develop. Alderfly eggs (Sialidae: *Sialis*) are off-white, turning dark brown. They are deposited in a compact mass containing 300 to 900 eggs, most often on the underside of a leaf, and may either stand upright or lie horizontally. Larvae make a jagged tear in the eggshell when they emerge, and a round hole likely indicates the emergence of *Tri-*

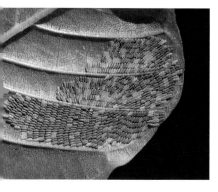

Eggs of an alderfly (Sialidae: *Sialis*). The dark ones are parasitized by chalcid wasps (Trichogrammatidae: *Trichogramma semblidis*). The mass is 17 mm across. (MA)

chogramma semblidis (Trichogrammatidae), a chalcid egg parasitoid. Fishflies (Corydalidae: Chauliodinae) lay their eggs in one to five layers. See page 15 for a description of the conspicuous covered eggs of dobsonflies.

Snakeflies

Snakeflies (Raphidioptera; W) deposit clusters of up to 100 yellowish white eggs under loose tree bark and in bark crevices.

Brown Lacewings, Dustywings, and Antlions

Neuropteran eggs other than the ones already mentioned are unlikely to be noticed. Brown lacewings (Hemerobiidae) lay white eggs, turning cream-colored, gray, pink, or brown, singly or in groups, usually attaching them on their sides to the undersides of leaves. They may also be deposited on buds or in bark crevices. Under magnification, the chorion (eggshell) is densely studded with glossy bumps. Dustywings (Coniopterygidae) lay tiny, flattened, oblong eggs singly on leaves or bark of trees and shrubs. They may be placed among colonies of mites or small insects. Antlions (Myrmeleontidae) deposit rows of 5 to 12 elliptical white eggs, stuck together, in sand.

True Bugs (Heteroptera), Terrestrial

Eggs of true bugs are often distinctively shaped. Many have circular perforations or caps that the nymphs push open when they hatch. Several also have characteristic spines or projections at the top.

Stink Bugs

Stink bug eggs (Pentatomidae) are more or less barrel-shaped and are deposited in compact clusters of a dozen or so (up to about 40 eggs per cluster in some cases), standing upright, on vegetation and other exposed surfaces. The circular lid at the top often has a ring of spines around the edge. These may be too tiny to see with the naked eye, but they are large and prominent in the bronze-colored eggs of *Podisus* species, such as the spined soldier bug (*P. maculiventris*). The eggs are hard-shelled and can be found intact long after they hatch, with the lids neatly pushed open. An irregular hole chewed in the top indicates the emergence of a chalcid or platygastrid wasp parasitoid. Eggs of some are pale green at first, later turning reddish or gray. These include the green stink bug (*Acrosternum*

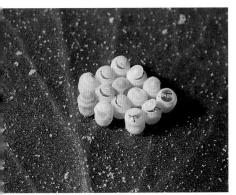

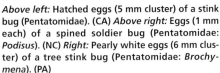

Above left: Hatched eggs (5 mm cluster) of a stink bug (Pentatomidae). (CA) *Above right:* Eggs (1 mm each) of a spined soldier bug (Pentatomidae: *Podisus*). (NC) *Right:* Pearly white eggs (6 mm cluster) of a tree stink bug (Pentatomidae: *Brochymena*). (PA)

hilare), rice stink bug (*Oebalus pugnax*), and conchuela (*Chlorochroa ligata*). Eggs of the tree stink bugs (*Brochymena*) are pearly white. The harlequin bug (*Murgantia histrionica*), on plants in the mustard family, lays striking white eggs with two black bands around the circumference.

Assassin Bugs

Eggs of assassin bugs (Reduviidae) come in a variety of forms, but they are generally elongate-cylindrical, tapering somewhat toward the top, and deposited standing upright. They always have a definite cap at the top, often with a whorl of raylike projections, giving the appearance of a tiny flower. Generally, as in *Sinea* species, the body of the egg is brown and the "flower" is a light tan. Eggs of wheel bugs, among others, are basically similar but are encased in a resinlike substance (see page 10).

Eggs of an assassin bug (Reduviidae) laid on a screen door. (TN) Photo by Kris Light.

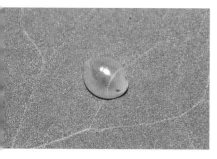

An *Acanthocephala*-style egg (2 mm) of a leaf-footed bug (Coreidae). (OK) Photo by Sam Houston.

Leaf-Footed Bugs

Eggs of leaf-footed bugs (Coreidae) come in a variety of shapes and arrangements, but they are always deposited on their sides. Some are more than 3 mm long. *Acanthocephala* eggs are large, oval, and somewhat three-sided in cross section. They are laid singly or in small groups. Rather than a distinct cap, the egg has a perforated ring at one end, forming a line of weakness where the chorion is torn when the nymph emerges. Squash bug (*Anasa*) eggs are similarly shaped but smaller, laid singly or in loose groups of 15 to 50 on leaves or stems of cucurbits. They are shiny and range from pale yellow to brown.

Other leaf-footed bug eggs have a definite circular lid, which is off-center relative to the axis of the egg. *Chelinidea* eggs are oval and brown with whitish blotches. They are laid several in a row along a prickly pear spine, with the lids facing up at an angle from the spine. The western conifer

Below: Leaf-footed bug (Coreidae) eggs (about 1.3 mm each) on a cholla spine, similar to those of *Leptoglossus*. (AZ) *Below bottom:* Eggs (1 mm each) of *Chelinidea*, a leaf-footed bug (Coreidae), one of which has hatched. (AZ)

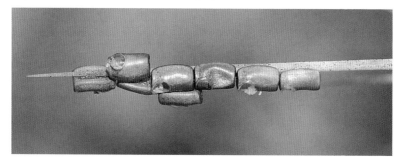

seed bug (*Leptoglossus occidentalis*) lays brown, truncated, cylindrical eggs end to end in a long chain on a pine needle. The circular cap is immediately adjacent to one end of the egg, facing straight up from the needle.

Scentless Plant Bugs

The eastern boxelder bug (Rhopalidae: *Boisea trivittata*) egg is oval with an off-center cap like those of some leaf-footed bugs. It has a round depression on either side, giving it a distinctive shape. The eggs are laid in loose, irregular clusters on a variety of substrates. Freshly laid eggs are red, and the empty shells are golden brown. Eggs of other scentless plant bugs are similar.

Eggs (1 mm each) of a scentless plant bug (Rhopalidae). (MA)

Seed Bugs

The large milkweed bug (Lygaeidae: *Oncopeltus fasciatus*) lays loose clusters of about 15 small, red eggs on its host plant. They are elongate and have three downcurved projections near the tip.

Lace Bugs

Lace bugs (Tingidae) lay their eggs in loose groups on the undersides of leaves, often along the midrib or prominent veins. The eggs are extremely tiny, shaped like kegs with tapered ends. The bottom tip is inserted in a slit in the leaf, and the top has a distinct flip-top lid. Often plant juices ooze from the slits and cover the eggs, drying to form small stalactitelike projections from the leaf.

True Bugs (Heteroptera), Aquatic

All aquatic true bugs attach their eggs to solid objects, usually underwater but sometimes just above the surface. They range from oval to spindle-shaped, and some are on short stalks. On a microscopic level, they often have a hexagonally reticulate pattern on the surface and a prominent micropylar knob.

Giant Water Bugs

The eggs of giant water bugs (Belostomatidae) are the largest aquatic insect eggs, usually around 5 mm long, in some cases swelling to about 7 mm. They are pale brown and capsule-shaped, about twice as long as wide. Eggs found attached to plants or other objects above the water belong to *Lethocerus*. They stand upright, tightly packed, and may be in masses of 100 or more. The eggs of *Abedus* and *Belostoma* are similarly arranged but are carried by the males on their backs, and in the smallest species they

Left: Giant water bug (Belostomatidae: *Abedus*) eggs, attached to the back of the male, whose face is visible peeking out of the sediment in the stream bottom. The bug on top of the 1.1-inch (28-mm) mass is a hatchling. (CA) *Right:* A 23-mm mass of hatched giant water bug eggs found at the bottom of a stream, having sloughed off the male's back. (CA)

are only 2 mm long. You might find them after they have hatched and sloughed off the male's back, still firmly fused in a single mass.

Water Measurers

Water measurers (Hydrometridae) attach their eggs to objects at or just above the surface of the water. They are spindle-shaped, about six times as long as wide, brown, and attached to the substrate by slender stalks.

Water Striders

Water striders (Gerridae) lay elongate brown eggs, usually longer than 1 mm, on their sides, on objects just below the water surface. Several are often placed side by side, parallel but not touching. Eggs of broad-shoul-

dered water striders (Veliidae) are laid in similar locations, but they are oval, white, less than 1 mm, and are laid singly or in irregular clusters. Eggs in both families have a thin, gelatinous coating.

Backswimmers

Notonecta backswimmers (Notonectidae) deposit 2-mm elongate (a little over two and a half times as long as wide), white eggs on their sides, along plant stems and

Eggs (1 mm each) of *Trepobates*, a water strider (Gerridae). (MA)

Eggs (2 mm each) of *Notonecta*, a backswimmer (Notonectidae). (MA)

on other underwater surfaces. They turn brown before hatching. Although they are not tightly packed, many may be laid close together, covering several inches of a stem. Eggs of creeping water bugs (Naucoridae) are also deposited horizontally on submerged objects. They are twice as long as wide, with a buttonlike micropyle, and they change from cream-colored to gray. Eggs in both families develop red eyespots as the embryos mature.

Water Boatmen

The eggs of water boatmen (Corixidae) are small, but they can be conspicuous because they are laid in very large numbers, sometimes forming a dense crust on plants and other submerged objects. The individual eggs are ovoid and somewhat asymmetrical, with a conspicuous micropylar knob at the tip, and attached to the substrate by a very short stalk at the base.

Other Aquatic True Bugs

Several aquatic true bugs lay their eggs out of water, at the bases of clumps of grass or moss. Those of the velvet water bugs (Hebridae) are elongate with rounded ends, surrounded by a gelatinous mass. Eggs of shore bugs (Saldidae) are elongate, tapering and slightly bent toward the tip. Velvety shore bug eggs (Ochteridae) are white, broadly oval, and deposited singly.

Eggs (0.5 mm each) of water boatmen (Corixidae) covering a rock at the edge of a lake. (ND)

True Flies (Diptera), Terrestrial

Eggs of true flies range from oval to long and skinny, often somewhat curved. They are almost always either white or black; a few are yellow or orange. They usually look featureless to the naked eye, but some show beautiful textures when magnified. The tiny spaces in the surface of the eggs trap air and help them breathe when they get wet. Many flies lay eggs on decaying matter, but some deposit them on vegetation or other surfaces where they are easily noticed.

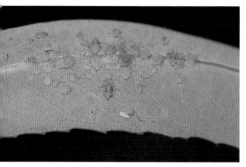 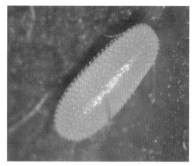

Left: The egg (1 mm) of a syrphid fly (Syrphinae), deposited on the underside of a willow leaf beside a cluster of aphids. (TN) *Right:* A highly magnified egg (1 mm) of a syrphid fly (possibly *Syrphus rectus*). (MA)

Hover Flies

A fun egg to look for, though certainly not the most conspicuous, is that of a hover fly (Syrphidae: Syrphinae) with aphid-eating larvae. These white eggs, about three times as long as wide, are laid singly (rarely two side by side) on their sides, near clusters of aphids, mealybugs, or scale insects. They are distinctively patterned under magnification, and Short and Bergh (2005) illustrate how three species can be separated by the eggs alone: *Heringia calcarata* has longitudinal ribs extending along its whole length; *Eupeodes americanus* is covered with very short longitudinal ribs; and *Syrphus rectus* is covered with blunt, tubular projections. There are at least ten aphid-eating syrphine genera, with others including *Baccha*, *Paragus*, *Pipiza*, and *Toxomerus*.

A non–aphid-eating genus of syrphid flies, *Helophilus*, has aquatic larvae and a distinctive way of laying its eggs. *Helophilus* eggs are similar to those of other syrphids but are laid in neat clusters of several dozen, standing on end, on the undersides of leaves overhanging water.

Horse and Deer Flies

Horse flies and deer flies (Tabanidae), like *Helophilus*, lay their eggs in masses on the undersides of leaves and other objects over water, or over damp ground, to which the larvae drop down when they hatch. A mass contains 100 to 1,000 eggs, 1 to 2.5 mm long and about one-fifth as wide. The eggs are at first creamy white but darken to brown and finally jet black. The eggs often

Two deer fly (Tabanidae: *Chrysops*) egg masses on the undersides of leaves overhanging a pond: freshly laid (left) and somewhat older. (MA)

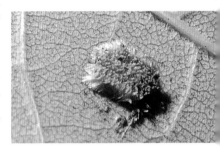

Above: A deer fly egg mass of the more spread-out variety. (MA) *Right:* An older egg mass (about 8 mm) of the species shown on page 56. (MA) *Lower right:* A hatched, single-layer mass (3 mm) of deer fly eggs. (TN)

stand on end (sometimes bent at the base) in a flat-topped compact mass, and typically additional layers are added to this, forming a rounded mound of stacked eggs. Some deer fly (*Chrysops*) eggs are laid nearly horizontally, overlapping each other like shingles.

Aquatic Soldier Flies

Eggs of aquatic soldier flies (Stratiomyidae) are also deposited over water in masses of several hundred. They are elongate, about 1 mm long, pale yellow or cream-colored at first but darkening as they develop. They can appear similar to deer and horse fly eggs but often have a distinct yellow tinge. In the examples we have seen, they are somewhat less elongate (about four times as long as wide) and are always deposited horizontally, though they may overlap or be piled in a mound.

Anthomyiid Flies

Anthomyiid fly eggs are often reticulated like those of some syrphids. The leaf-mining species oviposit on the undersides of

Aquatic soldier fly (Stratiomyidae) eggs, deposited just above the edge of a stagnant pool. The largest mass is 15 mm. (AZ)

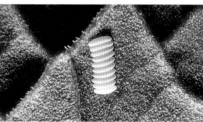

Above: Eggs (1 mm each) of a root maggot (Anthomyiidae: *Delia*) deposited in the charred bottom of a jack-o'-lantern. (MA) *Left:* Eggs (1 mm each) of *Pegomya* (Anthomyiidae), a leaf-mining fly, on the underside of a bitter dock leaf. (MA) *Lower left: Pegomya* eggs greatly magnified to show the reticulations. (MA)

the leaves of their host plants, sometimes singly but often in clusters of up to 8 or so, side by side like sardines. The larvae bore directly from the eggs into the leaf, and the chalky white eggshells remain, providing an easy way to verify the identity of the miner. The spinach leafminer (*Pegomya hyoscyami*) is common in gardens; several other *Pegomya* species lay eggs on *Rumex* (dock) leaves. Eggs of the seed and root maggots (*Delia*) can be found on decaying organic matter and on soil at the base of plants, laid one at a time or in masses. They have distinctive lateral flanges.

Bot Flies

Rodent and rabbit bot flies (Oestridae: *Cuterebra*) lay elongate, white eggs, about 1.5 mm long, in irregular aggregations on twigs and other objects, often near the nests and burrows of their hosts. The eggs stick to the animal's fur when it brushes against them, and the larvae either bore in or are ingested when the animal licks itself. Other bot flies lay their eggs directly on the host animal. See chapter 4 for details.

Small-headed Flies

Small-headed flies (Acroceridae) are internal parasitoids of spiders. Rather than locating a host, the female leaves this to the larvae and instead deposits her minute black eggs on stumps, fence posts, and especially the tips of twigs. They may be in small clusters or rows, or in extensive masses, with several females congregating at one site. Dead sagebrush twigs have been found covered with as many as 20,000 *Ogcodes adaptatus* eggs per linear foot.

Tachinid Flies

Some tachinid flies lay eggs directly on their hosts (see chapter 3 for details), but others deposit them on foliage. As with the small-headed flies, these are tiny (usally less than 0.2 mm long) and black, but they are not laid in large groups: they are meant to be inconspicuous. Like the eggs of trigonalid wasps, they do not hatch until they happen to be swallowed by a leaf-feeding caterpillar. Species with this habit include *Blepharipa pratensis* and *Hyphantrophaga virilis*.

Gall Midges

Although most gall midges (Cecidomyiidae) insert eggs into the tissues of their host plants, some lay elongate orange eggs on the surface of vegetation. Larvae of *Aphidoletes* species are predators of aphids, and as with syrphid flies, their eggs are laid singly among aphids. Eggs of the clover seed midge (*Dasineura leguminicola*) are laid singly or in clusters on or near clover heads, and those of the Hessian fly (*Mayetiola destructor*) are laid in grooves on the upper side of grass leaves.

Other Terrestrial Flies

Certain robber flies (Asilidae: Asilini) usually lay eggs in flowers and other plant crevices. The vast majority of the remaining flies with terrestrial larvae lay their eggs on soil, excrement, or decaying matter. The eggs of some fruit flies (Drosophilidae), although tiny, are distinctive. They have one or two respiratory "horns" that project above the moist food in which they are deposited. The house fly (Muscidae: *Musca domestica*) lays batches of about 100 elongate white eggs on garbage. The march fly *Bibio albipennis* (Bibionidae) digs into loose soil to deposit a mass of 200 to 300 eggs. A female bee fly (Bombyliidae) lays an egg near the entrance of a solitary bee or wasp burrow, where the larva will develop.

True Flies (Diptera), Aquatic

The most commonly noticed fly eggs in water are the gelatinous masses of midges already mentioned (see page 8). Deer and horse flies, soldier flies, and hover flies with aquatic larvae all lay their eggs on objects overhanging water, and they are discussed in the previous section.

The egg (0.5 mm) of a fruit fly (Drosophilidae: *Drosophila melanogaster*), with its characteristic respiratory "horns," on a rotten apple. (MA)

Mosquito (Culicidae) eggs (0.5 mm each) deposited in a dish of rainwater. (MA)

Mosquitoes

Some mosquitoes (Culicidae: *Culex*, *Culiseta*, and *Uranotaenia*) lay their spindle-shaped eggs in floating masses called "rafts," made up of 100 to 300 or more vertically oriented eggs packed together. They start out white, becoming darker as deer fly eggs do. *Anopheles* eggs float singly, equipped with air sacs on the sides. Other mosquito eggs, such as those of *Aedes*, are laid at or above the waterline, where they remain dormant until they become submerged. Look closely at the edges of rainwater-filled saucers neglected on your porch, and you will likely see a dense coating of small, black, pointy mosquito eggs.

Black Flies

Black flies (Simuliidae) lay clusters of tiny (less than 0.5 mm), oval eggs on rocks and vegetation in fast-moving streams. They may lay them at or above the water level, or they may dart in and out of the water to lay eggs on shallowly submerged rocks. Their eggs, too, start out whitish and darken as they develop.

Net-winged Midges

Net-winged midges (Blephariceridae), like black flies, develop in fast-moving streams. Females lay small clusters of eggs on rocks exposed when the water level is lowered or, in some species, crawl into the water and oviposit on submerged rocks. In aquatic entomologist Gregory Courtney's experience, the eggs are dark in color and are usually found in crevices and depressions.

Tiny eggs of black flies (Simuliidae) attached to a rock behind a small waterfall in a stream. (CA)

Brine Flies

Two species of brine flies (Ephydridae) breed only in the hot springs of Yellowstone National Park. *Ephydra bruesi* lays masses of elongate, bright pinkish orange eggs in neutral and alkaline springs, and *E. thermophila* does the same in acidic springs. The eggs are deposited on stones and other objects projecting from the microbial mats; they are most conspicuous in the winter when the mats fade from orange to dark green.

Beetles (Coleoptera)

Beetle eggs range from spherical to elongate, and a few are disc-shaped. They are usually plain-looking in shape and texture, although a few are brightly colored or have appendages. Case-bearing leaf beetle eggs are intricately patterned, but this is because a layer of excrement is packed around them. They are illustrated in chapter 5.

Ladybugs

Ladybugs (Coccinellidae) lay tight clusters of 5 to 50 elongate, bright yellow or orange eggs that stand upright. They tend to be more pointed than the leaf beetle eggs of similar color and size. Eggs of the predatory species may be on tree bark or near an aphid or scale insect colony. The herbivorous species lay eggs on their host plants: the Mexican bean beetle (*Epilachna varivestis*) on legumes, and the squash beetle (*E. borealis*) on cucurbits.

Eggs (7-mm cluster) of a ladybug (Coccinellidae) on a tree trunk. (MA)

Leaf Beetles

The eggs of leaf beetles (Chrysomelidae) are the other beetle eggs commonly seen attached to vegetation. They are attached to foliage of the host plant (usually the undersides of leaves) and are often accompanied by feeding sign of the adults, which are unusual among beetles (but similar to *Epilachna* ladybugs) in having the same feeding habits as their larvae. They are usually elongate and tend to be in tight, upright clusters similar to those of ladybugs. Many species have yellow or yellow-orange eggs, including the swamp milkweed leaf beetle (*Labidomera clivicollis*); three-lined potato

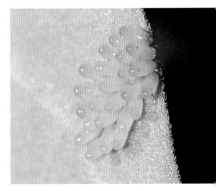

Eggs (cluster about 5 mm) of a three-lined potato beetle (Chrysomelidae: *Lema daturaphila*) on the underside of a jimsonweed leaf. (NV)

Left: Eggs (8-mm cluster) of *Calligrapha serpentina* (Chrysomelidae) on a globe mallow leaf, partially predated. (AZ) *Left center:* Eggs (1.2 mm each) of the common asparagus beetle (Chrysomelidae: *Crioceris asparagi*). (TN) *Left bottom:* Eggs (3-mm cluster) of the waterlily leaf beetle (Chrysomelidae: *Galerucella nymphaeae*). (MA)

beetle (*Lema daturaphila*) and Colorado potato beetle (*Leptinotarsa decemlineata*), both on various nightshades; dogbane leaf beetle (*Chrysochus auratus*); elm leaf beetle (*Xanthogaleruca luteola*); larger elm leaf beetle (*Monocesta coryli*; SE); cottonwood leaf beetle (*Chrysomela scripta*), in clusters of about 50; and spotted cucumber beetle (*Diabrotica undecimpunctata*), in soil near the food plant. The pea weevil (Bruchinae: *Bruchus pisorum*) glues oval, orange eggs, singly or paired, to the outsides of pea pods.

Some leaf beetle eggs are markedly different. *Calligrapha serpentina* (SW) deposits masses of striking reddish orange eggs on globe mallows. The common asparagus beetle (*Crioceris asparagi*) lays dark brown, upright eggs in spaced-out rows, whereas the spotted asparagus beetle (*Crioceris duodecimpunctata*) lays greenish eggs singly on their sides. Eggs of the argus tortoise beetle (*Chelymorpha cassidea*) are laid on morning glory leaves in clusters of 15 to 30, each attached by a pedicel. Golden tortoise beetle eggs (*Charidotella sexpunctata*), also on morning glories, have three spiny prongs. The waterlily leaf beetle (*Galerucella nymphaeae*) lays roughly spherical, whitish eggs in clusters on the upper surface of waterlily leaves. Eggs of the related purple loosestrife–feeding species (*Neogalerucella*) are similar. *Sumitrosis rosea*, whose larvae mine apple leaves, deposits rough, blackish, little eggs in clusters of 1 to 5.

Blister Beetles

Some blister beetles (Meloidae) deposit egg masses on various parts of flowering plants. Their larvae climb onto flowers and ride solitary bees back to their nests, where they complete their development. The eggs of at least some species are elongate with rounded ends, yellow-orange, and deposited sideways in a pile rather than in erect clusters.

Buprestids

The leaf-mining buprestids lay soft, disc-shaped eggs singly on the undersides of leaves of their host plants (see chapter 10 for examples). They are covered with a glistening transparent secretion that spreads over them and gives them the shape of a flattened dome. The hickory spiral borer (*Agrilus arcuatus*) lays similar eggs, about 1 mm long and pale yellowish green, on hickory twigs.

Other Eggs on Vegetation

Various other beetle eggs may be found on vegetation. *Holobus oviformis* (Staphylinidae), a rove beetle that preys on spider mites, deposits minute orange eggs singly on leaves. The clover weevil (Curculionidae: *Sitona hispidulus*) lays tiny, oval eggs on clover leaves and flowers. They start out yellowish and gradually turn black. The red-blue checkered beetle (Cleridae: *Trichodes nutalli*) lays eggs on flowers.

Eggs on Wood

Numerous beetles lay eggs in crevices of bark and wood. Many metallic wood-boring beetles (Buprestidae) and long-horned beetles (Cerambycidae) have elongate, white eggs, some of which are exceptionally large. Those of the introduced Asian long-horned beetle (*Anoplophora glabripennis*) are more than 5 mm. In addition to other wood-boring beetles, eggs on wood and bark may belong to stag beetles (Lucanidae; white and spherical), net-winged beetles (Lycidae), checkered beetles, fire-colored beetles (Pyrochroidae), flat bark beetles (Cucujidae; under bark), pleasing fungus beetles (Erotylidae), and wedge-shaped beetles (Rhipiphoridae).

Eggs (5.5 mm each) of the Asian long-horned beetle (Cerambycidae: *Anoplophora glabripennis*). (MA)

Eggs on or in the Ground

Other beetles lay eggs on or in the ground. Some blister beetles dig holes a few centimeters deep to bury clusters of 100 to 200 white, 2-mm elongate eggs with rounded ends. Soldier beetles (Cantharidae) deposit masses of pale yellow, oblong eggs in soil or among ground litter. Scarab beetles lay spherical or elongate eggs in soil, singly or in groups, in some cases several inches deep. Also deposited in soil are the eggs of click beetles (Elateridae), most ground beetles (Carabidae; usually singly), some carrion beetles (Silphidae), darkling beetles (Tenebrionidae), and root-feeding weevils, leaf beetles, and long-horned beetles. The eggs of

Pyrophorus click beetles (SW) are luminous, as are those of some fireflies (Lampyridae; in damp places) and possibly *Metophthalmus* minute brown scavenger beetles (Latridiidae; S).

Aquatic Beetles

Some aquatic beetles with gelatin-covered eggs have already been noted (see page 9). Perhaps the most distinctive aquatic beetle eggs are those of whirligigs (Gyrinidae). They deposit elongate, cylindrical eggs end to end in parallel rows (or sometimes in clusters) on submerged aquatic vegetation. Predaceous diving beetles (Dytiscidae) that do not insert their eggs may lay them singly on the surface of floating vegetation, in masses at the water's edge, or on various underwater objects. *Peltodytes* crawling water beetles (Haliplidae) lay yellow eggs on submerged vegetation. Some long-toed water beetles (Dryopidae) lay eggs on stems of aquatic plants. Skiff beetles (Hydroscaphidae) lay eggs one at a time on algae in streams. The 1-by-2-mm eggs of trout stream beetles (Amphizoidae; W) have been found loosely fastened in cracks on the underside of a piece of floating driftwood.

Bees, Wasps, Ants, and Sawflies (Hymenoptera)

Hymenopteran eggs are generally capsule- or kidney-shaped. A very small percentage of them are laid in exposed places. Those of social and solitary bees, wasps, and ants are laid in their nests. You can often see the oblong, white eggs of paper wasps (Vespidae: Polistinae) if you peek into their open nest cells. The tiny eggs of ants can be seen when their nests are exposed but should not be confused with their larvae and cocoons, which can appear egglike but are much larger. Most sawflies insert their eggs in vegetation, and most parasitoid wasps insert theirs into their hosts (or sometimes on or near the host, if it is concealed within a cocoon or plant tissue). There are, however, a few exceptions.

Sawflies

The pine false webworm (Pamphiliidae: *Acantholyda erythrocephala*) lays chains of straight, brown, elongate, capsule-shaped eggs, nearly 3 mm long, end to end along pine needles. Several other web-spinning sawflies lay straight or slightly curved elongate eggs, singly or in rows, on conifer needles. They are often white. The plum web-spinning sawfly (*Neurotoma inconspicua*) lays its eggs in a chain along the midrib on the underside of a plum or cherry leaf. The gooseberry sawfly (Tenthredinidae: *Nematus ribesii*) deposits elongate, flattened, cylindrical, whitish eggs end to end along veins on the undersides of currant and gooseberry leaves. Many other tenthredinid sawflies lay exposed eggs singly, such as the cherry fruit sawfly (*Hoplocampa cookei*; W), which deposits white, kidney-shaped eggs on developing cherry and plum blossoms.

Chalcids

Two families of parasitoid chalcid wasps lay their eggs on vegetation, accessing their hosts in roundabout ways reminiscent of the trigonalids.

Five tiny eggs (0.25 mm each) of *Perilampus chrysopae* (Perilampidae), deposited on an aphid-ridden leaf that also had two hover fly eggs. (MA)

The eggs are whitish, elongate ovals with somewhat tapered, curved tips, about 0.25 mm long. *Perilampus chrysopae* (Perilampidae) lays its eggs on aphid-infested foliage, where, with any luck, a green lacewing has also oviposited. The young larva attaches to a lacewing larva and eats it after the lacewing larva has spun a cocoon. *P. hyalinus* and others deposit their eggs on foliage near caterpillars. When the wasp larva encounters a caterpillar, it bores in and looks for the desired host: a braconid, ichneumonid, or tachinid parasitoid. Eucharitids deposit large numbers of tiny eggs on flower buds or the undersides of leaves (some insert them into the outer skin of fruits or other plant tissue). A successful hatchling attaches itself to either an ant or some small insect that is subsequently captured by an ant and gets a ride back to the nest, where the hatchling burrows into an ant larva and devours it after the larva pupates.

Grasshoppers, Crickets, and Katydids (Orthoptera)

Eggs of many orthopterans resemble grains of rice. The brown eggs of Mormon crickets (*Anabrus simplex*; W; actually in the katydid family, Tettigoniidae), about 7 mm long, are deposited in masses of up to 250 in sandy soil or grass clumps. The eggs of short-horned grasshoppers (Acrididae) encased in their "pods" are similarly shaped, though they may be substantially smaller. Carolina leaf-rolling crickets (Gryllacrididae: *Camptonotus carolinensis*; SE) lay their 4-mm eggs in bark crevices. Most true crickets (Gryllidae) lay roughly 2-mm eggs singly in soil or crevices. Jerusalem

Left: Egg (4 mm) of a clear-winged grasshopper (Acrididae: *Camnula pellucida*), deposited on the hood of a car following a fatal collision. (MT) *Right:* Eggs (2 mm each) of a house cricket (Gryllidae: *Acheta domesticus*). (MA)

crickets (Stenopelmatidae) and mole crickets (Gryllotalpidae) both excavate chambers several inches underground and deposit masses of eggs
that are oval, not elongate.

Pygmy Grasshoppers

Probably the most distinctively shaped eggs that are buried in soil are
those of pygmy grasshoppers (Tetrigidae). The eggs of *Tetrix* species have
been described as wine bottle–shaped, with each egg consisting of a 2-
mm-long elliptical portion and a narrower, 0.6- to 0.8-mm horn. They are
laid in clumps, covered with a secretion that at first gums them together
but cracks as they take up water and expand, allowing them to be separated easily. Sometimes the eggs are laid in patches of moss or lichens and
are not covered with soil. Being semiaquatic, pygmy grasshoppers also
sometimes lay eggs underwater.

Eggs (5 mm each) of an angle-wing
katydid (Tettigoniidae: *Microcentrum*). (WI)

Katydids

The eggs of katydids (Tettigoniidae) are
large (5 mm or so), flat ovals, very unlike
the eggs of any other insect. The slate gray
eggs of angle-wing katydids (*Microcentrum*) are especially distinctive because
they are deposited in a line, overlapping
each other like shingles, along a stem or
the edge of a leaf. Often there are two
rows side by side. Other katydids insert
their eggs into the edges of leaves or in
bark crevices.

Aphids and Their Relatives (Sternorrhyncha)

Eggs of scale insects and their relatives
(Coccoidea) are generally hidden under
their mother's remains or in an egg sac.
That leaves aphids, psyllids, and whiteflies
as the main members of this group whose
unprotected eggs you might come across.

Aphids

Although aphids give birth to live young
throughout the growing season, in the fall
they lay eggs that overwinter. These are
often in irregular clusters on the bark of woody plants, frequently a different
species from the summer host. But not always; the pea aphid (*Acyrthosiphon
pisum*), for instance, oviposits on the stems and leaves of alfalfa or clover.
Aphid eggs are oval, about three times as long as wide, hard-shelled, and
shiny black, although they may start out pale green or brown. They are often
more than 1 mm long, surprisingly large given the size of the mother, and

Above: Eggs (about 1.3 mm each) of white pine aphids (*Cinara strobi*). (MA) *Right:* Dogwood aphids (*Aphis cornifoliae*) and their eggs. (VT)

in some cases there is only one egg per female. The white pine aphid (*Cinara strobi*) deposits chains of about eight eggs end to end on pine needles. When you see chickadees and nuthatches picking tiny morsels off of bark in the winter, it is often aphid eggs they are after. Some ant species collect and store aphid eggs, then "pasture" the nymphs in the spring.

Psyllids

Psyllids lay eggs on leaves during the growing season, and in some cases on twigs or buds in early spring. Theirs are much smaller than aphid eggs, about twice as long as wide, pointed at one end, and generally yellow-orange. The potato psyllid (Triozidae: *Bactericera cockerelli*), on a variety of nightshades among other plants, attaches its egg by a hairlike stalk somewhat shorter than the egg itself. The redgum lerp psyllid (Psyllidae: *Glycaspis brimblecombei*), a fairly recent arrival to North America, lays its brightly colored eggs on eucalyptus leaves, either in clusters or side by side in neat, little lines.

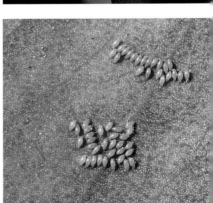

Eggs (0.3 mm each) of the redgum lerp psyllid (*Glycaspis brimblecombei*) on a eucalyptus leaf. (CA)

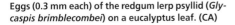

Whiteflies

Whitefly eggs (Aleyrodidae) are similar to psyllid eggs in size and shape, but they are typically pale yellow or brown. Each egg has a short, curved stalk that is inserted in the underside of a leaf. The greenhouse whitefly (*Trialeurodes vaporariorum*) usually deposits its yellowish green eggs side by side in a semicircular arc. The citrus blackfly's (*Aleurocanthus woglumi*) eggs are laid end to end in spirals.

Butterflies and Moths (Lepidoptera)

Eggs on vegetation that do not match any of the preceding descriptions probably belong to moths or butterflies. Their eggs come in a tremendous variety of colors, shapes, and textures. Some are extremely tiny—those of skippers, often deposited in small rows, may be less than 0.1 mm wide—whereas the eggs of giant silkmoths may be 3 mm across. It would take a whole book to do justice to the diversity of butterfly eggs alone. In addition to the different forms, the eggs of various species may be black, white, yellow, green, blue, purple, maroon, pinkish, orange, or brown. Yet there is amazingly little overlap in appearance between lepidopteran eggs and other insect eggs found on vegetation. They are often laid singly, but some are deposited in rows and others in masses of several hundred. Hatchlings typically eat most or all of their eggshells, which are often thin and transparent, upon emerging.

Freshly laid eggs (1 mm each) of a pipevine swallowtail (Papilionidae: *Battus philenor*). (TN)

Swallowtails

Eggs of swallowtails (Papilionidae: Papilioninae) are all more or less spherical and usually laid singly. At 1.2 by 0.8 mm, the egg of the eastern tiger swallowtail (*Papilio glaucus*), laid on the leaves of various trees, is exceptionally large for a butterfly. Pale, smooth, yellowish green eggs of the black swallowtail (*P. polyxenes*) and related species may be found on parsley, carrot, and related garden plants. Eggs of the pipevine swallowtail (*Battus philenor*) are bumpy with varying amounts of orange and purple. They are unusual in being laid in small clusters.

Tiger Moths

Tiger moth (Arctiidae) eggs are smooth and spherical and are often laid in flat

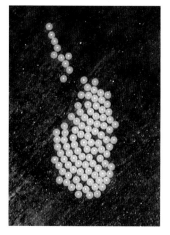

Smooth, spherical eggs of the isabella tiger moth (Arctiidae: *Pyrrharctia isabella*). (MA)

masses of up to several hundred. They are generally yellow or whitish, but those of the Virginia ctenucha (*Ctenucha virginica*) are green. Females in some species cover their eggs with hairs from their bodies. Many tussock moths (Lymantriidae) also lay spherical eggs, which are likewise covered with hairs and are often deposited on the female's cocoon.

Sphinx Moths

Sphinx moth (Sphingidae) eggs are smooth and may be perfectly spherical or somewhat compressed or oval. They are up to

Egg (1.5 mm) of a sphinx moth (Sphingidae) on a jimsonweed leaf. (NV)

about 2 mm across and are either colorless or green. The subspherical eggs often each have a large, round dimple in the top. Many species lay eggs singly, either on the upper or lower surface of a leaf of the host plant. The catalpa sphinx (*Ceratomia catalpae*) is an exception, laying moundlike masses of up to 1,000 translucent eggs, which are about 0.66 by 0.5 mm.

Giant Silkmoths

Eggs of many giant silkmoths (Saturniidae) are smooth, somewhat flattened ovals that lie on their sides. Cecropia moth eggs (*Hyalophora cecropia*) are 3 mm long and cream-colored with irregular brown blotches. Promethea moth eggs (*Callosamia promethea*) are similar but only 2 mm long. Io moth eggs (*Automeris io*) are marked with white and tan and have a conspicuous dot around the micropyle that turns black. They are laid in small masses. Buck moth eggs (*Hemileuca*) are laid in clusters around twigs,

Eggs (3 mm each) of a regal moth (Saturniidae: *Citheronia regalis*), deposited at a light. They would normally be laid singly or in small clusters. (TN)

Above: Eggs (2 mm each) of a promethea moth (Saturniidae: *Callosamia promethea*) on a brick wall. (TN) *Left:* Egg (2.5 mm wide) of a polyphemus moth (Saturniidae: *Antheraea polyphemus*) on the underside of a willow leaf. (MT)

Left: Eggs (1 mm each) of a New England buck moth (Saturniidae: *Hemileuca lucina*). (NH) Photo by Bonnie J. Caruthers. *Right:* Eggs (2 mm each) of an io moth (Saturniidae: *Automeris io*). (LA) Photo by Mark S. Fox.

where they overwinter. They are blue at first but turn olive green. The egg of the polyphemus moth (*Antheraea polyphemus*) is particularly round and flattened, nearly 3 mm across, and laid singly. It is white on the flattened faces and brown around the circumference.

Fall Cankerworm and Rusty Tussock Moth

The fall cankerworm (Geometridae: *Alsophila pometaria*) deposits flat-topped, cylindrical eggs on bark, often encircling a twig, in a tight mass of

Eggs of a rusty tussock moth, *Orgyia antiqua* (Lymantriidae), deposited on its cocoon inside a curled leaf. (VT)

several hundred. The top of each egg has a dark central spot and a dark ring around the edge. Eggs of the rusty tussock moth (Lymantriidae: *Orgyia antiqua*) are similarly marked but not as tall, and they are laid on top of the flightless female's cocoon.

Geometrid Moths

Eggs of many other geometrids are somewhat flattened and squared-off ovals that lie horizontally. They may be smooth, pitted, or otherwise textured, and sometimes have a large depression in the middle.

Cactus Moths

The eggs of cactus moths (Pyralidae: *Melitara* species, native and widespread; *Cactoblastis cactorum*, introduced in SE) are flattened and similar to some geometrid eggs, but their arrangement is distinctive. They are deposited on prickly pears in a "stick" of up to 100 or more, stacked one on top of another to produce a structure that looks like a curved, blunt-tipped cactus spine.

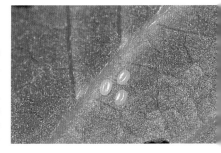

Aquatic Moths

The aquatic moth *Petrophila truckeealis* (Crambidae), common in western streams, lays flat, yellowish eggs on the surface of

Top right: Eggs of an unidentified geometrid (inchworm) moth. The cluster is about 1.5 mm across. (MA) *Right:* Egg (0.5 mm) of the bruce spanworm (Geometridae: *Operophtera bruceata*). (MI)

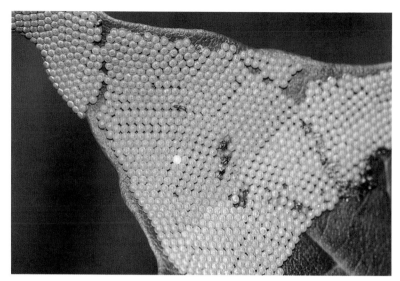

Eggs (0.5 mm each) of the large yellow underwing (Noctuidae: *Noctua pronuba*). (MA)

underwater rocks. They usually overlap slightly and tend to be on algae-covered rocks.

Owlet Moths

Eggs of noctuid moths tend to be shaped like compressed domes, with twenty-nine to fifty ribs converging on the micropylar opening in the center. They may be various muted shades of white, yellow, orange, or brown. Some species lay them singly, but some of the cutworms lay batches of up to 1,500, often in neat, diagonal rows. They are not always deposited on the host plant and sometimes are not even laid on vegetation.

Brush-footed Butterflies

Many butterfly eggs have similar longitudinal ribbing, often with (generally more subtle) horizontal cross lines as well. In most cases, they are laid singly, but mourning cloaks and many checkerspots (Nymphalidae: Nymphalinae) deposit large masses. The egg of the monarch (Nymphalidae: *Danaus plexippus*) is whitish, a little taller than wide, and rounded at the top. It is laid

Egg (about 1 mm) of a monarch (Nymphalidae: *Danaus plexippus*). (MA)

Eggs (about 0.75 mm each) of a painted lady (Nymphalidae: *Vanessa cardui*). The dark one is about to hatch. (MA)

on milkweed, as are the similar eggs of the queen (*D. gilippus*; S) and soldier (*D. eresimus*; Mexico and S tip of TX and FL). Most other brush-footed butterfly eggs are truncated at the top. The green eggs of question marks and commas (*Polygonia*) are sometimes stacked in vertical columns.

Whites and Sulphurs

Egg of a West Virginia white (Pieridae: *Pieris virginiensis*) on the underside of a toothwort leaf. (VT)

The longitudinally ribbed eggs of whites and sulphurs (Pieridae) are spindle-shaped, usually white, and stand more or less upright. Those of most whites (Pierinae) are laid singly on leaves in the mustard family. Examples include the white to pale yellow eggs of the cabbage white (*Pieris rapae*) and the greenish yellow to pale orange eggs of the falcate orangetip (*Anthocharis midea*). The pine white (*Neophasia menapia*; W) lays somewhat fatter, pale green eggs in rows near the tips of pine needles. Many sulphurs (Coliadinae) lay their eggs on legumes.

Other Butterflies

Eggs of admirals and viceroys (Nymphalidae: *Limenitis*) have a honeycomb pattern and are covered with little spikes. They are

Egg (about 1 mm) of a viceroy (Nymphalidae: *Limenitis archippus*) at the tip of a willow leaf. (TN)

laid at the tips of leaves. Eggs of parnassians (Papilionidae: *Parnassius*), metalmarks (Riodinidae), and gossamer-winged butterflies (Lycaenidae) are turban-shaped and finely textured.

Other Invertebrate Eggs

Eggs of most other invertebrates are deposited on or in the ground or underwater. The eggs of fleas, lice, and bot flies, which are found on mammal fur, are described in chapter 4.

Stick Insects

Stick insects (Phasmatodea) have distinctive, fairly large eggs with a definite circular "lid" reminiscent of those on true bug eggs. They are hard and thick-shelled, often described as seedlike. Unlike the eggs of any other terrestrial insect, they usually are simply dropped to the ground from above at random. Lutz (1948) described finding northern walkingsticks (Diapheromeridae: *Diapheromera femorata*) so abundant that the falling eggs sounded like rain. In this species, the eggs are oval, 2 to 3 mm long by 1 to 2 mm wide, with an oblique lid. They may be glossy black, brown, or gray. Eggs of other species are variously narrow, boxy, or rough-textured. Not all are simply dropped; the Colorado short-horned walkingstick (*Parabacillus coloradus*), for instance, glues its eggs to a substrate. It inhabits grasslands, and its smooth, gray eggs resemble grass seeds, 6.2 by 1.2 mm. Amisegine cuckoo wasps (Chrysididae) develop inside the eggs of walkingsticks.

Land Snails

The soft, gelatinous eggs of slugs and other land snails (Gastropoda: Pulmonata) are laid in clusters on or in the soil and are commonly found under logs and in similar places. They are frequently more than 2 mm long and may be spherical or oval. Some slime is often present to confirm their identity. Limacid and milacid slug eggs are translucent and essentially colorless. Those of the gray field slug (Limacidae: *Deroceras reticulatum*) are speckled with white calcium particles on the surface. Arionid slug eggs usually have a calcareous coating, which is at first white or yellow and may eventually turn brown. It can

easily be removed to reveal the translucent egg inside. Eggs of the Pacific banana slug (*Ariolimax columbianus*) are nearly spherical and about 7 mm across. Snail eggs have a thicker, calcium-rich shell, which the hatchlings eat to obtain calcium for their own shells. The oval eggs of Florida tree snails (Orthalcidae: Bulimulinae) are 7 by 5 mm. The Florida apple snail (Ampullariidae: *Pomacea palludosa*)

Tree snail (Orthalcidae: Bulimulinae) eggs (7 mm each). (FL)

Slug eggs (1.5 mm each). (MA)

is an aquatic species that deposits roughly 3-mm, spherical, whitish eggs in clusters on stems above the water. The introduced channeled apple snail (*P. canaliculata*) lays smaller eggs, which are a deep reddish color, in tightly packed masses.

Arachnids

Most arachnids have smooth, spherical eggs. Spiders enclose theirs in egg sacs, and various others carry theirs, guard them underground, or give birth to live young. Harvestmen (Opiliones) insert their tiny, white eggs in soil, vegetation, or other hidden places such as in bark crevices or under rocks. They may be single or in masses of up to several hundred. Engorged female hard ticks (Ixodidae) produce agglutinated masses of up to a few thousand translucent brown eggs and then die. Soft ticks (Argasidae) produce several small masses throughout their lives. The spherical eggs of spider mites (Tetranychidae), found on vegetation, are large, relative to a spider mite, at about 0.1 mm across. Some are colorless, and others are bright red, as are the slightly elliptical eggs of some false spider mites (Tenuipalpidae). They can occur

Spherical eggs (about 0.1 mm each) of spider mites (Tetranychidae). (MA)

Horseshoe crab (Limulidae: *Limulus polyphemus*) eggs (1 to 3 mm) washed up on a beach. (NJ)

in large enough numbers to give branches a reddish cast. Eggs of other mites, as small as 0.02 mm across, are often seen while examining objects under a microscope. The eggs of the predatory bdellid mites are elliptical, larger than spider mite eggs, and covered with clublike projections.

Horseshoe Crab

Piles of small (1- to 3-mm), blue-green, slightly irregular balls in Atlantic bays are the eggs of horseshoe crabs (Limulidae: *Limulus polyphemus*). These "crabs," which are actually most closely related to the arachnids, come ashore in huge numbers during spring high tides to spawn. Eggs are laid in clusters in bowl-like depressions dug in the intertidal zone, and many later wash up onshore, marking the tide lines with a bluish streak. If you look closely, you will see a good variety of color in the eggs, including reds, purples, yellows, blues, and greens. As the eggs develop, they expand with water and become translucent. Looking into a developed egg, you can clearly see an active miniature horseshoe crab spinning circles within.

Crustaceans

Crustaceans also have spherical eggs, but in general, the female carries them until they hatch. Those that inhabit temporary habitats such as vernal pools—ostracods, copepods, fairy shrimp (Anostraca), cladocerans, and clam shrimp (Diplostraca)—produce tiny, cold- and drought-resistant eggs that may lie dormant for years until water returns.

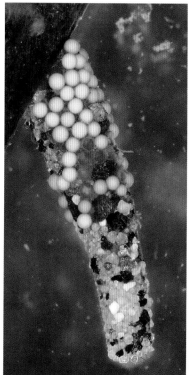

A caddisfly case (about 1 cm long) partially made of fairy shrimp (Anostraca) eggs. (OH) Photo by Judy Semroc.

Springtails

Springtail (Collembola) eggs are also spherical and are laid in batches. They are typically 0.1 to 0.2 mm across, but those of the smallest species are correspondingly smaller. They swell considerably during development.

Myriapods

Pauropod eggs are perfectly spherical, pearly white, and 0.17 mm in diameter, laid singly or in clumps of 3 to 12 in damp, decomposing vegetation. Centipede eggs are spherical, bun-shaped, or somewhat oval, deposited singly or in clusters. Many pseudocentipedes (Symphyla) deposit a clump of 3 to 25 eggs in a hollow in the soil and attach it by a stalk so that the eggs are not touching the soil. The millipede *Polyxenus lagurus* (Polyxenidae) lays its eggs in a string stuck together like beads, arranged in a disc-shaped spiral.

Silverfish

The firebrat (Lepismatidae: *Thermobia domestica*) deposits clusters of about 50 soft, spherical, opaque white eggs, which later turn yellowish. Other silverfish eggs may be oval.

Scorpionflies (Mecoptera)

Common scorpionflies (Panorpidae) deposit oval eggs in small masses in soil. Snow scorpionflies (Boreidae) lay theirs among mosses, on which their larvae feed. Hangingfly eggs (Bittacidae) are rectangular, with a depression in the center of each side, and are laid in marshy ground.

A centipede, *Scolopocryptops sexspinosus* (Scolopocryptopidae), guarding her eggs. (OH) Photo by Judy Semroc.

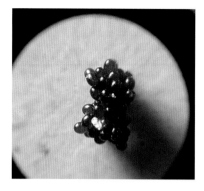

One of many perlid stonefly egg masses found attached to a flagpole, to which the stoneflies were attracted by the lights. This mass measures 3 mm. (PA)

Stoneflies

In inspecting man-made structures that are brightly lit at night, we have come across little blackberrylike masses, a few millimeters across, of soft, brown eggs. These are the doomed egg masses of stoneflies (Plecoptera), meant to be deposited in water but misplaced because their mothers were hypnotized by the lights. All stoneflies produce similar loose egg masses that dissipate in the water, with eggs sticking individually to submerged solid objects. In some species, the eggs are spherical and have a sticky coating. Eggs of other species lack this coating and instead have an adhesive plate; these eggs come in a variety of shapes and textures but are generally longer than wide.

Mayflies

Egg mass (1 mm) of a mayfly (Potamanthidae: *Anthopotamus neglectus*) attracted to gas station lights. (TN)

A closer look among the ill-fated stonefly eggs sometimes reveals yellow specks, just a millimeter long, which under magnification prove to be similar egg clusters, but more elongate in shape. These are the eggs of mayflies (Ephemeroptera), which, like stonefly eggs, would normally be dropped into the water. The yellow specks are not representative of all mayfly eggs, which can have a variety of shapes, microscopic patterns, and appendages. Some are laid individually on stems. *Heptagenia* (Heptageniidae) eggs have filaments at both ends that entangle aquatic vegetation and keep them from sinking to the bottom. *Baetis* (Baetidae) females crawl under the water in streams to lay eggs in distinctive 6-mm-square patches, containing up to 300 eggs, on the undersides of rocks.

Dragonflies

Eggs of dragonflies (Odonata: Anisoptera) are elliptical, up to about twice as long as wide, and about 0.5 mm long. They are whitish at first, turning brown, and may or may not be suspended in a gelatinous matrix. Most species deposit them directly in the water. Some lay eggs one or a few at a time, the female hovering and repeatedly dipping her abdomen into the water. Common skimmers (Libellulidae) often deposit their eggs on shin-

Eggs (0.5 mm each) of blue dasher dragonflies (Libellulidae: *Pachydiplax longipennis*). (TN)

ing objects such as floating leaves and algae-covered rocks. They sometimes mistake shiny surfaces such as the tops of cars for water and deposit their eggs there.

Egg Predators and Parasitoids

Some parasitoids of particular kinds of eggs have already been mentioned, but this section briefly summarizes egg parasitoids as a group. Tiny wasps in the families Mymaridae, Trichogrammatidae, and Platygastridae oviposit in, and complete their development entirely within, the eggs of other insects and spiders. They use a wide variety of hosts, and some members of all three families crawl or even swim underwater to oviposit in eggs of aquatic beetles and true bugs. Often every egg in a clutch is parasitized. Sometimes 50 or more trichogrammatids will emerge from a single egg. A

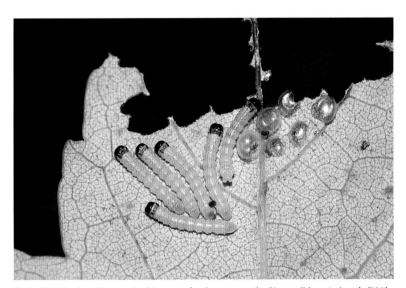

Typical hatched moth eggs, in this case of oakworm moths (Saturniidae: *Anisota*). (MA)

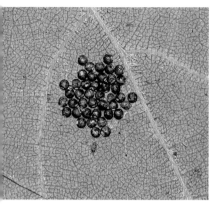

Moth eggs parasitized by trichogrammatid wasps; one of the wasps is visible below the eggs. (TN)

few other chalcids are egg parasitoids, and still others, as well as some braconids and ichneumonids, oviposit in eggs but do not complete development until the host's larval or pupal stage.

The basic sign of these parasitoids is a small, irregular, roughly round hole chewed in the eggshell rather than the typical mode of emergence, such as a neatly popped lid in a stink bug egg or a partially eaten shell in a moth egg. Also, caterpillars that are about to hatch typically secrete enzymes that dissolve much of the shell, making it thin and transparent. Parasitized eggs darken, and the shells of moth eggs stay thick. Eggs containing platygastrids usually turn gray or grayish brown, or occasionally black, and those with trichogrammatids usually turn black.

Several platygastrids have been observed to mark each parasitized egg by using their ovipositors to scratch circles around the point of insertion, as a warning to others that the egg is already taken. Females in this family may stay with the parasitized eggs until their offspring emerge as adults.

Eggs may also fall prey to external predators. When a green lacewing larva feeds on an egg, it leaves the egg intact except for a puncture on either side from its sharp mandibles. Many of the wasps that oviposit in eggs also destroy eggs by piercing them with their ovipositors and then drinking the contents. Some hover flies lay their eggs among ladybug or leaf beetle eggs, and their larvae suck the eggs dry, leaving the soft, collapsed eggshells stuck to the leaf. Ladybug larvae often feed on egg masses of other insects, leaving them munched rather than just drained.

Pupae and Exuviae **2**

Every arthropod, throughout its preadult life, periodically sheds its exoskeleton so that it can continue to grow. Sometimes, as with many caterpillars and millipedes, the cast skin is then eaten to recover the lost nutrients. In other cases, these cast skins, or *exuviae* (always plural, like *pants*), are left in prominent locations and can be the most obvious sign of the animal's presence. Exuviae of crabs and horseshoe crabs are common objects on beaches. Some exuviae are more hidden, or simply very small, but they can be important clues to look for in interpreting feeding sign and other mysteries.

If you ever catch a spider in the act of shedding its skin, stop and watch. It's amazing to see a limp, white, spindly creature extract itself leg by leg, with a slow pumping action, from its old dangling exoskeleton. Exposed, the fresh, vulnerable spider will hang there until it hardens. (We once got a crowd of customers at a rural Tennessee gas station excited about a spider molting on the door.) In general, molting is a dangerous time for inverte-brates. It usually takes a while for the new exoskeleton to harden, and while the crea-ture waits, it is both without its armor and unable to move effectively. Therefore invertebrates tend to choose secluded places out of the reach of predators to shed their skins. A mass emergence of periodi-cal cicadas is an excellent opportunity to witness molting in action. You will see adults burst out of their old skins a pale white color and darken as they harden

Exuviae of a brown recluse (Sicariidae: *Loxosceles reclusa*). (TN)

Exuviae (3 mm) of a carpet beetle larva (Dermestidae) found in the mud nest of a spider wasp. (MA)

over the course of an hour. As with any newly emerged winged adult insect, a cicada must pump blood through its wings to expand them before they dry. Any obstacles to speedy expansion of the wings can leave them permanently malformed.

As a general rule, an insect emerges from its old exoskeleton through a longitudinal slit that opens in the middle of the thorax. The head capsule of a caterpillar often pops off separately because it is harder than the rest of the skin. A woodlouse molts the front and back halves of its exoskeleton at different times. In spiders, the old skin splits along the sides of the body, just above the legs and mouthparts, and the carapace lifts off like a lid. Most spiders hang upside down from a thread, or a few threads, to molt; some spin silken molting chambers. Millipedes also create special chambers in which to molt.

Each life stage between molts is called an *instar*, and there is usually a set number of instars for each species. Tiny spiders, for example, may molt only twice, whereas a tarantula may require more than twenty molts to reach maturity. In insects with *simple*, or *incomplete*, metamorphosis, the immature forms are called *nymphs*, or *naiads* if they are aquatic. They generally look just like smaller, wingless versions of the adults, as is the case with grasshoppers, but sometimes the resemblance is not obvious, as with dragonflies. There are stumpy "wing buds" where the wings will eventually be. In virtually all cases, the final immature instar is as active as the previous ones, and the adult insect simply emerges from the last nymphal skin.

In insects with *complete* metamorphosis, the immature forms usually look nothing like the adults. A major transformation takes place during the final immature stage, which is less active than the others, if not completely inactive. This is the *pupal* stage; the form is called a *pupa*, and all the previous immature forms are called *larvae*. The act of becoming a pupa is called *pupation*. When the larva stops feeding and its body begins to contract, it is referred to as a *prepupa*. *Exarate* pupae have free appendages (legs and antennae), and in some cases, the pupal skin might be confused with that of a nymph. *Obtect* pupae do not have free appendages, and they are more cryptic objects. This is the form of nearly all butterfly and moth pupae. Certain fly larvae retain their last larval skin when they pupate, and it hardens to form a *puparium*. Fly puparia may be nearly featureless but can be recognized by a pair of more or less prominent projections, called *spiracles*, which are respiratory structures.

Adult insects do not molt, with the exception of jumping bristletails (Microcoryphia). Among some of the more primitive spiders, long-lived mature females may continue to molt, which, as with spider molting in general, offers an opportunity to gradually replace missing limbs. Some myriapods gain legs in early molts: young millipedes have only six legs, and centipedes in Lithobiomorpha and Scutigeromorpha start with just seven pairs, gaining the rest when they molt. Many insect larvae that feed on dry materials, such as clothes moths and carpet beetles, may continue to molt and become smaller with each molt if the food supply is limited.

Naiad Exuviae

Exuviae of dragonfly, damselfly, stonefly, and mayfly naiads are often found clinging to rocks and vegetation along water bodies. A mature naiad crawls a short distance out of the water in which it has developed, holding firmly on to whatever surface it finds so that the winged adult is able to climb out of its old skin. Usually this occurs within a few feet of the water, but dragonfly naiads have been observed crawling up to 150 feet (45 m) from the water and up to 20 feet (6 m) vertically before settling on a spot. We once found a tiny stonefly skin clinging to a twig on a bluff more than 100 feet (30 m) above a river.

Stoneflies

Stonefly naiads (Plecoptera) have long antennae and a pair of long caudal filaments ("tails"), although these may be broken in the exuviae. Stoneflies take more than a year to mature, so their presence is evidence of a permanent stream.

Stonefly (Plecoptera) exuviae. (ID)

Mayflies

Mayfly naiads (Ephemeroptera) are somewhat similar to those of stoneflies, but they have shorter antennae and usually three (but sometimes only two) caudal filaments. The surest way to distinguish them is by the paired gills along their

Mayfly (Ephemeroptera) exuviae. (MA)

Damselfly (Odonata: Zygoptera) exuviae (1.1 inch [2.8 cm]). (UT)

abdominal segments. These are obvious in a living naiad, because they are loose and feathery-looking in the water, but to see them in the exuviae may require closer inspection.

Damselflies

Damselfly naiads, instead of long caudal filaments, have three flat, elongate gills projecting from the tip of the abdomen. The head tends to be wider than the thorax and abdomen.

Dragonflies

Dragonfly naiads come in a variety of forms but always lack the prominent filaments and gills that characterize the other naiads. The head tends to be narrower than the thorax and abdomen. Naiads of darners (Aeshnidae) have elongate, cylindrical bodies; skimmers (Libellulidae) are more squat; clubtails (Gomphidae) are somewhat flattened. Dragonfly exuviae are often, but not always, evidence of a permanent water body; some species have an annual life cycle and are able to live in vernal pools.

Exuviae of an aeshnid (darner) dragonfly (Odonata: Anisoptera). (CA)

Aquatic Pupae

True bugs undergo simple metamorphosis, and the immature forms look similar to the adults. Megaloptera (dobsonflies, fishflies, and alderflies) and nearly all aquatic beetles leave the water before pupating; in fact, dobsonfly larvae often travel more than 35 feet (10 m) from the water's edge and may even climb buildings. Therefore, the only pupae normally found in water, besides those of a few beetles and moths enclosed in cocoons, belong to caddisflies and true flies.

Caddisflies

Caddisflies (Trichoptera) usually pupate in the water, either within the larval cases or in separate cocoons. When mature, the adult may emerge underwater, or the pupa may swim to the surface before molting. A few crawl onto the shore as naiads do. In any event, the pupal skin may be found floating or resting at the water's edge afterward. It is an exarate pupa, with long, fully free antennae and legs, conspicuous jaws, four prominent wing buds, and often filamentous gills on the thorax and abdomen. It is quite unlike anything else you may find floating in the water.

Pupal skin (2 cm) of a limnephilid caddisfly (*Limnephilus rhombicus*). (MA)

Mosquitoes and Midges

The pupae of mosquitoes and midges (Culicomorpha) generally continue to swim like the larvae, but wing buds and the shape of the adult's head and thorax are evident on close inspection. A pair of respiratory spiracular horns project from the front of the thorax. The adults may emerge at the water surface, or the pupae may first "beach" themselves on the shore or floating objects.

This mosquito (Culicidae: *Ochlerotatus*) has just emerged from one of the three 8-mm pupae that have come to rest on the floating leaf. (MA)

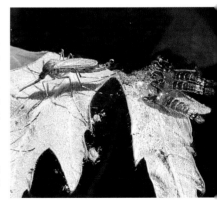

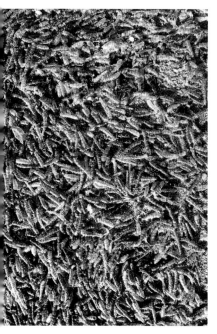

Pupae of brine flies (Ephydridae: *Ephydra*) on the shore of the Great Salt Lake. (UT)

Shore Flies

Shore flies (Ephydridae) form floating puparia, which sometimes clump together in masses. The puparia of *Ephydra* brine flies regularly wash up on the shore of the Great Salt Lake in huge numbers.

Black Flies

The pupae of black flies (Simuliidae) rest in translucent, conical, pocketlike cocoons that are affixed to rocks and other substrates in fast-moving streams. The cocoon is closed at first, but its end is popped off once the larva has pupated. Instead of little horns, the pupa has a pair of distinctive, branched, filamentous gills that project from the cocoon's broad opening, which faces downstream. The adult emerges underwater and rises to the surface in a bubble. Larvae of some dance flies (Empididae) in the genera *Roederiodes* and *Wiedemannia* prey on black fly pupae and then pupate in their cocoons, or sometimes in nearby crevices.

Net-winged Midges

Net-winged midges (Blephariceridae) have strange, flattened pupae that look nothing

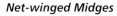

Left: Black fly (Simuliidae) pupae (about 5 mm each) in their pouchlike cocoons, behind a small waterfall in a stream. (CA) *Below:* A single black fly pupa (4 mm). (ID)

Pupae (3 to 4 mm) of net-winged midges (Blephariceridae) attached to a rocky stream bottom. (PA)

like the larvae or adults. They are blackish with pale spiracular horns and are firmly affixed to submerged rocks in fast streams. As with black flies, the adult usually rises to the surface in a bubble. The related mountain midges (Deuterophlebiidae; W) also have broad, flattened pupae attached to underwater rocks. Theirs are a golden brown color.

Water Pennies

Water pennies (Psephenidae) are beetle larvae with a flat, oval to nearly circular carapace, up to about 1 cm long. They look like little pennies as they cling to stones in streams. When mature, the water penny leaves the water and firmly attaches its carapace to a substrate, anywhere from a few inches to a few feet from the water's edge (or rarely underwater), and pupates beneath it.

Exuviae Clinging to Terrestrial Vegetation and Other Exposed Surfaces

Various immature terrestrial insects molt just as naiads do, leaving their exuviae clinging to vegetation and other objects above the ground. Those of cicadas are most conspicuous, but if you look closely, you will see all sorts of shed skins. As noted above, you occasionally may even find naiad exuviae far from water.

Cicadas

After spending its whole immature life sucking on roots underground, a cicada nymph (Cicadidae) emerges from the ground and clings to an object so that the adult insect can climb out of its old skin. This may happen close to the ground or high in a tree. The exuviae of these stocky creatures are easily recognized by their thick, cylindrical bodies and large forelegs adapted for digging.

Exuviae (about 2 cm) of a periodical cicada (*Magicicada septendecim*). (MA)

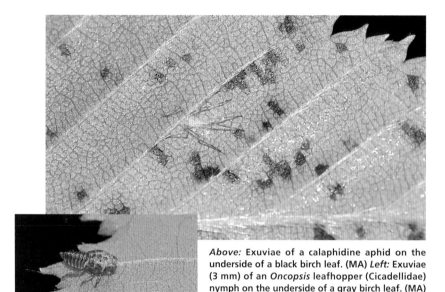

Above: Exuviae of a calaphidine aphid on the underside of a black birch leaf. (MA) *Left:* Exuviae (3 mm) of an *Oncopsis* leafhopper (Cicadellidae) nymph on the underside of a gray birch leaf. (MA) *Lower left:* Exuviae (7.5 mm) of a pine spittlebug (Cercopidae: *Aphrophora*). (WA)

Foliage-sucking Insects and Mites

The tiny relatives of cicadas, such as leafhoppers, spittlebugs, and treehoppers, similarly leave their exuviae clinging to foliage (often the undersides of leaves) and stems. Looking for these is a good way to confirm the cause of feeding damage. Aphid exuviae are left in clusters at feeding sites and can be recognized by their long antennae. On an even tinier scale, spider mites leave their cast skins on the undersides of leaves, often near a vein or midrib, and when many skins have accumulated, they can give the leaf a silvery appearance.

Orthoptera

Grasshoppers and crickets cling upside down to vegetation, using gravity to help them escape their old skins. This position distinguishes exuviae at a glance from victims of "summit disease," a pathogenic fungus that compels orthopterans to climb

Exuviae of a slant-faced grasshopper (Acrididae: Gomphocerinae). (AZ)

to the tops of stems before dying, oriented right side up (see chapter 3).

Neuropterida

The pupa of a green lacewing has well-developed legs and may crawl some distance from its cocoon, after biting its way out, before clinging to a stem and eclosing (*eclosion* is the term for "hatching" from a pupa). Technically, it is not the pupa doing the biting and crawling, but the *pharate* adult, still wearing the pupal skin. The cast skin is transparent and delicate, with the antennae and abdomen curled under it. Brown lacewings, mantidflies, and snakeflies have similar habits.

Mayflies

Mayflies are unique among insects in having wings in the penultimate life stage. This immature winged form is called the *subimago* (the adult form of any mature insect is called the *imago*). The subimago emerges from the naiad skin and flies a short distance before molting a final time, within a minute or two or up to a couple of days after leaving the water. In some species, the subimagos all emerge within a few days of each other and exuviae are left in large clusters.

Right: Pupal skin (11 mm) of a snakefly (Raphidioptera: Raphidiidae). The curved structure is an ovipositor, indicating a female. (CA) *Below:* Exuviae (4 mm) of a green lacewing (Chrysopidae). (TN)

Pupae Attached to Vegetation and Other Exposed Surfaces

Certain insects pupate with part of the body firmly attached to vegetation or other objects, not merely clinging with their legs as is done by the nymphs, naiads, exarate pupae, and subimagos noted previously. The best known of these are butterflies, whose chrysalises are discussed in the next section, followed by moth pupae, which may or may not be in exposed places.

Whiteflies

Whiteflies (Aleyrodidae), although not classified among insects that undergo complete metamorphosis, have an inactive, nonfeeding fourth instar that is referred to as a pupa. These small, oval, flattened pupae are attached to the undersides of leaves in groups and could easily be confused with eggs or scale insects. The pupae of some species are pale green (or transparent when they have eclosed) and featureless to the naked eye. Others are black and ringed with a white, waxy fringe, which may be very narrow, as in the citrus blackfly (*Aleu-*

Left: Pupae and pupal skins of whiteflies (Aleyrodidae) on the underside of a pale touch-me-not leaf. (VT) *Below:* Pupal skins of mulberry whiteflies (Aleyrodidae: *Tetraleurodes mori*) on the underside of a mountain laurel leaf. (MA)

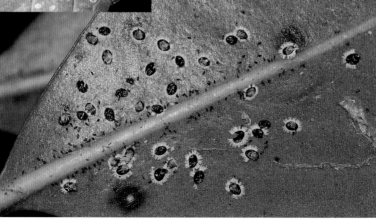

rocanthus woglumi), or quite substantial, as in the mulberry whitefly (*Tetraleurodes mori*). (It should be noted that adult *Cerataphis* aphids, found on palms and orchids among other plants, strongly resemble mulberry whitefly pupae.) The adult whitefly emerges through a T-shaped slit in the pupa.

Eulophid Wasps

The tiny (2-mm), seedlike, black or brown pupae of *Eulophus* wasps (Eulophidae) are found attached to leaves in clusters, lying on their backs. The larvae feed inside a caterpillar, and when mature, they emerge and pupate close to its remains, for which they have been nicknamed "tombstone pupae." Beside each pupa is a tiny cluster of round, yellow fecal pellets, the larva's accumulated wastes, which are expelled all at once just before pupation. *Colpoclypeus florus*, a European species with similar habits, has recently become established in Washington apple orchards. It specializes in leaf-rolling caterpillars (Tortricidae), and consequently, the pupae are found in the host's webbing rather than on exposed leaf surfaces.

Hover Flies

The mature larva of an aphid-eating syrphid fly (Syrphinae) adheres along the length of its body to a leaf and hardens to form a pale, teardrop- or pear-shaped puparium, which may be about 5 mm long. Whereas many fly puparia are dark and opaque, those of syrphids become translucent as the fly develops within, and a darkening of the skin indicates the presence of a parasitoid wasp such as an ichneumonid, figitid, encyrtid, or pteromalid. This darkening happens within a few hours of puparium formation. Puparia parasitized by *Bothriothorax* (Encyrtidae) have a characteristic lumpy appearance

Eulophid wasp (*Eulophus*) pupae (2 mm) found on the underside of a leaf. The yellow clusters are fecal material deposited by the larvae before pupating. (TN)

Puparium (5 mm) of a syrphid fly (Syrphinae). (TN)

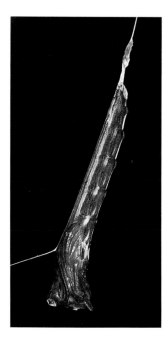

Pupa (9 mm) of a fungus gnat, *Leptomorphus hyalinus* (Mycetophilidae). (MA)

caused by the presence of up to thirty wasps developing inside (parasitoids in the other families are solitary).

Crane Flies

Certain crane fly larvae (Tipulidae: *Liogma* and *Cylindrotoma*) feed like caterpillars on the leaves of wetland plants. Their long, slender pupae can be found clinging to the food plants. Other crane flies pupate underground, wriggling to the surface and leaving the pupal skins protruding from the ground when they emerge.

Fungus Gnats

Other flies that pupate in the open include *Leptomorphus* fungus gnats (Mycetophilidae). The larvae live and feed on the undersides of bracket fungi, and when mature, they each spin a line of silk near where they have been feeding. The larva positions itself somewhere in the middle of its line and pupates there, hanging upside down. When an adult male emerges, he locates a female pupa and hangs under it, mating with the adult when she emerges.

Ladybugs

When a ladybug larva (Coccinellidae) is ready to pupate, it attaches the tip of its abdomen to a leaf or other surface. The spiny larval skin is either

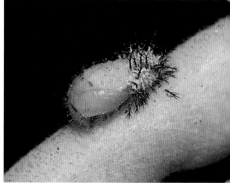

Left: Pupa of a multicolored Asian lady beetle, *Harmonia axyridis* (Coccinellidae). (MA)
Right: Pupa (6 mm) of a Mexican bean beetle (Coccinellidae: *Epilachna varivestis*). (MA)

bunched up at the base of the pupa or retained, loosely surrounding the pupa. Ladybug pupae are colored with varying amounts and patterns of black and orange or pink. The legs are free, but the pupa is usually curled forward, so they are not easy to see. Most ladybug pupae have transverse clefts near the base of the back that can be used to "bite" ants and other attackers when the pupa is disturbed and suddenly straightens. Pupae of the herbivorous ladybugs (Epilachninae: *Epilachna* spp. and *Subcoccinella vigintiquatuorpunctata*) lack these clefts and are instead adorned with tiny glandular hairs for protection.

Tortoise Beetles

Tortoise beetle pupae (Chrysomelidae: Cassidinae: Cassidini) are broad and flattened, somewhat similar to ladybug pupae. They may retain the messy-looking "fecal shield" that is carried on the larva's back. *Chelymorpha* pupae are 1 cm long, dark with pale mottling, and covered with a whitish powder that resembles mold. They have a row of narrow spines along each side of the abdomen and more spines at the anterior end. Other tortoise beetle pupae have broader, leafy-looking marginal spines, such as the pale green pupa of the clavate tortoise beetle (*Plagiometriona clavata*).

Pupa (6 mm) of a clavate tortoise beetle (Chrysomelidae: *Plagiometriona clavata*). (VT)

Other Leaf Beetles

Various other leaf beetles also pupate with the posterior end attached to the host plant. Willow and cottonwood leaf beetles (*Chrysomela* spp.) have tapered, brown pupae that hang from the undersides of leaves. On either side of the pupa's middle are white defense glands. The skeletonizing leaf beetles (Galerucinae) usually do not pupate in the open, but the waterlily leaf beetle (*Galerucella nymphaeae*), having nowhere else to go, pupates on the upper surfaces of waterlily leaves. *Lebia* ground beetle larvae (Carabidae) feed on leaf beetle pupae and pupate near or within the remains of the host.

Pupa of a cottonwood leaf beetle (Chrysomelidae: *Chrysomela scripta*). (FL)

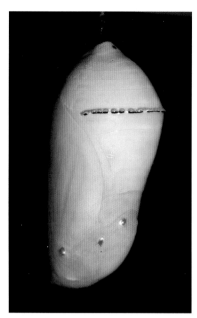

Chrysalis (22 mm) of a monarch (Nymphalidae: *Danaus plexippus*). (MA)

Butterfly Chrysalises

The largest and most conspicuous pupae attached to vegetation or other exposed objects are those of butterflies, which are better known as *chrysalises*. The pupa is secured to the substrate by a short projection at the tip of the abdomen, called the *cremaster*, which is implanted in a thin sheet of silk spun over the substrate. All chrysalises are obtect, with no sign of legs. The shape of the compacted wings is more or less visible, and sometimes the shapes of the antennae and face are as well. Many species can modify the color of the chrysalis according to the background the caterpillar sees before pupating.

Brush-footed Butterflies

All butterfly chrysalises that hang freely, attached only by the cremaster, are those of nymphalids (brush-footed butterflies). One of the most familiar is that of the

Left: Chrysalis of a Milbert's tortoiseshell (Nymphalidae: *Aglais milberti*). The black object is the caterpillar's last shed skin. (MA) *Right:* Eclosed chrysalis (23 mm) of a variegated fritillary (Nymphalidae: *Euptoieta claudia*). (TN)

Above: Chrysalis (1 inch [2.5 cm]) of a question mark (Nymphalidae: *Polygonia interrogationis*). (MA) *Right:* A viceroy (Nymphalidae: *Limenitis archippus*) emerged from the chrysalis on the left, and a white admiral (*L. arthemis*) from the one on the right. The chrysalises are 24 mm each. (VT) *Lower right:* Chrysalis (1.1 inches [2.8 cm]) of a mourning cloak (Nymphalidae: *Nymphalis antiopa*). (MA)

monarch (*Danaus plexippus*), which is 22 mm long, compact, bluish green, and studded with gold dots, some of which form a horizontal line across the abdomen. Those of the other milkweed butterflies (Danainae) are similar. The goatweed leafwing (*Anaea andria*), typical of the Charaxinae, has a similarly compact, leaf green chrysalis, without the gold dots, but with a plain, whitish, horizontal line corresponding with the monarch's. The chrysalis of the American snout (Libytheinae: *Libytheana carinenta*) is yellowish green and angular, wedge-shaped at the anterior end. Chrysalises of the emperors (Apaturinae) are also green, with a pair of pointed anterior lobes. Satyrine chrysalises are generally plain green or brown, smooth with a rounded abdomen, and usually found among grasses and sedges. They are sometimes hidden among leaf litter.

Other nymphalids have more elaborate chrysalises, with various projections or bright colors. Like butterfly eggs, these deserve a book all to themselves. Those of the variegated fritillary (*Euptoieta claudia*) and several checkerspots (*Chlosyne* and *Euphydryas*) are white with black markings and orange studs. The mottled brown chrysalis of the mourning cloak (*Nymphalis antiopa*) has red-tipped spikes. Chrysalises of question marks and commas (*Polygonia*) are brownish with a few metallic markings and a prominent finlike projection, as well as smaller pointed bumps. They look a bit like dead leaves. Viceroy and admiral chrysalises (*Limenitis*) lack small points or studs but have a rounded disk projecting from the middle. They are brown and white, resembling bird droppings.

Other Butterflies

Chrysalises in the four other butterfly families (excluding skippers) are attached to the substrate by the cremaster, as well as by a "girdle" consisting of a cord of silk looped around the thorax. When attached to vertical substrates such as stems and walls, this results in the head pointing up rather than hanging down as in nymphalids. Swallowtail chrysalises (Papilionidae: Papilioninae) are an inch or more long, have two points at the anterior end, and tend to be green or brown, without bold markings. Chrysalises of whites and sulphurs (Pieridae) have a single spine at the anterior end and are sometimes less than an inch long. Those of the gossamer-winged butterflies (Lycaenidae) are smooth, rounded, and compact, sometimes covered with short hairs, and typically about a centimeter long or even smaller. They are often formed in ground litter but may be found on the undersides of leaves. Metalmark chrysalises (Riodinidae) are also short and fat and often hairy. Although they are supported by a

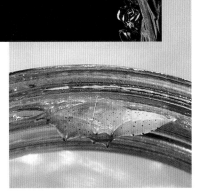

Left: Chrysalis (1.2 inches [3 cm]) of a black swallowtail (Papilionidae: *Papilio polyxenes*). (MA) *Lower left:* Chrysalis (19 mm) of a cabbage white (Pieridae: *Pieris rapae*). (VT) *Right:* Eclosed chrysalis (1.06 inches [2.7 cm]) of a palamedes swallowtail (Papilionidae: *Papilio palamedes*). (GA)

silk girdle, they hang with the head down. They are usually speckled brown, with two orange spots on the thorax and numerous projections.

Skippers

Chrysalises of skippers (Hesperiidae) are often covered with a waxy, white powder or bloom. Some are hairy, and others are smooth with no waxy covering. They generally are found in loose cocoons within leaf shelters. Some are supported by silken girdles. The giant skippers (Hesperiinae: Megathymini) pupate within chambers they excavate in leaves and stems of agaves and yuccas. Their chrysalises are unique among butterflies in that they move freely within their chambers, rather than being fixed in place by the cremaster.

Moth Pupae

The majority of moth pupae are hidden in the ground, in cocoons (see chapter 7), or in rolled leaves, plant stems, and similar shelters. They tend to be uniformly colored, most often reddish brown, and smooth without obvious distinguishing features. Mature pupae of many of the microlepidoptera are thrust out of their cocoons or leaf mines to allow the adult moths to emerge, leaving the protruding pupal skins as evidence that they successfully completed their metamorphosis. Similarly, pupal exuviae of the wood-boring clearwing (Sesiidae) and carpenter (Cossidae) moths may be found protruding from holes in trees. Small spines on the head and downward-pointing rows of spines on the abdominal segments help sesiid and cossid pupae work their way out.

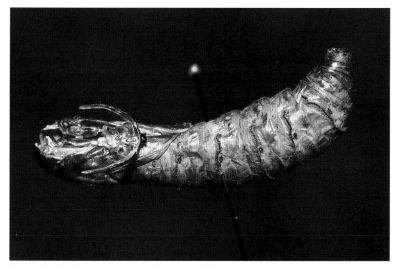

Pupal skin (4 cm) of a leopard moth (Cossidae). (MA)

Left: Pupa (13 mm) of an ailanthus webworm (Yponomeutidae: *Atteva punctella*) in its webbing. (MD) *Above:* Pupa (1 cm) of a common tan wave (Geometridae: *Pleuroprucha insulsaria*). (TN)

Plume Moths

Some plume moth pupae (Pterophoridae) are attached to vegetation by the tips of their abdomens as nymphalid butterfly chrysalises are. They are around 5 to 10 mm long and are often hairy like the caterpillars that produce them. *Geina* species (such as the grape plume moth, *G. periscelidactylus*) have a hairless pupa that is more or less green, truncated at the anterior end, and has a prominent pair of pointed horns arising from the middle of the back, along with other small spines and bumps. It projects from the leaf at an angle of about 40 degrees.

Other Exposed Pupae

Various other moth pupae may be found in exposed places. Pupae of the ailanthus webworm (Yponomeutidae: *Atteva punctella*), marked with a few

longitudinal stripes, hang among the webbing produced by the larvae. We collected a small, green, two-horned pupa that was attached to the underside of a mimosa leaf by a silken girdle like a butterfly chrysalis, and what emerged was a geometrid moth called the common tan wave (*Pleuroprucha insulsaria*). A few other geometrid pupae are known to hang exposed like a chrysalis.

Tussock Moths

Gypsy moths (Lymantriidae: *Lymantria dispar*) sometimes pupate in ground litter,

Pupa of a gypsy moth (Lymantriidae: *Lymantria dispar*). (MA)

Eclosed pupa (21 mm) of a satin moth (Lymantriidae: *Leucoma salicis*). (VT)

but their pupae often instead hang from
tree trunks and other exposed objects,
attached by a few loose threads. They are
sparsely covered with tufts of golden-
brown hair. The pupa of the related satin
moth (*Leucoma salicis*) is somewhat more
thickly covered with white and yellow hairs
and surrounded by loose webbing.

Plain, reddish brown pupae, about 2
cm long, found while digging in the garden are likely cutworms, also
known as owlet moths (Noctuidae). Large pupae on or in the ground, 1.6
inches (4 cm) or longer, likely belong to royal moths (Saturniidae: Ceratocampinae) or sphinx moths (Sphingidae). Pupae of *Manduca* sphinx
moths, such as tomato and tobacco hornworms, are distinctive not just
because of their very large size, around 2.8 inches (7 cm), but also in having a looped, handlelike appendage. This is the sheath that contains the
developing moth's proboscis (mouthpart). A hornworm pupa also usually
has a scar corresponding with the larva's posterior horn.

Right: Typical pupa (about 2 cm) of an owlet moth
(Noctuidae), found in garden soil. (VT) *Below left:*
Pupa (7 cm) of a tomato or tobacco hornworm
(Sphingidae: *Manduca*). (AZ) *Below right:* Pupae
(about 5.5 cm) of regal moths (Saturniidae: *Cithero-
nia regalis*). (MD) Photo by Bonnie J. Caruthers.

Not a pupa, but the larva of a crowned slug moth (Limacodidae: *Isa textula*). (MA)

Slug Moth Caterpillars

When resting, some of the slug caterpillars (Limacodidae) could easily be mistaken for pupae. They have no visible head or legs, and many look like smooth, interestingly patterned lumps. The crowned slug (*Isa textula*), ringed with feathery spines, is quite reminiscent of a tortoise beetle pupa. If you flip one over (carefully, as the hairs of the spiny ones can sting), you will see the opening into which its head is retracted, unlike anything you would see on an actual pupa.

Fly Pupae

Fly pupae come in two basic styles: those that are naked, and those that are surrounded by puparia, the hardened skins of the larvae. The first group includes nearly all of the "Nematocera" (in quotes because fly taxonomy is currently in flux), the slender, mosquitolike flies. An exception is the Hessian fly (Cecidomyiidae: *Mayetiola destructor*), a gall midge that forms a seedlike puparium beneath the leaf sheath of grasses. The "Orthorrhapha" are generally stockier flies, and with the exception of soldier flies (Stratiomyidae), they also do not form puparia. The most familiar examples are the horse and deer flies (Tabanidae), robber flies (Asilidae), and bee flies (Bombyliidae). Naked fly pupae are usually obtect, and some are fairly similar to moth pupae, but they do not come to a single point (cremaster) at the tip of the abdomen. Also, moth pupae are usually easily recognized by the impression of their long antennae, visible between the wing pads. All the remaining flies belong to the "Cyclorrhapha," and their pupae are enclosed in puparia. Apart from the aquatic pupae already described, most flies pupate in the ground or other hidden places.

Gall Midges

Certain gall midges (Cecidomyiidae) pupate within plant tissue rather than dropping to the ground to do so. When mature, the tiny pupae are thrust out, and the exuviae are left sticking out of the plant, just as some moth pupae protrude from leaves or wood. Some species form no externally visible galls, and their pupal skins are the most obvious sign of their presence. *Calamomyia* species, for instance, leave their skins sticking out of stems of cordgrass and other grasses, with no other external sign except for sometimes a bit of black discoloration from a symbiotic fungus. Pupal

Pupal skins (2 mm) of *Neolasioptera martelli* (Cecidomyiidae) projecting from an agave leaf. (TX)

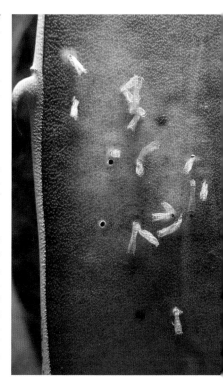

exuviae protruding from a yellowish patch in an agave leaf belong to *Neolasioptera martelli*.

Bee Flies

Larvae of some bee flies (Bombyliidae) parasitize the nests of carpenter bees, mud daubers, and other solitary bees and wasps. When they emerge, they leave their pupal skins protruding from the nests. Other bee flies, such as *Anthrax analis*, which parasitizes tiger beetle larvae, leave the exuviae poking out of the ground. The pupae have several small spikes or curved hooks on the front of the head, as well as varying amounts of bristles on the abdomen, both of which help them bust and wriggle their way out of the confined spaces where they have developed. Robber fly pupae (Asilidae), which also protrude from the ground when mature, are similar.

Left: Pupal skins of bee flies (Bombyliidae: *Xenox tigrinus*), which have emerged from a carpenter bee nest. (TN) *Right:* Another view of a *Xenox tigrinus* pupal skin (15 mm). (TN)

Puparium (3 mm) of a fruit fly (Drosophilidae). (MA)

Fruit Flies and Scuttle Flies

If you have ever waited a little too long to take out the compost, you are probably familiar with the puparia of fruit flies (Drosophilidae), which are found stuck to various objects near the decomposing matter in which the larvae develop. They are about 3 mm long, pale brown, and have a prominent pair of horns at the anterior end. Scuttle fly (*Phoridae*) puparia are similar and may be found in similar places—and sometimes seemingly more sanitary situations, such as rinsed bottles. They may also be found in empty snail shells. They too have a pair of anterior horns, but these are not at the tip and are actually part of the pupa poking through the puparium.

Tachinid Flies

Anyone who has raised many caterpillars has probably seen the puparia of parasitoid tachinid flies. They are dark reddish brown, smooth, and capsule-shaped, almost featureless except for two very small anterior spiracles. The larvae generally exit the caterpillar before pupating, and normally drop to the ground to do so, although some may pupate on vegetation near the host remains.

Puparia of tachinid fly larvae, which emerged from a tiger moth caterpillar. (FL) Photo by Jeff Hollenbeck.

Bot Flies

Less commonly encountered, but very distinctive, are the puparia of bot flies (Oestridae). They are about 2 cm long, coarsely textured, and blackish with a pair of yellow anterior spiracles. Noah has found several *Cuterebra fontinella* puparia in the carpet

A rodent bot fly (Oestridae: *Cuterebra fontinella*) lies beside the puparium from which it has just emerged, clinging to the puparium of its sibling. Both puparia measure 2 cm. (MA)

and other nooks around his house, the larvae having emerged from mice that were killed and brought in by his pet cat.

Emergence and Parasitoids

Flies that do not form puparia generally emerge through a longitudinal slit that opens near the anterior end of the pupal skin. When a fly emerges from a puparium, it pops open a neat, circular lid at the anterior end. In most cases, this is accomplished by the sudden expansion of a balloonlike structure in the front of the fly's head, called the *ptilinum*. In some species, the lid actually pops off; in others, it snaps back in place, making it difficult to see that anything has emerged.

A puparium that has opened in any other way has probably fallen prey to a parasitoid. Likely suspects include aleocharine rove beetles (Staphylinidae), velvet ants (Mutillidae), and the following wasps: alysiine and opiine braconids, cryptine ichneumonids, eucoiline figitids, and diapriids. A wasp parasitoid hatches from an egg inserted within its host, so there is no entry hole in the puparium. It pupates in a cocoon within the puparium. A rove beetle larva, on the other hand, bites its way into the puparium and seals the small entry hole with a secretion. After consuming the entire host pupa, it may pupate either inside or outside the puparium.

Other Pupae

Virtually all other pupae are exarate, looking essentially like pale, wingless versions of the adults, curled into a fetal position. Therefore, they are more or less recognizable if you are familiar with the characteristics of the adult: the constricted waist of a wasp; the long snout of a weevil or scorpionfly; the antennae of a long-horned beetle; the "neck" and man-

Top right: Pupa (6 mm) of a *Trirhabda*, a leaf beetle (Chrysomelidae). (MA) *Above left:* Pupae of ants (Formicidae: *Formica fusca* group). (TN) *Above right:* A small long-horned beetle (Cerambycidae) pupa (6 mm) in its cell within a dead twig. (GA)

Above left: Pupa (3 mm) of a gouty oak gall wasp (Cynipidae: *Callirhytis quercuspunctata*). (MA) *Above right:* Pupa (5 mm) of a boll weevil (Curculionidae: *Anthonomus grandis*). (TX) *Left:* Pupa (about 12 mm) of a soldier beetle (Cantharidae: *Cantharis livida*). (MA)

dibles of a dobsonfly; and so on. Most, as with many moths and flies, are hidden in unlined cells in the ground or under rocks and other objects on the ground. Wood-boring insects typically pupate in their galleries or cells excavated just beneath the bark; bean weevils and many true weevils pupate inside seeds or seedpods. Hymenopteran pupae may be found in their nests, galls, or their host's remains, according to the larva's lifestyle. Many pupae are concealed within cocoons, which are the subject of chapter 7.

Parasitism, Predation, and Other Causes of Death

3

Insects and other invertebrates are victims of a wide variety of diseases, predators, and parasites, many of which are also invertebrates. Pathogenic fungi, bacteria, and viruses often cause insects to behave and die in characteristic ways. Recognizing signs of predators may not be possible beyond identifying broad groups, but there are some exceptions. True parasites do not kill their hosts, and when we talk about parasitism of (and by) invertebrates, we are often really talking about *parasitoids*. They live for a while (sometimes months or even years) as parasites, but then kill the host in their final stages. Parasitoids are often quite host-specific, and the identity of the victim combined with the associated sign may indicate a particular family, genus, or even species of parasitoid. *Hyperparasitoids* are parasitoids that specialize in parasitizing other parasitoids. *Ectoparasitoids* are those that live on the surface of their hosts. *Endoparasitoids* live inside their hosts, but some have structures that are externally visible, and these are discussed here with the ectoparasitoids. Signs of parasitoids in eggs, pupae, and cocoons are covered in the corresponding chapters (1, 2, and 7).

Dismemberment and Predation with Chewing Mouthparts

Invertebrate predators with chewing mouthparts leave their prey mangled or dismembered. Insects dispatched in this way may be victims of arachnids, centipedes, wasps, ants, beetles, dragonflies, or mantises. Conclusively determining which of these is responsible may not be possible, but knowing the habits and habitats of the suspects can help narrow it down.

Most spiders have toothed chelicerae, which they use in combination with their movable fangs to mash their prey into a small, unrecognizable mass. Prey killed by hunting spiders such as tarantulas and wolf spiders have no silk on them, whereas orbweavers swaddle their prey with a thick layer of white silk. Jumping spiders and others eating soft-bodied flies may leave only the wings behind.

Centipedes hold their stunned prey speared on their fangs while their jaws chew the victims. They only eat the soft parts, leaving the harder parts behind.

Praying mantises lurk among vegetation, where they are well camouflaged, and seize insects when they come near. When they catch a butterfly or grasshopper, they consume everything except the wings. Dragonflies are similarly efficient but are more likely to drop remains from a prominent perch, or over open ground when they consume their prey while still in flight.

Adult tiger beetles are likely suspects when mangled remains of ants and other small insects are found on bare ground. They kill their prey by banging their victims repeatedly on the ground, then chew them up and drink their juices.

Nibbled remains of snails and slugs are probably the work of firefly larvae (Lampyridae). They often kill a number in rapid succession.

The luminescent larvae of glowworm beetles (Phengodidae) feed exclusively on millipedes, which (at least the species with well-developed chemical defenses) have few other predators. The larva bites the millipede and paralyzes it by injecting digestive fluid, then consumes its innards one segment at a time. The millipede is reduced to a heap of chitinous rings, with everything but the poison glands removed.

Ants normally bring their prey back to their nests. Sometimes, however, they have fierce territorial battles with each other, leaving the ground strewn with dead and dismembered ants that have been killed but not consumed.

Spider wasps (Pompilidae) in the tribe Auplopodini usually remove one or more of a spider's legs before carrying it back to the nest. Grass wasps (Sphecidae: *Isodontia*) similarly bite off the antennae of their cricket or katydid prey. Katydid wasps (*Sphex*), which provision their nests with katydids and leaf-rolling crickets but not with crickets, leave the antennae intact. This is most likely because katydid wasps are larger and do not find the antennae as cumbersome.

Mutilated or missing wings on a restless bush cricket (Gryllidae: *Hapithus agitator*; SE) are a sign not of attempted predation, but of successful mating. Males in northern populations, rather than singing, allow females to feed on their wings while they mate.

Predation with Piercing Mouthparts

Predators with piercing mouthparts suck their victims' fluids, leaving the dead bodies in one piece. These include true bugs such as assassin bugs (Reduviidae), damsel bugs (Nabidae), and stilt bugs (Berytidae); neuropteran larvae; and certain flies and spiders.

Predatory stink bugs (Pentatomidae: Asopinae) dangle their caterpillar prey from vegetation as they feed, from a distance giving the impression of a caterpillar infected with a bacterium or virus. Other true bugs similarly dangle their prey.

Lacewing and syrphid fly larvae often specialize in aphids. A mature syrphid larva may consume more than fifty aphids a day.

The prey of antlions lie scattered around their pits, having been tossed out after being drained of their contents.

Robber flies (Asilidae) are adept at catching other insects in midair, often bringing them to a favorite perch to suck the juices. The ground below this perch may be littered with bodies of other flies, bees, wasps, beetles, leafhoppers, or even dragonflies.

Aquatic predators with piercing mouthparts include water striders (Gerridae), backswimmers (Notonectidae), giant water bugs (Belostomatidae), waterscorpions (Nepidae), and predaceous diving beetle larvae (Dytiscidae). Dytiscids feed on mollusks and worms as well as insects.

Dead insects on flowers are likely victims of ambush bugs (Reduviidae: Phymatinae). These well-camouflaged predators rest on

This monarch caterpillar is becoming "deflated" by a predatory stink bug (Pentatomidae: Asopinae). (MA)

Dead insects lying on top of flowers generally indicate the presence of ambush bugs (Reduviidae: Phymatinae). (VT)

A butterfly or bee hanging under a flower likely indicates the presence of a thomisid crab spider. (NB)

flowers and seize flies, bees, day-flying moths, and other pollinators. Often several discarded prey insects can be seen on a given flower head, and a close look may reveal the killer. Certain crab spiders (Thomisidae: *Misumena, Misumenoides, Misumenops*) have similar habits, but they often move to the edge or underside of the flower to eat their meal (sometimes a large bumblebee or butterfly), dropping it to the ground when they are through.

Thomisid crab spiders are among only a few spider families that leave their prey apparently intact. The only external wound left is a pair of microscopic holes where the fangs were inserted. The spider pumps digestive fluid through these holes, sucking out the insect's tissues as they dissolve. An empty exoskeleton is all that is left. Cobweb spiders (Theridiidae) feed similarly but first wrap the prey in silk as is done by most web-spinning spiders, dropping it to the ground when through feeding. Their silk wrapping is not nearly as thick as that of orbweavers. Spitting spiders (Scytodidae: *Scytodes*) catch their prey by spitting strands of sticky material from their venom glands; these quickly harden, attaching the insect to the substrate. The poison kills the victim, and the spider drags it a short distance from the sticky mass, digesting it as a thomisid would. Pirate spiders (Mimetidae) invade the webs of other spiders, sucking them dry through their legs, one after another. They also sometimes wait by nests of spider wasps and mud daubers, stealing the paralyzed spiders brought by the wasps.

A fly predated by the common house spider (Theridiidae: *Parasteatoda tepidariorum*): swaddled in silk, sucked dry, and discarded. (MA)

Female parasitoid wasps make tiny punctures when laying eggs in their hosts. Sometimes they drink the juices that ooze from the wound, and some ichneumons, braconids, and chalcids make punctures with their ovipositors solely for this purpose. Many small insects and insect eggs are killed this way. *Aphelinus* species (Aphelinidae) typically make feeding punctures in first– and early-second–instar aphids, ovipositing in larger ones. A few chalcids have been observed to kill host insects by making repeated punctures without ovipositing or feeding.

Some female chalcids and braconids construct feeding tubes when drinking the juices of concealed hosts that they cannot reach directly. The host may be a scale insect or an egg, larva, or pupa inside a host plant or cocoon. The female creates the tube by secreting a fluid around her inserted ovipositor. When this fluid dries and the ovipositor is removed, the host's juices rise by capillary action, and the female is able to drink from this "straw."

Endoparasitoids

Endoparasitoids of insects and other invertebrates include wasps, flies, roundworms (Nematoda), and horsehair worms (Nematomorpha: Gordioidea). They can cause observable changes in the behavior of their hosts. Parasitized larvae may become sluggish, or agitated and twitchy. Sometimes more specific behaviors are induced, with clear benefits for the parasitoid. Certain fungi and other pathogens also affect insects' behavior, in some cases causing them to climb and die in prominent locations, as discussed in later sections. Generally victims with hard exoskeletons are left hollow but more or less intact, whereas soft-bodied hosts shrivel up. A caterpillar may become discolored and start to look shriveled while it is still alive and the parasitoid is still inside. The best hope for determining which parasitoid is responsible, if it is an insect, is finding its pupa or cocoon inside or nearby. Parasitoids are mostly quite host-specific, so the identity of the host is an important clue. A few endoparasites that partly protrude from living hosts are discussed in the next section, as they may appear to be ectoparasites.

Worms

Horsehair worms (Nematomorpha: Gordioidea) are parasitic in grasshoppers and other terrestrial and aquatic arthropods. They lay eggs in water, and the larvae either actively enter hosts or, if in temporary pools, become encysted and are consumed along with vegetation or detritus in the drying pool. The worm develops in the host's body cavity, later compelling the host to return to water. A nonaquatic insect such as a cricket may leap into the water, where the worm emerges and the insect soon dies.

Mermithid roundworms are very similar to horsehair worms and parasitize arthropods as well as a few other invertebrates. Symptoms in parasitized spiders include a lopsided or dramatically swollen abdomen and

This yellowjacket (Vespidae: *Vespula vidua*) is pumping its abdomen furiously into the wet soil at the edge of a reservoir, trying to relieve itself of a parasitic worm. (MA)

abnormally shortened and thickened legs. Eventually the worm's coiled form may be visible through the spider's skin as it fills its host's body cavity. The spider becomes sluggish and unresponsive, at the same time growing very thirsty and seeking out a water source. The life cycles of mermithids are not well known, but at least some lay eggs in aquatic habitats, so the spider's thirst would seem to benefit the parasitoid.

The parasitic worms that get all the attention are the horsehair worms and nematodes noted above, which burst from their doomed hosts with astonishingly long, looping bodies. Others are more subtle. We have watched yellowjackets (Vespidae: *Vespula*) come to the edge of water bodies, do a peculiar abdomen-wiggling dance, excrete a small worm of some kind, and fly away apparently unharmed.

If you find an ant with its mandibles clamped to the top of a blade of grass, it is likely a victim of the lancet liver fluke (Dicrocoeliidae: *Dicrocoelium dendriticum*). This is just one step in the flatworm's complex lifecycle. A grazing mammal accidentally eats the ant, and the worms mature in its liver. Their eggs are excreted, then ingested by a snail that feeds on the mammal's droppings. They hatch and develop into juveniles in the snail's digestive tract, then become encysted and excreted. When an ant feeding on the snail's slime trail swallows a cyst, most of the worms mature in its gut, but one takes control of its nerves. The ant is compelled to climb up and bite onto the top of a plant every night, from dusk to dawn, until a mammal comes along and swallows it. (Note that if you find a solitary bee hanging by its mandibles from a leaf, it is probably just sleeping.)

Wasps

There are wasp parasitoids for virtually every kind of insect, including the wasp parasitoids themselves. It may be possible to learn to distinguish the signs of the different species that attack a particular host, but that level of detail is impossible here. Thousands of species are involved, many of which have not been described or have little or nothing known about their habits. Just a few examples with especially distinctive signs are given here.

Numerous ichneumon wasps are endoparasitoids of caterpillars, but they tend to let the host pupate before killing it. After pupating within the moth pupa, the adult wasp chews a somewhat irregular hole near one end to emerge. Campoplegines are the major exceptions; most of them exit the caterpillar and spin distinctively patterned cocoons. Like other ichneumons, they usually consume virtually the entire host, so only a flimsy skin of the caterpillar is left next to the solitary wasp cocoon.

Exit hole of an ichneumon wasp in the chrysalis of a spicebush swallowtail (Papilionidae: *Papilio troilus*). (NH) Photo by Bonnie J. Caruthers.

Many braconid wasps are solitary or gregarious endoparasitoids of caterpillars, usually killing the host before it pupates. Some, particularly *Meteorus* and species in the Microgastrinae, leave much of the host uneaten. With the exception of *Aleiodes* species, the larvae bore out of the host before pupating, leaving an exit wound that is often dark and obvious. The caterpillar may live for several more days, but it stops feeding and gradually shrinks and dries up. Some braconids spin their cocoons standing upright on top of the

Right: A catalpa sphinx caterpillar covered with the cocoons (3 mm each) of *Cotesia congregata* (Braconidae) larvae that have emerged after feeding within its body. (TN)

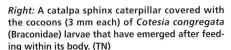

A caterpillar with the cocoon of a braconid parasitoid (*Microplitis*). The wasp larva's dark exit hole is visible just to the right of the cocoon. (MN) Photo by David E. Reed.

Above: The remains of a caterpillar and the cocoons of the three braconid wasps (*Cotesia*) that emerged from it. The adult wasps have emerged from the cocoons. (AZ) *Left:* A unicorn caterpillar (Notodontidae: *Schizura unicornis*) perched atop a bundle of braconid cocoons. Several of the wasp larvae's exit holes can be seen in the side of its body. (NC) Photo by Lynette Schimming.

host, others in a pile under it, and still others move a short distance before making a cocoon. Grosman et al. (2008) demonstrated that host caterpillars of *Glyptapanteles* wasps (Braconidae) act as "bodyguards" of the wasp pupae. The caterpillar stops feeding and remains near the cocoons of the parasitoids that have left its body, swinging violently at any potential predator that approaches, until its own untimely death.

The "mummy-wasps" (Braconidae: *Aleiodes*) kill their host caterpillars in a characteristic way. When mature, they puncture the host's underside, causing it to leak fluids that dry and firmly attach it to the substrate. The

Dagger moth caterpillars (Noctuidae: *Acronicta*) riddled with exit holes of stigmata mummy-wasps (Braconidae: *Aleiodes stigmator*). (ME)

Left: A victim of the tent caterpillar mummy-wasp (Braconidae: *Aleiodes malacosomatos*). (MA) *Right:* A darling underwing caterpillar (Erebidae: *Catocala cara*) mummified by Cameron's pitted mummy-wasp (Braconidae: *Aleiodes cameronii*). (MA)

caterpillar becomes hardened, or "mummified." The larvae pupate in minimal cocoons inside it, then chew small, round holes to emerge. Most species are solitary, exiting from the top of the caterpillar near the rear end. The only gregarious eastern species is the stigmata mummy-wasp (*A. stigmator*), which leaves various hairy noctuid and notodontid caterpillars riddled with evenly spaced exit holes, mainly on the top. Irregular holes in the sides or bottom of a mummy are made by hyperparasitoid chalcids or ichneumonids. Shaw (2006) has provided an excellent guide to the mummies produced by eastern mummy-wasps.

Braconids in the subfamily Aphidiinae are solitary endoparasitoids of aphids, and they do the same thing to their hosts that mummy-wasps do to caterpillars. Affected aphids are killed in their final nymphal instar, becoming hollow, bloated, and brownish or whitish. *Praon* species pupate in a tentlike cocoon beneath the aphid mummy. *Aphidius*, *Lysiphlebus*, and others pupate inside the aphid, then emerge through a round hole chewed in the aphid's back. Chalcids in the genus *Aphelinus* (Aphelinidae) also do this, but they cause the aphid mummy to turn black. *A. mali* mummifies woolly aphids (*Eriosoma*). Some charipine figitid wasps, among others, are parasitoids of both aphidiines and aphelinids.

Euphorine braconids are solitary or gregarious endoparasitoids of adult insects or, in the case of true bugs and barklice, nymphs that may or may not reach maturity. One of the more commonly encountered examples is *Dinocampus coccinellae*, which parasitizes a variety of ladybugs

Above: Aphids parasitized by *Aphelinus abdominalis* (Aphelinidae; left) and *Aphidius* (Braconidae: Aphidiinae). (ON) © Queen's Printer for Ontario, 2005. Reproduced with permission. *Left:* A 2-mm cocoon of *Praon* (Braconidae: Aphidiinae) under the aphid in which the larva developed. (TN)

(Coccinellidae). The larva feeds on only a small portion of the beetle's interior, without killing it. Before exiting and spinning its cocoon beneath the beetle, it first immobilizes it by cutting the nerves to its legs. In this way, the wasp uses its host's warning coloration and defensive reflex bleeding to protect itself while it transforms into an adult. Other euphorines include parasitoids of bark beetles (*Cosmophorus* and others), various other beetles (*Microctonus*), stink bugs (*Aridelus*), lace bugs (*Holdawayella*), plant bugs (*Leiophron* and *Peristenus*), damsel bugs (*Wesmaelia pendula*), barklice (*Euphoriella*), green lacewings (*Chrysopophthorus americanus*), and bumblebees and ichneumons (*Syntretus*).

A rove beetle larva with *Exallonyx* wasp (Proctotrupidae) pupae, about 10 mm each. (NY) Photo by Taro Eldredge.

Proctotrupid wasps are mainly endoparasitoids of beetle larvae, particularly those (such as ground, rove, and click beetles) that inhabit leaf litter and similar habitats. The wasp larvae may be solitary or gregarious. When mature, larvae of at least some species pupate projecting from the host's body, without spinning cocoons.

Typical dryinid wasp parasitism is described in the next section, but *Crovettia theliae* is unique (as far as is known) in completing its development inside its host, a treehopper (Membracidae). It is also unusual in being polyembryonic: one egg divides to produce up to seventy larvae.

Many chalcid wasps are also polyembryonic. Larvae such as caterpillars that are parasitized by encyrtids have a characteristic distended or lumpy appearance caused by the presence of as many as a hundred wasps developing inside.

The fairly rare parasitic wood wasps (Orussidae) are solitary endoparasitoids of metallic wood-boring beetle larvae (Buprestidae).

Flies

All tachinid fly larvae are internal parasitoids, usually solitary but not always. Many are highly host-specific, but there are exceptions. *Compsilura concinnata* was first introduced to North America in 1906 to control gypsy moths and is an extreme example of the dangers of careless attempts at biological control. It has since been documented as parasitizing more than two hundred hosts, including twenty lepidopteran families as well as sawfly and beetle larvae. The majority of tachinid species develop in caterpillars and their pupae or in beetle adults and larvae. Cucumber beetles (Chrysomelidae: *Diabrotica*) are often parasitized by *Celatoria*

This mourning cloak caterpillar was killed by a tachinid parasite just when it was preparing to pupate. The white shell of the fly egg is visible on the caterpillar's back. (MA)

Left: Five eggs of the winsome fly, *Istocheta aldrichi* (Tachinidae), on a Japanese beetle. (MA) *Right:* This cecropia caterpillar died in the process of pupating within its cocoon. The eggs on its skin indicate that it contains more than twenty larvae of the fly *Winthemia cecropia* (Tachinidae). (MI) Photo by Bonnie J. Caruthers.

diabroticae. Other tachinid hosts include Orthoptera, true bugs, earwigs, and crane fly larvae. *Loewia foeda* parasitizes centipedes.

Some tachinid flies lay white, hard-shelled, flattened, oval eggs, up to 1 mm long, on the bodies of beetles, true bugs, or caterpillars, most often near the head, where the insect cannot reach them. Depending on the species, the larvae either burrow directly from the eggs into the host or push a cap from the top of the egg and then bore in. The eggs of feather-legged flies (*Trichopoda*) are often seen on squash bugs (*Anasa*) and other true bugs. The winsome fly (*Istocheta aldrichi*) lays eggs on the thoraxes of Japanese beetles (Scarabaeidae: *Popillia japonica*). *Carcelia* species parasitize hairy caterpillars and attach soft, stalked eggs to their hairs. At least one nontachinid, the humpbacked fly *Megaselia aletiae* (Phoridae), deposits elongate eggs haphazardly over its host, the elder shoot borer (Noctuidae: *Achatodes zeae*).

Other tachinids lay eggs on their host's food plant, and the larvae hatch after the host swallows them. Still others (such as *Compsilura concinnata*) have ovipositors with which they puncture the skin of caterpillars and deposit eggs or larvae directly inside. In some species, the host produces hard, dark scar tissue around the larva, forming a structure called the "respiratory funnel." The larva obtains oxygen through the tip of this funnel, either from one of the host's respiratory structures or directly from the air at the point of entry. In the latter case, the tip of the funnel is visible as a dark spot in the caterpillar's skin. Sometimes tachinids pupate in their host's remains—for example, *Trichopoda* species do if they mature in the fall—but usually full-grown larvae chew their way out and pupate on or in the ground. BugGuide.net contributor Jeff Hollenbeck observed a tiger moth caterpillar (Arctiidae) chew a hole in its cocoon before dying two days later without pupating. Four tachinid flies later emerged, which, having no chewing mouthparts, would have been trapped inside the cocoon if the hole had not been made.

Pyrgotid flies are endoparasitoids of June bugs (*Phyllophaga*) and other scarab beetles. A female lands on a feeding beetle's back, causing it to fly, and inserts an egg in soft tissue exposed by the spreading of its wings. The larva feeds until it is 1 cm long, then pupates inside. The beetle dies soon after.

Most big-headed flies (Pipunculidae) are parasitoids of nymphal leafhoppers, spittlebugs, and planthoppers. Females scoop up the host insects and oviposit in them while in flight, then drop them. The larva grows inside until it completely fills the host's body cavity, then breaks out through a split between two abdominal segments or between the thorax and abdomen. It pupates either on nearby vegetation or in the ground. *Nephrocerus* larvae parasitize adult crane flies, causing their abdomens to swell conspicuously.

Thick-headed flies (Conopidae) parasitize adult bees and wasps. Females wait on flowers and seize the hosts in midair to lay an egg on them. The larva kills the host by consuming the entire contents of its abdomen, and then pupates inside it.

The flesh flies *Kellymyia kellyi*, *Neobellieria cooleyi*, and *Servaisia falciformis* (Sarcophagidae) are endoparasitoids of various grasshoppers. The female of *K. kellyi* deposits a larva under the host's hind wing while it is in flight, whereas *S. falciformis* larviposits in the hind femur, from which the larva migrates to the thoracic cavity. Insects parasitized by flesh flies usually do not survive long.

Tangle-veined flies (Nemestrinidae) in the subfamily Trichopsideinae are also endoparasitoids of grasshoppers. They lay eggs in cracks and crevices of wood, and the larvae seek out grasshoppers and bore inside, leaving a small, brown scar at the point of entry between abdominal segments. When full grown, they emerge and pupate in the ground. *Hirmoneura* species (Hirmoneurinae) instead bore into scarab beetle larvae. The larvae leave their last shed skins in the soil above the remains of the host's pupa, with their own pupae protruding vertically from the ground.

The related small-headed flies (Acroceridae) also lay eggs apart from their hosts, but their larvae bore into spiders. They mostly attack species that do not spin large webs. When mature, the larva bursts out and pupates nearby, sometimes among silk produced by the dying spider. Larvae are usually solitary, but a dozen or more may emerge from a large tarantula.

The woodlouse flies (Rhinophoridae) are endoparasitoids of woodlice. The first-instar larva finds a host and enters between segments, causing the formation of a respiratory funnel like those of tachinids. The orange-yellow puparium of *Melanophora roralis* occupies the entire body space of its host's remains.

Two species of *Endaphis* midges (Cecidomyiidae), one known from Florida and one from British Columbia, are endoparasitoids of aphids. Eggs are laid among aphids, and the larva searches out an aphid and bores into its back. When mature, it emerges and drops to the ground to pupate.

Larvae of many marsh flies (Sciomyzidae) feed on snails, both terrestrial and aquatic. Most lay their eggs on vegetation, but some deposit them on the snails' shells. Many leave to pupate in the ground or floating in the water, but *Pteromicra varia* pupates in a puparium that is coiled to fit inside the spiral of its host's shell.

The cluster fly (Calliphoridae: *Pollenia rudis*) is a parasitoid of earthworms. The larva hatches from an egg laid in the soil, finds a worm, and enters it through a body opening. It consumes most of the worm's interior, then exits to pupate in the soil.

Ectoparasites and Externally Visible Endoparasites

Ectoparasites technically are not invertebrate sign, since they are the organisms themselves, but because they tend to be fairly nondescript and difficult to identify out of context, this section briefly mentions them, along with other objects that may be seen attached to or protruding from various arthropods.

Red or orange objects on insects and arachnids that appear at first glance to be eggs are in fact parasitic mites, almost always larvae in the suborder Parasitengona. There are many species, with varying degrees of

The red objects on this daddy-long-legs are not eggs but mite larvae (Erythraeidae: *Leptus*). (TN)

host specificity. Most aquatic species parasitize adult nematoceran flies, but *Hydrachna* (Hydrachnidae) is found on aquatic true bugs; *Arrenurus* (Arrenuridae) on dragonflies and damselflies; and *Eylais* (Eylaidae) on adult aquatic beetles.

Some mesostigmatid mites also spend part of their lives on beetles and other terrestrial insects, not as parasites but as "hitchhikers." This habit is called *phoresy*. Some are obviously legged and mobile, and unlikely to be mistaken for eggs, such as the *Poecilochirus* species (Parasitidae) that ride carrion beetles to carrion, where they feed on fly eggs and larvae. Uropodid nymphs, however, produce colorless anal excretions that harden to form a pedicel by which they attach to the insect. These nymphs are brown and disc-shaped, and they tuck in all their legs while they ride. Tiny, whitish, nonfeeding nymphs in the suborder Acaridia similarly ride insects to favorable habitats, where they develop into feeding adults. Sometimes hyperphoretic acarid nymphs can be found riding uropodid nymphs. Bee lice (Braulidae: *Braula coeca*) are brown, mite-size, wingless flies that get around by riding honeybees. They cling between the bee's thorax and abdomen, periodically moving to the head to drink saliva from the bee's mouthparts.

Larvae of twisted-winged parasites (Strepsiptera) are internal parasites of other insects. When mature, the larva pupates inside its skin, forming a largely featureless puparium that protrudes between the host's abdominal segments. Female puparia are flattened; those of males are rounded and much more conspicuous. The winged adult male removes the cap of its puparium, flies to a female (which never leaves her host), and mates. Several thousand larvae hatch inside her body and emerge as tiny, legged crea-

Puparia of two male twisted-winged parasites (Strepsiptera: Stylopidae: *Xenos*) protrude from the abdomen of a northern paper wasp (Vespidae: *Polistes fuscatus*). (OK) Photo by Sam Houston.

tures, which enter another host insect's body and develop inside it. The Stylopidae parasitize bees and wasps; the Corioxenidae develop in true bugs; the Elenchidae in delphacid planthoppers; and the Halictophagidae in various "hoppers" (Auchenorrhyncha) as well as pygmy mole crickets (Tridactylidae). In the Myrmecolacidae, which include two extreme southern species, males develop in ants, whereas females parasitize Orthoptera and mantids. Strepsipterans generally do not kill their hosts, but they feed on reproductive organs, usually sterilizing the host and often causing it to change color. "Stylopized" bees and wasps may acquire characteristics of the opposite sex.

Dryinid wasps are parasitoids of leafhoppers, delphacid planthoppers, and other Auchenorrhyncha. The female temporarily paralyzes the host by stinging it, then lays an egg between two overlapping sclerites (plates of the exoskeleton), often on the abdomen but sometimes close to the head. The larva develops here, eventually forming a conspicuously protruding, brown to black sac (soft and yellowish in *Aphelopus*) composed of its cast skins. The sac balloons out from the host, making it easily distinguishable from the tip of a strepsipteran puparium. When full grown, the larva leaves the sac to pupate in a white cocoon away from the host (on foliage or in ground debris), which usually dies firmly attached to vegetation. *Ismarus* species (Diapriidae) are wasps that parasitize dryinid larvae.

Left: A leafhopper (Cicadellidae: *Ponana*) parasitized by a dryinid wasp larva. (NJ) Photo by John R. Maxwell. *Right:* A planthopper parasitized by a planthopper parasite moth larva (Epipyropidae: *Fulgoraecia exigua*). (AR) Photo by Edward Trammel.

A caterpillar with *Euplectrus* wasp larvae (Eulophidae). (TN)

The first-instar larva of the planthopper parasite moth (Epipyropidae: *Fulgoraecia exigua*) attaches to the abdomen of a planthopper, where it feeds beneath the wings as an ectoparasite, sucking body fluids, until ready to pupate. It secretes white wax that covers its body, making it quite conspicuous as it grows and displaces the host's wings.

Larvae of many ichneumonids, braconids, chalcids, and other wasps are ectoparasitoids, but virtually all of them develop on hosts in enclosed situations, such as in galls, leaf mines, cocoons, or galleries in wood. The only known exceptions among chalcids are *Euplectrus* and a few other eulophids, which live externally on free-living caterpillars. The larvae, which are sometimes a striking bluish green, congregate in a ball on the host's back. When mature, *Euplectrus* larvae spin loose, wispy, white

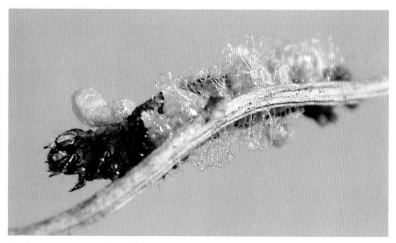

Euplectrus larvae and their flimsy cocoons spun between their host caterpillar and the substrate. (FL) Photo by Jeff Hollenbeck.

cocoons under the host larva so that it is attached to the substrate and retained as a protective covering. Sometimes they are arranged in a neat row. Just before pupating they deposit their meconium (waste) pellets, which may be found attached to the outside of the cocoons.

Bethylid wasp larvae are gregarious ectoparasitoids of moth and beetle larvae in concealed situations. These include wood borers, seed feeders, casebearers, leafrollers, leafminers, and soil dwellers. The female usually stings the host repeatedly so that it is permanently paralyzed, then either leaves it where it is or stashes it in a crevice. Mature larvae spin capsule-shaped, fuzzy, white or brown cocoons similar to those of some braconids.

Certain pimpline ichneumonid larvae are solitary ectoparasitoids of spiders, attaching to the upper side of the host's abdomen. These have distinctive paired, fleshy projections along their length. The larva of the spider wasp *Minagenia osoria* (Pompilidae) lives as an ectoparasitoid of a wolf spider (Lycosidae). Rhopalosomatid wasp larvae are external parasitoids of cricket nymphs. Scoliid wasp larvae are ectoparasitoids of June bug (*Phyllophaga*) and other scarab larvae. The female burrows into soil or rotting wood, stings the host larva, digs a small chamber around it, and deposits an egg on it.

Larvae of most cedar beetles (Rhipiceridae: *Sandalus*) are ectoparasitoids of cicada nymphs.

The larva of the humpbacked fly *Cataclinusa pachycondylae* (Phoridae) coils around the neck of a panther ant larva (Formicidae: *Pachycondyla harpax*) and steals food that worker ants bring to feed it.

Symbiocladius midges (Chironomidae) are parasites of mayfly nymphs. The larva spins a silken sac under the nymph's wing pads, making a small hole in its skin and sucking its juices.

Branchiobdellid worms live exclusively on the bodies of crayfish. Their egg cases are about 1 mm across, whitish, and nearly perfectly spherical. They are deposited on the crayfish's exoskeleton, generally in fairly protected nooks, and often in groups of three or more. The water boatman *Ramphocorixa acuminata* (Corixidae) also often attaches its eggs to the bodies of crayfish. Neither of these are actually parasites; in fact, there is evidence that the worms are beneficial.

Sacculina (Sacculinidae), a relative of barnacles, is parasitic on crabs. It is visible as a fleshy sac attached to the underside of the host's abdomen. This strange creature gets its food by permeating the inside of the crab with a system of rootlike structures.

Pathogenic Fungi

Many insects and spiders meet their end as a result of infection by pathogenic fungi, which are often highly host-specific. Infection generally begins with a fungal spore simply landing on the host. The spore germinates, and the fungus grows internally until it kills the host, at which

The distinctive fruiting body of a *Cordyceps* fungus projects from its victim, an ant. (MS) Photo by Mark S. Fox.

point spore-bearing structures usually emerge from the corpse. There are many unrelated groups of pathogenic fungi, and they come in a variety of forms, but the few that are described here account for the majority of the conspicuous and commonly seen types.

Tropical species of *Cordyceps* (Clavicipitales) are famous for compelling ants and other insects and spiders to climb up vegetation and cling to it, thereby improving the chances of spore dispersal. After mummifying the victim and absorbing its nutrients, these fungi produce distinctive long, clublike fruiting bodies that project from the host, either singly or in a cluster. Many *Cordyceps* species occur in North America, especially in areas with warm, humid summers. Although some compel their hosts to climb, as just described, the most abundant examples are on shallowly buried insects, such as larvae and pupae of moths, scarabs, click beetles, and crane flies. Some infect scale insects. The fruiting bodies range from about 8 mm tall in aerial species to 4 inches (10 cm) high in those growing from the ground. They may be whitish, yellow, orange, brown, or blackish.

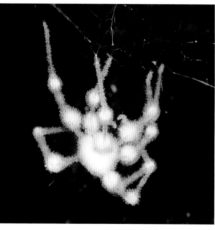

A cellar spider (Pholcidae) killed by the fungus *Torrubiella pulvinata*. (MA)

A related but very different-looking fungus, *Torrubiella pulvinata*, kills cellar spiders (Pholcidae). It first appears as white, fluffy spheres surrounding the body and each of the leg joints, eventually forming a complete covering of white fuzz.

The most commonly encountered arthropod pathogenic fungi belong to the order Entomophthorales. Many of these, like *Cordyceps*, cause insects to climb vegetation and clasp it tightly, an affliction often referred to as "summit disease." Rather than producing stalked structures, these fungi release spores through the host's membranes, such as between abdominal segments, where the fungal body often visibly bulges out. Many species attach infected insects to vegetation by white structures called *rhizoids*.

Above: A snipe fly (Rhagionidae: *Rhagio*) fused to the underside of a leaf by the fungus *Furia ithacensis*. (MA) *Right:* The fungus *Entomophthora muscae* caused this fly to die hanging by its mouthparts. The whitish coloring on its abdomen is all part of the fungus. (NH)

The *Entomophaga grylli* species complex infects various grasshoppers, and its effects are conspicuous because of the size of its victims, which die clasping vegetation head-up. *Entomophthora muscae* causes various types of flies to stick to walls and other objects by rhizoids emerging from the proboscis and legs. One summer in Vermont, it seemed as if the underside of every leaf had a snipe fly (Rhagionidae: *Rhagio*) that appeared to have melted onto it, a victim of *Furia ithacensis*. Adult caddisflies found stuck to the undersides of stones in streams are victims of *Erynia rhizospora*. *Entomophaga maimaiga* causes gypsy moth larvae (Lymantriidae: *Lymantria dispar*) to die hanging vertically along tree trunks with their prolegs extended to the sides.

This grasshopper is a victim of a fungus in the *Entomophaga grylli* species complex. (TN)

Left: A forest tent caterpillar (Lasiocampidae: *Malacosoma disstria*) killed by the fungus *Furia crustosa.* (VT) *Right:* The bottom of this beech is coated with the corpses of fungus-killed forest tent caterpillars. (VT)

A "friendly fly" (Sarcophagidae: *Metoposarcophaga aldrichi*) killed by the fungus *Pandora bullata.* (MA)

Periodical cicadas missing the ends of their abdomens, a characteristic sign of the fungus *Massospora cicadina*. (TN)

Furia crustosa causes massive die-offs of forest tent caterpillars (Lasiocampidae: *Malacosoma disstria*). The victims become attached to tree bark by their stiffened prolegs, the front ends of their bodies drooping backward. The spores are released later in the season as the shriveled, brittle caterpillars begin to disintegrate. In tent caterpillar outbreak years, this carnage is compounded, as "friendly flies" (Sarcophagidae: *Metoposarcophaga aldrichi*), which are parasitoids of the caterpillars, succumb in large numbers to a fungus of their own, *Pandora bullata*. They become mummified and attached to the tips of twigs of understory shrubs.

Some of the Entomophthorales release spores from the ruptured bodies of living hosts, which continue to go about their business as if nothing is wrong. *Strongwellsea castrans* infects *Delia* spp. flies (Anthomyiidae), ejecting spores through a neat hole in the side of the abdomen. *Entomophthora erupta* erupts from the backs of active green apple bugs (Miridae: *Lygocoris communis*) and other mirine plant bugs. *Massospora cicadina* causes the abdominal segments of periodical cicadas (*Magicicada septendecim*) to break off one at a time as the insects continue to fly, call, and attempt to mate. This species has somehow managed to get on a seventeen-year emergence cycle to match that of its host.

Bacteria and Viruses

Bacteria such as *Bacillus thuringiensis* are common causes of death in caterpillars and other larvae. Symptoms of bacterial infections include sluggishness, reduced feeding activity, and rectal and oral discharges. Once dead, larvae quickly darken, usually becoming soft and limp, losing their shape. The skin stays intact for a while and is stretchy rather than brittle. The innards are viscous and foul-smelling. *B. popilliae* and *B. lentimorbus* cause scarab larvae to turn white, symptomatic of an affliction known as "milky disease." Other bacteria can turn insect larvae red or yellow. Larvae that are limp with spasmodic convulsions may be infected with *Rickettsia*.

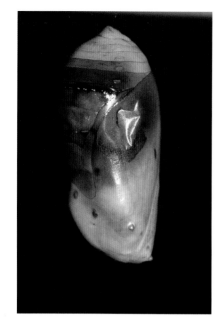

This monarch chrysalis has succumbed to a nuclear polyhedrosis virus. (MA)

Baculoviruses are highly species-specific pathogens, mostly of lepidopteran larvae, but also of sawfly and other insect larvae. Their symptoms are similar to those caused by bacteria, including wet discharges from both ends, but no foul smell is produced when the larva dies, and its skin breaks apart easily. Its decomposition releases more virus onto vegetation, to be consumed by other larvae. There are two types of baculoviruses: granulosis viruses and nuclear polyhedrosis viruses (NPV). Granulosis viruses cause the victim's blood to become more opaque, which can make the larva appear dramatically whitened externally. NPV-infected larvae may become discolored, often growing restless and climbing high up in a tree, where they die hanging limply by the prolegs, turning black as they decay. Viruses causing these effects are sometimes called "caterpillar wilt" or "treetop disease." A chrysalis infected with NPV develops brown splotches, eventually shriveling and turning completely black.

The less well-known cytoplasmic polyhedrosis viruses cause the infected larva's gut to malfunction, resulting in a shrunken and starved appearance. In contrast to a baculovirus infection, the larva generally becomes weak and drops to the ground before dying, rather than staying attached to vegetation. Contamination of foliage comes from cream-colored droppings that the larva produces for a while before dropping to the ground.

A gypsy moth caterpillar infected with a nuclear polyhedrosis virus hangs beside another that has successfully pupated. (NY)

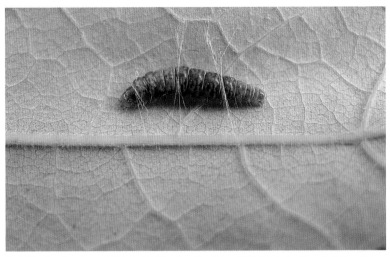

An iridovirus has turned this tortricid caterpillar blue. (NH) Photo by Bonnie J. Caruthers.

Iridoviruses produce a bluish tinge under the skin of fly, beetle, and lepidopteran larvae. Infected woodlice can become uniformly bright blue or purple. Note that a dramatic color change is not always a sign of disease. Many leaf-rolling and -tying caterpillars normally change from green to bright pink just before pupating.

Other Causes of Insect Death

Sometimes insects end up dead and stuck in prominent places for reasons having nothing to do with predation, parasitism, or pathogens.

One very conspicuous phenomenon is the masses of dead aquatic snipe flies (Athericidae) found on twigs or other objects overhanging streams. Numerous *Atherix variegata* females are attracted to one spot, where they each deposit an egg mass and stay with it until they die. They may form a ball several inches across surrounding a twig, or a much larger but flattened mass on a flat surface such as the underside of a bridge. Some accounts state that the larvae feed on the corpses until the mass falls into the water; others say the larvae simply drop into the water when they hatch, leaving the mass suspended above. The latter appeared to be the case in the example we found.

Dead insects are sometimes found on milkweed flowers. The flowers are complex structures with the pollen sacs hidden in slits. Pollination depends on an insect's leg slipping into one of the slits and picking up one of the sticky pollen sacs, then slipping into a slit in another flower and leaving the pollen sac there. Some insects become trapped and die with their legs stuck in the slits.

Part of a large mass of female aquatic snipe flies (Athericidae: *Atherix variegata*) that have laid eggs and died on the ceiling of a culvert. (MN)

Female horntails (Siricidae), which insert their ovipositors into dead trees to lay eggs, sometimes cannot get them back out and end up dying stuck in the tree as a result. The giant ichneumons (*Megarhyssa*) that parasitize horntail larvae sometimes suffer the same fate. You may find just an ovipositor sticking out of a tree, indicating that a bird or mammal either scavenged the dead insect or took advantage of its vulnerable state while it was in the act of ovipositing.

Sign on Vertebrates

4

Invertebrates can leave characteristic sign when they feed on vertebrates, either externally or internally, and when they bite or sting in self-defense. As you are most likely to notice this kind of sign when it involves you, we begin this chapter with a discussion of invertebrate sign on humans. This is followed by a summary of parasitism and predation sign on nonhuman vertebrates, and finally a brief look at invertebrates associated with vertebrate remains and droppings.

Sign on Humans

Identification of invertebrates by the sign left on human skin is complicated by changes that take place as the lesions (tissue abnormalities) age, and also by the variability in immune responses among individuals. Lesions without pain suggest species using human-specific anesthetics, and ones without itch point to those with anti-inflammatory proteins. Pain blunts the perception of itch. Thus skin lesions can be broadly divided into three categories: those with instantaneous pain (usually followed by varying degrees of itchiness once the pain diminishes); those with itch but no pain; and those with no significant sensation. Sign from other organs, including systemic allergy, can be linked to specific groups of invertebrates but may not be identifiable without other evidence.

Instantaneously Painful Skin Lesions

Ants, Bees, and Wasps

The "stingers" of ants, bees, and wasps (Hymenoptera) are complex structures containing a smooth central stylet and two lancets bearing recurved barbs that alternately scissor deeper into the skin. Except in the case of honeybees, the barbed lancets can be shielded by the stylet, allowing for

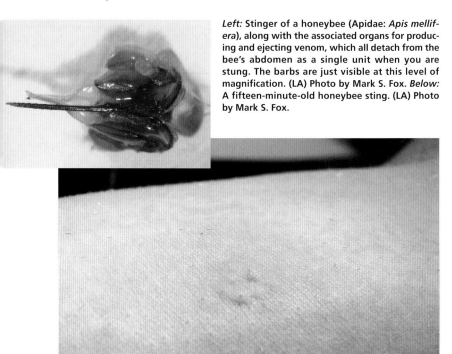

Left: Stinger of a honeybee (Apidae: *Apis mellifera*), along with the associated organs for producing and ejecting venom, which all detach from the bee's abdomen as a single unit when you are stung. The barbs are just visible at this level of magnification. (LA) Photo by Mark S. Fox. *Below:* A fifteen-minute-old honeybee sting. (LA) Photo by Mark S. Fox.

removal once venom has been injected. When a wasp is forcibly removed midsting, however, the stinger may remain lodged in the skin. With honeybees, the large, recurved barbs cannot be sufficiently shielded and thus cannot be withdrawn. In addition, the posterior section of the abdomen, containing the venom sac, is designed to tear away and thus is left behind as the bee departs. Examination of the retained material under a microscope can help determine whether the insect was a honeybee or another species. Differentiation is of great value in selecting the correct venom to use in desensitization for those that have experienced life-threatening reactions to stings.

Schmidt (1990) has worked out a vividly descriptive scale to compare the pain induced by the various Hymenoptera species. For example, for a paper wasp, he writes: "3.0. Caustic and burning. Distinctly bitter aftertaste. Like spilling a beaker of hydrochloric acid on a paper cut." Venom from social species functions to deter mammals that endanger their nests and therefore is generally more painful than venom of solitary Hymenoptera, which is primarily used to immobilize invertebrate prey. When multiple painful stings have occurred, a disturbed nest is likely to be nearby. The amount of pain produced by a species is not fixed, because the protein content of venom changes over a season, and the quantity of venom injected is variable. Reactions also depend on whether a person's immune system has developed tolerance or sensitivity to previous stings. It is

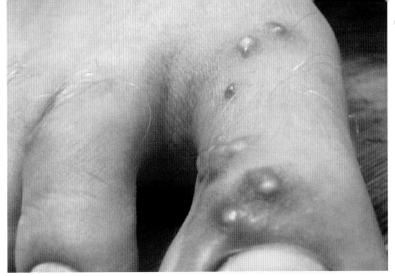

Sterile pustules caused by stings of imported fire ants (Formicidae: *Solenopsis*). (LA) Photo by Thomas Gage.

unclear why some individuals develop hypersensitivity while others become more tolerant; allergy to venom does not appear to be related to other types of allergies, nor is it inherited. Large local reactions to venom—swelling continuous with the sting site but spreading beyond the normal extent—do not increase the risk for systemic allergy, involving respiratory, cardiac, gastrointestinal, or diffuse skin symptoms.

Ant species with venom may inject it by stinging or releasing it into a wound inflicted by biting. Wounds occur on skin closest to the ground, in contrast with stings from flying Hymenoptera, which preferentially target the face. Imported fire ants (*Solenopsis invicta*) leave characteristic clusters of sterile pustules—small, smooth, white, blisterlike bumps—that appear within twenty-four hours. The clustering occurs when the ants bite with their mandibles, then rotate their bodies to repeatedly sting and inject their unique alkaline venom.

Blood-feeding Flies

Animals that feed primarily on nonhuman blood (*zoophilic* species) lack salivary anesthetics effective for humans and therefore trigger pain receptors when they attempt to feed. Concurrent or subsequent itch occurs as a result of a reaction to salivary proteins used to maintain blood flow. The sudden pain and inflammation can be difficult to distinguish from a hymenopteran sting in the case of day-feeding tabanids

Typical bite of the "yellow fly of the Dismal Swamp" (Tabanidae: *Diachlorus ferrugatus*). (VA)

(deer flies and horse flies), which have slicing, serrated mandibles, although there is more bleeding due to salivary anticoagulants. Sand flies (Psychodidae: *Lutzomyia*), black flies (Simuliidae), and biting midges (Ceratopogonidae) are very small flies that produce correspondingly smaller itching lesions that are mildly painful during the bite. Stable flies (Muscidae: *Stomoxys calcitrans*) are between tabanids and other biting flies in size. Thrips (Thysanoptera) are small insects that will bite humans for unknown reasons. Their bites are most similar to those of biting midges, in both their intensity and the difficulty of identifying the tiny insect responsible. Some of these may be important vectors for spread of disease to humans and other vertebrates. In Mexico, for instance, sand flies transmit skin and gut forms of leishmaniasis. The dreaded mucocutaneous form of this disease can cause severe facial disfiguration.

True Bugs

Assassin bugs (Reduviidae) can inflict painful bites with their large sucking proboscises. Members of the conenose subfamily (Triatominae) feed primarily on vertebrate blood, and many of these inject an anesthetic to lessen the pain, though the bites may still itch later. Feeding bites usually occur at night, often on soft parts such as lips. For this reason, conenose bugs are also called "kissing bugs." From coastal Mexico down through South America, conenoses are important vectors for the potentially fatal Chagas disease, which some blame for killing Charles Darwin. Bugs acquire the disease by feasting on an infected person and transmit it through feces left while feeding on another person. Streaks of liquid feces on sheets or walls are seen in infested homes.

Giant water bugs (Belostomatidae) and other predatory aquatic Heteroptera inject neurotoxins into their prey. Bites can be excruciatingly painful, despite the absence of redness and swelling. After experiencing giant water bug and creeping water bug (Naucoridae) bites, John gained an appreciation of Schmidt's inclusion of wild descriptions in his scale. The pain was so pure that it can only be described as electrical. There was no sign of the bite, during the pain or afterward, except for the puncture mark where the proboscis entered. He would rate the magnitude of pain as equivalent to a yellowjacket sting, but so pure that it was actually much less bothersome—it was mostly just remarkable. A friend's similar experiences with other water bugs suggest that this is a characteristic of the aquatic Heteroptera as a group. Although it is believed that Heteroptera inject necrotic enzymes into prey to liquefy the tissue, John experienced no inflammation or discoloration, perhaps because the enzymes are not very effective on human tissue. There are scattered reports, however, of permanent damage being done to people who let them feed for too long.

Caterpillars

The few species of venomous caterpillars are cryptically colored. The severity of the reaction in the victim is highly dependent on whether breakaway spines are retained in the skin. Retained spines are likely if blisters form.

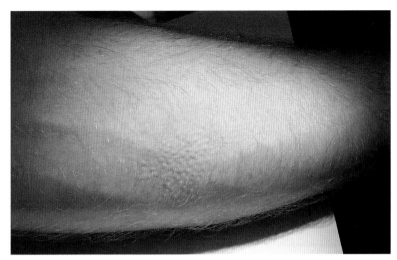

Two-minute-old urtication marks from brief contact with the top side of a puss caterpillar (Megalopygidae: *Megalopyge*). (LA) Photo by John C. Carlson.

These spines inject histamine, which generates itching welts at the site of contact, in addition to species-specific toxins. Most reactions occur to species of slug caterpillars (Limacodidae), flannel moth caterpillars (Megalopygidae), and giant silkmoth caterpillars (Saturniidae). For most species (e.g., io moths, *Automeris io*), symptoms subside within minutes or hours. Puss (Megalopygidae: *Megalopyge*), saddleback (Limacodidae: *Acharia stimulea*), and buck moth (Saturniidae: *Hemileuca*) caterpillars induce intense local pain and swelling that can last for days, sometimes followed by aching at lymph nodes draining the area envenomated (for example, armpit for arm envenomations, groin for leg envenomations). When John placed a puss caterpillar on his arm, the aching in the armpit was much more bothersome than the sharp pain on the arm. The inflamed impressions of spines are particularly prominent in puss caterpillar envenomations. Saddleback caterpillars can induce a fleeting paralysis in the affected limb, lasting about five seconds when we timed the reaction on a human.

Blister Beetles

Male blister beetles (Meloidae) produce a defensive fluid containing a blistering agent (cantharidin), which is transferred to females during mating. It is released when beetles feel threatened. Blisters are generally larger than those seen in caterpillar envenomations.

Arachnids and Centipedes

Scorpion sting reactions are highly variable and depend on both the quantity and type of venom injected. In severe cases of neurotoxin injection by Arizona bark scorpions (*Centruroides sculpturatus*), pain is accompanied by tremors of the affected muscles.

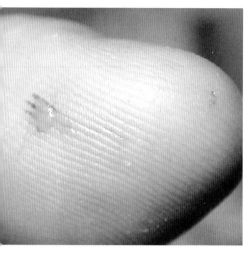

Fresh bite of a Carolina wolf spider (Lycosidae: *Hogna carolinensis*). Note the two puncture wounds about 1 cm apart. (FL) Photo by Jeff Hollenbeck.

Bites of both centipedes and spiders consist of two closely spaced punctures (visible if inspected early), whereas other arthropods typically produce a single puncture. Members of these two groups inject venom with a pair of specialized appendages near the mouth (*chelicerae* in spiders, *forcipules* in centipedes). The spacing between the chelicerae or forcipules determines the spacing of the skin punctures. Reactions to bites of most centipedes and spiders (e.g., wolf spiders, Lycosidae) are typically minor, with pain and swelling dissipating within a couple of days. House centipedes and hunting spiders bite when they are sheltering in shoes or clothes that are put on without giving them a chance to escape. After putting on a shirt that had been left on the floor, one of us experienced the surprising, painful pinch of a house centipede, which produced a dark red, marble-sized bump that lasted for three days.

Though the small bites of brown recluse spiders (Sicariidae: *Loxosceles reclusa*) are often painless, their venom can sometimes lead to significant inflammation of a purplish hue indicating necrosis (dying flesh), which usually heals without incident. Brown recluses rarely bite people, and they are falsely blamed for many other unrelated skin problems. Many spiders will bite when trapped, but black widow spiders (Theridiidae: *Latrodectus*) are the most dangerous North American species. Their bites are very painful and are occasionally followed by systemic reactions to the injected neurotoxin, such as cramping, nausea, and other symptoms.

Itching Lesions

In species adapted to feeding on human blood, the saliva often contains anesthetics and substances that promote blood flow so that feeding is brief and painless. Sensation is generally absent until the arthropod has departed, at which time itching and inflammation develop in reaction to the salivary proteins. The classic lesion induced by blood-feeding insects is termed *papular urticaria*: a small, raised bump with a central puncture mark at the site of proboscis insertion. "Satellite" papules may be seen as well.

A person's history of previous insect bites has a strong influence on the extent and duration of inflammation surrounding a bite. Your immune response depends in part on how many times you have been bitten by the species, and partly on the peculiarities of your own unique body. Generally, through a lifetime of repeated exposure to a particular insect species, your reaction starts out mild, gets more intense, then becomes mild again. Young children can develop large, intensely inflamed mosquito bite reactions, accompanied by fever, referred to as "skeeter syndrome." With continued exposure, the reactions subside, becoming rare in adolescents. The first time you are ever bitten by a mosquito, you will have no reaction, because your immune system has not yet developed any antibodies to mosquito proteins. As time goes by and you are bitten by more and more mosquitoes, your body builds up more and more mosquito-specific antibodies. The twist is that there are two types of antibodies that act in distinct ways. One set of antibodies (IgE) causes you to become more and more sensitive to the bites. Mosquito bites become increasingly inflamed and irritating as you become more sensitive. The other set of antibodies (IgG) actually blocks the first set of antibodies, thus suppressing the response and making you more tolerant to the bites. This sequence of sensitization followed by tolerance differs for each person and for each group of insect species. If you have developed tolerance to mosquitoes, you can still become miserably sensitized to fleas or any other kind of biting arthropod. At the height of sensitization, bites can cause the nearest glands to swell and your whole body to grow weary.

The most intensely itchy bites are produced by species that leave foreign proteins in your skin for a long time, such as chiggers, scabies, and zoonotic hookworms. When organisms such as mosquitoes bite, fewer proteins are left behind, so the reaction tends to be more fleeting and less intense.

Mosquitoes

Mosquitoes feed for a relatively short time and are among the arthropods that tend to produce less inflamed, less colorful bites. Itching begins within a few minutes of being bitten and often fades faster than with chiggers. As with all bites, individual reactions are highly variable. Mosquito females of most species are very active at dusk and dawn, with variation in daytime

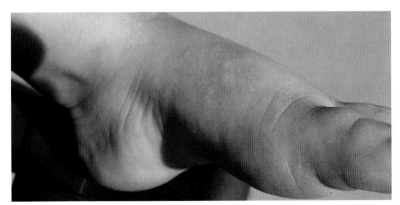

Classic papular urticaria from mosquito (Culicidae) bites. Note the "satellite" lesions, which are smaller bumps that appear near the main bump. These tend to itch less and go away sooner. (LA) Photo by John C. Carlson.

and nighttime feeding patterns. They follow carbon dioxide to the vicinity of warm-blooded animals, and then use airborne chemicals to locate skin. These chemicals vary from person to person and between sites on an individual. Thus mosquitoes preferentially feed on a given area (e.g., the lower legs) of a particular member of the group (e.g., a nonvegetarian). Species that feed on birds and humans may transmit encephalitis viruses, of which West Nile virus is the most common. These infections may have no symptoms or cause a flulike condition. Rarely, confusion and other signs of encephalitis develop. In Mexico, mosquitoes also carry dengue and malaria.

Chiggers and Other Mites

The intensely itchy bites of larval chiggers (Trombiculidae: *Trombicula*) are familiar to people who venture outdoors during summer in southeastern states. Chiggers crawl over your skin before they settle into constricted areas such as armpits, groins, beneath clothing elastic, and the backsides of knees to feed. There, the tiny mites (less than 0.2 mm) inject saliva that breaks down skin cells and forms a hard feeding tube (stylostome), through which they slurp out a soup of cell fluids. Undisturbed, they might feed for several hours to a couple days before dropping off. The chiggers are easily brushed off by the swipe of your hand, but the stylostome remains behind as your body slowly breaks it down. Chigger bites tend to produce large, hard, red bumps that peak in itching a day or two after exposure and may persist for several weeks until the stylostome has been reabsorbed. The itching is typically most noticeable at night while you are trying unsuccessfully to sleep through it. Other mites that can be problematic for people include those that parasitize home-invading animals such as birds and rodents, as well as predatory itch mites (e.g., *Pyemotes tritici* and *P. herfsi*).

Ticks

Ticks generally feed without being noticed, although their bites can sometimes be painful or become itchy on repeated exposure. Itchiness might protect against infection by tick-borne diseases by prompting the person to remove the tick early. Lyme disease is thought to be transmitted by ticks only after twenty-four hours or more of attachment. Secondary infection at the bite can occur if mouthparts are left in the skin during tick removal. Diseases carried by ticks sometimes produce characteristic rashes, such as spots on hands and feet due to Rocky Mountain spotted fever, a bull's-eye caused by Lyme disease, or a similar-looking bull's-eye from southern tick–associated rash illness (STARI). Some tick species can induce a progressive paralysis when feeding, but removal of the tick leads to recovery.

Female hard ticks (Ixodidae) lay eggs in one large mass (up to 20,000 eggs), which hatch into a mass of tiny larvae known as "seed ticks." If you are curious about seed ticks, take a walk through a middle Tennessee forest with thick undergrowth in late August, when the lone star ticks (*Amblyomma americanum*) are hatching. They will crawl right through the fabric

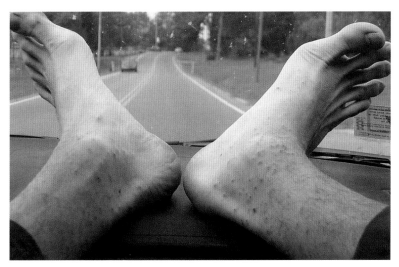

Bite marks from immature lone star "seed ticks" (Ixodidae: *Amblyomma americanum*). (TN)

of your socks for an easy meal. If you do not remove them soon enough, the next day you will find hundreds of red welts on each leg, like small, itchy chigger bites. If you discover them right away, scraping your ankles with your fingernails will lodge dozens of ticks under each nail. The concentration of bites on the lower legs and ankles is characteristic of seed ticks, though these will be evident and itchy only if your immune system is properly sensitized. It is possible for newly hatched seed ticks to acquire infectiousness from their mothers, but ticks most often transmit diseases as older nymphs or adults.

Bed Bugs

Bed bugs (Cimicidae: *Cimex lectularius*) are true bugs that superficially resemble ticks and feast on vertebrate blood. They produce red bumps similar to mosquito bites, with swelling related to sensitization. They feed on exposed skin, such as the back of a shirtless person sleeping facedown. Bed bugs tend to feed, walk a bit, then feed again. This often results in a row or cluster of several bites near each other. Bed bugs emit an odor that has been described as sickly sweet. The reddish fluid that they excrete can be seen on bedding and clothing. It can be difficult to locate the bugs, which hide in mattresses or other nearby locations during the day.

Fleas

Fleas (Siphonaptera) vary with regard to the length of time they attach to feed. The vast majority of flea bites on humans, dogs, and cats are caused by the cat flea (Pulicidae: *Ctenocephalides felis*). As with most fleas that bite humans, this species is incapable of completing its life cycle on human blood, and attempts to feed are brief but potentially persistent. Reactions similar to "skeeter syndrome" are common into adulthood.

Lice

Head lice (Pediculidae: *Pediculus humanus capitis*), contrary to popular belief, rarely cause significant itching. John has observed that people often start scratching only after they are told that they have head lice. He also sees scratching among large groups of uninfested people when he gives talks about lice. Infestations are suggested by finding eggs (nits) cemented onto hair shafts within 1 cm of the scalp, primarily above the ears to the back of the head. Past infestations are suggested by finding light-colored (empty) nits attached farther than 15 mm from the scalp. Pubic lice (Pthiridae: *Pthirus pubis*) and their nits, though typically restricted to the pubic area, can be found on head and facial hair, including the eyelashes when infesting children. Two nits per follicle are not unusual for this species. Small blue spots and itching may be seen at the site of feeding. In Mexico, body lice and other arthropods can transmit typhus.

Scabies

Human scabies mites (Sarcoptidae: *Sarcoptes scabiei hominis*) create short (5- to 15-mm), straight or curved burrows just under the skin, typically with a small raised area at the end where the mite resides. This sign is frequently obscured by scratching. Common sites include the webs of the fingers and groin. Dog scabies mites (*S. scabiei canis*) can cause itching in humans where skin contact is made with an infested animal, but these mites cannot maintain an infestation in humans who have an intact immune system.

Other Causes of Itch

Sometimes people think their itching rashes are from "bug" bites when they are not. Here are some common alternate explanations for biteless bumps. Scratching can lead to irritation that triggers additional itch as it heals, resulting in the "itch-scratch cycle." A bite reaction remains centered at the site of the bite, in contrast to hives that move over the course of minutes to hours. The "id reaction" is a diffuse, intensely itching rash with individual bumps that lack a central puncture. It results from nonspecific immune activation triggered after prolonged exposure to scabies, lice, and other irritants.

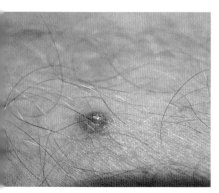

Lesion associated with "swamp itch," at the entry point of a hookworm (Nematoda: Ancylostomatidae: *Ancylostoma*). (LA) Photo by John C. Carlson.

Hookworms (Nematoda: Ancylostomatidae: *Ancylostoma*) of domesticated animals occasionally enter human skin that contacts contaminated soil. These hookworm species are unable to enter the bloodstream. Instead, they migrate through the skin in a graceful, looping pattern, inducing an intensely itchy red trail called *cutaneous larval migrans* as they travel.

"Swimmer's itch" from bird flukes (Platyhelminthes: Schistosomatidae: *Schistosoma*) and "swamp itch" from hookworms of nutria and raccoons result from immune destruction of these parasites at the site where they enter human skin. An itchy, inflamed lesion of variable size (depending on the degree of prior sensitization) develops at the site of each worm, sometimes becoming filled with clear or cloudy fluid. The distribution is consistent with uncovered skin exposed to fresh water.

"Sea bather's itch," in contrast to swimmer's itch, occurs in areas covered by clothing. It is caused by defensive actions of the larvae of jellyfish and sea anemones that become trapped in the clothing.

Loose, floating hairs from some caterpillars (e.g., gypsy moths, Lymantriidae: *Lymantria dispar*), when they occur in great numbers, have caused outbreaks of itching rashes on exposed skin. Rarely, airborne hairs or scales shed from the adults' wings can cause respiratory and other systemic symptoms.

Relatively Painless and Itchless Skin Lesions

Leeches

In our experience, leech (Hirudinea) bites are surprisingly painless, and we are often unaware that we have been bitten until long after we leave the water and look down to see leeches sucking on our legs. It seems that researchers have not yet found anesthetics in leech saliva to explain this lack of pain, so perhaps it is due to small mouthparts and the numbing effects of cold water. Larger species and terrestrial species on other continents are said to be more painful. Special proteins contained in leech saliva do prevent blood from clotting. When a leech is removed, blood flows freely until the anticoagulants have worn off, which might take several hours. North American jawed leeches (Hirudinidae) all have three jaws that leave a characteristic Y-shaped wound. (The terrestrial leeches on other continents are two-jawed.) Jawless leeches for the most part can extract blood only through preexisting wounds, but some (Glossiphoniidae: *Placobdella*) are able to pierce skin between fingers and toes with their proboscises. For a few days following removal of a leech, bites may itch or develop local bruising.

Millipedes

Millipedes (Diplopoda) produce defensive fluids when alarmed that are ineffective against human skin. Contact with this fluid causes no pain in humans, but it oxidizes the skin color to a mahogany brown. Because the curved shape of the marks left by millipedes can resemble whiplashes,

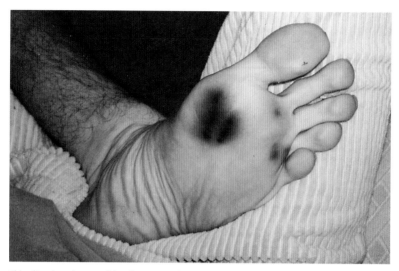

Skin discoloration resulting from stepping on a millipede (Diplopoda). (TN)

child abuse has been suspected on seeing these marks. In addition to the unique color, close examination may reveal segmentation of the marks, corresponding with the millipede's body segments.

Sign or Reactions in Other Organs and Hair

Eyes

Stick insects (Phasmatodea), and rarely other arthropods, emit a defensive spray that can induce severe reactions in the eyes. Airborne tarantula or caterpillar hairs are capable of piercing into the eye. Initially the eye's surface is inflamed. Chronic reactions against the internal hairs can lead to blindness. Superficial irritation has been reported in humans from the worm *Thelazia californiensis* (Nematoda: Thelaziidae), which can infest the tear ducts of mammals in the western United States.

Hair

Roaches will consume hair on sleeping people in heavily infested buildings, resulting in loss of eyelashes and eyebrows over time.

Intestines and Stomach

With the exception of pinworms, intestinal roundworms (Nematoda) are rare in the United States. Those that parasitize the small intestines (Ascarididae: *Ascaris*; Strongyloididae: *Strongyloides*; hookworms) can be asymptomatic to painful, sometimes interfering with digestion, resulting in frequent, loose stools that float in water. Infestation of the large intestine with whipworms (Trichuridae: *Trichuris trichiura*) can result in symptoms that range from absent to significant pain, and can lead to prolapse of the rectum and bleeding. Pinworms (Oxyuridae: *Enterobius vermicularis*) can induce significant itching as the females migrate out of the anus to deposit their eggs at night. Infestation of the female genital tract can occur when adult worms migrate inappropriately after laying eggs. Rare reports of anisakiasis occur in the United States, caused by marine mammal parasites (Anisakidae: *Anisakis*) attaching in the stomachs of humans who consume raw fish and associated with varying degrees of abdominal pain, occasionally requiring endoscopic removal. The roundworm *Gnathostoma* (Gnathostomatidae) can be ingested when eating uncooked snails, among other sources. Once in the body, they can migrate around, causing problems such as meningitis.

Intestinal tapeworms (Cestoda) are flatworms contracted from pork, beef, and dog excrement. They are probably less of a problem than the other intestinal worms, but they can encyst in the brain and other tissues, causing significant problems.

Allergic Reactions

Among the most common triggers for allergic asthma and nasal reactions is the inhalation of dust containing proteins from dead cockroaches and dust mites, as well as their waste products. Likewise, when any species is present in large numbers, such as emergence swarms of chironomid midges, congregations of multicolored Asian lady beetles (Coccinellidae: *Harmonia axyridis*), or infestations of grain mites (e.g., Glycyphagidae: *Lepidoglyphus destructor*), those exposed may develop severe respiratory and nasal allergies. A friend reports having developed an intense allergy to one particular species of tarantula that he kept as a pet when he was younger, even though he now regularly handles other species. A variety of inhaled substances can lead to other types of destructive immune activation in the lungs, such as hypersensitivity pneumonitis seen in workers exposed to proteins from granary weevils (Curculionidae: *Sitophilus granarius*), who develop fever, wheezing, and other symptoms.

Anaphylaxis is a life-threatening, systemic allergic reaction that occurs within minutes of exposure to a protein to which the immune system has previously been sensitized. Each year, forty to fifty people in the United States die from anaphylaxis to hymenopteran venom. Anaphylactic reactions frequently involve multiple organ systems. Reactions may include hives; diffuse redness; diffuse itching; swelling of the extremities, face, or mouth; difficulty swallowing, speaking, or breathing; nausea and vomiting; and lowered blood pressure, evidenced by confusion, weakness, headache, or passing out. Anaphylaxis has been well documented after exposure to the venom of bees, wasps, and ants; saliva of western conenoses (Reduviidae: *Triatoma protracta*); and consumption of crustaceans and mollusks. Anyone who has developed hives within an hour of these triggers is at increased risk for anaphylaxis with future reexposure. Life-threatening delayed reactions, starting more than a day after exposure, are rare but include *Arthus reactions*, in which venom-antibody complexes in the blood cause aches, fever, and damage of internal organs. Because allergic reactions can become worse after each reexposure, prompt evaluation by a physician is recommended if hives or other systemic reactions occur.

Parasites of Nonhuman Vertebrates

Nonhuman vertebrates are afflicted with many of the same sorts of parasites as we are, as well as others. These can be divided into the ones that live in or on their skin, *ectoparasites*, and those that live inside their bodies, *endoparasites*.

Ectoparasites

Ectoparasites of other vertebrates include familiar creatures such as ticks, mites, lice, and fleas. Some lesser known examples include leiodid beetles, hippoboscid flies, and a few invertebrates that specialize in fishes.

Ticks

Ticks (Ixodida) are parasitic on mammals, birds, and reptiles. They usually have little effect on their hosts but may cause serious inflammation and swelling.

Mites

A number of different types of mites infest the skin of mammals. *Psoroptes ovis* (Psoroptidae) causes "wet mange" on sheep, cattle, horses, and other animals. The mites feed on the surface of the skin, causing scabs to form. This species is believed to be eradicated from the United States. Ear mange mites (*Otodectes cynotis*) live in the ears of dogs, cats, and wild animals, feeding on the soft skin near the eardrum. Infested animals run around wildly, shaking their heads. *Sarcoptes scabiei canis* (Sarcoptidae), closely related to the mite responsible for scabies in humans, causes sarcoptic mange in various other mammals. Unlike psoroptid mites, these burrow under the skin, making it inflamed and itchy. Large patches of hair may fall out as a result of repeated scratching of the area. Follicle mites (Demodecidae: *Demodex*) live deep in hair follicles or oil glands, often around the eyes. They can lead to hair loss and thickening of skin, or the formation of red, pus-filled pimples or nodules, which in cattle may be up to the size of a chicken egg, although, as with similar species in humans, these common mites rarely cause problems.

Some parasitic mites are specific to birds. The species leaving the most distinctive sign is the scalyleg mite (Knemidokoptidae: *Knemidokoptes mutans*), which tunnels under the scales of birds' legs. The scales stand up, and rough swellings and encrustations form. The depluming mite (*Neocnemidocoptes laevis*) burrows into the skin at the base of the tail feathers. Infected birds pull out their tail feathers in response to the intense irritation this causes. *Dermanyssus gallinae* (Dermanyssidae) sucks the blood of resting birds at night, hiding in cracks and crevices during the day. Infested chickens become listless and are poor egg layers, and young ones may be killed. Chigger mites (Trombiculidae) feeding on birds favor the anal region and the area between the wing and thigh.

Lice

Chewing lice in the families Menoponidae, Philopteridae, Laemobothriidae, and Ricinidae are all ectoparasites of birds. Some species, such as *Myrsidea rustica* (Menoponidae), chew holes in feathers, making them ragged and disheveled. All other lice, both sucking and chewing, feed on various groups of mammals. Eggs (nits) of lice are typically white and have a circular cap, as with true bug and walkingstick eggs. They are elongate and glued singly to hairs or feathers. Eggs of some bird lice are bizarrely shaped, with a long, skinny appendage on the top and a whorl of flat projections around the cap.

Fleas

Adult fleas (Siphonaptera) also feed on both mammals and birds. They defecate while feeding, and the material dries in the animal's fur or feathers, resulting in "flea dirt" that appears red when reconstituted (see chapter 5). Most lay their white, oval eggs, 0.5 mm long, in dirt or the host's nesting area, but some lay eggs directly on the host's fur or feathers. Eggs in the latter case eventually fall off, and the wormlike larvae develop off the host, feeding on the flea dirt and other material that falls to the ground where the animal sleeps.

Beetles

The beaver parasite beetle (Leiodidae: *Platypsylla castoris*) creates small skin lesions on young beavers and feeds on the exudates. Other leiodids are found on various small rodents and insectivores.

Flies

Louse flies (Hippoboscidae) are ectoparasites of birds and mammals. The most obvious sign of their presence is their smooth, egg-shaped puparia, which are glued to feathers or fur. The best-known species is the sheep ked (*Melophagus ovinus*), found on sheep.

Fish Parasites

Fish lice (Argulidae: *Argulus*) are small crustaceans that are ectoparasites on fish. They have piercing mouthparts that inject an enzyme into the fish, thereby digesting the tissue externally before sucking it up. They cause obvious, irregular wounds, and in heavy infestations, they gradually weaken the fish.

Piscicolid leeches attach their spherical egg cases to their host fish.

The tiny larvae of freshwater mussels (Unionoida) spend their first few weeks as parasites of fish. Less than 0.5 mm long, they attach to gills or fins, becoming encysted and feeding on the fish's blood. Once they have become juveniles, they release from the fish and burrow into the sediment. Some generalist species may attach to salamanders instead of fish.

Endoparasites

The endoparasites that typically produce externally visible sign in mammals, birds, and reptiles are bot flies (Oestridae), blow flies (Calliphoridae), and flesh flies (Sarcophagidae). The infestation of live vertebrates with fly larvae is known as *myiasis*.

Bot Flies

Bot flies are large endoparasites of mammals. Females lay eggs either on the host's fur or near its nest, and depending on the species, either the host ingests the eggs by licking or inhaling, or the larvae bore into the skin. The larvae cause tumorous swellings of the skin called *warbles*, each with a small, round hole through which the larva breathes. When fully grown, the larva emerges from the skin, leaving an obvious exit wound, and pupates in the ground. *Cuterebra* species parasitize rodents and rabbits, often infesting the groin. *Hypoderma* species form warbles on the backs of cattle and bison. Because they migrate there internally from the hind legs, where the white eggs are laid, they may damage organs or cause paralysis by damaging the spinal cord. *H. tarandi* infests caribou similarly. The human bot fly (*Dermatobia hominis*) occurs in Mexico and Central America. It lays its eggs on mosquitoes, and the larvae hatch when the mosquito lands

on a person or other animal. This species is most often found around cattle.

The sheep bot fly (*Oestrus ovis*) lives in the sinuses of sheep, goats, and deer, feeding on mucus and blood. Larvae cause inflammation of the mucous membranes and a nasal discharge. Infested animals shake their heads, sneeze, and may hold their noses to the ground. *Cephenemyia* species are also nose bots, with *C. jellisoni* parasitizing deer and *C. trompe* infesting caribou. Horse bot flies (*Gasterophilus*) live in the horse's digestive tract and leave no external sign while developing. *G. intestinalis* glues its elongate, white eggs to hairs, usually on the horse's front legs, where the animal is likely to lick them up while grooming. *G. nasalis* attaches its eggs to the horse's throat, and the larvae find their own way into its mouth. *G.*

Exit wound of a bot fly (Oestridae: *Cuterebra fontinella*) in a white-footed mouse (Muridae: *Peromyscus leucopus*) killed by a cat. (MA)

The wound in this box turtle's (Emydidae: *Terrapene carolina*) neck contains at least two larvae of *Cistudinomyia cistudinis* (Sarcophagidae), a flesh fly that specializes in living turtle flesh. (TN) Photo by Adam Charney.

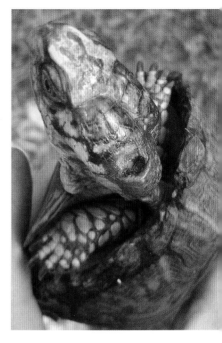

haemorrhoidalis lays them on the horse's lips. Each species develops in a different part of the digestive tract. The mature larvae pass out with excrement and pupate in the ground.

Blow Flies and Flesh Flies

Certain blow flies and flesh flies also cause myiasis in mammals. *Wohlfahrtia vigil* larvae (Sarcophagidae) are deposited on young mammals, where they bore into the skin individually and cause boils to form. The screw-worm fly (Calliphoridae: *Cochliomyia hominivorax*) lays a mass of creamy white eggs on the dry skin of a mammal at the edge of a small preexisting sore or wound, or by a mucous membrane. When the larvae hatch, they invade the tissue in this vulnerable spot, creating a smelly, open sore that attracts other blow flies. As with bot flies, the mature larvae drop to the ground to pupate. This species has largely been eradicated north of Mexico.

Some other blow flies and flesh flies are obligate endoparasites of birds and reptiles. *Protocalliphora* species (Calliphoridae) breed in nestling birds, sometimes killing them. *Cistudinomyia cistudinis* (Sarcophagidae) is a parasite of turtles and tortoises. Larvae enter through small existing openings or weak spots, such as the edge of scar tissue from old tick bites, creating large swellings and wounds with a black discharge. In occasional extreme cases, an infestation of more than a hundred larvae may kill the host.

Predators of Vertebrates

Small aquatic vertebrates regularly fall prey to certain invertebrates. Dragonfly and stonefly naiads prey on small fish and frogs. "Water tigers," the larvae of predaceous diving beetles (Dytiscidae), catch tadpoles, salamanders, and small fish, sucking their juices through the tips of their sicklelike jaws. Giant water bugs (Belostomatidae) kill fish several times their size, as well as snakes. Fishing spiders (Pisauridae: *Dolomedes*) sometimes capture small fish, taking them to a dry spot on land to feed.

Predation of vertebrates on land is less common but certainly occurs. Some fire ants (*Solenopsis*), among others, have been known to kill young mammals and birds. Praying mantises (*Mantis religiosa*) sometimes prey on small frogs and lizards, and one was observed clutching a short-tailed shrew. A very large darner (Aeshnidae) was seen picking up small frogs and eating them. The common house spider (Theridiidae: *Parasteatoda tepidariorum*) has reportedly caught, lifted, and subdued mice, small snakes, and other vertebrates in its web. Hutchins (1966) stated that "there is a case on record of a woodpecker being found in a tree with a giant water bug attached to it."

Sign on Vertebrate Remains and Dung

So far this chapter has dealt exclusively with sign on living vertebrates, but there is an equally diverse suite of invertebrates that feed on vertebrate remains and dung. Those that develop in carcasses may appear at very specific stages of decomposition, an important concept in the field of forensic entomology. Only a few of the groups discussed below leave obvious sign by which they can be identified with certainty, but others are included to provide a list of suspects to consider when pondering mysteries involving remains and dung.

Carrion

Many flesh flies and blow flies lay eggs on freshly killed meat. As decomposition ensues, anthomyiid, phorid, and sepsid flies are attracted, as well as carrion beetles (Silphidae), hister beetles (Histeridae), rove beetles (Staphylinidae), and sap beetles (Nitidulidae). These insects do not tend to leave distinct, recognizable sign as they break down a carcass. The pupae of phorids are often found attached to bones and other sources of decay-

A mouse in the process of being buried by a pair of tomentose burying beetles (Silphidae: *Nicrophorus tomentosus*). (MA)

ing organic matter on which the larvae have fed. Eggs and pupae of these other flies and beetles may be in evidence as well.

Burying beetles (Silphidae: *Nicrophorus*) have the distinctive habit of burying dead mice and other small animals to prevent them from drying out and to keep flies away. A pair works together to excavate the ground beneath a carcass until it sinks below the surface and is completely concealed. They then strip away the fur or feathers and work the carcass into a compact ball. The female lays eggs above it, and both parents regurgitate partially digested food into a depression at the top of the ball, continuing to feed the larvae throughout their development. The burial site is difficult to detect unless you catch them midburial, when you may see a foot or tail still protruding from the ground.

Dry and Stored Animal Products

Insects that feed on old, dry animal remains include dermestid beetles, trogid beetles, sap beetles, checkered beetles (Cleridae), darkling beetles (Tenebrionidae), crickets (Gryllidae), and piophilid flies. Many of these also infest carpets, wool clothes, hides, and other stored animal products indoors. The shed skins of dermestid beetle larvae (see page 82) are often found on carpets and in collections of naturalists, where the larvae reduce dried animal products (vertebrate or otherwise) to powder. The cheese skipper (Piophilidae: *Piophila casei*) breeds in preserved meats and cheese. Its larvae have been known to eat out a cavity in a large ham without showing any trace on the surface.

At least four groups of terrestrial invertebrates are able to chip away at bones. Dermestid beetles are capable of pitting bone surfaces, tunneling through them, and excavating small chambers in which to pupate. Termites (Isoptera), surprisingly, also may eat bone. Their work produces irregular patches of rough, shallow pits, sometimes more than 15 mm wide. Larval clothes moths (Tineidae) eat keratin, such as in horns and hair. Both termites and clothes moths produce a hard covering for protection while feeding. Clothes moths use hardened feces, keratin, and bone fragments held together with silk, whereas termites use a mixture of soil, feces, and saliva. Submerged bones may be tunneled by pale burrower mayfly naiads (Polymitarcyidae). These mayflies have very hard mandibles that allow them to bite their way through bone and wood. The resultant burrows have the U shape typical of other mayfly naiads that burrow in soil, with two entrance holes near each other at the substrate surface. Britt (2008) provides a table to distinguish the work of these four invertebrate groups, based in part on microscopic features left by different types of mandibles.

Dung

The best-known invertebrate users of vertebrate dung are the dung beetles (Scarabaeidae: Scarabaeinae). Tumblebugs (Canthonini) are famous for rolling spherical balls of dung, in which they have laid eggs, to a suitable nesting site. They leave a distinct spherical depression in the dung from which the ball is removed. *Copris*, *Dichotomius*, *Onthophagus*, and *Phan-*

This human scat is being divided into pieces by tumblebugs (Scarabaeidae: *Canthonini*). Note the large chunk missing from the center and the beetle rolling away the ball in the lower right of the frame. (TX)

Aphodius rubripennis, an aphodiine dung beetle (Scarabaeidae), boring a hole in a deer pellet. (VT)

aeus remove similar balls but bury them near or under the dung, leaving loose, excavated soil as evidence of their digging. The aphodiine dung beetles, which tend to be smaller, simply burrow into dung and lay eggs there, without any additional preparation. Some of these, such as *Aphotaenius carolinus* and species of *Aphodius* and *Dialytes*, specialize in deer droppings, excavating a chamber with an obvious, irregular entrance.

In addition to scarabs, other beetles that may be found in dung include water scavenger beetles (Hydrophilidae), carrion beetles, rove beetles, darkling beetles (Tenebrionidae), hister beetles, false clown beetles (Sphaeritidae), and handsome fungus beetles (Endomychidae). Larvae (and therefore eggs, galleries, and pupae) of many fly families may also be found in dung. These include anthomyiids, bibionids, calliphorids, chironomids, chloropids, heleomyzids, lauxaniids, muscids, psychodids, rhagionids, sarcophagids, scatopsids, sepsids, sphaerocerids, stratiomyids, and syrphids.

Droppings, Secretions, and Protective Coverings without Foreign Materials

5

Invertebrates produce a wide variety of droppings (excrement), as well as various other liquid, frothy, or waxy secretions, which can be important clues in interpreting other types of sign. The word *frass* is commonly used to refer to any debris left behind by insects, including droppings, dust from wood boring, and other waste products. It is the German word for "animal feed," and therefore its use in reference to pure excrement should be avoided, as this is not only imprecise but is really the opposite of the word's original meaning. You will likely see it used in this way elsewhere, but in this book, *frass* refers to the miscellaneous debris of insects, which may or may not include droppings.

Leaf-mining insects often deposit their droppings in characteristic patterns within the mine, which is discussed in chapter 10. Similarly, the frass of wood borers is most logically discussed in the context of the galleries where it is found and is covered in chapter 14. Castings of earthworms and various marine invertebrates are deposited at their burrow entrances, and these are described in chapter 16. Some marine worm tubes are made entirely of secretions, but these seem best placed along with the other worm tubes in chapter 8. Silk is such a versatile secretion that the next two chapters are devoted to it, and it crops up in many others as well.

Liquid Deposits

Many invertebrates have a liquid diet, which may include nectar, plant juices, or the juices of other invertebrates. Their droppings are likewise liquid and for the most part are inconspicuous and rarely seen. In some cases, however, they are quite noticeable, on vegetation or around man-made structures. Various other wet substances produced by certain invertebrates provide a clue to their presence.

Sooty mold, a fungus that grows on the honeydew produced by plant-feeding insects. (MA)

Honeydew

Many insects that feed on plant sap excrete a sweet, sticky substance called honeydew, which contains all the sugars and other nutrients that they do not need as they process large amounts of sap. It is colorless but visibly glistens on the leaves where it accumulates. Its presence becomes quite conspicuous when sooty mold, a black fungus specific to honeydew, begins to grow on it, sometimes covering a whole plant and the ground below it. There are many species of sooty mold, some of them growing only on the honeydew of a particular insect species. Producers of honeydew include aphids, soft scale insects, leafhoppers, treehoppers, mealybugs, psyllids, whiteflies, and caterpillars of lycaenid butterflies such as blues and azures. The sweet substance attracts flies, bees, wasps, butterflies, and most notably ants, which often tend honeydew-producing insects like cattle, "milking" them and in some cases even bringing them into their nests to overwinter. Some cynipid oak galls also exude honeydew that is harvested by ants.

Brown Specks

Other foliage-feeding insects leave brown fecal specks on leaves. Such specks generally accompany feeding sign of lace bugs (Tingidae), as well as some plant bugs (Miridae) and thrips (see chapter 9 for examples). Asparagus beetle larvae (Chrysomelidae: *Crioceris asparagi*) excrete a black fluid that stains the plant. Some sawfly adults are said to leave fecal specks as well, but presumably not in quantities that would normally be noticed.

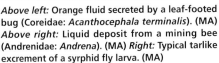

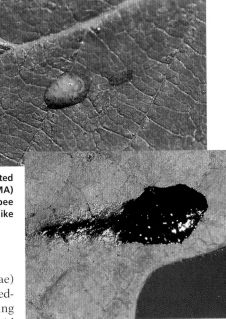

Above left: Orange fluid secreted by a leaf-footed bug (Coreidae: *Acanthocephala terminalis*). (MA) *Above right:* Liquid deposit from a mining bee (Andrenidae: *Andrena*). (MA) *Right:* Typical tarlike excrement of a syrphid fly larva. (MA)

Colorful Drips

We have seen leaf-footed bugs (Coreidae) deposit small amounts of transparent, reddish brown fluid, and once saw a mining bee (Andrenidae: *Andrena*) leave a liquid droplet loaded with bright yellow pollen on a leaf, though it was not clear which end of the bee it came from. Syrphid fly larvae leave droppings on leaves in the form of a black, tarlike smear.

Butterflies, on emerging from their chrysalises, eject a bright red fluid called *meconium*, the metabolic waste resulting from pupation. Those emerging from chrysalises attached to man-made structures can leave conspicuous stains on the floor below.

Spiders

Spiders have milky white to dark brown liquid excrement, which can look like tiny bird droppings. The common house spider often chooses a partic-

Left: Fresh droppings of a jumping spider (Salticidae: *Phidippus*). The largest puddle is 2 mm wide. (MS) *Right:* Dried droppings (1 to 2 mm) of a common house spider (Theridiidae: *Parasteatoda tepidariorum*) on a house plant. (MA)

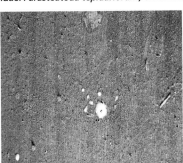

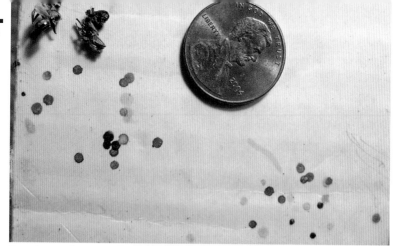

Droppings and prey remains from a cellar spider (Pholcidae). (MA)

ular spot to which it retreats when consuming its prey, and its dried droppings accumulate in clusters of small, round spots on whatever surface is below this. A purseweb spider ejects its droppings through the open top of its tube, shooting them several inches away.

Wasps

Males of many types of apoid and vespoid wasps establish sheltered communal roosting sites not far from their mating territories. They sleep in the same spot, night after night (sometimes year after year), and they stain the surface below with their fecal discharges. This spot may be a particular branch, or with paper wasps and mud daubers, it is often a particular corner under the shelter of a roof. Paper wasp (*Polistes*) droppings range from off-white to brown and have some body to them, but because they are generally dropped from a considerable distance, they mostly take the form of an amorphous splat, like tiny bird droppings.

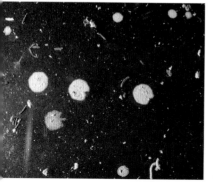

Accumulated droppings from communally roosting organ pipe mud daubers (Crabronidae: *Trypoxylon politum*) on the back of a chair in an abandoned cabin. (TN)

Carpenter Bees

The drippings of large carpenter bees (Apidae: *Xylocopa*) are obvious when they nest in man-made structures. Wax and yellow-

Wax and droppings of large carpenter bees (Apidae: *Xylocopa virginica*) accumulating on the roof of a car below a nest. (TN)

ish liquid wastes drip out of the burrow entrances, often staining the surfaces below. Solid, elongate fecal pellets may be associated with these drippings, also with a yellowish tinge because of the diet of pollen.

Smelly Secretions

Cockroaches secrete a sticky, smelly brown fluid that is sometimes left on foods or other household items. Some earwigs are able to shoot a foulsmelling liquid several inches. Certain true bugs, such as stink bugs (Pentatomidae), bed bugs (Cimicidae), and leaf-footed bugs (Coreidae), also possess scent glands.

Slime

Terrestrial snails and slugs leave slime trails wherever they go, and this glistening substance is usually apparent where they have been feeding. In the Pacific Northwest, the sides of buildings are sometimes covered with large "slime prints" where banana slugs have rested for a while. On occasion, what looks like a slime trail of a slug or snail may in fact have been left by a land planarian (flatworm in the suborder Terricola). Fungus gnat larvae (Mycetophilidae) leave narrow slime trails on the surface of the fungi on which they feed.

Above: A slug leaving a narrow slime trail. (MA) *Above right:* Slime stains left by banana slugs (Arionidae: *Ariolimax*) on the side of a house. The top one is 4.7 inches (12 cm) long. (CA) *Right:* Slime from a banana slug (Arionidae: *Ariolimax*) glistens in the sun. (WA)

"Spittle" of the meadow spittlebug (Cercopidae: *Philaenus spumarius*). The froth mass is 15 mm long. (MA)

Frothy Secretions

A number of insects produce frothy secretions for various reasons. Mantids, grasshoppers, and certain tussock moths and robber flies cover their eggs with a hard-drying froth, which is further described in chapter 1.

Spittlebugs

The "spittle" produced by spittlebugs (Cercopidae), which suck plant juices, is often very conspicuous. The nymphs surround themselves with a white, bubbly mass by forcing air into excreted sap. The air issues from a chamber beneath the abdomen, and the sap is mixed with a waxy substance that causes the bubbles to last for hours. Each mass may contain one or more nymphs, sometimes accompanied by certain fruit fly larvae (Drosophilidae: *Cladochaeta*) that develop exclusively in spittlebug spittle. The froth keeps them moist and protects them from predators. Eventually it shrinks down and hardens, but the nymphs keep making new froth every day until they mature.

Dance Flies

Dance flies (Empididae) are sometimes called balloon flies because of the "nuptial balloons" that males of some species bring females as part of courtship. The balloon consists of a captured prey insect covered in frothy secretions, and the male carries it under his abdomen until mating. In some species, the insect gift is left out, and the female is presented with an empty mass of froth.

Droppings with Definite Form

Foliage-feeding invertebrates that take bites, rather than just sucking juices, have more solid droppings, often with very distinct and recognizable forms. In fact, within a given habitat and region, it is possible to identify many droppings to species, based on features such as size, texture, and host plant. Morris (1942) provided a key to the droppings of common spruce defoliators in central New Brunswick, and Hodson and Brooks (1956) presented one for droppings from forest trees in the north-central

United States and Canada. Some non–foliage-feeding invertebrates with chewing mouthparts also leave more or less solid droppings.

Caterpillars and Sawfly Larvae

The most easily recognized droppings of foliage feeders are the grooved, cylindrical pellets made by many moth caterpillars. In addition to six longitudinal grooves, the pellets often have several more or less conspicuous transverse grooves. The largest pellets are from giant silkworms (Saturniidae) and hornworms (Sphingidae). Those of cecropia moth caterpillars (*Hyalophora cecropia*) can be up to about 8 mm long; the similarly large pellets of tomato and tobacco hornworms (*Manduca*) are a common sight in gardens. Most other caterpillar droppings are less than 4 mm long. Other caterpillars with similar droppings include tussock moths (Lymantriidae) and prominents (Notodontidae). Pellets of some prominents and oakworms (Saturniidae: *Anisota*) are tapered at one end rather than perfectly cylindrical.

In some lepidopteran families, some species make grooved pellets and others

Right top: Tapered droppings of white-streaked prominent caterpillars (Notodontidae: *Oligocentria lignicolor*). (MA) *Right center:* Droppings (4 mm by 5 to 7 mm) of polyphemus moth caterpillars (Saturniidae: *Antheraea polyphemus*). (MA) *Below left:* Droppings (about 3 mm long) of forest tent caterpillars (Lasiocampidae: *Malacosoma disstria*). (MA) *Below right:* Droppings of catalpa sphinx caterpillars (Sphingidae: *Ceratomia catalpae*). (TN)

Droppings (2 to 2.5 mm) of gypsy moth caterpillars (Lymantriidae: *Lymantria dispar*). (NJ)

do not. For instance, the forest tent caterpillar (Lasiocampidae: *Malacosoma disstria*) produces clearly ridged droppings, whereas those of the eastern tent caterpillar (*M. americana*) are irregularly lumpy cylinders. Dagger moth (*Acronicta*) pellets are ridged, but those of many other noctuids are not. Caterpillars of nymphalid butterflies such as the mourning cloak (*Nymphalis antiopa*) and question mark (*Polygonia interrogationis*) make longitudinally grooved pellets, but monarchs (*Danaus plexippus*) do not.

Droppings of some caterpillars are cylindrical with a few transverse constrictions and no longitudinal grooves. These include tiger moths such as the neighbor moth (Arctiidae: *Haploa contigua*), owlet moths such as the black zigzag (Noctuidae: *Panthea acronyctoides*; on conifers), and butterflies such as the red admiral (Nymphalidae: *Vanessa atalanta*; on net-

Left: Droppings of a black swallowtail caterpillar (Papilionidae: *Papilio polyxenes*). (MA) *Below:* Cylindrical, segmented droppings of neighbor moth caterpillars (Arctiidae: *Haploa contigua*). (MA)

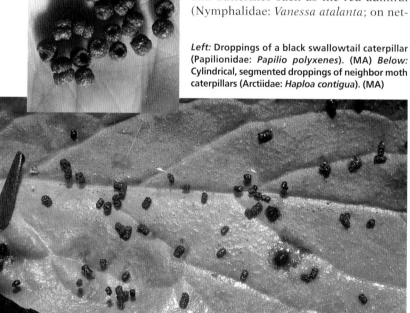

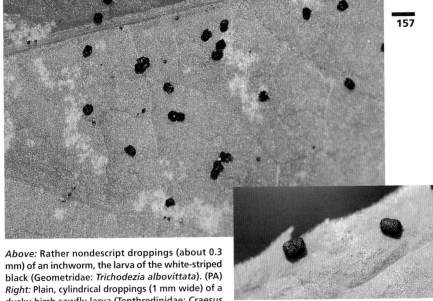

Above: Rather nondescript droppings (about 0.3 mm) of an inchworm, the larva of the white-striped black (Geometridae: *Trichodezia albovittata*). (PA) *Right:* Plain, cylindrical droppings (1 mm wide) of a dusky birch sawfly larva (Tenthredinidae: *Craesus latitarsus*). (MA) *Lower right:* Droppings (2 to 3 mm) of introduced pine sawfly larvae (Diprionidae: *Diprion similis*). (MA)

tles). In fresh droppings of monarchs (on milkweeds) and black swallowtails (Papilionidae: *Papilio polyxenes*; on plants in the parsley family), the segments are rounded and have a prominent circular depression in the middle of one side. Larger droppings are often broken into individual bowl-shaped segments.

Other lepidopteran larvae, as well as sawfly larvae, leave more or less cylindrical pellets without grooves or constrictions. Examples include inchworms (Geometridae), many owlet moths (Noctuidae), and *Limenitis* species such as viceroys (Nymphalidae). Pellets of conifer sawflies (Diprionidae) are usually in the form of distinct parallelograms, with the needle fragments neatly arranged in transverse rows. Pellets of conifer-feeding inchworms consist of large pieces of needles stuck together irregularly at different angles, with no visible matrix between the pieces.

Elongate Droppings

Very few lepidopteran or sawfly droppings are more than twice as long as wide. Morris (1942) described the pellets of web-spinning sawflies (Pamphiliidae) that feed on spruce as about three times as long as thick. Droppings this elongate, or more so, are typical of Orthoptera and stick insects. Bush katydid (Tettigoniidae: *Scudderia*) pellets we have seen were about 3 by 1 mm; those of short-horned grasshoppers (Acrididae) can be up to four

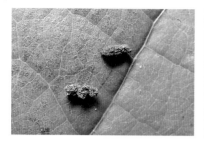

Top left: Droppings (2.5 by 1 mm) of a bush katydid (Tettigoniidae: *Scudderia*). (TN) *Top right:* Fecal pellet of a red-legged grasshopper (Acrididae: *Melanoplus femurrubrum*). (VT) *Center left:* Droppings (about 10 by 2 mm) of a two-striped grasshopper (Acrididae: *Melanoplus bivittatus*). (MA) *Bottom left:* Droppings (6 mm) of the common walkingstick (Diapheromeridae: *Diapheromera femorata*). (MA)

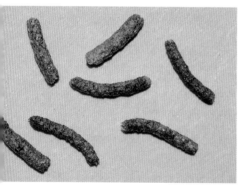

times as long as wide, and perhaps longer. Droppings of the common walkingstick (Diapheromeridae: *Diapheromera femorata*) are typically 6 to 7 mm long and 1 mm wide. This species feeds high in trees, as a rule, making it difficult to find the source of the distinctive droppings littering the ground below.

"Frass Chains"

Some early-instar caterpillars of nymphalid butterflies have the peculiar habit of building a straight rod of excrement bound together with silk, called a "frass chain" (despite what we said earlier), off the margin of a leaf where they are feeding. A common length is 6 mm, but a chain may be up to 1.2 inches (3 cm) or so long. The larva perches on it when not feeding, as a refuge from ants, and builds a new one when it moves to another feeding spot. A hatchling's first frass chain is typically at the tip of the midrib, and can appear to be part of it, but subsequent ones may be just about anywhere on the leaf margin. Frass chains are generally not built after the second instar. Caterpillars with this behavior include viceroys and admirals (*Limenitis*) on willow and poplar; California sisters (*Adelpha californica*) on oak; ruddy daggerwings (*Marpesia petreus*) on fig; American snouts (*Libytheana carinenta*) on hackberry; and leafwings (*Anaea*) on croton.

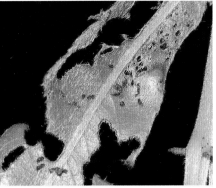

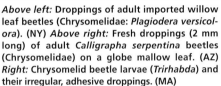

Above left: Droppings of adult imported willow leaf beetles (Chrysomelidae: *Plagiodera versicolora*). (NY) Above right: Fresh droppings (2 mm long) of adult *Calligrapha serpentina* beetles (Chrysomelidae) on a globe mallow leaf. (AZ) Right: Chrysomelid beetle larvae (*Trirhabda*) and their irregular, adhesive droppings. (MA)

Beetles

We find beetle droppings stuck to vegetation, particularly the undersides of leaves, much more often than caterpillar droppings. This is partly because of their initial softness and partly because many caterpillars have a structure called an "anal comb," which is used to flick fecal pellets

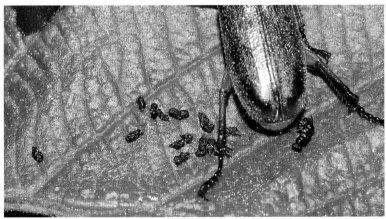

Droppings (about 1 mm) of a June bug, *Dichelonyx* (Scarabaeidae: Melolonthinae). (MA)

Left: Droppings (4 mm) of an adult cactus long-horned beetle (Cerambycidae: *Moneilema*). (AZ) *Center:* Droppings (1 mm by 2 to 3 mm) of a margined blister beetle (Meloidae: *Epicauta pestifera*). (AR) *Right:* Droppings (5 mm) of a June bug larva (Scarabaeidae: Melolonthinae) in garden soil. (MA)

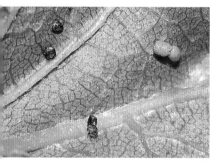

Above top: Droppings (1 mm) of a small millipede on the underside of a leaf. (WA) *Above bottom:* Droppings (4 by 3 mm) of a large millipede, *Narceus americanus* (Spirobolidae). (MA)

out of sight. Droppings of leaf beetles (Chrysomelidae), both larvae and adults, tend to be soft, elongate, and highly irregular, often thin and twisted. Those of adults may appear more regularly cylindrical when fresh, but they do not retain this shape as they dry. Droppings of adult long-horned beetles (Cerambycidae) are similar but larger. The droppings of adult June bugs (Scarabaeidae: Melolonthinae) and blister beetles (Meloidae) we have seen have been more thick and solid, but still too irregularly lumpy to be confused with nonbeetle foliage feeders. They were also unusually dark. We have found similar dark, cylindrical droppings in garden soil, produced by June bug larvae.

Millipedes

Millipede droppings are short, rounded cylinders, often with one blunt end and one pointy end. They look something like tiny deer pellets. They are normally found in leaf litter and under rotten logs, but we found a small millipede leaving similar droppings on leaves of a shrub in Olympic National Park.

Cockroach droppings (about 1 mm) found on top of a cabinet. (TN)

Cockroaches

Cockroach droppings tend to be small and irregular, and are often said to look like ground black pepper. They may be up to 3 mm long, with discernible longitudinal ridges.

Fleas

Fleas have surprisingly distinctive droppings. They are dark, elongate, and of constant diameter, often curved into a C shape or coil, about 1 mm across. Some are more stretched out and J shaped. Flea larvae do not feed on blood directly but obtain it by eating the droppings of their parents.

Slugs and Snails

Slugs and snails leave distinctive droppings in the form of a long, continuous rope, which is generally coiled in a fairly compact mass. A rope of banana slug excrement may be 3.5 mm or more thick.

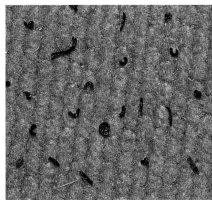

Droppings (1 to 3 mm) of cat fleas (Pulicidae: *Ctenocephalides felis*) found on a sofa. (VT)

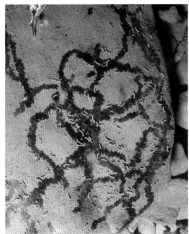

Left: Droppings (1.2 inches [3 cm] across) of a banana slug (Arionidae: *Ariolimax*). (CA)
Right: Droppings (0.4 mm wide) of aquatic snails alongside the trails where they have been scraping algae from a submerged rock. (TN)

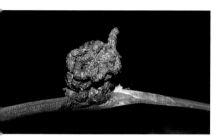

Snail droppings. (MA)

Hiking in Olympic National Park one day, we happened to catch a banana slug in the act. Having never given slug anatomy much thought before, we were surprised to see the droppings issuing from an opening on its right side, toward the front of its body. The rope came out extremely slowly, settling in one direction until the tension caused it to slump back the other way. In this manner, it continued to slump back and forth, creating the characteristic coiled heap. In addition to this distinctive shape, slug and snail droppings can usually be recognized by the presence of glistening traces of slime. Droppings of some aquatic snails are deposited in shorter sections that are curved but not coiled.

Meconium

Many insects besides butterflies void meconium as part of metamorphosis, but it is solid rather than liquid. It may not look like much on its own, but it may be noticed in association with pupae or pupal skins. In all of these insects, unlike butterflies, it consists of everything the larva has eaten up until that point; it is held in until then because these larvae live in enclosed places that need to be kept clean. In ants and other social Hymenoptera, the enclosed space is a nest cell; in cynipid wasps, it is a gall; in parasitic Hymenoptera, it is the body of the host. Some nonhymenopteran parasites, the louse flies (Hippoboscidae) and the twisted-winged parasites (Strepsiptera), also have this habit. Eulophid wasps do as well, even ectoparasitoids that do not live in enclosed places. *Eulophus* larvae deposit masses of tiny, round, yellow or pale brown pellets just before pupating. The black meconium of *Euplectrus* larvae may be found stuck to their flimsy cocoons.

Some neuropterans deposit pellets on emerging from the pupa. We found a brown, 1-mm-long, capsule-shaped pellet in a container in which a green lacewing had emerged from a cocoon. Why the free-living larva of a green lacewing would need to retain its wastes until then is a mystery to us. The meconium of *Climacia* spongillaflies is also a single, dark brown pellet. The hard, reddish or pinkish, cylindrical or biscuit-shaped meconial pellets of antlions were mistaken for eggs by early observers. Interestingly, the wormlions (Vermilionidae), which are fly larvae that mimic antlions in making pitfall traps, mirror them in this habit as well, except that they void their dark meconium just before pupating.

Meconial pellet (about 1 mm) of a green lacewing (Chrysopidae). (TN)

Droppings Issuing from Holes in Vegetation

Some larvae that feed within plant tissues cause conspicuous clumps of droppings to issue from small holes in flowers, fruits, and stems. Many of these are olethreutine tortricids, including the oriental fruit moth (*Grapholita molesta*) and codling moth (*Cydia pomonella*) in apples and other fruits; the sunflower bud moth (*Suleima helianthana*) in sunflowers; and the cypress bark moth (*C. cupressana*) in cones and bark of Monterey cypress. A *Rhopobota* species accumulates a curved "stick" of droppings, about 4 mm long, which projects from a small blotch mine on the underside of winterberry and mountain holly leaves. The larva later abandons the mine and folds or rolls the leaf. *Scrobipalpa scutellariaeella*, a gelechiid (which may soon find its name changed to *Euscrobipalpa*), similarly protrudes frass from mines in the undersides of skullcap leaves. The droppings in this case surround a small silken tube from which the larva makes feeding forays. The squash vine borer (Sesiidae: *Melittia cucurbitae*) pushes soft yellowish droppings out

Right: Droppings of cypress bark moth larvae (Tortricidae: *Cydia cupressana*) pushed out of a Monterey cypress cone. (CA) *Lower left:* Droppings pushed out of a sunflower head by a sunflower bud moth larva (Tortricidae: *Suleima helianthana*) feeding within. (TX) *Lower right:* The 4-mm tube of droppings projecting from the bottom of this winterberry leaf was made by a *Rhopobota* (Tortricidae) larva. The larva started out life in a small blotch mine, then rolled the leaf as other tortricids do. (MA)

Left: The droppings pouring out of this squash vine are a sure sign of a squash vine borer larva (Sesiidae: *Melittia cucurbitae*) feeding within. (MA) *Right:* Droppings of a larval cactus long-horned beetle (Cerambycidae: *Moneilema*) collect outside its hole in a cholla cactus. (TX)

of holes near the base of squash vines. The droppings of larval cactus long-horned beetles (Cerambycidae: *Moneilema*) form black, crusty deposits on cholla cacti. See chapters 13 and 14 for notes on frass issuing from holes in trees and shrubs.

Excrement-covered Eggs

Some beetles and millipedes, as well as timemas, use their droppings or similar secretions as coverings for their eggs. In many cases, this involves laying eggs on a leaf and then depositing excrement on top, but in others, each egg is carefully and thoroughly coated with packed excrement.

Leaf-mining Beetles

Leaf-mining buprestids lay their eggs singly on the undersides of leaves. They are covered with a transparent secretion that gives them a low, dome-shaped form. The female

A pair of goldenrod leafminers (Chrysomelidae: *Microrhopala vittata*). The female has just finished covering her eggs with soupy excrement. (OH) Photo by Judy Semroc.

often then conceals them with lumps of excrement. Some leaf-mining chrysomelids share this habit. The goldenrod leafminer (*Microrhopala vittata*) deposits eggs on the undersides of goldenrod leaves, usually in groups of 3 to 4 near the tip, and partially covers them with a soupy, brown substance. The locust leafminer (*Odontota dorsalis*) does the same on locust leaves. A brown spot appears on the upper leaf surface above the eggs. The plantain flea beetle (*Dibolia borealis*) lays yellow eggs in small holes chewed in the upper surface of plantain leaves, partially covering them with blackish excrement.

Tortoise Beetles

The palmetto tortoise beetle (*Hemisphaerota cyanea*) deposits a single, oval, yellow egg on its side on a palmetto leaf, then carefully covers it with brown fecal pellets. The egg is about 2 mm long.

Case-bearing Leaf Beetles

The case-bearing leaf beetles (Chrysomelidae: Cryptocephalinae) take the art of excrement-covered eggs to a whole new level. Each egg is coated with a compact covering, which may have a wafflelike pattern (as in some of the Clytrini) or imbricate scales like a pinecone (some members of all three tribes, and perhaps all of the Chlamisini). The Chlamisini and some of the Clytrini attach their eggs to plants, whereas the Cryptocephalini and most Clytrini drop them to the ground. Some species attach their eggs by short stalks, and others suspend them from long, silklike threads, just as is done by green lacewings. Members of the closely related Lamprosomatinae (of which the only species known to occur north of Mexico is *Oomorphus floridanus*, common in south Florida) cover eggs with long, narrow scales that project outward.

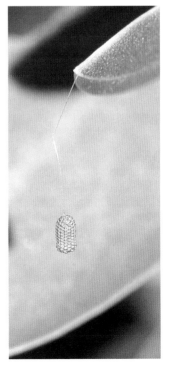

Above right: Cluster (3.5 mm) of case-bearing leaf beetle eggs (Chrysomelidae: Cryptocephalinae: Clytrini), encrusted with excrement, on a cholla spine. (AZ) *Right:* Excrement-covered egg (1 mm) of a case-bearing leaf beetle (Chrysomelidae: Cryptocephalinae: Clytrini), suspended from an ocotillo leaf by a 5-mm string. (AZ)

Millipedes

Most millipedes produce a covering for their eggs by eating earth and mixing it with a rectal secretion as they excrete it. As discussed in chapter 8, some use this excrement to line an earthen chamber in which multiple eggs are laid. Others, including some pill millipedes (Oniscomorpha), use it to make a small, spherical chamber for each individual egg. A female *Narceus* (Spirobolidae) coats each 1-mm, oval egg in chewed, regurgitated leaf litter and compacts it in her rectum. The finished product looks something like a fecal pellet, but it is perfectly spherical, has a coarser texture, and is lighter in color. The nymph eats its capsule when it hatches. Groups of females have been found among large deposits of fecal pellets along with hundreds of egg capsules.

Timemas

Timemas (Timematidae: *Timema*) are stocky stick insects that live in California and the adjacent states. Their eggs have a cap like those of other phasmids, but the females coat them as millipedes do, by ingesting soil and defecating it onto them. Some species drop their eggs to the ground, and others carefully place them.

Larval Coverings and Cases Made of Fecal Matter

A number of different insect larvae have the charming habit of building shelters for themselves out of their own droppings. The larva of an *Epicypta* fungus gnat (Mycetophilidae) wears a soft sheath of molded excrement, eventually pupating within it. *Phronia* larvae produce similar coverings, but theirs are said to be hard. Larvae of certain *Bittacus* hangingflies (Bittacidae) swallow soil and then spray it all over themselves, mixed with a glutinous anal secretion.

Leaf Beetles

The larvae of three subfamilies of leaf beetles (Chrysomelidae) have distinctly different variations on this theme. Members of the Criocerinae,

Left: This three-lined potato beetle larva (Chrysomelidae: *Lema daturaphila*) has piled its excrement on its back. (NV) *Right:* A clavate tortoise beetle pupa (Chrysomelidae: *Plagiometriona clavata*) with the retained fecal shield of the larva. (MA)

Above left: The fecal covering (8 mm across) of a palmetto tortoise beetle (Chrysomelidae: *Hemisphaerota cyanea*). (GA) *Above right:* Case (5 mm) of *Exema*, a case-bearing leaf beetle, with the egg covering retained at the tip. (TN) *Right:* Case (5 mm) of another case-bearing leaf beetle (Chrysomelidae: *Neochlamisus eubati*). (MA)

such as the three-lined potato beetle (*Lema daturaphila*) and the introduced lily leaf beetle (*Lilioceris lilii*), simply pile their moist droppings on their backs. Tortoise beetle larvae (Cassidinae) have a tail-like structure, called a *fecifork*, with which they hold a shield of excrement and cast skins over their body. This is usually an irregular, dark brown lump, but it takes different forms in different species. The palmetto tortoise beetle larva (*Hemisphaerota cyanea*) extrudes long, wiry, segmented, pale brown fecal strands, which coil and completely cover its body, and under which it pupates. Larvae of the case-bearing leaf beetles (Cryptocephalinae; most are actually detritivores living on the ground) live in hard, portable cases made of excrement, sometimes incorporating other bits of debris. These are up to about 5 mm long. The shape varies somewhat, but they are generally rounded and often somewhat contracted toward the sole opening, from which the larva extends its head and legs. Larvae begin by simply wearing the fecal covering from the egg, and in some species (such as *Exema*, on goldenrods) this is retained as a nipple at the tip of the case. The larva withdraws into its case when disturbed and eventually attaches it to a twig or other object and pupates inside it. The Lamprosomatinae have similar habits.

Octagonal Casemaker

A very different portable case is made by the octagonal casemaker moth (*Coleophora octagonella*). It is up to about 1 inch (2.5 cm) long and is straight, narrow, and tapered to a point, something like a unicorn horn. Close inspection reveals it to be octagonal in cross section, composed of

The case of this octagonal casemaker (*Coleophora octagonella*) measures about 1 inch (2.5 cm). (TN) Photo by Kris Light.

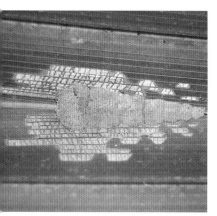

This "house" of the palm leaf housemaker (Batrachedridae: *Homaledra heptathalama*) is 2.4 inches (6 cm) long. (FL)

neatly arranged elongate fecal pellets. This species will soon have a different genus name, because Dr. Jean-François Landry has determined that it belongs in the family Batrachedridae, not Coleophoridae.

Palm Leaf Housemaker and Skeletonizer

Another batrachedrid, the palm leaf housemaker (*Homaledra heptathalama*), makes a very distinctive "house" of droppings. The larva feeds on the underside of a palmetto leaf, making a firm, smooth shelter of fecal pellets webbed together with silk. As it grows, it builds successively larger, squarish chambers, all connected in a row, and pupates inside the last one. The finished structure has seven or eight sections and is about 2 inches (5 cm) long. The closely related palm leaf skeletonizer (*H. sabalella*) feeds gregariously on the upper surfaces of palmetto leaves, making irregular channels that are covered with a roof of looser pellets with no particular form.

Watershield Midge

A midge larva (Chironomidae: *Polypedilum braseniae*) that feeds on watershield leaves has a lifestyle essentially similar to that of the *Homaledra* species. It excavates meandering, linear channels on the upper surface of a leaf, neatly covering the channels with a uniformly wide roof of droppings. It pupates in a slight enlargement at the end of a channel, leaving the pupal skin partly protruding when the adult emerges.

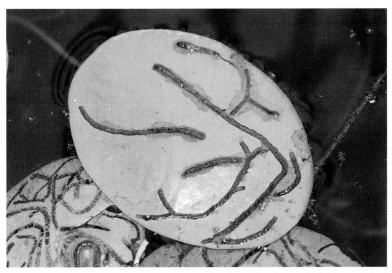

Excrement-covered channels made by larvae of *Polypedilum braseniae* (Chironomidae) in watershield leaves. (MA)

Pine Webworm

Many kinds of caterpillars feed on trees and shrubs in webbing that gradually fills with their droppings. Certain pyralids frequently take this so far that their nests become solid masses of excrement with little or no webbing visible. A common example is the pine webworm (*Pococera robustella*; E).

Leaf Crumpler Moth and Relatives

Some moth larvae bind their excrement with silk to build stationary tubes that they use as retreats while they feed on the surrounding foliage. The many *Acrobasis* species (Pyralidae) live in conical or cornucopia-shaped cases, up to 1 inch (2.5 cm) or more long, within clusters of webbed-together leaves. In some species, the larva moves its case to a twig in the fall and fas-

An old, excrement-filled web (1.8 inches [4.5 cm]) of pine webworms (Pyralidae: *Pococera robustella*). (GA)

Above: Larval case (about 2 cm) of the leaf crumpler moth (Pyralidae: *Acrobasis indigenella*) on an apple twig. (MA) *Left:* Three cases of *Acrobasis comptoniella* (Pyralidae), each about 2 cm long, on a sweetfern twig. (MA)

tens it there to overwinter (sometimes in aggregations of several cases), moving it again in the spring to resume feeding for a while before pupating. The twisted case of *A. indigenella*, the leaf crumpler moth, is found on apple and related trees. *A. caryae* and *A. juglandis*, among others, feed on pecan, hickory, and walnut, making more oval overwintering cases. Other species include *A. comptoniella* on sweetfern; *A. rubrifasciella* on alder and hazelnut; and *A. betulella* on birch.

Tortricid Moths

A few tortricids make similar tubes. The maple trumpet skeletonizer (*Catastega aceriella*) feeds beneath a sheet of silk on the underside of a crumpled maple leaf from within a long, narrow tube. *C. timidella* does the same

Tube (2 cm) of the maple trumpet skeletonizer (Tortricidae: *Catastega aceriella*). (MA)

on the undersides of oak leaves. The eye-spotted bud moth larva (*Spilonota ocellana*), found on a variety of hosts, makes a short, slightly curved silken case attached to a leaf, loosely covered with fecal pellets. *Acrolepiopsis heppneri* (Acrolepiidae; E) skeletonizes the undersides of greenbrier leaves from within a cylindrical silk tube, covered with black fecal pellets, placed alongside a vein.

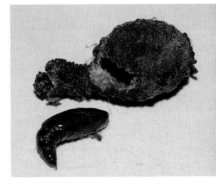

An extremely tough excrement-encrusted cocoon (1 cm) of an unknown moth, torn open to reveal the pupa. (MA)

Other Moths

Other moths build tough cocoons of silk and excrement when they are ready to pupate. These include some of the hooded owlets (Noctuidae: *Cucullia*). The oblong cocoon of the peach tree borer (Sesiidae: *Synanthedon exitiosa*) is composed of a mixture of droppings and other materials.

White Fluff

Masses of white, cottony fluff are produced by aphids, adelgids, mealybugs, scales, whiteflies, psyllids, and planthoppers. Many of these insects are host-specific, so identifying the host plant is often the easiest way to reach a probable identification. The fluff is secreted wax, which may completely conceal the insects that produce it. It keeps them from drying out and apparently is disagreeable to most potential predators, but there are several that specialize in attacking these insects.

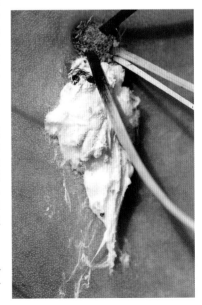

Cochineal Insects

Matted, white fluff on prickly pear cacti hides cochineal insects (Dactylopiidae: *Dactylopius*). The body fluid of the insects is a deep red and is used in dyes and food coloring. The larvae of *Laetilia coccidivora*, a pyralid moth, feed on cochineal insects (as well as other scale insects) and pupate under their white covering.

This white mass (about 15 mm across) on a prickly pear conceals several cochineal insects (Dactylopiidae: *Dactylopius*). (AZ)

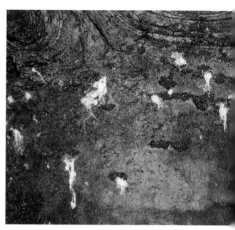

Left: Hemlock woolly adelgid (*Adelges tsugae*) on the underside of an eastern hemlock twig. (MA) *Right:* Pine bark adelgid (*Pineus strobi*) on white pine. (MA)

Adelgids

Tufts of white fluff on conifers are made by female adelgids. The hemlock woolly adelgid (*Adelges tsugae*), introduced from Japan, has killed whole stands of eastern hemlocks. It is found only among foliage, in contrast to other adelgids, which may be found on the bark of trunks and branches

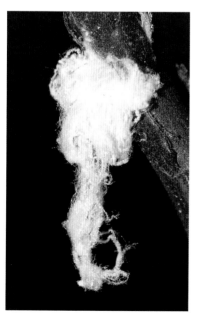

as well. The introduced balsam woolly adelgid (*A. piceae*) is found on balsam and Frasier fir, and the woolly pine adelgids (*Pineus*) are found on various pines and spruces. Pale, yellow, elongate eggs are laid in masses under the waxy coverings. Balsam twig aphids (*Mindarus abietinus*) produce white fuzz at the tips of balsam fir shoots, not as thick as the wool of adelgids, and with longer filaments.

Psyllids

Psyllid nymphs produce waxy filaments that in some cases conceal their bodies. Small tufts on alder leaves may conceal nymphs of cottony alder psyllids (*Psylla floccosa*) or American alder psyllids (*P. alni*; CA, NV). Other psyllids may cover

Fluff (about 12 mm across) produced by the manzanita psyllid (Aphalaridae: *Neophyllura arctostaphyli*). (CA)

Mojave seablite covered with sticky white fluff produced by psyllids. (NV)

vegetation with extensive white "cotton" that is sticky to the touch.

Whiteflies

Older nymphs and pupae of the woolly whitefly (*Aleurothrixus floccosus*) and giant whitefly (*Aleurodicus dugesii*) are also covered in white wool and form masses on the undersides of leaves. Both are introduced species found in southern Florida and California (the latter also in Texas) on a variety of plants. The wool of giant whiteflies is in tall strands, whereas woolly whiteflies make low, matted clumps. The flattened, oval nymphs of various other whiteflies exude white fibers that partially or completely conceal individual nymphs but do not form dense masses.

Aphids

Some woolly aphids secrete long, often coarse wax filaments, sometimes up to 2 inches (5 cm) long, and groups of them form large, dense masses on twigs and leaves. Common examples include the woolly alder aphid (*Paraprociphilus tessellatus*), which has silver maple as an alternate host, and the beech blight aphid (*Grylloprociphilus imbricator*), which is also found on cypress. *Eriosoma* species spend part of the year on elms and part on apple and other rosaceous trees and shrubs. The five *Stegophylla* species produce fine, woolly mats on oak leaves. *Prociphilus fraxinifolii* and *P. americanus* are woolly aphids on ash leaves, and *P. caryae* is on shadbush leaves; most members of this genus spend the summer on conifer

These tufts of waxy fluff (about 4 mm each) on the underside of an arrowwood leaf conceal whitefly nymphs (Aleyrodidae). (MA)

A colony of woolly alder aphids, *Paraprociphilus tessellatus*. (VT)

roots. The introduced woolly beech aphid (*Phyllaphis fagi*) is found primarily on European beech varieties, mostly on foliage (not forming dense masses on twigs as the beech blight aphid does). Fluffy tufts on hackberry leaves conceal Asian woolly hackberry aphids (*Shivaphis celti*).

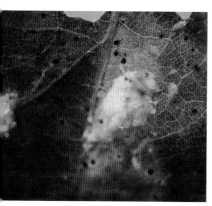

Cottony fluff of mealybugs (Pseudococcidae) containing round droplets of honeydew. (MA)

The caterpillar of the harvester butterfly (Lycaenidae: *Feniseca tarquinius*) lives among woolly aphids and feeds on them, concealing itself in webbing that incorporates their empty woolly skins. At least one species of green lacewing larva has been observed to similarly disguise itself with woolly aphid fluff.

Mealybugs

About 280 species of mealybugs (Pseudococcidae) are found in North America, and these too create messy masses of white fluff, on a wide variety of plant species. Some overwinter under bark in small cocoons of the same substance, and in some species, the last nymphal instar of males is a nonfeeding stage enclosed in a similar cocoon. Some create elongate, cottony egg sacs, as described in chapter 1.

Felt Scales

Felt scales (Eriococcidae) can be similar to mealybugs, but the body is generally bare or only lightly covered with wax. The female and her eggs are often enclosed in a white, oval, feltlike sac, however, and like mealybugs, the males transform in (smaller) oval cocoons. The introduced beech scale (*Cryptococcus fagisuga*) forms masses on beech bark and is quite covered with white fluff.

Other Insects

A few sawfly and ladybug larvae have coverings of white, waxy filaments similar to those of woolly aphids, as do planthopper nymphs. The butternut woolly worm (Ten-

The introduced beech scale (Eriococcidae: *Cryptococcus fagisuga*). (MA)

thredinidae: *Eriocampa juglandis*), when full grown, looks like an elongate, cottony mass, about 25 mm long and 15 mm tall. It feeds on leaves of butternut, walnut, and hickory. The mealybug destroyer larva (Coccinellidae: *Cryptolaemus montrouzieri*) secretes long filaments that make it look much like a mealybug, as do the larvae of *Hyperaspis* and *Scymnus* ladybugs. Some planthopper nymphs (Fulgoroidea) simply have a "tail" of waxy filaments, but others are more generally covered with cottony fluff. In some cases, plants become coated with this fluff as well.

Scale Insects

Scale insects (Coccoidea) have rounded, largely featureless bodies and thus may appear to be some sort of secreted covering when in fact you are looking at the insect itself. Some cover themselves with waxy secretions, but apart from the felt scales, these are usually smooth and solid rather than fibrous and fluffy. In cottony scales and cottony cushion scales, the female produces a large, white, cottony

Right: Magnolia scale (Coccidae: *Neolecanium cornuparvum*), one of the largest scale insects, at up to 12 mm. (MA) *Lower left:* Terrapin scales (Coccidae: *Mesolecanium nigrofasciatum*) on a sassafras twig. These scales each measure 2 mm. (MD) *Lower right:* A 1-cm wax scale (Coccidae: *Ceroplastes*) on a spicebush twig. (GA) Photo by Carmen Champagne.

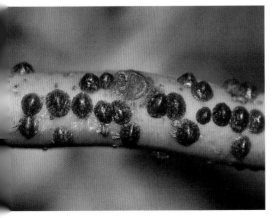

Elongate hemlock scales (Diaspididae: *Fiorinia externa*), introduced from Japan. (MA)

egg sac, and her much smaller body often remains attached at one end. Some spider egg sacs and *Enchenopa* treehopper egg masses might be confused with scale insects.

About a thousand species of soft scales (Coccidae) exist in North America. They tend to be oval and flattened, swelling to a dome when the females have laid eggs, which may be white or red. The largest are about 12 mm long, but most are much smaller. The female's body functions as an egg case after she dies. Most scales range from yellowish brown to reddish brown. The wax scales (*Ceroplastes*), however, have a thick coating of smooth, whitish wax, often with distinctive projections. They are mostly tropical but occur in parts of the southern United States. Gall-like scales (Kermesidae) are large, globose, and found on oak twigs and trunks.

The Margarodidae are basically similar to soft scales. This family includes the giant coccids, some up to 1 inch (2.5 cm) long, which occur in the tropics. The pinyon needle scale (*Matsucoccus acalyptus*) is common in the Southwest, where pinyon needles are often spotted with the flat, black, oval nymphs, about 2 mm long. The cottony cushion scale (*Icerya purchasi*) usually has a white, waxy covering and is easily recognized by its large, fluted egg sac. The larvae of an imported fly, *Cryptochetum iceryae* (Cryptochetidae), feed inside cottony cushion scales, leaving large, round exit holes when they emerge. The oval, black puparia are found either within or beside the host.

Pit scales (Asterolecaniidae) are so named because they feed on developing twigs, causing a sunken area, or pit, to form around each scale. The five species of false pit scales (Lecanodiaspididae: *Lecanodiaspis*) have similar habits; the covering of adults is a thick, whitish, waxy dome.

Armored scales (Diaspididae) are distinctly different from other scale insects. They are 2 to 3 mm long and secrete a hard, waxy, white or brown cover, which is separate from the body and enlarged by adding threads of wax around the outer edge. Males usually have smaller, more elongate coverings than females, whose coverings eventually become the egg case. A round or oval, light brown area at one end of the covering is the insect's exuviae, and it may have several bands indicating successive molts. In some of the elongate white species, this looks something like a tiny version of a cottony scale with an extruded egg sac. Pine needle scales (*Chionaspis pinifoliae*) are a common example of this type and are found on pine needles across North America; the similar pineleaf scale (*C. heterophyllae*) is found in the southeastern United States. Their eggs are reddish purple, numbering around 40. Oystershell scales (*Lepidosaphes*) are narrow and brown, resembling tiny oyster shells. The covering may con-

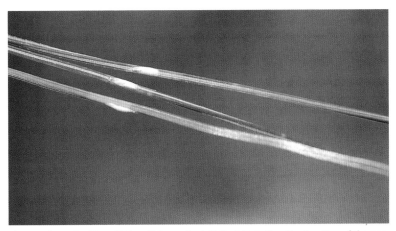

Pine needle scales (Diaspididae: *Chionaspis pinifoliae*). Note the discoloration of the needles as a result of their feeding. (MA)

ceal 40 to 100 oval, white eggs. Some species, such as the San Jose scale (*Quadraspidiotus perniciosus*), are more circular, with nipplelike exuviae close to the center instead of at one end. These species add to their waxy coverings by rotating their bodies, whereas the elongate species do so by moving their bodies from side to side.

Parasitoids

Aphytis chalcids (Aphelinidae) insert a single minute, yellow egg, with a long stalk at one end, under armored scale coverings onto the body of the scale. The wasp larva feeds on the scale, pupates under its covering, and after metamorphosing, chews a small, round hole in the covering to escape. Many other aphelinids have similar habits. Exit holes of *Comperiella bifasciata* (Encyrtidae; CA, FL) are larger and more irregularly shaped. Exit holes in other types of scale insects may be from eunotine pteromalids or certain mymarids that feed as larvae on the eggs. Some *Coccophagus* species (Aphelinidae) that feed on scale insects are among the very few chalcids to pupate within cocoons.

Lerp Psyllids

Some Australian psyllid nymphs live under hollow, white domes called *lerps*, which can superficially resemble some armored scales but lack the brown exuviae. They are made of crystallized honeydew rather than wax. The redgum lerp psyllid (*Glycaspis brimblecombei*) feeds on eucalyptus and has recently become established in California and Florida. The lerps are round and somewhat conical, sometimes with distinct concentric rings.

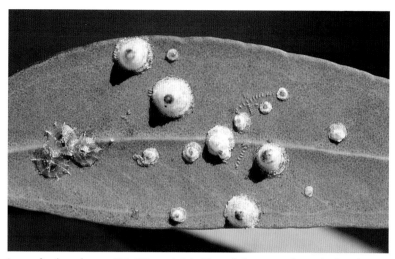

Lerps of redgum lerp psyllids (*Glycaspis brimblecombei*) on a eucalyptus leaf, each up to about 4 mm across. The orange nymphs are visible through the more transparent ones. Also note the rows of hatched eggs. (CA)

Old lerps become brown and moldy. The spotted gum lerp psyllid (*Eucalyptolyma maideni*), also now found in southern California, makes tapering lerps that resemble little rib cages, up to about 6 mm long and 3 mm wide. They are found on lemon gum as well as spotted gum eucalyptus.

Webs and Other Silken Constructions

6

Spiders are probably what come to mind when you think of webs, and theirs certainly are among the most artful silken constructions. Many insect orders have at least some silk-producing members, however, as do several other arthropod groups. Neuropteran larvae and certain beetles produce silk from posterior glands as spiders do. The webspinners (Embiidina) and some male dance flies secrete it from their feet. Barklice and larvae of butterflies, moths, caddisflies, true flies, bees, wasps, ants, and fleas spin silk from salivary glands.

The use of silk in spider egg sacs and the egg coverings of certain insects was discussed in chapter 1, and the silken cocoons that many insects spin are the subject of the next chapter. Later chapters cover portable debris cases that are held together with silk; shelters made by binding leaves with silk; burrows lined with silk; and various other invertebrate sign where silk is involved. This chapter covers the phenomena, other than egg coverings and cocoons, in which silk is the most prominent feature.

Unstructured Silk Lines

Isolated strands of silk, or loose collections of unstructured silk strands, may be sign of spiders, caterpillars, or fungus gnat larvae.

Spiders

Virtually all spiders lay down a continuous line of silk, called a *dragline*, as they travel. It is fastened to the substrate at regular intervals by a small cluster of looped threads called an *attachment disc*. This allows the spider to return to a spot from which it has fallen, or jumped in the case of a jumping spider. Cobwebs in houses are largely made up of accumulated draglines.

Spiderlings disperse by climbing trees and other objects, each then releasing a line of silk that is picked up by the wind, floating them away with it. This is called *ballooning* and is also employed by adults in small species such as dwarf spiders (Linyphiidae: Erigoninae). Sometimes the threads of many ballooning spiders coalesce into large sheets known as gossamer.

Stick spiders (Uloboridae: *Miagrammopes*) are common in Mexico and may be found in Texas in the lower Rio Grande Valley. Their web consists of a single horizontal line, about 4 feet (1.2 m) long, stretched between two twigs. The middle third or so is thickened with sticky silk, forming an attractive resting place for flying insects. The spider positions itself near one end of the line and holds it taut. When an insect lands, the spider lets go, and the sudden movement and loosening of the thread helps entangle its prey.

A bolas spider (Araneidae: *Mastophora*; S) spins a horizontal line on the underside of a twig, then hangs from this and dangles another line, about 2 inches (5 cm) long. At the end of this line is a sticky drop that imitates a moth pheromone. Male moths are attracted, and the spider catches them by swinging the thread. The many old silk lines form a coating on the leaves and twigs where the spider rests.

On the North Carolina barrier islands, we came across a mysterious silken spider construction whose maker and purpose we would love to have identified. It consisted of a central taut strand of slightly wavy silk stretched horizontally between two branches of a shrub. Loosely wound around this line like a corkscrew was another, thicker strand of silk. At either end, the lines of silk diverged, wrapping around the branches and anchored with other silk strands.

Caterpillars

Many kinds of caterpillars are able to drop down from their food plants on silken threads. They may do this to escape predators, climbing back up when the danger has passed. It can also be a way to descend from a tree quickly, to find either a new food source or a secluded place to pupate. This is the main dispersal method for tussock moths (Lymantriidae), whose females are poor fliers, if not completely wingless. Young caterpillars dangle from treetops and let the wind carry them somewhere new. Many inchworms (Geometridae), some of which also have wingless mothers, have similar habits. Both inchworms and tussock moth caterpillars can sometimes be so abundant that shade trees or large patches of forest are conspicuously strewn with their tangled silk lines.

Fungus Gnat Larvae

Some fungus gnat larvae (Sciaroidea) lay down a line of silk as they travel, which may visibly glisten with their slime. Particularly conspicuous are the lines left by certain dark-winged fungus gnat larvae (Sciaridae) that move across the ground by the hundreds in snakelike masses. Also conspicuous are the strong lines from which *Leptomorphus* species (Mycetophilidae) suspend themselves from bracket fungi when they pupate.

Sperm Webs

Before mating, a male spider spins a tiny web called a *sperm web*, measuring just a few millimeters across. He deposits a drop of sperm on this, then drinks it with his palps (leglike mouthparts), which are later inserted into his mate's twin openings, in some cases after first tying her down with more silk threads. In *Xysticus* crab spiders (Thomisidae), the sperm web is a rectangular ribbon, about 4 mm long. In others, such as the green lynx spider (Oxyopidae: *Peucetia viridans*), it is triangular. In either case, the web is made up of very fine threads neatly framed with a border of thick threads. It may be spun on the ground or suspended in vegetation.

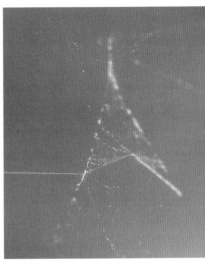

Sperm web of a green lynx spider (Oxyopidae: *Peucetia viridans*). (FL) Photo by Jeff Hollenbeck.

A male centipede also spins a sperm web, but the spermatophore that he places on it is picked up directly by the female. The web is a roughly circular pad of many crisscrossing threads, not neatly framed like those of spiders, and may be over 10 mm in diameter. The small millipede *Polyxenus lagurus* (Polyxenidae) spins a sperm web using zigzag movements, adding a pair of 15-mm signal threads that lead the female to it. Sperm webs among millipedes are unique to the Polyxenida.

Webbing on Fungi

Certain fungus gnat larvae spread a film of webbing over the surface of the fungi on which they feed. Some, such as *Leptomorphus*, spin a flat sheet under bracket fungi so that it catches the spores as they are released. The larva moves around under the sheet, eating the spore-laden silk and repairing the holes it makes as it does so. Some of the Keroplatidae instead use the silk to catch insect prey.

Irregular Webbing on Vegetation (Insects and Spider Mites)

Irregular webbing on vegetation may be a product of spiders, caterpillars, sawfly larvae, barklice, or spider mites. It is usually straightforward to distinguish spider webs from the rest, by looking for clues such as egg sacs,

Left: Webbing of *Aaroniella* barklice (Philotarsidae) on a highbush blueberry stem. Two silk-covered egg clusters are visible. (MA) *Right:* Webbing of *Graphopsocus cruciatus* barklice (Stenopsocidae) on the underside of a leaf. Note the exuviae and dark specks of excrement suspended in it. (TN)

caught prey, and spider exuviae, as well as a lack of the droppings and feeding sign associated with most insect and mite webs.

Barklice

Many barklice spin irregular webbing over bark of trees and shrubs, using it as a shelter under which they feed on molds, algae, lichens, and debris. The webbing produced by *Archipsocus nomas* (Archipsocidae) in the southeastern United States is particularly extensive. The introduced *Graphopsocus cruciatus* (Stenopsocidae) spins small, flat webs on the undersides of leaves. Exuviae and tiny, dark specks of excrement accumulate in the webbing.

Webbing of spider mites (Tetranychidae) on a house plant. (MA)

Spider Mites

Some spider mites (Tetranychidae) spin webbing for a shelter as barklice do. Their webs can be conspicuous when spun among multiple leaves, occasionally covering an entire plant. Often, however, they are flat and hidden on leaf undersides like those of *Graphopsocus cruciatus*. *Oligonychus bicolor* spins webbing on the upper surfaces of pin oak leaves. Unlike barklouse webs, those of spider mites are associated with discoloration of leaves from their feeding activities.

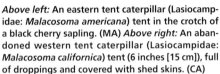

Above left: An eastern tent caterpillar (Lasiocampidae: *Malacosoma americana*) tent in the crotch of a black cherry sapling. (MA) *Above right:* An abandoned western tent caterpillar (Lasiocampidae: *Malacosoma californica*) tent (6 inches [15 cm]), full of droppings and covered with shed skins. (CA)

Tent Caterpillars

Among the numerous species of gregarious, web-spinning caterpillars, the webs of tent caterpillars (Lasiocampidae: *Malacosoma*) are distinctive. Rather than webbing together the leaves on which they feed, they spin a tent in a fork or crotch of two or more branches. They rest in this tent when not feeding and deposit their droppings and shed skins there. They make forays out to feed on leaves, trailing silk behind them like a spider's dragline, which accumulates thickly on well-used routes. The eastern tent caterpillar (*M. americana*) feeds on

A black cherry sapling showing the accumulated silk trails of a colony of eastern tent caterpillars. (MA)

cherry and apple; the Pacific (*M. constricta*) and Sonoran (*M. tigris*) on oaks; the southwestern (*M. incurva*) on willow, poplar, and *Prunus*; and the western (*M. californica*) on various trees and shrubs. The tent of the Pacific can be distinguished from those of the western feeding on oaks because the former is much smaller, used only as a molting mat and not as a shelter. The forest tent caterpillar (*M. disstria*) makes no tent.

Fall Webworm

The webs of fall webworms (Arctiidae: *Hyphantria cunea*) are among the most conspicuous caterpillar webs. This widespread, gregarious species feeds on leaves of more than a hundred deciduous trees, including cherry,

Communal web of fall webworms (Arctiidae: *Hyphantria cunea*). (MA)

willow, walnut, and ash, although it is often found on just one species in a given season and location. The webbing covers the ends of branches, surrounding all of the leaves on which the caterpillars feed, sometimes spanning a few feet. Masses of dirty webbing persist long after the caterpillars are gone.

Other Moth Larvae

Archips cerasivorana (Tortricidae; N) is called the "uglynest caterpillar" because of the webs it makes, full of droppings and dead leaves, but certainly other species are worthy of this title. It is most common on chokecherry but is found on various other trees and shrubs. Rather than simply engulfing the ends of branches with webbing as fall webworms do, these caterpillars tie the leaves together tightly, often resulting in long, narrow nests. They make their loose cocoons within the webbing, instead of dispersing to pupate as fall webworms and tent caterpillars do.

Many other caterpillars web leaves together, and it is difficult to draw a line between those where the webbing is the most conspicuous feature and those that belong in chapter 11 along with the other leaf tiers. At any rate, there are far too many to list them all, and all produce basically similar silk nests with varying amounts of leaves and droppings. In addition to other tortricids, caterpillars that web leaves include pyralids, crambids, elachistids, plume moths (Pterophoridae), and ermine moths (Yponomeutidae). The parsnip webworm (Elachistidae:

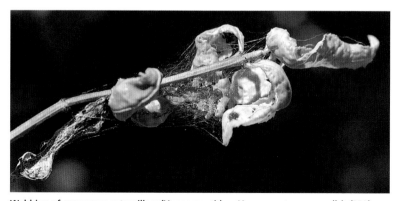

Webbing of euonymus caterpillars (Yponomeutidae: *Yponomeuta cagnagella*). (MA)

Depressaria pastinacella) makes webbing in the flower heads and seeds of parsnip and other plants in the parsley family. Ermine moths include the ailanthus webworm (*Atteva punctella*) and several species that make webs on plants in the bittersweet family.

Butterfly Caterpillars

Some nymphaline butterfly caterpillars also live in silk nests, where in some cases they overwinter. These include Harris's checkerspot (*Chlosyne harrisii*) on flat-topped aster; the Baltimore checkerspot (*Euphydryas phaeton*) on turtlehead; and Milbert's tortoiseshell (*Aglais milberti*) on nettles. Whereas these examples are gregarious, some *Vanessa* species make solitary silk nests, in which they often form their chrysalises: the red admiral (*V. atalanta*) on nettles; the west coast lady (*V. annabella*) on mallows and nettles; the American lady (*V. virginiensis*) on everlastings and related composites; and the painted lady (*V. cardui*) on composites such as thistle.

Web-spinning Sawflies

Most of the web-spinning sawflies (Pamphiliidae) are rare or are solitary leafrollers. Two more common gregarious species are the plum web-spinning sawfly (*Neurotoma inconspicua*) and cherry web-spinning sawfly (*N. edwardi*). Both are eastern and web the tips of *Prunus* branches in a manner similar to the uglynest caterpillar, but they drop to the ground to spin cocoons. Rusty willow sawfly larvae (Cimbicidae: *Cimbex rubidus*; W) spin webs on willow branches and drag leaf fragments into these shelters to feed.

Webbing on Conifers

More than twenty species of pamphiliid sawfly larvae (*Acantholyda* and *Cephalcia*) feed among webbed-together conifer needles. Many are gregarious and feed on older needles, leaving characteristic terminal tufts of new growth that resemble feather dusters beyond the defoliated portions bearing their excrement-filled webs. Some *Cephalcia* species are solitary, living in inconspicuous silk tubes along twigs and small branches.

Webs of the pine webworm (Pyralidae: *Pococera robustella*; E) can be similar to those of the gregarious sawflies, but this species does not share their preference for older needles. Its nests are usually about 2 inches (5 cm) long but sometimes reach 6 inches (15 cm). The silver-spotted tiger moth (Arctiidae: *Lophocampa argentata*) makes webs on various conifers in the Pacific Northwest like those of its relative, the fall webworm, on hardwoods. The Douglas-fir tussock moth (Lymantriidae: *Orgyia pseudotsugata*), with a similar range of hosts and in the same region, produces looser webbing that does not retain frass in the same way.

Other moth larvae make little silk nests incorporating conifer needles that have been mined, cut, or both. The spruce needleminer (Tortricidae: *Taniva albolineana*) mines in the bases of the previous year's spruce needles, making a dense web full of droppings and cut needles and pupating in a cocoon within this mass. The European spruce needleminer (*Epinotia nanana*) does the same, but its webbing is less dense, and it usually pupates in a cocoon on the ground. The spruce budworm (*Choristoneura fumiferana*) webs together cut needles at the tips of shoots. Many other tortricids and gelechiids leave various combinations of such sign on spruces and other conifers (see chapter 10).

Webbing on Fern Pinnae

Stathmopoda species (Batrachedridae) make small but conspicuous "blisters" of webbed-together spores on the upper surfaces of ferns. The larva feeds in a sorus (spore cluster) on the underside of the frond, in the shelter of a small web, and constructs the blister to use as its retreat. It pupates in a dense, white cocoon, which may be within the web.

Matzo crumbled and webbed together by Indianmeal moth larvae (Pyralidae: *Plodia interpunctella*). One can be seen pupating in its cocoon in the chunk in the foreground. (TN)

Webbing in Dried Plant and Animal Products

A number of types of moth larvae may be responsible for webbing found in food and other stored materials. The Indianmeal moth (*Plodia interpunctella*), the Mediterranean flour moth (*Ephestia kuehniella*), and the meal moth (*Pyralis farinalis*) are all pyralids that feed on stored cereals and other dry foods. All three spin extensive webbing, the last two feeding from silken tubes, and pupate in silken cocoons. These and certain other pyralids also make webbing in other dried plant materials, such as tobacco and hay. The larvae of the European grain moth (Tineidae: *Nemapogon granella*) can also be found making webbing in vegetable matter, sometimes boring in wine corks, but tineids are more typically associated with animal products. Tapestry moths (*Trichophaga tapetzella*) construct silken galleries in carpets and materials made from animal hides, and they have also been found in owl pellets. The more common webbing clothes moth (*Tineola bisselliella*) feeds on wool products, making disorganized webbing rather than distinct galleries.

Silken Galleries and Tubes

Long tubes of silk may be the work of moth larvae, webspinners, or spiders. For the insects, they function as protection from predators, but the tubes of spiders are used as places to lurk while waiting for prey.

Silken gallery of webspinners (Embiidina), revealed when loose bark sloughed off the log. The stretch visible in the photo is about 8 inches (20 cm) long, with the tunnel having an internal diameter of 2 mm. (CA)

Pyraloid Moths

Various pyraloid moth larvae live in silken galleries. In addition to those found in stored products, as listed above, several species live in beehives, which are discussed in chapter 8. A number of crambids are known as sod webworms because they form tubes of webbing at the base of grasses or moss on which they feed, on or below the ground surface. In the New Jersey Pine Barrens, *Prionapteryx nebulifera* makes a tube of silk and sand leading from an underground retreat into sand myrtle and huckleberry plants. At night, the larva emerges to cut pieces of the leaves and carry them into its burrow, where it feeds on them during the day. Burrowing webworms (Tineoidea: Acrolophidae) feed on grass roots and detritus, constructing silken tunnels that may extend 2 feet (60 cm) underground.

Webspinners

The other makers of silken tunnel systems are the webspinners (Embiidina), an order of gregarious insects found in the southern United States and Mexico. They are mostly around 1 cm long and feed primarily on dead plant materials. They spin their narrow, interconnecting galleries where their food is found: under bark and stones; in crevices of bark and soil; and among lichens, moss, dry grass, debris, and epiphytic plants. In dry regions, they extend deep into the soil. Fungus gnat larvae may also make silken tunnels in soil, but these are in moist environments and not so clearly defined. Some silk-lined spider burrows might be construed as galleries, and these are discussed in chapter 16.

Purseweb Spiders

Purseweb spiders (Atypidae) are small eastern mygalomorphs that make webs that are unmistakable if you are lucky

The web (13 inches [33 cm] high) of a red-legged purseweb spider (Atypidae: *Sphodros rufipes*) stands among poison ivy vines against a tree trunk, masterfully camouflaged to match the pattern of moss on the bark. (MS)

enough to spot one. Like other tarantula relatives, a purseweb spider makes a burrow in the ground, but in this case at the base of a tree. From this burrow, the spider extends a papery silken tube up the side of the tree; the tube also extends underground as the burrow's lining. Depending on the size of the spider, the tube ranges from 0.4 to 2 inches (1 to 5 cm) wide and 6 to 12 inches (15 to 30 cm) tall. The web of a tiny juvenile *Sphodros niger* found attached to a grass blade in a lawn measured only 2 cm high and 1.5 mm wide. Sometimes an adult female's tube has several small tubes of her offspring side by side on the same tree. As the spider excavates the burrow, it disposes of some soil pellets out the top of the tube and presses some particles outward through the walls, until the outside is well camouflaged and looks much like a truncated vine. The spider hides at the burrow entrance, then rushes up the tube when an insect lands on it, bites through the wall, and pulls its prey inside. After eating, it pushes the remains of its meal out through the top and repairs the hole. *S. rufipes* is the most widespread species but is nowhere common. *S. niger*, a northeastern species, is unusual in that its tubes typically lie flat on the ground, where they may be entirely concealed by grass or leaf litter. These webs are only 10 to 12 mm wide and average around 5 inches (13 cm) long, but may be longer than 24 inches (60 cm). Examples of *S. atlanticus* with semihorizontal tubes have also been found.

Complex Spider Webs

Everyone is familiar with the snare webs spiders spin to catch their prey. Even if you have never paid much attention to them, you can surely call to mind at least two kinds: the classic *orb web*, with a sticky thread spiraling over a number of other threads that radiate from one central point, and those messy-looking ones that show up in the corners of your house. Actually, there is tremendous diversity in the form of spider webs, and often the web alone can be used to identify the family or genus, and sometimes even the species. Even when the spider is present, looking at the web's structure may tell you more than looking at the spider itself. (As with many invertebrates, precise spider identification generally requires collecting the animal and examining it under a microscope.)

Spider webs are believed to have originated with egg sacs. If the randomly placed draglines around an egg sac occasionally stopped or slowed insects that were passing through, this would have led to the construction of more elaborate mazes of threads. From here, more effective designs were developed, with innumerable variations. Besides irregular and orb webs, the basic categories include webs that consist mainly of a tubular retreat; sheet webs; and funnel webs, which combine the two.

In addition to the variations in form, two new types of silk arose that make webs more effective in ensnaring insects. Some spiders spin threads that are studded with sticky droplets; others make silk that has no glue but is structurally sticky, something like Velcro. This type is called *cribellate* silk because it comes from an organ called the *cribellum*, and it gets its woolly structure from being combed by a structure on the hind leg called the *calamistrum*. The woolliness is microscopic, but the cribellate threads are combined with regular threads, and the resulting "hackled bands" are visibly thicker, fuzzy-looking, and often have a bluish cast. It is thought that many of the spiders that spin sticky threads are descended from spiders that made cribellate silk but have lost the structures that produce it. Spiders without a cribellum are referred to as *ecribellate*.

Irregular Webs

Many spider webs have no definite design, or at least do not have an easily recognized pattern or shape. Some have distinctive features that serve to identify them, and others can at least be narrowed down based on their location, but many cannot be reliably identified. Spiders that make irregular webs often hang their egg sacs in them or nearby, so these can be important clues to look for.

Cobweb Spiders

The Theridiidae, of which there are more than two hundred North American species, have officially been given the title of cobweb spiders. Most are small and make inconspicuous webs on plants or hidden in burrows or under debris. A typical theridiid web has dry strands extending irregularly in all directions. The strands increase in density and frequency of branching at the center of the web. In many webs, this part includes a densely woven silk retreat. There are also sticky strands, anchored to the substrate, that break when an insect hits them, pulling the prey in toward the center.

The most conspicuous and commonly seen theridiid webs are made by the common house spider (*Parasteatoda tepidariorum*). They are found in

Web of the common house spider (Theridiidae: *Parasteatoda tepidariorum*), with several egg sacs. (VT)

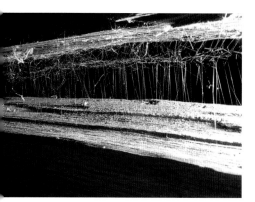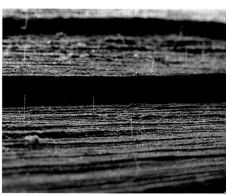

Left: Web (1.6 inches [4 cm] high) of *Steatoda* (Theridiidae). (TN) *Right:* Detail of the 2-mm sticky bases of a few of the strands in the same web. (TN)

any dry structure, including houses, basements, and barns, as well as under natural "roofs" such as overhanging ledges. These webs often include a more densely woven tent that serves as a retreat. The webs of black widows (*Latrodectus*) look similar, but they are generally in more concealed places and composed of extremely strong, coarse threads.

Certain cobweb spiders incorporate various materials into the central retreat as camouflage. The webs of *Achaearanea rupicola* are often found around houses. This spider's retreat, which may be in the form of an inverted cup, is camouflaged with leaves and debris, or sometimes grains of sand. *Theridion pictum* makes a bowl of dry spruce needles or other plant parts sewed together with silk, beneath which the female hides her egg sacs and young. In *Tidarren* species, common in the South, the female lives in a curled leaf or cluster of leaves suspended in the middle of the web.

In *Steatoda* webs, the denser central area forms a sort of sheet, but it is loose and irregular compared with the sheets of linyphiids. Often most of the anchoring threads below this horizontal sheet are vertical, with sticky droplets just at the base, especially suited to ensnaring walking prey. When an ant or other insect walks into the sticky base, the thread's connection to the surface below breaks easily. The prey is then suspended helplessly, becoming increasingly entangled as it tries to get free. *S. triangulosa* webs are common in basements and are usually built in lower corners, whereas common house spider webs are usually in upper corners.

Cave Spiders

The webs of cave spiders (Nesticidae), usually in dark, moist places, are similar to those of *Steatoda*. A typical web is a loose platform beneath which vertical threads, often with forks near the ends, anchor to the substrate. As with *Steatoda*, these threads have short zones of sticky droplets at the base. Besides caves, they are found in deep leaf litter, among boulders, and in moist crevices of cliffs.

Cellar Spiders

Cellar spiders (Pholcidae) generally inhabit dark places such as ledges, caves, cellars, and poorly lit corners in houses. They make loose, highly irregular webs, sometimes with a distinct, more closely woven sheet. Pholcids vibrate their webs when disturbed and to help entangle their prey. *Pholcus phalangioides* often covers the ceiling and walls of cellars and neglected rooms with its large, loose web. It may be flat and horizontal when space permits, or irregular when conforming to surrounding objects. *Neotama mexicana* (Hersiliidae) spins similar webs on trees in southern Texas and Mexico.

Recluse Spiders

The recluse spiders (Sicariidae: *Loxosceles*) make large, irregular webs in dark places, usually in dry habitats. They are generally hidden in crevices, but the silk may extend beyond the retreat. The strands are thick and very sticky, somewhat resembling cribellate silk. Common web locations include holes in the ground, caves, and under logs and stones. The brown recluse (*L. reclusa*) is strongly associated with man-made structures, especially in the northern parts of its range, and often makes its webs under boards and similar hiding places.

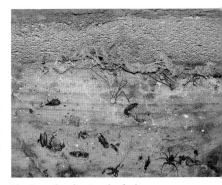

The irregular sheet web of a brown recluse (Sicariidae: *Loxosceles reclusa*), found between two boards. (TN)

Meshweb Weavers

Webs of many dictynine meshweb weavers (Dictynidae) are made on foliage, flowers, branches, and dead stalks of plants. Some are made in and around small crevices between boards in fences and buildings. The web consists of a framework of plain threads supporting an irregular mesh of cribellate silk, and the distinctive "hackled" appearance distinguishes it from most other irregular webs found in the open. A silken retreat may be in the center. The webs often take the form of loose sheets with a more or less symmetrical lattice. Some webs are spun across a single curled

Web of a meshweb weaver (Dictynidae: Dictyninae) at the top of a meadowsweet bush. The web measures 1.4 by 3 inches (3.5 by 7.5 cm). (MA)

Web of *Callobius* (Amaurobiidae), a hacklemesh weaver, on redwood bark. (CA)

leaf. Others surround the ends of twigs and weeds, with the foundation lines strung from stem to stem and the hackled bands woven over this foundation. *Badumna longinqua* (Desidae), an Australian species with a web very similar to this latter design, is now abundant in some coastal urban areas in California.

Hacklemesh Weavers

The cribellate hacklemesh weavers (Amaurobiidae) also generally make irregular webs, but theirs tend to be in dark, damp situations, rather than in the sunny, exposed locations frequented by the cribellate dictynids. Their webs are usually loose, with no apparent plan, but they may form more definite sheets. In the webs of some species, the hackled band is particularly coarse, and in fresh webs, the loose bands can be seen running irregularly about on the other threads. The conspicuous amaurobiid webs tend to be in crevices in vertical surfaces such as rocks and tree trunks; those of *Callobius* are very common on redwood bark in California. Most amaurobiid webs are under stones or logs and hidden from view. *Titanoeca* (Titanoecidae), *Zorocrates* (Zorocratidae; SW), and *Metaltella simoni* (Amphinectidae; introduced in CA and SE) also make irregular cribellate webs under objects on the ground.

Nursery Web Spiders

When a nursery web spider's (Pisauridae) spiderlings are ready to emerge, she hangs the egg sac in a web of irregularly crisscrossing threads, the "nursery." The web is easily recognized by the torn-open egg sac. Some orbweaver (Araneidae) spiderlings, upon emerging from their egg sac, communally spin a similar-looking nursery of their own.

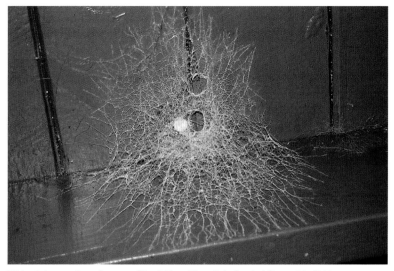

Web of the southern house spider (Filistatidae: *Kukulcania hibernalis*). (GA)

Webs with a Tubular Retreat

A variety of webs incorporate some sort of funnel or tube in which the spider hides, including those of some of the hacklemesh weavers just mentioned. Some webs consist of little more than a silk-lined crevice; others are broad sheet webs that taper into funnels. This section covers the former, and the latter are described in the next section.

Crevice Weavers

The crevice weavers (Filistatidae) make conspicuous webs surrounding central tubular retreats. They can be similar to those of *Callobius*, but the thick covering of cribellate silk is laid down on a framework of lines that radiate from the retreat, giving the web a more symmetrical and structured, albeit unkempt, appearance. They commonly extend over 1 foot (30.5 cm) in diameter. The southern house spider (*Kukulcania hibernalis*) is one of the commonest spiders in the Southeast, often building its wild, frizzy-looking webs around crevices on the sides of buildings. Smaller individuals frequently use abandoned mud dauber tubes as retreats. *Filistatinella* species in Texas and the Southwest make similar, but smaller webs between stones and on houses in moist environments.

Tube Web Spiders

Ariadna bicolor and other tube web spiders (Segestriidae) build small tubes of silk in crevices such as cracks in rocks and trees. Usually only the mouth of the tube is visible, and its diameter ranges from 1 to 10 mm or so, just wide enough for the spider to fit. One example we saw built along the outside of a brick wall, in the depression between two bricks, had a tube 1.8

Above left: Entrance to the tube web of *Ariadna bicolor* (Segestriidae). (VA) *Above right:* A segestriid web with several of the radiating threads (up to 2.8 inches [7 cm] long) visible. The retreat is 5 mm wide. (CA) *Left:* An atypically exposed *Ariadna bicolor* web. The spider was uninterested in this woodlouse, but it rushed out and seized a firefly that arrived later. (TN)

inches (4.5 cm) long. A silken "collar" extends in a circle around the mouth of the tube from just a few millimeters up to around 1.2 inches (3 cm) in diameter. In a complete web, twenty or so long silk strands radiate out in all directions from the opening, extending several centimeters beyond the collar. Each of these radii is supported by a few short silken pillars so that it does not quite lie flat. The spider waits near the entrance to the tube, springing out when something touches one of these signal lines. These radii have been absent or difficult to see in most examples we have found, perhaps because they were old, abandoned tubes.

Plectreurids

Plectreurids are little-known spiders of the desert Southwest. They spin tubular retreats in dark places such as under rocks, bark, and debris, and in crevices of stone walls and bridges. The small entrance is fringed with an irregular tangle of silk. *Prodidomus rufus* (Prodidomidae) is a fairly rare southeastern spider that makes a tubular web in cellars and dark closets.

Funnel Webs

Some spiders have expanded the webbing around their tubular retreats to form well-defined sheets of silk. The most frequently encountered of these are the funnel-web spiders (Agelenidae), but there are several other possibilities.

Funnel-Web Spiders

The web of many agelenids consists of a flat, slightly concave silken sheet that curves abruptly into a funnel-shaped retreat at one end. The spider hides in the funnel, poised to dart out and seize any insects that land on the sheet. Many, but not all, funnel webs are built close to the ground, often in grass. The sheet is composed of dry silk (not sticky), and there may be an irregular maze of threads above it. The spider continues to enlarge the sheet throughout its life, which may be several months. A dragline is continually laid down whenever the spider runs across the sheet, so it becomes ever thicker and more finely woven. Webs of this sort made by grass spiders (*Agelenopsis*) are very common on grass, but they may also be found in shrubs and corners of buildings. Some southern agelenids make larger, more truly funnel-shaped webs; one we measured in Mississippi was 17.7 inches (45 cm) tall with a mouth 19.7 inches (50 cm) wide, tapering gradually to a 1.2-inch (3-cm) base. The barn funnel weaver (*Tegenaria domestica*), known in Great Britain as the common house spider, lives almost exclusively in cellars and neglected buildings. Its web is basically similar to the grass spider's, but the tube is generally smaller and less funnel-shaped (straighter) where it enters the web. Often the sheet sags to form a deep pocket instead of being flat. The web may form a shelf in a corner or spread out along a beam.

Web of a grass spider (Agelenidae: *Agelenopsis*). (FL)

Funnel-Web Wolf Spiders

Across the southern United States and in Mexico, large, permanent, agelenidlike webs are made by the funnel-web wolf spiders (Lycosidae: *Sosippus*). *S. floridanus* spins its funnel retreat under beach debris in southern Florida, with its sheet spread over dry sand. Other species are found in wetlands, grasslands, deciduous forests, and deserts.

Funnel-Web Mygalomorphs

Two families of small mygalomorphs also make basically similar horizontal funnel webs on the ground. *Megahexura fulva*

A more funnel-shaped agelenid web, 1.2 inches (3 cm) wide at the base; the whole web was 18 inches (45 cm) high and 20 inches (50 cm) wide. (MS)

(Mecicobothriidae) makes its webs in holes and crevices in the banks of ravines in California, usually in the shade of trees. The other mecicobothriids make webs that are mostly hidden under rocks, wood, or litter, attached to complexes of silken tubes. Two *Hexura* species are found in the Northwest, and three *Hexurella* species in the Southwest. The five species of Dipluridae make small, irregular sheet webs that are likewise mostly or entirely hidden from view. The tubular retreats are irregular and flattened, often branching. Three *Euagrus* species are found from southern Texas to Arizona, usually hiding most of the web under a rock, with some of it extending into the surrounding leaf litter. *Microhexura idahoana* webs are common in or under rotting logs and other organic debris in the Northwest. *M. montivaga* is a federally endangered species, making its webs under moss mats on rock outcrops in the southern Appalachians.

Ecribellate Amaurobiids

Coras and *Wadotes* are ecribellate amaurobiids (the common name "hacklemesh weavers" does not really apply to them), formerly considered to belong to the Agelenidae. They spin sheet webs with one or more retreats. *C. medicinalis* is a common forest species that often makes an extensive, somewhat sagging, platformlike web beneath overhanging rock ledges. Webs may also be in various crevices, curving according to their location and not flat like a grass spider's.

Desertshrub Spiders

The webs of desertshrub spiders (Diguetidae: *Diguetia*) are common among cacti and other desert vegetation in the Southwest. The centerpiece of the web is a vertical silk tube, up to a few inches long, which is covered with bits of leaves, prey remains, and other debris. The base of the tube flares out into a broad, conical, coarsely woven sheet. An irregular maze of

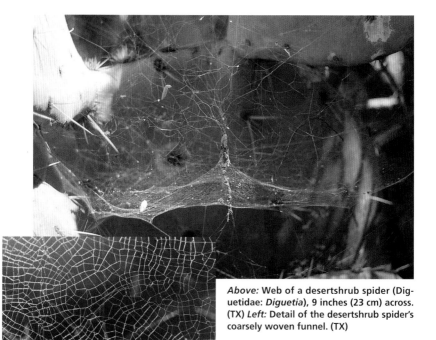

Above: Web of a desertshrub spider (Diguetidae: *Diguetia*), 9 inches (23 cm) across. (TX) *Left:* Detail of the desertshrub spider's coarsely woven funnel. (TX)

threads surrounds the funnel, some emanating from the closed top of the tube. The spider moves along the underside of the sheet and captures insects intercepted by the maze. In the winter, you may find the suspended retreat intact with the spider hiding inside but no sheet web beneath.

Cybaeids

The webs of the Cybaeidae (W, Appalachians) have not been well documented, but according to Ubick et al. (2005), they are best described as a type of funnel web and are small, probably functioning primarily as retreats. Ubick et al. describe a *Cybaeus* web as a "lacy, loosely woven squarish basket with an opening at each corner and a pair of long silk threads (signal lines?) extending from each opening." Webs of other genera apparently are more clearly funnel-shaped. All are fairly inconspicuous, found under objects on the ground and among forest litter.

Flat Sheet Webs

Other spiders spin flat sheets, made up of irregularly crisscrossing lines, without any funnel-like structure. These vary in texture, but they never have the finely woven appearance that funnel-web spiders achieve by constantly adding more silk as they run over the surface. Some insects and spider mites could be said to spin sheet webs of sorts, but these should be easy to distinguish for reasons already explained.

Sheet webs are characteristic of the Linyphiidae, commonly called the sheetweb spiders. A linyphiid usually hangs on the underside of its sheet, which typically is supported by irregular threads above and below. Insects become trapped between the irregular threads above the sheet, and the spider shakes the web until they fall onto the sheet. When one reaches the sheet, the spider bites through the web and pulls it through. After feeding, the spider repairs the web, and it uses the same web for a long time.

Pimoids

Pimoa species (Pimoidae; formerly in Linyphiidae), found from California to Alaska, build large sheet webs close to the ground, sometimes covering as much as 11 square feet (1 square m). They are in sheltered places such as hollow tree trunks or cavities in banks, or sometimes in sheds and outhouses. Several species are found in caves. The webs are maintained for long periods and may show obvious signs of repair. The spider hangs from the underside of the sheet like a linyphiid at night, hiding in a retreat at the web's margin during the day.

Sheetweb Spiders

Hammock spiders (*Pityohyphantes*) are among the most common sheetweb spiders in the East. Their web may be more than 1 foot (30.5 cm) across and often has a four-sided outline, but this depends on where it is built. It can be found on herbaceous plants, in shrubs, and on man-made objects. We have found them in the wheel wells of neglected vehicles and in the lower branches of trees, where they can be very contorted from their nor-

Left: Web of a hammock spider (Linyphiidae: *Pityohyphantes*). The "hammock" is 8 by 10 inches (20 by 25 cm). (MA) *Right:* A less regular hammock spider web, with the "hammock" bending to the available attachment points. (MA)

mal flat shape in order to conform to the arrangement of twigs and leaves. The web may have a corner that extends under a stone or some other hiding place, or else the spider uses a curled leaf or builds a little silk tent.

Other flat sheet webs are difficult to tell apart, but the location can offer clues to their identity. *Megalepthyphantes nebulosus* makes large, flat webs in damp and shady places. They are often found in cellars and similar places

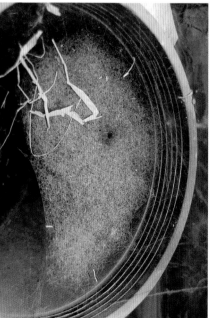

around houses, where the web may cover the opening of a foot-wide box or bucket. *Porrhomma cavernicola* makes small webs on the walls and ceilings in dark, damp recesses of caves. *Drapetisca* makes fine, vertical webs on tree trunks. *Bathyphantes* makes very delicate sheets under stones or in leaf litter.

Various other linyphiids, such as *Neriene clathrata* and *Helophora insignis*, build flat sheet webs among grass or other low vegetation. Platform spiders (*Microlinyphia*) spin a web 3 to 6 inches (7.6 to 15.2 cm) across and usually 2 to 6 inches (5 to 15.2 cm) from the ground. Above the sheet is a labyrinth of delicate threads. The spider usually hangs below the center of the platform, in contrast to other members of this family that drop to the ground and run away when disturbed.

Web of *Megalepthyphantes nebulosus* (Linyphiidae), built in a bucket in a garage. (VT)

A dwarf spider (Linyphiidae: Erigoninae) web, about 2.4 inches (6 cm) across, made visible by the morning dew. (AZ)

Dwarf Spiders

Dwarf spiders (subfamily Erigoninae) make particularly small sheet webs, about 2 inches (5 cm) across, on or close to the ground. These may be found in grass, moss, or dead leaves, or suspended over water. They are so delicate that they are invisible except when covered with dew. As they are described, webs of *Neoantistea* (Hahniidae) evidently are indistinguishable. They are much less common than those of dwarf spiders but are sometimes found in abundance. These webs are most often found among moss or in animal footprints and other such depressions in moist soil and snow. The spider hides in the soil at the edge of the web.

Flatmesh Weavers

Still smaller sheet webs are made by the flatmesh weavers (Oecobiidae). Several *Oecobius* species are found around houses in California and across the southern United States. The main part of the web is a very fine sheet, often starlike in outline and usually less than 1 inch (2.5 cm) in diameter. It is made on the side of a building over a crack or angle or over a small projection such as the head of a nail. The spider rests beneath this sheet, either atop a smaller sheet or in a tube.

Ogre-Faced Spider

A rare and very unusual southeastern species, the ogre-faced spider (Deinopidae: *Deinopis spinosa*), spends the day hanging from a small platform of nonsticky silk. At night, this long-legged spider spins a sparse scaffolding across which it extends its body, and across four of these silk lines it spins a sticky, rectangular patch of webbing about the size of a postage stamp. The spider holds each corner of this rectangular net with the tips of its four front legs and hangs downward. When a flying insect approaches, it holds out the net to intercept its prey. This net is woven of thick, white,

The discarded net of an ogre-faced spider (Deinopidae: *Deinopis spinosa*). (FL) Photo by Jeff Hollenbeck.

cribellate silk that is conspicuous in the daylight, and if it is left hanging, it can be the most obvious clue to this well-camouflaged spider's presence.

Other Flat Sheet Webs

Many dictynids spin very small, flat, delicate, inconspicuous sheet webs, which function mainly as retreats. Ecribellate species such as *Cicurina* make theirs on the ground, under rocks and logs or among moss. *Zanomys*, *Parazanomys*, and *Cavernocymbium* are western amaurobiids that hang upside down from small cribellate sheet webs. Leptonetids (W, S) and telemids (NW) hang from small, finely woven sheets of about 1.2 to 1.6 inches (3 to 4 cm). They are found in damp situations such as in ground litter and especially in caves. Spitting spiders (Scytodidae) usually make no webs but may spin thin, flat sheets in crevices or on leaves. Tarantulas spin sheets of silk over their burrow entrances when they are not hunting.

Curved Sheet Webs

Several spiders make distinctive curved, three-dimensional shapes in their webs. Unlike many of the webs described above, most of these can reliably be identified to genus, if not species, by the web architecture alone.

Sheetweb Spiders

The bowl and doily spider (Linyphiidae: *Frontinella communis*) got its name because its web includes one sheet, curved upward like a shallow bowl, positioned slightly above a less curved sheet, which could be imagined to be a saucer or doily that the bowl is sitting on. As in other linyphiid webs, an irregular maze of threads anchors the sheet webs above and

Web of the bowl and doily spider (Linyphiidae: *Frontinella communis*). The "bowl" is 3.5 inches (9 cm) wide. (MA)

Left: Web of the Sierra dome spider (Linyphiidae: *Neriene litigiosa*), 10 inches (25 cm) across. (CA) *Right:* Web of the filmy dome spider (Linyphiidae: *Neriene radiata*), about 4 inches (10 cm) across. (NJ)

below and deflects flying insects, in this case into the bowl. The spider hangs under the bowl, and the "doily" protects it from attacks from below. The web is usually in low shrubs, up to 4 feet (1.2 m) or so above the ground, and the bowls we have seen have ranged from 2.4 to 3.5 inches (6 to 9 cm) across. A similar but much less common web is made by *Florinda coccinea* in the Southeast. It tends to be lower to the ground, with a finer mesh and shallower bowl than that of the bowl and doily spider.

The filmy dome spider (*Neriene radiata*) spins a sheet in the form of a dome that is 3 to 5 inches (8 to 13 cm) wide, again usually near the ground and with an associated maze of irregular threads. The spider hangs from the top of the dome and pulls insects through as other sheetweb spiders do. Often the threads are difficult to see, and the web appears as many points of light coalescing into a dome shape, which presumably is how the "filmy" got in the name. When the dome is damaged beyond repair, the spider pulls it down and spins a new one, and sometimes the remains of several flat and torn old domes can be seen hanging below a fresh one. A strictly western species, the Sierra dome spider (*N. litigiosa*), makes a similar but much larger web, with the dome up to 24 inches (60 cm) wide and 5 to 8 inches (13 to 20 cm) tall.

Basilica Spider

Another web that appears similar from a distance is made by the basilica spider (Araneidae: *Mecynogea lemniscata*). On

Web of the basilica spider (Araneidae: *Mecynogea lemniscata*), about 8 inches (20 cm) across. Note the "clothesline" from which its string of egg sacs is suspended over the center. (MS)

close inspection, it is revealed to be a tightly woven horizontal orb web that has been pulled into the shape of a dome. As with the linyphiid domes, this web is surrounded by an irregular maze of threads.

Holocnemus pluchei

Holocnemus pluchei, a common pholcid in California's Central Valley, makes a distinctive spherical web about 2 inches (5 cm) in diameter. These are built only by egg-carrying females and are found attached to outdoor ceilings on buildings or in junipers and other shrubs. The female remains inside the sphere until the eggs hatch, and the spiderlings stay until their first molt.

Lampshade Weavers

The aptly named lampshade weavers (Hypochilidae: *Hypochilus*) make unmistakable lampshade-shaped webs attached to the undersides of over-hanging ledges and other similar surfaces. A typical web we measured in the Smoky Mountains was 3.1 inches (8 cm) in diameter at its circular attachment to the ledge, with the clearly visible "lampshade" mesh of cribellate silk measuring 2 inches (5 cm) tall and 4.7 inches (12 cm) wide. Beyond this, the web flares out into a much larger network of threads, which are not as easily seen. The spider typically rests pressed against the rock in the center of the web. White, circular "web scars" are visible on former web locations.

Web of a lampshade weaver (Hypochilidae: *Hypochilus*). The visible portion is 5 inches (12 cm) across. (TN)

Calymmaria

Another very distinctive web is made by spiders in the hahniid genus *Calymmaria*. It is a thick, finely woven sheet in the form of a conical bag, anchored with supporting lines above and below. These bags hang from rocks and exposed root systems in steep stream banks, road cuts, and similar places. The spider hangs above the open bag from a thin sheet spun on the surface from which the bag is hanging. A number of species are found west of the Rockies, and two occur in the Appalachians, all making essentially identical webs.

Orb Webs

Last but not least are *orb webs*, the classic two-dimensional spider webs consisting of several lines of silk radiating from a central point, with an evenly spaced spiral built over these lines. Webs of this sort are built by just a few of the roughly seventy families of spiders found in North America: Araneidae (orbweavers), Tetragnathidae (long-jawed orbweavers), Uloboridae (hackled orbweavers), Theridiosomatidae (ray spiders), Nephilidae (one species, the golden silk orbweaver), and three others too rarely encountered to have

Web of *Calymmaria* (Hahniidae), 4 inches (10 cm) across. (CA)

common names. There are many variations on the basic pattern, one of the more extreme being that of the basilica spider shown on page 201.

Construction of a typical orb web begins with the spinning of a single horizontal thread, called the *bridge*, which may be reused many times to construct new webs in the same location. The spider strengthens the bridge by walking back and forth across it and laying down more silk. Next it goes to the middle of the bridge, attaches a line to one of the component strands, and drops down. This causes the strand from the bridge to stretch, and together with the new line, it forms a Y-shaped figure. The three lines are the first *radii*, and their intersection will be the web's *hub*. The spider fastens the line to a support and returns to the hub.

To create each additional radial thread, the spider attaches a line to the hub, walks to the end of one of the existing radii, moves some distance around the web's perimeter, and finally tightens the line and attaches it to a support. It spins *frame threads* between the ends of the radii, delineating the edge of the web and serving as attachment points for more radii. Once the frame is complete, the spider spins a mesh of additional lines at the center to form the hub.

The penultimate step is to spin a temporary, widely spaced *scaffolding spiral* out from the hub, which stabilizes the radii for the construction of the remainder of the web. All of the lines spun so far have been dry silk. Finally, beginning at the outside of the web, the spider lays down closely spaced, sticky threads that spiral in toward the hub, discarding or eating the scaffolding spiral as it goes. Once this is complete, some species then bite out the threads in the center or add various kinds of decorations. Ordinarily the whole process takes between half an hour and an hour, and most species rebuild the web each day or night. Depending on the species, the spider rests on the hub or off to the side of the web, and when an insect is caught, the spider darts over to it and wraps it like a mummy.

Nonaraneid Orb Webs

Orb-weaving spiders that are not in the Araneidae all have their own twist on the web's design. A couple of atypical araneid webs are also mentioned here for convenience.

Ray Spiders

The two species of ray spiders make small orb webs, 2.5 to 5 inches (6 to 13 cm) wide, with no hub. Instead of all converging at the center, the radii are united in four groups of three or four, and each group is connected to the center by a single "ray." The spider holds on to the four rays with its back four legs, and with its front four it holds a strand of silk roughly perpendicular to the plane of the web and pulls the web into a cone. When an insect hits the web, the spider lets go of this strand, staying on the web as it springs back and further entangles the prey. *Theridiosoma gemmosum* is a widespread eastern species that prefers dark, damp places; the orientation of its web varies but is most often vertical. *T. savannum* makes horizontal webs on the ground in southeastern forests, with the tension line attached to the leaf litter. Its web has a tightly spaced central spiral that occupies only about the central fourth of the area of the radii.

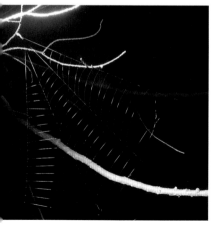

Triangle Spiders

The concept of a triangle spider (Uloboridae: *Hyptiotes*) web is similar to that of a ray spider's, except it consists of only a 45- to 60-degree sector of a complete orb web. It is vertically oriented, with just four radii, 12 to 20 inches (30 to 50 cm) long, which converge on a single line that the spider holds taut. The spider may rest somewhere in the middle of the line, bridging a gap between two threads, or it may rest on a

Web of a triangle spider (Uloboridae: *Hyptiotes*). Note the spider at upper left, holding the web taut. (MA)

Horizontal web of a feather-legged orbweaver (Uloboridae: *Uloborus*), 4 inches (10 cm) across. (MS)

twig, where it can easily be mistaken for a bud. When an insect hits the web, the spider releases the tension, and it may tighten and snap the line a few times before securing it and approaching its prey.

Feather-Legged Orbweaver

With the exception of the triangle spiders, uloborids build small, horizontally oriented (sometimes slightly inclined) webs, which distinguishes them from most other orbweavers. They are also the only cribellate orbweavers, so on close examination, the individual strands appear uniquely "hackled" and have no sticky droplets. This distinguishes their webs in the rare instances when they are vertically oriented. The feather-legged orbweaver (*Uloborus glomosus*), the most common and widespread species in the East, makes a horizontal web 4 to 6 inches (10 to 15 cm) across, usually close to the ground. The spider may decorate the web with thickened silk in a variety of patterns, including a narrow, scalloped band crossing through the center of the hub; four ribbons forming a cross; or concentric circles around the hub. The horizontal web of *Philoponella arizonica* (SW) is sometimes drawn up in the center by threads attached to the hub, giving it a slightly domed appearance, and often the radii are not all in one plane, making the orb look pleated.

Lined Orbweaver

The lined orbweaver (Araneidae: *Mangora gibberosa*) makes a horizontal orb web that might be mistaken for a uloborid's. *Mangora* webs are extremely tightly woven, however, with fifty to sixty radii (whereas *Uloborus* webs would have thirty or so) and a similar number of spirals. The webs are very delicate and measure 6 to 12 inches (15 to 30 cm) across. The hub is sometimes decorated with an open or closed white cir-

Detail of the delicate horizontal web of the lined orbweaver (Araneidae: *Mangora gibberosa*). The circular stabilimentum is 6 mm across. (NJ)

Typical web of a long-jawed orbweaver (Tetragnathidae: *Tetragnatha*), over water and inclined, with an open hub and a broad free space. (CA)

cle of thickened silk. In examples we saw in a New Jersey fen, the overall orb was folded down in a saddle shape. The only horizontally level part was the prominent central ring, 6 mm in diameter. The webs were virtually invisible except for the tiny rings, which seemed to float in midair.

Long-jawed Orbweavers

The long-jawed orbweavers make complete orb webs with an *open hub*, a circular gap in the center where the radii have been removed; relatively few radii (generally twelve to twenty); and relatively few, widely spaced spirals. The webs are usually inclined and near water or in wetlands. The orchard spider (*Leucauge venusta*), found throughout the eastern United States and very common in southeastern swamps, makes a more or less horizontal web, sometimes more than 1 foot (30.5 cm) across, often with an extensive, irregular maze of threads below it, and hangs under the hub. *Tetragnatha* species with moderate-size to large inclined or horizontal webs, about 2 feet (61 cm) across, are common near water across North America. Their webs sometimes have a broad free space, without sticky spiral threads, around the open hub. *T. elongata* often makes its web over running water and frequently perfectly horizontal. *T. laboriosa* is common in meadows and makes a more or less vertical web between grass stems. *Glenognatha foxi* builds a delicate orb web among vegetation in hot, dry situations (though it is found in wet areas as well); the web is usually horizontal and about 2 inches (5 cm) above the ground. *Meta ovalis* makes webs in dark places, often in caves. The web is usually inclined, but varies from vertical to horizontal, and has a wide, clear space as in some *Tetragnatha* webs. *Larinia directa* is a southern araneid that also makes an inclined web. It is found in sunny, grassy areas and is often particularly messy and irregular.

Golden Silk Orbweaver

The golden silk orbweaver (*Nephila clavipes*) is a tropical species with a range extending into the southeastern United States. Its web has several distinctive aspects, one being the sticky silk's golden color for which it is named. The web is exceptionally large, up to 3.3 feet (1 m) or more in diameter, and slightly inclined. The radii branch periodically, so that they

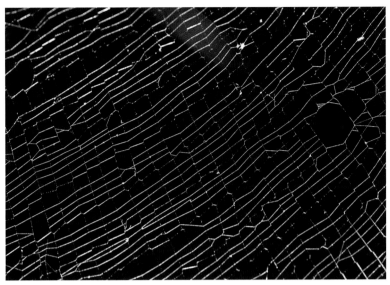

Detail of a web of the golden silk orbweaver (Nephilidae: *Nephila clavipes*). The spiral strands are about 2 mm apart. (LA)

are just about as close together toward the outside of the web as they are near the hub, which tends to be off-center. The radii are pulled out from their normal position at intervals, resulting in periodic interruptions in the spacing of the spiral strands. This species is also unusual in that it uses the same web for a long time, repairing the sticky strands as needed. Many of the webs we have seen were accompanied by a *barrier web*, a tangle of lines built on one or both sides of the orb web.

Bizarre Variations

Four additional species, in three different families, make webs that bring to mind those experiments in which orbweavers were given various drugs to see how it affected their web building. All make small webs that are largely hidden in hollows among leaf litter or similar spaces. *Anapistula secreta* (Symphytognathidae) is found in humid microhabitats from the extreme southern United States to Colombia. It spins horizontal orbs 0.8 to 1.6 inches (2 to 4 cm) wide, with numerous sticky spirals and what appear to be hundreds of radii. It is thought that this tiny spider might be a vegetarian, using its finely meshed web to collect spores and pollen from the air. *Maymena ambita* (Mysmenidae), also in the southeastern United States, makes a horizontal orb web with the hub pulled up by one or several radii that project at angles out of the plane of the web. The sticky spiral sporadically departs from its circuit around the primary radii to attach to these additional ones. The webs of *Gertschanapis shantzi* (Anapidae) in California and Oregon are similar and may sometimes be found in somewhat more exposed places, such as among fern fronds.

From the outside, the web of *Microdipoena guttata* (Mysmenidae; E) appears to be a sphere of sticky silk. If the outer "rind" is teased apart, it is revealed to have an internal structure of radii emanating in all directions from the center, with no spiral strands.

Araneid Orb Webs

An orb web not matching any of the above descriptions is the work of an araneid. Almost all araneids spin vertical or nearly vertical orb webs, but there are many variations that can be used to identify the genus or species.

Some araneids decorate their webs with thick bands of silk, as *Uloborus* does. These decorations are called *stabilimenta* (singular: stabilimentum), because they were initially believed to function in stabilizing the web, though this is no longer thought to be the case. The "intended" purpose is still debated, but it has been experimentally demonstrated that stabilimenta benefit the spiders that make them because they are visible to birds that would otherwise fly through and wreck the web. In some cases, it is clear that the spider also uses the stabilimentum to camouflage itself. These decorations are made only by species that spend most of their time resting on the hubs of their webs.

Garden Spiders

The garden spiders (*Argiope*) make large webs up to 2 feet (60 cm) across, with distinctive zigzag stabilimenta in the middle. The orb web may be

 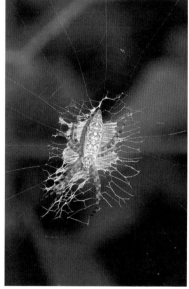

Left: Typical stabilimentum of the black and yellow garden spider (Araneidae: *Argiope aurantia*). (NC) *Right:* Broad stabilimentum of an immature black and yellow garden spider. (NC)

Web of a trashline orbweaver (Araneidae: *Cyclosa*). (MA)

accompanied by a barrier web. The black and yellow garden spider (*A. aurantia*) makes a long, narrow, vertical zigzag, extending above and below the hub; it may be up to 1.2 inches (3 cm) wide and 13.8 inches (35 cm) long but usually is much smaller. Immature spiders make a wide, short stabilimentum, oval or nearly circular, up to 2.4 inches (6 cm) across; it may be composed of several distinct, curved zigzags. The stabilimenta of adult and immature banded garden spiders (*A. trifasciata*) are similar. The silver (*A. argentata*) and Florida (*A. florida*) garden spiders make four zigzag stabilimenta, one in line with each pair of legs, forming an X.

Trashline Orbweavers

The trashline orbweavers (*Cyclosa*), which are much smaller spiders, also make a vertical stabilimentum, but not a zigzag. They usually decorate it with prey remains, their own shed skins, other debris, and eventually their egg sacs. The spider is well camouflaged resting in the middle of this "trashline," and it has been demonstrated that the decorated webs trap significantly more insects than do undecorated webs. The webs are very fine-meshed, with many radii; we counted fifty-seven in one example.

Spiny Orbweavers

The spiny orbweavers (*Gasteracantha* and *Micrathena*) also often make some kind of stabilimentum. Their webs tend to be somewhat inclined, and although the spiral portion of the web may not be particularly large, the attachment strands often span a few meters. The spinybacked orb-

Top: Web of the spinybacked orbweaver (Araneidae: *Gasteracantha cancriformis*), showing the distinctive flocculent tufts. (FL) *Above:* Web of the spined micrathena (Araneidae: *Micrathena gracilis*). The web measures 7.5 inches (19 cm) across, 10 feet (3 m) including anchoring threads (not shown). (MS)

weaver (*G. cancriformis*) makes a web with a large free zone in the middle and decorates one to five radii with a series of well-spaced fluffy, white tufts. It also thickens some of the attachment strands at intervals, particularly the lower ones, creating dashed, white lines. The *Micrathena* species spin particularly tight, compact webs, about 1 foot (30.5 cm) in diameter, with open hubs like those in tetragnathid webs. They usually make a small stabilimentum above the hub, reminiscent of those made by garden spiders.

Web of *Zygiella* (Araneidae). (WA) Photo by Lynette Schimming.

Zygiella and Others

Zygiella webs usually have a wedge in the upper part of the orb missing, as if it has been borrowed by the triangle spider. In this open wedge is a radial strand that extends from the hub to a silken tube at the edge of the web, in which the spider hides during the day. This strand acts as a signal line, alerting the spider when an insect has hit the web.

Many species of *Araneus* and *Neoscona* use a signal line as *Zygiella* does, attaching it to a silken retreat, usually in a curled leaf or several woven-together leaves at the periphery of the web. *A. pegnia* and *A. thaddeus* webs sometimes also have a missing (or partly missing) sector. *A. pegnia* makes an irregular network of threads next to the orb web. *A. thaddeus* has a distinctive cylindrical retreat with a latticed pattern, giving the spider its common name, the lattice orbweaver.

Labyrinth Spider

The labyrinth spider (*Metepeira labyrinthea*) is another species that uses a signal line

Web of a western relative of the labyrinth spider (Araneidae: *Metepeira*). The orb is 8 inches (20 cm) across. Note the signal line leading from the hub to the retreat of silk and plant debris. (CA)

(often multiple signal lines) and also sometimes has a missing sector. Like *Araneus pegnia*, it makes a tangle of irregular webbing in addition to the orb web. In this species, the irregular webbing is particularly extensive, usually both behind and above the orb web. In the middle of this "labyrinth," the spider hangs a leaf or a few leaves to use as its retreat. It may also make a more substantial debris tube, similar to the ones made by desertshrub spiders. The string of egg sacs is incorporated into the retreat, and the labyrinth becomes a nursery for the spiderlings. Other *Metepeira* species make similar webs.

Other Variations

Scoloderus, in the extreme southern United States and Mexico, makes a tall, skinny, ladderlike orb web. It is thought that this is specially adapted for capturing moths. Ordinarily, when a moth or butterfly runs into an orb web, the sticky threads manage to catch only some scales from its wings, and the insect is able to escape, sometimes leaving a hole, or "moth scar." When a moth hits the top of a *Scoloderus* web, however, it tumbles down the ladder, losing scales as it goes, and by the time it gets to the bottom, it has lost enough scales that it sticks to the web.

Several other araneids have various idiosyncrasies about their webs that help identify them. The six-spotted orbweaver (*Araniella displicata*) makes a particularly tiny web, which often occupies the space created by bending a single leaf. *Mangora* species make especially finely meshed webs, as described earlier; *M. gibberosa*'s is horizontal, but others may be verti-

Web of the starbellied orbweaver (Araneidae: *Acanthepeira stellata*), showing the scaffolding spiral and the aborted outer portion of the sticky spiral. (NH)

cal or nearly so. *Larinioides* species are the orbweavers most commonly found around man-made structures. They make webs that are frequently more than 3 feet (91.4 cm) across, usually with fewer than twenty radii. *L. cornutus* and *L. patagiatus* tend to hide in a cocoonlike retreat at the periphery of the web during the day. The starbellied orbweaver (*Acanthepeira stellata*), among other species, often leaves the web unfinished, with the scaffolding spiral still covering a large part of it.

Kleptoparasites

Some cobweb spiders in the subfamily Argyrodinae are *kleptoparasitic*, building their irregular webs near the webs of orbweavers (and sometimes others), attaching their own signal lines to the hub, and stealing freshly wrapped prey. The argyrodine may also eat the host spider's egg sacs or spiderlings, or even the spider itself.

Balls of Silk

You may notice little balls of silk associated with the webs of certain orbweavers. If these are not egg sacs or wrapped prey, they are most likely old, dismantled webs. Many spiders often eat their old webs, but the spinybacked orbweaver, labyrinth spider, and others at least sometimes collect the silk into a lump, which they then place in a remaining part of the web or on nearby vegetation, or simply drop.

A ball of silk found near water may have been dropped by a dance fly (Empididae). As noted in chapter 5, males court females by offering them gifts surrounded by frothy secretions. Those in the genus *Hilara* instead wrap the prey insect with silk, or sometimes present a ball of silk with nothing inside.

Underwater Silk

Some insects spin silk underwater, most notably the caddisflies. Those that make firm cases are discussed in chapter 8, but there are some whose silk creations clearly belong here with the spider webs. All of the insects described below live in fast-moving streams.

Net-spinning Caddisflies

The net-spinning caddisflies (Hydropsychidae) spin intricate, rectangular-mesh nets that strain algae, fine organic particles, and small aquatic invertebrates from the current. A typical net is affixed to a rock or sometimes a log, forming a pouch against the surface. The open end faces upstream, and the net is bowed by the current so that its shape resembles a bowl cut in half and glued to a wall. Often it is well coated with algae, strands of which may hang downstream. The net is sometimes the only conspicuous

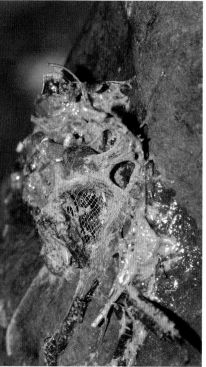

Above: An aggregation of algae-filled hydropsy-chid caddisfly nets, each about 15 mm wide. (MA) *Left:* Retreat (2 cm) of a net-spinning caddisfly larva (Hydropsychidae), found on the underside of a rock in a stream. (WY)

structure, but there may be a camouflaged retreat at the base made of gravel, sand, plant detritus, or some combination of these. The larva periodically emerges from its retreat to feed on whatever the net has caught. In warm southern waters, this type of net is very abundant in shallow rapids of rivers and streams, such as where water passes the bedrock or spills over dams or waterfalls. In Wyoming and North Dakota, the nets we encountered tended to be stretched taut across a prominent three-dimensional framework made of pebbles and debris.

Trumpetnet and Tubemaker Caddisflies

The trumpetnet and tubemaker caddisflies (Polycentropodidae) make a variety of retreats, all of which consist entirely of a silken net, without the other materials used by hydropsychids. *Nyctiophylax* retreats consist of a broad silken roof, up to 15 mm or so long, built over a depression in a rock or log, forming a cylindrical chamber open equally at both ends. They are soon camouflaged by silt and diatoms that are caught in the silk. A loose network of threads is attached to the entrance, and the predaceous larva emerges to attack anything that disturbs them. The retreats of *Polyplectropus* (TX, Mexico) and *Cernotina* are similar. The retreat of *Cyrnellus fraternus* (E; about 2 cm across) is roughly circular in outline and has a flat roof with a small, round exit hole at either end. Some *Polycentropus* species construct a narrow cylindrical tube, up to about 2 cm long, with one or both ends flared out into an irregular maze of threads. *Neureclipsis* makes a distinctive trumpet-shaped net that is held open by the current. The flared opening is up to 1.6 inches (4 cm) wide, and the net tapers to a slender, recurved tube that may be more than 4.7 inches (12 cm) long, in which the larva hides.

Fingernet Caddisflies

Fingernet caddisflies (Philopotamidae) make elongate, fingerlike pouches that are held open by the current, without the trumpetlike opening of *Neureclipsis* nets. They are up to 2.4 inches (6 cm) long by 5 mm wide and have an extremely fine mesh. It has been estimated that a net of one species incorporates over 3,280 feet (1 km) of silk strands and has more than one hundred million mesh openings. Large numbers of them are often found

Nets of fingernet caddisflies (Philopotamidae). Each net is about 1.4 inches (3.6 cm) long and 6 mm wide. (TN)

close together. The larvae feed from within on the fine particles caught in the net.

Aquatic Moths

Aquatic moth larvae in the genus *Petrophila* (Crambidae: Nymphulinae) spin dense silken mats across the exposed surfaces of submerged stones. They live beneath these, grazing on algae and eventually pupating there.

Black Flies

Black fly larvae (Simuliidae) spin networks of silk threads that help them move around on the surfaces of stones without being swept downstream. When they move downstream, they pay out silk as they go, just like a spider in the wind. The threads accumulate small debris particles, making them easy to spot against a light background.

Cocoons

7

A cocoon, as defined in this book, is the silken case a larva spins around itself before pupating. The egg sacs of spiders and egg cases of earthworms are sometimes referred to as cocoons, but for clarity, we have chosen to follow the stricter definition. Many insects pupate in debris cases in which they have spent their whole larval lives. These are addressed in chapter 8, as are those that construct pupal cells of foreign materials with little or no silk. Some arachnids make silken structures that are similar to cocoons in form and function, and these are discussed below. The most conspicuous and familiar cocoons are made by moths; others are made by Hymenoptera, Neuroptera, beetles, true flies, fleas, caddisflies, and thrips.

Silken Retreats of Arachnids

Many spiders, of both hunting and web-spinning varieties, spin silken retreats or nests. These may serve as protective hiding places when the spiders are waiting for prey, resting, molting, hibernating, mating, or guarding eggs. Regardless of the purpose, they are generally of thin, finely woven, white silk. They come in a variety of forms—even within a given species, depending on the purpose—but they are generally either tubes or flattened bags, and none of them closely resemble the oval cocoons of caterpillars or other insects. They are found in the same sorts of places as cocoons—in crevices, rolled or folded leaves, or ground litter; under rocks and logs; and in nooks of man-made structures.

A spider's old molting chamber, containing its exuviae. (MA)

Left: The 1.6-inch (4-cm) retreat of a bold jumper (Salticidae: *Phidippus audax*). (MA)
Right: A long-legged sac spider (Miturgidae: *Cheiracanthium inclusum*) in its hibernation retreat, found inside a folded tarp. The sac measures 1.1 inches (2.8 cm). (MA)

Probably the most distinctive arachnid retreat is the one made by the lattice orbweaver (Araneidae: *Araneus thaddeus*). It is a cylindrical tube, an inch or so long and half as wide, built in the shelter of a curled leaf or a few leaves tied together. Its walls are full of holes, giving it a latticelike appearance.

Many hunting spiders make flat, tubular retreats, open at both ends. These include the clubionid sac spiders, ghost spiders (Anyphaenidae), prowling spiders (Miturgidae), jumping spiders (Salticidae), and recluses (Sicariidae). Those of jumping spiders are often thick and opaque from many layers of silk, tapering slightly at either end. The papery, translucent bags of the long-legged sac spider *Cheiracanthium inclusum* (Miturgidae) are common objects on crops and in houses. *Paratheuma insulana* (Desidae; FL) is an intertidal species that makes its retreats in abandoned barnacle shells. A spider guarding an egg sac may construct a completely sealed retreat, without any openings.

The nursery web spider (Pisauridae: *Pisaurina mira*) sometimes makes a sac, much larger than that of sac spiders, on the underside of a leaf to use as a shelter while she constructs her egg sac.

Pseudoscorpions also spin silk retreats in hidden places, such as the undersides of rocks, for molting, hibernating, or brooding. Sometimes they mix soil with the silk.

Silken Retreats of Moth Larvae

Certain moth larvae spin silk structures that are functionally similar to those of arachnids described above. The excrement-covered tubes of some species are discussed in chapter 5; the two examples here are of pure silk.

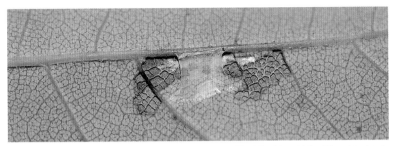

The distinctive silk tent of an early-instar gold-striped leaftier (Amphisbatidae: *Machimia tentoriferella*). The patch of skeletonized leaf tissue is 9 mm long. (MA)

The gold-striped leaftier (Amphisbatidae: *Machimia tentoriferella*; E) feeds on leaves of a wide variety of hardwood trees and constructs a distinctive shelter on the underside of the leaf on which it feeds. It spins a flat, slanting sheet of silk supported by the midrib, creating a little tent that is open at both ends. The sheet is very tightly woven, transparent, and glossy. An early-instar larva feeds by extending its head from either side of the tent, skeletonizing the leaf surface. Later, it leaves its tent to feed on the edge of the leaf. At this point, the tent is up to about 12 mm long and may cause a slight bulge in the upper side of the leaf. The larva may eat its existing tent before moving on to make a new one. It pupates beneath the last one.

Ribbed cocoon-makers (Bucculatricidae: *Bucculatrix*) also spin little patches of webbing on the undersides of leaves, a few millimeters across. Theirs, however, are closed structures and are whiter and more coarsely textured. These are molting cocoons—shelters built each time the larva molts, and nothing like the ribbed pupation cocoons that give them their name. Leaves with these molting cocoons also have patches that have been skeletonized by the larvae.

Round, Flat Cocoons

Most round, flat silken structures are spider egg sacs. A few kinds of insects make cocoons of this shape, however. In the first three described below, the cocoon consists of two distinct layers, one envelope nested within another.

The larva of the moth *Neurobathra strigifinitella* (Gracillariidae) mines leaves of oaks and related trees, then drops down on a silk strand to spin its cocoon. It almost always makes its cocoon on the underside of a leaf, which may or may not be on the host tree. Both layers are white but transparent, and the pupa is plainly visible inside. The outer envelope is oval, 14 mm long, with four to ten small, pearl-like globules along the middle. The inner layer is separated by a space of 1 to 1.5 mm on all sides.

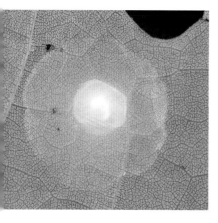

A mysterious cocoon (11 mm across), similar to that of *Neurobathra strigifinitella* (Gracillariidae). (TN)

We have found several flat, circular double cocoons on the undersides of sugar maple leaves in Tennessee and a similar one on a snowberry leaf in California. All had a 4-mm inner envelope, not quite transparent enough to make out the details of the larva or pupa inside, and a perfectly transparent outer envelope, 8 to 12 mm across. They lacked the pearly decorations described for *N. strigifinitella*, but we have been unable to find a better match. We suspect they belong to a related leaf-mining moth.

Dustywings (Coniopterygidae) are tiny relatives of lacewings, no more than 3 mm long. Their cocoons are white or yellow, often near the midrib on the underside of a leaf, but they may be on the upper surface, in a bark crevice, or among moss. They usually have two finely woven layers, but the cocoon of *Heteroconis picticornis*, introduced in California, has a tightly woven inner layer, a lacy second layer, and a very loose and lacy third layer. The whole cocoon is roughly circular, 2.5 to 3 mm across, and 0.5 mm thick.

The cocoon of the grape leaf skeletonizer (Zygaenidae: *Harrisina americana*) is dirty white, tough, flattened, and oval. Clusters of them may be found on grape leaves or the bark of vines.

Nepticulids are among the tiniest moths. The larvae spin dense, flattened cocoons that may be whitish, yellowish, greenish, or brownish, depending on the species. The cocoon has a mouthlike opening at one end that allows the mature adult to emerge. It extends about a third of the way down the cocoon and is inconspicuous, but sometimes its edges are continued as a projecting rim around the whole circumference. Although they are often made on the ground, *Stigmella pomivorella*, which mines in leaves of rosaceous trees, makes its 3-mm, oval, brown cocoon on the host tree's bark, often in a crotch. It is said to resemble a scale insect.

Lacy Cocoons

A number of unrelated insects spin distinctive cocoons with a lacy mesh, which may enclose a denser inner cocoon or an otherwise naked pupa. A few giant silkmoth cocoons are similarly lacy and are described along with the rest of that family's cocoons.

Moths

The bumelia webworm moth (Urodidae: *Urodus parvula*; SE) spins a delicate, golden cocoon with a very coarse, rectangular mesh, suspended from

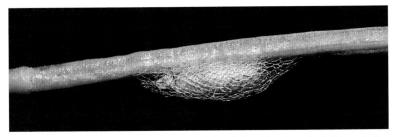

A 9-mm cocoon of the diamondback moth (Plutellidae: *Plutella xylostella*), with the cocoon of a parasitoid ichneumon wasp inside. (ID)

the food plant by a thread. The pupa within is not at all concealed, and it protrudes from the cocoon when the adult emerges. *Wockia asperipunctella*, only recently discovered in Ontario, makes a similar cocoon on aspen and willow.

The cocoon of the chain-dotted geometer (Geometridae: *Cingilia catenaria*) is similarly sparse, but the mesh is less regular and the silk is white to yellowish green. The pupa is as nicely decorated as a butterfly chrysalis; it is white with scattered black markings and has yellow bands around the abdomen.

The diamondback moth (Plutellidae: *Plutella xylostella*) makes an elongate, white, gauzy cocoon with tapered ends. It is generally attached to the mustard plants on which the caterpillar feeds. The green or yellow pupa is clearly visible inside. The cocoon of *Prays atomocella* (Yponomeutidae), which feeds on hoptree, is similar. Moths in the related family Acrolepiidae make similar cocoons with coarser, brown silk, although they may start out white. *Acrolepiopsis* species feed on greenbrier, leeks, lilies, and related plants. *Digitivalva clarkei* (SE) feeds on nightshades. These cocoons all range from about 7 to 10 mm long. The three species of *Schreckensteinia* (Schreckensteiniidae) make superficially similar cocoons of white silk. Unlike all the yponomeutoids just mentioned, their pupae protrude from the cocoon when the adult emerges. The caterpillars feed on sumac, raspberry, and Indian paintbrush.

Beetles

The clover leaf weevil (Curculionidae: *Hypera zoilus*) spins a cocoon about 8 mm long with an irregular mesh of coarse, brownish threads. The mesh can be fairly fine, but as with the above moths, it is not fine enough to obscure the beetle's dark pupa. Other *Hypera* species spin similar cocoons (e.g., *H. rumicis*, about 5 mm long,

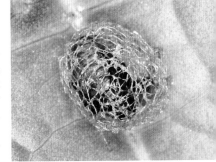

Cocoon (about 5 mm) of *Hypera rumicis* (Curculionidae), a weevil. (OH) Photo by Judy Semroc.

Cocoon (6 mm) of *Climacia* (Sisyridae), a spongillafly. (OK) Photo by Charles Lewallen.

on plants in the buckwheat family), either on the host plant or on the ground. Leaf beetles (Chrysomelidae) in the genus *Ophraella* make similar cocoons on vegetation, but the pupae are a light yellowish color rather than dark brown. Each species feeds on, and therefore makes its cocoon on, a different species of plant in the aster family.

Neuropterans

Spongillafly larvae (Sisyridae) emerge from water bodies where they have been feeding on freshwater sponges and spin their cocoons, either hidden or attached to objects in the open, within 50 feet (15.2 m) or so of the water. The cocoons are 3 to 7 mm long, with a densely woven inner cocoon and a separate delicate outer net that are both oval in shape. The inner cocoon is about half the diameter of the outer one. In *Sisyra* cocoons, the outer net is made of simply crisscrossed fibers, whereas in *Climacia* cocoons, it has a beautiful hexagonal mesh. When mature, just a few days after cocoon construction, the pharate adult chews a hole through both layers and then emerges from its pupal skin, leaving it either protruding from the cocoon or wadded in one end.

The cocoons of brown lacewings (Hemerobiidae) are also double-walled, but the outer portion is very loosely woven and does not form a definite mesh. The inner cocoon is elliptical, nearly twice as long as wide, and although it is denser, it is still very thin, with the pupa visible inside. The outer portion is more spherical. Brown lacewing cocoons are usually formed in protected spots such as under bark or in rolled leaves.

Other Neuropteran Cocoons

Many of the Neuroptera have oval to nearly spherical cocoons. Those of some are encrusted with sand or debris, and these are discussed in chapter 8.

The 3-mm, oval cocoons of green lacewings (Chrysopidae) are very common on vegetation and other objects. They are white (yellowish green in *Chrysoperla harrisii*), closely woven, and parchmentlike, opaque or somewhat transparent, with loose webbing anchoring them to the substrate. When ready to emerge, the pharate adult chews a neat circular lid, which is often left attached, and crawls some distance before emerging from its pupal skin. Cocoons with less neat openings may have been parasitized by wasps such as *Dichrogaster* (Ichneumonidae; also parasitizes brown lacewing cocoons), *Helorus* (Heloridae), or anacharitine figitids.

Right top: Green lacewing (Chrysopidae) cocoon (3 mm) in a cluster of pine needles. (VA) *Right bottom:* Another 3-mm green lacewing cocoon, with a neatly cut circular lid indicating successful emergence. (TN)

The round, whitish cocoons of mantid-flies (Mantispidae) are larger than those of green lacewings and not quite as densely woven. Because the larvae are mostly predators of spider eggs and bee and wasp larvae, the cocoons are usually made within spider egg sacs and in hymenopteran nests (see page 46).

Giant Silkmoth Cocoons

The giant silkmoths (Saturniidae) are our largest moths and, not surprisingly, are the makers of the largest cocoons. They are 1.5 to 4 inches (4 to 10 cm) long, usually tough and papery, and often incorporate leaves. Once the cocoon is made, the caterpillar secretes a substance that makes the inner surface hard and shiny.

The cecropia moth (*Hyalophora cecropia*) is the largest North American moth. Its cocoon is 3 to 4 inches (8 to 10 cm) long by 1 inch (2.5 cm) or somewhat wider and made of tough, brown, paperlike silk that may weather to gray. The size alone should be enough to distinguish it, but it is also characteristically attached to a twig along one entire side. Leaves or twigs may or may not be incorporated into its structure. It may be compact and spindle-shaped or more plump and egg-shaped. Inside is a second tough cocoon, separated by an air space with loose strands of silk.

Left: A 4.1-inch (10.5-cm) cocoon of a cecropia moth (Saturniidae: *Hyalophora cecropia*), incorporating beech leaves. (VT) *Right:* Two cecropia cocoons of the baggier variety. (ME)

Promethea moth (Saturniidae: *Callosamia promethea*) cocoon, about 2 inches (5 cm). (MA)

The cocoons of the other two *Hyalophora* species are similar. The ceanothus silkmoth (*H. euryalus*) replaces the cecropia moth on the Pacific Coast. Its cocoon is oval to nearly spherical, about 2 inches (5 cm) long, with the ends usually free rather than fused to the twig. *H. columbia* cocoons are 2 to 2.4 inches (5 to 6 cm) long and are brown with prominent silvery or golden striations. Eastern ones (subspecies *columbia*) are made on tamarack bark or adjacent undergrowth. Western ones (subspecies *gloveri*) are tapered at both ends. *H. euryalus* and *H. c. gloveri* sometimes hybridize, making intermediate cocoons.

The promethea moth (*Callosamia promethea*) has a distinctive habit of wrapping its elongate cocoon in a single leaf and winding silk around the petiole so that it stays fastened to the twig throughout the winter. The silk may cover the leaf. The cocoon is about 1.8 to 2 inches (4.5 to 5 cm) long and 0.5 to 0.8 inches (1.5 to 2 cm) wide and tapers somewhat at each end. It is usually compact, but in cocoons found in the southern Appalachians, a layer of loose silk often separates the outer wall from the inner cocoon, creating a baggy appearance. As in the *Hyalophora* cocoons, a valvelike structure at the upper end allows the adult to emerge without having to make a hole in the cocoon.

The introduced cynthia moth (*Samia cynthia*) makes a similar cocoon, which may be found in New York City and scattered other urban areas along the East Coast in association with its food plant, ailanthus. The cynthia moth's cocoon tends to be paler and fatter than the promethea moth's, and the outer wall is loosely corrugated. The tuliptree silkmoth (*C. angulifera*) also makes a similar cocoon, but it is a darker brown and the petiole is not usually fastened to the twig, so the cocoon falls to the ground in the autumn and is therefore much less conspicuous. The cocoon of *C. securifera* (SE) has a similar structure to the baggy Appalachian promethea cocoons, but it is found on sweetbay and usually incorporates several additional leaves. These leaves become detached from the plant but stay attached to the cocoon, which remains secured to the host plant.

Polyphemus moth (Saturniidae: *Antheraea poly-phemus*) cocoon, about 1.6 inches (4 cm). (NJ)

Polyphemus moth (*Antheraea polyphemus*) cocoons sometimes stay fastened to twigs but more often fall to the ground in the autumn. They are pale, 1.5 to 1.8 inches (4 to 4.5 cm) long, tough like other saturniid cocoons, and usually enclosed in one or several leaves, but they are oval rather than elongate. The cocoon also differs from the preceding ones in being closed at both ends. When ready to emerge, the pupa secretes a fluid that dissolves the hard, gummy substance binding the silk together, until the moth is able to push the fibers aside and work its way out.

The luna moth (*Actias luna*) makes a similar oval cocoon that is also usually found on the ground and enclosed in leaves, but it is loose-fitting, irregular, and very thin. It does not have a well-defined escape valve, but the overall flimsiness allows the adult to escape. The cocoon of the io moth (*Automeris io*) is thin and flimsy like the luna's, but it is made of darker and coarser silk and tends to be more boxy rather than oval. The io's cocoon is about 1.5 inches (4 cm) long. The other *Automeris* species are found in Mexico, with restricted ranges in the southern United States. They also pupate among ground litter, in more or less substantial cocoons. The cocoon of *A. patagoniensis* (in very southern AZ) has a precut diagonal slit through which the adult emerges.

Some Saturniids spin plain, smooth cocoons without incorporating any leaves. The cocoon of the calleta silkmoth (*Eupackardia calleta*) is attached to a low twig by a short silken loop. It can be found from Mexico into southern Arizona and

Luna moth (Saturniidae: *Actias luna*) cocoon (1.4 inches [3.5 cm]), from which the adult moth has emerged. (NH) Photo by Bonnie J. Caruthers.

Texas. *Rothschildia* species, with a similar range, suspend their cocoons from the host plant by a strongly hooded peduncle. *Saturnia albofasciata*, found in West Coast chaparral, makes a small, compact, tightly woven, ellip-

Calleta silkmoth (Saturniidae: *Eupackardia calleta*) cocoon, 1.5 inches (3.7 cm). (AZ)

tical cocoon, 19 to 22 mm long. It is cream-colored to pale brown and is attached to a stem by its side, with its ends free. It has the typical saturniid escape valve.

Other western and southwestern species make very different cocoons, but their size easily identifies them as belonging to giant silkmoths. *Agapema* (SW) species make a beige, loosely woven, open mesh cocoon, surrounding another, more tightly woven but still open mesh cocoon, with the pupa visible inside. The open construction is thought to facilitate airflow, preventing overheating. The Rocky Mountain agapema (*A. homogena*) makes its cocoons in crevices of tree trunks, among rocks, or on buildings. The other species make their cocoons on branches of shrubs, sometimes in large clusters. *Saturnia mendocino* and *S. walterorum*, again endemic to West Coast chaparral, make similar cocoons that are solitary and dark brown, 1 to 1.6 inches (2.5 to 4 cm) long.

If a giant silkmoth cocoon contains a viable pupa, it will rattle when shaken gently. If it does not rattle, an empty pupal skin may be inside, indicating that the moth has emerged, but often there will be signs of parasitoids inside. Some of the most common parasitoids of saturniids are ichneumon wasps in the genus *Gambrus*. Eggs are laid in the caterpillar while it is spinning the cocoon, and it does not pupate. On opening the cocoon, you may find it packed full of ichneumon cocoons, or it may hold a shriveled, blackened caterpillar and a small cluster of cocoons. To emerge, the adult wasps chew one or more exit holes in the side of the moth cocoon, rather than escaping through the exit valve if there is one.

Greasewood moth (Saturniidae: *Agapema galbina*) cocoon, 1.6 inches (4 cm). (AZ)

Cluster of *Gambrus nuncius* (Ichneumonidae) cocoons found packed in one end of a promethea moth cocoon. (ME)

Hairy Moth Cocoons

Some moth families with hairy caterpillars incorporate the larval body hairs into the cocoons. Although this is the case with some of the slug and flannel moths, whose cocoons are described in the next section, cocoons that seem to be composed primarily of larval hairs likely belong to tiger moths (Arctiidae) or tussock moths (Lymantriidae). Those of both families are oval to somewhat elongate.

Left: The cocoon in which a woolly bear caterpillar transforms into an Isabella tiger moth (Arctiidae: *Pyrrharctia isabella*). (FL) Photo by Jeff Hollenbeck. *Right:* Cocoon (22 mm) of a Virginia ctenucha (Arctiidae: *Ctenucha virginica*), composed entirely of the caterpillar's hairs. (MA)

Tiger moths mostly pupate in loose cocoons under debris on the ground or in other sheltered nooks. They generally have a very minimal framework of silk. The hairy cocoons of lichen moths (Lithosiinae) may be found attached to rocks or tree trunks, close to the lichens on which the larvae feed. A *Ctenucha* caterpillar makes its cocoon entirely out of its yellow and white hairs, without spinning any silk; they are held together by the tiny spines.

Other hairy cocoons are made by tussock moths (Lymantriidae). These, too, are fairly loose. They may be found attached to tree bark or nooks in man-made structures, and sometimes the cocoon is in a curled leaf that is secured to the twig in

Partially complete, 1.3-inch (3.2-cm) cocoon of the definite tussock moth (Lymantriidae: *Orgyia definita*), composed of both silk and hairs. (MA)

the same way a promethea moth's is. The females of some species are wingless and deposit their eggs on top of their cocoons. The white-marked tussock moth (*Orgyia leucostigma*) covers its eggs with a white, frothy substance. In this species, the female's cocoon is about 1 inch (2.5 cm) long, and the male's is 0.5 inch (13 mm).

Other Moth Cocoons

Bee moth cocoons (Pyralidae: *Aphomia sociella*) found between two boards. The cocoons are 5 mm wide, with variable lengths. (WV) Photo by Claire Stuart.

Planthopper parasite moth (Epipyropidae: *Fulgoraecia exigua*) cocoon, 8 mm. (OH) Photo by Diane P. Brooks.

Many other moths pupate in cocoons. Often, as with some noctuids, geometrids, sphingids, and notodontids, they are nondescript or consist of loose webbing with no definite form. Some, however, are quite distinctive.

Bee Moth

The bee moth (Pyralidae: *Aphomia sociella*) is an introduced species whose larvae live gregariously in nests of bees and social wasps, feeding on nest materials, stored food, and waste products. They have also been found in mouse nests, bird nests, and human dwellings. When mature, they form soft but extremely tough, elongate cocoons in a densely packed mass. These are about 5 mm wide and up to 2 inches (5 cm) long.

Planthopper Parasite Moth

The cocoon of the planthopper parasite moth (Epipyropidae: *Fulgoraecia exigua*) is as unusual as the larva's feeding habits. It is white, about 8 mm long, and saturated with wax from the larva's body. Oval and somewhat laterally compressed, the cocoon has a row of scoop-shaped projections along the top. Because of these, it has been likened to the Sydney Opera House. When the moth is ready to emerge, the pupa is partially protruded from a slit at one end.

Tent Caterpillar Moths

Tent caterpillars (Lasiocampidae: *Malacosoma*) spin soft, white cocoons, about 2 cm long and tapered somewhat toward both ends. Before pupating, they secrete a substance that dries as a yellow or whitish powder on the surface, giving it the appearance of plaster gauze. The cocoons may be found just about anywhere, often in groups, surrounded by varying amounts of loose webbing. When the moth is ready to emerge, it secretes

Eastern tent caterpillar (Lasiocampidae: *Malaco-soma americana*) cocoon, 22 mm. Note the ragged opening at the right end, from which the moth emerged. (VT)

another fluid that dissolves part of the cocoon, allowing it to exit through a small, ragged hole at one end. The "friendly fly" (Sarcophagidae: *Metoposarcophaga aldrichi*) deposits its larvae on tent caterpillar cocoons, and they bore in and feed on the contents.

Ermine Moths

Many ermine moth larvae (Yponomeutidae) form delicate, white, spindle-shaped cocoons that are suspended in the webbing they make on their host plants. These are about 1 cm long.

Ribbed Cocoon-maker Moths

Moths in the genus *Bucculatrix* (Bucculatricidae) make slender, white cocoons, about 5 mm long, with distinctive longitudinal ribbing. They are attached securely along their whole length and may be found on any kind of vegetation, because the larvae often drop down from their food plants before constructing them. The larva begins by spinning a very delicate, elliptical "fence" of vertical silk strands, which apparently protects it while it is spinning the cocoon. The cocoon is spun in the center of the area enclosed by the fence, which is soon weathered away without a trace. The ribbing is normally obvious, but parasitized larvae often make incompletely ribbed cocoons. As with many of the smaller moths, the mature pupa is thrust through the end of the cocoon, and the projecting pupal skin is evidence of a successful emergence.

Euonymus caterpillar (Yponomeutidae: *Yponomeuta cagnagella*) cocoons, about 1 cm long. (MA)

Ribbed cocoon-maker moth (Bucculatricidae: *Bucculatrix*) cocoon (4 mm), complete with delicate silk "fence." The adult moth has emerged, and its pupal skin is protruding from the right side of the cocoon. (TN)

Marmara

Cocoons of *Marmara* (Gracillariidae) are flattened, about 6 mm long, and may be white or yellowish. The larva excretes pearly globules and pushes them through the wall of the cocoon, decorating the surface. These are something like the decorations made by *Neurobathra*, but more brilliant, and there may be more than a hundred of them.

Slug Caterpillar Moths

Slug caterpillars (Limacodidae) overwinter in dense, dark brown, nearly spherical cocoons. Those that have stinging bristles incorporate them into the silk so that they continue to be protected from predators. The cocoon has a circular lid that pops open when the adult emerges. Most species conceal their cocoons, but the well-armed cocoon of the monkey slug (*Phobetron pithecium*) is attached to a leaf or twig in plain view.

Flannel Moths

Cocoons of flannel moths (Megalopygidae) are tough, brown, and parchmentlike. They are oval, around 13 to 14 mm long, with a flat, hinged, circular lid at one end, similar to the one on a slug caterpillar's cocoon. The cocoon of the southern flannel moth (*Megalopyge opercularis*) has a peculiar structure that looks like a pair of lips, in the middle of the side of the cocoon opposite the surface to which it is attached. A freshly spun cocoon may be covered with an additional thin sheet of silk that extends beyond the lid, making it appear longer and more spindle-shaped.

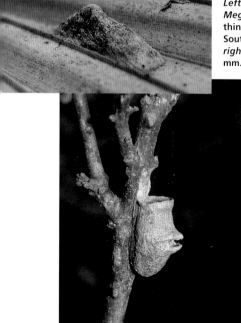

Left: A southern flannel moth (Megalopygidae: *Megalopyge opercularis*) cocoon covered with a thin, 1.2-inch (3-cm) silken sheet. (FL) *Below left:* Southern flannel moth cocoon, 13 mm. (FL) *Below right:* Flannel moth (Megalopygidae) cocoon, 14 mm. (AZ)

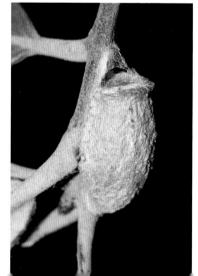

Sawfly Cocoons

Sawflies are wasplike insects with caterpillarlike larvae that feed on vegetation. They are very common but often overlooked, and their cocoons may be noticed more often than the insects themselves. These are generally brown, smooth, and parchmentlike, similar in texture to those of flannel moths. The larvae usually overwinter in them and pupate in the spring. Shrews, voles, and mice collect the cocoons and store them for later consumption. It has been estimated that a single short-tailed shrew consumes twenty-three thousand pine sawfly cocoons in a year.

The largest sawflies are the cimbicids, and the largest of these is the elm sawfly (*Cimbex americana*). Its cocoon is 1 inch (2.5 cm) long and is formed in leaf litter or underground. *Trichiosoma* cocoons, on the other hand, are attached lengthwise to twigs. They are tough, brown, elongate, and capsule-shaped, 15 to 19 mm long, and may be wrapped in a leaf or have the imprint of a formerly attached leaf. The cocoon of the honeysuckle sawfly (*Abia inflata*), made on the ground, is pale yellowish.

Yellowish cocoon (9 mm) of an unknown sawfly. The green larva is somewhat visible inside, with its head at the top. (MA)

The cocoons of conifer sawflies (Diprionidae) are more perfectly capsule-shaped and about 7 to 10 mm long. They can often be found in large numbers attached to vegetation below the coniferous trees in which the larvae feed.

The tough, papery, brown cocoons of tenthredinid sawflies are usually formed in leaf litter or underground. *Pristiphora appendiculata*, which feeds on currant and gooseberry, is one exception, spinning its cocoon on the host plant.

Packard (1878) described *Arge* (Argidae) as forming a "gauzy, doubly enveloping cocoon," but we have not found illustrations of this. Some birch sawfly larvae (*A. pectoralis*) that we kept in a jar made 12-mm cocoons that could be described as gauzy; they were of the usual tough, brown

Cocoons of *Trichiosoma*, a cimbicid sawfly. A sawfly emerged from the cocoon on the left (18 mm), and an ichneumon from the one on the right (15 mm). (ME, MA)

Conifer sawfly (Diprionidae) cocoons, 8 to 10 mm. An introduced pine sawfly (*Diprion similis*) emerged from the leftmost cocoon; an ichneumonid (*Exenterus*) from the middle one; and numerous chalcids (Torymidae) from the rightmost. (MA)

Captive birch sawfly (Argidae: *Arge pectoralis*) cocoon, 12 mm. (MA)

sawfly material, but thinner and riddled with tiny holes. If there was a second, inner layer, it was not evident from the outside. An unspecified sawfly cocoon that appears in Frost (1959) looks similar, but with an added covering of very loose, irregular, coarse and squiggly threads, which may be what Packard was describing.

When an adult sawfly emerges from its cocoon, it chews in a circle at one end to create a flip-top lid, which often stays attached after the sawfly is gone. An off-center circular hole chewed near one end, a few millimeters across, likely indicates that an ichneumonid parasitoid emerged. A tiny hole about 1 mm across is the opening through which chalcidoid parasitoids emerged. A cleptine cuckoo wasp (Chrysididae) chews a small hole in a sawfly cocoon, deposits an egg on the larva, and then closes the hole with a mucilaginous material. The cuckoo wasp larva feeds on the sawfly larva, then makes its own cocoon inside its host's cocoon. Its exit hole is presumably similar to an ichneumonid's, but the sealed oviposition hole should be distinctive.

Ichneumonid Wasp Cocoons

The cocoons of some campoplegine ichneumonids, up to 6 mm long, are capsule-shaped and parchmentlike, very similar to some sawfly cocoons. They are marked with distinctive blotches of white or gold, however, which often form attractive banding patterns, like little Easter eggs. The cocoon is usually attached to the host caterpillar's food plant and may be found beside the host's withered remains. *Hyposoter* cocoons are frequently formed within the host's remains. Some species, such as *Charops*, suspend theirs from single long threads. A few, such as *Spudastica*, *Bathyplectes*, and *Phobocampe*, are able to make their cocoons jump before they have pupated; some of these cocoons are more squat and oval in shape, smooth, and have a single pale band around the middle. The unusual features of campoplegine cocoons are all adaptations for defense against predators—including the pale blotches, which are made by incorporating fecal material and are thought to mimic bird droppings.

Above top: Campoplegine ichneumonid cocoon, 6 mm. (CA) *Above bottom:* Another campoplegine cocoon, 5 mm. (MA)

Other ichneumonids allow their hosts to pupate or spin cocoons before killing them. They then spin their own cocoons inside the hosts' pupae or cocoons. Generally these are brown and parchmentlike, but the appearance can vary, even within a species. Some make flimsier, paler cocoons in the summer and tougher, darker ones to overwinter. *Dusona* and some other campoplegines make cocoons inside their host caterpillars' cocoons that are similarly shaped to those of others in the subfamily, but often plainly colored. The oval cocoons of ophionines are typically brownish with a paler central band. The Banchini (Banchinae) spin shiny, black, oval cocoons in the pupal chambers of moth larvae. Cocoons of the Tryphoninae are usually black, somewhat leathery, and at least in some cases very slender. They are found in the cocoons and pupal chambers of sawfly and moth larvae. The Metopiinae and others spin flimsy cocoons inside moth pupae.

Braconid Wasp Cocoons

Although they are small (usually about 3 mm long), some of the most commonly noticed cocoons are those of braconid wasps. Species in the Microgastrinae are all parasitoids of caterpillars, and in some cases eighty or more larvae will emerge from one caterpillar and spin their elongate, fuzzy cocoons on its back while it is still alive. Others spin cocoons on the outside of the host's cocoon or attach solitary cocoons to vegetation. (See chapter 3 for illustrations of cocoons that are found in association with

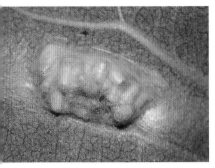

Cluster (13 mm) of 3-mm cocoons of *Cotesia glomerata* (Braconidae), made by larvae that emerged from a cabbage white caterpillar. The yellow silk was spun by the wasp larvae, and the white silk by the caterpillar. (TN)

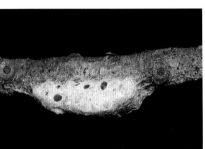

Cocoon bundle of several braconid wasp larvae (probably *Cotesia diacrisiae*), formed beneath the caterpillar from which they emerged. The bundle is 13 mm long and is composed of two rows of 4-mm-long cocoons. (MA)

host remains.) The mature wasp emerges from a neatly cut circular lid at one end of the cocoon, as a sawfly does. An irregular, off-center exit hole indicates the emergence of a chalcid or other hyperparasitoid wasp.

Cotesia congregata forms masses of woolly, white cocoons that stand upright on the backs of tobacco hornworms (Sphingidae: *Manduca sexta*). Braconids making similar cocoons on other sphinx moth caterpillars are currently considered to be the same species, but research is showing that *Cotesia* species are highly host-specific, so they may turn out to be a suite of nearly identical species, each with its own particular hornworm.

Other species spin similar cocoons, but in an irregular cluster on vegetation rather than attached to the host. Often such cocoon masses are formed beneath the caterpillar, which later drops off the plant. The masses of fuzzy yellow cocoons of *Cotesia glomerata* are a common sight in gardens because this species parasitizes cabbage white caterpillars (Pieridae: *Pieris rapae*). In another fascinating example of behavior modification by parasitoids (see chapter 3), the caterpillar covers the *C. glomerata* cocoons with a protective sheet of its own white silk. *Glyptapanteles* is another microgastrine genus that makes clusters of soft, woolly cocoons, which may be white or brown. Some *Macrocentrus* species (Macrocentrinae) are also gregarious parasitoids of caterpillars, but their cocoons tend to be very elongate, brown, and more shiny and papery.

Other braconid larvae pupate underneath their host, spinning their cocoons in a semicircular "logpile" configuration with a common covering. The dead or dying caterpillar may sometimes be found still perched atop this cocoon mass. *Cotesia diacrisiae*, which usually parasitizes tussock moths (Lymantriidae: *Orgyia*), is a common species with this habit.

Microplitis species make oblong cocoons, 3 to 6 mm long, with more or less distinct longitudinal ribbing. They are whitish and somewhat delicate at first, becoming hard and tough, and darkening to a dingy yellow or a deeper brown. There are both solitary and gregarious species, and the cocoons may

Ribbed, 5-mm cocoon of *Microplitis* (Braconidae), with the cap cut off by the emerging adult. (MA)

either project from the caterpillar (usually a noctuid) or be attached to vegetation.

Cotesia melanoscela is a solitary species that has been introduced to control gypsy moths (Lymantriidae: *Lymantria dispar*). Its 5-mm-long, off-white, elongate cocoons may be abundant on the bark of infested trees.

Some *Meteorus* species (Meteorinae) spin a 4- to 5-mm-long, glossy, papery, brown, spindle-shaped cocoon, which is usually suspended from vegetation by a thread a few centimeters long. These should not be confused with the banded or mottled, oval or capsule-shaped cocoons of campoplegine ichneumonids that are similarly suspended.

As noted in chapter 3, the capsule-shaped, fuzzy, white or brown cocoons of bethylid wasps are similar to those of some braconids. They parasitize moth and beetle larvae that develop in concealed situations and pupate near their remains. Soon after emerging from their own cocoons, the males tear open their sisters' cocoons. Torn-open cocoons combined with a concealed location may be the best clues to look for in distinguishing between cocoons of braconids and bethylids.

Cocoon (5 mm) of *Cotesia melanoscela* (Braconidae), a parasitoid of the gypsy moth, attached to the trunk of a tree. (NY)

Other Hymenopteran Cocoons

Many other hymenopterans pupate in cocoons, but virtually all are hidden in nests. Social bee and wasp larvae form cocoons by capping the cells in which they have developed. Solitary species spin gen-

A 5-mm *Meteorus* cocoon (Braconidae), found hanging by a thread from a fall webworm web. (MA)

Thin, papery cocoon (13 mm) of the black and yellow mud dauber (Sphecidae: *Sceliphron caementarium*). The dark plug at the end is the larval meconium. (AR)

Spring tiphia (Tiphiidae: *Tiphia vernalis*) cocoon, 2 cm. (MI)

Cocoons (2 mm) of *Lasius* ants (Formicidae). (MA)

erally thin, papery cocoons within their cells, whether in aerial mud nests, between partitions in a stem, or underground.

The spring tiphia (Tiphiidae: *Tiphia vernalis*) is an introduced parasitoid of the Japanese beetle. In its host's underground cell, it spins a distinctive, parchmentlike cocoon, up to 2 cm long, that is widest near one end and tapers gradually toward the other end. This species is unusual in overwintering as an adult inside its cocoon. The cocoons of scoliid wasps, which parasitize other scarab larvae, are also elongate but symmetrical and widest at the middle.

Most of the so-called "higher" ants have naked pupae, but other ants pupate in smooth, tough, capsule-shaped cocoons. You can often see these when an ant colony is disturbed, such as when you flip over a rock, and they are frequently mistaken for eggs.

Virtually no chalcids spin cocoons. Exceptions include *Euplectrus* (Eulophidae), which spins flimsy cocoons under the host caterpillar, and some *Coccophagus* species (Aphelinidae), which pupate under the coverings of scale insects. Askew (1971) also mentions *Systasis* (Pteromalidae) and a few encyrtids as making cocoons, but these may or may not occur in North America.

Dryinid wasp larvae pupate in tough silken cocoons. These may be either among leaf litter or attached to the plant on which the larva emerged from the host leafhopper.

Fly Cocoons

A few types of flies pupate within silken cocoons. The pouchlike, underwater cocoons of black flies are described in chapter 2. Members of a few families use silk to make cocoons that are covered with foreign materials, and these are mentioned in chapter 8.

Possibly the only fly cocoons attached to vegetation belong to certain gall midges (Cecidomyiidae). Pitch and resin midges (*Cecidomyia*) feed externally on branches, twigs, and needles of pines and a few other conifers. When mature, they form somewhat elongate, 3- to 5-mm-long, white cocoons near where they have been feeding. These may be completely surrounded with hardened resin. A few other gall midges form cocoons on vegetation, at their feeding sites, and many more do so on or in the ground. When an adult emerges, it leaves the pupal skin protruding.

Fungus gnats (Mycetophilidae) generally pupate in silken cocoons, usually underground. They may be densely woven or very slight. In some cases, they are formed within the host fungus. Dance flies (Empididae) and long-legged flies (Dolichopodidae) also spin cocoons, which generally are covered with debris. The long respiratory horns of long-legged fly pupae often protrude from their cocoons.

Above top: Resin midge (Cecidomyiidae: *Cecidomyia*) cocoon, less than 5 mm. (NC) Photo by Lynette Schimming. *Above bottom:* Cocoon (5 mm) of a resin midge, surrounded with hardened resin. (MA)

Beetle Cocoons

Apparently the only silken beetle cocoons formed on terrestrial vegetation are the open mesh ones made by *Hypera* and *Ophraella*. Members of several other families spin cocoons in stored products, underground, under bark, or underwater.

Cocoons of various death-watch and spider beetles (Anobiidae), among others, may be found in households. Spider beetles (Ptininae) make nearly spherical cocoons, about 3 mm long, in flour and other cereal products. The cigarette beetle (*Lasioderma serricorne*) and drugstore beetle (*Stegobium paniceum*) make silken cocoons in dry stored foods as well as tobacco, herbarium specimens, and even books, among the powdery frass they produce. Flat grain beetles (Laemophloeidae: *Cryptolestes*), about half the size, also spin cocoons among stored grains. Ham beetles (Cleridae: *Necrobia*) are instead found on dried animal products and are most often encountered on museum specimens. Their glistening, white, papery cocoons are actually composed of dried globules of the larvae's saliva.

Larvae of aquatic leaf beetles (Chrysomelidae: Donaciinae) obtain oxygen by tapping the submerged stems or roots of waterlilies. They pupate in tough cocoons in the same locations, still using oxygen from the plant.

American spider beetles (Anobiidae: *Mezium americanum*) and their 3-mm cocoons in a bin of flour. (MA)

Often several can be found in a row. At least one species of *Lixus* weevil (Curculionidae) does the same on stems of aquatic smartweeds, and the burrowing water beetles (Noteridae) do so on various plants, presumably while buried in the mud.

Some other weevils pupate in silk cocoons underground. The obscure rove beetles (Staphylinidae: Aleocharinae) also spin cocoons. These poorly known beetles live in a variety of hidden habitats, often involving some sort of decay, and their cocoons are no doubt found in the same places.

Other Cocoons

A few other kinds of insects make silken cocoons as well. Flea larvae (Siphonaptera) spin theirs among the debris where they develop, in cracks and crevices such as between floorboards. When the adults are ready to emerge, they may lie dormant for months until stimulated by vibrations of a potential host moving nearby, and then they spring into action. Male scale insects and mealybugs (Coccoidea) complete their development in flimsy cocoons that look like tiny cotton balls. Most thrips (Thysanoptera) transform in cocoons, apparently underground for the most part. The only confirmed example of one we have seen belonged to a captive *Franklinothrips* (Aeolothripidae). It was a delicate oval of white silk, twice as long as wide, surrounded by a halo of more loosely woven silk. The pupa was clearly visible within.

Coverings, Cases, Retreats, and Nests Made from Foreign Materials

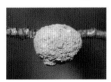

8

Invertebrates build an impressive variety of structures using foreign materials. For the most part, these can be divided into four groups based on function: protection for pupating insects; portable protection for mobile insects; fixed dwelling structures for solitary animals; and protection built by parents for their eggs and developing larvae. In most instances, it is straightforward to decide in which category a given object belongs. Cocoons and pupal cells are generally oval and form closed compartments. Most are found in concealed locations. Portable cases tend to be tubular in form, although there are exceptions. Most are eventually converted to stationary pupal cases, which are often attached to objects in the open. The third group includes tubular structures made by aquatic organisms, as well as retreats of a few spiders that do not settle for just concealing themselves with silk. Some of these retreats are found on the undersides of objects on the ground, and others are normally suspended in webs but may be found loosely attached to vegetation long after the webs are gone. The final category comprises nests of bees, ants, and wasps. Some are quite elaborate, whereas others are simple partitions built in hollow stems and similar cavities. A few miscellaneous paper constructions made by ants are lumped with nests in this chapter.

To maintain some kind of logical organization in this book, we included some objects in other chapters that employ foreign materials in their construction, and some in this chapter that do not. Debris-covered spider egg sacs are described along with the other egg sacs in chapter 1; a few of these could potentially be confused with cocoons, but they have foreign materials packed or fastened onto the outside, rather than simply incorporated into the silk, which is what a larva does when building a cocoon around itself. Leaf-covered cocoons of giant silkmoths are included with those that are pure silk (see chapter 7). The "sand collars" made by moon snails do not fit well in any category, and it seemed best to place them along with the other strange egg-related objects that wash up on the beach (chapter 1). There are casebearer moth and caddisfly cases made entirely of silk, and worm tubes made entirely of other secreted substances, all of which are best discussed here along with the other cases and tubes. The nests of social bees are also made largely of secreted materials but clearly belong with the rest of the nests.

Miscellaneous Earthen Structures

A few earthen structures made by invertebrates do not quite fit into the categories just outlined. The mud tubes and coverings made by termites are unlikely to be mistaken for anything else. Millipedes build chambers of soil and other organic matter for two different purposes; these are most likely to be confused with pupal cells of insects, which are the subject of the next section.

Termite Encrustations and Tubes

Desert termites (Termitidae: *Gnathamitermes tubiformans*) surround herbaceous and woody vegetation with tubes and sheetings of mud, which protect them from predation and the elements as they feed on the surface of the vegetation they have covered. In addition to living plants, they encrust all kinds of plant debris and even animal droppings. They mostly work close to the ground, but we have measured their tubes extending as high as 32.3

inches (82 cm) up the stem and branches of a desert shrub.

Subterranean termites (Rhinotermitidae) occur throughout North America and make somewhat similar shelter tunnels to those of desert termites. All termites in this family live in colonies in the soil and travel through tunnels or mud tubes to the above-ground wood on which they feed. Often these tubes are inconspicuous, on the undersides of logs. When these termites infest houses, however, they may construct long, slender, vertical tubes across foundations or other surfaces that lie between the ground and the wood they seek. Partially constructed tubes, made largely of wood particles and measuring more than 3 feet (91.4 cm) long, may be found hanging freely from ceilings near ground level. There are variations in the construction of

Vegetation encrusted with mud tubes by desert termites (Termitidae: *Gnathamitermes*). (TX)

This log was lying on top of leaf litter, so the earth stuck to the underside is all the work of eastern subterranean termites (Rhinotermitidae: *Reticulitermes flavipes*), concealing their galleries in the wood. (MA)

these tubes; for instance, those of desert subterranean termites (*Heterotermes aureus*) are more circular in cross section, and those of the western subterranean termite (*Reticulitermes hesperus*) are flattened in cross section. In the tropics (including southern Mexico), termite shelter tunnels extend many feet up tree trunks, and some species build large, spherical arboreal nests surrounding branches.

Millipede Nests and Molting Chambers

Many millipedes make discrete earthen nests for their eggs. Some pill millipedes (Glomerida and Sphaerotheriida) construct nests in the form of hollow spheres, which are rough and irregular on the outside but have smooth, even inner linings of dried excrement.

Polydesmus angustus, among others in the Polydesmida and Colobognatha (the group comprising Platydesmida, Polyzoniida, and Siphonophorida), builds a thin-walled, dome-shaped structure on a firm substrate such as a stone, a leaf, the inside of an acorn cap, or the inner surface of a piece of bark. At the top of the dome is a narrow, tubular chimney. The circumference of the nest is slightly greater than the length of the mother's body. She stays coiled around it for about a week, keeping it covered with bits of debris. Most of the Juliformia (i.e., Julida, Spirobolida, and Spirostreptida) build a very crude, dome-shaped nest, mostly from the inside, by plastering with excrement an underground space cleared in the loose soil above a rock.

Some millipedes also build earthen structures in which they shed their skins. The exuviae are usually eaten to restore lost calcium, so they are

A xystodesmid millipede's molting chamber, about 1.2 inches (3 cm). (MA)

unlikely to be left behind as a clue to the identity of the structure. Molting chambers of the Polydesmida and Juliformia are often roughly spherical and basically similar to their nests, made from soil or decaying wood moistened with saliva and sometimes lined with fecal material. The largest, about 2.4 inches (6 cm) across, are made by the desert millipede *Orthoporus ornatus* (Spirostreptidae) and are also used as hibernacula. The common eastern species *Narceus americanus* (Spirobolidae) forms its chamber by burrowing into a log, sealing the entrance with chewed wood. Other millipedes simply molt in existing structures, such as seed capsules, or shallow depressions they make in the soil.

Cocoons and Pupal Cells

Many insects construct cells of soil, wood fibers, and other debris in which they pupate. These are mostly formed in hidden locations such as under bark, in rotting wood, under objects on the ground, or underground. Few can be identified with much specificity without examining the exuviae inside. Those found near or in water likely belong to caddisflies and are discussed along with the portable cases these insects make.

Cocoons

As defined in the previous chapter, cocoons are pupal chambers that are composed at least partly of silk. Many moths and a few other insects make silk cocoons that incorporate other materials, sometimes to the point of completely obscuring the silk.

Antlions and Owlflies

Myrmeleon antlions (Myrmeleontidae) pupate within roughly spherical cocoons that are encrusted with sand grains. The larva spins its cocoon while buried up to 4 inches (10 cm) deep in the sand, first spinning a hemisphere over itself, then another below, and finally uniting the two. The completed cocoon is up to 14 mm across. The pharate adult exits through a

Empty, predated cocoon (about 1 cm) of an antlion (Myrmeleontidae), encrusted with sand grains. (MI)

neatly cut circular door just as is done by green lacewings, then wriggles to the surface of the sand. Given this natural history, an intact antlion cocoon is unlikely to be found without digging, but we have found empty ones exposed by the shifting sand of dunes.

Owlfly larvae (Ascalaphidae) spin cocoons similar to those of antlions. Living on the surface of the ground rather than under it, they cover the cocoons with bits of leaves, twigs, and other debris rather than sand. The cocoons are hidden in crevices in bark or soil. Presumably antlions other than *Myrmeleon*, which do not live under sand, make cocoons similar to those of owlflies.

Moths

Many prominents (Notodontidae) pupate in flimsy cocoons among ground litter, incorporating bits of earth and debris. Some geometrids, such as the spring cankerworm (*Paleacrita vernata*), spin more substantial debris-covered cocoons underground. Many noctuids have similar habits, some making thin cocoons (e.g., the eight-spotted forester, *Alypia octomaculata*) and

others very tough ones (e.g., some hooded owlets, *Cucullia*) that may also incorporate droppings. Tough silk and soil cocoons of the squash vine borer (Sesiidae: *Melittia cucurbitae*) may be found buried in gardens. There are no doubt moths in other families that also incorporate debris into their cocoons on or in the ground.

Loose debris cocoon (2 cm) of an unknown moth. (TN)

Some dagger moths (Noctuidae: *Acronicta*) make silken cocoons, about 1.2 inches (3 cm) long, that are coated with bits of chewed wood. The caterpillar gnaws a shallow trench in a wooden surface and incorporates the excavated material. Certain other owlet moths make similar cocoons. Some tentacled prominents (Notodontidae: *Cerura*) pupate in cavities in rotten wood or under bark in tough, brown cocoons of silk mixed with wood particles.

Codling moth larvae (Tortricidae: *Cydia pomonella*) usually overwinter on trunks of fruit trees in cocoons that incorporate bits of bark. In the spring, they may either leave to spin a thinner cocoon elsewhere or break open the hibernaculum and reseal it with thinner silk that will allow the mature pupa to push through. The peach twig borer (Gelechiidae: *Anarsia lineatella*; on various *Prunus* trees) similarly hibernates in a bark crevice, usually in

Predated cocoon (1.3 inches [3.3 cm]) of a dagger moth (Noctuidae: *Acronicta*) on a hemlock trunk. The caterpillar's hairy skin is bunched at one end. (MA)

a crotch. A small chimney projects from its cell of silk, bark fragments, and excrement.

The peach tree borer (Sesiidae: *Synanthedon exitiosa*) usually leaves its burrow and makes its oblong cocoon of excrement, bark fragments, resin, and silk low on the trunk. The pupa protrudes from the end of the cocoon when the moth is ready to emerge. Other wood-boring clearwing moth larvae generally pupate within their galleries, in similar cocoons incorporating wood chips. The habits of carpenter moths (Cossidae) are much the same. Horntails and wood wasps (Siricoidea) make thin cocoons of silk and bark chips in their galleries. They leave their pupal exuviae inside the cocoon, unlike the wood-boring moths.

Flies

Long-legged flies (Dolichopodidae) spin cocoons that incorporate soil and organic debris. Aquatic species glue together sand or mud with a tough, gelatinous substance. Others may be found in galleries in wood. The pupae have elongate respiratory horns that frequently protrude from the cocoons. According to Chu (1949), the related dance flies (Empididae) pupate in cocoons that are densely coated with wood particles. Fungus gnats (Mycetophilidae) often incorporate soil particles into their underground cocoons.

Sawflies and Wasps

Various sawflies are said to pupate in earthen cells. Presumably these involve silk, as cocoon spinning is the general rule among sawflies.

Although we have seen no literature that mentions anything of the sort, BugGuide.net contributor Claude Pilon photographed a dryinid wasp larva building a debris-covered cocoon. The larva crawled down the stem on which it had emerged from its leafhopper host, stopping a centimeter from the base when it encountered organic debris that was stuck to the stem. It stopped here and loosely surrounded itself with the debris as it spun its cocoon.

Pupal Cells without Silk

Many authors, when summarizing insects' natural histories, refer vaguely to pupation in a cell in the ground. This sometimes means that the larva simply forms a cavity by pressing the earth around it in all directions, perhaps using saliva or other secretions to hold it in place. The Megaloptera and many flies, moths, and beetles pupate in cells of this sort. The pupal cells of some insects, however, are discrete objects formed of earth or organic materials without the use of silk. Some of these are made on or in the ground, and others are made in wood or under bark. With just one exception that we have found, cells of this sort are all made by beetles. Many more families of beetles than the ones mentioned here pupate in some kind of constructed cell.

Sand Wasps

The pupal cells of *Bembix* sand wasps (Crabronidae) are unmistakable. Each cell is blimp-shaped and about an inch long, consisting of a thin, tough shell of fine sand bound together with saliva, with several small, dark projections in a ring around the middle. The empty cells, opened neatly at one end, can be found in abundance after they have been exposed by the shifting of the dunes in which they are buried.

Aquatic Beetles

Whereas most aquatic beetles make their pupal chambers under objects or in the ground, whirligigs (Gyrinidae) construct dome-shaped pupal cases in exposed locations. They may be built on the ground at

Sand cocoons (2 cm) of *Bembix* sand wasps (Crabronidae). (UT)

the water's edge or attached to rocks or plant stems 2 to 4 inches (5 to 10 cm) above the waterline. They are formed of mud, pieces of vegetation, and other debris mixed with an adhesive substance. *Dineutus* larvae build their cells around themselves, one piece at a time; *Gyrinus* larvae carry the whole mass in one load, attach it to a surface, burrow into it, and close the opening. Lutz (1948), unlike other accounts, implied the use of silk, saying *Gyrinus* larvae "spin" a grayish cocoon that is pointed at both ends. Whatever their appearance, they are rarely seen. Late summer is the time to look for them, as they are formed in August and the adults emerge a month later. Larvae of some bombardier beetles (Carabidae: *Brachinus*) parasitize whirligig pupae, as do numerous wasps such as *Pleurogyrus* ichneumons.

Pupal cell of a predaceous diving beetle (Dytiscidae: *Dytiscus verticalis*), found under a log near a stream. The larval skin is at the right end of the cell, and the pupal skin is at the bottom. The cell is 2.8 inches (7 cm) long, and its interior is 1.6 inches (4 cm) long. (MA)

Left: Ribbed pine borer (Cerambycidae: *Rhagium inquisitor*) pupal cell, about 1.4 inches (3.5 cm). (MA) *Above:* Pupal cell (15 mm) of an unknown beetle on the side of a tree, composed entirely of wood fibers. (NH)

A few other aquatic beetles may form exposed pupal cells, but these are even less likely to be seen. Some minute moss beetles (Hydraenidae: *Ochthebius*), which are less than 3 mm long, make mud cells on the sides of stones. Trout stream beetles (Amphizoidae; W) may form protective cases of twigs on the ground.

Cells Made of Wood Fragments

Some beetle larvae that develop in wood form pupal cells of chewed wood fragments. Perhaps the most distinctive are those made by the ribbed pine borer (Cerambycidae: *Rhagium inquisitor*). In the fall, it burrows out of the wood until it is just under the bark, and there it excavates a flattened chamber. It removes the wood in long shreds, which it arranges in a wide, oval ring around the chamber, about 1.4 inches (3.5 cm) long. The adult emerges from the pupa and stays in this shelter through the winter. Pine weevils (Curculionidae: *Pissodes*) also use long fibers in making pupal cells in their tunnels under pine bark, but their cells are compact and a fraction of the size. Other long-horned beetles construct pupal cells out of short chips of wood. Flat bark beetles (Cucujidae) also pupate under bark, in circular cells using small particles of decaying bark and wood.

Scarab beetle (*Osmoderma scabra*) pupal cell, measuring 1.6 inches (4 cm), found in a flying squirrel latrine in a hollow pine. (NH) Photo by Dan Gardoqui.

Osmoderma scarab larvae feed on rotten wood in the hollows of various trees. In the fall, they make firm, oval cells of wood fragments cemented together with saliva, in which they pupate and overwinter. These may be up to 1.6 inches (4 cm) or so long. Stag beetles also live in rotten wood and make pupal cells of chewed wood fragments. The adult beetles range from 0.3 to 2.4 inches (8 mm to 6 cm) long, and the size of their cells varies accordingly.

Terrestrial Case-bearing Insects

True case making among terrestrial insects is mostly limited to moth larvae. The one exception is the case-bearing leaf beetles, which make their cases largely of their own droppings. A couple other types of immature insects, however, conceal themselves with disorganized debris coverings.

Loose Debris Coverings

Masked hunter nymphs (Reduviidae: *Reduvius personatus*) secrete a sticky substance that causes them to become coated in dust, lint, and other debris. This helps conceal them from their prey, but the general form of an assassin bug is still clearly discernible.

A 6-mm "trash-carrying" green lacewing larva (Chrysopidae), completely concealed except for a couple of legs. (NC)

In contrast, the larvae of some green lacewings (Chrysopidae), known as "trash carriers," cover themselves with fluffy heaps of debris that completely conceal their bodies. The covering may include plant matter and the remains of aphids and other prey items. It is held in place by hooked spines or bristles on the larva's body. When in motion, the larva's legs and large mandibles can be seen on close inspection.

Camouflaged loopers (Geometridae: *Synchlora*) are inchworms that cover themselves with bits of the flowers on which they feed, attached with silk. They are most often found on flowers in the aster family. Their shed skins retain the covering of flower pieces, and when they pupate, they make loose cocoons that incorporate them.

This camouflaged looper (Geometridae: *Synchlora*) has covered itself with smartweed flowers. (TN) Photo by Kris Light.

Bagworms and Their Relatives

Bagworms are moth larvae in the family Psychidae. The larva, 0.6 to 1.6 inches (16 mm to 4 cm) in most species, carries around a case made of silk and covered with bits of twigs, leaves, or other debris. The case is fastened down to the food plant when the larva is molting, and shed skins (as well as excrement) are pushed out through the top. When mature, larvae disperse and fasten their cases to twigs or other objects to pupate. The adult males emerge, leaving their pupal skins protruding from the cases, and fly to females, which are wingless and legless and never leave their cases. After mating, the female lays her yellowish eggs in the case and dies—or may even die with the eggs still inside her. When the larvae hatch, they emerge from the case, soon wearing tiny versions of their parents' cases, which they enlarge as they grow. Since there are fewer than thirty North American species (north of Mexico, that is), we will give a complete summary here, drawn mostly from Davis (1964), which illustrates them all. We have omitted some species that are known from only one specimen, which in some cases has been lost and may actually belong to another species. Bear in mind that the size ranges given are only for full-size (pupal) cases.

Cases over 1.2 inches (3 cm) long almost always belong to species of *Oiketicus* and *Thyridopterix*. Abbot's bagworm (*O. abbotii*; up to 2.8 inches [7 cm]), a coastal southeastern species, is unique among bagworms north of Mexico in placing twigs around its bag transversely. It does not always use twigs, however. When feeding on oak, it usually covers the bag heavily with projecting leaf fragments, and when on mangrove, the case may be largely

Left: Abbot's bagworm (Psychidae: *Oiketicus abbotii*) case, 1.6 inches (4 cm). (GA) *Center:* Cases (2.4 inches [6 cm]) of evergreen bagworms (Psychidae: *Thyridopterix ephemerae-formis*) feeding on arborvitae. (TN) *Right:* A 2.4-inch (6-cm) case of an evergreen bagworm feeding on boxelder. (TN)

bare silk with just a few attached leaves. Bags on acacia may have a thin sheet of silk on the outside. The evergreen bagworm (*T. ephemeraeformis*; up to 2.4 inches [6 cm]) is the only other large eastern species. It feeds on many different plants but is often seen on cedars, making its case out of the leaves from its food plant. When twigs are incorporated, they are aligned parallel to the length of the case.

The other large species are all southwestern. *O. townsendi* (up to 4.5 inches [11.5 cm]) makes a spindle-shaped case, usually with half of the underlying silk exposed and the remainder covered with short, longitudinally arranged twig (or

Psyche casta (Psychidae) case, 12 mm. (MA)

sometimes leaf) fragments. Cases in Texas may be heavily covered with twigs, somewhat loosely attached at the upper ends, giving them a shaggy appearance. *O. toumeyi* (up to 3.5 inches [9 cm]; AZ, Mexico) makes narrow cases that also often leave the silk exposed. The sparsely applied material may be tightly attached leaf fragments or longitudinally arranged twig pieces. *T. meadi* (up to 1.6 inches [4 cm]) is largely associated with creosote bush. Its case is completely covered by small, flat, firmly attached leaf fragments or short, somewhat spirally arranged, obliquely placed twig fragments. The case of *T. alcora* (S AZ; up to 1.6 inches [4 cm]) is also completely covered with obliquely arranged stem or twig pieces, but the pieces are longer and their ends often diverge from the bag, giving it a bulky appearance.

Hyaloscotes pithopoera (NW, ME, QC) makes a gradually tapering case, 21 to 27 mm long, that is covered longitudinally with short pieces of leaves and grass blades. *H. fragmentella* (along with two other poorly known species that are probably actually synonymous) makes a similar case and is restricted to northern California.

The case of *Astala confederatra* (E; 15 to 20 mm) is composed of silk interwoven with minute plant fragments, overlaid with a number of longitudinal pieces of stems that usually extend most of the bag length. The pieces are attached firmly toward the front and diverge somewhat as they project backward. *Psyche casta* is an introduced species with a somewhat similar but smaller case (9 to 13 mm). It is heavily covered by longitudinal pieces that may diverge or be closely appressed, and they often project irregularly beyond the case. This species is often found attached to the sides of houses.

The remaining species that incorporate plant fragments are all restricted to the southeastern coastal plain. The case of *Basicladus tracyi* (NC to MS; 1 to 1.2 inches [2.5 to 3 cm]) varies considerably in width. It is usually covered with overlapping, longitudinally applied leaves and stems of grasses and sedges. *B. celibatus* (NC to FL; 11 to 15 mm) covers its slender, cylindri-

Left: Snailcase bagworm (Psychidae: *Apterona helix*) case, about 4 mm. (VT) *Right: Dahlica triquetrella* (Psychidae) case, 7 mm. (MA)

cal case with thin flakes of pine bark and usually a number of longitudinally arranged pieces of pine needles or stems. It is generally found low on tree trunks. The stout case of *Cryptothelea gloverii* (SC to Mexico; 15 to 23 mm) may be fairly bare or covered with pieces of bark, leaves, fruit rinds, or scale insects. The case of *C. nigrita* (FL, AL, MS; 18 to 20 mm) is often somewhat shaggy looking, with a dense covering of spreading, backward-projecting pieces of grass leaves—a smaller version of *B. tracyi*. It is sometimes almost bare silk.

Other bagworm cases have very fine-textured coverings. The introduced snailcase bagworm (*Apterona helix*) has a tiny, coiled case, no more than 5 mm across, covered with fine particles of earth. The similar *A. helicoidella* has recently turned up in British Columbia. *Dahlica triquetrella* is another introduced species. Its case is straight and elongate, up to about 8 mm long, tapered at both ends and distinctly three-sided in cross section. It is covered with sand grains, bits of lichen, and other small debris, and sometimes has a very regular, smooth outline. This species, too, has a look-alike (*D. lichenella*) that has been found in British Columbia. The related species *Siederia walshella* (7 to 10 mm), native in the Northeast, makes a spindle-shaped case with a similar covering. If it is three-sided, Davis does not mention this.

The case of *Prochalia pygmaea* (SC to TX; 13 to 16 mm) is also covered with sand and tiny fragments of lichen and bark. It tapers posteriorly and appears smooth to the naked eye. *Zamopsyche commentella* (DE to MS; 11 to 15 mm) is similar. The much larger *Astala polingi* (AZ, Mexico; up to 1.4 inches [3.5 cm]) has a similarly smooth case, embedded with very small plant fragments. It is narrow and nearly cylindrical, tapering slightly, and

A 7-mm case of a case-making clothes moth (Tineidae: *Tinea pellionella*) with the pupal skin projecting from the top, indicating that the moth has emerged. (MA)

usually has a few larger plant pieces attached longitudinally to the posterior end. *A. edwardsi* (OK, TX; 0.9 to 1.1 inches [23 to 27 mm]) is similar.

Portable cases of moth larvae in the related family Tineidae are often found inside houses. The household casebearers (*Phereoeca* spp.) in southern states make cases out of small particles of sand, plaster, insect droppings, fibers, and other debris. They mostly eat spider webs, along with wool and other animal products. The case is elliptical, usually with a short, straight, tubular projection at either end. A mature larva's case is up to 14 mm long and 5 mm wide in the middle. The widely distributed case-making clothes moth (*Tinea pellionella*) makes a cylindrical case, up to about 1 cm long, out of wool from the fabrics on which it feeds.

Coleophorids

Coleophora moth larvae (Coleophoridae), known as casebearers, make cases in a variety of forms, ranging from about 0.2 to 1.2 inches (5 mm to 3 cm) long. There are more than 140 described North American species

Left: Tubular silk case (8 mm) of an unknown *Coleophora* (Coleophoridae). (AZ) *Right:* A 1-inch (2.5-cm) tubular silk case of a possibly undescribed aster-feeding *Coleophora* species, decorated with sand grains. (MT)

and about three times as many still waiting to be named. The cases use various combinations of plant material, silk, and other secretions, and it is sometimes difficult to recognize what the composition is. The rear end has two or three valves for ejection of droppings. Unlike bagworms, casebearers tend to be highly host-specific, and noting the plant species on which they are found is critical to their identification. They may overwinter or pupate attached to something other than their host plant, so this is not always possible. Bucheli et al. (2002) list the known North American species and their host plants, grouped by the eight case types described below. Given the large number of species that are unaccounted for, identifications made using this reference should not be considered definitive.

Tubular silk cases begin as a case of pure silk, and they may be left at that or decorated with bits of plant material. Cases of most mature larvae have three valves at the rear end, but immature larvae—and mature larvae of a few species—have two. The larvae feed on various herbaceous plants, hollowing out developing seeds or mining from the undersides of leaves. *C. astericola*, which feeds on gray goldenrod, completely encrusts the outside of its case with sand grains.

Pistol cases are tubular in front and bent at the rear end, which often has a large, rounded projection something like the butt of a pistol. They are made of silk hardened with a secretion. The larvae all feed on leaves of woody plants, mostly trees, except for an undescribed species that feeds on vetch. Whereas all the other groups feed in the same ways as those with tubular silk cases, these species "graze" on the upper surfaces of leaves.

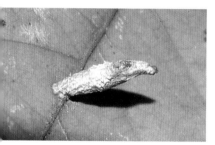

A pistol casebearer, probably *Coleophora querciella*. (NH)

Some larvae begin by wearing a hollowed-out floret or seed and then add material to it, creating what are called *seed cases*. *C. trifolii* feeds on sweetclover, and others feed on clovers and rushes.

Tubular leaf cases are made by mining inside a leaf and then cutting out a single piece, reinforcing it with silk. They are, naturally, tubular, with three valves at the rear end. *C. klimeschiella* (W) was introduced to control Russian thistle and is now widespread and abundant. When staying at a friend's house in Utah, we were asked to figure out what all the little "porcupine quills" stuck to the outside of the house were, and they turned out to be cases of this species. The larch casebearer (*C. laricella*) was also introduced, but unintentionally. It overwinters in a case consisting of the tip of a single hollowed-out

Tubular leaf case (12 mm) of *Coleophora klimeschiella*. (UT)

larch needle. In the spring, it adds small pieces of leaves to the sides of the case to enlarge it. *C. serratella* feeds on birch, alder, sweetfern, sweetgale, and willow. *C. irroratella* feeds on hawthorn, and two others feed on rose.

Spatulate leaf cases are similar in construction, but they are laterally compressed, with two valves at the rear end. The larvae feed on leaves of various trees and shrubs. The species with unique hosts (barring discovery of new species or host associations) are *C. affiliatella* on azalea and Labrador tea; *C. cornella* on dogwood; *C. corylifoliella* on hazelnut; *C. glaucella* on manzanita;

Spatulate leaf case (12 mm) of *Coleophora cornella*. (MA)

C. juglandella on walnut; *C. ostryae* on hophornbeam; and *C. umbratica* on plum.

Whereas species with tubular and spatulate leaf cases make a whole new case when they outgrow the existing one, *composite leaf cases* are enlarged by neatly wrapping additional leaf sheets around the front end and gluing them down with silk. Species of this type include *C. canadensisella* on bunchberry; *C. cornivorella* on dogwood; *C. rupestrella* on strawberry and cinquefoil; and *C. viburniella* on viburnum.

Lobe cases are also enlarged by adding more leaf pieces, but these project irregularly rather than being neatly wrapped. *C. accordella* makes lobe cases on trefoil and sweetvetch; *C. kearfottella* on willow; *C. ledi* on leatherleaf and Labrador tea; *C. perisimplexella* on sweetfern and birch; and an undescribed species on wormwood.

Annulate cases are enlarged incrementally by adding little leaf rings to the front end. These rings are cut from the holes the larva makes in the undersides of leaves in order to mine inside them. The rings gradually increase in size as the larva grows. As a result of this unique construction, the cases are annulated and taper toward the rear. Most species of this type feed on plants in the aster family, with two feeding on mints and one on phacelia.

Simple Cases of One, Two, or a Few Leaf Pieces

Various other larvae make simple cases out of cut pieces of leaves. These may be formed by a single section that the larva has mined inside, or by two or more pieces fastened together.

The shield bearers (Heliozelidae) spend their larval lives feeding between the layers of a single leaf. When mature, they cut out a neat, 3- to 4-mm elliptical piece of

A 3-mm pupal case of *Coptodisca*, a heliozelid leafminer. (UT)

the leaf, attach it to some object, and pupate within it. These little ovals may be seen dangling from trees by long silk threads when the larvae are descending to the ground. Some leaf-mining buprestid beetles similarly make circular pupal cases cut from a leaf, but they simply pupate wherever they land. *Cycloplasis panicifoliella* (Heliodinidae) mines in deertongue grass and forms a semicircular pupal chamber by cutting a circle out of the upper epidermis and folding it in half.

Adela fairy moths (Adelidae) start out feeding in the flowers or seeds of milkweed and other plants, and in later instars, they feed on foliage, living in cases each made from two oval pieces of leaf. They pupate inside these cases.

The maple leafcutter (Incurvariidae: *Paraclemensia acerifoliella*) lives sandwiched between flat, elliptical pieces of sugar maple leaves. The piece on one side is always slightly larger than the piece on the other, and the larva feeds with the smaller side down, periodically enlarging the case by attaching a new piece to the bottom and then flipping it over. The finished case is 1 cm or so across (see page 304).

The sack-bearers (Mimallonidae) feed on leaves beneath coarse webbing when young, but later instars construct open-ended portable cases using two or more irregular but roughly elliptical leaf pieces. The interior of the case, which is generally made of oak leaves, is a tough, tightly woven sleeve of silk. Each end is closed with a circular silken lid when the caterpillar is ready to pupate. One case of a scalloped sack-bearer (*Lacosoma chiridota*) measured about 1 inch (2.5 cm) long and 1 cm thick.

Case-bearing Leaf Beetles

The habits of case-bearing leaf beetles (Chrysomelidae: Cryptocephalinae) are described in chapter 5. Some species incorporate considerable amounts of foreign material into their cases of excrement. *Neochlamisus platani*, which feeds on sycamore, completely covers its case with trichomes (hairs) from the leaves. *N. bebbianae*, on willow and maple, often does as well. The Clytrini incorporate chewed leaf fragments, bark, and soil. At least some of them feed on debris in ant nests and are rarely seen.

A 5-mm case of *Neochlamisus platani* (Chrysomelidae: Cryptocephalinae), a case-bearing leaf beetle, covered with trichomes from sycamore leaves. (TN) Photo by Christopher G. Brown.

Aquatic Case-bearing Insects

Caddisfly larvae, along with a few aquatic moth larvae in the tribe Nymphulini, are the aquatic equivalents of bagworms and casebearers. About 1,400 caddisfly species are found in North America, most of which construct portable cases that they carry around with them throughout their lives. Each of these species uses a particular set of materials to build cases with a characteristic shape. Some cases are pure silk; others incorporate mineral fragments, plant debris, or a combination of the two. When the larva is mature, it may attach the case to a rock and pupate within it; sometimes many do this in a large aggregation. Wiggins (1996) is an excellent reference that illustrates a representative case or retreat from each of the 149 genera. The descriptions given here are largely based on that book. Because pupal cells of free-living larvae are similar in form to some portable cases (which may be converted to pupal cells), all are discussed together here. Long, tubular retreats that clearly have never been portable are discussed in the next section.

Microcaddisflies

Microcaddisflies (Hydroptilidae) include the smallest caddisflies, some of which have cases only 2.5 mm long when they are full-grown. Most are around 6 mm, with the largest being 8 mm long. They are free-living until the final instar, at which point most make portable, laterally compressed, two-valved cases with a slotlike opening at each end. A number are symmetrical and made entirely of parchmentlike silk or silk with some algae incorporated. *Orthotrichia* cases (up to 3.5 mm) have unique longitudinal

Cases (5 mm) of microcaddisflies (Hydroptilidae), probably *Agraylea*. (CA)

The cases (about 4 mm long) above and to the right of this unidentified caddisfly larva belong to *Leucotrichia pictipes* microcaddisfly larvae (Hydroptilidae). (WI)

ridges on the dorsal half. *Oxyethira* cases are bottle-shaped, tapering to a round opening at one end. Those of *Palaeagapetus* are covered with small pieces of liverworts. *Ochrotrichia* cases are covered with sand grains; *Hydroptila* cases are as well but differ in having a straight ventral edge and curved dorsal edge.

Leucotrichia (widespread) and *Zumatrichia* (W) make flattened, elliptical silk retreats that are firmly fixed to rocks, resembling leech egg cases. The structure has a circular, rimmed opening at each end rather than the usual slots.

Two genera have tiny, cylindrical cases, no more than 2.5 mm long, that are slightly tapered. *Mayatrichia* cases are pure silk and somewhat curved. Those of *Neotrichia* are covered with tiny sand grains.

Other Silk Cases

Apart from the microcaddisflies, cases of pure silk are unusual among caddisflies. *Sericostriata surdickae* (Uenoidae; MT, ID) is an uncommon species with a tapered, curved case, up to 8 mm, of tough, dark silk with longitudinal ridges. *Leptocerus americanus* (Leptoceridae; E) makes a slender case entirely of silk, up to 9.5 mm, which at the posterior end is strongly tapered and slightly curved. *Micrasema* cases (Brachycentridae) may be similar but are less slender and include some sand or plant materials. *Amiocentrus aspilus* (W; up to 10 mm) and *Brachycentrus* (up to 17 mm) may make straight, tapered, cylindrical cases composed largely or entirely of silk. *Ceraclea* species (Leptoceridae) that feed on freshwater sponges make cone-shaped cases of nearly pure silk, sometimes with pieces of sponge incorporated, up to 13 mm long.

Plain, Tubular Mineral Cases

Many kinds of caddisflies make portable tubular cases of mineral fragments. Substantial variation exists in the amount of curvature and taper among the cases of different genera. The distinguishing features among similar cases, if there are any, can be subtle. The shape and position of the posterior opening of the case are often important distinguishing features.

A few mineral cases are covered with an outer layer of silk. The silk-covered case of *Moselyana comosa* (Apataniidae; OR; up to 8.5 mm) is strongly tapered and curved. Its posterior opening has several silken points radiating toward the center. *Parthina* (Odontoceridae; W; up to 10 mm) has a similar case, but the posterior opening starts out wide open, then has a single pebble attached to one side in the final instar, and eventually is completely covered with a sheet of silk. Some western uenoids make very slender, curved cases of sand grains, up to 14 mm long, lined inside and outside with thin sheets of silk. The case of *Farula* is so slender that it could be mistaken for a conifer needle, and the case of *Neothremma* is only slightly stouter.

Brachycentrus echo (Brachycentridae; W) makes a straight, tapered case of pebbles, up to 18 mm long, that is circular in cross section. Other *Brachycentrus* species may make similar cases. Some *Micrasema* cases (up to 10 mm) are made of sand and are also cylindrical and tapered, straight or curved. The posterior end may be reduced with silk to a three- or four-lobed opening. Some *Nectopsyche* cases (Leptoceridae; up to 1.2 inches [3.1 cm]) are slender, tapered, and made almost entirely of mineral materials or diatoms.

Many other caddisflies make more or less curved and tapered, cylindrical cases of rock fragments, including the following, in order of increasing size of finished cases: *Lepania cascada* (Goeridae; OR, WA; up to 5.5 mm) makes a curved, strongly tapered case with a chevron-shaped posterior opening. *Goerita* (Goeridae; E; up to 6.5 mm) fashions a smooth case of sand grains, with the posterior opening reduced to a slightly off-center hole. *Pedomoecus sierra* (Apataniidae; W; up to 7 mm) constructs a strongly tapered case, with the posterior opening reduced to a small, central circular opening. The case of *Theliopsyche* (Lepidostomatidae; up to 7 mm) is smooth in outline and has a large, circular posterior opening. *Setodes* (Leptoceridae; E; up to 8.5 mm) builds a case with hardly any taper and an unconstricted posterior opening about the same size as the anterior opening. The case of *Oligophlebodes* (Uenoidae; W; up to 8.5 mm) is strongly tapered and curved, often incorporating relatively large pieces, and has a posterior silken membrane with a distinctly off-center circular opening. *Beraea* species (Beraeidae; E; up to 10 mm), which are rare and live in small streams or wet organic muck, have a curved and tapered case that is smooth, with the posterior opening reduced to an oblong slot. The case of *Rossiana montana* (Rossianidae; NW; up to 10.5 mm) does not taper much and has a small, circular, central posterior opening. *Oecetis* cases (Leptoceridae; up to 15 mm) are often irregular in outline, made of both sand

Plain, tubular mineral cases (1.02 inches [2.6 cm]) of limnephilid caddisflies. (CA)

grains and larger stones. Some *Lepidostoma* cases (Lepidostomatidae; up to 15 mm) are made of sand grains and taper somewhat at both ends.

The Sericostomatidae make a somewhat larger case of the same style, with the posterior opening substantially reduced with silk to a circular or oval central hole. *Agarodes* cases (E; up to 24 mm) are made of moderately coarse but uniform rock fragments. Those of *Fattigia pele* (SE; up to 18 mm) are similar. *Gumaga* cases (W; up to 29 mm) are made of finer sand grains and are often long, slender, and strongly curved.

The strongcase maker caddisflies (Odontoceridae) also make round, curved cases that are more or less tapered. The rock particles are very uniform in size. There is often an obvious transverse discontinuity where new pieces are added to enlarge the case. The larvae are mostly burrowers and make their cases extremely strong. Instead of the continuous interior lining of silk typical of caddisfly cases, most odontocerids have individual silken bands between adjacent rock pieces on the inside. The case of *Pseudogoera singularis* (up to 10 mm) has the posterior end reduced with silk to a several-lobed opening. In *Psilotreta* (E; up to 20 mm), the case has the posterior opening reduced with both rock fragments and silk to a small, off-center hole. In a *Marilia* case (S, W; up to 24 mm), the opening is reduced with silk to an oval hole at the dorsal edge. In *Nerophilus californicus* (OR, CA; up to 25 mm), it is reduced to a kidney-shaped central opening. The case of *Namamyia plutonis* (OR, CA; up to 30 mm) has a sievelike closure of rock fragments at the posterior end.

A plain, tubular mineral case that does not perfectly match any of the above descriptions has a good chance of belonging to a limnephilid. A number of genera make cases of this type, and it may not be possible to distinguish them from one another, or from the less distinctive cases of other families. To further complicate things, some species in other families that primarily make cases of plant materials may make mineral cases in early instars (e.g., some *Lepidostoma* species) or just before pupating (e.g., Phryganeidae: *Yphria californica*). A case made entirely of tiny snail shells is likely the work of *Philarctus quaeris* (NW).

Tubular Mineral Cases with Hoods, Flanges, or Other Prominent Features

Some caddisflies build cylindrical or conical cases of rock fragments with modifications to the shape that clearly set them apart from the ones in the previous section.

Ceraclea species (Leptoceridae) make strongly tapered, cone-shaped cases of sand, up to 13 mm, usually with an overhanging dorsal lip. In some species, this lip is extended along both sides, creating a broad, shieldlike structure. Cases with these pronounced lateral flanges are otherwise unique to the Molannidae. *Molanna* cases are up to 1.1 inches (27 mm) and have a prominent lateral flange and anterior hood. There may be some organic materials in addition to rock fragments, and some species incorporate a marginal row of larger pieces into their cases. *Molannodes tinctus* cases (AK, YT), up to 20 mm, have smaller flanges and hoods. They incorporate more pieces of plant material and sometimes are made entirely of detritus.

A 1-cm case of *Goera* (Goeridae). (MT)

The curved, tapered case of *Allomyia cidoipes* (Apataniidae; W; up to 13 mm) has a ridge of small stones along each side. Some *Apatania* cases (up to 9.5 mm) have larger pieces arranged on each side. In the finished case of all species in this genus, the dorsal edge is extended so that the anterior opening faces downward.

Neophylax (Uenoidae; E) makes a relatively short and thick case, up to 15 mm, of coarse rock fragments with several larger stones along each side. Cases of *Goera* (Goeridae; up to 14 mm) are similar but usually have only two larger stones on each side. A silken membrane reduces the posterior opening to a very small central hole. Cases are enlarged in the same manner as by glossosomatids (see below), so they are sometimes much longer. *Goeracea* cases (W; up to 8 mm) are curved and tapered, with a row of several larger pebbles along each side and often also a ridge of small stones along the top. A silken membrane reduces the posterior opening to a small, off-center hole.

Allomyia scotti (Apataniidae; W; up to 13 mm) has an abrupt constriction in the rear quarter of its curved, tapered case.

Other Mineral Cases

The cases of the snailcase caddisflies (Helicopsychidae: *Helicopsyche*) are among the easiest to recognize. A larva in this family makes a smooth tube of sand grains or pebbles, coiled in a spiral that looks much like a snail shell. It may be up to 7 mm across and completely covers the larva as it grazes on rock surfaces, usually in clear, fast-moving streams.

Saddlecase maker caddisflies (Glossosomatidae) are very common and also make easily recognizable cases. The case

Snailcase caddisfly (Helicopsychidae: *Helicopsyche borealis*) case, about 6 mm. (FL) Photo by David Almquist.

An 8-mm case of a saddlecase maker caddisfly (Glossosomatidae). (PA)

Pupation shelter (1 cm) of a net-spinning caddisfly larva (Hydropsychidae). (MT)

is a dome of pebbles, up to 12 mm long, something like a tiny turtle shell. On the underside is a broad strap of sand grains, like a turtle's plastron, with an equal opening at each end through which the larva can extend its head and legs. As with the snailcase caddisflies, the larva is completely concealed by the case while it grazes on rocks. Whereas most caddisfly larvae continually enlarge their cases as they grow, a glossosomatid builds a new, larger case at one end of the existing case, then cuts off the old one, each larva leaving several small cases behind in its lifetime.

The Rhyacophilidae (widespread) and Hydrobiosidae (SW, Mexico) have free-living larvae, but they use pebbles to build dome-shaped pupal cells up to 1 inch (2.5 cm) long, attached to rocks. Alternatively, the larva may make an enclosure by placing a ring of pebbles between two rocks. Inside this, it spins a tough, dark brown, oval cocoon. Spaces are left between the pebbles for circulation. Most of the fixed-retreat makers (Annulipalpia) make similar domes, which are sometimes only 1 cm long. Unlike the closed cocoons of the free-living caddisflies, theirs have small openings at each end.

Net-spinning caddisflies (Hydropsychidae) in the genus *Macrostemum* build domes of sand grains. The dome has one opening at the upstream end and two at the downstream end, with a curved partition between the downstream openings that partially divides the shelter into two chambers. One is a narrow chamber in which the larva rests, depositing its droppings out the opening. A silken net is spun across the larger chamber, in the middle of the dome, to catch small organic particles on which the larva feeds.

Tubular Cases of Mixed Materials

Certain caddisfly larvae normally construct cases that incorporate both mineral and plant materials. Some simply integrate the two; others build complete cases of rock fragments and then add plant pieces. Genera other than the ones mentioned below, such as *Limnephilus*, may also sometimes make tubular cases of mixed materials.

A number of long-horned caddisflies (Leptoceridae) typically make cases of mixed materials, up to 1.2 inches (3 cm) long. *Mystacides* species make coarse-textured, straight tubes of rock, mollusk shell, or plant pieces,

A limnephilid caddisfly larva (possibly *Ecclisomyia*) and its 1.06-inch (2.7-cm) case of sand grains and conifer needles. (CA)

usually with twigs or conifer needles extending well beyond the front end. *Nectopsyche* cases similarly have twigs or needles extending beyond one end, but the cases are long, slender, and tapered. The mineral cases of *Oecetis* are also often combined with bark or leaves.

Ecclisomyia (Limnephilidae; up to 1.2 inches [3.1 cm]) makes a slender, straight tube of rock fragments with some long plant pieces, similar to that of *Mystacides*, but the plant pieces do not necessarily project forward. The larvae are found in western mountain streams. *Psychoglypha* cases (N; up to 1.7 inches [4.3 cm]) are similarly straight but less slender, with a random mixture of rock and wood fragments. *Manophylax annulatus* (Apataniidae; ID; up to 10 mm) constructs a curved, tapered case entirely of rock fragments, then adds bits of twigs and leaves to the outside.

Yphria californica (Phryganeidae; NW) makes a case up to 1.3 inches (3.3 cm) long, incorporating rock fragments, bark, and twigs. The rock fragments are mostly placed at the front end, extending some distance on the underside. Cases of *Frenesia* (Limnephilidae; NE; up to 21 mm) are made mostly of rock fragments but often incorporate a few randomly distributed bits of wood. *Goereilla baumanni* (Rossianidae; MT, ID; up to 11 mm) makes curved cases of sand grains with several pieces of debris mixed in. The posterior opening is somewhat reduced with silk to form a many-lobed central hole.

Heteroplectron californicum (Calamoceratidae; W) has been found using stone cases of other caddisflies, with small pieces of wood added to the front end.

A case of Molannidae may incorporate both mineral and plant material, but it is easily recognized by the distinctive lateral flanges and anterior hood.

Cases of Plant Materials

Aquatic cases made of plant materials may be the work of either caddisflies or moths. Cases of the latter tend to be simple constructions, and there are only a few caddisfly cases that resemble them.

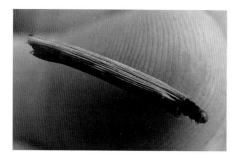

An aquatic moth larva (Crambidae: Nymphulinae: Nymphulini) and its simple case (11 mm). (MA)

Moth larvae in the Nymphulini (Crambidae: Nymphulinae) are aquatic and build portable cases or tubes of green pieces cut from living plants. Some of these larvae lack gills and depend on the bubbles of air that surround them in their cases. Sometimes a case is made of a single piece of a hollow plant stem. Many consist of two leaf pieces fastened together, and some are made of three or more pieces arranged longitudinally or otherwise. They range in size from 1 cm to about 1 inch (2.5 cm) long. Some larvae simply fasten two living leaves together without cutting them from the plant.

Agrypnia pagetana (Phryganeidae) sometimes uses a simple piece of hollow stem as a case, as is done by some Nymphulini. *Heteroplectron* (Calamoceratidae) makes its case by excavating a chamber through the center of a twig and lining it with silk. *Amphicosmoecus* (Limnephilidae; W; up to 1.3 inches [3.3 cm]) uses a hollow twig or stem, which it may chew so that it tapers at each end, and often adds a small turret of bark pieces at the front end.

Anisocentropus pyraloides (Calamoceratidae; SE) presumably gets its name from its case's resemblance to those of some Nymphulini (which are pyraloid moths). It uses two oval leaf pieces, a smaller ventral piece fastened to the middle of a larger dorsal piece (up to 1.4 inches [3.5 cm]), with a flattened chamber in between. *Phylloicus* cases (Calamoceratidae; TX, AZ; up to 1.6 inches [4 cm]) are flattened and straight, composed of pieces of bark, wood, or thick leaves fastened together along the edges. The case often has a protective hoodlike piece overhanging the anterior opening. *Chyranda centralis* (Limnephilidae; N; up to 1.4 inches [3.5 cm]) and *Clostoeca disjuncta* (W; up to 18.5 mm) construct similar cases, with the edges pinched together to form a prominent lateral flange. Immature larvae of *Nemotaulius hostilis* (N) also make flat cases of leaf pieces, but the edges are not neatly aligned as in the others. They are common in ponds.

Caddisflies in two families make cases of plant debris that are tapered and distinctly square in cross section. Eastern species of *Lepidostoma* (Lepidostomatidae) make four-sided cases, up to 15 mm long, out of square or rectangular pieces of bark or dead leaves. Many brachycentrids make four-sided cases, but the component pieces are elongate, stacked transversely as

A 2.4-inch (6-cm) case of an immature *Nemotaulius hostilis* (Limnephilidae). (MA)

Four-sided case (8.5 mm) of a pupating *Brachycentrus* (Brachycentridae), found attached to the underside of a rock. (WA)

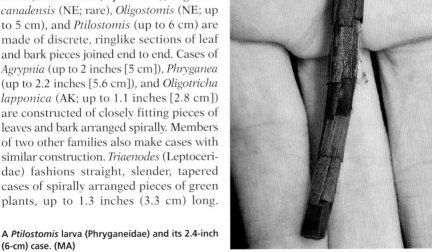

in a log cabin. Very neat cases of this type, up to 17 mm long, likely belong to *Brachycentrus*. In this genus, part of the case may be circular in cross section and made only of silk. The case of *Eobrachycentrus gelidae* (NW mountain springs; up to 13 mm) is largely composed of moss, with loose ends often left projecting from the sides, and has a four-lobed posterior opening. The case of *Adicrophleps hitchcocki* (E; up to 7 mm) is similar, but the posterior opening is circular.

Some brachycentrids make tapering cases that are circular in cross section, with thin ribbons of plant material wrapped around the circumference. They may include rock fragments and are sometimes largely of silk alone. The cases of *Micrasema* species (up to 10 mm) may be straight or curved, and the posterior end may be reduced with silk to a three- or four-lobed opening. *Amiocentrus aspilus* (W; up to 16 mm) makes a straight case with a round posterior opening that is not reduced with silk.

Giant caddisflies (Phryganeidae) mostly live in still water and make large, cylindrical cases, up to 6 cm long, that are round in cross section. Those of *Beothukus complicatus* (north central; up to 4 cm), *Hagenella canadensis* (NE; rare), *Oligostomis* (NE; up to 5 cm), and *Ptilostomis* (up to 6 cm) are made of discrete, ringlike sections of leaf and bark pieces joined end to end. Cases of *Agrypnia* (up to 2 inches [5 cm]), *Phryganea* (up to 2.2 inches [5.6 cm]), and *Oligotricha lapponica* (AK; up to 1.1 inches [2.8 cm]) are constructed of closely fitting pieces of leaves and bark arranged spirally. Members of two other families also make cases with similar construction. *Triaenodes* (Leptoceridae) fashions straight, slender, tapered cases of spirally arranged pieces of green plants, up to 1.3 inches (3.3 cm) long.

A *Ptilostomis* larva (Phryganeidae) and its 2.4-inch (6-cm) case. (MA)

Case (2 cm) of a limnephilid caddisfly, possibly *Limnephilus indivisus*. (MA)

Ylodes cases are similar, up to 22 mm. Some *Lepidostoma* (Lepidostomatidae) cases are similarly spiraled but are no more than 15 mm long.

Two additional phryganeid genera make spiraled cases, but with distinctive differences. In *Banksiola* cases (up to 1.8 inches [4.5 cm]) some of the pieces often have loose, trailing ends. In *Fabria inornata* cases (NE; up to 2.2 inches [5.5 cm]) the pieces all have trailing ends, giving the case a bushy appearance.

Arctopora (Limnephilidae; up to 1.1 inches [2.7 cm]) arranges longer pieces of grass and sedge leaves longitudinally, in no particular pattern. Cases of *Sphagnophylax meiops* (Arctic; up to 17 mm), *Grammotaulius* (N; up to 1.6 inches [4.1 cm]), *Limnephilus* (up to 2 inches [5.1 cm]), *Lenarchus* (N; up to 2.2 inches [5.5 cm]), and *Nemotaulius hostilis* (N; up to 2.8 inches [7 cm]) are similar.

Some *Oecetis* species (Leptoceridae) make cases of short lengths of stems, twigs, or spruce needles placed transversely, up to 15 mm long. The ends of the pieces project beyond the sides of the case, not making neat corners as in brachycentrid cases. Some *Lepidostoma* cases (Lepidostomatidae) are similar but shaggier-looking. Larger cases of transversely arranged leaf pieces likely belong to limnephilids such as *Platycentropus* (up to 1 inch [2.5 cm]) or *Limnephilus*. Those of *L. indivisus* are abundant in vernal pools. *Phanocelia canadensis* (N; up to 10 mm) has been found in bogs, making tubes of transversely arranged sphagnum moss pieces.

Cryptochia cases (Limnephilidae; W; up to 13 mm) are also made of transversely arranged materials, but their shape is distinctive. They are strongly tapered, with a smooth, flattened posterior end.

As with the mineral cases, chances are good that a case that does not match any of these is from a limnephilid. *Anabolia* cases (up to 2 inches [5 cm]) are generally made of pieces of twigs and other plant material arranged lengthwise. Various others make cylindrical cases of irregularly arranged leaf and bark pieces. Those of *Homophylax* (NW; up to 1 inch [2.5 cm]) have distinctively smooth and thin, often flexible walls. The irregular cases of *Hydatophylax* (N) may be up to 3 inches (7.6 cm) long, the largest known cases in North America.

Stationary Aquatic Retreats and Tubes

Invertebrates in both freshwater and marine aquatic environments create stationary homes for themselves. In freshwater habitats, this behavior is found in several insects and a few worms. In the ocean, there are many different kinds of tube-dwelling worms, as well as some crustaceans that live in similar structures.

Freshwater Retreats and Tubes

Members of four caddisfly families spend their whole larval lives in stationary tubular retreats of silk covered with sand grains or other materials. Those in three other families live in retreats that consist of, or are adjacent to, nets or tubes of pure silk. These silken structures were discussed in chapter 6. Some fly larvae and worms also live in tubes, which for the most part bear little resemblance to those of caddisflies.

Caddisfly Larvae

The tube-making caddisflies (Psychomyiidae) make sand- or debris-covered silk tubes on the surfaces of rocks or wood, generally in cool, running water. The well-camouflaged retreat of *Lype diversa* (E) is a slightly arched roof of small pieces of detritus, about 8 mm long and less than 2 mm wide, built over a groove in a submerged piece of wood. *Tinodes* species (W) make flattened tubes of small rock fragments, about 3 mm wide and often several centimeters long, usually on rock surfaces. The meandering tubes of *Psychomyia*, also attached to rocks, are covered with sand grains and may be about 4 mm wide. Western tubes are several centimeters long, but those of

Retreat (about 4 mm wide) of a tube-making caddisfly (Psychomyiidae), probably *Psychomyia*. (CA)

Tubes (3 mm wide) of *Phylocentropus* caddisflies (Dipseudopsidae). (MA)

eastern species are only about 1 cm long. The similar family Xiphocentron-idae is largely restricted to Mexico. The tubes of *Xiphocentron mexico*, which occurs into southern Texas, are up to 2.5 mm wide and 2 inches (5 cm) long, often extending several centimeters above the water surface on wet substrates. *Austrotinodes texensis* (Ecnomidae) is a recently described species, also in southern Texas, with similar habits.

Phylocentropus caddisflies (Dipseudopsidae; E) construct tough, branching, sand- and detritus-covered tubes that are mostly buried in sandy deposits along the margins of streams and lakes. The main tube is up to 6 inches (16 cm) long, and part of it extends more or less vertically from the substrate. The side branch diverges diagonally underground and has its opening at ground level, usually downstream from the other opening. Near the base of the side branch is a bulbous portion containing a net of randomly arranged silk strands. The larva feeds on small organic particles caught in the net as the current flows through the tube. There are often additional, nonfunctional side branches that are sealed off at the base.

Fly Larvae

Most midge larvae (Chironomidae), which range from 2 to 30 mm long, live in delicate tubes of fine particles of silt, algae, or other debris held together with silk. Each genus makes tubes out of particular materials in a particular aquatic habitat. They are usually open at both ends and can have an internal diameter of up to 3 mm. These are usually on or in the bottom sediment, oriented either horizontally or vertically, but tubes of some species are conspicuously attached to plants, rocks, and other solid submerged objects. Some species have movable cases. A larva normally

Tubes (each about 1 mm wide) of chironomid midge larvae on a submerged leaf. (MA)

never leaves its tube, but it may occasionally reach out to gather food. In some cases, a larva spins a tiny net across the inside of the tube to catch food particles, then eats the net, similar to the feeding style of some fungus gnats. Others stretch sticky threads between two arms that stand up at the front of the tube. Larvae pupate inside their tubes.

Antocha crane fly larvae (Tipulidae) live in well-aerated water inside tubes that evidently are similar to those of midges, silk tubes or cases that are open at both ends and often covered with fine debris, small stones, and other materials. Various other crane fly larvae live in silk cases or make them when they are ready to pupate.

Worms

Sludge worms (Naididae) live in stagnant water, where they glue sediment together into short, vertical tubes at their burrow entrances. These are about 1 to 2 mm wide and 2 to 5 mm high. The worms, which are up to about 2 cm long, project most of their bodies out of the tops of their tubes, eating whatever food is within reach.

Manayunkia speciosa (Sabellidae), a polychaete worm, is found in rivers and lakes. It is no more than 5 mm long, but its mud tubes, which are attached at one end to rocks, logs, and other submerged objects, may be several times that length. They are cylindrical, somewhat annulated, straight or bent, and may have up to five branches.

Marine Tubes

A wide variety of invertebrate tubes may be found washed up on beaches or sticking out of the sand at low tide. Just as silk is the foundation for most freshwater tubes, marine tubes are made of various secreted substances, which may or may not have an additional covering of sand or other materials. Most are made by various polychaete worms (Annelida), but horseshoe worms (Phoronida), ribbon worms (Nemertea), and certain crustaceans also make tubes. Many tubes cannot be reliably identified without the organism itself or other clues, but some are distinctive.

A plumed worm (Onuphidae: *Diopatra cuprea*) peeks out of its 15-mm-wide tube at low tide. (MA)

Parchment Tubes Covered by Coarse Debris

Many polychaete tubes are lined with parchmentlike chitinous material and may wash up onshore. At low tide on flat Atlantic beaches, the tubes of plumed worms (Onuphidae: *Diopatra cuprea*) rise above their burrows like upside down Js (inner diameter 5 to 8 mm). The worms glue rocks, shells, and other objects onto the outside to help catch debris to feed on. If you sit and wait by a tube, you might see a tentacled head poke out. The burrows are lined with a tough chitin and extend as much as 39 inches (1 m) below the surface. In Florida, *Americonuphis magna* builds tubes that are similar but tougher, and along the Pacific coast, *D. ornata* and *D. splendidissima* build tubes far out in the very low tide range. Shingle tube worms (Oweniidae: *Owenia fusiformis*) build similar structures, but the shells and sand on their flexible tubes are carefully arranged in an overlapping pattern like roof shingles. Some terebellids also build tubes with attached debris, but these tend to stick straight up rather than curving over.

Parchment Tubes Covered with Fine or No Sediment

Parchment worms (Chaetopteridae: *Chaetopterus*) have tapered tubes that project from either end of their U-shaped burrows. *Mesochaetopterus taylori* builds rusty brown, parchmentlike tubes coated with fine sand, 8 mm in diameter, that stick up 1.2 to 1.6 inches (3 to 4 cm) and extend 6.6 feet (2 m) down. This species is less com-

A 1.5-mm-wide tube of a cellophane tube worm (Chaetopteridae: *Spiochaetopterus*). (WA)

mon than other polychaetes but can be found on both coasts. Dense clusters of 1-mm-wide parchment tubes sticking out of crevices or pilings may be the work of the Pacific species *Phyllochaetopterus prolifica*. Shiny, translucent, grayish tubes 1 to 2 mm in diameter and up to 1 foot (30 cm) long, with distinctive regularly spaced rings, often wash up on Atlantic and Pacific shores. These are the work of cellophane tube worms (Chaetopteridae: *Spiochaetopterus*), which bury their tubes vertically in muddy intertidal and subtidal sand flats. A cellophane tube worm builds its tube one section at a time, rotating as it secretes material from one side of its head. The older sections are the thickest, as the worm continually reinforces the inner walls of its tube with new secretions.

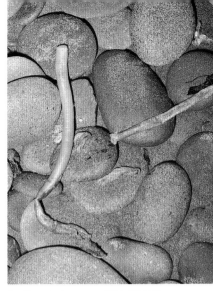

Feather duster worm (Sabellidae) tubes, about 1 cm wide. (WA)

Feather duster worms (Sabellidae) also make leathery tubes that may wash up on the shore. Pencil-thick tubes 8 inches (20 cm) long made by *Schizobranchia insignis* are abundant in northern Pacific harbors. Tubes of northern feather duster worms (*Eudistylia vancouveri*) are more than 1 cm wide. *Myxicola infundibulum* builds thick tubes bound together by transparent mucus and buried in sediment.

The exposed portion of the tubes made by the West Coast *Pista* spaghetti worms (Terebellidae) flares into a mass of tiny tubes like many thin fibers. The worms extend their noodlelike tentacles through these small tubes to feed. Tubes of the Atlantic *Lanice conchilega* are similar. Other terebellids make less distinctive structures, such as the sand-coated tubes that *Thelepus crispus* makes under rocks and the clay tubes of *Neoamphitrite robusta* (both on the Pacific coast).

Horseshoe worms (Phoronida) secrete parchmentlike tubes with sand grains and other material embedded in them. These include the chitinous burrows (4 inches [10 cm] long) of *Phoronis psammophila*.

A few ribbon worms (Tubulanidae: *Tubulanus* and Lineidae: *Micrura*) live in thin, fragile, cellophanelike tubes attached to the undersides of rocks.

Thin, Sandy Tubes

Soda straw worms (Onuphidae: *Kinbergonuphis jenneri*; SE) build sand tubes 5 mm wide that stick a few centimeters straight up out of anaerobic beaches. On the ground around them, you may find the worms' small, dark droppings, which have been described as closely resembling the chocolate sprinkles used on cupcakes. The tubes are lined with thin, grayish parchment. *Onuphis eremita* makes tubes that are similar but smaller. Those of *Mooreonuphis nebulosa* are harder and more irregular, and also incorporate shells.

Tubes like these 5-mm-wide ones are made by a variety of polychaete worms. (MA)

Vertical sand or mud tubes made by bamboo worms (Maldanidae) are much more fragile; they will break easily if you pull on them, whereas tubes of soda straw worms are fairly stretchy. Polychaetes that feed with the head end up may intentionally build tubes that project above the surface of the sediment, but maldanids feed head-down, and they have no need to reach high up into the water column. Their tubes typically form as burrows belowground, becoming more visible as the sediment around them is eroded away. Dark fecal deposits accumulate around maldanid tubes as the worms suck sediment from below and expel their wastes out the top. Some bamboo worms, such as *Clymenella torquata*, also use their hind ends to scrape surface sediments toward their burrows, making series of traces like spokes on a wheel. *Petaloproctus socialis* produces dense, hard reefs of adjacent sandy tubes in coarse-sand flats.

The fragile, slightly curved, cone-shaped sand tubes of trumpet or "ice cream cone" worms (Pectinariidae: *Pectinaria*) can be found washed up on beaches. They are one sand grain thick, with the larger particles at the wider end, and are up to 2 inches (5 cm) long. When occupied, just the tip sticks out of the sand near the low-tide mark in intertidal flats.

Hard Tubes Attached to Submerged Objects

Limy tube worms (Serpulidae) secrete hard, white, calcareous tubes. When one retreats into its tube, it seals off the entrance with a specialized flap. Sometimes they bore into rock beneath their tubes. *Hydroides* tubes are loosely coiled. *Serpula vermicularis* has a coiled, rambling tube up to 4 inches (10 cm) long. *Filograna implexa* forms tangled networks of long, thin tubes, the whole bundle under 6 mm in diameter. *Ficopomatus enigmaticus*, introduced from Australia, is even found in freshwater lakes near the California coast. Its 2-mm-wide tubes, flared at both ends, occur in

Tube (2 cm) of a limy tube worm (Serpulidae) on an oyster shell. The holes were made by a boring sponge. (MA)

large aggregations. Serpulid tubes could be confused with the shells of worm snails (Vermetidae), but the snail shells have shiny interiors and three shell layers instead of two.

The related Spirorbidae make similar calcareous tubes, but these are in the form of tightly coiled, flat spirals, no more than 3 mm across. *Spirorbis spirillum* and *S. violaceus* make counterclockwise coils (starting from the center). *S. borealis* makes smooth clockwise coils, whereas *S. granulatus* makes clockwise coils with two to three longitudinal ridges.

Sabellariids build strong, rigid, interconnected tubes of sand and mud that coat any hard object in the water, even beverage cans. Those of *Neosabellaria cementarium* are typically found in oyster bed communities. Colonies of *Sabellaria*, known as sand builder worms or mason worms, construct reeflike aggregations out of many well-cemented sand tubes. Colonies more than 1 foot (30 cm) wide can be found in California and southeastern Florida.

Soft Tubes

Soft tubes made of mud or other sediment, either buried or attached to rocks, are made by several types of polychaetes, including the mud worms (Spionidae) and fringed worms (Cirratulidae). Members of the Ampharetidae build tubes of mud or other debris attached to sponges, mollusk shells, or colonial sea squirts. Clam worms (Nereididae: *Nereis*) construct sandy tubes held together by mucus on clam shells. The oyster mud worm (*Polydora websteri*) forms its tube on the inside edge of a live oyster shell, provoking the oyster to build shell over the tube and enclose the worm in a blister.

Crustacean Tubes

Marine tubes may also be the work of amphipods. Ampeliscids build flattened, gray, parchmentlike tubes that project a few centimeters out of the sediment at the bases of plants in seagrass meadows. These and other amphipods may form large aggregations of tubes. Corophiids make crude, fragile tubes of mud and algae, and their colonies form thick mats on submerged objects. *Leptocheirus pilosus* (Aoridae) builds a short, flattened tube out of mud and tiny debris particles on a smooth surface of seaweed or a rock. It is about 4 mm long, open at both ends, with the substrate forming the bottom wall. *Amphitoe* (Melitidae) uses a silklike substance to bind together coarse debris into a straight, cylindrical tube attached to seaweed.

Tanaids are another group of small (up to about 5 mm), tube-building crustaceans. Some leptocheliids can be extremely abundant in muddy areas, where they build soft tubes of detritus.

The 1.4-inch (3.5-cm) retreat of a desertshrub spider (Diguetidae: *Diguetia*). (AZ)

Spider Retreats

Several unrelated kinds of spiders use foreign materials to build retreats. Some of these are part of webs and were described in chapter 6. The vertical debris tubes of desertshrub spiders (Diguetidae: *Diguetia*), up to a few inches long, may be found hanging from cacti and desert shrubs when nothing else is left of the web. Retreats of the more broadly distributed *Metepeira* species (Araneidae; labyrinth spiders and their relatives) can be similar. These may have fuzzy balls of silk incorporated in them, which are the old, dismantled orb webs. Two other spiders build distinctive shelters on the undersides of objects.

Cicurina bryantae (Dictynidae) constructs unique retreats of organic debris on the undersides of rotting logs in the Smoky Mountains. The retreat is a tube, up to about 20 mm long, with an opening at each end. The openings are often turretlike, and they both face down (away from the log) rather than away from each other. Sometimes short silk strands connect the turrets to the substrate, and these may alert the spider to passing prey. Retreats of immature spiders may be as small as 2 mm.

Zodarion rubidum (Zodariidae) is a tiny ant-eating spider that has been introduced from Europe to scattered locations in the United States and Canada. It constructs 2- to 3-mm igloo-shaped retreats on the undersides of rocks and sometimes logs, usually near the entrance to an ant nest.

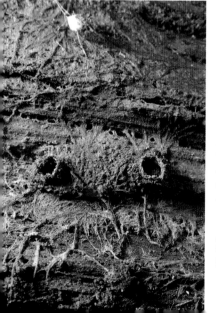

A small spider, *Cicurina bryantae* (Dictynidae), built this 18-mm-long retreat on the underside of a log. (TN)

Retreat (about 3 mm) of the tiny spider *Zodarion rubidum* (Zodariidae), on the underside of a rock. (CO) Photo by Paula E. Cushing, Denver Museum of Nature & Science.

These retreats are largely made of tiny pebbles, but may incorporate plant material, built on a framework of silk. Some retreats have visible entrance openings, but some spiders plug their entrances with pebbles or soil particles. The retreats are used for resting, molting, and concealing the tiny egg sacs.

Nests of Bees, Ants, and Wasps

Bees, ants, and wasps prepare many different kinds of structures for rearing their offspring. Many dig burrows for this purpose, which are discussed in chapter 16. Others use secreted wax, collected mud, manufactured paper, or other materials to build single nest cells or elaborate multicelled nests. The cells are provisioned either with pollen and nectar or with various insect or spider prey, each species having a particular type of prey that it collects. Therefore, in the less distinctive nests, prey remains are an important clue to the identity of the builder.

Wax Nests of Social Bees

Social bees (Apidae: Apinae) make nests using wax secreted from their abdomens. The only social bees in North America are bumblebees (*Bombus*), which make their cells from a mixture of pollen and wax, and the introduced European honeybee (*Apis mellifera*), which uses almost pure wax, sealing small gaps with propolis, a sticky substance derived from plants. Both usually nest in concealed places.

A queen bumblebee begins a nest by constructing a roughly spherical cell containing pollen paste and several eggs. She also builds a cup-shaped "honey pot," which she fills with nectar that she feeds on. The larvae feed on the pollen, and after a while, she makes an opening in the cell and feeds them a mixture of pollen and honey. When mature, they spin thin

The nest of a bumblebee, *Bombus perplexus* (Apidae), in the fiberglass insulation of a house wall. (MD) Photo by David Inouye.

A honeybee (Apidae: *Apis mellifera*) nest, exposed when a hollow tree was cut. (MA)

Silken galleries of wax moths (Pyralidae: Galleriinae) in a honeybee nest. (MA)

cocoons, emerging as workers that forage and build more brood cells and honey pots while the queen continues to lay eggs. The brood cells are often built in parallel lines, but the nest basically looks like an irregular mass of round, yellowish brown balls. After cells have produced adults, they are cleaned out, strengthened with wax, and used to store pollen and honey. Nests are typically on or below the ground and may be in abandoned mammal burrows, in bird nests, or under rocks. Sometimes they are made in the insulation between walls of houses or in the space under neglected lawn mowers. Species in the subgenus *Psithyrus* make egg cells in the center of other bumblebee nests, and their offspring are raised by their hosts.

Unlike bumblebees and social wasps, a honeybee queen begins her nest not alone, but with the help of a swarm of workers from an existing colony. The nest consists of vertically aligned slabs of honeycomb, each one being two flat layers of open hexagonal cells constructed back to back. The small cells are used to raise workers or store pollen. Larger cells are built for drones and to store honey. Queen cells are still larger and are separate oval structures, something like bumblebee brood cells, and they hang down vertically from the comb. Larvae are fed for several days, then the cells are capped and the larvae spin cocoons in which to pupate. Wild honeybees usually build their nests in cavities such as hollow trees, but if they are unable to find a suitable one, they make exposed combs suspended from a branch.

Larvae of several pyralid moths infest bee nests. Greater wax moth larvae (*Galleria mellonella*) tunnel through the wax and spin silken galleries in which they hide, feeding mostly on debris and remains of cocoons rather than on the wax itself. They then pupate in their own tough, white cocoons on the side of the hive. The lesser wax moth (*Achroia grisella*) has similar habits. Healthy bees are able to defend themselves, so these larvae mostly occur in weakened or abandoned hives. They are, however, common pests of commercial beehives, and their burrowing drains the honey. Bee moth larvae (*Aphomia sociella*) live in nests of both bees and wasps, spinning long, soft, and woolly, but extremely tough cocoons in which they pupate. *Vitula edmandsii* is also recorded as feeding on bumblebee nest cells.

Bee lice (Braulidae: *Braula coeca*) are tiny, wingless flies that develop in honeybee hives. Females lay white eggs, which are oval with two lateral flanges, in various places in the hive. Only those that are laid on caps of honey cells hatch, and the larvae make tunnels that look like fine fractures on the inner surfaces of the caps. In heavily infested combs, these tunnels are visible from the outside, as are the tiny exit holes made by emerging adults.

Paper Constructions

Social vespid wasps build their nests out of paper that they make by chewing wood pulp and mixing it with a proteinaceous secretion from their labial glands. They apply the pulp in lines that are visible as different shades of gray or brown in the walls of the nest. Certain ants produce a similar papery material. The paper made by both wasps and ants is known as *carton*.

Paper Wasps

Paper wasps (Vespidae: Polistinae) make a nest in the form of a horizontal cluster or disc of paper cells, similar in form to honeycomb. This hangs from a central stalk that is dark and shiny, composed mainly of the labial

Left: Nest of *Polistes metricus* (Vespidae), a paper wasp. Two eggs and a larva are visible in the cells. (NJ) *Right:* A *Polistes annularis* nest. The domed-over cells contain pupae. (MS)

Left: Nests of red wasps (probably *Polistes perplexus*) suspended from old nests from a previous year. (TN) *Right: Mischocyttarus mexicanus* (Vespidae) nest (2 cm) on the underside of a palm frond. (FL)

gland secretion. One or more overwintering females begin a nest, and one becomes dominant and is the only one to lay eggs or eats the others' eggs. The larvae are generally fed prechewed caterpillars, and they spin domes of silk over their cells when they are ready to pupate. *Polistes* nests are usually gray and composed mostly of long wood fibers. The individual cells are larger than 3 mm wide. Some species lay their eggs in the nests of other *Polistes* species. *Mischocyttarus* species (S, W) are smaller, and their nest cells are no more than 3 mm wide. They may be gray or brown and are composed mostly of short chips rather than long fibers.

Yellowjackets and Hornets

Yellowjackets and hornets (Vespinae) construct discs of cells similar to those of paper wasps, but they are surrounded by an envelope of paper with an entrance at the bottom. Generally, nests that hang in exposed places, such as from branches or eaves of houses, belong to *Dolichovespula* species; *Vespula* species usually build theirs in underground cavities or hollow logs and other concealed places close the ground (occasionally in more elevated places such as the hollow walls of houses). Rarely, *Dolichovespula* species make underground nests and *Vespula* species make aboveground nests in somewhat exposed places such as dense shrubs. In the spring, an overwintering queen begins by making a few hexagonal cells, with an egg laid in each one and a round paper covering 1 inch (2.5 cm) or so in diameter. The initial offspring, when mature, enlarge the nest and tend additional larvae, feeding them prechewed insect prey. They eat away the inner layers of the envelope and add it to the outside along with new material. The nest soon has a thick, many-layered envelope and a stack of several *Polistes*-like combs

Left: Small, aborted "queen nest" of an aerial yellowjacket (Vespidae: *Dolichovespula arenaria*). (MA) *Right:* "Queen nest" of a bald-faced hornet (*Dolichovespula maculata*), with the beginnings of an entrance tube. The nest is 2.4 inches (6 cm) high. (MA)

on the inside. Nests are killed off by freezing temperatures, with just the queens overwintering to found new ones, but in warm climates, a nest can survive for several years and grow to be many feet high. Small, aborted "queen nests" are commonly seen, resulting from the queen being eaten or otherwise meeting an untimely end.

Dolichovespula nests are grayish and durable, made of strong fibers from weathered wood such as fence posts. Several

Right: A more ragged-looking aerial yellowjacket nest. (VT) *Below left:* Mature bald-faced hornet nest. (MA) *Below right:* Aerial yellowjacket nest. (TN)

Underground nest of downy yellowjackets (Vespidae: *Vespula flavopilosa*). The exposed portion is 3 inches (7 cm) across. (MA)

characteristics distinguish the nests of the two common species. A bald-faced hornet (*D. maculata*) nest that is just being started usually has a long, narrow entrance tube at the bottom, lacking in the young nests of aerial yellowjackets (*D. arenaria*). The outer envelope of an older bald-faced hornet nest usually has a scalloped appearance, especially near the top, whereas aerial yellowjacket nests usually are not scalloped. A bald-faced hornet nest also has larger stripes than an aerial yellowjacket nest.

The introduced German yellowjacket (*V. germanica*) occasionally nests in the open, making nests with gray paper as *Dolichovespula* species do, sometimes more than 39 inches (1 m) across. The arcs of paper in the envelope are usually less than 4 inches (10 cm) wide and overlapping, whereas *Dolichovespula* nests often have independent arcs that are wider than that or even extend all the way around. Dissection of *Dolichovespula* nests reveals that the envelope has a smooth, nearly continuous inner surface, and the combs are usually curved upward somewhat at the edges. A German yellowjacket nest envelope usually has a rough, pocketed inner surface, and the combs (as with other *Vespula* species) are flat.

In addition to the German yellowjacket, *V. pensylvanica* and *V. squamosa* also make concealed nests with supple, bluish gray envelopes. The other *Vespula* species make brownish, brittle paper from decayed wood fibers. The European hornet (*Vespa crabro*; introduced in E), too, makes a brown, brittle nest; it is usually concealed in an aboveground cavity such as a hollow tree or man-made structure, but it may be exposed or, rarely, underground. Whereas yellowjacket nests are usually completely enclosed by their envelopes, hornet nest envelopes often have broad openings below the combs and may consist only of sheets closing the opening to the cavity in which the nest is built. In a very sheltered site, the envelope may be missing entirely, whereas an exposed hornet nest has a complete paper covering. The older cells in a hornet nest are mostly over 6 mm across, but they are usually less than 5 mm across in yellowjacket nests.

Mexican Honey Wasp

The Mexican honey wasp (*Brachygastra mellifica*), common in Mexico and southern Texas, also makes aerial nests with a papery covering. They tend to be about 1 foot (30.5 cm) across, with an envelope consisting of a single sheet. Rather than containing horizontal combs inside, the nest is a series of concentric spheres, each with a layer of hexagonal cells that uses the previous outer wall as its base. A typical nest has fifty thousand cells, some of which are used to store honey. There are several entrances, and spiral passageways connect the layers of cells. Two *Polybia* species have been found as far north as Nogales, Arizona. Their nests are of similar construction, but with a single exit hole on the side or bottom.

A Mexican honey wasp (Vespidae: *Brachygastra mellifica*) nest. Note the new layer of brood cells being started on the bottom. (TX) Photo by Jason Penney.

Ants

A few ants in the genus *Crematogaster* also manufacture a papery material from plant fibers. *C. atkinsoni* makes carton nests on vegetation in southeastern freshwater and salt marshes. They are often more or less spherical and around the size of a tennis ball, but the first nest described was elongate, about 18 inches (45 cm) tall and 12 inches (30 cm) in circumference. The material is light gray, similar to the color of paper nests made by vespid wasps, but darker internally. The walls are thicker, and the nest's overall appearance is lumpier and more irregular than that of wasp nests. The nests may be up to a few feet from the ground, keeping the ants high and dry in their wetland habitat. In southwestern mountains, *C. emeryana* often constructs carton structures under rocks. Texas shed-builder ants (*C. lineolata*; E) build shedlike shields of chewed vegetable matter over the honeydew-producing insects (such as aphids, mealybugs, scale insects, and lycaenid caterpillars) that they tend. These small, cardboardlike structures usually surround twigs. Imported fire ants (*Solenopsis*) in the Southeast construct sheds somewhat similar to these, but theirs are flimsy structures made by loosely attaching bits of dead plant debris. Wesson and Wesson (1940) described a large carton nest of *C. lineolata* found in a clump of grass in an open meadow as "a thick, flaky and rather fragile . . . upright cigar-shaped struc-

The distinctive carton nest of *Crematogaster atkinsoni*, an acrobat ant (Formicidae). This nest measures about 2.4 inches (6 cm). (FL) Photo by Pete Diamond.

ture about 18 cm high, bluntly pointed above, about 10 cm in diameter at the widest point a little below the middle and with the narrower bottom resting in the middle of the base of the clump."

Some eastern *Dolichoderus* ants also make carton nests. The nest of *D. plagiatus* may consist of a curled dead leaf or a hollowed stem with the gaps sealed with carton. *D. pustulatus* nests can be more substantial, consisting of an irregular, oval or oblong carton chamber about 1 inch (2.5 cm) long, with a 6- to 18-mm entrance tube sticking out of the side, built at the base of a grass clump. The material is hard and firm, thinner and made of finer particles than *Crematogaster* nests.

A few other ants make less conspicuous use of manufactured carton. *Liometopum* species (W) nest under bark, in crevices of trees, or under objects on the ground, subdividing their nest chambers with a network of paperlike material. *Camponotus ulcerosus* (TX, AZ, Mexico) nests in soil under rocks. Ants of this species build a carton shield at the nest entrance, with an opening just the right size for a worker to plug with its head to keep out intruders.

Mud Cells Attached to Rocks, Vegetation, or Other Objects

Several kinds of solitary wasps and bees attach more or less conspicuous mud or clay structures to various objects. These nests are made from little balls of mud carried one at a time from wet places nearby. Some are very distinctive, whereas others are best distinguished by the food stored inside. Smaller mud cells may be eggs of ground beetles.

Black and Yellow Mud Dauber

The widespread black and yellow mud dauber (Sphecidae: *Sceliphron caementarium*) constructs cylindrical cells, up to about 1.6 inches (4 cm) long and around 15 mm wide, and stuffs each one full of paralyzed spiders before laying an egg on one of them and sealing it. Often a row of several

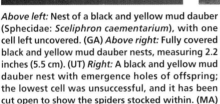

Above left: Nest of a black and yellow mud dauber (Sphecidae: *Sceliphron caementarium*), with one cell left uncovered. (GA) *Above right:* Fully covered black and yellow mud dauber nests, measuring 2.2 inches (5.5 cm). (UT) *Right:* A black and yellow mud dauber nest with emergence holes of offspring; the lowest cell was unsuccessful, and it has been cut open to show the spiders stocked within. (MA)

parallel cells is built, and another parallel row may be stacked on top. Generally the artistry of the individual cells is hidden by a smooth or lumpy blanket of additional mud that covers the whole nest. The larva within each cell feeds on the spiders, spinning a thin, papery, reddish brown cocoon when it is mature. In the spring, it pupates, becomes an adult, and chews through the side of the cell to emerge. These nests may be in hidden places such as the undersides of rocks but are often conspicuously placed under the shelter of overhanging ledges or roofs of man-made structures. *S. assimile*, found in Mexico and Texas, evidently makes similar nests.

Organ Pipe Mud Dauber

The organ pipe mud dauber (Crabronidae: *Trypoxylon politum*; E) gets its name from the parallel rows of long mud tubes that it

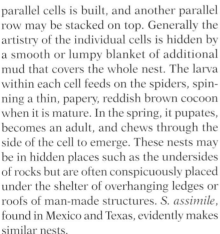

An organ pipe mud dauber (Crabronidae: *Trypoxylon politum*) nest, 6 inches (15 cm) long. (NC)

A pollen wasp (Vespidae: *Pseudomasaris*) nest, about 1 inch (2.5 cm). Look closely and you will see the outline of six or so stacked cells, aligned parallel to the stem. (CA) Photo by Kolby Kirk.

builds. Each tube is built similarly to *Sceliphron* cells, by applying mud in a series of slanted arches, but the tubes are partitioned into multiple cells and may be up to around 6 inches (15 cm) long. The tubes are not covered with additional mud. As with *Sceliphron*, each cell is stocked with several spiders, and an egg is laid on one of them.

Pollen Wasps

The nests of pollen wasps (Vespidae: *Pseudomasaris*; W) are most similar to those of *Sceliphron*, but they are substantially smaller and stocked with pollen and nectar rather than spiders. They consist of one or more elongate, parallel, cylindrical cells. Among the nests that have been described, all have been attached to the sides or undersides of rocks except for those of *P. vespoides*, which may attach its nests to twigs. The cells are often arranged in small, stacked clumps, but on rock surfaces, a dozen or so may be found in a row with their tops perfectly aligned. They often are covered with additional soil, obscuring the individual cells, as with *Sceliphron* nests. The nests of *P. edwardsii* have been most clearly described. Each cell is 14 to 21 mm long and 5 to 6 mm wide, with thin walls of even thickness (0.25 to 1 mm) and a smooth, flat, somewhat thicker cap, flush with the end of the cell. The cells that are attached to the substrate are incomplete cylinders, with the rock forming part of the wall.

Potter Wasps

Potter wasps (Vespidae: Eumeninae) in the genus *Eumenes* make conspicuous aerial mud nests attached to twigs or other objects. *E. fraternus* and most others in the genus build roughly spherical nests, about 12 mm wide, that are usually attached to twigs. When first built, the nest has a distinctive flared opening suggestive of the mouth of a jug. As with all potter wasp nests, the mother stocks it with caterpillars or sometimes larvae of sawflies or leaf beetles. She then lays a single egg near the entrance (the habit of

Left: Nests of a potter wasp (Vespidae: *Eumenes*). The one on the left has not yet been closed, and part of a green caterpillar is visible in the opening. The nests each measure 13 mm. (TN) *Right:* Finished nest (14 mm) of a potter wasp (*Eumenes*) made from sandier mud. (SC)

laying an egg on the wall of the cell rather than on the stored prey distinguishes vespids from sphecids) and seals it with a last mud pellet. Sometimes several are built in a row. The nest of *E. verticalis* is attached to a rock surface and differs from other described *Eumenes* nests in being a hemispherical dome rather than a complete spheroid.

Some other potter wasps are known to build exposed aerial nests, and again, the nests of many species have not been described. *Ancistrocerus lutonidus* (E) nests appear externally as irregular lumps of coarse clay built around small twigs. They are 1 inch (2.5 cm) or so across and may be lumpy or have a fairly smooth, continuous covering. The cells are near the center, arranged somewhat radially, and have a thin silky lining. A nest may have six to twenty or more cells, and the mature wasps emerge through round openings gnawed in the clay. The number of wasps that emerge is generally greater than the number of exit holes. Frost (1959) attributed identical nests to *Stenodynerus anormis*, but this appears to have been an error. The only described nest of *Euodynerus annectens* (SE) apparently was similar, 2.3 inches (6 cm) across, containing twenty-one kidney-shaped cells that surrounded a twig. *Parancistrocerus vagus* also makes multicellular mud nests attached to branches.

This 2-cm-wide potter wasp (Vespidae: Eumeninae) nest consists of three cells built into pits in a wall and obscured by a thick covering of additional mud. (VT)

Spider wasp nests (Pompilidae: Auplopodini) found between logs in a wood pile. The nests are each about 15 mm. (MI) Photo by Tamar Charney.

Spider Wasps

Spider wasps (Pompilidae) in the genus *Auplopus* make thimble-shaped mud cells, about 10 to 15 mm long and 7 to 10 mm wide, often under stones or bark but sometimes in crevices on walls. Some build their cells in cavities such as the abandoned cells of paper wasp and mud dauber nests. Unlike *Sceliphron* and *Trypoxylon*, they stock each cell with just one spider and usually amputate one or more of its legs. The closely related *Phanagenia bombycina* (E) makes similar nests. *Ceropales* species sneak an egg into a spider captured by these and other spider wasps before it has been placed in the nest. The *Ceropales* larva eats the host's egg and then feeds on its spider.

Pison koreense (Crabronidae), introduced from Asia, makes oval to cashew-shaped mud nests, fairly similar to those of spider wasps but smaller. They are 6 to 10 mm long and 4 to 5 mm wide, constructed singly or in variably arranged clusters of up to a dozen. Each is provisioned with twenty or more small spiders.

Mason Bees

Osmia mason bees (Megachilidae) construct small, earthen cells, singly or in clusters. They may be located on twigs, on or under stones, in burrows, or inside twigs, empty galls, rotting wood, or other hidden places. Some are made of pure clay, and others may include plant fragments. They are about 12 mm long and 7 mm wide, oval, and somewhat contracted at the upper end just before the flattened, oblique lid. Each one contains a single developing larva and is provisioned with pollen and nectar. The larvae spin tough cocoons before pupating inside.

Packard (1878, 1892) described similarly shaped *Osmia simillima* and *Ancistrocerus catskill* (Eumeninae) cells found in old oak apple galls. They are about the same length, but the *Ancistrocerus* cells are narrower, with a corrugated appearance, and thinly lined on the inside with silk, rather than parchmentlike on the outside and "shining mahogany-colored" on the inside. The mature wasp makes a hole in the end of its cell to emerge, whereas the mature bee cuts out a longitudinal ovate lid almost as large as one side of the cell, attached to the posterior end by a hinge. *A. catskill* sometimes builds its nests in exposed locations, but this is more typical of *A. waldenii*. In both species, exposed nest clusters may have mud smeared over them so that individual cells are poorly defined.

Ground Beetles

Certain ground beetles (Carabidae) enclose their eggs in distinctive mud cells, which may be attached to rocks, stems, bark, or the undersides of leaves up to several feet above the ground. Some *Chlaenius* species enclose each egg in its own smooth, oblong cell, 2.5 to 5 mm long, with a distinct lid or flap. Others may enclose up to about 20 eggs in a single cell. Similar mud cells are also made by *Brachinus* (bombardier beetles), *Calosoma*, *Carabus*, *Galerita*, and *Pterostichus*.

Mud Partitions in Old Wasp Nests, Hollow Stems, and Other Cavities

Many wasps and bees, rather than constructing complete mud cells, make nests in existing cavities by building simple mud partitions. For the most part, looking for remains of the provisions—one spider, multiple spiders, caterpillars, or pollen and nectar—is the only way to tell these nests apart. Examining the wasp's cocoon is also helpful in some cases.

The blue mud dauber (Sphecidae: *Chalybion californicum*) often reuses old nests of black and yellow mud daubers, packing a cell full of spiders just as its original maker did. One individual was observed to open an active nest, remove the spiders, and replace them with her own, and this has often been mistakenly reported as the normal mode of operation. A refurbished nest can be recognized by the glob of mud used to seal the original inhabitant's exit hole, often a different color or texture than the rest of the cell. *C. zimmermanni* (S) has similar habits.

Trypoxylon species other than *T. politum* are known as "keyhole wasps" because they nest in small preexisting cavities such as keyholes, knotholes, wood borings, hollow stems, and chinks in walls, sealing the openings with mud or clay. They sometimes use old mud dauber nests, but they are usually much smaller than *Chalybion* species (which can also be found nesting in these other cavities), and they make mud partitions within the mud dauber cells to produce cells more suited to their size. (*T. clavatum* (E), however, is large enough that it does not need to make partitions.) They similarly partition stems and larger chinks, and store many small spiders in each cell. Those in the subgenus *Trypoxylon* spin delicate silken cocoons in their cells, except for *T. johnsoni* (E), which makes a brittle cocoon incorporating sand from the cell partition. Species in the subgenus *Trypargilum* make cocoons incorporating silk, other salivary secretions, and mud from the cell partitions, and as far as is known, each species makes a distinctly different cocoon. *Pisonopsis birkmanni* (SW) makes linear series of cells in hollow stems, similar to those of related *Trypoxylon* species.

Left: Cavities in a hose rack neatly filled with nests of an *Ancistrocerus* potter wasp (Vespidae: Eumeninae; probably *A. catskill*). The triangles are each 1 cm tall. (WA) Photo by Lynette Schimming. *Right:* A potter wasp nest (Eumeninae) built over a screw in a car's license plate fixture. The wasp that developed inside has emerged. (MA)

Other than *Eumenes* and the other species already noted, most potter and mason wasps (Vespidae: Eumeninae) make mud cells in preexisting cavities, such as crevices in rocks, empty galls, sawfly cocoons, old insect burrows in the ground, and abandoned mud dauber or paper wasp cells. Many, such as *Monobia quadridens* and *Pseudodynerus quadrisectus*, make mud partitions in wood borings or hollow stems. Like their relatives, they stock their cells with moth, leaf beetle, or sawfly larvae, and the head capsules of the larvae may remain in old nests as a clue to their inhabitants. Whereas *Eumenes* species nearly finish their "pots" before filling them, these species collect their prey first. We once came upon a small pile of beetle larvae in a round cavity in a rock and watched as a potter wasp made many trips from a nearby stream, applying clay spirally from the edges of the opening until it had created a flat disc, flush with the surrounding rock surface, that completely walled them in. We have since seen similar nests in knotholes of pine boards and covering a screw in a car's license plate fixture.

Hoplitis producta, a mason bee (Megachilidae), nests in the hollow stems of sumac and other pithy plants, excavating the pith if necessary. It uses a mixture of clay and plant material to partition off a few cells at the bottom of the tunnel. Each cell contains one egg and is supplied with pollen and nectar. A space is left between the last cell and the entrance, which is walled off. Some *Osmia* mason bees, in constructing their mud nests, may plaster over natural and man-made cavities with openings much larger than themselves.

Nest Cells Using Materials Other Than Mud

Many other bees and wasps make nest cells in pithy stems (such as sumac, blackberry, and elderberry) and wood borings by building partitions of plant matter or various other materials.

Nest of a grass wasp (Sphecidae: *Isodontia*) in an abandoned carpenter bee hole. (TN) Photo by Adam Charney.

Grass Wasps

Three species of grass wasps (Sphecidae: *Isodontia*) use grass stems and blades to construct their nests in wood borings, hollow stems, and old burrows of ground-nesting bees. The grass used to plug the entrance hole is sometimes very conspicuous. Spanish moss and fibrous inner bark may also be used. Nests of *I. auripes* (E) consist of one large brood chamber containing several larvae; *I. elegans* (W) makes individual nests separated by partitions. *I. mexicana* (E, SW) usually uses the former construction but occasionally separates the larvae with flimsy partitions. This species sometimes nests in pitcher plants. All three provision their nests mostly with tree crickets, but at times with other crickets or katydids.

Leafcutter and Resin Bees

The cylindrical, rounded cells made by *Megachile* leafcutter bees (Megachilidae) are unmistakable. Each cell is a neat little packet, about 1 cm long, consisting of several layers of oval and circular pieces of leaves or flower petals.

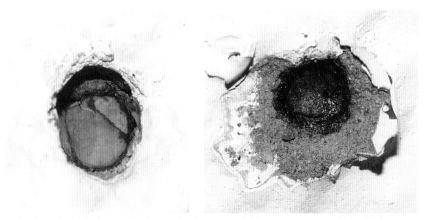

Left: The end of a leafcutter bee (Megachilidae: *Megachile*) nest cell (6 mm wide), visible at the opening of a hole in a wall. (MA) *Right:* Another leafcutter bee nest hole in the same wall, sealed over with resin. This one is 4 mm wide. (MA)

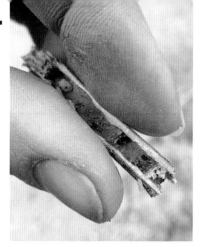
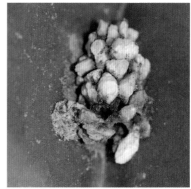

Left: Nest partitions of a resin bee (Megachilidae) in a 5-mm-wide palo verde twig. (AZ)
Right: The 1-cm single-cell nest of a resin bee (Megachilidae: Anthidiini), attached to the side of a cactus. (AZ)

They may be found in ground burrows, under stones, or in other nooks, as well as in hollow stems. Waiting in line at an auto shop, we once watched leafcutter bees carrying leaf fragments into circular holes in the cinder-block walls of the building. From the outside, green leaves were apparent blocking the holes just a few millimeters deep, although in some holes the leaves were obscured by a dark yellowish substance, and others had not yet been stuffed full. As with all solitary bee nests, each cell contains one developing larva and is provisioned with a paste made from pollen and nectar.

Other megachilid bees use irregular leaf pieces in cell construction. Some (e.g., some *Anthidium* species) use down from hairy stems and leaves to construct their nests. Still others (known as resin bees) use resin, sometimes mixed with sand or other materials, in the construction of cells and plugging of entrance holes. Some western *Anthidiellum* and *Dianthidium* species make oval, 1-cm-long, single-celled nests of resin that are more or less covered with pebbles. These may be attached to leaves, twigs, or exposed rock faces, or may be in more hidden places such as the undersides of rocks.

The use of resin does not always indicate the work of resin bees. *Passaloecus cuspidatus*, an aphid wasp (Crabronidae: Pemphredoninae), nests in 3- to 5-mm-wide preexisting galleries in wood, using pine resin to make partitions between its cells, which are stocked with aphids. Before constructing her cells, the female spreads resin in a ring around the nest entrance, and when she is done, she plugs it with resin. She then camouflages it by placing wood and bark fragments on the sticky surface.

Plasterer Bees

Yellow-faced bees (Colletidae: *Hylaeus*) nest in cavities such as preexisting burrows or hollow stems, generally in the outer few inches. They line their cells with saliva, which dries as a thin, glistening, transparent, cellophane-like material. Cellophane bees (*Colletes*) make cells of the same substance, but in burrows they dig in the ground.

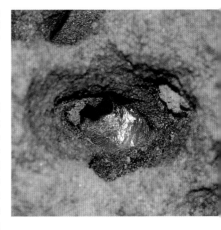

"Cellophane" of a yellow-faced bee (Colletidae: *Hylaeus*) at the entrance to its nest in an old *Macrotera opuntiae* burrow. The patch of "cellophane" measures 5 mm across. (CA)

Small Carpenter Bees

Small carpenter bees (Apidae: *Ceratina*) hollow out pithy-stemmed plants such as elderberry, blackberry, or lilac, often to a depth of 6 to 7 inches (15 to 18 cm). They then construct three to six cells, about 3 mm wide, using bits of pith to make the partitions and provisioning them with a paste of pollen and nectar. When a female has finished making her nest, she sits in the space above the last cell and waits until her young have become adults and chewed through the partitions. The stem is cleaned out, and one of the daughters reuses it to make her own nest. Small carpenter bees are unable to bore into the sides of stems and twigs, and thus require a cut or broken stem to access the pith. They may also use cavities of wood-boring insects, cracks between shingles, or crevices of stone walls.

Wasps

Aphid wasps (Crabronidae: Pemphredoninae) make partitions in pithy stems similar to those of small carpenter bees but provision them with aphids. In wider stems, they make branching tunnels rather than excavating all of the pith. The tunnels are 3 to 5 mm wide, and the cells are about 8 to 9 mm long. Partitions made of bits of pith may be absent or may be up to 1.1 inch (27 mm) thick. The square-headed wasps *Crossocerus* and *Ectemnius* (Crabroninae) make nests in pithy stems that they provision with flies, and *Lestica* does the same with moths. Some members of each of these genera, as well as some aphid wasps, excavate branched galleries in rotting wood, making partitions of sawdust and beetle frass. *Mimumesa* species (Pemphredoninae) do the same, provisioning with leafhoppers.

Leptochilus erubescens and *L. periallis* (Eumeninae; W) nest in pithy stems and are unusual among potter and mason wasps in abandoning mud and using only

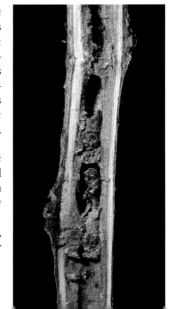

Small carpenter bee (Apidae: *Ceratina*) nest cells, one of which contains a dead bee, in an 8-mm-wide sumac twig. (MA)

chewed pith to construct partitions. The former stocks cells with beetle larvae, and the latter with moth larvae. *L. rufinodus* and related species make composite partitions, each consisting of a layer of mud or sand on top of a layer of chewed pith. The cells are stocked with leaf-mining beetle larvae. After consuming these, the mature wasp larva moves through the pith layer into the earthen layer and incorporates the soil particles into its silken cocoon.

Dipogon spider wasps make linear series of nest cells in preexisting cavities in wood. The nest partitions consist of debris, such as bits of leaves and wood, dead insects, and caterpillar droppings, with an outer layer of packed soil. As with other pompilid nests, each cell contains a single spider.

Parasites of Bee and Wasp Nests

In investigating bee and wasp nests, you are likely to encounter sign of various nest parasites. Those that are specific to social bees were noted earlier, and the distinctive pupae of bee flies were described in chapter 2. Although the pupae and cocoons of other nest parasites are not described here, the following are potential suspects to consider when you encounter something amiss in a nest.

Wedge-shaped beetles (Rhipiphoridae) lay their eggs among flowers. The first-instar larvae ride solitary and social bees and wasps back to their nests, where they are at first internal parasites of the larvae, later external. They pupate in the host's cell. This may seem like an exceptional strategy, but the larvae of some blister beetles (Meloidae) and checkered beetles (Cleridae) also ride bees and wasps back to their nests and feed on the contents.

Sapygid wasps and many velvet ants (Mutillidae) and cuckoo wasps (Chrysididae) lay their eggs in bee and wasp nests, in some cases chewing holes in mud cells to gain access. Their larvae feed on the eggs or larvae of their hosts as well as their provisions, then spin cocoons in their cells.

Leucospids (*Leucospis*) are small wasps that parasitize resin bees, mason bees, and other solitary bees. The female inserts her ovipositor through the host's nest cell, depositing an egg that is suspended by a slender stalk. The larva feeds externally on the host larva, pupates in the cell, and chews its way out as an adult.

Gasteruptiid wasps parasitize solitary bees and sphecid wasps that nest in wood. The female lays an egg on the host's egg or larva. The larva eats the host and whatever is left of the cell's provisions, often breaking into one or more neighboring cells and feasting some more before finally pupating.

Many flesh flies (Sarcophagidae) in the tribe Miltogrammini develop in the nests of bees and wasps. They feed primarily on the nest provisions but result in the death of the host just the same, either by eating the egg or by causing the larva to starve to death.

Other insects commonly occur as scavengers in nests. Some syrphid fly larvae (e.g., *Volucella*) feed on excrement, dead inhabitants, and other debris in bee and wasp nests. Dermestid beetle larvae are also very common, as they are anywhere that dried animal remains are found. Their distinctive exuviae are obvious signs of their presence.

Sign on Algae, Fungi, and Plants

9

This and the next several chapters focus on sign from feeding and other activities on vegetation. Leaf mining, the modification of leaves to form shelters, galls, boring and cutting of stems and twigs, and wood boring are all specialized activities that deserve their own chapters (or books, in most cases). This chapter includes general invertebrate sign from herbivorous feeding, as well as other sign on vegetation that does not fit any of these categories.

Studying the nature of damage to vegetation can give you a general sense of what insect (or other invertebrate) group is responsible. Droppings, other secretions, and exuviae are important clues to look for in addition to the pattern of damage. Identifying the host plant can often lead to a more specific identification. A given plant species may have only a few insects that commonly feed on it, and it may be possible to learn to distinguish their sign, but it is not possible to go into that level of detail here. Johnson and Lyon (1988), Cranshaw (2004), and the three books by Eastman and Hansen listed in the References are all excellent resources that allow you to look up which insects are associated with a particular plant, often with good descriptions or illustrations of the sign they leave. There are various online databases of species and their host plants for particular groups of insects, which are very useful in generating a list of suspects. Certain generalist feeders can confuse things a bit, but once you have identified the insect responsible for a particular type of damage to a particular type of plant, you can usually be reasonably confident that when you see the same sign again, you are seeing the work of the same species.

Before diving into the plant kingdom, we will briefly mention some feeding sign that may be found on algae and fungi.

Radular tooth marks of snails (Stylommatophora) scraping algae from a picnic table. (TN)

Sign on Algae

Long, winding trails are often visible in the algal film covering light-colored surfaces such as birch bark and propane tanks. On smoother surfaces, when you look closely, you will see that these trails have a beautiful, intricate pattern. It consists of rows of short lines, parallel to the length of the trail, broadly meandering from side to side. From a distance, the trails are suggestive of a slug or snail's track, but the presence of these apparent tooth marks might cause you to reconsider. Nevertheless, that is exactly who is responsible. Like other mollusks, slugs and snails possess a *radula*, a straplike organ inside the mouth that is covered with many small, sharp teeth. As the animal slowly glides across the surface, it moves its head from side to side while scraping up algae with its radular teeth. We have found this pattern scraped into algae-coated mud in dirt roads, and we expect that close inspection of any surface where algae might grow could reveal this sign. Limpets feeding on marine algae are said to make a similar pattern, sometimes even carving grooves into the rock substrate beneath. Some millipedes also graze on the algae on tree trunks, but it is unlikely that they leave recognizable patterns.

Aquatic snails make trails on the surfaces of submerged rocks that are similar to those of their terrestrial counterparts, though we have never seen an example where the actual tooth marks were visible. The calico crayfish (Cambaridae: *Orconectes immunis*) has been observed scraping the algal growth from rocks, and various aquatic insects also eat algae. We are unaware of any arthropods that leave distinguishable sign when feeding on algae.

Sign on Fungi

A number of beetles, flies, and other invertebrates feed exclusively on fungi. Others, such as slugs, are generalists that commonly include fungi in their diets. Very little has been documented about the sign left by these animals, but there is much variety among them in features such as the type of fungus chosen, the pattern of damage (including size of tunnels, if present), the nature of the frass, and presence or absence of substances such as silk and slime.

Slugs

Slugs are the most conspicuous eaters of mushrooms. They make characteristic large, irregular pits where they feed, generally leaving some amount of slime behind as well. They seem to prefer the mushrooms that are edible to humans. By no means are we suggesting that it is safe to eat any mushroom you see a slug eating, but a conspicuous lack of slug feeding often indicates an especially toxic species.

Slug (Stylommatophora) feeding sign on a bolete. (MA)

Flies

Networks of small tunnels inside a mushroom are often the work of fly larvae, specifically fungus gnats (Mycetophilidae), dark-winged fungus gnats (Sciaridae), and scuttle flies (Phoridae, including *Megaselia halterata*, known as the "mushroom fly"). The presence of slime or silk indicates one of the fungus gnat families (species that spin sheets of silk on the undersides of bracket fungi are noted in chapter 6). Their eggs are laid at the base of a mushroom stalk, and the larvae tunnel up to the cap. Other fly larvae feeding in fungi include certain flat-footed flies (Platypezidae), lance flies (Lonchaeidae), crane flies (Tipulidae), gall midges (Cecidomyiidae), sphaerocerids, and heleomyzids.

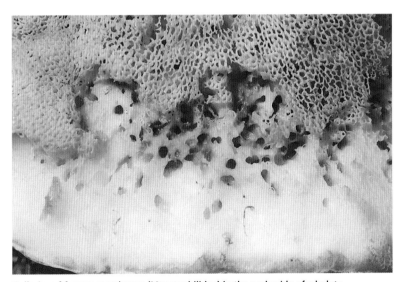

Galleries of fungus gnat larvae (Mycetophilidae) in the underside of a bolete.

Beetles

Beetles are the other major fungus feeders. Some feed in fleshy fungi, including sap beetles (Nitidulidae; several genera each feed in a different type of fungus), cross-toothed rove beetles (Staphylinidae: *Oxyporus*; large galleries), obscure rove beetles (Aleocharinae), pleasing fungus beetles (Erotylidae; *Triplax* is common in soft bracket fungi such as oyster mushrooms), hairy fungus beetles (Mycetophagidae), silken fungus beetles (Cryptophagidae), round fungus beetles (Leiodidae), and bark-gnawing beetles (Trogossitidae). *Caenocara* death-watch beetles (Anobiidae) and *Lycoperdina* handsome fungus beetles (Endomychidae) develop in puffballs.

Many more beetles feed in harder fungi. Minute tree-fungus beetles (Ciidae) are among the most prominent of these, particularly in smaller dry bracket fungi. Larvae and adults, often of multiple species, live gregariously within a fruiting body, making narrow, branching galleries of varying widths, around 1 mm wide. Bolitophagine and diaperine darkling beetles (Tenebrionidae) often leave a hard shelf fungus fairly intact on the outside but completely destroyed and filled with fecal pellets on the inside. The forked fungus beetle (Bolitophaginae: *Bolitotherus cornutus*), a common eastern species, leaves perfectly round holes, about 5 mm wide.

If you are very familiar with both the beetles and the fungi in a given area, it may be possible to learn to distinguish the sign of different beetles based on the type of fungus, the size of galleries, frass characteristics, and so on. Lest we give the impression that this is an easy task, consider that fungus-feeding beetles (adults or larvae), in addition to other members of the families noted above, also include fungus weevils (Anthribidae), tooth-necked fungus beetles (Derodontidae), false darkling beetles (Melandryidae), polypore fungus beetles (Tetratomidae), dry-fungus beetles (Sphindidae), false skin beetles (Biphyllidae), cylindrical bark beetles (Zopheridae: Colydiinae), and others.

Other Arthropods

Various other arthropods also feed on fungi. *Scardia* species (Tineidae), relatives of the clothes moths, are unusual among moths in being fungus borers. They make messy, frass-filled silken galleries in dry fungi. Harvestmen sometimes eat the gills of mushrooms. Other fungivores, habitual or occasional, include springtails, woodlice, millipedes, and certain mites.

Sign on Vegetation

Apart from galls, most damage to vegetation can be divided into two categories: feeding damage caused by invertebrates with piercing-sucking mouthparts, in which only juices have been removed; and damage caused by those with chewing mouthparts, in which tissue has been removed. Distinguishing between the two is usually straightforward, and various characteristics can help narrow down the suspects within either group.

Some insects make holes in vegetation for laying eggs, either by piercing with an ovipositor or by chewing with mandibles. Thick, fleshy plant parts, such as fruits and tubers, provide opportunities for boring and tunneling, a special case of feeding with chewing mouthparts. Mining just below the epidermis can be thought of as a special type of boring.

Damage Caused by Sucking Mouthparts

Herbivores with piercing-sucking mouthparts puncture leaves and stems and drink the juices, but they do not remove tissue. Therefore, their feeding sign does not include holes or missing portions but various patterns of discoloration: bleaching, bronzing, silvering, stippling, or streaking. The discoloration may result from injected enzymes that dissolve the tissue, as well as from the actual draining of fluids. Heavily attacked leaves may curl and distort, or even blacken and dry to a crisp. Concen-

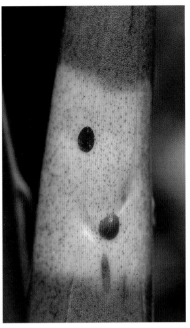

Discoloration of an agave leaf caused by soft scales (Coccidae). (TX)

trated feeding on stems by aphids, spittle-bugs, and scale insects can cause attached leaves to yellow and droop. Plants may be further affected by the transmission of diseases.

All hemipterans have beaklike sucking mouthparts, and the foliage feeders include leafhoppers, lace bugs, plant bugs, aphids, psyllids, stink bugs, leaf-footed bugs, stilt bugs, scentless plant bugs, seed bugs, planthoppers, scale insects, adelgids, whiteflies, mealybugs, and treehoppers. Thrips feed similarly, as do spider mites and false spider mites. All of these groups leave more or less similar feeding sign, and an affected leaf's appearance can have as much to do with the plant species as with the type of insect or mite that has sucked its juices. Members of some families, however, leave distinctive enough sign to be recognized by it.

Lace Bugs

Lace bugs (Tingidae) generally feed on foliage of trees and shrubs, sucking juices from the undersides. The upper side of the leaf becomes speckled with yellow, grayish, or pale brown discoloration, and the underside is characteristically peppered with brown excrement. These symptoms tend to cover the whole leaf, as lace bugs feed in groups. They are fairly host-specific, with common species including the basswood lace bug (*Gargaphia tiliae*), oak lace bug (*Corythucha arcuata*), sycamore lace bug (*C. ciliata*), hawthorn lace bug (*C. cydoniae*; on various rosaceous trees and shrubs), hackberry lace bug (*C. celtidis*), andromeda lace bug (*Stephanitis takeyai*),

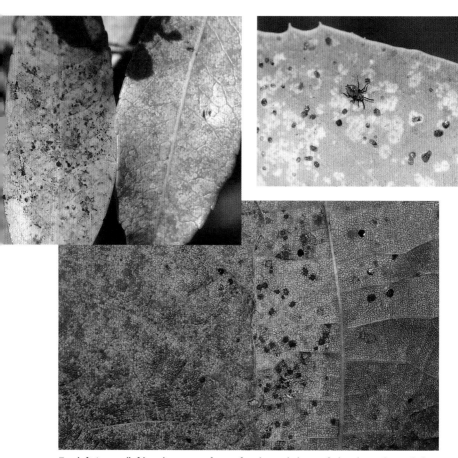

Top left: Lower (left) and upper surfaces of andromeda leaves fed on by andromeda lace bugs (Tingidae: *Stephanitis takeyai*). (MA) *Top right:* Nymph and feeding sign of *Teleonemia montivaga* (Tingidae) on a Palmer's penstemon leaf—an example of a lace bug that feeds on the upper surface. (UT) *Above:* Upper (left) and lower surfaces of a basswood leaf fed on by basswood lace bugs (Tingidae: *Gargaphia tiliae*). (WI)

azalea lace bug (*S. pyrioides*), and rhododendron lace bug (*S. rhododendri*; also on mountain laurel). The chrysanthemum lace bug (*C. marmorata*) feeds on various plants in the aster family and may be found on either the upper or lower leaf surface, depending on temperature and intensity of sunlight.

Other True Bugs

The four-lined plant bug (Miridae: *Poecilocapsus lineatus*) is a common generalist feeder that causes sunken light or dark patches to appear on leaves. These are often accompanied by some distortion of the leaf, and sometimes the whole leaf withers and drops. The apple red bug (*Lygidea mendax*) creates stippling on apple leaves.

An elderberry leaflet with feeding damage of the four-lined plant bug (Miridae: *Poecilocapsus lineatus*). (NY)

Yucca plant bugs (*Halticotoma*) cause yellow stippling on yucca leaves, depositing small puddles of brown excrement. *Caulotops* species make similar stippling on agave, yucca, and similar plants, but in the United States, they are found only in Arizona, except for one species recently introduced into Florida. The giant agave bug (Coreidae: *Acanthocephala thomasi*) leaves brown, circular patches where it has fed on agave leaves, generally less concentrated than the spots of discoloration caused by the tiny, gregarious plant bugs.

Leafhoppers

Leafhoppers (Cicadellidae), like lace bugs, generally feed on the undersides of leaves. Their feeding sign often appears as discrete clusters of little, pale dots on the upper side of the leaf, rather than more evenly distributed mottling as left by lace bugs. They excrete colorless honeydew instead of brown excrement, and the cast skins of nymphs can often be found stuck to the undersides of leaves. More than

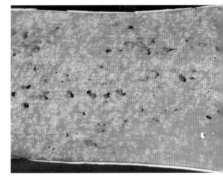

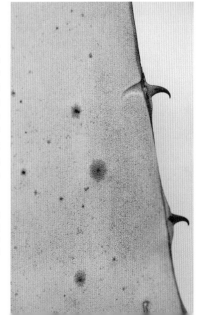

Above right: Feeding sign and excrement of yucca plant bugs (Miridae: *Halticotoma valida*) on a yucca leaf. (TN) *Right:* Feeding punctures on agave made by giant agave bugs (Coreidae: *Acanthocephala thomasi*). The largest spot is 4 mm across. (TX)

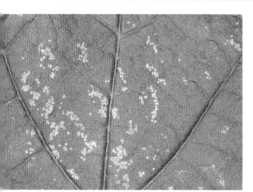

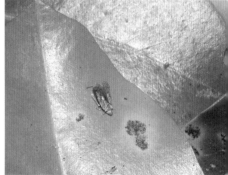

Top: These colorful spots on lambsquarters leaves are caused by feeding of *Norvellina chenopodii* (Cicadellidae) leafhopper nymphs. (MA) *Above left:* Stippling on a sugar maple leaf caused by leafhopper (Cicadellidae) feeding. (TN) *Above right: Catonia,* an achilid planthopper, and its feeding sign on the underside of a mountain laurel leaf. (MA)

twenty-five hundred species occur in North America, most of them fairly host-specific. Leaves of some plants can become stunted, curl, or wilt and fall off. The term "hopperburn" is sometimes used to describe the symptom of leaf edges and tips curling, yellowing, and finally becoming brown and brittle. The potato leafhopper (*Empoasca fabae*) commonly causes this type of damage. *Norvellina chenopodii* nymphs make distinctive crimson spots on lambsquarters.

Aphids

While many foliage feeders can cause leaves to twist or wither as they kill the tissue, certain aphids distort developing leaves in a more distinct way, keeping the tissue alive, at least at first. Affected leaves thicken and pucker or curl in ways that seem designed to provide some shelter for the aphids, like a crude sort of gall. Spiny witch hazel gall aphids (*Hamamelistes spinosus*) cause characteristic corrugations in birch leaves and live within the crevices formed on the leaf undersides. We often see shadbush leaves that are puckered and rolled downward by woolly aphids (*Eriosoma*) and blackberry leaves crumpled by *Aphis rubifolii* into bunches that completely conceal the

Above: **A blackberry leaf distorted by the feeding of *Aphis rubifolii* aphids on the underside. (MA)** *Top right:* **Feeding sign of calaphidine aphids on a black birch leaf: discoloration but no distortion. (MA)** *Right:* **A black birch leaf corrugated by spiny witch hazel gall aphids (*Hamamelistes spinosus*). (MA)**

aphids. The currant aphid (*Cryptomyzus ribis*) causes a similar downward puckering of currant leaves, though generally not as severe.

Thrips

Thrips (Thysanoptera), in addition to sucking mouthparts, have a single mandible that they use to saw and scrape the leaf surface to get at the juices. Although this happens on a very small scale, the thrips damage we have seen is suggestive of this feeding style, with leaves appearing to be wounded in small or large patches, rather than at discrete points as found

Some thrips (2 mm) and their feeding sign on the underside of a spicebush leaf. (MA)

 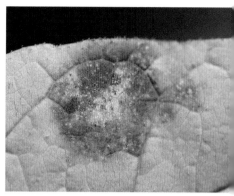

Left: Upper (left) and lower surfaces of phlox leaves on the undersides of which spider mites (Tetranychidae) have been feeding. (MA) *Right:* A 1-cm patch on the upper surface of a white ash leaflet discolored by spider mites (Tetranychidae) feeding on the underside. (MA)

where a hemipteran inserted its beak. The resulting discoloration sometimes has a silvery appearance. Like lace bugs, thrips often leave brown drops of excrement, and as with leafhoppers and others, they may cause leaf tips to curl and wither.

Spider Mites

Spider mites (Tetranychidae), like lace bugs, feed in groups usually on the undersides of leaves, resulting in discoloration on the upper surface. Unlike the distinct stippling caused by lace bugs and leafhoppers, however, spider mites tend to produce a more diffuse "bronzing" where they have been feeding. They usually, but not always, spin some amount of light webbing on the underside of the leaf, or sometimes over the whole leaf, and their tiny accumulated exuviae look like white powder. They are not usually host-specific, but they may have favorite plants in a given area. Every year, we see spider mites turn all the phlox plants yellow in a garden where there is no sign of them on any other plant. Various species are found on foliage of hardwoods, conifers, and herbaceous monocots and dicots. False spider mites (Tenuipalpidae) produce no webbing but otherwise may cause similar symptoms, although there often are no symptoms at all.

Nematodes

Leaf and bud eelworms (Aphelenchoididae: *Aphelenchoides*) are tiny roundworms that feed on leaves of a wide variety of plants, either externally or internally. They cause patches of discoloration that are delimited by the leaf veins. In leaves with strong side veins branching off a central midrib, affected areas are often partitioned from healthy tissue by the veins, resulting in discrete color patches with V-shaped boundaries. Presence of nematodes can be confirmed by tearing open a leaf in a dish of water and looking for them the next day with a hand lens.

Oviposition Wounds

Insects that insert their eggs in vegetation are summarized in chapter 1. In some cases, the inserted eggs are clearly visible, either bulging under the plant epidermis or partially protruding. In others, the sign is inconspicuous at best, and you probably will not see it unless you are looking for it. Certain insects, however, cause noticeable damage to plant tissues that you might not immediately recognize as being associated with eggs. Oviposition holes in fleshy fruits are discussed in the "Fleshy Fruits" section of this chapter, and those in stems and twigs are discussed in chapter 13.

Sawflies

Sawflies often cut very neat slits in leaves, so that what you mainly see is a bulge in the shape of the oval or oblong egg, perhaps with part of the egg exposed. In the midribs of leathery, evergreen leaves, however, we have found rough, ragged-looking scars containing sawfly eggs.

Thrips

Thrips, like sawflies, have sawlike ovipositors, which can cause scars much larger than the tiny, kidney-shaped eggs. Egg slits may be made in stems, leaves, fruits, corms, and other plant tissues.

Sawfly eggs inserted in the underside of a leaf midrib. The scar measures 12 mm. (FL)

Treehoppers

The common treehopper *Publilia concava* (Membracidae) inserts masses of eggs into the midribs of leaves of goldenrods and related plants. The midrib is visibly swollen where the eggs are, and the female often stands guard until the nymphs erupt out of the leaf tissue, at which point ants arrive to tend them. *Entylia carinata* does the same, also on plants in the aster family.

Leafhoppers

Leafhoppers may insert as many as 35 eggs into a single growing leaf, causing it to become distorted and curled as if damaged by feeding.

Midrib of a sugar maple leaf damaged by a thrips (Thysanoptera) inserting eggs. The affected area is 1 cm long. The two black specks are thrips excrement. (TN)

A female *Publilia concava* treehopper (Membracidae), her egg mass, and hatchlings, tended by ants (*Formica* sp.). (TN)

Left: Oviposition holes (each about 3 mm across) in a yucca leaf, believed to be from a tree cricket (Gryllidae: Oecanthinae). (UT) *Right:* The eggs (about 4 mm long) found in the leaf tissue beneath one of the holes. (UT)

Tree Crickets

We investigated some conspicuous, irregular holes in the undersides of fleshy yucca leaves in Utah and found that each one contained a few long, curved, yellowish eggs. The best explanation we can find is that these belonged to a western tree cricket (Gryllidae: *Oecanthus californicus*). The holes appeared to be chewed, rather than pierced or slit with an ovipositor, but each had a smaller puncture within the irregular hole. A tree cricket would seem to be the only option, given the method of oviposition combined with the shape of the eggs (see chapter 13 for more on tree cricket oviposition).

Leafminer Flies

Females of some leafminer flies (Agromyzidae) have found a second use for their ovipositors, using them to puncture the leaves of their host plants and then drinking the juices that ooze from the holes. The punctures tend to be large and conspicuous, but some species leave only small, discolored dots. They are most easily recognized when found on the same leaf as the larval mines. The oak shothole leafminer (*Japanagromyza viridula*; E) makes these punctures in oak leaves in early spring when the new leaves are still expanding. These tiny holes enlarge as the leaves continue to grow, and in mature leaves, they are frequently several millimeters wide, sometimes up to a centimeter or so. They are often very regularly spaced. They may be roughly circular, irregular, or oblong, but the edges are characteristically smooth, without any evidence of chewing. On close inspection, some of the holes may have a tiny knob along the rim, indicating where

Left: Feeding punctures in an ailanthus leaflet made by a female agromyzid fly, likely *Phytomyza ilicicola*, given the abundance of larval mines nearby. Note the small discs of brown tissue indicating where the ovipositor was inserted. (MD) *Right:* Holes caused by feeding punctures of adult female oak shothole leafminers (Agromyzidae: *Japanagromyza viridula*). (NH)

the ovipositor was inserted. Other agromyzids, such as holly-mining *Phytomyza* species, sometimes cause similar holes, but these are made later in leaf development and do not expand as the ones in oak leaves do.

Round Cuts in Leaves

Several types of insects chew round or elliptical holes in leaves without consuming the tissue. These include leafcutter bees, leafcutter ants, tree crickets, and certain moth larvae, and they do it for very different reasons. Certain leaf-mining species cut out neat, little circles or ovals to form pupal cases that drop to the ground. Because these are always associated with mines, and are the easiest way to recognize them, they are discussed in chapter 10 (see Heliozelidae).

Leafcutter Bees

The work of *Megachile* leafcutter bees (Megachilidae) is widespread and easily recognized. They cut both circular and oval pieces from the edges of leaves, which they use to make cells in their nests. The bee first forces several circular pieces into the bottom of a burrow to form the base of a cell, lines the sides with several oblong pieces, and then packs in several more circular pieces to close the cell, creating a thimblelike capsule. The bees often return to the same plant again and again, giving the leaves distinctive perforated margins. Many types of leaves are used, including rose, blackberry, grape, redbud, ash, and hibiscus. Some other megachilids also cut pieces of leaves, but they make jagged cuts with no particular shape.

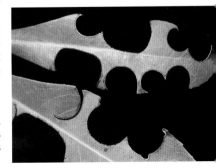

Leaves showing the various shapes cut out by leafcutter bees (Megachilidae: *Megachile*). Note the aborted cut in the lower leaf. The smallest circles are 8 mm across. (GA)

A Texas leafcutter ant (Formicidae: *Atta texana*) finishing a second cut. (TX)

A male two-spotted tree cricket (Gryillidae: *Neoxabea bipunctata*) chirps through the hole of about 1 cm that he has chewed in an oak leaf. (TN) Photo by Kris Light.

A maple leafcutter (Incurvariidae: *Paraclemensia acerifoliella*) feeds beneath the round piece it has cut from a sugar maple leaf. (VT)

Leafcutter Ants

Atta leafcutter ants are found in southern Louisiana, Texas, and Mexico. The leaf fragments they cut are not as perfectly rounded as those of leafcutter bees. They chew in a broad arc, so that something like a half oval is removed from the edge of a leaf. A single ant may cut several overlapping pieces from the same leaf in one session, dropping them down for others to carry back to the nest. The shape of the leaf fragments is not important to the ants, because they merely use them as a medium on which to cultivate the fungus that they feed their larvae. The related species *Trachymyrmex septentrionalis*, which occurs in the East as far north as New York, sometimes similarly cuts leaves but is also content to grow its fungus on insect droppings and other debris.

Two-Spotted Tree Cricket

Most male crickets (Gryllidae) "sing" by rubbing the edges of their wings together. To amplify his song, the two-spotted tree cricket (Oecanthinae: *Neoxabea bipunctata*) chews a hole in the middle of a leaf and rubs his wings below it. The hole is slightly oval, about a centimeter long, and has a finely ragged margin, as is generally the case with leaves cut by orthopterans. Often several leaves on a single plant each have a hole of identical size and shape, in the same location on the leaf, made by the same male on different nights.

Maple Leafcutter Moth

The maple leafcutter (Incurvariidae: *Paraclemensia acerifoliella*) is a moth larva that feeds on sugar maple leaves. After mining within the leaf for about ten days, it cuts an elliptical piece from the leaf and places this piece over its back. It then ties the leaf piece down with silk around the edges, creating a shelter under which it feeds on the surface of the leaf. When it begins to outgrow this, it cuts a larger piece and ties this new piece to the outer edges of the first one. The larva may travel a bit, sandwiched between the two pieces, before settling down to feed again with the larger piece on top. It forms characteristic ringlike patches of feeding damage, feeding only in the area that is covered by the larger piece but not the smaller piece. Sometimes many of the leaves on one sugar maple are riddled with the holes cut to make these cases (the larger ones more than 1 cm long), and we have seen them show up on neighboring trees such as red oak and basswood.

Other Holes in Leaves

Tortoise and Flea Beetles

Besides the nonfeeding holes already discussed, most holes in leaves of somewhat regular shape and size are made by leaf beetles (Chrysomelidae). Certain adult tortoise beetles (Cassidinae) cut very smooth-edged but irregular-shaped holes in morning glory leaves, several millimeters across. Adult flea beetles (Alticini) often riddle leaves with more or less round holes 0.5 to 2.5 mm in diameter. Examples include the grape flea beetle (*Altica chalybea*) and eggplant flea beetle (*Epitrix fuscula*), the latter of which often eventually kills the leaves.

Slugs and Snails

Leaves riddled with holes that are highly irregular in shape and size are most often the work of beetles or snails (note that snails include slugs). Slugs and snails

Right: An eggplant leaf killed by eggplant flea beetles (Chrysomelidae: *Epitrix fuscula*). (MA) *Below left:* A hedge bindweed leaf with characteristic feeding holes of the golden tortoise beetle (Chrysomelidae: *Charidotella sexpunctata*). (MA) *Below right:* Adult grape flea beetles (Chrysomelidae: *Altica chalybea*) made these 1- to 2-mm holes in a Virginia creeper leaf. (MA)

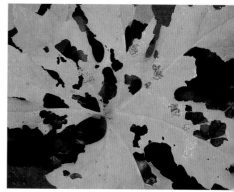

Left: Snail feeding sign on the underside of a white vervain leaf. Note the droppings and the spot of glistening slime. (VT) *Right:* Feeding sign of banana slugs (Arionidae: *Ariolimax*) on an Arctic sweet coltsfoot leaf. (CA)

almost always leave slime or droppings that reveal their identity. They generally leave the main veins intact, unless feeding on more delicate leaves—but so do beetles, so their secretions are the definitive sign to look for. They are by no means host-specific, although like any herbivore, they may show preferences in a given area.

Other Beetles

Both adults and larvae of many leaf beetles make similar patterns of irregular holes, and most feed exclusively on members of a particular plant family. Smaller larvae tend to skeletonize leaves, eating between the smaller veins, whereas older larvae and adults eat larger holes and may eventually consume everything but the midrib and main veins. Droppings, especially of the larvae, can often be found stuck to the damaged leaves. Some common examples, among the thousand or so North American species, include the elm leaf beetle (*Xanthogaleruca luteola*); viburnum leaf beetle (*Pyrrhalta viburni*); imported willow leaf beetle (*Plagiodera versicolora*) and various *Chrysomela* species on poplars and willows; the waterlily leaf beetle (*Galerucella nymphaeae*) and various *Donacia* species on waterlilies, the latter feeding on submerged leaves; various tortoise beetles (Cassidinae) and *Lema* species on nightshades; adult cranberry rootworms (*Rhabdopterus picipes*) on cranberry and blueberry; adult grape rootworms (*Fidia viticida*) on grape leaves; and *Trirhabda* species on goldenrods and other composites. Cereal leaf beetles (*Oulema melanopus*) chew long, straight strips from leaves of oats and other grasses, paralleling the veins.

The damage caused by chrysomelids is nearly unique among beetles. *Epilachna* ladybugs (Coccinellidae) are herbivorous, however, and cause similar damage—the Mexican bean beetle (*E. varivestis*) on legumes, and the squash beetle (*E. borealis*) on cucurbits. At least one adult scarab, the Japanese beetle (*Popillia japonica*), makes similar irregular feeding holes. It is a generalist but is especially enthusiastic about grape and raspberry

Top left: Feeding sign of young *Chrysomela* leaf beetle larvae (Chrysomelidae) on a willow leaf. (MA) *Top right:* Viburnum leaf beetle larvae (Chrysomelidae: *Pyrrhalta viburni*) and their damage to an arrowwood leaf. (VT) *Center left:* Feeding holes of the imported willow leaf beetle (Chrysomelidae: *Plagiodera versicolora*). (NY) *Center right:* A waterlily leaf beetle (Chrysomelidae: *Galerucella nymphaeae*) and its feeding sign on a watershield leaf. (NH) *Bottom left:* Feeding sign of three-lined potato beetles (Chrysomelidae: *Lema daturaphila*) on jimsonweed. (NV) *Bottom right:* Feeding damage of yellow-margined leaf beetles (Chrysomelidae: *Microtheca ochroloma*) on a cabbage leaf. (TN)

leaves. Adults of the leaf-rolling weevil *Himatolabus pubescens* (Attelabidae) eat long, narrow holes between the main veins of alder leaves. The holes have notched outlines because the ends of small cross veinlets are left sticking into them.

Certain adult weevils (Curculionidae) also make holes in leaves. The yellow poplar weevil (*Odontopus calceatus*) eats holes in sassafras and tuliptree leaves similar to those made by flea beetles, and the flea weevils

Irregular holes chewed in a raspberry leaflet by Japanese beetles (Scarabaeidae: *Popillia japonica*). (MA)

(Rhamphini) do the same in their host plants. The grape curculio (*Craponius inaequalis*) makes characteristic short, curved slits in grape leaves, usually in groups. Southern corn billbugs (*Sphenophorus callosus*) feed on corn seedlings, causing regular series of transverse holes to appear when the leaves open. Various other weevils cause similar damage by nibbling on buds and tender shoots.

Caterpillars and Sawfly Larvae

Early-instar caterpillars and sawfly larvae, as well as grasshopper nymphs, may eat small holes in leaves, but they tend to eat the smaller veins, making clean holes at least a few millimeters across, without the tight clusters of tiny holes often present in the beetle damage described above. Hollyhock sawfly larvae (Argidae: *Neoptilia malvacearum*) are one exception, skeletonizing mallow leaves in a very beetlelike way. Probably the most commonly seen irregular holes in foliage caused by a caterpillar are those of the cabbage white (Pieridae: *Pieris rapae*) on broccoli and other mustards. Sawfly larvae that commonly make small, rounded holes in leaves include the raspberry sawfly (Tenthredinidae: *Monophadnoides rubi*), imported currantworm (*Nematus ribesii*), and strawberry sawfly (*Empria maculata*). We have seen one photo of unidentified young sawfly larvae eating meandering channels in a leaf, suggestive of the ones some adult beetles cut from the edges of leaves.

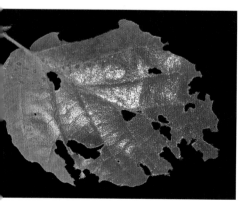

Left: A witch hazel leaf fed on by an inchworm (Geometridae). (MA) *Right:* Feeding sign of early-instar neighbor moth caterpillars (Arctiidae: *Haploa contigua*) on a beebalm leaf. (MA)

A distinctive feeding pattern on oak leaves is made by the scalloped sack-bearer (Mimallonidae: *Lacosoma chiridota*). Early instars spin a coarse meshwork of silk covering a roughly circular area on the upper side of the leaf, centered over the midrib or a main vein. The larva eats holes in the leaf throughout the area covered by the shelter, except for a central patch surrounding the vein, on which it rests when not feeding.

Litter moths (Erebidae: Herminiinae) such as the common idia (*Idia aemula*) feed on a wide range of organic matter. They often eat dead, fallen oak leaves, consuming all the tissue between the veins and leaving them as lacelike skeletons.

Leaf Edge Feeders

Other insects feed primarily from the edges of leaves. This is the usual pattern for most sawfly and lepidopteran larvae, grasshoppers, and nonchrysomelid beetles. All of them can also eat holes in the middle of leaves, but these tend to be more extensive than the holes made by beetles, with the insect expanding the hole by feeding in the same way it would if it were feeding along the leaf edge.

Caterpillars and Sawfly Larvae

Caterpillars and sawfly larvae tend to make arcing movements with their heads as they feed, making several munches in each arc, resulting in a characteristic scalloped pattern on the leaf margin. When they make holes, these show the same scalloped pattern. They commonly eat everything except the main veins, but they may leave only the midrib or ultimately consume the entire leaf. Early-instar viceroy and admiral caterpillars

Right: A monarch caterpillar (Nymphalidae: *Danaus plexippus*) on a milkweed leaf, showing the typical leaf-edge feeding pattern of larger caterpillars. (MA) *Below:* Bits of sugar maple leaves accumulate on the ground from forest tent caterpillars (Lasiocampidae: *Malacosoma disstria*) feeding above. (MA)

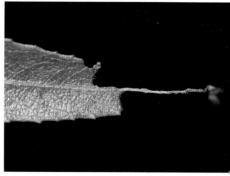

Left: Gregarious sawfly larvae, such as these birch sawfly larvae (Argidae: *Arge pectoralis*) on a yellow birch leaf, attack all the edges of a leaf at once, until eventually only the midrib remains. (MA) *Right:* A young viceroy or white admiral caterpillar (Nymphalidae: *Limenitis*) has eaten both sides of this willow leaf's midrib and extended the tip with a "frass chain." (MA)

(Nymphalidae: *Limenitis*) characteristically eat both sides of the outer end of a leaf and leave the midrib intact. See the discussion of "frass chains" (page 158) for more on this behavior. Promethea moth caterpillars (Saturniidae: *Callosamia promethea*) also tend to leave the midrib but often cut off the uneaten portion of the leaf at the petiole, making their feeding sign less conspicuous.

Grasshoppers and Katydids

Grasshoppers and katydids typically leave a more ragged or finely serrated edge, rather than the smooth, scalloped edges left by caterpillars and sawfly larvae. They may occasionally produce a scalloped pattern, but for the most part, this is in isolated portions of the damaged leaves and not the dominant pattern. Feeding sign of walkingsticks is presumably similar.

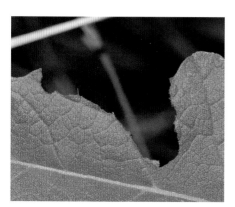

Left: Feeding sign of an arid lands spur-throat grasshopper nymph (Acrididae: *Melanoplus aridus*). (AZ) *Right:* Hole in a grape leaf eaten by a greater angle-wing katydid (Tettigoniidae: *Microcentrum rhombifolium*). Leafhopper feeding sign is also visible. (UT)

Beetles

With the exceptions of *Epilachna* ladybugs (Coccinellidae) and a few weevils (e.g., Curculionidae: *Hypera*), nonchrysomelid beetles eat leaves only as adults, if at all, generally feeding from the margins and producing ragged, irregular edges similar to those left by grasshoppers. In some cases, their sign may be difficult to distinguish from that of grasshoppers, but some beetles leave recognizable notches or channels in leaves. Long, narrow, crooked, and sometimes branching channels are typical of some broad-nosed weevils (Curculionidae: Entiminae), including the introduced *Oedophrys hilleri*, which feeds on maple leaves. Dogbane leaf beetles (*Chrysochus auratus*) are unusual among chrysomelids in producing somewhat similar channels. Before laying eggs, females of the recently introduced Asian long-horned beetle (Cerambycidae: *Anoplophora glabripennis*) cut characteristic ragged channels in maple leaves, eating just the main veins rather than the tissue between them. Hickory spiral borers (Buprestidae: *Agrilus arcuatus*) chew elongate notches and slits in the edges of leaves.

  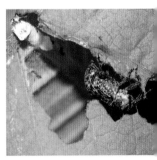

Top left: Oedophrys hilleri, a broad-nosed weevil (Curculionidae: Entiminae), chewed these 2-mm-wide channels in a sugar maple leaf. (TN) *Top right:* A dogbane leaf beetle (Chrysomelidae: *Chrysochus auratus*) and its feeding sign on a dogbane leaf. (VT) *Bottom left:* Typical feeding sign of a female Asian long-horned beetle (Cerambycidae: *Anoplophora glabripennis*) in a sugar maple leaf. (MA) Photo by Robert D. Childs. *Bottom center:* A milkweed leaf with a notched tip: characteristic feeding sign of an adult milkweed longhorn (Cerambycidae: *Tetraopes*). Note how the midrib has been nipped to cut off the flow of latex. (MA) *Bottom right:* This milkweed weevil (Curculionidae: *Rhyssomatus palmacollis*) has cut off the flow of sticky latex from the central vein (upper left corner) and is now eating an irregular hole in the middle of the leaf. (MA)

Left: Feeding sign of the margined blister beetle (Meloidae: *Epicauta pestifera*) on devil's walkingstick leaflets. (AR) *Right:* An alder leaf showing sign of feeding by *Dichelonyx* beetles (Scarabaeidae: Melolonthinae). (MA)

Adult milkweed longhorns (Cerambycidae: *Tetraopes*) make characteristic notches in the tips of milkweed leaves, nipping the midvein beforehand to cut off the flow of gummy latex. We have found milkweed weevils (Curculionidae: *Rhyssomatus palmacollis*) using the same trick, but nipping the vein closer to the base and eating an irregular hole in the middle of the leaf. (Many other insects also cut veins before feeding on milkweed and other latex-producing plants.) Blister beetles (Meloidae) and melolonthine scarabs (June bugs and their relatives) are other common leaf edge feeders.

Other Insects

A few terrestrial crane fly larvae (Tipulidae: Cylindrotominae) eat leaves in a caterpillarlike way. *Liogma nodicornis* and *Cylindrotoma* species feed on plants in boggy habitats. Adult stoneflies (Plecoptera) also may occasionally feed on young leaves of terrestrial plants, and earwigs (Dermaptera) sometimes eat foliage and other plant parts.

Surface Skeletonizers

Some insects with chewing mouthparts only eat partway through the leaf. This is typical of many leaf-rolling, -folding, and -tying caterpillars, which are discussed in chapter 11. It is also done by early instars of some leaf beetle and moth larvae that later eat all the way through leaves, especially on thicker-leaved plants. Insects that feed in this way generally leave the larger veins intact; in other words, they skeletonize only one side of the leaf. The word *skeletonize* is often used vaguely, without indicating whether the leaf is eaten all the way through. When we say a leaf is skeletonized, we mean it is eaten all the way through unless we specify that just one surface is skeletonized.

"Slug" Sawfly Larvae

Larvae of the "slug" sawfly species (Tenthredinidae: Heterarthrinae: Caliroini) characteristically skeletonize the undersides of leaves. The patches where they have fed are more translucent than the rest of the leaf, making

Top right: A pear leaf with parts of the underside skeletonized by pearslugs (Tenthredinidae: *Caliroa cerasi*), as seen from the upper surface. (MA) *Bottom right:* Oak slug sawfly larvae (Tenthredinidae: *Caliroa*) skeletonizing the underside of an oak leaf. Note the several exuviae. (MA)

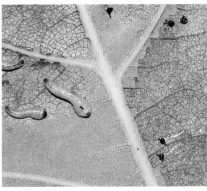

their sign easy to notice from above. At least five *Caliroa* species feed on oak leaves. Others include the pearslug (*C. cerasi*) on various rosaceous trees, *C. liturata* on *Prunus* species, *C. labrata* (W) on willow, *C. annulipes* on paper birch, *C. lorata* on chestnut, *C. nyssae* on tupelo, and the rose-slug (*Endelomyia aethiops*) on rose.

Moth Larvae

The grapeleaf skeletonizer (*Harrisina americana*) and western grapeleaf skeletonizer (*H. metallica*) are common examples of moth larvae that feed in this manner. The young larvae feed gregariously on the undersides of leaves, eating the surface tissue between the small veins as the "slug" sawflies do. Older larvae eat all the way through, leaving only the main veins. Larvae of the ribbed cocoon-maker moths (Bucculatricidae: *Bucculatrix*) start out as leafminers, then switch to skeletonizing patches on the lower leaf surfaces. Their feeding sign can be recognized by the associated "molting cocoons" they spin each time they molt. Common examples include the apple bucculatrix (*B. pomifoliella*; NE; on various rosaceous trees), birch skeletonizer (*B. canadensisella*), oak skeletonizer (*B. ainsliella*; E), oak ribbed skeletonizer (*B. albertiella*; W), and cotton leaf perforator (*B. thurberiella*). Little skeletonized patches at both ends of an open-ended silk tent spun against the midrib are the work of early-instar gold-striped leaftiers (Amphisbatidae: *Machimia tentoriferella*; E; see page 219).

Leaf Beetles

Leaf beetles feeding on thicker leaves, particularly young larvae, often skeletonize one side of a leaf. This is also common among adult flea beetles. Adult sweet potato flea beetles (*Chaetocnema confinis*) eat long, narrow grooves out of upper leaf surfaces along the veins. Adult locust leafminers

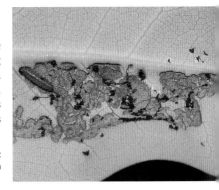

A skeletonizing leaf beetle larva (Chrysomelidae: Galerucinae), its feeding sign and droppings on the underside of a rhododendron leaf. (MA)

(*Odontota dorsalis*) eat small, oblong holes in young locust leaves, but eat only partway through older ones. Adult *Oberea* long-horned beetles (Cerambycidae) often eat the undersides of leaf midribs along their whole length, causing them to curl downward.

Garden Springtail

Few springtails feed on living plant tissue, and those that do rarely leave a noticeable sign. The garden springtail (Bourletiellidae: *Bourletiella hortensis*) chews tiny pits, which may be visible as brown specks, in the leaves and stems of tender shoots and seedlings. Thin leaves may have irregular holes eaten all the way through them. In extreme cases, seedlings can be deformed or killed.

Conifer Needles

Conifer needles may turn yellow because of feeding by scale insects and adelgids, or they may be chewed off by various sawfly, butterfly, and moth larvae. Balsam twig aphids (*Mindarus abietinus*) cause balsam fir needles to twist and curl. Several *Pleroneura* sawflies (Xyelidae) mine in the tips of fir buds. The shoots are still able to grow, but many of the needles are characteristically bowed and fused together at their tips.

The most distinctive feeding sign on pine needles (aside from those involving mining or silk, discussed in chapters 10 and 11) is that of the pine needle weevils (Curculionidae: *Pachyrhinus*) in western states. Rather than nibbling the needles down to stubs as other insects do, they chew characteristic notches intermittently along a needle's length. The needle generally dies and turns brown beyond the lowest notch.

Left: Balsam fir needles twisted by the feeding of balsam twig aphids (*Mindarus abietinus*). (MA) *Below:* Characteristic feeding notches of pine needle weevils (Curculionidae: *Pachyrhinus*). (AZ)

Top left: A staghorn cholla moth caterpillar (Noctuidae: *Euscirrhopterus cosyra*) and its feeding sign. (AZ) *Top right:* Scars on a prickly pear caused by feeding of leaf-footed bugs (Coreidae). (FL) *Right:* The top of this cholla was nibbled by an adult cactus long-horned beetle (Cerambycidae: *Moneilema*). (AZ)

Cacti

Sign of external feeding on cacti is similar to sign on other types of vegetation, but the list of suspects is fairly short. Mottling on prickly pears and other cacti, eventually becoming circular, brown scars, is likely the result of feeding by *Chelinidea* and *Narnia* leaf-footed bugs (Coreidae). Adult cactus long-horned beetles (Cerambycidae: *Moneilema*) nibble on the edges of prickly pear pads and the tips of other cacti. The feeding sign of the staghorn cholla moth caterpillar (Noctuidae: *Euscirrhopterus cosyra*) on *Cylindropuntia* cacti can be similar, and droppings are the best way to distinguish it. The stringy droppings of the beetles are usually stuck to the cactus spines right at the feeding site, whereas the pellets of the caterpillar may be found on the ground below.

Flower Buds

Many insects that feed on foliage also feed on flower buds, but the sign of the strawberry weevil (Curculionidae: *Anthonomus signatus*), also known as the strawberry clipper, is distinctive. The female chews a hole in a strawberry bud and lays a single egg in it. She then cuts the pedicel so that the bud either hangs down or falls to the ground. The larva completes its development within the damaged bud, pupating inside it. Many other weevils develop inside and kill flower buds, common examples including the cranberry weevil (*A. musculus*; also in blueberry, chokeberry, and huckleberry) and rose curculio (Attelabidae: *Merhynchites bicolor*). A number of tortricid moth larvae also frequently feed in buds. See chapter 12 for examples

Holes chewed in a chrysanthemum by the oriental beetle (Scarabaeidae: *Anomala orientalis*). (MA)

of insects and mites that distort buds rather than simply killing them.

Flowers

The same general suite of insects that feed on foliage also feed on flowers, and their sign is similar. Hemipterans such as plant bugs, stink bugs, aphids, leafhoppers, and seed bugs suck the juices of flowers. Some thrips scrape flower petals and feed on the juices, causing portions to turn brown; colorful flowers become mottled with white. Common examples are the flower thrips (Thripidae: *Frankliniella tritici*) and gladiolus thrips (*Thrips simplex*). Beetles, caterpillars, and sawfly larvae eat holes in flowers or feed on the edges of petals. The introduced oriental beetle (Scarabaeidae: *Anomala orientalis*) often eats little holes in daisies and other garden flowers. Gray hairstreak caterpillars (Lycaenidae: *Strymon melinus*) feed primarily on flowers, especially of legumes and mallows, but many others

as well. Female dobsonflies (Corydalidae: *Corydalus*) tear apart flowers to feed on the nectar.

A type of damage unique to flowers is the holes made by "nectar robbing" insects. Flowers with long corolla tubes or nectar spurs, such as snapdragon, jewelweed, columbine, and trumpet creeper, have coevolved with insects with elongate mouthparts that can reach the nectar from the flower's intended entrance. In accessing the nectar hidden deep within the flower, the insect does the plant a service by picking up pollen and transporting it to other flowers. Some insects that lack these specialized mouthparts, and are too big to simply crawl inside the flower, access the nectar by making a hole in the corolla tube near the nectary. This is considered "robbing" because in doing so, they bypass the pollen, giving the plant nothing in return

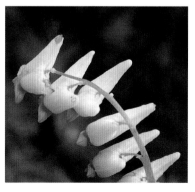

Top: The 5-mm slit at the base of this flower was made by a nectar-robbing carpenter bee (Apidae: *Xylocopa*). (TX) *Left:* The holes in these dutchman's breeches flowers were likely chewed by nectar-robbing bumblebees (Apidae: *Bombus*). (VT)

for the meal. Large carpenter bees (Apidae: *Xylocopa*) are frequent nectar robbers, and their sign is distinctive: the bee uses its proboscis to cut a narrow slit several millimeters long, whereas other nectar robbers tend to bite more or less round holes. Short-tongued bumblebees, such as *Bombus ternarius*, *B. terricola*, *B. affinis*, and *B. lucorum*, are most often responsible for these holes; other bumblebees have long tongues and can get at the nectar in the intended way. There have been reports of eastern yellowjackets (Vespidae: *Vespula maculifrons*) biting through, or off, the spurs of jewelweed flowers, and soldier beetles (Cantharidae) robbing false foxglove. An Egyptian ant has been observed biting holes near the base of vetch flowers, so ants should be considered potential suspects as well. In addition to insects, orioles have been observed robbing golden currant flowers, and hummingbirds sometimes bite off columbine spurs that are otherwise accessible only to sphinx moths. Various bees and other insects act as secondary nectar robbers, accessing nectar through the holes made by primary nectar robbers. In defense of nectar robbers, they often still do pollinate the flowers, either by incidentally brushing the reproductive parts as they crawl around or by collecting pollen from the flower before or after robbing it.

The clover head caterpillar (Tortricidae: *Grapholita interstinctana*) feeds on developing seeds, mostly of red clover. The affected florets are stunted and open on only one side, often with one side turning pink while the other side stays green. The caterpillar pupates in a silken cocoon in the flower head or at the base of the plant. Clover seed midge larvae (*Dasineura leguminicola*) similarly cause aborted florets in red clover, and *D. gentneri* in white and alsike clovers.

Seeds and Seedpods

Surface damage to seeds and seedpods is similar to feeding sign on other plant parts. External feeding on pea pods by aphids can cause them to become stunted and only partly filled with peas. Most seed bugs (Lygaeidae) suck juices from developing or mature seeds and their pods. Mexican

Mexican bean beetles (Coccinellidae: *Epilachna varivestis*) and their feeding sign on a green bean. (MA)

bean beetles (Coccinellidae: *Epilachna varivestis*) eat irregular patches on the surfaces of bean pods. Slugs hollow out wheat grains, leaving an irregular, somewhat round hole in a grain. In addition to examples such as these, there are many insects that develop exclusively within the seeds or seedpods of particular plants. In general, the sign of their presence is exit holes, and in some cases aborted seeds or pods.

McAtee (1908) described finding a bladdernut on which many of the pods had an irregular hole. Most had a loosely constructed door made of bits of pod and a network of silk. Each pod contained a Carolina leaf-rolling cricket (Gryllacrididae: *Camptonotus carolinensis*; SE). The crickets had not fed on the pods at all and had modified them purely for use as daytime shelters.

Beetles

A number of weevils (Curculionidae) develop inside dry seeds and seedpods. The females lay eggs in holes bored in fruits with their long snouts, sometimes creating a visible wound. In some species, the mature larva chews a circular hole to emerge and pupates in the ground; in others, the larva pupates within the seed or fruit, chewing a similar hole to emerge as an adult. The boll weevil (*Anthonomus grandis*) is well known for causing cotton bolls to abort and turn brown. It pupates within the fruit, as does the mullein weevil (*Gymnetron tetrum*). Cowpea curculio larvae (*Chalcodermus aeneus*; E) develop within green seeds of cowpeas and closely related legumes, cutting a hole in the pod and dropping to the ground to pupate.

The granary weevil (*Sitophilus granarius*) and rice weevil (*S. oryzae*) infest various stored grains, sealing their oviposition holes with a gelati-

The aborted cotton boll on the right contains a developing boll weevil (Curculionidae: *Anthonomus grandis*). (TX)

Exit holes of *Algarobius prosopis* bean weevils (Chrysomelidae: Bruchinae) in screwbean mesquite pods. (CA)

nous secretion. Larvae pupate inside and chew round exit holes like those of other weevils. Larvae of the lesser grain borer (Bostrichidae: *Rhyzopertha dominica*) feed on dust from the adults' borings in loose grain, then bore into damaged grain to pupate. The large grain borer (*Prostephanus truncatus*) is sometimes found in stored corn in the southern United States.

Chrysomelids in the subfamily Bruchinae are known as seed beetles or bean weevils. The larvae live in seeds, usually of legumes. Females may lay eggs at any stage of development, from flower to mature seed, but in most cases, they lay eggs on pods while the seeds are developing, and the newly hatched larva bores in, feeds and develops within a seed, and pupates inside it. The new adult beetle emerges through a round exit hole. *Acanthoscelides obtectus* and *Bruchus rufimanus* develop in various cultivated legumes, including in dried, stored beans, usually with multiple larvae in a single bean. The pea weevil (*B. pisorum*) develops in peas, usually just one larva per pea. *B. brachialis* develops in vetch seeds, and *Amblycerus robiniae* in locust seeds (both *Robinia* and *Gleditsia*).

Larvae of the eleven species of short-winged flower beetles (Kateredidae) also develop in seed capsules of various plants. Dusky sap beetle larvae (Nitidulidae: *Carpophilus lugubris*) feed inside the kernels at the tips of ears of sweet corn.

Chalcids

Although most chalcid wasps are parasitoids of other insects, some develop within seeds, chewing tiny, round exit holes after metamorphosing. Many use seeds of fleshy fruits, and examples of these are given in that section (page 324). *Bruchophagus* species (Eurytomidae) develop in leguminous seeds. They include the clover seed chalcid (*B. gibbus*; also in sweetclover), alfalfa seed chalcid (*B. roddi*), and trefoil seed chalcid (*B. platypterus*). Others developing in seeds of dry fruits include *Systole* species in seeds of the parsley family; *Eurytoma seminis* in skunkbush sumac; *E. ceanothi* in desert ceanothus; *E. squamosa* in other western *Ceanothus* species; and *Torymus atheatus* (Torymidae) in globe mallow.

Moths

The famous Mexican jumping beans are inhabited by larvae of the jumping bean moth (*Cydia deshaisiana*). They are, in fact, not beans but carpels (sections) of the dry, three-part fruit of a shrub, *Sebastiania*. The larva hatches from an egg laid on the fruit and bores in, hollowing out a carpel and lining it with silk. When the carpel falls to the ground, the larva rolls it by snapping its body until it reaches a shady place, safe from the scorching heat of the desert floor. Eventually it chews a circular escape hatch partway through the wall, then pupates. In the spring, the pupa pushes out through this door, and the moth emerges.

Other tortricids—less well known but more widespread—also feed on seeds. Pea moth larvae (*Cydia nigricana*) bore into pea pods, spin webbing, and feed on the peas. *Endothenia hebesana* develops in seedpods of plants in the iris and snapdragon families, among others.

The lima bean pod borer (Pyralidae: *Etiella zinckenella*) bores into pods of lima beans, lupine, and other legumes. The entry hole heals, and there is no external sign until the larva chews an exit hole to pupate in the ground. The larva of the rattlebox moth (Arctiidae: *Utetheisa ornatrix*) chews a circular hole to enter a rattlebox pod (or occasionally the pod of another legume) and feeds on the seeds within.

The very presence of a viable yucca seed capsule is almost a sure sign of yucca moths (Prodoxidae: *Tegeticula*), as yucca plants depend on these moths for pollination. A female yucca moth inserts her eggs into a yucca ovary, then takes a mass of pollen she has gathered from other flowers and thrusts it into the stigma. As the capsule develops, her offspring feed on some of the seeds, and the rest are left to produce other plants. They chew prominent exit holes in the capsule when they are mature. Bogus yucca moth larvae (*Prodoxus*) feed in the flower stalks and sometimes the fleshy parts of the capsules.

A Mexican jumping bean that never jumped: the adult moth (Tortricidae: *Cydia deshaisiana*) exited through this 2-mm hole while the fruit was still attached to the plant. (AZ)

The Angoumois grain moth (Gelechiidae: *Sitotroga cerealella*) feeds in stored grains of all kinds. The larva spins a small web and bores into a grain. Before pupating in a cocoon within the grain, it cuts a circular hole partway around to form a flap so that it will be able to emerge when it becomes an adult. It has a few seed-feeding relatives in the wild. Burdock seed moth larvae (*Metzneria lappella*) feed on burdock seeds and hibernate in the burs. Pink bollworm larvae (*Pectinophora gossypiella*) bore in buds and fruits of cotton and other mallows, feeding on the developing flowers, seeds, and fibers.

The corn earworm (Noctuidae: *Helicoverpa zea*) feeds at the tips of ears of corn, producing large amounts of excrement. Various casebearers (Coleophoridae) live in seed heads, and some fairy moth larvae (Adelidae: *Adela*) feed on milkweed seeds. The larvae of *Ectoedemia sericopeza* (Nepti-culidae) mine in Norway maple keys.

Flies

Wheat midge larvae (Cecidomyiidae: *Hyperdiplosis tritici*) crowd around developing wheat seeds, sucking the juice and causing them to become shriveled and aborted. They leave many molted skins among the seeds before dropping to the ground to pupate. The sorghum midge (*Contarinia sorghicola*) likewise causes sorghum seeds to dry up. The bromegrass seed midge (*C. bromicola*) is a pest of bromegrass, and various other *Contarinia* species feed similarly in native grasses, all of them pupating in the florets. Some frit fly larvae (Chloropidae) also feed on developing grains.

Some tephritid fruit fly larvae feed and pupate in seed heads of the aster family. *Neotephritis finalis* develops in sunflowers, among many other plants. *Neaspilota alba*, *N. vernoniae*, and *Tomoplagia obliqua* are all specific to ironweed.

Conifer Cones and Seeds

As with other kinds of seeds, conifer seeds are fed on by chalcid wasps, tortricid moths, gall midges, and various beetles.

Gall Midges

Many gall midges are found in conifer cones. Some *Resseliella* larvae live gregariously in pine cones, stimulating resin flow that sticks the scales together and pupating within the cone. In northwestern fir cones, larvae of two *Resseliella* species feed along the surface of scales, causing discolored necrotic areas; *Dasineura abiesemia* lives within swollen scales; and an undescribed *Dasineura* species overwinters and pupates within aborted seeds. Another *Resseliella* species lives in tamarack seeds. In white spruce, *Dasineura carpophaga* lives in swollen, discolored seeds, and a *Plemeliella* species inhabits externally unaffected seeds. Spruce cone axis midge larvae (*Kaltenbachiola rachiphaga*) live gregariously in the axis, lining their tunnel with silk and spinning cocoons inside it, and spruce cone gall midge larvae (*K. canadensis*) live singly in swollen scales. The Douglas-fir cone gall midge (*Contarinia oregonensis*) lives in swollen scales, and the Douglas-fir cone scale midge (*C. washingtonensis*) tunnels in unswollen scales, sometimes killing them and damaging seeds. *Janetiella siskiyou* larvae feed and spin cocoons among scales of Lawson's cypress, and *Mayetiola thujae* larvae do the same in western redcedar. In both cases, cones may be slightly deformed. *Sequoiomyia taxodii* causes swollen, aborted bald cypress seeds, emerging from them in the spring.

Tortricid Moths

Several *Cydia* species (Tortricidae) live in the axes of conifer cones, feeding on the maturing seeds. These include the ponderosa pine seedworm (*Cydia piperana*) in ponderosa and Jeffrey pines and Douglas-fir; the fir seed moth (*C. bracteatana*) in western firs and redwood; the spruce seed moth (*C. strobilella*) in western spruces; the eastern pine seedworm (*C. toreuta*) in jack, red, and Virginia pines; and the cypress bark moth (*C. cupressana*) in California cypresses.

Beetles

Bark beetles (Curculionidae: Scolytinae) in the genus *Conophthorus* also develop in the axes of various pine cones, causing them to die before reaching full size. The female excavates a brood gallery through the axis of the cone, laying many eggs along it, just as other scolytines do under bark. The flat-headed cone borer (Buprestidae: *Chrysophana placida*) develops in cones of knobcone and ponderosa pines. At least two species of deathwatch beetles (Anobiidae) in the genus *Ernobius* also develop in pine cones, killing them in the process.

Chalcids

Various species of *Megastigmus* chalcids (Torymidae) develop in seeds of members of the pine family, including pines, spruces, hemlocks, firs, Douglas-firs, and tamarack.

Nuts

When squirrels partially eat acorns, they are often really going after a developing beetle larva inside. Acorns processed by these larvae may later be colonized by *Temnothorax* ants that specialize in living inside damaged acorns.

The ants appear to finish the work of emptying the contents, and such acorns that we have inspected seemed slightly lighter weight than a typical grub-eaten acorn.

Weevils

Nut and acorn weevil larvae (*Curculio* spp.) develop within acorns and other nuts. Adults drill into nuts with their long beaks

Exit hole of an acorn weevil larva (Curculionidae: *Curculio*). (FL) Photo by David Almquist.

to feed on the meat, and in early summer, the female uses hers to drill tiny holes in which to lay her eggs. She plugs each oviposition hole with a fecal pellet, which dries and turns white. When the fully grown nuts fall to the ground, the mature larvae chew circular exit holes about 3 mm across and hibernate in the soil. Most species feed on acorns, but *C. caryae* feeds in pecans and hickory nuts and *C. obtusus* in hazelnuts. The larger chestnut weevil (*C. caryatrypes*) has a similar life cycle to the others, but the lesser chestnut weevil (*C. sayi*) lays eggs in mature chestnuts, and the larvae hibernate within the nuts. *C. caryae* adults feeding on immature hickory nuts can cause them to drop prematurely. There may be a brown stain around the feeding puncture in the husk, and the nut shrivels and blackens. Prematurely dropped nuts may also be caused by the hickory nut curculio (*Conotrachelus hicoriae*), which lays eggs in shallow, crescent-shaped punctures in the husks of pecans and hickory nuts. Brown sap bleeds from the point of entry, and mature larvae exit through a hole about 1.5 mm across. The walnut curculio (*Conotrachelus juglandis*) causes premature drop of butternuts and walnuts, as well as hickory nuts.

Moths

A few tortricid moth larvae feed on nuts. The hickory shuckworm (*Cydia caryana*) tunnels in the husks of pecans and hickory nuts, preventing the normal separation from the nut. Codling moth larvae (*C. pomonella*) sometimes tunnel in walnut husks. The filbertworm (*C. latiferreana*) feeds in acorns and hazelnuts, usually making its cocoon where it has been feeding, rather than leaving as the other species do. Larvae of the acorn moth (Coleophoridae: *Blastobasis glandulella*) feed inside acorns and chestnuts that have already been attacked by other insects, such as acorn weevils and filbertworms.

Pecan nut casebearer larvae (Pyralidae: *Acrobasis caryae*) bore into pecans, destroying very young ones but only feeding in the husks of more developed ones. Silk and black excrement are often visible outside the nuts. The navel orangeworm (*Amyelois transitella*) bores into almonds, walnuts, and many other nuts and fruits, either after the husk is cracked or using an entry hole made by another insect. It pupates in a cocoon inside the nut and constructs a tube leading to the exit hole.

Walnut Husk Fly

The walnut husk fly (Tephritidae: *Rhagoletis completa*; W) inserts a dozen or so eggs near the stalk of a developing walnut. The larvae develop as they burrow in the husk, then tunnel out and drop to the ground to pupate. The walnut shell may become stained, but the nut is not otherwise damaged.

Wasps

A number of gall wasps (Cynipidae) induce galls on acorns or in some cases cause them to be stunted or lopsided. The introduced pistachio seed chalcid (Torymidae: *Megastigmus pistaciae*) is a pest of pistachio nuts in California.

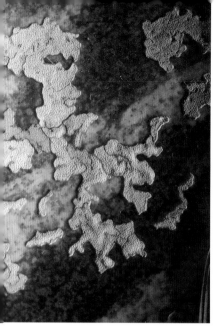

Scarring on the surface of a watermelon caused by feeding of striped cucumber beetles (Chrysomelidae: *Acalymma vittatum*). (MA)

Fleshy Fruits

Many of the same insects that feed on foliage and flowers feed similarly on the surfaces of fleshy fruits. Some stink bugs, plant bugs, scentless plant bugs, and leaf-footed bugs suck juices of developing fruits, and weevils make round punctures to feed on the flesh. Any of these may cause droplets of resin to appear and eventually result in the fruit becoming blemished, gnarled, and distorted. The false spider mite *Brevipalpus lewisi* (Tenuipalpidae) causes scars on lemons. Fork-tailed bush katydids (Tettigoniidae: *Scudderia furcata*) sometimes damage developing oranges by nibbling holes through the rind, and tree crickets (Gryllidae: Oecanthinae) have been observed chewing round pits in plums, peaches, and grapes. Slugs feeding on strawberries bite out rounded chunks in a pattern similar to their sign on mushrooms. Striped cucumber beetles (Chrysomelidae: *Acalymma vittatum*) eat extensive patches on the surfaces of melons and other cucurbits, which form brown scar tissue. The green fruitworm (*Lithophane antennata*) and other noctuids chew broad, round cavities in the surfaces of young apples and other fruits, sometimes causing them to drop. Various scarab beetles, scorpionflies, and woodlice also occasionally eat fleshy fruits.

In addition to these mostly generalist surface feeders, many insects feed inside fleshy fruits. Many of those mentioned here make small punctures in fruit skins to insert eggs, as do some thrips and leafhoppers. The leafhopper *Draeculacephala mollipes* makes crescent-shaped cuts in apple skin, 3 to 4 mm long and each containing up to 20 or more eggs. Well over a hundred punctures may be made in a single apple.

Moths

A few leaf-mining moths sometimes make long, winding, linear mines in the skins of fruits, just like the ones they normally make in leaves or stems. *Marmara pomonella* mines in apple skin. Both *M. gulosa* and *Phyllocnistis citrella* mine in the skins of citrus fruits. The completed mines are easily distinguished, because *Marmara* leaves the mine to pupate, whereas *Phyllocnistis* pupates in a cocoon within a slightly enlarged space at the end of the mine.

Larvae of some tortricid moths bore in fleshy fruits, leaving droppings and webbing as evidence in addition to the tunnels. In some cases, they make tunnels just under the skin; these appear on the surface as brown lines, unlike the whitish trails left by leafminers tunneling within the skin. Often droppings accumulate at the entrance hole. Lesser appleworms (*Grapholita prunivora*) tunnel in apples and other rosaceous fruits. Larvae of the oriental fruit moth (*G. molesta*) and codling moth (*Cydia pomonella*) do as well, both sometimes also turning up in unrelated fruits. Codling moth larvae work their way to the core, often eating the seeds, and fill their burrows with excrement. The cherry fruitworm (*G. packardi*) bores in blueberries and cherries, as well as larger rosaceous fruits. The larvae leave conspicuous exit holes, which are sealed with silk plugs. The orange tortrix (*Argyrotaenia citrana*)

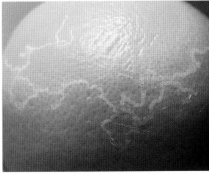

Mines of *Marmara gulosa* (Gracillariidae) in an orange.

burrows in ripe oranges, and the grape berry moth (*Paralobesia viteana*) spins webbing between grapes, eating both pulp and seeds.

The cranberry fruitworm (Pyralidae: *Acrobasis vaccinii*) bores into cranberries, blueberries, and huckleberries, causing them to shrivel. Clusters of berries become encrusted with webbing and brown excrement. The destructive pruneworm (*A. scitulella*) bores into cherries and plums. The gooseberry fruitworm (*Zophodia grossulariella*) causes full-grown gooseberries and currants to turn prematurely red and dull whitish. It consumes the insides of several berries, connecting them with silk and depositing its droppings out a hole in each berry.

The fruitworm moths (Carposinidae) also bore in fleshy fruits. They include the currant fruitworm (*Carposina fernaldana*; also in apple and hawthorn fruits) and peach fruit moth (*C. sasakii*; in a variety of rosaceous fruits). The tomato pinworm (Gelechiidae: *Keiferia lycopersicella*; S) bores pinholes in the developing buds and fruits of tomatoes, usually near the stalk. The corn earworm also sometimes tunnels into tomatoes.

Beetles

A number of weevil species (Curculionidae) are associated with fleshy fruits, laying eggs when the fruits are still green and developing. The plum gouger (*Coccotorus scutellaris*) makes round punctures in plums; these are conspicuous because of the resin that exudes in abundance. The larva develops in the pit and usually pupates there as well. The plum curculio (*Conotrachelus nenuphar*) also oviposits in plums, among many other rosaceous fruits (apples, peaches, nectarines, apricots, cherries, pears, and quince) and even blueberries. After depositing a single egg in a round puncture, the female makes a diagonal, crescent-shaped cut, separating a little flap that includes the egg. This apparently serves to prevent the growing fruit from crushing the egg. Plums drop prematurely, but cherries ripen; apples and pears ripen but are deformed. The larva packs its droppings into a cavity in the fruit, and when mature, it bores out and pupates in the ground. Apple curculio larvae (*Anthonomus quadrigibbus*) develop and pupate in the flesh

Hole in an aging strawberry made by a sap beetle (Nitidulidae: *Glischrochilus*).

of apples. A grape that appears to be ripening prematurely may contain a larval grape curculio (*Craponius inaequalis*) feeding on the flesh and seeds within. The mature larva drops to the ground to pupate.

Spotted asparagus beetle larvae (Chrysomelidae: *Crioceris duodecimpunctata*) feed inside ripening asparagus berries. Larvae of the raspberry fruitworm beetle (Byturidae: *Byturus unicolor*) feed in the cups of raspberries, causing them to drop. *Glischrochilus* sap beetles (Nitidulidae) are not typically found in fruit that is in good condition, but they are common in fruit that is damaged or past its prime.

Flies

The pear midge (*Contarinia pyrivora*) causes pears to grow faster than normal at first, then stop at about 1 cm long. At this point, the larvae, which have developed in the core, exit and drop to the ground to pupate. Chokecherry midge larvae (*C. virginianiae*) develop gregariously in the centers of wild cherries, which grow to twice the normal size but without developing a pit. *Cecidomyia grossulariae* causes gooseberries to become enlarged and deformed and to turn red and drop prematurely.

Some female fruit flies (Tephritidae) insert eggs in ripening fruits. The larvae make winding burrows, sometimes visible through the skin as dark lines or slight depressions, then leave to pupate in the ground. The apple maggot (*Rhagoletis pomonella*) develops in apples, plums, peaches, cherries, hawthorn fruits, cranberries, and dogwood fruits. Several related species are more specific to cherries, and walnut husk flies sometimes develop in peaches. *R. mendax* is the blueberry maggot, and *Euphranta canadensis* is the currant and gooseberry fruit fly. The pepper maggot (*Zonosemata electa*) breeds in a variety of nightshade fruits; other *Zonosemata* species are restricted to *Solanum* species, such as tomato and eggplant.

The Drosophilidae are also known as fruit flies, and these are most often what people are referring to when they use this common name. These small flies, also known as pomace flies or vinegar flies, do not oviposit in developing fruit. Instead, they lay eggs, and their larvae develop, in rotting fruit or other decaying organic matter.

Chalcids and Sawflies

A number of chalcids develop in seeds of fleshy fruits. The female's long ovipositor is inserted through the flesh of the developing fruit, and her offspring usually emerge as adults after the fruits have decayed. *Eurytoma vitis* and *Prodecatoma cooki* (Eurytomidae) both develop in grape seeds, the latter also in Virginia creeper. *Bephratelloides cubensis* (FL) develops in cherimoya and other custard-apples. Torymids that inhabit fruit seeds include *Torymus rugglesi* in American holly; *T. thompsoni* in plum; *T. varians* in apple, hawthorn, pear, and mountain-ash; and various *Megastigmus* species in rose hips and other rosaceous fruits.

Just as yucca fruits are a sign of yucca moths, figs are a sign of pollinating fig wasps (Agaonidae: Agaoninae). Figs are dependent on fig wasps for pollination, and some agaonid species have been imported to make fig cultivation possible. Fig inflorescences include two types of flowers, one of which develops into seeds, with the others becoming tiny galls containing wasp larvae; all of these are contained within the fig.

Hoplocampa sawflies (Tenthredinidae) oviposit in the ovaries of rosaceous fruits. The larva tunnels and feeds in the flesh, exiting through a hole when mature; at this point, the fruit usually drops. Species include the cherry fruit sawfly (*H. cookei*; W; also in plum), pear fruit sawfly (*H. brevis*), and apple fruit sawfly (*H. brevis*). Adults of other species have been found on flowers of shadbush, hawthorn, and other related plants, so these are likely hosts as well. The dock sawfly (*Ametastegia glabrata*; N) also occasionally bores round holes in apples. Many other tenthredinids sometimes bore into apples and other fleshy fruits, not to feed, but to overwinter and pupate.

Seedlings

Certain insects are notorious for damaging tender shoots in gardens and cultivated fields. For the most part, they cannot be reliably identified by their feeding sign alone, but most are larvae that live in the soil, so with a little digging, you may find the culprits or their pupae. In addition to the insects noted here, woodlice and millipedes sometimes feed on young seedlings or may cause them to wilt by feeding on the taproots. All of these arthropods are generalists, eating a variety of plant species.

Numerous noctuid caterpillars (e.g., *Agrotis*, *Feltia*, *Nephelodes*) are known as "cutworms" because they chew off young shoots just above or below ground level. They are active at night, hiding underground during the day. Many species drag the shoots into their burrows before feeding on them. Others just eat the base of a plant, leaving most of the severed shoot lying on the ground. Plants killed in this way may also be the result of feeding by "white grubs," the larvae of June bugs and their relatives (Scarabaeidae: Melolonthinae). They feed on roots, often cutting taproots just below the ground surface. "Leatherjackets" (Tipulidae: Tipulinae) are crane fly larvae that primarily feed on roots as well. On evenings when it is humid or the ground is covered with dew, they may feed at the ground surface, cutting young plants down as cutworms do. Both larvae and adults of the introduced vegetable weevils (Curculionidae: *Listroderes*; S) feed on the aboveground portion of young shoots, the adults often cutting them off at the base.

The introduced seedcorn maggot (Anthomyiidae: *Delia platura*) feeds on a variety of decomposing matter, but also on very young living plants.

The larvae feed on germinating seeds and tunnel in young stems, cotyledons, and leaves while they are still underground. If the plant succeeds in sprouting, the first true leaves may have holes or be missing entirely, rendering it unable to grow any further.

Roots and Other Underground Plant Parts

Many insects and nematodes feed on roots and other underground plant parts. Most of the time, they do so without having any visible effect aboveground, so they are unlikely to be noticed except in plants we dig up to use for food. Plants with heavy infestations may have stunted growth or develop a general sickly appearance and eventually die.

Beetles

Various leaf beetle larvae feed on underground parts of plants. Most likely to be noticed are the dark tunnels of tuber flea beetles (*Epitrix tuberis*; W) in potatoes and the shallow, winding tunnels of sweet potato flea beetles (*Chaetocnema confinis*) on the surfaces of sweet potatoes. Striped cucumber beetle larvae (*Acalymma vittatum*) feed in cucurbits, hollowing out the upper part of the root and the underground portion of the stem. Larvae of several *Diabrotica* species bore in the roots of corn and other grasses and are known as corn rootworms. The grape rootworm (*Fidia viticida*) eats smaller grape roots and tunnels in larger ones.

Chrysomelids are by no means the only subterranean herbivores among beetles. Some click beetle larvae (Elateridae), known as wireworms, tunnel in carrots, potatoes, and roots of many other plants, sometimes causing serious damage. "White grubs," the larvae of June bugs, Japanese beetles, and other scarabs, primarily feed on roots. There have been reports of these occurring in lawns in such high densities that they completely severed the roots, so that the turf could be rolled up like a carpet. Many weevil larvae (Curculionidae) feed on roots of herbaceous plants, particularly broad-nosed weevils (Entiminae) and baridines; some of them induce galls. *Sphenophorus* billbug larvae feed on the bulbous roots of grasses and sedges. Carrot weevils (*Listronotus oregonensis*) oviposit in carrot and parsley stems, and the larvae tunnel into the roots. Some ironclad beetles (Zopheridae) bore into rootstalks of agave. Larvae of burrowing water beetles (Noteridae) feed on submerged roots of aquatic plants, as do aquatic leaf beetle larvae (Chrysomelidae: Donaciinae). Some darkling beetles (Tenebrionidae) also feed on roots.

Flies

Although the seedcorn maggot feeds only on tender shoots, some of its relatives feed in roots of older plants. The onion fly (Anthomyiidae: *Delia antiqua*) lays eggs on onion and related plants at all stages of development. The maggots crawl down behind the leaf sheaths and feed on the roots, killing seedlings and causing developing bulbs to become misshapen. They bore into mature onions left on the ground to dry. Cabbage maggots (*D. radicum*) at first feed on fibrous root hairs, later tunneling into roots and stems. Damaged cabbages often wilt, but radishes and turnips do not, and the maggots' feeding is likely to go unnoticed until the roots are harvested.

Two types of introduced syrphid flies develop in flower bulbs. The larva of the narcissus bulb fly (*Merodon equestris*) enters at the base of a bulb, leaving a sunken brown splotch there, and eats a large cavity in the center of the bulb. Lesser bulb flies (*Eumerus*) usually enter and begin excavating a cavity at the neck of the bulb. Their feeding in association with bacteria and fungi turns bulbs to mush. They also feed on potatoes.

Some picture-winged fly larvae (Ulidiidae) feed on roots. The best known is the sugarbeet root maggot (*Tetanops myopaeformis*; W), which feeds on the root surface, causing it to turn black. Older sources mention the black onion fly (*Tritoxa flexa*) and barred-winged onion fly (*Chaetopsis aenea*) feeding within and destroying onions, but we have found no mention of this in recent literature.

Larvae of some winter crane flies (Trichoceridae: *Trichocera*) feed inside potatoes. "Leatherjacket" crane fly larvae (Tipulidae: Tipulinae) feed on various kinds of roots just below the soil surface. They are sometimes abundant enough to cause bare, brown patches in fields. March fly larvae (Bibionidae) also feed on roots, sometimes killing large patches of grass. The carrot rust fly (Psilidae: *Chamaepsila rosae*) lays eggs at the base of carrot and other plants in the parsley family. The larva feeds at the top of the root, girdling it and excavating rusty red tunnels, causing the plant to turn yellow and wilt. Some gall midges and tephritid fruit flies also develop in roots.

Moths

Many noctuids in the genus *Papaipema* bore in roots, rhizomes, and the lower portions of stems. A number of these are on various states' rare species lists. Several feed in fern rhizomes, including the bracken borer moth (*P. pterisii*), chain fern borer moth (*P. stenocelis*), osmunda borer moth (*P. speciosissima*; in cinnamon, interrupted, and royal ferns), sensitive fern borer moth (*P. inquaesita*), and ostrich fern borer moth (not yet formally described). Others include the columbine borer moth (*P. leucostigma*), pitcher plant borer moth (*P. appassionata*), and various species feeding in burdock, sunflowers, and other plants in the aster family. The buffalo moth (*Parapamea buffaloensis*) bores in the roots of lizard's tail. Iris borer caterpillars (*Macronoctua onusta*) bore into iris leaves and make their way into the rhizome, eventually killing the plant. Some cutworms are strictly subterranean, feeding externally on roots and other underground plant parts, rather than cutting off shoots near the surface.

Larvae of clearwing moths (Sesiidae) are all borers in plant tissue, and certain species feed in roots. These include the grape root borer (*Vitacea polistiformis*), raspberry crown borer (*Pennisetia marginata*), strawberry crown borers (*Synanthedon bibionipennis*), manroot borer (*Melittia gloriosa*; also in wild gourds), and eupatorium borer (*Carmenta bassiformis*; in ironweed and Joe-Pye weed). At least some of these leave their pupal skins protruding from the bases of the stems when they emerge as adults.

The triangle-backed eucosma (Tortricidae: *Eucosma dorsisignatana*) bores in goldenrod roots. Many others in this genus, and a few other olethreutines, bore in roots of various other plants in the aster family.

The potato tuberworm (Gelechiidae: *Phthorimaea operculella*) tunnels in stored potatoes, filling them with webbing and excrement.

Other Invertebrates

Many soil-dwelling nematodes feed on roots and cause pronounced necrosis at their feeding sites. Their feeding can directly introduce viruses, as well as create wounds through which bacteria and fungi can enter the plant, and the sign of these pathogens is more obvious than the actual feeding sign.

Several different mites feed on bulbs. Onion mites (Eriophyidae: *Aceria tulipae*) live between the layers of onion, garlic, and tulip bulbs, causing them to shrink and dry out. The presence of bulb scale mites (Tarsonemidae: *Steneotarsonemus laticeps*) leads to similar symptoms in bulbs of narcissus and others in the amaryllis family. Bulb mites (Acaridae: *Rhizoglyphus*) enter a wide variety of already damaged bulbs, quickly turning them to a rotten pulp.

Slugs eat bulbs and tubers, and are among the most important pests of potatoes. They often make a small, round hole that opens up into a large chamber. This is the opposite of typical cutworm damage, which consists of more extensive feeding on the surface, becoming narrower as it goes deeper.

Cicada nymphs suck sap from tree roots. Certain aphids and scale insects feed on roots as well.

Stored Dry Plant Matter

Death-watch beetles (Anobiidae) such as the drugstore beetle (*Stegobium paniceum*), cigarette beetle (*Lasioderma serricorne*), and spider beetles (Ptininae) are commonly found in stored vegetable matter, reducing it to powder as they feed. They may infest spices (including cayenne pepper), tobacco, herbarium specimens, flour, seeds, and books. One white-marked spider beetle (*Ptinus fur*) was credited with boring in a perfectly straight line through twenty-seven large books. The presence of silken cocoons (see page 237) indicates these rather than other beetles that infest stored products, such as mealworms (Tenebrionidae) or the coffee bean weevil (Anthribidae: *Araecerus fasciculatus*). *Oryzaephilus* grain beetles (Silvanidae), except when in fine materials such as flour, construct a thin pupal cell of food particles held together with sticky oral secretions. Moth larvae feeding in stored products can be recognized by the webbing they produce; see chapter 6 for details. Flour mites (Acaridae: *Acarus siro*) infest flour, grains, and dried fruits and vegetables. They leave only the husks when feeding on grains. The mites give foods a sickly sweet smell and make them unpalatable.

10

Leaf Mines

Leaf mining is a distinctive style of foliage feeding in which a larva lives between the two epidermal layers of a leaf, feeding on the tissue in between. The vast majority of leafminers are moths and flies, but a few are sawflies and beetles. It is often possible to identify a leafminer to species based solely on the host plant and the characteristics of the mine. This is, in fact, usually much more straightforward than examining the larvae, as most are wormlike and fairly nondescript. Sometimes even the adult insects are best distinguished by the mines from which they have emerged. Note, however, that of the several hundred known species of leaf-mining agromyzid flies, the host plants have been identified for fewer than half, so it may not be possible to determine which agromyzid is responsible for a particular mine without rearing the larva and examining the adult. The other three groups include numerous species that likewise have not been linked to a host plant or that have a known host plant but their mine has not been described. Some nematodes could be considered leafminers, but their feeding sign is more similar to that of externally feeding insects with piercing-sucking mouthparts and was described in the previous chapter. A few insects mine in petioles, and some giant skippers bore in the fleshy leaves of agave, but these habits are more akin to stem boring and are discussed in chapter 13.

Leaf mines can take two basic shapes: *linear* mines, in which the larva plows ahead through the leaf tissue as it feeds, forming a narrow trail, and *blotch* mines, in which the larva excavates a broad patch. There are variations within these types and intergradations between them. In addition to the shape of the mines, key features to notice include their location on the leaf (top or bottom, middle or edge), the type and placement of excrement, the presence or absence of a pupa or cocoon, and in a few cases the presence of conspicuous eggs.

In distinguishing mines, it is useful to understand the anatomy of a leaf. The *epidermis*, the outer layer, is by definition not eaten by leafminers (although some may eventually stop mining and feed externally). The interior is called the *mesophyll* and consists of veins and *parenchyma*. The parenchyma, in turn, is made up of two layers: the upper *palisade* layer, which is most nutritious but dense and difficult to penetrate, and the lower *spongy* layer, which is relatively easy to penetrate. *Full-depth* miners consume all the parenchyma, making the mine equally visible from both sides.

Most leafminers do not have common names. Those that have been suggested, such as the "cherry leafminer," are often confusing because they could describe any number of species. Unless otherwise noted, the families listed here are moths. Given the existence of hundreds of leaf-mining species, this chapter can only scratch the surface of the subject. The most comprehensive account of North American leafminers is Needham et al. (1928). Forbes (1923) is very useful for identifying mines of northeastern moths. Both of these are full of out-of-date names and have a number of misidentifications, and many species have been discovered since they were written. This tends to be the case with older references in general, but they remain excellent resources despite these shortcomings. Various comprehensive works describe and illustrate mines for a single family or smaller group, such as Braun (1908) for Lithocolletinae (Gracillariidae); Braun (1917) and Wilkinson and Scoble (1979) for Nepticulidae; Braun (1972) for Tischeriidae; and Spencer and Steyskal (1986) for agromyzid flies. Spencer (1990) lists all of the world's agromyzid flies with known hosts, grouped by host plant. Literature published before Spencer's monograph is full of misinformation, and it is best to ignore any names or host records that conflict with what it says.

Linear Mines

Included in this section are linear mines that remain narrow for their full length, such as those of *Phyllocnistis* and *Marmara*, as well as some that gradually increase in width and may end in a blotchlike enlargement. *Serpentine mine* has been defined by some authors as describing this latter type, but more commonly this term is used interchangeably with *linear*, although it is not really appropriate to apply it to the occasional linear mines that do not follow a sinuous course. Not included here are the many blotch miners, such as anthomyiids, agromyzids, eriocraniids, lyonetiids, *Phyllonorycter* species, and certain sawflies, that often begin with a linear mine but soon expand it into a blotch, which may or may not obliterate the linear portion. Finished mines that typically have both a distinct linear portion and a pronounced blotch (some of which might be considered serpentine) are covered in the next section.

Gracillariidae

Phyllocnistis species (Gracillariidae) always make a long, tortuous linear mine that never becomes a blotch. These larvae are unusual among leaf miners in that they feed only on sap. They cut through just the outer cells of the mesophyll, drinking the liquid contents. Because it takes a long time to obtain enough nutrients from this to become a moth, they grow slowly and make particularly long mines that widen very gradually. The excrement is, naturally, liquid and may be a dark central line (commonly referred to as a "frass line," even though it is pure excrement) or invisible. The mine may appear whitened or may just be a bit shinier than the rest of the leaf. Whereas most leaf mines are more pronounced when backlit, these are so shallow that there is little or no difference. When it is done growing, the larva pupates in a silken chamber formed in a slightly widened space at the end of the mine. The adult leaves the pupal skin projecting from the mine when it emerges.

The *Phyllocnistis* species can mostly be distinguished by host plant. *P. populiella* mines in poplar leaves; *P. liquidambarisella* in sweetgum; *P. liriodendronella* in tuliptree; *P. magnoliella* in magnolia; *P. citrella* in citrus; *P. intermediella* in false mastic; and *P. ampelopsiella* in Virginia creeper. In grape leaves, *P. vitifoliella* leaves a dark frass line, whereas *P. vitegenella* makes a subtle, shining mine with no visible excrement. *P. finitima* mines in southwestern ragworts, *P. insignis* in fireweed and other eastern asteraceous plants including ragwort.

Marmara is another genus of sap-feeding gracillariids that make very long, tortuous mines. Unlike *Phyllocnistis*, the larva leaves the mine to pupate. *M. smilacisella* mines the upper surface of *Smilax* leaves, leaving a narrow central frass line. *M. arbutiella* makes pure white mines in madrone and manzanita leaves, sometimes mining through the petioles and under

Left: Mine of *Phyllocnistis insignis* in a golden ragwort leaf. (MA) *Right:* Mine of *Phyllocnistis liquidambarisella* in a sweetgum leaf. (VA)

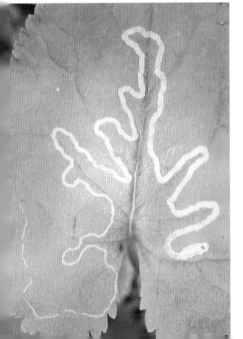
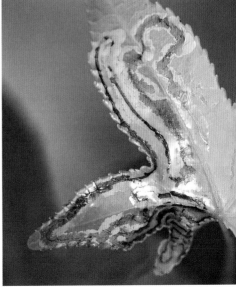

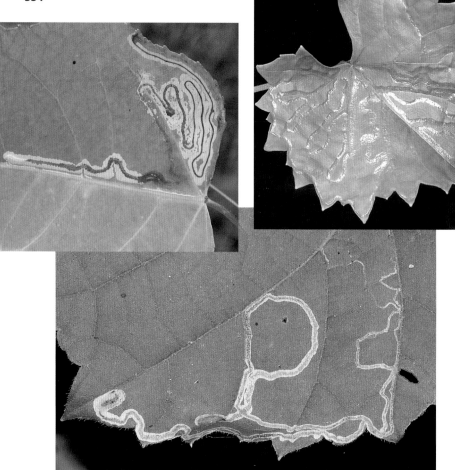

Top left: Mine of *Phyllocnistis populiella* (Gracillariidae) in a poplar leaf. (VT) *Top right:* Mine of *Phyllocnistis vitegenella* in a grape leaf. Typical of this species, the larva is pupating in a small fold at the edge of the leaf. (NC) *Above:* Two mines of *Phyllocnistis vitifoliella* in a grape leaf, with cocoons at the ends. (TN)

the bark of twigs. The other species mine under the cuticles of young twigs or semiherbaceous stems rather than in leaves, or sometimes in the skins of fruits.

Neurobathra strigifinitella makes a unique mine in oak, chestnut, and beech. It begins by making a short, irregular linear mine on the underside of the leaf. It then bores into a side vein, and finally into the midrib. When mature, it descends on a silk strand to spin its equally distinctive cocoon.

Nepticulidae

Virtually all nepticulid moth larvae mine in leaves of deciduous trees and shrubs. Their mines tend to be linear or serpentine, but some widen into blotches in later instars (sometimes abruptly), and a few have no linear component. The excrement is usually deposited in a black central line or sometimes a zigzag. The mines that remain narrow like those of *Phyllocnistis* are easily distinguished, because the larvae are tissue feeders and consume much of the parenchyma, making the mines more transparent; the excrement is also more solid and well defined. Another difference is that a nepticulid larva leaves through a small hole cut in the epidermis to spin a cocoon elsewhere, usually on the ground.

Nepticulids with mines that remain narrow for their entire length include *Stigmella tiliella* in basswood; *S. juglandifoliella* in butternut and walnut; *S. apicialbella* in elm; *S. pallida* on the undersides of willow leaves; *S. intermedia* in sumac; *S. rhoifoliella* in poison ivy; *S. castaneaefoliella* in chestnut; several *Stigmella* species in oaks; *S. condaliafoliella* in leadwood; *S. prunifoliella* in cherry and plum; *S. chalybeia* in pear (often less than 2 cm long); *S. amelanchierella* in shadbush (rather broad and irregular); *S. rosae-*

Right: Mine of **Stigmella tiliella** (Nepticulidae) in a basswood leaf. The track is 1 to 1.5 mm wide. (MA)
Below: Mine of **Stigmella crataegifoliella** in a hawthorn leaf. The track is up to 2 mm wide. (MA)

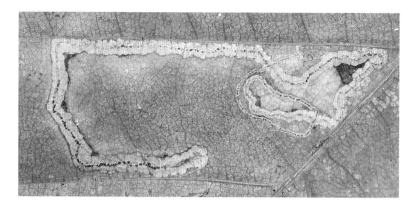

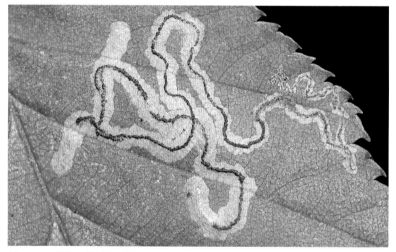

Above top: Mine of *Stigmella castaneaefoliella* in a chestnut leaf. The track is up to 2 mm wide. (MA) *Above:* Mine of *Stigmella corylifoliella* in a black birch leaf. (MA)

foliella in rose; *S. villosella* in blackberry; *S. corylifoliella* in hazelnut, birch, alder, witch hazel, blueberry, huckleberry, cranberry, and ninebark; *S. ostryaefoliella* in hophornbeam, musclewood, hickory, and bayberry; *S. ceanothi* in hairy ceanothus; *Acalyptris punctulatus* in buckbrush and California buckthorn; *Trifurcula saccharella* in maples; and *Ectoedemia pteliaeella* in hoptree (very contorted; sometimes blotchlike). In hawthorn, *S. crataegifoliella* makes a mine that follows the edge of the leaf for part of its length, eventually widening to 2 mm or so; the mine of *S. scintillans* is only up to about 1 mm wide, often crossing under itself.

Bucculatricidae

The ribbed cocoon makers (Bucculatricadae: *Bucculatrix*) make narrow, brown, serpentine mines in the upper surfaces of leaves until around the first molt. At this point, most species emerge and skeletonize the lower leaf surfaces, as described in the previous chapter, spinning special molting cocoons each time they molt. Their mines have a central frass line, somewhat like nepticulid mines, but can be recognized by their short length (about 2 cm) as well as by these associated signs. *B. staintonella* completes its development inside the mine. It makes a full-depth linear mine in a new leaf of heart-leaved aster, in very early spring or even late winter. The ribbed cocoons in which *Bucculatrix* species pupate are spun away from their feeding sites more often than not. There are around a hundred species, a few examples of which were given in the last chapter.

Gelechiidae

Chrysoesthia drurella (Gelechiidae) makes coarse, tightly meandering linear mines in leaves of lambsquarters and orache, with excrement scattered throughout. They bear little resemblance to the neat mines of the moths noted above. The larva may exit the leaf and reenter at another point.

Agromyzid Flies

Some agromyzid flies make long, narrow, linear mines. Examples include *Ophiomyia quinta* in asters and goldenrods; *Liriomyza eupatoriella* in white snakeroot; and *L. smilacinae* in starry false Solomon's seal. The excrement, if visible, may be in discrete specks or a thin, disjointed, and irregularly meandering drizzle. A few species make mothlike continuous central frass lines. Some may pupate inside the mine, but most drop to the ground to do so. Often the distinctive feeding punctures of the females are present. *Phytomyza opacae* makes long, linear mines in American and English hollies. When *P. ilicicola* oviposits in English holly, the larva

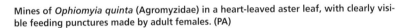

Mines of *Ophiomyia quinta* (Agromyzidae) in a heart-leaved aster leaf, with clearly visible feeding punctures made by adult females. (PA)

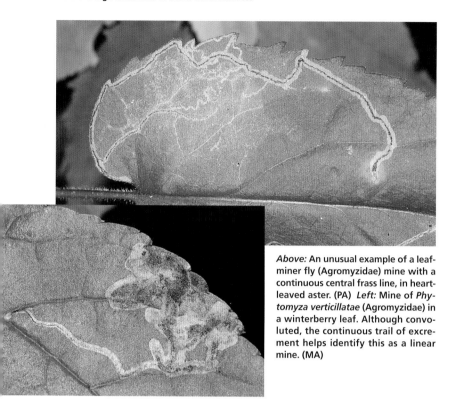

Above: An unusual example of a leaf-miner fly (Agromyzidae) mine with a continuous central frass line, in heart-leaved aster. (PA) *Left:* Mine of *Phytomyza verticillatae* (Agromyzidae) in a winterberry leaf. Although convoluted, the continuous trail of excrement helps identify this as a linear mine. (MA)

Mines of *Liriomyza eupatoriella* (Agromyzidae) in a white snakeroot leaf. (PA)

makes a narrow linear mine, and then dies without producing the blotch it would normally make in American holly. The mine of *P. verticillatae* in winterberry is generally an irregularly linear one, but it may become blotchlike at the end. At least one agromyzid commonly makes a linear mine in raspberry and blackberry.

Other agromyzids make broader serpentine mines, which tend to be pale with clearly visible specks or strips of black excrement. *Phytomyza persicae* makes a very distinctive mine in peach leaves, with the excrement in a single neat row of dots. The mine of *P. minuscula* in columbine has conspicuous strips of excrement, whereas that of *P. aquilegivora* may have strips or scattered grains. The latter, at least, may attach its puparium to the outside of the leaf. *P. aralivora* mines in wild sarsaparilla.

Most agromyzids are restricted to one species or genus of plants, or perhaps to several genera in a family or several families in an order. A few generalist *Liriomyza* species, however, often make irregular-looking serpentine mines in a variety of garden plants, particularly in the southern United States. The vegetable leafminer (*L. sativae*) feeds in leaves of legumes, nightshades, cucurbits, and onions, among others. The American serpentine leafminer (*L. trifolii*) is found in all of these, as well as the parsley family, but is especially common in chrysanthemums and other composites. The pea leafminer (*L. huidobrensis*; W) mines leaves of at least ten different families. Its mine usually follows the midrib or a main vein. Although the first two sometimes mine in plants in the mustard family, the most likely suspect for mines in these plants is the cabbage leafminer (*L. brassicae*). In addition to mustards, this species mines in leaves of caper, cleome, and nasturtium, which belong to other families in the same order.

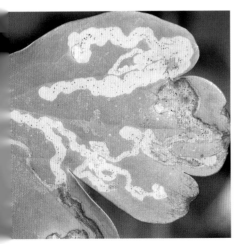 

Left: Serpentine mines of *Phytomyza aquilegivora* in a garden columbine leaf. (TN) *Right:* Serpentine mine of *Phytomyza aralivora* in a wild sarsaparilla leaf. (MA)

Mines of plantain flea beetle larvae (Chrysomelidae: *Dibolia borealis*) in common plantain. (MA)

Leaf Beetles

Most beetle mines are blotches, but some chrysomelid larvae make distinctly linear mines. The plantain flea beetle (*Dibolia borealis*) makes irregular linear mines on common plantain leaves. Often there are multiple larvae in one leaf, and their mines run into one another, sometimes occupying the whole leaf and causing it to wither. *Mantura* species make short linear or serpentine mines in dock leaves, and *Phyllotreta* species make similar mines in mustards.

Linear-Blotch Mines

Mines covered in this section begin with a distinct linear portion and end with a distinct blotch. There are some gray areas between these and some of the serpentine mines in the previous section, as well as the trumpet mines of the next section. Flea weevils, some gracillariids, and many lyonetiids start by making a narrow linear track that may or may not be visible in the finished blotch; they are discussed in the section on blotch mines below.

Nepticulidae

Many nepticulids make mines of this type, with a distinct central frass line at least in the linear portion. *Stigmella fuscotibiella* makes mines on the upper surfaces of willow leaves that gradually widen, often becoming blotches at the ends. *S. populetorum* and the virtually identical *S. aromella* make similar mines in poplar leaves. The linear mine of *S. quercipulchella* in oak widens dramatically but maintains a narrow central frass line throughout its length. Other nepticulids with linear mines that expand into definite blotches include *S. argentifasciella* in basswood (the linear portion is mainly visible

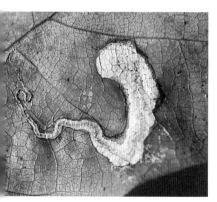

Mine of *Stigmella quercipulchella* (Nepticulidae) in a red oak leaf. (MA)

on the underside); *S. rhamnicola* in lanceleaf buckthorn (linear portion on underside, blotch on upper surface); *S. slingerlandella* in cherry and plum; *Ectoedemia trinotata* in hickory; *E. similella* in pin oak; *E. ulmella* in elm; *E. rubifoliella* in blackberry; *E. nyssaefoliella* in tupelo; *E. canadensis* (BC) in alder; *E. clemensella* in sycamore (a long linear mine that suddenly broadens into a small terminal blotch); and *E. quadrinotata* in musclewood, hophornbeam, hazelnut, and yellow birch. *S. scinanella* and *S. pomivorella* both feed in apple leaves (the latter also in hawthorn), forming a linear mine that suddenly broadens about halfway through its length.

A distinct variation on a linear-blotch mine is made by *Ectoedemia argyropeza* in poplar leaves. The larva begins by mining in the petiole, causing some amount of swelling. Once in the leaf blade, it forms a blotch mine.

Tischeriidae

Tischeria ceanothi (Tischeriidae) mines in ceanothus leaves. The mine begins with a gradually widening linear portion with a black central frass line. It then expands into a blotch, which may cover part of the linear portion, with the excrement fairly evenly distributed. The typical mine of *T. bifurcata*, also in ceanothus, begins with a linear part that curves until it hits the midrib, follows it for some distance toward the base of the leaf, and then expands irregularly on either side of the midrib.

Agromyzid Flies

Some agromyzid flies make an abrupt change from a linear mine to a blotch after the first (sometimes second) instar. The native *Phytomyza ilicicola* (E) mines in American holly; the introduced *P. ilicis* in English holly; and *P. glabricola* (E) in inkberry. They pupate inside the leaf. *Agromyza aristata* mines in elm leaves in very early spring. It begins at the edge of the leaf and makes a pale green linear track until its second molt, at which point it forms a narrow brown blotch about 1 inch (2.5 cm) long, with excrement arranged in two rows of dots. The oak shothole leafminer (*Japanagromyza*

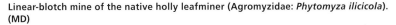

Linear-blotch mine of the native holly leafminer (Agromyzidae: *Phytomyza ilicicola*). (MD)

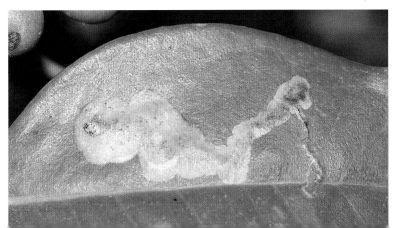

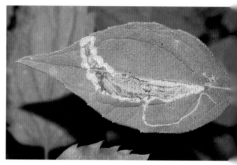

Top: Mines of *Phytoliriomyza melampyga* (Agromyzidae) in a jewelweed leaf, with feeding punctures made by adult females. (MA) *Above left:* Mine of *Agromyza aristata* (Agromyzidae) in an American elm leaf. (MA) *Above right:* Linear-blotch mine of *Liriomyza philadelphivora* (Agromyzidae) in a mock orange leaf. (PA)

viridula) usually makes a linear mine along a leaf vein, then expands it to a blotch when it reaches the edge of the leaf. *Agromyza frontella* mines in clover and alfalfa; *Amauromyza pleuralis* in catalpa; *Phytoliriomyza melampyga* in jewelweed; and *Liriomyza philadelphivora* in mock orange.

Trumpet Mines

Trumpet mines are intermediate between linear-blotch and blotch mines. They expand in one direction from an obvious starting point, but without an extended linear portion. Mines of this form are characteristic of certain tischeriids. The mine of *Coptotriche fuscomarginella* (E), in chestnut and various oaks, is translucent and has the excrement retained and packed in an elongate mass in the narrower portion. The pupal chamber is usually constructed over a lateral vein, and there are many fine folds in the upper epidermis marking its location. *C. castaneaeella* (E) makes a similar mine

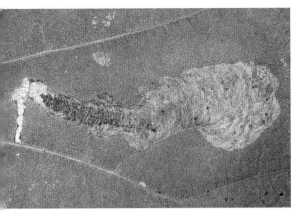

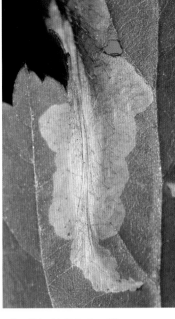

Above: Trumpet mine of *Coptotriche castaneaeella* (Tischeriidae) in a red oak leaf, 1.3 inches (3.3 cm) long. (MA) *Right:* Trumpet mine of *Coptotriche aenea* in a northern dewberry leaflet. (MA)

in various oaks, but the mine is grayish and marked by characteristic concentric crescents in the upper epidermis. *C. malifoliella* (E) makes a trumpet mine in apple and hawthorn, and *C. aenea* (E) in blackberry (the finished mine may have prominent longitudinal folds); the mine of *C. splendida* (CA) in Pacific dewberry apparently is similar. Two species in this genus have been reared from mines radiating from the midribs of cultivated strawberry leaflets in California.

Bucculatrix angustata (Bucculatricidae) mines in aster, fleabane, and goldenrod. Rather than making a linear mine and abandoning it to feed externally as its relatives do, it makes a trumpet mine with a central frass line, emerging just before spinning its ribbed cocoon.

The floatingheart waterlily moth (Crambidae: *Parapoynx seminealis*) is said to make a trumpet-shaped mine on the lower surface of floatingheart leaves in its second instar.

Digitate Mines

Digitate mines are blotch mines with distinct fingerlike lobes. They are characteristic of *Parectopa* species (Gracillariidae) that feed on legumes. *P. robiniella* mines along the midrib in leaflets of black locust. Before making the digitate mine on the upper side, it excavates a small chamber in the underside into which it deposits all its droppings and sometimes its exuviae. *P. lespedezaefoliella* makes a similar mine in bush clover, although according to Annette Braun in Forbes (1923), the frass is "thrown outside through a hole on the under side." Both species have been reared from

Digitate mines of *Parectopa* (Gracillariidae) in a tick trefoil leaf. (MA)

mines in tick trefoil. *P. occulta* mines in sweetclover, and *P. thermopsella* in prairie thermopsis.

Epinotia heucherana (Tortricidae) makes digitate mines in the leaves of American alumroot.

The native cabbage leafminer (Drosophilidae: *Scaptomyza adusta*) is a fly that mines mostly in plants of the mustard family, but also some unrelated species such as pea. The larvae are gregarious and make small digitate mines, usually on the upper side of the leaf, depositing their excrement in the fingerlike projections.

Blotch Mines

Blotch mines are made by representatives of each of the four leaf-mining orders. Although these mines may seem nondescript and difficult to tell apart at first, there are many features that help narrow down which group is responsible (in some cases, however, these are present only in finished mines). A mine with an elliptical hole cut out of the leaf belongs to the Heliozelidae. *Cameraria* species (Gracillariidae) and certain tischeriids form distinctive circular chambers, and one birch-mining sawfly pupates in a disc-shaped cocoon within the mine. Weevils spin distinctive spherical cocoons. Others pupating inside their mines include lithocolletine gracillariids, tischeriids, buprestids, and a sunflower-mining crambid. Lyonetiids tend to pupate strapped with silken bands to the outsides of the leaves in which they developed. Gelechiids often have an associated silk tube inside or outside the mine, which may or may not be covered with excrement.

Mines in which the lower (or sometimes upper) epidermis buckles to form a "tent" are characteristic of certain gracillariids. Several tischeriids make mines along the leaf margin that cause the leaf to curl over them. Distinctly puffy mines in leaves of woody plants likely belong to beetles, sawflies, or eriocraniids; those in herbs may belong to *Parectopa* (Gracillariidae; in asters and others), leaf beetles (in aster family), tephritid fruit flies (in parsley family), or anthomyiid flies (in docks and goosefoots). Certain mines are characteristically free of excrement, including those of coleophorids, cosmopterigids, most tischeriids, certain lyonetiids, and bedelliids (also see *Parectopa* in the earlier section on digitate mines). In other mines, the consistency and distribution of excrement within can be diagnostic. If these clues do not help, it becomes a matter of finding out which insects mine the plant species in question and systematically ruling out possibilities—or, if the larva or pupa is still present, waiting to see what emerges.

Heliozelidae

Moths in the family Heliozelidae are called "shield bearers" because when a larva is done making its small blotch mine, it cuts a neat, elliptical piece out of the leaf, 3 to 4 mm long. It drops to the ground, protected by this "shield," and pupates within it. Some species begin with a short linear mine, forming what might be called linear-blotch or trumpet mines. A substantial portion is filled with excrement.

A number of *Antispila* species mine in grape leaves. (*Heliozela aesella* does as well, but it forms a blister gall.) Several more mine leaves in the dogwood family, including *A. freemani* in bunchberry and *A. nysaefoliella* in tupelo. *A. argentifera* mines in birch; *A. eugeniella* in *Eugenia*; and *A. hydrangaeella* in hydrangea.

Coptodisca powellella and *C. quercicolella* mines are found in oaks; *C. juglandiella* in black walnut; and *C. ella* and *C. lucifluella* in hickory and

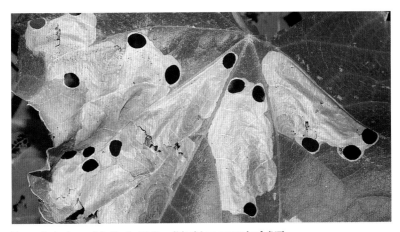

Evacuated mines of *Antispila* (Heliozelidae) in a grape leaf. (UT)

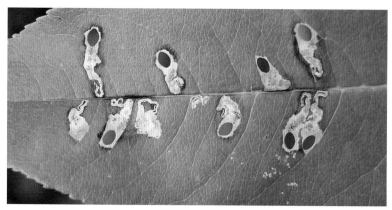

Evacuated mines of *Coptodisca splendoriferella* (Heliozelidae) in a black cherry leaf. (MA)

pecan. Several species mine in leaves of the heath family: *C. arbutiella* in madrone; *C. kalmiella* in sheep laurel; *C. magnella* in huckleberry; *C. matheri* in farkleberry; and *C. negligens* in cranberry. Each of the remaining species mines plants of a different family, except for two in the Rosaceae: *C. condaliae* in leadwood; *C. diospyriella* in persimmon; *C. ostryaefoliella* in hophornbeam; *C. ribesella* in wax currant; *C. saliciella* in willow; *C. cercocarpella* in mountain mahogany; and *C. splendoriferella* in apple, pear, plum, cherry, quince, and hawthorn.

Some British buprestids and weevils make similar round cuts in their mines, but as far as is known, no North American species do so. See the section on mines in grass and sedge leaves (page 359) for two moth species that cut circles after mining in deertongue grass.

Gracillariidae

Blotch mines are the rule in the Gracillariidae, a large family with at least 275 North American species—*Marmara* and *Phyllocnistis* being the major exceptions. They have been given the common name of leaf blotch miner moths, but as discussed below, many other moth families make blotch mines as well.

Underside tentiform mines are characteristic of several genera in the Lithocolletinae. The larvae are sap-feeding at first, but later feed on the tissues within the same area, spinning silk across the loosened epidermis and causing its surface to buckle and become tentlike. Depending on the species, they may feed on the tissue from the circumference of the mine inward, from one end to the other, or haphazardly in small patches. The ultimate result is a full-depth mine, although the upper epidermis may not be picked as clean as the lower. Most of the many *Phyllonorycter* species make underside tentiform mines in leaves of woody plants. The droppings may be collected in a ball at one side of the mine (as in *P. lucidostella*, in sugar maple) or scattered around the edge of the mine (as in *P. lucetiella*, in basswood; the mine of this species remains flat rather than becoming tentiform). Some have more or less naked pupae; others have loosely woven cocoons taking up nearly half the mine (e.g., *P. albanotella* in oak and *P. robiniella* in black locust); still others spin a ringlike silken wall within which they pupate; some make oval cocoons covered with droppings (e.g., *P. caryaealbella* and *P. olivaeformis* in hickory; *P. aeriferella* in oak); *P. basistrigella* (in oak) makes an oval cocoon with a narrow outline of droppings. Sometimes these quirks are useful in distinguishing species with the same host. For instance, in hophornbeam, *P. ostryaefoliella* (usually along the leaf margin) incorporates excrement into its cocoon, whereas *P. obscuricostella* (usually between two veins) pupates in a thin silken web.

Below: Mines (each about 15 mm across) of *Phyllonorycter lucetiella* (Gracillariidae) in basswood, as seen from below (left) and above. The larvae have not yet finished eating the palisade tissue. (MA) *Bottom left:* Underside tentiform mines of *Phyllonorycter robiniella* in black locust, as seen from below (left) and above. (VT) *Bottom right:* The silhouette of an excrement-covered cocoon is visible in this backlit blotch mine in a hickory leaflet. It could belong to either *Phyllonorycter caryaealbella* or *P. olivaeformis.* (MA)

Several small lithocolletine genera comprise species that make underside tentiform mines in herbaceous plants. The five *Cremastobombycia* species mine in composites. They pupate in white, spindle-shaped cocoons suspended in the mines. *Protolithocolletis lathyri* mines in beach pea and veiny pea. *Porphyrosela desmodiella* mines in legumes such as tick trefoil and bush clover.

Caloptilia species (Gracillariinae) typically make an underside tentiform mine (which may be preceded by a linear mine), and then abandon it to feed within a characteristic asymmetrical "cone" rolled in the corner of a leaf. Examples are given in chapter 11. *C. scutellariella* mines in skullcaps and is atypical in completing its development in the mine, leaving when it is ready to construct its cocoon. It makes a puffy underside mine in hoary skullcap but a full-depth mine in heartleaf skullcap.

Parornix species (Gracillariinae) make blotch mines, some of them underside tentiform and some on the upper surface. Like *Caloptilia*, they abandon the mines before pupating. The larva then makes a small flap at the edge of a leaf, which may or may not be the leaf with the mine. It may continue to feed by skeletonizing the inside of the flap, or it may spin its cocoon there without feeding. Many of the more than twenty species mine in rosaceous plants, with a few in birches and ericaceous shrubs. *P. geminatella* forms underside tentiform mines in the leaves of apple, shadbush, and other rosaceous trees. *P. inusitatumella* makes nearly circular, whitish blotches on the upper sides of hawthorn leaves, which become tentiform. *P. kalmiella* makes pale orange blotches on the upper sides of sheep laurel leaves.

Cameraria, with *Phyllonorycter*, is the other large genus in this family. *Cameraria* species make blotch mines on the upper sides of leaves of woody plants. Like the other lithocolletines, they start out as sap feeders, but the later tissue-feeding instars continue to expand the mine rather than revisiting the same area. The mines are therefore relatively large and stay flat rather than becoming tentiform. If a mined leaf is backlit, the part mined by the earlier instars will be distinctly darker than the rest because it contains more tissue. In many species, multiple larvae share one mine. *Cameraria* excrement is somewhat viscous and tends to be smeared indiscriminately on the floor of the mine, although the borders are generally fairly clean as the larvae feed outward from the center. An exception is *C. tubiferella* (on oak), which makes elongate mines that are about as wide as the larva is long. It feeds on alternate sides of the mine, and as it does so, its excrement ends up forming a line along either edge. *Cameraria* larvae spin flat, oval cocoons, and the mature pupa is thrust through the top of the leaf. Most overwintering larvae spin a distinctive chamber that appears as a ring on the upper side of the leaf and as an oval or hemispherical projection on the underside.

Chrysaster ostensackenella makes yellowish mines in black locust leaves similar to those of *Cameraria*. They are sometimes on the underside. This species is unusual among lithocolletines in that the larva abandons the leaf to pupate.

Above: Mines of *Cameraria guttifinitella* (Gracil-lariidae) in a poison ivy leaf. (VT) *Right:* Group mine of *Cameraria hamameliella* in a witch hazel leaf, in which some larvae have formed circular overwintering chambers. (MA)

In addition to the species making digitate mines on legumes, some *Parectopa* species mine in composites and other herbs. They begin by making narrow, winding, frass-filled mines, then expand them into distinctly puffy blotch mines. Upon emerging, they spin dense, semi-transparent, somewhat flattened white cocoons, either in a fold of the leaf or elsewhere. *P. pennsylvaniella* mines in heart-leaved aster; *P. plantaginisella* in both fleabane and plantain (underside); *P. geraniella* in spotted geranium; and *P. albicostella* in vetch.

Micrurapteryx salicifoliella makes a flat blotch mine on the upper surface of a willow leaf. The larva exits through a hole chewed in the bottom and spins a distinctive cocoon, often on the upper side of the leaf. It is flat, oblong, and fairly transparent, with many small, white flecks decorating the middle.

The two *Leucanthiza* species make flat, irregular, whitish blotches on the upper sides of leaves, each of which may contain one or several larvae. When there are multiple larvae, their feeding in different directions can make the mine somewhat digitate. They leave the mine and pupate in cocoons. *L. amphicarpeaefoliella* mines in hog peanut and *L. dircella* in leatherwood.

Tischeriidae

Linear-blotch and trumpet mines of tischeriids are described above; the rest of the mines of this family are blotches with little or no linear portion. They are usually on the upper surface of the leaf. Whatever the form, tis-

Mine of *Leucanthiza amphicarpeaefoliella* (Gracillariidae), containing two larvae, in a hog peanut leaf. (MA)

cheriid mines are unusual in being carpeted throughout with silk, and in all cases, the larva pupates in a silken chamber inside the mine, thrusting the pupa through the epidermis upon emerging. Most species eject their droppings through a small hole at the beginning of the mine, which is marked by the white empty eggshell.

Coptotriche citrinipennella is found throughout the East in a variety of oaks as well as chestnut. Its mine is usually very elongate and is along the margin of the leaf, which curls and partly conceals the finished mine. A number of others in this genus make similarly curling marginal mines in oak leaves, of various shapes and sizes, but this is the only one occurring north of Ohio and New Jersey. *C. crataegifoliae* makes curling marginal mines in hawthorn leaves; *C. amelanchieris* in shadbush; *C. agrimoniella* in agrimony; and *C. insolita* in blueberry. Two species make mines that curl the edges of rose leaflets: *C. roseticola* makes a very narrow, elongate mine along the margin, whereas the broad mine of *C. admirabilis* often extends across the midrib.

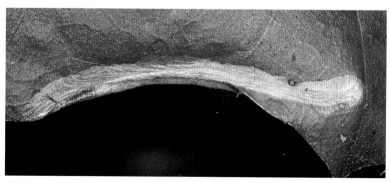

Mine of *Coptotriche citrinipennella* (Tischeriidae) in a red oak leaf. (MA)

C. badiiella (E) primarily feeds in white oak leaves, with the mine beginning at a vein. In the mature mine, the beginning portion becomes wrinkled and the leaf bends somewhat. The mine of *C. zelleriella* (E), in chestnut and various oaks, is at first trumpet-shaped but spreads out into an irregular blotch. The droppings are retained in patches, concentrated toward the beginning of the mine. The upper epidermis is drawn into several folds and torn at either end of the silk-lined pupal chamber.

The mine of *Tischeria quercitella* (E) is unique among oak- and chestnut-feeding tischeriids in having a circular, slightly bulging, silk-lined chamber (nidus) that the larva uses as a retreat and eventually a pupal chamber. Several composite-mining species also make a nidus. *Astrotischeria solidagonifoliella* mines in goldenrod; *A. heliopsisella* in false sunflower and ragweed; and *A. ambrosiaeella* in ragweed. Finished mines of these last two differ in that the nidus of *A. heliopsisella* is white, having a thick lining of silk just below the upper epidermis, whereas that of *A. ambrosiaeella* is green, remaining covered by uneaten palisade tissue. *A. astericola* mines in heart-leaved and other eastern asters; the other aster-mining species, *A. occidentalis*, is known from Wyoming and makes a noticeably larger nidus, about 7 mm across.

Astrotischeria helianthi makes a blotch mine in the underside of sunflower leaves. It begins at the junction of two veins, and the elongate, silk-lined pupal chamber is eventually constructed here. *A. gregaria* makes a similarly placed underside mine on five-nerve helianthella.

The mine of *Tischeria ceanothi* in hoaryleaf ceanothus may be an elongate blotch rather than the linear-blotch mine previously described. The loosened epidermis is raised in a low ridge through the middle of the mine. The short blotch of *T. ambigua* in hairy ceanothus has numerous radiating ridges.

Astrotischeria omissa makes a whitish, translucent blotch in hollyhock and native western mallows. Like other tischeriids, it pupates in a wrinkled, silk-lined chamber.

Lyonetiidae

Most lyonetiids begin with a narrow, linear mine but later expand it into a blotch, which may or may not obliterate the linear portion. Some make a blotch mine right from the beginning. The larva consumes nearly all of the tissue and produces a large amount of excrement, which in most cases accumulates in the mine, making it appear brownish or blackish. Some species extrude their droppings through a hole, so that the mine is clean and transparent. When mature, the larva leaves the mine, and its pupa is generally attached to the leaf with silk, either naked or in a cocoon. Most species mine leaves of woody plants.

Proleucoptera smilaciella makes large, messy, reddish brown blotches on the upper sides of greenbrier leaves, often with up to five larvae in the same mine. The mature larva cuts a hole in the upper epidermis and pupates on top of the leaf, in a white cocoon strapped down with a 1-cm-long H-shaped silken harness. *Paraleucoptera heinrichi* (W) pupates under a similar H-shaped tent on hollyleaf cherry. *Paraleucoptera albella* makes a very dirty, somewhat puffy, excrement-filled mine on poplar and willow. This species, too, is often gregarious, and the mine may take up the whole leaf. Each cocoon is attached to the leaf, usually against the midrib, by two short, transverse bands of silk. *Leucoptera pachystimella* (W) attaches its cocoon with similar bands to a leaf underside of Oregon boxleaf, after covering the leaf with a mine that has the excrement packed at one end. *Lyonetia alniella* (NE) makes large, brownish blotch mines in alder. *L. latistrigella* (E) makes a large, brown blotch in great laurel, and *L. candida* in western rhododendrons. The naked pupa of the former is suspended by a few silken threads stretched across the leaf; the latter spins a slight white cocoon.

Lyonetia speculella is a widespread species making small blotch mines on the upper surfaces of grape, apple, cherry, plum, birch, and ceanothus leaves. The larva cuts several holes in the lower epidermis and pushes its droppings out; they stick together like little sausage links at first, later becoming a dense mass. The leaf becomes slightly curled, and the larva spins a somewhat tubular, white cocoon on the underside. *L. saliciella* (BC) makes a similar mine in willow.

Bedelliidae

The morning glory leafminer (Bedelliidae: *Bedellia somnulentella*) mines in various species in the morning glory family but also has been found in paper birch, willow, eggplant, and London rocket. Its habits are similar to those of *Lyonetia speculella*. The larva at first makes a linear mine with a central frass line, but then leaves the mine and reenters the leaf elsewhere to form a blotch. There are usually several larvae per leaf, each making one or more small, full-depth blotch mines. They spin silk over the leaf surface as they move around on it. Each larva extrudes stringy, black excrement through its mine's entrance hole, causing a small pile to accumulate just outside. When mature, the larva leaves the mine once more and pupates suspended in a hammock of silk. *B. minor* (S), the only other North American bedelliid, is only known to mine in *Ipomoea* morning glories, which include sweet potato.

Cosmopterigidae

Some species of *Cosmopterix* (Cosmopterigidae), primarily mining herbaceous plants, also keep their blotch mines clean by ejecting their droppings through one or more holes. The larva leaves its mine to spin a thin, flattened cocoon. *C. pulchrimella* mines in clearweed leaves, causing them to twist and crumple. It may make a series of mines in different leaves. Other species include miners of morning glories (*Ipomoea*), grasses, and sedges.

Coleophoridae

Many of the casebearers (Coleophoridae: *Coleophora*) live in leaf mines, but only during their first instar. After this, the larva cuts pieces of the mined leaf to make its portable case. A number of species then proceed to

A 17-mm-long blotch mine on the underside of a gray birch leaf, excavated by a case-bearer moth larva (Coleophoridae: *Coleophora comptoniella* or *C. lentella*). Note the entrance hole near the middle of the mine. (MA)

feed by making blotch mines on the undersides of leaves without leaving their cases. The mine therefore has a radius that is no longer than the larva's reach, with a conspicuous entry hole in the middle. Because the larva does not fully enter the mine, it is completely free of excrement and exuviae (even just outside the entrance, where droppings often accumulate in species that push them out of their mines). Host plants of some species are listed in chapter 8.

Nepticulidae

A few nepticulids make small blotch mines without a linear portion. *Stigmella stigmaciella* forms a blotch at the edge of a hawthorn leaf, with the excrement in a broad central patch. *Ectoedemia lindquisti* makes a more or less rectangular mine between two birch leaf veins. *E. platanella* makes a relatively large, round blotch in sycamore, preceded by a very short linear mine.

Gelechiidae

Mines of gelechiids tend to be more or less blotchlike. Some sort of constructed shelter is often associated with the mine. *Recurvaria ceanothiella* (CA) spins a short tube of silk on the underside of a ceanothus leaf, at the entrance to its mine. The mine is linear at first but is expanded into a blotch. *Scrobipalpa scutellariaeella*, as noted in chapter 5, mines the undersides of skullcap leaves and constructs an external silk-lined tube of excrement that serves as a retreat and eventually a cocoon.

The potato tuberworm (*Phthorimaea operculella*) mines in leaves of tobacco, potato, and other nightshades. When it begins the mine, it spins a tent of silk between a vein and the surface of the leaf. It makes an irregular mine that often distorts the leaf, either storing its excrement in one part of the mine or depositing it outside. The tomato pinworm (*Keiferia lycopersicella*) specializes in tomato but is also found on various other nightshades.

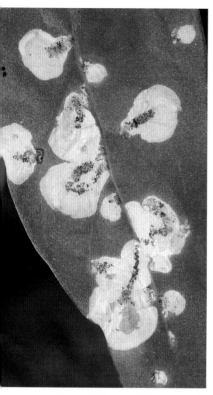

It makes a similar silk tent but produces only small blotch mines before emerging to tie leaves and feed externally. The mine of the eggplant leafminer (*K. glochinella*) is easily recognized by the dense, excrement-covered silk tube constructed within it. The mine is always at the edge of the leaf and causes the leaf to distort. There is no silk on the leaf surface. *Aristotelia physaliella* mines leaves of ground cherry, without a special shelter inside or outside the mine.

Chrysoesthia sexguttella makes a distinctive mine in lambsquarters and possibly other goosefoots. It is a full-depth, transparent blotch, with the black excrement deposited in a wide stripe in the middle.

In Florida, *Nealyda kinzelella* makes circular, puffy, full-depth blotch mines in leaves of *Guapira* trees. The mine becomes partially detached and hangs down from the leaf, with the moth developing in a thin, white cocoon inside.

Crambidae

Frechinia helianthiales (Crambidae) makes large blotch mines in sunflower leaves. The excrement is scattered mostly on one side, and the pupa can usually be found inside the mine.

Mines of *Chrysoesthia sexguttella* (Gelechiidae) in a lambsquarters leaf. (VT)

Eriocraniidae

The Eriocraniidae make full-depth blotch mines, mostly in leaves of the Fagales: birch, hazelnut, oak, chestnut, and beech. Their mines become puffy like those of sawflies and beetles, and they contain distinctive long, dark, irregularly curled strings of frass. The mature larva cuts a semicircular slit in the upper epidermis and leaves to pupate in the ground.

Sawflies

The leaf-mining sawflies (Tenthredinidae) make blotch mines that are usually very transparent. They leave faint remnants of the leaf veins attached to the upper cuticle, in contrast to the sap-feeding lepidopteran blotch miners, which leave the cuticle very clean. There is usually more tissue left attached to the lower cuticle, especially in thicker-leaved plants. The mines contain large amounts of dark, cylindrical fecal pellets and are often somewhat bulged because the larvae are not as flattened as most leaf miners. In several species, multiple mines on one leaf may combine to form a single con-

Puffy mines of *Metallus* sawfly larvae (Ten-thredinidae) in a raspberry leaflet. (MA)

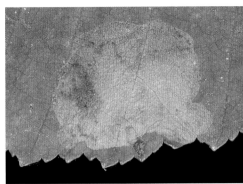

Blotch mine of a sawfly, *Fenusella nana* (Tenthredinidae), in a paper birch leaf. The larva is visible in the upper right, trailed by fecal pellets attached by a string of silk. (MA)

tinuous blotch. The cast skins of the larvae are usually in one piece, whereas lepidopteran miners leave the head capsules separate from the rest. Most cut a hole in the upper epidermis and pupate in cocoons on the ground.

The mines of *Metallus rohweri* and *M. capitalis* can be found in the leaves of blackberry and other *Rubus* species; *Fenusella populifoliella* in Fremont cottonwood; *Fenusa dohrnii* in alder (mostly confined between lateral veins); *F. ulmi* in elm (begin as serpentine mines, becoming blotches); *Profenusa canadensis* in hawthorn and cherry (usually close to margin); and *P. alumna* in oak (upper side).

Several introduced sawfly species mine in birch leaves. *Fenusa pumila* and *Profenusa thomsoni* both begin the mine near the midrib and extend it toward the leaf edge. The former mines in tender, terminal leaves (often with several larvae forming one large, common mine), whereas the latter uses thicker, older leaves. *Fenusella nana* begins its mine at the leaf edge. *Heterarthrus nemoratus* also mines at the edge, but the mine has several distinguishing features: the older part is typically reddish brown; there is relatively little frass, because the larva ejects it through a slit; and the larva pupates within the mine in a disc-shaped cocoon.

Schizocerella pilicornis mines in purslane and is the only known North American leaf-mining argid sawfly. A single larva mines out a number of different leaves (the habit of leaving one leaf and entering another is unusual among sawflies), and it may bore into the stem when it has exhausted the available leaves.

Beetles

Most leaf-mining beetles also make blotch mines that tend to be puffy and blisterlike. Except for a few chrysomelids, beetle larvae pupate in the mine, unlike nearly all sawflies.

Leaf Beetles

Leaf-mining chrysomelids (Cassidinae: Chalepini) usually make full-depth mines and are mostly active in spring and early summer. Larvae in many species often desert a mine in one leaf and migrate to another leaf to start a new mine. *Odontota dorsalis* often does extensive damage to black locusts. Several larvae enter a leaflet from an excrement-covered egg mass on the underside and together form a common mine, before dispersing to make individual mines in other leaflets. Their mines are usually on the outer edge of the leaflet and are most visible from the underside. *Baliosus nervosus* makes blotch mines primarily in basswood, but it may also be found in oaks, willows, or rosaceous trees. *Microrhopala* species mine in goldenrods and other composites.

Zeugophora species (Megalopodidae) make large blotch mines, which turn dark brown or black as they age, on the upper sides of poplar leaves. Eggs are inserted into small holes chewed in the underside of the leaf, rather than deposited on the surface and covered with excrement as is done by the related chrysomelid leafminers.

Buprestids

The small buprestids *Brachys*, *Trachys*, *Taphrocerus*, and *Pachyschelus* (Agrilinae: Trachyini) are leafminers as larvae. They make full-depth blotch mines (sometimes very broad linear mines) that are bounded by the main veins, with the excrement heaped toward the center. The mine is often puffy enough that the pupa rolls around loosely inside it.

Brachys species mine in various hardwoods. The egg, which is laid on the underside of the leaf, is covered with a glistening, transparent secretion that is conspicuous long after the beetle has emerged. *B. ovatus* makes a large mine in oak leaves, sometimes crossing the midrib. The larva overwinters in the fallen leaf, pupating in the spring. *B. aeruginosus* makes a small, oval mine between two veins of a beech leaf. *B. aerosus* mines in elm and oak; Needham et al. (1928) also listed hickory, poplars, and basswood as hosts, but they may actually have been referring to other *Brachys* species.

Pachyschelus laevigatus forms an irregular, meandering mine in tick trefoil or bush clover. The egg is inserted in a pocket in the underside of the leaf. The larva pupates within a thin, tough, parchmentlike cocoon in its mine, about 4 mm across, which causes a conspicuous swelling. It overwinters inside the cocoon. Several other species have the same host plants. *P. purpureus purpureus* mines in geraniums, and *P. p. uvaldei* in copperleaf or three-seeded mercury. *P. fisheri* was reared from mouse's eye in the 1940s but has not been seen since.

Weevils

The fourteen species of flea weevils (Curculionidae: Rhamphini) mine in willow, poplar, elm, alder, hazelnut, birch, musclewood, apple, cherry, hawthorn, shadbush, and probably other trees. At least one species mines in leaves of two different families, and there is much overlap in hosts.

The female chews a tiny, oval hole in the midrib or a main vein and lays an egg in it, which may cause the vein to swell and bend. Upon hatching, the larva begins by making a narrow, full-depth linear mine, then expands to a puffy blotch, often reaching the tip or edge of the leaf. It spins a firm, nearly spherical cocoon in the inflated part of the mine. The mined portion of the leaf may eventually shrivel up.

The yellow poplar weevil (*Odontopus calceatus*) makes full-depth blotch mines in leaves of tuliptree, magnolia, and sassafras, often covering nearly half the area of the leaf. At least in the first two hosts, the mine starts near the apex. The cocoon, similar to those of the flea weevils, is covered with droppings and causes a conspicuous bulge in the leaf. A single mine may contain as many as ten larvae. The mine becomes puffy when dry.

Flies

Blotch mines may be made by a few anthomyiids and tephritids, as well as agromyzids. The first two are found exclusively in herbaceous plants, and the vast majority of blotch-mining agromyzids are as well.

Anthomyiid Flies

The large, blisterlike blotch mines of anthomyiid flies are easily recognized by the conspicuous white eggs that remain attached to the underside of the leaf. These are oblong and may occur singly or with several arranged side by side like sardines. Several *Pegomya* species mine gregariously in dock leaves, often covering the whole leaf. Others, such as the spinach leafminer (*P. hyoscyami*) and beet leafminer (*P. betae*), mine leaves of spinach, beet, and other goosefoots. Because these leaves are succulent, the large mines often cause them to wilt, forcing the larvae to migrate to new leaves. Dark, liquid excrement is smeared messily throughout the mines.

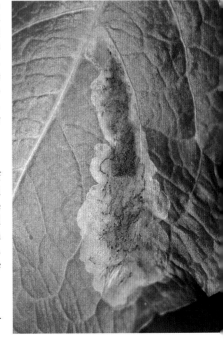

Tephritid Fruit Flies

Euleia (Tephritidae) mines in members of the parsley family, such as honewort, wild parsnip, and cow parsnip. Several larvae form a large, puffy, irregular communal mine, which has scattered spots of blackish excrement and is often filled with moisture. The leaf curls up as it dries, and the larvae may pupate inside it or on the surface.

Large blotch mine of *Pegomya* fly larvae (Anthomyiidae) in a bitter dock leaf. (MA)

Agromyzid Flies

Some agromyzid fly larvae also make pure blotch mines. *Liriomyza asclepiadis* makes a small, fairly regular mine in milkweed, with diffused greenish excrement. *Galiomyza violivora* makes irregular blotches in violet leaves. *Phytomyza aquilegiana*, *P. aquilegioides* (W), and *P. columbinae* all form blotches in columbine leaves. Other agromyzids mine leaves of larkspur, monkshood, and various composites, sometimes causing them to wilt.

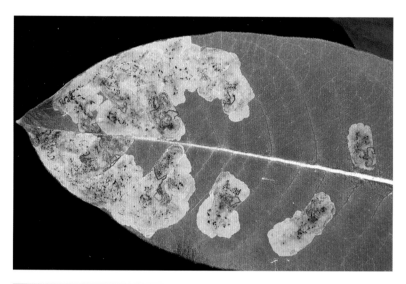

Above top: Blotch mines of *Liriomyza asclepiadis* (Agromyzidae) in a milkweed leaf. (MA) *Above:* Blotch mines of *Phytomyza* fly larvae (Agromyzidae) in a garden columbine leaf. (MA)

Noctuid Leafminers and Stem Borers

Larvae of several noctuid species start out as leafminers (linear, blotch, or somewhere in between), then transition to stem boring. Most are found in aquatic plants.

The larva of the white-tailed diver (*Bellura gortynoides*) feeds in yellow pond lily leaves, making mines in the upper surface that may be linear, digitate, or irregular blotches. The mined portion begins to disintegrate after a few days, and when the larva becomes too large to mine, it bores down into the stalk. It periodically returns to the surface to deposit its droppings in a conspicuous heap by the entrance hole. The cattail borer moth (*B. obliqua*) deposits a distinctive hairy egg mass on a cattail leaf, and when the larvae hatch, they bore directly into the leaf. They mine more or less straight downward, side by side. After traveling up to 2 feet (61 cm), they exit their mines, later becoming stem borers. The pickerelweed borer moth (*B. densa*; SE) has similar habits, feeding in cattail, pickerelweed, and water hyacinth.

Larvae of the oblong sedge borer moth (*Archanara oblonga*) make irregular, meandering mines in leaves of both cattail and bulrush. They later bore in stems below the waterline. Two other *Archanara* species have similar habits and hosts, and *A. laeta* mines in bur-reed. Iris borer caterpillars (*Macronoctua onusta*) bore into iris leaves and make their way into the rhizome, eventually killing the plant.

Mines in Grass and Sedge Leaves

Mines in grass and sedge leaves may be the work of moth, fly, or buprestid beetle larvae. They are grouped together here for ease of comparison.

Moths

A few species of *Cosmopterix* (Cosmopterigidae) make blotch mines in grasses and sedges. Like others in the genus, they keep the mine clean by ejecting their excrement through a hole. *C. gemmiferella* mines the basal leaves of cypress panicgrass in the spring, consuming virtually all of the mesophyll. When mature, it enters a lower stem leaf and makes a mine slightly larger than itself, in which it pupates. *C. clandestinella* makes an irregular blotch in deertongue grass. It forms a pupal case, in which it drops to the ground, by cutting a circular piece out of the upper epidermis (not a hole all the way through the leaf, as a heliozelid would make) and folding it in half. *Cycloplasis panicifoliella* (Heliodinidae), curiously, does exactly the same thing in the same host plant. Before making its irregular blotch, however, this species makes a long, threadlike mine beginning at the base of the leaf.

Larvae of nearly all the roughly sixty elachistine elachistids make blotch mines in grasses and sedges. The mine generally extends from the tip of the leaf toward the base, widening to a blotch. The larva's excrement is scattered throughout the mine, which distinguishes these mines from the others just mentioned. Some species overwinter in their mines, moving to another leaf in early spring. The larva leaves the mine to pupate, often against the midvein of a leaf of the host plant. Some pupae are completely naked, but others are covered by a loose sheet of silk.

Asymmetrura graminivorella (Xyloryctidae) feeds on bottlebrush grass, Canada bluegrass, and other grasses. Its mine is an elongate, transparent blotch with a broad tube of silk at the entrance. One larva usually makes several mines before pupating.

Flies

The corn blotch leafminer (Agromyzidae: *Agromyza parvicornis*) mines in corn, wheat, and other grasses. It usually begins at the tip of the leaf and makes a broad linear mine, or sometimes a blotch, which may alternate between the upper and lower leaf surfaces as it progresses toward the base. The mines of several larvae may unite. The larvae leave the mines to pupate. As with other agromyzids, the presence of feeding punctures of the female can help confirm the mine's identity. A number of other agromyzids mine in grasses and grasslike plants.

Hydrellia shore flies (Ephydridae) are all leaf and stem miners of grasses and other aquatic plants, as far as is known. The mines are often linear, running parallel to the midrib, but they may also form blotches. The larvae pupate within their mines, inserting their respiratory spines into the leaf veins.

Beetles

Taphrocerus gracilis (Buprestidae) makes a variable full-depth blotch in the leaves of river bulrush and shortbristle horned beaksedge. Its naked pupa is found among its droppings and exuviae in the center of the mine. According to Needham et al. (1928), the egg is covered with a hardened, transparent secretion, but Macrae (2004) describes it as a black, tarlike substance. The mines are often abundant, with the leaves jagged-edged from adults feeding on their margins. The other *Taphrocerus* species also mine in various sedges.

Needle Mines

Moths in a few different families mine in conifer needles. Because the larvae do not have much leaf surface to work with, there is little variation in the appearance of their mines, which generally look like a brown, dead tip, or sometimes occupy the whole needle. Apart from the larch casebearer, the needleminers belong to Gelechiidae, Yponomeutidae, and Tortricidae.

Larch

The larch casebearer (Coleophoridae: *Coleophora laricella*) adopts the first or second larch needle it mines as a portable case. It then proceeds to mine in other needles as far as it can reach without leaving its case, making a conspicuous hole in each, in the manner of other casebearers that mine the undersides of leaves. A single larva may mine more than a hundred needles.

Hemlock

The green hemlock needleminer (Gelechiidae: *Coleotechnites apicitri-punctella*; NE) mines hemlock needles until it is too large to fit inside. It then webs several needles together and feeds by eating grooves in their undersides. The brown hemlock needleminer (*C. macleodi*; NE) does the same and is distinguished by the color of the larva, as indicated by the common name.

Fir

The white fir needleminer (Tortricidae: *Epinotia meritana*) mines several needles of white or red fir, spinning webbing among them. The mined needles often become detached and dangle in bunches from the webbing.

Spruce

The orange spruce needleminer (Gelechiidae: *Coleotechnites piceaella*) mines in various spruces, especially ornamental ones. It takes two years to develop, overwintering in either a needle or a silk shelter at the base of the needles. It pupates inside a mined needle. *C. ducharmei* mines in red, white, and black spruces. *Epinotia piceafoliana* (Tortricidae) mines in needles of black spruce, then pupates close to the twig in a dense, white cocoon between the needles. The European spruce needleminer (*E. nanana*) mines the bases of spruce needles, then pupates in a loosely webbed-together mass of mined needles and excrement. Another tortricid, *Taniva albolineana*, cuts its mined spruce needles and webs them together in a small mass, where it overwinters in a cocoon.

Pine

The pine needle sheathminer (Yponomeutidae: *Zelleria haimbachi*; N) starts out mining pine needles, entering them from the base. Later it feeds from a silk tube at the base of the needles, inserting the front of its body into the needles in the same way that casebearers feed. The needles are cut and left hanging by the silk. *Argyresthia pilatella* apparently mines only in Monterey pine needles. *Exoteleia pinifoliella* (Gelechiidae) mines in needles of eastern pines, pushing its excrement out through the entrance holes. The larva pupates inside the needle, sealing the hole with silk. Several *Coleotechnites* species also mine in needles of various pines, generally entering around the middle or beyond it.

Cypress Family

A number of species of *Argyresthia* (Yponomeutidae) mine the tips of arborvitae, cypress, cedar, and juniper. In the Northeast, mined arborvitae tips may also be the work of the brown arborvitae leafminer (Gelechiidae:

Mined arborvitae tips such as these could be the work of *Coleotechnites thujaella* (Gelechiidae) or several species of *Argyresthia* (Yponomeutidae). (VT)

Coleotechnites thujaella). A few *Argyresthia* species pupate in a white cocoon attached to the foliage, but in the absence of this, the only way to distinguish the mines is by examining the larva, which is green in *Argyresthia* species rather than brown. Several western *Coleotechnites* species mine the tips of juniper and Monterey cypress needles, at least one of which forms a shelter by tying mined needles together with silk. *C. juniperella*, on juniper, is also found in the East. *Stenolechia bathrodyas* mines in juniper and cypress along the southern coast of California.

Parasitoids

Like all insects, leaf-mining larvae are attacked by a variety of parasitoids. Keep an eye out for their pupae, cocoons, and droppings when investigating mines.

Pholetesor ornigis (Braconidae) parasitizes leaf-mining moth larvae and spins its cocoon within the mine. The cocoon is 3 mm long and 1 mm wide, suspended like a hammock by threads at either end. It is smooth and white, with a dark central band about 0.5 mm wide where the silk is thinner than at the ends.

Some eulophids, such as *Diglyphus* and *Chrysocharis*, pupate within the mines of their hosts. The larva first constructs a circle of fecal pillars around itself to prevent the mine from collapsing on it as the plant tissue dries. These two genera have mostly been reared from agromyzid fly mines, but species of the latter are known to parasitize moths and sawflies as well.

Leaf Shelters

11

Many types of insects and spiders roll, fold, tie, or crumple leaves. Spiders and some insects use these shelters they create solely as hiding places, but most insects also feed on the leaf tissue within. The first feature to consider in identifying a leaf shelter is whether silk was involved in its making.

Leaf Shelters without Silk

Most of the leaf shelters that do not involve silk are covered elsewhere in this book. The cylindrical cells leafcutter bees make from pieces of leaves were discussed in chapter 8. The feeding of aphids can cause a leaf to pucker and curl around them; this is illustrated in chapter 9. Leafminers live between the layers of a single leaf; they are the subject of chapter 10. Leaf galls, which are very specialized leaf shelters, are discussed with the other galls in chapter 12. That chapter includes the small, simple folds that certain midges and sawflies induce in leaves. This leaves just one type of silk-free leaf shelter, and it is a masterpiece of insect origami.

Leaf-rolling weevils (Attelabidae: Attelabinae) have the unique habit of rolling the ends of leaves into neat, compact, little cylindrical packets, called *niduses*, about 5 mm long. *Nidus* literally means "nest," and this name is also given to the shelters built by certain leaf-mining moth larvae. The female makes a straight cut across each side of a leaf blade, with the two cuts meeting at the midrib, and then proceeds to roll and fold the severed portion, laying a single egg in the middle. She uses no silk, making periodic bites and tucks to hold the roll in place. The finished nidus may be left attached to the rest of the leaf or cut and dropped to the ground. The larva feeds on the leaf tissue within the nidus, then pupates underground. *Attelabus nigripes* uses leaves in the sumac family; the other species use oaks, birches, hickories, and related plants. The thief weevil (*Pterocolus ovatus*) works its way into another attelabid's nidus, eats the spherical yellowish egg, and replaces it with one or more of its own smaller, more oval, and

Two 5-mm niduses of leaf-rolling weevils (Attelabidae: Attelabinae). Both have been parasitized by chalcids; an exit hole is visible in the upper one. (VA)

whitish eggs. The larvae then feed as the original larva would have. Both male and female adults are said to eat nothing but the eggs of other atte-labids. A tiny, round hole in a nidus, with little or none of the tissue consumed, indicates the emergence of a chalcid parasitoid of the egg or larva.

Leaf Shelters Made with Silk

Leaves may be fastened together with silk by spiders, the Carolina leaf-rolling cricket, and the larvae of moths, butterflies, and pamphiliid sawflies. The first two do so exclusively to create places to hide themselves or their eggs, whereas the rest generally feed on the foliage within or adjacent to this shelter. In all cases, strategically placed silk strands shrink as they dry, pulling two leaf surfaces closer together. Moth larvae often construct short, thick bands of silk for this purpose, as do skipper caterpillars. The foliage feeders can mostly be divided into leaf folders, leaf rollers, and leaf tiers, although individuals of some species may differ in which of these they do. They generally skeletonize the inner surfaces of the leaf shelter, filling it with droppings. Many of these insects are fairly host-specific and make a consistent style of shelter, so once you determine which species makes a particular type of shelter on a particular plant, you may be able to identify it by its sign alone. This type of sign is not nearly as distinctive as leaf mines, however, and multiple species may make similar shelters on a given host plant. Tortricid moths are the primary suspects, with more than a thousand species, and quite a few—especially those in the Tortricinae—are generalist feeders, adding further uncertainty to identification of their shelters. Crambids, gelechiids, and gracillariids are also responsible for many folded, rolled, and tied leaves, but a complete list of suspects would include members of many other moth families, in addition to certain butterflies and sawflies.

Leaf Folders, Feeding Inside

Leaf folders simply form a single crease along one leaf, attaching strands of silk from side to side across part of it until it curls and eventually is folded flat. Many species of Tortricidae, Gelechiidae, and Crambidae have this habit. Caterpillars of some swallowtail butterflies fold leaves that they use only for shelter, employing a very different method of silk spinning, which is described with the other non-feeding shelters.

Grape leaves are folded by grape plume moth larvae (Pterophoridae: *Geina periscelidactylus*) in the spring, grapevine epimenis larvae (Noctuidae: *Psychomorpha epimenis*) later in the season, and grape leaffolders (Crambidae: *Desmia funeralis*) throughout the year. Leaf-folding gelechiids include the redbud leaffolder (*Fascista cercerisella*); *Anacampsis lupinella* on lupine; *Filatima serotinella* on black cherry; and *Aristotelia roseosuffusella* on clover. *Agonopterix robi-*

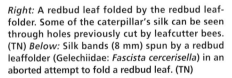

Right: A redbud leaf folded by the redbud leaffolder. Some of the caterpillar's silk can be seen through holes previously cut by leafcutter bees. (TN) *Below:* Silk bands (8 mm) spun by a redbud leaffolder (Gelechiidae: *Fascista cercerisella*) in an aborted attempt to fold a redbud leaf. (TN)

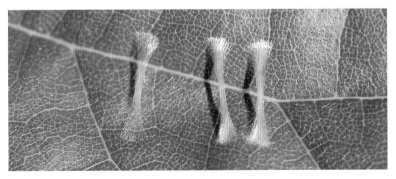

niella larvae (Elachistidae) live in longitudinally folded leaves of black locust, and *A. pulvipennella* in goldenrod, nettle, and *Eupatorium.*

Gracillariid Moths

Some gracillariids leave their blotch mines to feed within a small flap at the edge of a leaf; often there are a few of these on the same leaf. This is characteristic of the genus *Parornix*, with many species on rosaceous trees and shrubs; several on birches; *P. kalmiella* on sheep laurel; and *P. preciosella* on highbush blueberry. A similar fold on apple could also be from *Callisto denticulella. Caloptilia blandella*, on black walnut, is atypical for its genus in making a simple fold rather than a cone. Marginal leaf folds are also made by moths of other families such as Tortricidae.

Tortricid Moths

Leaf-folding tortricids include species of *Ancylis* and *Olethreutes*, among others. Some species, rather than making a neat, flat fold, instead cinch together part of the middle of a leaf from the underside, causing it to crumple. The easiest of these to recognize is the maple trumpet skeletonizer (*Catastega aceriella*), which constructs a tapering tube of excrement within its silk shelter. The sycamore leaffolder (*A. platanana*)

Below: A witch hazel leaf folded and skeletonized by a tortricid moth larva. (MA) *Below bottom:* Black cherry leaves folded and skeletonized by tortricid larvae. (MA)

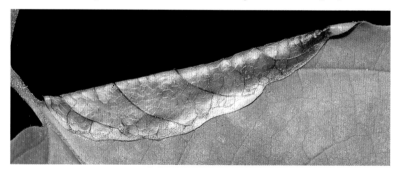

Sugar maple leaves crumpled by maple trumpet skeletonizers (Tortricidae: *Catastega aceriella*). (MA)

produces similar folds but lives in a tube of clean white silk.

Skippers

Many skipper caterpillars (Hesperiidae) live in a leaf that is folded or curled by attaching thick bands of silk like those made by moth larvae. Rather than skeletonizing the inside of the shelter, they either chew off the tip of the leaf and bring it inside to consume, or leave the shelter at night to feed on other leaves. They keep their shelters free of droppings. A common example in the South is the "bean leafroller" (*Urbanus proteus*), the larva of the long-tailed skipper, which chews two cuts in a legume leaf to make a flap that it folds over for its hiding place. Most of the grass skippers (Hesperiinae) feed on grasses and sedges, hiding in a longitudinally folded leaf.

Leaf Rollers, Feeding Inside

Leaf rollers also use a single leaf but cause it to become distinctly rolled by making a series of successive folds beginning at the edge of the leaf. Sometimes the leaf is cut, and a small flap is rolled into a cone. Most leaf rollers are tortricid moths, but a few pamphiliid sawflies and certain members of several other moth families also have this habit.

Tortricid Moths

Ancylis brauni is one example of a tortricid with a distinctive, recognizable leaf roll. The larva makes a little roll toward the tip of a buckthorn (*Rham-*

A staghorn sumac leaflet rolled by a tortricid larva, possibly *Episimus argutanus*. (MA)

A basswood leaf cut and rolled by a basswood leafroller moth larva (Crambidae: *Pantographa limata*). (MA)

nus) leaf, and its feeding style is more akin to that of some skippers than to other tortricids: rather than skeletonizing, it feeds on the outer end, extending the roll toward the base of the leaf as it continues to feed. Many species of *Archips* and *Argyrotaenia*, on the other hand, are generalist feeders, rolling single leaves of all sorts of plants in early instars, later webbing several leaves together.

Crambid Moths

The basswood leafroller (Crambidae: *Pantographa limata*) makes a cut halfway across a basswood leaf and with this piece makes a large and conspicuous roll. It overwinters elsewhere on the leaf in a small, simple fold lined with silk. The grape leaffolder sometimes also rolls leaves.

Gelechiid Moths

Gelechiid leaf rollers include *Telphusa latifasciella* and *Neotelphusa querciella* on oaks; *Pseudotelphusa betulella* on birch; *P. belangerella* on alder; and *Helcystogramma hystricella* on bottlebrush grass. *Anacampsis innocuella* rolls a poplar leaf and usually cuts the petiole when nearly mature, finishing its feeding on the ground.

Gracillariid Moths

As noted previously, gracillariids in the genus *Caloptilia* start out as leafminers but then roll a corner of the leaf into a short, stout, usually asymmetrical cone. Sometimes the larva cuts the leaf to form a flap with which to make the cone. In addition to the shape (tortricid rolls tend to be more long, narrow, and symmetrical), their cones differ from most others in rarely having externally placed straps of silk along the fold. The elongate, white cocoon may be spun within the cone or elsewhere; if within, the mature pupa is thrust through the cocoon as well as the leaf tissue to allow the moth to escape. Examples include *C. azaleella* on azalea; *C. syringella* on lilac, privet, and occasionally ash; *C. fraxinella* on ash; *C. sassafrasella* on sassafras; *C. stigmatella* on willow and poplar; *C. ostryaeella* on hophornbeam; *C. superbifrontella* on witch hazel; *C. rhoifoliella* on sumac; *C. negundella* on boxelder; several species on maples; and *C. violacella* on tick trefoil. *Povolnya quercinigrella* makes a similar cone on black oak, and *Parornix strobivorella* is said to do so on mountain-ash. *Her-*

petogramma (Crambidae) and certain
other moth larvae can make superficially
similar rolls.

Caloptilia belfragella rolls dogwood
leaves, usually lengthwise rather than in
the transverse cone typical of its genus.
Olethreutes connectum (Tortricidae) also
rolls dogwood leaves lengthwise, so look
for associated underside tentiform mines
to confirm the identity of the former.

Leaf Tiers, Feeding Inside

Leaf tiers differ from leaf folders and leaf
rollers in using more than one leaf. They
may simply attach two leaves together, or
they may pull in multiple leaves, as well as
other plant parts. Leaf crumplers (Pyralidae: *Acrobasis*) are leaf tiers that live in
conical, curved and twisted tubes of silk and droppings. These are discussed in chapter 5.

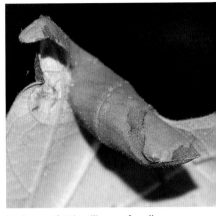

Leaf cone of *Caloptilia sassafrasella*
(Gracillariidae) on sassafras. (MD)

Two-Leaf Shelters

Olethreutes ferriferana (Tortricidae) ties together two terminal hydrangea
leaves, enclosing the flower bud. The larva feeds on both the flower and
the inner surfaces of the leaves. Some *Agonopterix* species (Elachistidae)

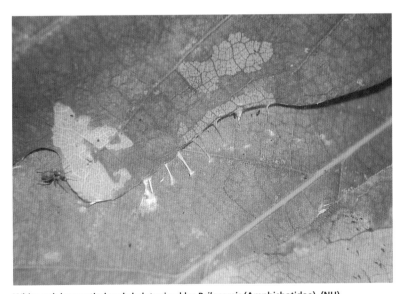

White oak leaves tied and skeletonized by *Psilocorsis* (Amphisbatidae). (NH)

Black locust leaflets tied by *Filatima pseudacaciella* (Gelechiidae). They have been separated to show the skeletonizing of the lower leaflet. (VT)

similarly tie together two terminal leaves of St. Johnswort, enclosing and feeding on the flowers. *Psilocorsis* species (Amphisbatidae) tie together neighboring leaves of oaks and related trees, thoroughly skeletonizing the inner surfaces. Other two-leaf tiers include *Stilbosis tesquella* (Cosmopterigidae) on hog-peanut; *Filatima pseudacaciella* (Gelechiidae) on black locust; and sometimes the redbud leaffolder.

Tied Conifer Needles

The shelter of the pine tube moth (Tortricidae: *Argyrotaenia pinatubana*) is easily recognized. The larva feeds on white pine, and as its name suggests, it ties together several pine needles to make a tube in which it lives. It feeds on the tips of the needles that make up the tube and overwinters as a pupa inside its second or third tube.

Shelter of a pine tube moth larva (Tortricidae: *Argyrotaenia pinatubana*). The larva is feeding on the needle that is protruding from the tube. (MA)

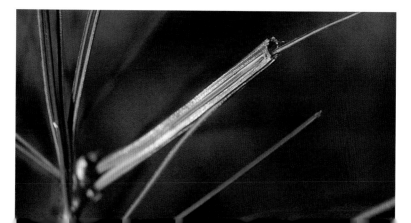

The cypress leaftier (*Epinotia subviridis*) feeds on cypress and related trees on the West Coast. It lives in a silk-lined tube that incorporates living and dead foliage as well as its droppings.

Various other tortricid and gelechiid moths start out as needleminers, then later tie needles together with silk. They are discussed in chapter 10.

Skippers

Some skipper caterpillars (Hesperiidae) draw several leaves together, rather than using a single leaf. As with those that fold leaves, their shelters differ from those of most moth larvae in that they chew leaf edges rather than skeletonizing, and they keep the space clean rather than letting it fill with excrement. The widespread silver-spotted skipper (*Epargyreus clarus*) feeds on various legumes. When on black locust, it makes a distinctive chamber by fastening several pairs of leaflets together below the leafstalk. At night, it feeds on the leaflets at either end of this shelter. Palmer's metalmark (Riodinidae: *Apodemia palmeri*; SW) makes a similar shelter out of mesquite leaflets.

Other Leaf Tiers

Some gelechiid moths tie together the terminal growth of herbaceous plants. Examples include *Frumenta nundinella* on horse nettle; *Scrobipalpula artemisiella* on wormwood; and *Dichomeris nonstrigella* on asters. *Depressaria cinereocostella* (Elachistidae) ties leaves of plants in the parsley family.

Many types of moth larvae live gregariously on woody plants in tents of several leaves tied together, often forming conspicuous masses of brown, dead leaves. An example is the poplar tentmaker (Notodontidae: *Clostera inclusa*), on willow as well as poplar. The larvae of scallop shells (Geometridae: *Rheumaptera*) make tight clusters of leaves at the ends of cherry twigs, tying in additional leaves as they need them. Some other examples, in which the webbing is conspicuous, are given in chapter 6.

A number of tortricids (e.g., *Archips*; *Argyrotaenia*; *Platynota stultana*) and crambids (e.g., *Herpetogramma*) are generalist leaf tiers on a variety of herbaceous and woody plants. Other moth larvae, in these and additional families, may web together leaves of a particular species, genus, or family of plants. In general, they all produce tight masses of leaves, which when teased apart are found to be full of droppings.

Excrement-filled rolled tips of Christmas fern such as this one are the work of *Herpetogramma aeglealis*, a crambid moth larva. (MA)

Rolled, Folded, or Tied Leaves without Feeding Damage Inside

Some insects and spiders roll or fold leaves solely to make shelters in which to hide (or hide their offspring, in the case of some spiders). Unlike other leaf shelters, therefore, these do not involve consumption of the leaf tissue, although with caterpillars, there may be feeding damage adjacent to the shelter. If taking a peek inside does not reveal the creature, the method of construction may reveal its identity.

Simple Folds

Certain lepidopteran larvae and a variety of spiders create simple nonfeeding shelters by making a single fold in a leaf.

Moths

Parornix species, as noted above, make small folds at the edges of leaves. Although only some species feed in these folds, most or all make their cocoons in them. The cocoon is usually reddish or brownish and somewhat mottled. It is firm and opaque, and the pupa is thrust through it when the moth emerges. Larvae of the grape berry moth (Tortricidae: *Paralobesia viteana*) pupate in little leaf folds lined with white silk. Rather than simply folding over the leaf edge, they cut a round flap for this purpose. When doing so away from the leaf edge, they make two cuts and draw the resulting flaps together. Many other caterpillars may fold a whole leaf to create a shelter in which to spin a cocoon.

Morning glory leafcutters and their relatives (Crambidae: *Hahncappsia*) chew partway through the petioles of morning glories and various

Pupation chamber of *Rhopobota* (Tortricidae), similar to that of the grape berry moth. (MA)

other plants, causing the leaves to hang down and wilt. For whatever reason, they prefer to feed on a leaf in this condition rather than a fresh one. The larva either folds the edge of a single leaf or draws together several small ones. It stays in this shelter during the day, emerging to feed in the evening.

Swallowtails

Some swallowtail caterpillars (Papilionidae: *Papilio*) make shelters for themselves by folding a leaf in half longitudinally. Quite different from other lepidopteran leaf shelters, the caterpillar does this by spinning a fine silken mat along the middle of the upper side of the leaf, with no silk strands attached to the leaf edge. The contracting of the silk as it dries causes the leaf to fold upward. The caterpillar uses this shelter when not feeding, keeping it clean by brushing out its droppings. Species with this habit include the spicebush swallowtail (*P. troilus*; E) on leaves in the laurel family; the pale swallowtail (*P. eurymedon*; W) on buckthorns, buckbrush, and wild plum; and the three tiger swallowtail species on cherry, aspen, and other trees.

Spiders

Many spiders may make a silken retreat within a single curled or folded leaf. These include certain orbweavers (Araneidae) that monitor the web with a signal line that transmits vibrations from the web's hub. Other spiders conceal egg sacs within folded leaves, including some orbweavers, cobweb spiders (Theridiidae), jumping spiders (Salticidae), ghost spiders (Anyphaenidae), and crab spiders (Thomisidae, Philodromidae, and Sparassidae). Some thomisid crab spiders suspend the egg sac like a hammock in a retreat formed of folded or drawn-together leaves. *Philodromus minutus* makes its egg sac near the tip of a leaf; the tip bearing the egg sac is folded back and fastened down to the body of the leaf by many silken threads, and the spider then remains on guard near the folded part of the leaf.

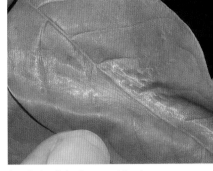

A spicebush leaf opened to show the fine mat of silk, spun by a spicebush swallowtail caterpillar (Papilionidae: *Papilio troilus*), that caused it to fold. (PA)

This jumping spider (Salticidae: *Zygoballus rufipes*) was coaxed out from under her leaf fold, where she was guarding her egg sac. (PA)

Grasslike Leaves with Two Folds

The sac spider *Clubiona riparia* (Clubionidae) folds a grass blade or cattail leaf transversely twice to form a three-sided chamber up to about 1.8 inches (4.5 cm) long, which she lines with silk, sealing herself in with her egg sac. The cattail caterpillar (Noctuidae: *Simyra insularis*) constructs a shelter that is 1 inch (2.5 cm) long in the same way, spinning its cocoon inside.

Petioles Fastened with Silk

A young viceroy caterpillar (Nymphalidae: *Limenitis archippus*) overwinters in a small tube made from the base of a willow, poplar, or other tree leaf. The larva feeds on both sides of a leaf's midrib, beginning at the tip, saving a portion next to the petiole around 12 to 15 mm long. It curls the leaf fragment into a narrow, silk-lined tube a few millimeters thick, secur-

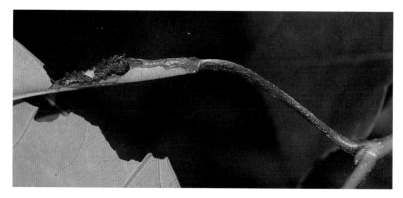

Above top: This viceroy caterpillar (Nymphalidae: *Limenitis archippus*) has prepared its cottonwood leaf hibernaculum and is ready for winter. (MA) *Above:* A red-spotted purple (*Limenitis arthemis*) hibernaculum as it appears in winter. (OH) Photo by Judy Semroc.

ing the petiole to the twig by winding silk around both. This shelter stays attached to the twig all winter, concealing the caterpillar as it waits to resume feeding in the spring. Other *Limenitis* species also have this habit, including the red-spotted admiral (*L. arthemis*; includes the white admiral and red-spotted purple), Lorquin's admiral (*L. lorquini*), and Weidemeyer's admiral (*L. weidemeyerii*).

Although the cut-leaf tube is unique to *Limenitis* caterpillars, several moth larvae

The webbing holding this dead apple leaf to the twig was spun by the rusty tussock moth caterpillar (Lymantriidae: *Orgyia antiqua*) whose cocoon is hidden within. (VT)

This tightly rolled birch leaf (11 mm long) contains the overwintering egg sac of an orbweaver (Araneidae). (MA)

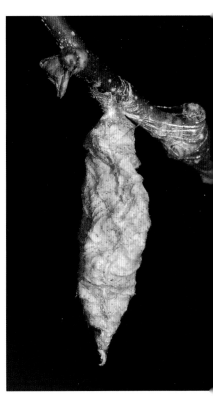

and spiders also use the trick of fastening a leaf to a twig so that it will stay attached through the winter. Promethea moth and related saturniid caterpillars do this when making their cocoons; see chapter 7 for more about these. Tussock moth caterpillars (Lymantriidae: *Orgyia*) also wind silk around the petioles when they make their hairy cocoons inside curled leaves. Some orbweavers (Araneidae) and perhaps other spiders conceal their egg sacs in tightly rolled leaves that they attach similarly. The spined micrathena (*Micrathena gracilis*) lays a clutch of more than 250 eggs near the center of a leaf's underside, then folds the leaf transversely and seals it tightly, forming a triangular packet with the petiole likewise fastened to the twig.

Other Leaf Shelters

The Carolina leaf-rolling cricket (Gryllacrididae: *Camptonotus carolinensis*; SE) hunts aphids at night and spends the day in a tubelike leaf shelter it constructs. There is much variation in the construction. One method is for the cricket to cut two slits in a leaf and pull the resulting flap over itself. Alternatively, it may make two pairs of slits on opposite sides of the midrib, place itself between the cuts, and draw the two flaps together. Sometimes more than one leaf is used. The cricket manipulates the leaf or leaves with its feet and fastens the edges together with silk spun from its mouth, moving its head back and forth between them. It builds a new shelter after each night of hunting.

Other tied leaves without evidence of feeding are likely the work of spiders. A

Carolina leaf-rolling cricket (Gryllacrididae: *Camptonotus carolinensis*) shelter, about 1.4 inches (3.5 cm) tall. (TN) Photo by Nancy Collins.

Leaf shelter constructed by an orbweaver (Araneidae: *Zygiella*). (TN)

nursery web spider (Pisauridae) often webs several leaves together to make an enclosed nursery. The empty, torn-open egg sac is left to identify it after the spiderlings have dispersed. Members of the families mentioned in the section on simple folds above, among others, may also tie several leaves together in which they spin a web, retreat, or egg sac. Many other spiders may simply adopt leaf shelters made by insects, with or without adding silk of their own.

Galls

12

A gall is a plant deformity caused by another organism, which may be an insect, mite, fungus, bacterium, virus, or nematode. North America has more than 150 species of gall mites (Eriophyidae), several hundred gall wasps (Cynipidae), and still more gall midges (Cecidomyiidae). Galls are also caused by several dozen aphids and other Sternorrhyncha, as well as some beetles, moths, and other flies and hymenopterans.

Insects and mites cause galls by entering plant tissue while it is still forming. They stimulate the tissue not just to modify its growth, but also to produce more nutrients. As a result, galls serve as both shelter and food source for the developing larvae or nymphs. Gall formation benefits the plant as well, because it contains the damage in a relatively small space. Galls rarely cause significant damage to the host plant. An intriguing idea proposed by Pirozynski (1991) is that fleshy fruits originated from gall wasps modifying the heritable genomes of plants by ovipositing in their reproductive organs. This would cause the plants' descendants to continue producing galls around their seeds without the wasp stimulus, which would then become juicier and more nutritious over time as seed-dispersing vertebrates preferentially ate fruits with these qualities.

Gall-producing organisms are usually highly host-specific, inducing galls in one plant species or a few closely related species. Some insect galls are indistinct and may intergrade with leaf mining or stem boring, but many are very distinctive structures, which are often much easier to identify and distinguish than the actual insects that cause them. Many are formed not just in a specific plant, but in a specific part of that plant. So if you want to identify a gall, it is critical that you identify the host plant and the precise location on that plant: bud, fruit, leaf, stem, or root. If it is a leaf gall, is it on the petiole or blade? If on the petiole, is it in the middle or at one end? If on the blade, is it on the upper side, underside, or edge? Is it on a main vein, a side vein, or in the intervening tissue?

A complete treatment of the hundreds of North American galls is clearly impossible here. If you have collected the information just mentioned, you have a good chance of reaching a precise identification using resources such as Felt (1940), Weld (1957, 1959, 1960; cynipids), Keifer et al. (1982; mites), Gagné (1989; midges), and Russo (2006; western states). All of these resources are organized by host plant. Here, galls are grouped instead primarily by similarities in form, and by either plant species or type of insect (or mite) within these groups. This way, if a particular gall is not illustrated or described, you should still be able to get a sense of the likely suspects—even if you do not know what the plant species is. To make a sweeping generalization: if a gall is not addressed in this chapter and is on an oak, it almost certainly belongs to a cynipid gall wasp; rose galls have a good chance of belonging to cynipids in the genus *Diplolepis*; if a gall is on any other plant, it most likely belongs to a gall midge. This does not apply to simple stem and twig swellings, which can be caused by just about any of the gall-making insect groups.

If a gall is inhabited, it is often possible to collect it and see what emerges. Bear in mind, however, that what emerges may not be the insect responsible for the gall. Numerous parasitoids and inquilines are often "guests" in the galls of other insects, which may or may not kill the gall inducer.

Although a number of gall insects have been given common names, we have omitted many because they are ambiguous and only create confusion. For instance, the name "eastern spruce gall adelgid" gives the false impression that there is only one adelgid that causes galls on eastern spruces.

Leaf Galls

There is tremendous diversity in form among the galls that insects and mites induce in leaves. The leaf may be distorted into a fold or roll in which the gall maker lives, or the gall may be a flat, fuzzy area on an otherwise unmodified leaf. Some galls are simple pouches or lobes, open on one side of the leaf; others have a slit that widens to allow the mature insects to escape; and many are entirely closed, requiring the mature larvae or adults to bore their way out. The gall may be fully integrated into the leaf tissue, in the form of a flattened blister, swollen vein, or more pronounced projection from the leaf blade; or it may have a small attachment point and be fairly easy to remove from the leaf. Some insects form galls on the petiole rather than the leaf blade.

Leaves Distorted into Folds or Rolls

Certain mites, aphids, midges, sawflies, and moths create shelters by distorting leaves so that they fold or crumple around the arthropods. With aphids, it can be difficult to draw a line between gall forming and incidental feeding damage; the characteristic corrugations in birch leaves caused by spiny witch hazel gall aphids are certainly in the gray area. Leafhoppers can cause leaves to distort and curl, but as they are highly mobile, there is

Sign of a leaf-folding sawfly (Tenthredinidae: *Phyllocolpa*) on a bigtooth aspen leaf.
(MA)

no particular advantage to this and the curling is incidental, without taking any particular form. Folds involving silk are discussed in chapter 11.

Phyllocolpa sawflies (Tenthredinidae) cause longitudinal crimps and folds in the edges of willow and poplar leaves. This distorted growth is induced by the females when they oviposit. The larva feeds within the fold, eventually leaving it and feeding along the leaf edge. A gall midge, *Prodiplosis morrisi*, causes similar but much smaller marginal folds on poplar leaves; on less well-developed leaves, it causes much of the leaf to wrinkle and curl inward. The midge larva, having sucking mouthparts, does not leave any chewed surfaces as the sawfly larvae do. The midge *Dasineura plicata* crimps and curls willow leaves, causing them to become tightly rolled into tubes. Mature larvae of this species form cocoons in the leaves.

The midrib gall moth (Cosmopterigidae: *Sorhagenia nimbosa*) induces very distinctive galls in buckthorn (*Frangula*) leaves. The middle of the leaf crinkles upward so that the sides meet, forming a tight little pouch, while the base and tip of the leaf are more or less unaffected. These were

A buckthorn leaf distorted by a larva of the midrib gall moth (Cosmopterigidae: *Sorhagenia nimbosa*). The recently emerged adult can be seen resting on the leaf. (WA)

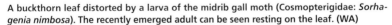

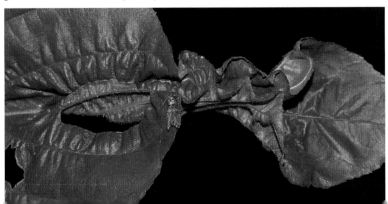

Marginal fold on a red oak leaf caused by *Macrodiplosis erubescens* (Cecidomyiidae). (MA)

the most abundant and conspicuous galls we came across in Olympic National Park.

Most other folds and rolls are induced by midges or mites. Marginal rolls in the edges of western snowberry leaves may be caused by either of these. The gall of the snowberry mite (*Phyllocoptes triacis*) is usually a paler green than the surrounding leaf surface, whereas that of the snowberry gall midge (of uncertain identity) may be green or purplish. The mite *Aceria caryae* causes elongate marginal rolls in pecan leaves.

Midge-induced small, marginal leaf rolls are mostly caused by species of *Contarinia* and *Dasineura*. In several cases, species of both genera have been reared from similar galls on the same host plant. Examples are found on maple, bramble, and spicebush leaves. Marginal folds on eastern oaks are caused by *Macrodiplosis erubescens*; several midges induce similar galls on western oaks. *Phylloxera nyssae* (Phylloxeridae) causes similar small, marginal folds on tupelo leaves.

The midge *Dasineura pudibunda* induces small, swollen folds in musclewood leaves, usually along lateral veins. A *Contarinia* species makes

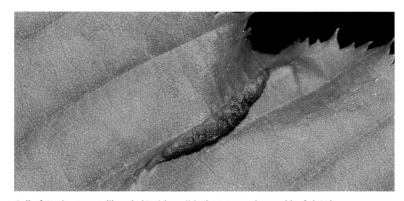

Gall of *Dasineura pudibunda* (Cecidomyiidae) on a musclewood leaf. (MA)

simple, little folds in chestnut leaves, between or across veins. The clover leaf midge (*Dasineura trifolii*) causes clover leaflets to fold in half and swell along the midveins. Up to twenty larvae feed in one leaflet. When mature, they spin cocoons either in the fold or underground.

Erineum Patches and Small Pouches

Erineum patches are densely fuzzy areas produced by gall mites on the upper or lower surface of a leaf. Some are essentially flat, and others are visible as a slight puckering on the opposite side. They may occur in small patches of a few millimeters or cover a large part of the leaf. Sometimes they significantly distort the leaf. Several species cause bright pink or red erineum patches on maple leaves. Most erineum is whitish to yellowish brown. Examples include *Aceria ferruginea* on beech; *A. fraxini* on ash; and *Colomerus vitis* on grape.

Many gall mites make small pouch galls, measuring just a few millimeters, that project from the upper surfaces of leaves. In some cases, they are very pronounced pouches; in others, they are more like small blisters. The underside of the gall looks like typical erineum, and there is a continuum rather than a clear line between erineum patches and pouch galls. Species that form distinct pouches include *Aceria campestricola* on American elm; *A. theospyri* on persimmon; *A. negundi* on boxelder; the alder beadgall mite (*Eriophyes laevis*); and the maple bladdergall mite (*Vasates quadripedes*). *Aculops rhois* causes small, red pouch galls on poison ivy, sometimes making it look like the plant itself has a bad

Right: Colored patches on a red maple leaf caused by erineum mites (Eriophyidae). (MA) *Below left:* Beech erineum galls caused by *Aceria ferruginea* (Eriophyidae). The leaf has been folded to show both sides of the galls. (MA) *Below right:* A white ash leaflet distorted by erineum mite (Eriophyidae) galls. (MA)

Above top: Pouch galls (3 mm) of *Aceria campestricola* (Eriophyidae) on American elm. (MA) *Above:* Galls of *Aceria theospyri* (Eriophyidae) on persimmon leaves. (VA) *Below left:* Galls of the alder beadgall mite (Eriophyidae: *Eriophyes laevis*). (MA) *Below right:* Poison ivy infested with *Aculops rhois* mites (Eriophyidae). (TN)

Galls of the maple bladdergall mite (Eriophyidae: *Vasates quadripedes*) on a silver maple leaf. (MA)

case of poison ivy. *A. tetanothrix* can similarly cover willow leaves with 2- to 3-mm warty galls that may be red or yellow-green, smooth or hairy.

Pronounced Pouches, Lobes, and Fingerlike Galls

A number of mite species produce finger galls, which are very narrow and open at the bottom. They have a fuzzy inner lining and represent the extreme end of the continuum noted above. Examples include the galls of *Eriophyes cerasicrumena* on black cherry; *E. emarginatae* on other cherries and plums; *E. tiliae* on basswood; and *Vasates aceriscrumena* on maple. A species of *Blaesodiplosis* midge makes galls on shadbush that are similar but thicker and without an opening. They are on the underside of the leaf, unlike the mite finger galls, which are all on the upper surface.

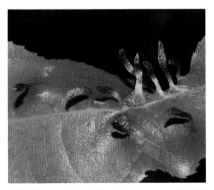 

Left: Finger galls on black cherry caused by *Eriophyes cerasicrumena* (Eriophyidae). (MA)
Right: Finger galls up to 3 mm long on basswood, caused by *Eriophyes tiliae* (Eriophyidae). (MA)

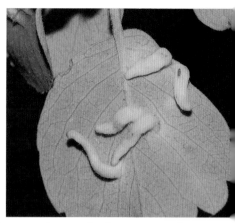

Left: Maple spindlegall mite (Eriophyidae: *Vasates aceriscrumena*) galls on sugar maple. (MA) *Right:* Galls (5 mm) of *Blaesodiplosis* (Cecidomyiidae) on the underside of a shadbush leaf. (UT)

The mite *Aceria parulmi* induces finger galls on elm, about 1 cm long. In addition to the small pouches of *A. campestricola* noted above, three species of aphids make pronounced pouches with distinctive shapes on the upper surfaces of elm leaves. *Kaltenbachiella ulmifusa* causes the slippery elm pouch gall, which is usually solitary. It is spindle-shaped and may be 0.8 to 1.4 inches (2 to 3.5 cm) tall, 6 to 10 mm wide at the middle. A crack opens in the side to let the aphids out. *Tetraneura ulmi* causes the elm sack gall, which is a stalked pouch, somewhat resembling a mushroom. It may be 1 inch (2.5 cm) long or less than a quarter of that size; there may be a single gall or more than thirty. They are often near, but not quite on, the midrib. In this gall, a circular hole opens in the side rather than a slit. Most distinctive is the elm cockscomb gall, caused by *Colopha ulmicola*. It is 12 to 15 mm long, about 8 mm tall, and laterally compressed, with a toothed crest somewhat resembling a cockscomb.

Left top: Elm sack galls (2 to 5 mm) of *Tetraneura ulmi*, an aphid. (MA) *Left:* An old 15-by-8-mm elm cockscomb gall of *Colopha ulmicola*, an aphid. (MA)

A grape leaf covered with galls of the grape phylloxera (Phylloxeridae: *Daktulosphaira vitifoliae*).

Hackberry nipple galls of *Pachypsylla celtidismamma* (Psyllidae), on the leaf underside. (VT)

Pouchlike galls on the undersides of grape leaves are caused by the grape phylloxera (Phylloxeridae: *Daktulosphaira vitifoliae*). These can cover the surface of the leaf and cause it to be crumpled and disfigured.

Hackberry nipple galls are pouchlike galls on the undersides of hackberry leaves, caused by a psyllid (*Pachypsylla celtidismamma*).

The sumac gall aphid (*Melaphis rhois*) makes large, reddish galls along sumac midribs, up to about 1.6 inches (4 cm) across. They look like apples on the outside but are soft, thin-walled, hollow pouches.

Galls of the sumac gall aphid (*Melaphis rhois*) on staghorn sumac. (MA)

Globular or Conical Galls with a Slit on the Underside

Aphid and phylloxera leaf galls can often be recognized easily by the presence of a slit, generally on the underside. As with the openings in the elm galls described above, this is a necessary feature to allow the mature insects to escape, as they do not have chewing mouthparts. Twenty or so *Phylloxera* species cause conical or rounded galls on hickory leaves, ranging in size from 0.5 mm (*P. minima*) to 12 mm (*P. caryae-*

Phylloxera (Phylloxeridae) galls (5 mm across) on a shagbark hickory leaf, as seen from below and above. (MA)

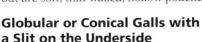

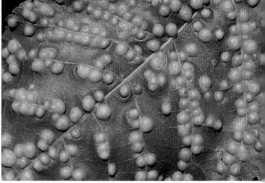

Left: Gall of the witch hazel cone gall aphid (*Hormaphis hamamelidis*). Its shadow points to a spot caused by an undescribed gall midge (*Contarinia* sp.). (MA) *Right: Phylloxera* galls (2 mm) on the upper surface of a bitternut hickory leaf. (TN)

Flat galls of the ocellate gall midge (Cecidomyiidae: *Acericecis ocellaris*) on a red maple leaf, along with a few galls of maple bladdergall mites. (MA)

Asteromyia carbonifera (Cecidomyiidae) galls (6 to 9 mm), containing a black symbiotic fungus. (MA)

globuli) across. Pointy cones on the upper surfaces of witch hazel leaves are caused by the witch hazel cone gall aphid (*Hormaphis hamamelidis*).

Spot and Blister Galls

A number of midges induce spot or blister galls, which are flat, slightly thickened, roughly circular areas, ranging from a few millimeters to more than a centimeter in diameter. A common example is the ocellate gall midge (*Acericecis ocellaris*), which lives exposed on the undersides of maple leaves, causing a red, green, or yellow spot on the upper surface, about 5 mm across. The spot turns brown after the larva drops to the ground to pupate. *Lasioptera spiraeafolia* causes a flat, circular spot on meadowsweet. *Resseliella liriodendri* causes circular blister galls on tuliptree leaves; *Sackenomyia commota* on viburnum; *Parallelodiplosis subtruncata* on dogwood; an undescribed *Contarinia* on witch hazel; and other undescribed species on greenbriers and various members of the lily family. At least five *Polystepha* species make blister galls on oak leaves, protruding from either side; *P. quercifolia* forms flat galls on oak leaves that are often reddish but otherwise inconspicuous. *Monarthropalpus flavus*, known as the boxwood leafminer, causes irregular blisters in boxwood leaves.

Hackberry blister galls of *Pachypsylla celtidisvesiculum* (Psyllidae). (VT)

Three midge species form blister galls on goldenrods. *Asphondylia solidaginis* creates a blister that involves two leaves stuck together, lined with a white symbiotic fungus. *Asteromyia modesta* makes a single-leaf, fungus-free gall on goldenrod and other composites. *Asteromyia carbonifera* forms galls containing a hard, black symbiotic fungus. Several other *Asteromyia* species cause galls with black fungus on other composites.

A few other insects and mites produce blisterlike galls. The moth *Heliozela aesella* (Heliozelidae) is responsible for lumpy, irregular blisters in grape leaves. When mature, the larva cuts an oval hole in the leaf to form its pupal case, just as its leaf-mining relatives do. Small blisters on hackberry leaves are caused by a psyllid, *Pachypsylla celtidisvesiculum*. Other small or irregular blisters may be the work of mites such as the pear leaf blister mite (*Eriophyes pyri*).

Elongate Vein Swellings

A number of midges cause elongate vein swellings in the undersides of leaves. Several of these have a longitudinal slit on the upper surface, through which the mature larvae leave the gall. *Dasineura tumidosae* induces large, succulent midrib and petiole swellings in the undersides of ash leaflets. *D. communis* causes elongate swellings on the undersides of maple leaves, which may crumple if the swellings

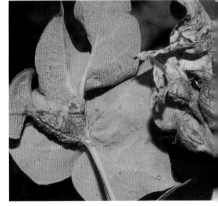

Undersides of sugar maple leaves distorted by galls of *Dasineura communis* (Cecidomyiidae). (VT)

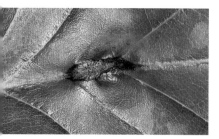

Left: A tuliptree leaf midrib swelling caused by *Resseliella tulipiferae* (Cecidomyiidae), as seen from above. (NC) *Right:* Purplish vein swellings on arrowwood caused by *Sackenomyia viburnifolia* (Cecidomyiidae). (MA)

form while they are still expanding. *Macrodiplosis* species are responsible for swellings in chestnut veins that may be either elongate or elliptical. *Resseliella tulipiferae* causes an underside swelling in tuliptree leaf midribs and veins. *Sackenomyia viburnifolia* induces striking purplish swellings on arrowwood veins (there is also a mite that causes much narrower purple swellings *between* the veins). Two *Polystepha* species have been reared from elongate vein swellings on oak leaves.

A 1-cm willow tooth gall, caused by a midge (Cecidomyiidae: *Iteomyia*). (CA)

Fleshy galls on grape leaves are caused by various gall midges (Cecidomyiidae). (MA)

Other Nondetachable Leaf Galls

Several species of *Pontania* sawflies (Tenthredinidae) form large, nearly spherical galls that protrude from both sides of a willow leaf. At least four *Iteomyia* midges also make galls on willow leaves. One causes the willow tooth gall, which has a rounded portion on the upper surface of the leaf and one or more bent, conical projections on the underside, like the roots of a tooth. The gall of *I. salicisverruca* has a similar setup, but it is very narrow, with a distinct beak. A third species makes 5-mm-long, dimpled, thimble-shaped galls that hang from the leaf underside, and *I. salicifolia* induces 2-mm spherical galls that likewise protrude from only one side of the leaf.

Most other nondetachable leaf galls not already described are also caused by midges—with the exception of those on oak, which are virtually all from cynipid

Left: Dasineura pellex (Cecidomyiidae) galls (3 mm) on a white ash leaflet. (MA) *Right:* Galls on a blackberry leaf induced by *Neolasioptera farinosa* (Cecidomyiidae). (MA)

wasps. Examples include succulent leaf swellings on grape leaves, caused by various species; globular swellings along the veins on the upper sides of ash leaflets, caused by *Dasineura pellex*; and swellings that become brown and woody in the fall, induced by *Neolasioptera farinosa* on blackberry leaves and petioles.

Detachable Leaf Galls

Some leaf galls are visible on only one surface of the leaf, and many of these have a small enough attachment point that they can be removed with little or no damage to the leaf. Once again, those that are not on oaks are likely the work of midges. Forty or so *Caryomyia* species make small galls on hickory leaves, often fully detachable and *dehiscent*, dropping to the ground before the leaves do. They come in a wide variety of shapes, including elongate cylinders (*C. tubicola*); broad cones with contracted bases (*C. sanguinolenta*); and tiny onion-shaped ones, both smooth (*C. caryaecola*) and hairy (*C. holotricha*). At least ten *Celticecis* species make dehiscent leaf and stem galls on hackberry with a similar variety of forms.

Left: Galls of *Caryomyia tubicola* (Cecidomyiidae) on a hickory leaf. (MA) *Above:* Celticecis unguicula (Cecidomyiidae) galls (4 mm) on a hackberry leaf. (MS)

Galls of *Polystepha pilulae* (Cecidomyiidae), among the few oak galls that are not caused by cynipid wasps. (MA)

Only two noncynipids are known to make detachable galls on oak, and both are eastern gall midges. *Polystepha globosa* makes thin-walled, 3-mm-wide spheres on black oak leaves, usually on the lower surfaces. *P. pilulae* makes hard, irregular galls of varying sizes on the upper surfaces of many kinds of oak leaves.

Numerous gall wasps make roughly spherical leaf galls on oaks. Species in several genera cause oak apples, which are large (up to 5 cm across), spherical galls that each have a single small cell containing a developing larva in the center. Sometimes the leaf is poorly developed or entirely consumed by the gall. In some species, spongy tissue fills the space between this cell and the outer wall; the galls of other species are largely hollow, with the cell suspended by many radiating fibers. In New England, there are two types that we commonly find detached, lying on the forest floor: *Amphibolips quercusinanis* and *A. quercusjuglans*. The former, of the "empty" variety, is bright green with red spots when fresh, becoming brown and papery when dry. The latter has dense, applelike flesh and actually forms on acorn caps rather than leaves. Roly-poly galls are smaller detachable galls, usually no more than 12 mm, each with a central cell that

Left top: Acorn plum galls (24 mm each) of *Amphibolips quercusjuglans* (Cynipidae). (MA) *Left center:* "Empty" oak apples (1.02 inches [2.6 cm] each) of *Amphibolips cookii* (Cynipidae). (MA) *Left bottom:* Oak pea gall of *Acraspis pezomachoides* (Cynipidae), on white oak. (MA)

rolls around freely inside. Many *Acraspis* species make loosely attached, spherical or oblong galls on white oak leaves that are many-faceted, either smooth or spiny.

Cynipid oak galls come in a wide variety of other forms. Some of the most striking ones are the bright pink, spiky galls of *Antron* species on blue oak and a few other western oaks. The spined turban gall of *A. douglasii* has up to ten or so spikes, and the red sea urchin gall of *A. quercusechinus* may have twenty or even as many as sixty.

Oak hedgehog gall of *Acraspis erinacei* (Cynipidae). (MA)

Petiole Swellings

A few different insects cause swellings on poplar petioles. The aphid *Pemphigus populitransversus* makes an oval gall near the middle of the petiole, with a transverse slit that opens like a mouth to let out the mature aphids. *P. populicaulis* makes a twisted gall with a similar but oblique opening, at the base of the leaf blade. A nepticulid moth larva (*Ectoedemia populella*) causes a small, closed, oval, ribbed gall in the same location.

The red sea urchin gall of *Antron quercusechinus* (Cynipidae) on blue oak. (CA) Photo by Monica Erhart.

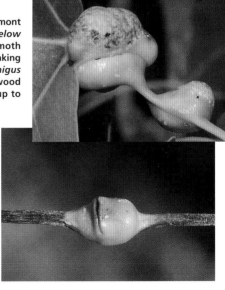

Right: Galls of *Pemphigus populicaulis* on Fremont cottonwood. The larger one is 2 cm. (UT) *Below left:* A 6-mm gall of the poplar petiolegall moth (Nepticulidae: *Ectoedemia populella*) on a quaking aspen leaf. (MA) *Below right:* Gall of *Pemphigus populitransversus* (Aphididae) on a cottonwood petiole, showing the slit that has opened up to allow the aphids to escape. (MA)

Hackberry petiole gall (12 mm) of *Pachypsylla venusta* (Psyllidae). (TN)

Large, woody swellings at the base of hackberry leaves are caused by a psyllid, *Pachypsylla venusta*. A few *Phylloxera* species cause galls on hickory petioles, which may be smooth, spiny (*P. caryaecaulis*), or have numerous long, fleshy filaments (*P. spinuloida*).

The midge *Neolasioptera vitinea* causes tapered swellings on grape petioles and tendrils. *N. impatientifolia* induces swellings on both petioles and midribs of jewelweed leaves.

At least two species of *Euura* sawflies (Tenthredinidae) induce conical galls on willow petioles. A sawfly that causes slight swellings in maple petioles is discussed in chapter 13.

Gall of *Neolasioptera vitinea* (Cecidomyiidae) on a grape petiole. (MA)

Swollen Buds

Mites and midges may cause buds to become swollen and then aborted. Mites include the taxus bud mite (*Cecidophyopsis psilaspis*; on yew) and blueberry bud mite (*Acalitus vaccinii*). Midges include

Upper left: A 16-mm gall of *Schizomyia impatientis* (Cecidomyiidae) on jewelweed. (MA) *Lower left:* An enlarged, aborted alder bud caused by *Dasineura serrulatae* (Cecidomyiidae). (MA) *Below:* Bud galls of *Schizomyia eupatoriflorae* (Cecidomyiidae) on white snakeroot. (VT)

Dasineura ulmea on elm; *D. serrulatae* on alder; and *Schizomyia eupatoriflorae* on white snakeroot. *S. impatientis* causes large, fleshy swellings in jewelweed flower buds that dangle like fruits. Some other galls that distort buds beyond all recognition are discussed in the section on detachable stem and twig galls below.

Dense Growth of Buds, Bracts, or Leaves

Certain mites and flies, instead of causing buds to abort, induce dense growth of buds, bracts, or leaves, sometimes resulting in more or less spherical, spiky galls. Abnormally dense growth can also be a result of other organisms, such as the fungus (*Pucciniastrum goeppertianum*) that causes "witches' brooms" on highbush blueberry. Witches' brooms on hackberry seem to be caused by a mite (*Aceria celtis*) in combination with a powdery mildew fungus.

The ash flower gall mite (*Aceria fraxiniflora*) causes dense growth of flower buds on male ash trees. This results in spiky balls that are often so abundant they could be mistaken for the tree's normal fruits, if you are not familiar with what ash samaras look like. *Aceria populi* causes dense growth of buds on poplars, and *Eriophyes betulae* on birch.

Several *Rabdophaga* gall midges induce dense terminal growths on willows. Three of these form tight, pineconelike galls. The gall of *R. strobiloides* is erect and closed at the top, with scales that are wider than long; that of *R. salicisstrobiliscus* has triangular scales that narrow toward the tip, forming an open "beak"; and that of *R. sal-*

Above top: Dense bud growth on black birch caused by *Eriophyes betulae* (Eriophyidae). (MA) *Above:* Galls (2 cm) induced by the ash flower gall mite (Eriophyidae: *Aceria fraxiniflora*). (MN)

The willow pinecone gall, caused by *Rabdophaga strobiloides* (Cecidomyiidae). (MA)

Above: Willow gall of *Rabdophaga saliciscoryloides* (Cecidomyiidae). (MA) *Right:* Willow gall of *Rabdophaga salicisstrobiliscus* (Cecidomyiidae). (MA)

icisgnaphaloides is small (no more than 1 cm long) and drooping. Three others form loose, leafy galls. The gall of *R. salicisbrassicoides* has leaves that are clearly longer than wide, whereas those of the remaining two are about as long as wide. The gall of *R. saliciscoryloides* is at least 2 inches (5 cm) wide, but that of *R. salicisrhodoides* is no more than 2 cm wide.

Other midges cause dense leafy growths on meadowsweet. Several species of *Oligotrophus* and *Walshomyia* produce conelike bud galls on western junipers. These may not look out of place on an evergreen, until you remember that junipers have berrylike fruits rather than cones. On creosote bush, the midge *Asphondylia foliosa* makes a single-celled twig gall covered with narrow, leafy bracts, about 7 mm across; *A. auripila* makes a similar but multicelled gall, up to 1 inch (2.5 cm) across.

Left top: Galls (about 15 mm) of an undescribed *Walshomyia* species (Cecidomyiidae) on Utah juniper. (UT) *Left:* A 1-inch (2.5-cm), multicelled gall on creosote bush, caused by *Asphondylia auripila* (Cecidomyiidae). (AZ)

Several *Rhopalomyia* species (Cecidomyiidae) cause leafy galls on goldenrod similar to this one. (MA)

Dense leafy growths on goldenrods that are 2 to 2.4 inches (5 to 6 cm) across are caused by *Rhopalomyia* midges; smaller growths may also be caused by these but could be from *Asphondylia monacha* (if the gall has a white inner lining of symbiotic fungus) or *Proceci-dochares* fruit flies (Tephritidae).

Detachable Stem and Twig Galls

Some insects cause buds to become greatly enlarged and mutated beyond all recognition. The result may be a smooth ball or spiky object, often appearing to be a fruit.

Galls of this type are not very common on herbaceous plants. The gall wasp *Gonaspis potentillae* causes galls on cinquefoil that are sometimes recognizable as bloated buds but may just look like round, hairy fruits. Another cynipid, *Liposthenes glechomae*, causes roughly spherical galls on ground ivy stems and petioles.

Hard, irregular, lumpy galls on blueberry twigs are caused by a chalcid wasp, *Hemadas nubilipennis* (Pteromalidae). Old galls stay attached for a long time, and the many tiny exit holes reveal that they are multicelled.

Above top: Gall of ***Gonaspis potentillae*** (Cynipidae) on cinquefoil. (MA) *Above:* Gall of *Liposthenes glechomae* (Cynipidae) on ground ivy. (MA)

Spiky galls on witch hazel are caused by the spiny witch hazel gall aphid, *Hamamelistes spinosus*. These galls are produced by aphids hatching from eggs laid on witch hazel in the fall. Some females of this species hibernate on birch trees, and they give birth to live young in the spring; these cause the distinctive corrugations in birch leaves. Many aphids have similar dual lives on two different host plants, although usu-

A 15-mm, multicelled gall of *Hemadas nubilipennis* (Pteromalidae) on blueberry. (MA)

Galls of the spiny witch hazel gall aphid (*Hamamelistes spinosus*). (VT)

ally they are found on one or the other at a given time of year. The same, incidentally, is true of some of the gall-forming fungi; for instance, the apple rust fungus (*Gymnosporangium juniperivirginianae*) also causes bizarre fruitlike galls that are purple with orange projections on juniper. Many gall wasps form two different types of oak galls at different times of year.

All detachable twig galls on oaks are made by cynipid wasps. Some are plain and spherical, like the hard bullet galls of *Disholcaspis quercusglobulus* on white oak, but they come in a wide variety of other shapes and textures. *Callirhytis seminator* causes the wool sower gall, a fluffy, white ball with pink spots, up to 2 inches (5 cm) across, consisting of many separate cells. *Andricus furnessae* causes a similarly fluffy, multicelled gall, white or pinkish, 3 to 4 inches (7.6 to 10.2 cm) across.

At least two *Diplolepis* species (Cynipidae) cause filamentous, green masses on

Left center: White oak bullet gall of *Disholcaspis quercusglobulus* (Cynipidae). (MA) *Left:* The wool sower gall on white oak, caused by *Callirhytis seminator* (Cynipidae). (MA)

Mossy rose gall of a *Diplolepis* gall wasp (Cynipidae). (MA)

rose plants, known as mossy rose galls. Felt (1940) called *D. rosae* "the" mossy rose gall, listed it as a twig gall, and gave the diameter as 2 to 4 inches (5 to 10.2 cm). Most books repeat this, sometimes adding that *D. bassetti* is a western species that causes a similar but much smaller gall. Russo (2006) contradicts this, showing *D. rosae* as a leaf gall. When we asked him about this, he replied that Felt was likely misled by a *D. rosae* specimen that had consumed a leaf bud before it opened. *D. bassetti* galls are made up of many 3- to 4-mm cells, forming masses up to 2 inches (5 cm) across, and may stay attached to a twig for years, because they develop from lateral stem buds. *D. rosae* galls are single-celled and, in Russo's experience, much smaller. They are typically on the upper surfaces of leaves, and when they do consume a whole leaf, appearing to be a twig gall, they will usually drop off when the other leaves do.

Terminal Twig Swellings

The very common beaked willow gall is caused by *Rabdophaga rigidae* (Cecidomyiidae). It is a tapered, terminal swelling in willow twigs. Gagné (1989) says it is a greatly swollen terminal bud, but whether or not this is true, it is woody and *appears* to be a swollen twig tip. New growth is aborted beyond the gall but may develop at the base. *Rhopalomyia californica* causes lumpy terminal swellings, which may have

Right: The beaked willow gall, caused by *Rabdophaga rigidae* (Cecidomyiidae). (MA) *Below left:* Coyote brush bud gall midge (Cecidomyiidae: *Rhopalomyia californica*) gall, measuring 1 cm. (CA) *Below right:* Gall of *Callirhytis clavula* (Cynipidae) on white oak. (MA)

leaves emerging from them, in coyote brush. *Callirhytis clavula* (Cynipidae) causes the white oak club gall, a globular terminal swelling with viable leaf buds protruding.

Herbaceous Stem Swellings

Many insect galls are simple, smooth swellings in stems. These may be caused by gall midges, tephritid fruit flies, agromyzid flies, moths, or gall wasps.

One of the most common examples is the nearly spherical goldenrod ball gall, an inch or so in diameter, caused by a fruit fly, *Eurosta solidaginis*

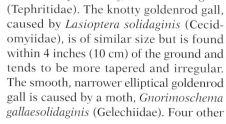

(Tephritidae). The knotty goldenrod gall, caused by *Lasioptera solidaginis* (Cecidomyiidae), is of similar size but is found within 4 inches (10 cm) of the ground and tends to be more tapered and irregular. The smooth, narrower elliptical goldenrod gall is caused by a moth, *Gnorimoschema gallaesolidaginis* (Gelechiidae). Four other

Left: The goldenrod ball gall, caused by *Eurosta solidaginis* (Tephritidae). (MA) *Lower left:* Goldenrod gall of a moth, *Gnorimoschema gallaesolidaginis* (Gelechiidae). (MA) *Lower right:* Another goldenrod gall from an unrelated moth, *Epiblema scudderiana* (Tortricidae). (MA)

Gall of *Neolasioptera convolvuli* (Cecidomyiidae) in a hedge bindweed stem. (VT)

moths (Tortricidae: *Epiblema scudderiana* and other *Gnorimoschema* spp.) cause oval or fusiform stem galls on goldenrod.

Irregular swellings on dandelion stems are caused by a cynipid wasp, *Phanacis taraxaci*. *Melanagromyza marellii*, an agromyzid fly, causes conspicuous blobby stem galls on alligatorweed (*Alternanthera philoxeroides*). The moth *Caloptilia murtfeldtella* (Gracillariidae) induces a gall near the base of penstemon stems, leaving its pupal skin protruding when it emerges.

Neolasioptera midges cause stem swellings in a wide variety of plants; these swellings may become woody in the fall, as in *N. convolvuli* in bindweed and *N. boehmeriae* in false nettle. Other examples include *N. portulacae* in purslane; *N. clematidis* in clematis; *N. lupini* in lupine; *N. menthae* in mint; and *N. monardi* in wild bergamot. In bugleweed, *N. lycopi* makes 1-cm galls that each hold a single larva, whereas *N. mitchellae* makes more elongate galls containing multiple larvae.

Woody Stem and Twig Swellings

Swellings in woody stems and twigs include a similar cast of characters to those in herbaceous stems—midges, agromyzid flies, gall wasps, and moths—but they may also be made by beetles or sawflies. Rough, lumpy, gall-like deformities can also result from external feeding by insects with piercing-sucking mouthparts, such as woolly aphids (*Eriosoma*) on rosaceous trees and elms, and balsam woolly adelgids (*Adelges piceae*) on fir. Still other swellings in trees may be caused by viruses, bacteria, or fungi. The large deformities known as burls usually do not involve another organism, but are outgrowths around dormant buds in response to some type of environmental stress.

More than twenty-five different species of *Euura* sawflies (Tenthredinidae) cause swellings in willow stems, along with members of several midge genera. Dissection of old sawfly galls, with exit holes up to 2 mm wide, will reveal droppings and one or more empty cocoons. These are not present in the midge galls, which may have pupal skins protruding from them. The widespread willow potato gall is caused by the midge *Rab-*

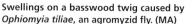

Swellings on a basswood twig caused by *Ophiomyia tiliae*, an agromyzid fly. (MA)

Poplar stem gall caused by a long-horned beetle (Cerambycidae: *Saperda*). (MA)

dophaga salicisbatatas. It is up to 1.6 inches (4 cm) long and 2 cm wide and may be shaped like a potato, often containing many larvae. It is yellow-green and soft at first but becomes hard and brown by the fall. *R. salicistriticoides* causes a foreshortening of the twig, so that there are many buds close together on the swollen portion: the wheat-ear gall. All the other midge galls are simple, tapered swellings, sometimes barely noticeable, whereas many of the sawfly galls are quite pronounced, often on just one side of the twig.

Small, oval or irregular twig galls on willow may also be caused by *Hexomyza* agromyzid flies. Similar galls are made by *H. schineri* on poplars and *Ophiomyia tiliae* on basswood.

Various wood-boring beetles are responsible for swellings in stems and twigs. Among the long-horned beetles (Cerambycidae), *Saperda fayi* causes oval swellings up to 2 inches (5 cm) long in hawthorn twigs; *S. obliqua* does the same in alder stems; and *S. inornata* and *S. populnea* in poplar stems. Weevils (Curculionidae) include the poplar and willow borer (*Cryptorhynchus lapathi*), which induces irregular, generally less pronounced swellings than those of *Saperda* species, and the grape cane gallmaker, which is discussed in chapter 13. *Podapion gallicola* (Brentidae), a straight-snouted weevil, causes small, rounded swellings in pine twigs. Metallic wood-boring beetles (Buprestidae) include the red-necked cane borer

Left: Black locust twig gall of *Ecdytolopha insiticiana* (Tortricidae). (VT) *Right:* A 17-mm-wide gall of the baccharis stem gall moth (Gelechiidae: *Gnorimoschema baccharisella*) on coyote brush. (CA)

(*Agrilus ruficollis*), responsible for slight, ridged swellings that are 1 inch (2.5 cm) long in bramble canes; *A. aurichalceus,* more elongate swellings in rose canes; *A. politus,* round swellings in hawthorn twigs; and *Eupristocerus cogitans,* irregular stem swellings in alder.

Moths in several different families induce twig galls. *Ectoedemia castaneae* (Nepticulidae) makes galls that encircle chestnut twigs. Elongate swellings on black locust twigs are caused by *Ecdytolopha insiticiana* (Tortricidae). Smooth, elliptical swellings on coyote brush, up to 1.4 inches (3.5

Old gall of *Neolasioptera linderae* (Cecidomyiidae) on a spicebush twig. (MA)

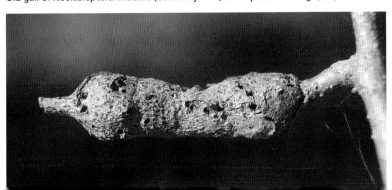

A small (1.2-inch [3-cm]) gouty oak gall, caused by *Callirhytis quercuspunctata* (Cynipidae). (MA)

cm) long, are induced by the baccharis stem gall moth (Gelechiidae: *Gnorimoschema baccharisella*). On the same host plant, the coyote brush stem gall midge (*Rhopalomyia baccharis*) causes a portion of the stem 2 to 3.5 inches (5 to 9 cm) long to become contorted and slightly swollen.

Woody stems and twigs are host to a number of *Neolasioptera* midges, just as herbaceous ones are. *N. linderae* causes elongate, irregular stem swellings in spicebush, with several larvae developing in a single gall. *N. viburnicola* induces similar ones in arrowwood, and *N. cornicola* in dogwood. *N. pierrei* is responsible for tapered swellings in elderberry; *N. fontagrensis*, irregular swellings in bittersweet; and *N. nodulosa*, swellings on brambles, sometimes ridged and usually near the tip of the stem.

Several *Lasioptera* midges have been reared from tapered swellings in oak twigs or petioles, although at least some of these are known to have been caused by wasps. With the exception of irregular, lumpy, ter-

Dewberry stem gall of *Diastrophus* (Cynipidae), containing many larvae. (MA)

minal swellings sometimes induced by mites, it appears that any other twig gall on an oak can safely be attributed to a cynipid wasp. One of the most conspicuous of the nondetachable variety is the gouty oak gall caused by *Callirhytis quercuspunctata*. These large (up to 5 inches [12.7 cm]), lumpy, irregular, woody swellings are found on twigs of a variety of oaks. They may appear to be some kind of burl, but old ones are riddled with exit holes of the numerous wasps that developed within.

Several species of *Diastrophus* (Cynipidae) cause pronounced swellings on blackberry stems (as well as roots), up to 6 inches (15.2 cm) long. The blackberry knot gall, induced by *D. nebulosus*, sometimes has several distinct longitudinal furrows.

Complex Integral Twig Galls

A number of the galls noted above are internally complex, with multiple larvae in separate chambers; there are also some integral (nondetachable) twig galls that are visibly multicelled on the outside. *Diastrophus cuscutaeformis* (Cynipidae) causes blackberry "seed" galls, dense aggregations of round cells surrounding blackberry stems; these galls may be densely covered with bristles. Pineapplelike swellings on bald cypress branchlets are induced by a midge, *Taxodiomyia cupressiananassa*.

Several different adelgids are responsible for multicelled twig galls on spruces. *Adelges abietis* causes nonterminal pineapplelike galls; those of *A. lariciatus* are simi-

Right: A 7-mm gall of *Taxodiomyia cupressiananassa* (Cecidomyiidae) on bald cypress. (LA) *Below:* Blackberry "seed" galls of *Diastrophus cuscutaeformis* (Cynipidae). (MA)

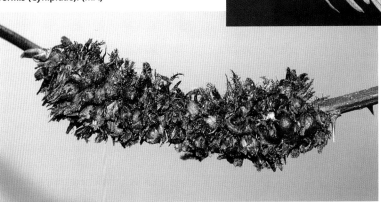

Above: Spruce galls of *Adelges abietis* (Adelgidae). (MA) *Left:* Spruce galls of *Pineus similis* (Adelgidae). (MA)

lar but with the needles stunted to less than a third of the normal length; those of *A. laricis* are terminal and usually found on black spruce. *Pineus similis* induces terminal galls that are concealed by scragglylooking dead needles. Those of *P. pinifoliae* are conelike, with the needles reduced to thin scales. The Cooley spruce gall adelgid (*A. cooleyi*) causes a terminal swelling up to about 2.4 inches (6 cm) long, with the needles unmodified and projecting outward as they normally would; *P. floccus* produces a much smaller gall of similar form, almost exclusively on black spruce.

Sign on Twigs, Stems, and Stemlike Structures

13

Insect sign on twigs and stems is generally related to either egg-laying activity of adults or boring and feeding by larvae. Both can weaken and kill stems and twigs, and dead or broken shoots or twigs with the foliage still attached are often the most conspicuous sign of these activities. Certain beetles girdle twigs and cause them to break off cleanly without first killing them, suggesting from a distance the work of squirrels or porcupines. Insects that produce pronounced swellings (galls) were discussed in chapter 12. This chapter includes a few insects that bore in petioles and fern rachises, which are technically leaf components but are stemlike in structure.

Bark Stripping

The European hornet (Vespidae: *Vespa crabro*), introduced in the eastern United States, leaves a sign on twigs and branches that is more likely to be mistaken for the work of rodents than of any other insect. Workers girdle sections of twigs and small branches by chewing off all the bark. It is often said that they do this to collect wood fibers for nest construction, but this is doubtful, because their nests are made primarily of decayed wood fibers. They have been seen feeding on sap from the wounds, and this would seem to be the purpose of the stripping. The exposed wood surface has a finely scratched-up appearance, without the clear paired incisor marks that rodents would leave. Lilac, birch, willow, and poplar twigs are some of the ones most frequently stripped by hornets.

Subcuticular Mines

Mine of a *Marmara* larva (Gracillari-idae) in a white ash sapling. (VT)

Species of *Marmara* (Gracillariidae) mine under the cuticle or "skin" of stems and twigs in the same way related leaf-mining moth larvae do under the epidermis of leaves. Like those of the leaf-mining *Marmara* species, these mines are linear, long, and tortuous. *M. arbutiella* mines in madrone and manzanita; *M. serotinella* in black cherry; *M. fasciella* in white pine and balsam fir; *M. oregonensis* in Douglas-fir and grand fir; and *M. guilandinella* in nicker bean. *M. fraxinicola* and two other species mine in ash. *M. pomonella* and *M. elotella* both mine in apple and pear. *M. salictella* mines in willow, as does *M. gulosa*, which also mines in oleander, cotton, and avocado. *M. apocynella* mines in dogbane stems, and *M. auratella* in coneflower and dahlia stems.

Marmara fulgidella produces similar mines in oak and chestnut. *Ectoedemia phleophaga* (Nepticulidae) makes a serpentine track in chestnut bark, and *E. heinrichi* a "characteristic, flattened-oval, spiral mine in the bark of young branches of pin oak" (Forbes 1923). We have not seen these but would expect the differences between the two genera to be similar to those of their leaf-mining counterparts.

The gooseberry barkminer moth (Opostegidae: *Pseudopostega quadristrigella*) is a member of a poorly known family closely related to the Nepticulidae. The larva mines the fibrous inner lining of currant and gooseberry bark.

Marmara opuntiella mines just under the surface of prickly pear pads, sometimes widening its winding, linear mine out into irregular blotches. Larvae of the pyralid cactus moths may also mine the surface of prickly pears at first, but they soon go deeper and hollow them out.

Many of the agromyzid flies that develop in stems bore on the inside without producing an externally visible sign, but some do make mines near the surface. Best known is the asparagus miner (*Ophiomyia simplex*), which sometimes girdles asparagus stems at the base and kills them. Related stem miners include *O. labiatarum* in mints; *O. texana* in mustards; *O. abutilivora*

Mines of *Marmara opuntiella* in a prickly pear pad. (TX)

in velvetleaf and other mallows; *O. coniceps* in sowthistle; and *O. chondrillae* in rush skeletonweed. Unlike stem-mining moths, these flies pupate at the end of the mine, with the anterior spiracles projecting through the epidermis. Stem miners are scattered in other agromyzid genera, including *Liriomyza angulicornis* in arrowgrass; *Phytoliriomyza arctica* in goldenrod; and *Phytomyza clematisella* in clematis.

Oviposition Scars

Tree crickets, cicadas, treehoppers, and certain leafhoppers produce characteristic scars when they insert their eggs in stems and twigs. Stem-boring weevils, long-horned beetles, and sawflies may also make conspicuous wounds when they oviposit; these are discussed along with sign of their larvae later in this chapter. See the sections on eggs inserted in terrestrial and aquatic vegetation in chapter 1 for other insects that may insert eggs in stems.

Tree Crickets

Tree crickets (Gryllidae: Oecanthinae) insert their eggs in saplings and stems of shrubs and herbaceous plants, generally in edge habitats. The female begins by chewing a small pit, then drills in with her ovipositor and deposits an elongate, slightly curved egg, about 3 mm long. The egg has a white cap at the end toward the opening, and depending on the species, the rest of the egg is white or yellow. She fills the small, round hole with a

Old scar and oviposition holes of a black-horned tree cricket (Gryllidae: *Oecanthus nigricornis*) on a red maple sapling. (MA)

mucilaginous substance, and most species finish by plugging the hole with bits of chewed bark. The holes are more obvious after the nymphs hatch out in the spring, and pronounced scars develop in woody plants as they grow. The arrangement of holes and choice of substrate vary considerably among species.

The black-horned tree cricket (*Oecanthus nigricornis*; west to MT, CO) makes punctures in compact lines, with seven to ten holes per centimeter. The female usually makes about thirty punctures, but there can be anywhere from two to eighty or more. She uses herbaceous or woody stems and twigs, almost always over 5 mm wide. Riley's tree cricket (*O. rileyi*; east to ID, AZ) makes similarly compact lines, usually in bramble stems, and the prairie tree cricket (*O. argentinus*; east to MN, OH, LA) does so in pithy herbaceous stems. The widespread four-spotted tree cricket (*O. quadripunctatus*) oviposits in 2- to 5-mm-wide herbaceous stems such as wild carrot. She also makes compact lines, but they are crooked and broken into groups of two to five, with each group separated by a 3- to 15-mm gap. Sometimes all the punctures are fairly well scattered. Forbes's tree cricket (*O. forbesi*; N central U.S.) is closely related to these species and also lays its eggs more or less in a line, but her preferences are not known. The pine tree cricket (*O. pini*; west to MI, TX) typically spaces the punctures about 3 mm apart and apparently oviposits only in pine twigs.

The broad-winged tree cricket (*O. latipennis*; E), rather than depositing a single egg in each puncture, inserts 4 to 12 eggs side by side, half above and half below the main hole. The opening is relatively large and conspicuous because of the repeated drillings and because she leaves it unplugged. The holes may be in a row, but they are 1 cm or more apart. The western tree cricket (*O. californicus*; east to ID, TX) oviposits similarly but with 2 to 6 eggs per puncture. There are usually several punctures in a stem, 7 to 20 mm apart, which may or may not be plugged with chewed bark. Both species typically use herbaceous stems, but the former also uses grapevines, and we have found eggs oviposited in fleshy yucca leaves that we suspect belonged to the latter (see page 302).

Whereas the above species all insert their eggs well within the pith, others insert theirs in the inner bark or cambium of trees and shrubs, never reaching the pith. The punctures are generally well scattered, and when there are several in a row, they are not in a compact line as in the first group. The snowy tree cricket (*O. fultoni*) usually oviposits in branches 1 to 3 inches (2.5 to 7.6 cm) wide, often in the lenticels. It plugs the holes with excrement rather than with chewed bark. Davis's tree cricket (*O. exclamationis*; E, AZ) has been observed to plug its holes with a combination of excrement and chewed bark. The narrow-winged tree cricket (*O. niveus*; E) often makes two oviposition holes in a V from a single puncture. The two-spotted tree cricket (*Neoxabea bipunctata*; E) also lays its eggs (4 mm rather than the 3 typical of *Oecanthus* species) singly in bark or cambium, placed similarly to those of the snowy tree cricket.

Bush crickets (Hapithinae; SE) also insert their eggs in plant stems. We have found no further information than this, so we assume that they do not leave a conspicuous sign.

Cicadas

Cicadas use their ovipositors to cut elongate slits that often run into one another, forming a continuous jagged line along the length of a twig or stem. There are often about half a dozen slits in a row, but they may number up to twenty or so. The length of the individual slits varies, since cicadas come in a range of sizes. We watched *Magicicada septendecim* periodical cicadas on Cape Cod, Massachusetts, making 1-cm slits in oak twigs, whereas those of smaller cicadas on mesquite in Tucson, Arizona, were only 4 mm. The slits are generally on the undersides of horizontal woody twigs but may be found in herbaceous stems such as goldenrods. Conifers are avoided, presumably because the sticky resin would interfere. In each slit, the female inserts closely packed eggs in two neat rows (a total of 10 to 28 eggs per slit in the case of *M. septendecim*). Upon hatching, the nymphs fall to the ground, where they burrow down and spend almost their whole lives sucking sap from roots. Twigs are sometimes killed by the oviposition slits, and the resulting bunches of dead, brown leaves become noticeable in the late summer.

Egg slits in an oak twig made by a periodical cicada (*Magicicada septendecim*). Each slit is about 1 cm long. (MA)

Scars on an apple twig caused by the paired egg-laying slits of a buffalo treehopper (Membracidae: *Ceresa*). (VT)

Treehoppers

Treehoppers (Membracidae) also cut slits in woody twigs to lay their elongate eggs and may kill the tip of the twig. The slits they make are either straight or crescent-shaped. When we looked beneath the alternating white egg masses of a two-spotted treehopper (*Enchenopa binotata*) on a bittersweet vine, we found that the 4-mm slit beneath each was very ragged-looking, itself made up of several tiny, alternating slits, each containing a few yellowish eggs. As with cicadas, treehopper nymphs drop to the ground upon hatching, but they feed on herbaceous plants instead of burrowing underground.

Buffalo treehoppers (*Ceresa*) cut paired slits that are either parallel or curved like parentheses, often on apple twigs, but also on elm, willow, and even herbaceous plants. The pairing of the slits slows down the growth of the wood fibers in between them, preventing the eggs from being crushed by the rapid growth of the twig. The slits are about 5 mm long, and there are usually a number of paired slits in succession along the twig. In each slit are 5 to 12 or more smooth, whitish, 2-mm-long eggs arranged in a row. According to Marlatt (1885–86), the eggs in each slit are actually inserted from the opposite slit, causing the outer bark to be cut loose from beneath. As the twig continues to grow, this strip of bark breaks, and each pair of slits becomes a single, irregularly circular scar, 3 to 6 mm in diameter, extending through the bark into the sapwood. These paired slits are usually reported as being characteristic of "the" buffalo treehopper, *C. alta*, but there are several very similar species, and the one Marlatt illustrated was quite possibly misidentified.

Leafhoppers

Oviposition wounds of leafhoppers (Cicadellidae) are not often described, but a number of species insert their eggs in woody stems or twigs to overwinter. Some may only produce small blisters under the bark, whereas others make obvious slits. Tree cricket enthusiast Nancy Collins collected a prickly-ash twig with a dashed line of a dozen 2-mm slits, each containing a single whitish egg. From these eggs, she raised what turned out to be leafhoppers in the genus *Gyponana*. The eggs were clearly visible inside the slits in May, but the slits were still tightly sealed in the twig pictured here, which was found on the same prickly ash the following March, and this twig had to be sliced open to see the eggs. Both twigs had an obvious bulge to one side of each slit, but this does not indicate the position of the egg.

Borers in Herbaceous Stems

Larvae of various flies, moths, sawflies, and beetles bore in herbaceous stems. Some leave characteristic sign, but many do not, or if they do it has not been described.

Beetles

Larvae of many weevils (Curculionidae) bore in the stems of herbaceous plants, typically pupating near the base. Females use

Oviposition slits of a *Gyponana* leafhopper (Cicadellidae) in a prickly-ash stem, 2 mm each. (WI)

their long snouts to chew holes in the stems, into which they deposit their eggs. They often make similar punctures when feeding. Milkweed weevils (*Rhyssomatus*) chew several holes in a vertical line in the lower part of a milkweed stem, laying an egg in each. The already conspicuous scar is made more so by gobs of sticky latex that ooze from the wounds. Sweet potato weevil larvae (Brentidae: *Cylas formicarius*) are root feeders, but clustered egg punctures near the base of vines are the best clue to their presence.

Larvae of the potato stalk weevil (*Trichobaris trinotata*; E) and tobacco stalk weevil (*T. mucorea*; SW) bore up and down the stems of various nightshades, causing them to wilt. Agave and yucca snout weevils (*Scyphopho-*

Oviposition pits chewed by a milkweed weevil (Curculionidae: *Rhyssomatus palmacollis*). (MA)

rus) lay their eggs at the base of their host plants' flower stalks, and larval feeding combined with pathogens entering through the egg pits soon cause the plants to collapse and die. The rhubarb curculio (*Lixus concavus*) and related species bore in dock, sunflower, and thistle (they feed on and oviposit in rhubarb stalks, but the eggs do not hatch). Larvae of the cabbage curculio (*Ceutorhynchus rapae*) develop in stems of wild mustards and occasionally in cabbage seed stalks.

Most long-horned beetle larvae (Cerambycidae) bore in woody plants, but some flat-faced longhorns (Lamiinae) develop in herbaceous stems. Soybean stem borers (*Dectes*) bore in ragweed and cocklebur stems, as well as soybean. The female lays an egg in a small pit chewed in the stem or a petiole, and the larva bores in, feeding on the pith as it makes its way down. It girdles the stem about 2 inches (5 cm) above the ground and overwinters below this point, plugging its burrow with frass. *Dorcasta*, *Hippopsis*, and *Mecas* species also bore in composites and other herbs. Milkweed longhorn larvae (*Tetraopes*) enter milkweed stems close to the ground and bore in the lower stem and roots.

Larvae of many lizard beetles (Languriidae) are stem borers, often in composites and legumes. Feeding of the clover stem borer (*Languria mozardi*) weakens its host, and the plant may swell and break off at the oviposition hole. A few leaf beetle (Chrysomelidae) and tumbling flower beetle (Mordellidae) larvae also are stem borers of herbaceous plants.

Flies

We often come across ferns of various species that have the tops conspicuously kinked and stunted. On breaking open an intermediate woodfern with this mutation, we found a larva inside, so we broke off several stunted fern tops and took them home. A few days later, several *Scaptomyza* fruit flies (Drosophilidae; apparently *S. pallida*) emerged. Oldroyd (1964) mentions that a few species in this genus are stem miners, but we have found no information on host plants of North American species. It seems unlikely that no one has discovered these fern-kinking flies before, but so far we have found nothing to suggest otherwise.

The top of this intermediate woodfern has been deformed by *Scaptomyza* fly larvae (Drosophilidae) feeding within the rachis. (MA)

Agromyzid flies bore in stems of a variety of herbaceous plants. Miners in grass stems also include frit flies (Chloropidae), shore flies (Ephydridae), long-legged flies (Dolichopodidae; e.g., *Thrypticus* in common reed), and opomyzid flies.

Moths and Skippers

Larvae of the squash vine borer (Sesiidae: *Melittia cucurbitae*) eat the pith of cucurbit stems near the base, causing the plant to wilt and die. Their soft fecal pellets pushed out of a hole in the vine are a sure sign of their presence before this happens.

Giant skipper caterpillars (Hesperiidae: Hesperiinae: Megathymini) feed exclusively on yuccas, agaves, and manfredas, boring in the stems, leaves, and rootstocks. Before pupating inside the plant, most of them build a trapdoor so that the adult can emerge. The much smaller larvae of bogus yucca moths (Prodoxidae: *Prodoxus*) feed in yucca flower stalks, also pupating inside, and leaving them riddled with round emergence holes.

The stalk borer (Noctuidae: *Papaipema nebris*) is an extreme generalist, having been found in more than 175 plant species, both herbaceous and woody. It may be common in corn, tomatoes, potatoes, ragweeds, and docks. The plant wilts above the point where the larva is boring, and the larva often leaves one plant to enter another. Eventually it may pupate within a stem (although apparently this species more often pupates underground), chewing an escape hole for the adult just before doing so. Other *Papaipema* species are borers with more specific tastes; several that are mentioned as root feeders in chapter 9 may also bore in the lower portions of stems. Some other stem-mining noctuids start out as leafminers and are mentioned in chapter 10. A number of tortricids, among other moth larvae, also bore in herbaceous stems, often expelling excrement from the entrance hole.

Sawflies

Some stem sawfly larvae (Cephidae: *Cephus*) bore in stems of wheat and other grasses. Eggs are inserted in the upper parts of the stems, and the larvae bore toward the bottom, where they overwinter in cocoons before chewing holes to emerge as adults.

Borers in Conifer Twigs and Leaders

The common borers in conifer twigs and leaders are weevils, xyelid sawflies, and various moths. Certain moth and midge larvae feed on the surfaces of twigs beneath conspicuous masses of pitch that form around them.

Weevils

A number of weevils (Curculionidae) kill the leaders and branch tips of pines and other conifers. The work of weevils can be recognized by the feeding and oviposition holes chewed by adults on the surface (the latter are plugged with chewed bark or wood fibers), which cause drops of resin to form. The widespread *Pissodes strobi* was formerly thought to be three different species: the white pine weevil, Engelmann spruce weevil, and Sitka spruce weevil. Many females may lay eggs in a single leader, and the feeding of the larvae inside kills the current and previous years' growth. This permanently changes the form of the tree by causing side branches to become the new leaders. Other *Pissodes* and *Cylindrocopturus* weevils (among others) cause similar damage, from either internal feeding by larvae or external feeding on young tips by adults. Adult *Phloeosinus* bark

Left: Two side branches of this pine have become leaders since the main stem was killed by larval white pine weevils (Curculionidae: *Pissodes strobi*). (MA) *Above:* An incense cedar twig tip killed by the feeding of an adult *Phloeosinus* bark beetle (Curculionidae: Scolytinae). (CA)

beetles often cause 6- to 12-inch (15- to 30-cm) tips of twigs in the cypress family to die and "flag," kinking at the point where the beetles have fed. They sometimes tunnel inside rather than simply nibbling the surface.

Sawflies

Several *Pleroneura* sawflies (Xyelidae) bore in terminal shoots of firs. Some cause them to die and turn brown; others leave little sign beyond an exit hole chewed in the side of an apparently healthy but hollowed-out shoot.

Moths

Many moth larvae bore in the tips of pine shoots, killing them from the tip down. Most of them are tortricids in the tribe Eucosmini, but some pyralids (*Dioryctria*) and gelechiids (*Exoteleia*) do the same thing. Some mine in the needles in early instars. Webbing may be mixed with the exuded resin, and in some species, the pupa can be found within the shoot. The juniper twig girdler (Cosmopterigidae: *Periploca nigra*) tunnels in juniper twigs and eventually kills them by cutting a circular groove under the bark.

Pitch Masses

Larvae of pitch twig moths (Tortricidae: *Retinia*) feed on pine twigs within large blobs of pitch. The larva overwinters in one blob, then moves and creates a second one, in which it completes its development and pupates. Its pupal skin is left protruding from the mass of pitch.

Resin and pitch midges (Cecidomyiidae: *Cecidomyia*) also form pitch masses on twigs. Some species feed gregariously on pines, pupate within the masses, and leave their pupal skins protruding when they emerge. Others, which may be either solitary or gregarious, leave their pitch masses to spin white cocoons on twigs and foliage nearby. Species with similar habits are found on spruce and Douglas-fir.

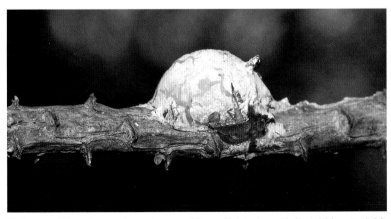

Pitch mass (12 mm) on a pine twig caused by a pitch twig moth (Tortricidae: *Retinia*), with the pupal skin protruding. (VA)

Borers in Stems and Twigs of Broad-leaved Woody Plants

The borers in stems and twigs of broad-leaved woody plants are mostly larvae of beetles, sawflies, and moths. Members of two or three of these groups may use a given host plant, but they are arranged here by type of insect in order to highlight the similarities among related species. Solomon (1995) is the best reference for further information on these insects and their sign.

Flies

The raspberry cane maggot (Anthomyiidae: *Pegomya rubivora*) is an unusual example of a fly larva that bores in the stems of shrubs. Eggs are laid in leaf axils of brambles and rose, and the larva tunnels down the middle of the young shoot. At some point, it works its way out to just under the bark, girdling the stem from within and causing the top of the plant to wilt. It then continues boring to the base of the plant, where it pupates and overwinters. Each of the other insects listed in this section, except for weevils, includes another borer in stems of raspberry and related plants.

Long-horned Beetles

Female *Oberea* long-horned beetles (Cerambycidae) girdle the stems and twigs in which they lay their eggs. The female chews two rows of punctures, 13 mm or so apart, around the stem of a new shoot, 6 to 8 inches (15 to 20 cm) from the tip, and inserts her elongate eggs in between. As with the buffalo treehopper's paired slits, this prevents the egg from being crushed by growth of the stem. The stem wilts above the girdle, and the larva bores downward when it hatches. Larvae in at least some species make occasional clusters of holes in the stem or twig, through which they push out frass. The frass contains cylindrical excrement pellets up to 1 mm long, which may be packed end to end in strands up to 1 cm long. Some species periodically cut off the end of the twig by girdling it from within. Species include the raspberry cane borer (*O. perspicillata*), dogwood twig borer (*O. tripunctata*), sassafras borer (*O. ruficollis*; also in spicebush), azalea stem borer (*O. myops*; also in rhododendron and mountain laurel), and several species that specialize in poplars. Both the raspberry cane borer and dogwood twig borer feed in a variety of shrubs and trees but prefer the hosts for which they are named.

The oak stem borer (*Aneflomorpha subpubescens*) is found in the eastern United States north to Pennsylvania and has somewhat similar habits, but without any girdling by the female. The larva hatches from an egg laid at the tip of an oak twig and bores down the center of the stem. It is typically found in saplings less than 3.3 feet (1 m) tall, and it may completely hollow out the stem as it makes its way to the base. It cuts round holes to eject frass, but rather than just a few, it makes a long, straight line of them

3 to 6 mm apart. The larva overwinters and pupates in the roots, usually after cutting the stem off at ground level. The sapling has often been cut or broken into two or more sections above this point. In the Mojave Desert, the boxthorn borer (*Anelaphus inflaticollis*) makes a similar line of holes, up to 2.5 mm in diameter, in stems of boxthorn and greasewood. At least one moth larva, the coyote brush borer, also makes lines of holes for the same purpose (see page 419).

The round-headed oak twig borer (*Styloxus fulleri*) causes dieback of twigs on trees, rather than saplings. The larva bores straight down the middle of the twig.

The currant tip borer (*Psenocerus supernotatus*) eats the pith all through the length of currant and gooseberry stems, filling them with fine, powdery frass. It may also be found in grapevines and occasionally kills terminal twigs of apple trees.

Elderberry borers (*Desmocerus*) lay their eggs low on elderberry stems. As with milkweed longhorns (one of the beetles listed earlier in the section on borers in herbaceous stems), the larvae bore down and feed in the roots.

Metallic Wood-boring Beetles

Unlike the long-horned beetles described above, larvae of metallic wood-boring beetles (Buprestidae) spiral around stems and twigs in the inner bark, rather than boring straight down the middle. Their burrows may be visible externally as raised ridges; if not, they can be seen by peeling off the bark.

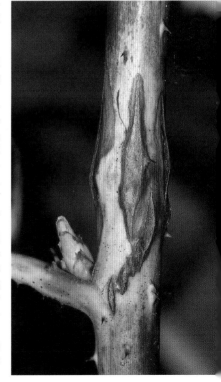

The red-necked cane borer (*Agrilus ruficollis*) bores in raspberry and blackberry stems and is unusual among stem borers in burrowing upward rather than toward the roots. It produces a characteristic gall-like swelling with longitudinal splitting. The spiral boring of the rose stem girdler (*A. aurichalceus*) causes dieback of rose, raspberry, and currant stems.

In California, scattered patches of dead foliage in oak trees are likely caused by the oak twig girdler (*Agrilus angelicus*). The larva burrows away from the tip of the twig in a typical corkscrew pattern, causing it to die, although it stays attached to the tree.

Swelling and splitting in a raspberry stem caused by a red-necked cane borer larva (Buprestidae: *Agrilus ruficollis*). (MA)

Having spent nearly two years in the twig, the larva eventually turns around and burrows up to 6 inches (15 cm) back toward the tip, pupates, and emerges as an adult. The two-lined chestnut borer (*A. bilineatus*) similarly girdles oak and chestnut twigs in the East. Various other *Agrilus* species feed in hardwoods, girdling twigs or spiraling in larger branches.

Weevils

Ampeloglypter weevils insert their eggs in small cavities chewed in grape and Virginia creeper vines, plugging the holes with excrement. The grape cane gallmaker (*A. sesostris*) deposits a single egg, then makes a series of ten or so additional cavities in a longitudinal line above the egg cavity. This produces a gall-like swelling up to 1.6 inches (4 cm) long, where the larva develops. The grape cane girdler (*A. ampelopsis*) also lays a single egg, but rather than a vertical line of cavities, she makes a circle of punctures to girdle the vine just below the egg cavity. She girdles it a second time several inches above the egg. The larva develops and pupates within the dying portion of the stem, which eventually breaks off.

Sawflies

Several stem sawflies (Cephidae) cause the ends of woody twigs to wilt and die back, hollowing them out and filling them with brown droppings. The larvae pupate at the bottom of their tunnels within a thin silken cocoon and chew a 1- to 3-mm circular hole in the stem to emerge as adults. Finding this cocoon will rule out long-horned or metallic wood-boring beetles as suspects.

The raspberry horntail (*Hartigia cressonii*; W) inserts its white eggs in young rose and bramble stems, causing slight swelling and obvious discoloration around the points of insertion. The larva begins by spiraling downward in the cambium for about 1.2 inches (3 cm), then bores upward in the pith, causing the shoot to wilt and die. Next it heads back down, pupates, and chews an exit hole upon becoming an adult. The rose shoot sawfly (*H. trimaculata*; mostly E) has the same host plants, but the larva begins by feeding in the succulent tips, causing them to wilt and die. It then tunnels downward in the pith, girdling the stem at frequent intervals, which may cause the stem to break at these points.

Female *Janus* sawflies girdle stems above the egg insertion point by inserting their ovipositors repeatedly in a circle around the twig. They do this just once, rather than both above and below the egg as in the punctures chewed by *Oberea* long-horned beetles, and often only a few centimeters from the tip of the shoot. The tip wilts and in some cases cleanly breaks off at the girdle. The larvae of different species vary somewhat in their boring patterns, but the girdling by the female is distinctive. The known species are the currant stem girdler (*J. integer*), viburnum stem sawfly (*J. bimaculatus*), willow shoot sawfly (*J. abbreviatus*; also in poplar), oak shoot sawfly (*J. quercusae*; SE; in red oak group), and white oak shoot sawfly (*J. rufiventris*; in Oregon white oak).

Moths

Stems bored by clearwing moth larvae (Sesiidae) can often be recognized by the pupal skin left protruding from the exit hole. The introduced currant borer (*Synanthedon tipuliformis*) feeds in the pith of currant stems, pupating in a silk-lined cavity just under the bark. The rhododendron borer (*S. rhododendri*) has similar habits. The dogwood borer (*S. scitula*; E) may be found in a variety of trees and shrubs in addition to dogwood. It enters a twig through an existing wound or scar and makes broad, blotchy tunnels in the inner bark. Fecal pellets may accumulate at the entry point.

The peach twig borer (Gelechiidae: *Anarsia lineatella*) was introduced from Asia more than a hundred years ago and is now found throughout North America. The larvae bore into the succulent shoot tips of rosaceous fruit trees, causing the terminal 0.4 to 2 inches (1 to 5 cm) to wilt.

The coyote brush borer (Pterophoridae: *Hellinsia grandis*) makes lines of excrement-disposal holes in coyote brush stems similar to those made by certain long-horned beetles in other woody plants. Other *Hellinsia* plume moth caterpillars bore in eastern baccharis species, but their droppings spill out of solitary entrance holes.

The stalk borer (Noctuidae: *Papaipema nebris*), noted above as a generalist borer of herbaceous stems, also bores in the terminal shoots of trees and shrubs such as sycamore, maple, boxelder, elm, ash, willow, poplar, sumac, elderberry, brambles, and fruit trees. The larva may enter a shoot at any point, usually boring toward the tip and expelling excrement from the entrance hole, which is about 3 mm across. Shoots containing these larvae suddenly wilt or break. Some other *Papaipema* species with similar habits bore in some of the same hosts. A number of tortricids also bore in shoots, cause them to wilt, and extrude excrement from the holes.

Petiole Borers

Probably the most conspicuous petiole mines are those of the maple petiole borer (Tenthredinidae: *Caulocampus acericaulis*), a sawfly larva. It causes the leaf blade to wilt and drop off, and the adjacent centimeter or so of the petiole goes limp. The rest of the petiole becomes slightly swollen and stays on the tree until late June. At this point, many bare petioles drop to the ground around the same time, and each larva exits through an irregular hole to pupate in the ground.

The hard maple bud miner (Nepticulidae: *Obrussa ochrefasciella*) is a tiny moth that lays its eggs singly on the petioles of terminal leaves of sugar maples. The larva bores into the petiole, making its way into a newly formed axillary bud, where it overwinters. In the spring, it feeds inside the terminal bud, then exits through a hole in the shoot just below it and drops to the ground to pupate. This usually kills the shoot, causing the axillary buds at its base to grow into branches.

Neatly Severed Twigs

White oak twigs cut by *Agrilus* larvae (Buprestidae). (MA)

Most of the insects mentioned in this chapter can cause stems and twigs to weaken and break, as can some gall-forming insects. Whereas these breaks are typically irregular, several different beetles sever hardwood twigs and branches by making characteristic cuts. It is usually possible to tell which beetle is responsible by examining the cut ends of twigs that have fallen to the ground after breaking in the wind.

Twig Girdlers

A broken twig with a ragged inner core but a smooth, neat cut around the outside is the work of a twig girdler (Cerambycidae: *Oncideres*). In these species, the female lays several eggs in slits chewed at the tip of a twig, then moves down it and cuts a circular groove around it. Eventually the twig dies and breaks off in the wind. The larvae develop within the twig for a year or more, making a few small, circular holes in the bark, through which they eject fecal pellets. The common twig girdler (*O. cingulata*) uses a variety of hardwoods and is found throughout the eastern United States. The other three species are restricted to Texas, Arizona, and Mexico: the mesquite twig girdler (*O. rhodosticta*; also girdles acacia), huisache girdler (*O. pustulata*; also girdles mimosa), and Arizona oak girdler (*O. quercus*).

Twig Pruners

A twig cut smoothly all the way across is likely the work of an oak twig pruner (Cerambycidae: *Anelaphus parallelus*). Despite the name, it feeds on a wide variety of eastern hardwoods. The female lays an egg in the tip of a twig, but unlike the twig girdler, her work is done at this point. The larva

A sure sign of an adult female mesquite twig girdler (Cerambycidae: *Oncideres rhodosticta*). (AZ)

A paloverde twig cut from within by an unknown long-horned beetle larva (Cerambycidae), likely related to the oak twig pruner. (AZ)

burrows into the twig and toward the center of the tree, until it reaches a point 8 to 35 inches (20 to 90 cm) from the tip and 8 to 20 mm in diameter. Here it chews in one plane, in progressively larger arcs, until only the bark of the twig is left. It then retreats into the severed twig, firmly plugging the central hole with fine, fibrous frass. The twig falls to the ground, and the larva overwinters as a pupa inside it, emerging in the spring.

We have found paloverde twigs in Arizona that were similarly cut cleanly from within but have not been able to determine what species was responsible. There are a number of southwestern twig-pruning species of *Anelaphus* and *Aneflomorpha* (a closely related genus), whose habits are poorly known.

Anelaphus villosus has been confused with *A. parallelus* in the past and is still known by the common name of twig pruner, even though it does not make pruning cuts, according to Solomon (1995). This species is also found in a variety of hardwoods, but it oviposits in dead and dying branches rather than healthy ones. The larva excavates a gallery up to 2 cm wide and often more than 3.3 feet (1 m) long, sometimes causing the branch to break off incidentally. Unfortunately, the confusion over the *Anelaphus* species appears to persist in Solomon's otherwise excellent book: of the white oak branch girdler (*Purpuricenus axillaris*), he states that "damage is similar to that of *Anelaphus villosus* except that *P. axillaris* prunes larger branches, often up to 50 mm in diameter." Evidently the intended comparison is with *A. parallelus*, because the white oak branch girdler larva does make pruning cuts in living branches. It prefers oaks in the white oak group but is also recorded from black oak, hickory, and chestnut.

Hickory Spiral Borer and Relatives

Twigs severed with a distinctly spiral cut are likely the work of the hickory spiral borer (Buprestidae: *Agrilus arcuatus*). This species primarily feeds in hickory and pecan but occasionally other hardwoods. Its life history is somewhat similar to the oak twig pruner's, but like other *Agrilus* species, the larva burrows just under the bark for most of its life, rather than down the middle of the twig. Also like other buprestids, it packs its rela-

A hickory twig cut by a hickory spiral borer larva (Buprestidae: *Agrilus arcuatus*). (MA)

Ends of white oak twigs cut by *Agrilus* larvae. (MA)

tively broad, flat gallery with fine wood dust. Late in its second autumn, the larva abruptly switches from burrowing along the length of the twig to cutting a circle around it, just under the bark. When this outer circle is complete, it makes a spiral cut into the center, severing the twig except for the bark and sometimes a few fibers in the center. It then mines back toward the tip of the branch, just under the bark again, for several centimeters and forms a pupal chamber, where it overwinters. The twigs mostly fall to the ground in early spring. They range from 20 inches to 8 feet (50 cm to 2.5 m) long, and 0.3 to 1.6 inches (8 mm to 4 cm) in diameter at the cut. The larva leaves through a D-shaped hole chewed in the bark.

Some other *Agrilus* species commonly prune small twigs of oaks and other deciduous trees in the Northeast. The break is rough, but often with a smoothly cut burrow arcing halfway around the perimeter. As with the hickory spiral borer, you can confirm that a buprestid was responsible by removing the bark and looking for the frass-packed galleries just under it.

Branch Pruner

Another species with similar habits is the branch pruner (Cerambycidae: *Psyrassa unicolor*), which, like the hickory spiral borer, favors hickory and pecan but sometimes uses other hardwoods. It cuts branches ranging from 0.4 to 2 inches (1 to 5 cm) thick and 2 to 12 feet (60 cm to 3.6 m) long. Also like the hickory spiral borer, the larva's tunnel is just under the bark or close to it, rather than in the center of the branch, and it is often plugged with frass. The larva starts out from an egg laid on a small side twig and tunnels down the center of this until it reaches the branch, at which point it makes the cut. Like the twig pruner, it makes a smooth, flat cut rather than a spiral, but because it cuts in the opposite direction, the center may

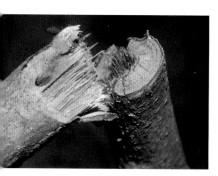

not be a clean break. The larva then burrows some distance toward the tip of the branch, usually beginning just under the bark near the base of the small side twig. Eventually it pupates just under the bark and leaves through an irregular hole.

A beech sapling cut cleanly by a branch pruner larva (Cerambycidae: *Psyrassa unicolor*). A remnant of the small side twig from which the larva originally came is visible behind the portion on the left. (MA)

Sign on and in Wood   **14**

Insect sign on wood may be on the surface, just under the bark, or mostly inside the wood. Each type of wood-boring insect makes galleries of a particular pattern, with a particular type of frass, in wood of a particular condition, and often of a particular type of tree. This chapter summarizes some common groups and especially distinctive sign and should not be taken for anything approaching a comprehensive treatment. Also note that individual species may diverge from the generalized descriptions of families given here. An excellent book for further reading on borers in hardwoods is Solomon (1995).

Shallow Pits, Grooves, and Scrapes

Several types of insects leave identifiable signs in the surface of wood. Some of these are related to wood boring, but others are connected with oviposition, pupation, and collection of nest materials.

Polistes paper wasps and *Dolichovespula* yellowjackets and hornets (Vespidae) collect fibers from sound, weathered wood to build their nests. A wasp walks along

Stripes on a weathered fence from bald-faced hornets (Vespidae: *Dolichovespula maculata*) collecting fibers for nest material. (MA)

423

A 1.3-inch (3.3-cm) groove chewed in the side of a snag by a dagger moth caterpillar (Noctuidae: *Acronicta*) before spinning its cocoon. (VT)

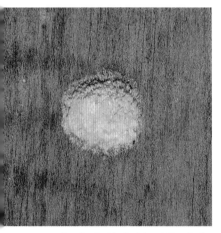

An aborted hole (about 1 cm) of a large carpenter bee (Apidae: *Xylocopa virginica*). (MA)

the wood surface in a straight line, scraping up a ball of fibers with its mandibles. On an old, gray fence post, this shows up as a narrow, vertical, brown stripe, up to a few centimeters long. Once a good source is located, it is used by many wasps again and again, and the surface is soon marked with many of these stripes. Material may also be collected from dead branches, dried herbaceous stems, or man-made paper objects, but the marks on fence posts are the most conspicuous.

Some insect larvae excavate a shallow depression in a wood surface to form the foundation for a pupal cell. This is usually done under bark, and in many cases, it may not be possible to tell which insect is responsible without other clues. Dagger moth caterpillars (Noctuidae: *Acronicta*), however, chew elongate grooves about 1.2 inches (3 cm) long on exposed surfaces of snags or even fence posts, over which they make their cocoons of silk and bits of wood. The cocoon eventually weathers away, leaving just the bare groove. In addition to the size, shape, and exposed location, these differ from grooves made by beetles in that they are not associated with other wood-boring activity. We once came across a snag in Vermont that had at least twenty of these grooves on it, ranging from 1 to 1.4 inches (2.5 to 3.6 cm) long and 6 to 10 mm wide.

A perfectly round depression chewed in a wood surface, about 1 cm across, is an aborted burrow of a large carpenter bee (Apidae: *Xylocopa*). Although there are several unrelated insects that might make a large hole coming *out* of wood, after having developed inside, these are the only large insects that bore *into* wood.

A chewed depression with a definite horizontal slit through the middle is likely the *egg niche* of a long-horned beetle (Cerambycidae). The female chews such a niche in bark to prepare a spot for insertion of eggs. The slit may be straight or somewhat crescent-shaped. Egg niches in pines, up to about 1 cm across, belong to pine sawyers (*Monochamus*) and may con-

Egg niches of Asian long-horned beetles (Cerambycidae: *Anoplophora glabripennis*), from the current (above) and previous year. The niches are 1.5 to 2 cm across. (MA) Photo by Mollie Freilicher.

tain 1 to 9 eggs. Niches of the introduced Asian long-horned beetle (*Anoplophora glabripennis*), on hardwoods, are up to 2 cm across. Those of some species, such as the round-headed apple tree borer (*Saperda candida*) and linden borer (*S. vestita*), are made just above ground level. Similar niches of other species, just a few millimeters across, such as those of the poplar gall saperda (*S. inornata*), can be found on smaller twigs.

Pitch Masses

Insects that bore in living conifers cause conspicuous masses of pitch to appear on the bark. Certain *Dendroctonus* and *Ips* bark beetles (Curculionidae: Scolytinae) frequently produce *pitch tubes* at their entry points. These may actually be open tubes or may just look like lumpy masses of pitch. Close inspection reveals that the pitch is mixed with brown dust from the beetle's excavations. A clean, whitish pitch tube indicates that the tree has succeeded in keeping out the beetle, and the tube is likely to have the beetle embedded within it. These certainly are not the only beetles that cause pitch masses to form on bark; the red pine flat-headed borer (Buprestidae: *Chrysobothris orono*), for instance, attacks living red and jack pines, and when the larva enters the tree, it causes a yellowish pitch mass on red pine and a white one on jack pine.

Pitch masses may also indicate the presence of certain clearwing moth larvae (Sesiidae). The sequoia pitch moth (*Synanthedon sequoiae*; W) and pitch mass borer (*S. pini*; E) both feed on the inner bark of

A frass-plugged "pitch tube" indicating where a mountain pine beetle (Curculionidae: *Dendroctonus ponderosae*) bored into a pine trunk. (MT)

pines and related trees (and not sequoia, as far as is known). The larva is concealed by a large accumulation of pitch and frass, and it pupates within this mass. Pitch twig moths (Tortricidae: *Retinia*) have similar habits but are typically found on small twigs, as are pitch midges (Cecidomyiidae: *Cecidomyia*).

Galleries under Bark

Some wood-boring insects limit their activities to just beneath the bark. Others spend some of their lives here but later disappear into the sapwood or heartwood; these are discussed in the next section. Moth larvae that make visible mines in the surface of bark were discussed in chapter 13, as they are typically found in twigs and saplings.

Bark Beetles

The most interesting, and most easily recognized, galleries under bark are made by bark beetles (Curculionidae: Scolytinae). They feed on the cambium, the layer of cells that divide to produce the wood and inner bark, making patterns in the inner bark and outer sapwood that are often distinctive enough to identify the species. They rarely penetrate into the sapwood more than a few millimeters. In most cases, they attack trees that are already injured or diseased. The tunnels made by these small beetles are usually no more than 3 mm wide.

The most basic type of bark beetle gallery begins with a mating chamber, from which the female excavates a linear tunnel of uniform width under the bark, either parallel or perpendicular to the grain of the wood. On either side of this tunnel, she chews alternating, evenly spaced egg niches, laying one egg in each. When the eggs hatch, each larva feeds by excavating its own tunnel away from the mother's, without interfering with any of its siblings. The angle of the larval galleries from their mother's is usually constant within a species, and it is important in distinguishing the galleries of different species that feed on the same type of tree. Also important are the host tree species, the position of the galleries (in just the bark, just the wood, or both), and the branch size. As the larva grows, the width of its gallery increases, and the larva pupates at the end, in a slightly enlarged chamber close to the bark surface, chewing its way out when it has metamorphosed. The pattern of emergence holes in the bark is characteristic. When the bark is removed, the combined galleries of the mother and all her offspring make a distinctive pattern that looks a bit like a giant house centipede. The parental gallery is deeper than those made by the larvae, and the mating chamber is visible as a slightly enlarged area at one end. When these beetles occur in high densities, the cambium is killed and the bark is loosened.

Beetles making this basic pattern with a vertical parental gallery (running with the grain) include the hickory bark beetle (*Scolytus quad-*

Two complete galleries of the European elm bark beetle (Curculionidae: *Scolytus multis-triatus*). The two thick, vertical grooves are the parental galleries, and each line radiating from these was made by one of the larvae. (MA)

rispinosus), fruit tree bark beetle (*S. rugulosus*), Douglas-fir engraver (*S. unispinosus*), and European elm bark beetle (*S. multistriatus*). Those with a horizontal parental gallery (going across the grain) include the fir engraver (*S. ventralis*; with a brown fungus stain in the feeding area) and native elm bark beetle (*Hylurgopinus rufipes*). Galleries in trees in the cypress family can be attributed to *Phloeosinus* species with near certainty.

In polygamous bark beetles, the male excavates a nuptial chamber and then initiates a parental gallery with each of two or more females. These radiate from the nuptial chamber, and each female and her offspring proceed as with the monogamous species. A common example is the two-toothed pine beetle (*Pityogenes bidentatus*). In this species, the male gnaws out a circular chamber, and four to six females excavate radiating galleries. The galleries of the pine engraver (*Ips pini*) and pinyon ips (*I. confusus*) are very similar. Males of polygamous species keep the galleries clean, in contrast to monogamous species, whose galleries are typically packed with bore dust.

There are many variations on these basic patterns. Adult spruce beetles (*Dendroctonus rufipennis*) excavate short, straight, wide, longitudinal egg galleries in the inner bark. Eggs are laid in masses in alternating elongate cavities. The larvae at first bore away from the central gallery together, later diverging. Adult western pine beetles (*D. brevicomis*) make winding egg galleries that crisscross each other. Adult red turpentine beetles (*D. valens*) excavate branching galleries in the inner bark of pines and other conifers. The larvae feed close together, creating one large, irregular, dust-

Galleries of two "harems" of two-toothed pine beetles (Curculionidae: *Pityogenes bidentatus*) in a white pine branch. The long grooves are brood channels, each branch excavated by a different female, and the alternating notches indicate where eggs were laid. The larvae tunneled mostly in the bark, leaving only faint marks on the wood. (MA)

filled chamber. After a male Monterey pine engraver (*Pseudips mexicanus*) creates a nuptial gallery, two or three females make sharply curved ovipositional galleries, creating egg niches on only the outside of the curve. They lay a few eggs in each niche, so that three to four larval galleries emanate from each niche.

Agromyzid Flies

Several species of *Phytobia* (Agromyzidae) are called cambium miners but actually mine the surface of the sapwood just below the cambium. The mines are usually not detectable unless the bark is removed. Larvae start out mining up into the branches, making narrow, threadlike mines that are difficult to see even with the bark removed. They then turn around and work toward the base of the tree, making distinct, vertical, straight or somewhat meandering mines. If they reach the bottom before they are ready to pupate, they reverse direction; this may happen a few times. When mature, the larva bores out of the trunk or a root to pupate. Because the mines are below the cambium, they become surrounded by wood as the tree grows. They are visible in cut lumber, as brown streaks in veneer and oblong or flattened blemishes in log ends. *P. setosa* mines in maples; *P. betulivora* in river birch; *P. pruni* in hawthorn, cherry, and plum; and *P. amelanchieris* in shadbush. An undescribed species mines in ash, with older larvae differing from those of other species in making distinct zigzags; they also sometimes disappear into the inner bark for several centimeters.

Galleries under Bark or in Wood

Larvae of metallic wood-boring beetles, long-horned beetles, and wood-boring moths feed just under the bark as well as deep in the wood. Each group has some species that complete their development just under the bark, others that bore into the wood as soon as they hatch, and many that spend part of their lives in both places. Regardless of the location, it is often possible to separate these groups by the frass they produce, and in some cases the pattern of their galleries.

Metallic Wood-boring Beetles

Many metallic wood-boring beetle larvae (Buprestidae) make broad, shallow, meandering galleries at the outer edge of the sapwood, just under the bark. The fronts

Top right: Classic zigzag gallery of a metallic wood-boring beetle larva (Buprestidae). (MA) *Above:* Meandering galleries of emerald ash borer larvae (Buprestidae: *Agrilus planipennis*). (MI)

 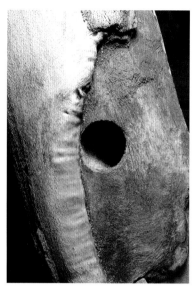

Left: A flattened exit hole is often a sign of a metallic wood-boring beetle (Buprestidae). (FL) *Right:* Exit hole of an Asian long-horned beetle (Cerambycidae: *Anoplophora glabripennis*). (MA)

of the larvae's bodies are flattened, giving them the name "flat-headed borers," and they have projections on the rear end that they use to grasp fecal pellets and pack them in the back of the tunnel. As a result, their galleries are flattened-oval in cross section and tightly packed with fine frass; little or no frass is ejected from the tree. Prior to pupation, the galleries turn into the sapwood, where eventually a pupal chamber is excavated. The exit holes are flattened or D-shaped, rather than circular.

Buprestid galleries often meander in a distinctive, regular zigzag, but this can vary within a species. The bronze poplar borer (*Agrilus liragus*) makes an increasingly compressed zigzag when in a healthy tree, but it meanders without a clear pattern if the tree is severely weakened. The bronze birch borer (*A. anxius*) spirals around branches, producing visible ridges in the bark surface.

Long-horned Beetles

Long-horned beetle larvae (Cerambycidae), with more than a thousand North American species, have a wide variety of habits and hosts. The ribbed pine borer (*Rhagium inquisitor*) is a common example of a species that does all of its feeding just under the bark, as well as pupating there. It makes large, irregular galleries and fills them with frass that contains both digested and undigested wood, with shredded splinters averaging 6 mm long. Others feed between the bark and wood but excavate their pupal chambers in the wood, and still others feed and pupate entirely in the wood. Many have fibrous frass like the ribbed pine borer, but some species

Characteristic sign of the sugar maple borer (Cerambycidae: *Glycobius speciosus*), with the larval gallery partially visible. (MA)

turn everything to powder as buprestids do. Known as the "round-headed borers," they tend to produce galleries that are rounder in cross section, and their exit holes can be perfectly circular. The galleries and exit holes of some species, however, are just as flattened as those of buprestids.

Some long-horned beetle larvae bore in characteristic patterns. The spotted apple tree borer (*Saperda cretata*) lays its eggs in pairs in larger limbs, and the two larvae mine in opposite directions. The sugar maple borer (*Glycobius speciosus*) partially encircles the trunk before working its way into the heartwood. This rarely kills the tree but produces a conspicuous horizontal scar. The poplar borer (*S. calcarata*), on the other hand, does kill poplars by girdling them before entering the heartwood.

Moths

Larvae of clearwing moths (Sesiidae) and carpenter moths (Cossidae; also known as carpenterworms) are wood borers. Their distinctive frass often accumulates on the surface of the host tree. The presence of occasional silk threads in it rules out any other wood borer, but it also has other dis-

Frass of a clearwing moth larva (Sesiidae). (MA)

tinguishing features. The wood fragments are in chips, not like the shreds or fine dust produced by many beetles. Frass of carpenterworms has a large proportion (50 to 100 percent) of cylindrical excrement pellets, which with full-size larvae are 5 to 7 mm long. The largest chips are of about the same size. Frass of clearwing larvae is less than half excrement pellets, which are only up to about 2 mm long, and the rest is relatively uniform-size wood chips 1 mm long or less. Larvae in both families pupate just beneath the bark, leaving the pupal skin protruding from the wood when the adult emerges.

Galleries Entirely in Wood

The insects in this section bore exclusively in sapwood and heartwood, without excavating any galleries between the bark and wood.

Bees

Large carpenter bees (Apidae: *Xylocopa*) bore into sound wood, including man-made structures, to make their nests. The perfectly circular entrance, about 1 cm wide, typically faces down, and in the absence of structural timbers, it is usually in the underside of a dead branch or a fallen tree. It may, however, be on the vertical surface of a tree trunk or even an agave stalk. It can be distinguished from the exit hole of a horntail or long-horned beetle by its beveled rim with evenly distributed chew marks. In contrast, an insect making its way out of a tree generally leaves a sharp-edged hole. Various bee-related drippings may also be in evidence, as well as "sawdust" accumulated below the hole, which is not produced in significant quantities by insects on their way out of wood.

After excavating about 1 inch (2.5 cm) into the wood, the bee turns and follows the grain of the wood for up to 1 foot (30.5 cm) or more. There may be a second tunnel heading the opposite direction from the entrance. The bee makes partitions out of wood chips stuck together with saliva, much like the partitions in other solitary bee nests, and provisions the cells with the usual paste of pollen and nectar.

A large carpenter bee (Apidae: *Xylocopa virginica*) looks out from its hole (about 1 cm) in a slanted porch ceiling. (MA)

Although "small carpenter bees" (*Ceratina*) excavate their nests in pithy stems, *Osmia bucephala* (Megachilidae) is a smaller bee that actually nests in the same way a large carpenter bee does. Packard (1878) described a nest tunnel in a maple tree that was more than 3 inches (8 cm) long, about 7 mm wide, and contained five cells, each 12 mm long. Nesting *Augochlora* sweat bees (Halictidae) excavate branching burrows in rotting wood.

Horntails

Horntails (Siricidae) excavate long, 6-inch to 10-foot (15-cm to 3-m), round galleries that meander through sapwood and heartwood and are tightly packed with fine frass. Females oviposit in dead or dying trees, in the process inoculating the tree with a fungus that rots the wood, making it possible for the larva to digest it. The egg is inserted 2 to 20 mm into the wood, and the young larva generally bores parallel to the surface for a while before tunneling in toward the heartwood, so there are no larval galleries immediately under the bark. The pigeon tremex (*Tremex columba*) uses maple, beech, and many other hardwoods. The larva pupates in its gallery in the sapwood, within a cocoon of silk and small wood chips, then excavates an empty exit tunnel that curves back to the surface, leaving through a perfectly round hole, 7 to 8 mm across. Exit holes of several adults are typically clustered in a localized part of the trunk. The other horntails bore in various conifers and generally excavate a pupation chamber 1 to 2 cm from the surface. A giant ichneumon larva (*Megarhyssa*) lives as an external parasitoid of a horntail larva, pupating in a transparent cocoon and leaving the tree through a circular exit hole somewhat smaller than the one its host would have made.

Ambrosia Beetles

The ambrosia beetles (Curculionidae: Scolytinae) are related, and similar in size, to the bark beetles, but rather than tunneling just under the bark, they tunnel into the wood, across the grain, often penetrating into the center of the heartwood. They also differ in that the larvae excavate no galleries and instead feed on the fungi, or "ambrosia," that grow in their

Bore dust from two ambrosia beetle (Curculionidae: Scolytinae) galleries. The entrance hole for one is visible above the pile on the left. (MA)

Compacted frass rods of ambrosia beetles found in a log of firewood. (MA)

"cradles." These fungi are carried in the digestive tracts of the females, and for the most part, each beetle species raises just one species of fungus. The tunnels made by the parents are long, round, of constant width (0.5 to 3 mm, depending on species), and usually stained black, often surrounded by a flamelike streak of discolored wood. The larvae develop in short tunnels, about 6 mm long, that come off at right angles and are clustered at the ends of the main tunnels. The adults feed their young bits of fungus from the larger tunnels, keeping the cradle entrances plugged. They remove the larvae's excrement and keep the tunnels free of wood dust. When they first bore into the wood, they eject loose "sawdust," but later they push out curious-looking rods of compacted frass. The tunnels are never overlapping and dense, as with some other wood-boring insects.

Ambrosia beetles mostly attack hardwoods, usually only dead or unhealthy trees. Examples include the apple wood stainer (*Monarthrum mali*; E; also in oak, other hardwoods, and even conifers), whose larval cradles are in long, secondary tunnels that branch off the main nuptial chamber; and the European shot-hole borer (*Xyleborus dispar*; NW; in fruit trees). The several species of pinhole borers (Platypodinae) have similar habits.

Carpenter Ants

Carpenter ants (Formicidae: *Camponotus*) make large, irregular cavities in partially decayed wood. Like carpenter bees, and unlike all the other insects mentioned here, they do not eat the wood. It is merely the medium in which they excavate their nests, and as a result, they produce large amounts of excavated "sawdust." Just like ants that nest in the ground, many workers each carry out one tiny piece at a time and deposit it outside the gallery. The dust often accumulates conspicuously at the base of the tree. In addition to being free of frass, carpenter ant galleries are characterized by their complexity, with series of chambers excavated for eggs, larvae, and pupae. Various other ants may nest in more thoroughly rotten wood or preexisting galleries of wood-boring insects.

Left: "Sawdust" collects at the base of a hollow tree, excavated by carpenter ants (Formicidae: *Camponotus*). (CA) *Right:* A carpenter ant gallery (Formicidae: *Camponotus*). (MA)

Termites

Termite galleries, like those of carpenter ants, are free of sawdust, but this is because they eat all of it, not because they remove it. Subterranean termites (Rhinotermitidae) are widespread in North America. They live underground and construct earthen tunnels leading to the wood in which they feed. Their galleries go with the grain of the wood, typically leaving the harder wood that was formed in the summer. The spaces between these thin layers of intact wood are packed with soil.

Drywood termites (Kalotermitidae; S) live inside the wood and do not require contact with the soil, although they occasionally construct a narrow tube of cemented-together fecal pellets to bridge two pieces of wood. They cut across the grain, eating both spring and summer wood. They keep their tunnels clear, either depositing their fecal pellets in old tunnels or making small holes, which are later sealed over with a secretion, to dump them outside the wood. These small, seedlike pellets can accumulate in large piles and differ from those of death-watch beetles in having concave surfaces.

Dampwood termites (Termopsidae) are found along the Pacific Coast. They do not require contact with the ground but do require moisture in the wood. They primarily feed in rotting logs but may be found in man-made structures in foggy coastal areas.

Powderpost Beetles

Powderpost beetles (Bostrichidae) are so named because larvae of some species feed in hardwoods until there is nothing left but a thin veneer with the interior reduced to fine powder. Before it gets to this stage, they begin by tunneling mostly with the grain, later boring haphazardly and crossing each other's galleries, and pushing their bore dust out of the wood. The surface becomes riddled with their round exit holes, which are typically 2 to 3 mm wide. They are primarily found in dry, dead trees but sometimes invade seasoned wood and structural timbers of houses.

Death-Watch Beetles

Death-watch beetles (Anobiidae), along with powderpost beetles and dry-wood termites, are the other insects that commonly feed in dry wood. Unlike powderpost beetles, they produce definite fecal pellets, which have convex faces unlike those of drywood termites. They get their name from a ticking sound the adults make by tapping the wood repeatedly with their heads.

Galleries in Marine Wood

Wood that finds its way out to sea has its own set of invertebrate borers, which include both bivalves and crustaceans. Before discussing these, it is worth noting one beetle species that is common in wood right along the shore.

Wharf Borer

The wharf borer (Oedemeridae: *Nacerdes melanura*) is a false blister beetle, introduced from Europe, whose larvae are found especially in wood wetted with salt water. Inland, this includes wooden fences and telephone poles on which dogs have urinated, but they are common in docks, pilings, and other wood at the high-tide mark. The larvae excavate galleries that are irregular in size and shape, plugged in places with long shreds like those made by some long-horned beetle larvae.

Gribbles

Several crustaceans bore and feed in floating or sunken wood in the ocean. Of these, the most common are the gribbles (Limnoriidae: *Limnoria*), which look like small woodlice about 4 mm long. Where present, they occur in abundance, making 1- to 2-mm-wide burrows that go a centimeter or so deep, then run parallel to the surface for a few centimeters. Periodic ventilation tunnels lead to the surface from the main gallery. Much like bark beetles, the males do little while the females construct the galleries, from which their offspring make side burrows, dispersing to other wood when they reach the water. Eventually the outer layer of wood becomes so riddled with holes that it turns spongy and sheds off, and the gribbles begin working on a new layer. It is said that each year, softwood pilings can lose up to 1 inch (2.5 cm) in diameter because of gribbles, resulting in hourglass-shaped timbers that constrict at the water level. Other isopods (Sphaeromatidae: *Sphaeroma*) make holes in wood up to 9 mm wide and 3.5 cm deep, not to feed but simply for hiding places. Some amphipods (e.g., Cheluridae: *Chelura terebrans*) are also known to bore in wood.

Shipworms

Driftwood full of porcelain-lined tunnels is a sure sign of shipworms (Teredinidae), odd-looking bivalves with tiny shells and long, wormlike bodies. They use their shells to rasp tunnels through wooden ships, piers, and driftwood, digesting wood with specialized internal organs. Shipworms are considered the primary decomposers of marine wood. The free-swimming larvae find wood and create small entry holes, which they enlarge inward as they grow. They tunnel much more deeply than gribbles do, producing galleries more than 8 inches (20 cm) long and up to 15 mm wide. Although the tunnels do not typically cross each other, they twist and turn and may occasionally branch. Most shipworm species line part or all of the tunnel walls with a calcareous material that is used for attachment points. The end of the tunnel in contact with the ocean sometimes forms a calcite valve that is used for filter feeding. Both branching tunnels and the external cap occur more frequently when the wood is overcrowded with

Galleries of two common borers in marine driftwood. The small tunnels (1 mm wide) are made by gribbles (Limnoriidae: *Limnoria*). The larger ones (5 mm), in the lower right, are the work of shipworms (Teredinidae) and contain fragments of their characteristic white porcelain lining. (CT)

shipworms and individuals must search out unused wood and nonwood food sources. Exposed galleries in pieces of driftwood may have the calcium material eroded away. Shipworms are credited with drilling so many holes in Christopher Columbus's ship that he was marooned in Jamaica for a year. The bottoms of ships more than twenty-four hundred years ago were coated with arsenic, sulfur, and oil, presumably to deter shipworms.

Piddocks

The piddocks (Pholadidae) are a related family of bivalves that also bore in wood. Unlike shipworms, piddocks (also known as angelwings) have a classic clamlike body plan, and they use their wood burrow only as an anchor point, not for food. Like those of shipworms, piddock burrows tend to widen as they get deeper. The most widespread in our range are *Martesia* species, which live in warm waters from North Carolina and Baja California south. Their holes are not much deeper than their shell length (to 2 inches [5 cm]) because they have short feeding siphons. Species in the Xylophaginae live in deeper waters, 115 feet to 2.2 miles (35 to 3,500 m), and dig wormlike tunnels up to eight times longer than their shells, which can be up to 4.7 inches (12 cm) long. As with shipworms, calcium is sometimes deposited on the tunnel walls, but the calcium lining in piddock tunnels is only on the back half of the tunnel and is typically thinner and less complex.

Sign on Rocks and Shells   **15**

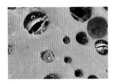

Various marine invertebrates have the ability to bore into rocks and shells. Some holes in shells may be related to predation, whereas other holes in both shells and rocks are made by animals solely to anchor or conceal themselves. At least two terrestrial arthropods also bore holes in relatively soft rock.

Feeding Holes

Snails are usually responsible for the large (6- to 10-mm), single, smooth, round holes in marine bivalve shells. The primary boring snails are moon snails (Naticidae) and rock snails (Muricidae, including oyster drills). Boreholes on burying clams are generally the work of moon snails, which cruise along sand flats just under the surface searching for buried prey, whereas rock snails do not burrow as readily. The snails grab their live bivalve prey with a large foot and drill a hole through the shell to suck out their meal. They use a combination of chemical etching and scraping with a rotating radula to bore through shells at a rate of 0.5 mm per day. Dark bivalves may show signs of chemical bleaching around the hole. On thick-walled bivalves, rock snail boreholes tend to be shaped like straight cylinders, whereas moon snail holes are shaped like broad parabolic bowls with much larger outer diameters. On thin-walled bivalves, rock snail

A 3-mm hole in a clam shell bored by a predaceous moon snail (Naticidae). (MA)

439

and moon snail borings are both somewhat parabolic. In incomplete rock snail boreholes, the bottom is bowl-shaped, whereas a moon snail hole has a central hump that rises up from the bottom. Sometimes the snail will stop boring before completing a full circular puncture in the bottom, leaving an odd-shaped hole that presumably is sufficient for feeding. The outer edges of moon snail holes are usually beveled (countersunk), whereas the edges of rock snail holes may or may not be noticeably beveled. Although the walls of the holes appear smooth, under magnification the radula marks are apparent at the edges. Baby snails bore holes less than 1 mm in diameter on tiny shells. Moon snails and rock snails are the dominant shell borers, and all members of these families have this habit, but a few cap shells (Capulidae) and tritons (Ranellidae) also bore through shells. Incidentally, there are also some Central American land snails (Oleacinidae) that bore much more ragged holes than these other groups.

Flatworms (Turbellaria) bore through young oyster valves, sometimes producing a small keyhole shape. Octopuses (Cephalopoda) may rasp a series of jagged holes or pits in a mollusk in order to inject venom. Smooth, round, beveled holes in serpulid worm tubes may be the work of nudibranchs.

Anchor Holes

Bivalves are responsible for most of the larger and deeper holes bored into intertidal rocks. Primary boring bivalves initially carve out the holes, then a succession of bivalves and other secondary inhabitants appropriates the burrows. Calcareous substrates such as limestone, shell conglomerates,

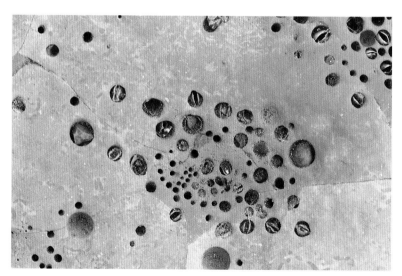

Piddock (Pholadidae) holes, measuring 2 to 10 mm, in soft mudstone. (Costa Rica)

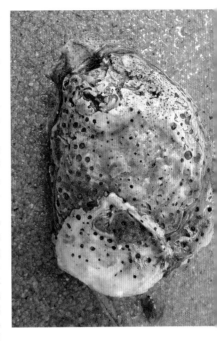

An oyster shell pitted with numerous holes made by a boring sponge (Clionaidae: *Cliona*). (MA)

mollusk shells, and coral are bored by the Atlantic rock borer (Petricolidae: *Rupellaria typica*), mytilid mussels (*Adula*, *Lithophaga*), and some piddocks (Pholadidae: *Diplothyra*). Several other piddocks (e.g., *Penitella penita*, *Parapholas californica*, *Zirfaea pilsbryi*) commonly bore into shale, creating burrows that may exceed 8 inches (20 cm) deep. As piddocks bore, they spin like a drill bit, producing smooth, round holes.

Many other marine organisms leave smaller holes in rocks and shells where they anchored themselves. The burrowing isopod *Sphaeroma quoyanum* (Sphaeromatidae), introduced to the Pacific coast from Australia, reportedly can dig burrows in sandstone up to 9 mm wide and 1.4 inches (3.5 cm) deep. Some limpets (Patellogastropoda) maintain spots on intertidal rock to which they return after browsing on nearby algae. A limpet's resting place may appear as a small depression or circular groove in the rock. Some sea urchins (e.g., the purple sea urchin, Strongylocentrotidae: *Strongylocentrotus purpuratus*) gradually enlarge existing hollows in soft rock. Boring sponges (Clionaidae: *Cliona*, and a few related genera that are restricted to coral reefs) root themselves in mollusk shells (or anything made of calcium carbonate, such as limestone or coral) by chemically boring. They produce a series of small holes perpendicular to the surface, along with a network of interconnecting horizontal tubes at many layers through the material. Bryozoans etch a series of tiny holes (less than 0.1 mm) in oysters and other objects where they live. Limy tube worms (Serpulidae) may also excavate some rock under their tubes. Other organisms that bore in calcium carbonate include some feather duster worms (Sabellidae), eunicid worms, horseshoe worms (Phoronida), and peanut worms (Sipuncula).

Terrestrial Rock Borings

Smooth, round holes in sandstone bluffs are likely to be burrows of the mining bee *Macrotera opuntiae* (Andrenidae; W). These bees, which collect pollen exclusively from prickly pears, construct their rock burrows much like other solitary bees do in the ground. Their branching tunnels go up to 4 inches (10 cm) into the rock, with several entrances leading to a common network. Generation after generation may continue to excavate tun-

This sandstone cliff is riddled with 4- to 5-mm-wide holes made by *Macrotera opuntiae* mining bees (Andrenidae). (CA)

nels in the same site, until there is a large, open chamber of pulverized stone containing two hundred or more larvae in their mudlike cells. The entrance holes are initially around 5 mm wide, but they may erode to be 1 cm or so. They are left open, but when they face up at an angle, they are sometimes filled with loose, excavated sand. Eventually, a protected cliff side can become riddled with hundreds of burrows, with parts of old tunnel systems becoming exposed as the rock breaks apart.

Banks (1906) described a species of rock-boring mite (Cymbaeremaeidae: *Scapheremaeus petrophagus*) that was found in a moist limestone cliff near Ithaca, New York. The rock surface had many small cavities of varying sizes, each of which contained a mite about the size of the pit. The full-size mites were 4 mm long. In most cases, the opening was smaller than the inside of the cavity. Banks speculated that the mites fed on algae growing on the surface of the rock, excavating the pits as shelters so they would not be washed away from their exposed habitat in storms.

Burrows and Mounds

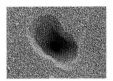

16

Virtually every insect order has members that dig or burrow in the earth at some point in their life cycle, as do many other types of invertebrates. Beetles and others dig temporary burrows to escape hot sun or strong winds. Numerous larvae of moths, beetles, flies, and sawflies burrow into the ground to pupate. Some scorpionfly larvae (Panorpidae: *Panorpa*) rest at the top of shallow burrows in the soil, making excursions on the surface to scavenge for food. Grasshoppers make holes with their abdomens when laying eggs in the ground. Windscorpions burrow into loose sand when at rest or to lay and guard their eggs. Vinegaroons and some scorpions and crickets make shallow resting burrows under rocks and other objects. Often these burrowers make nondescript holes that cannot be identified other than by digging and finding the inhabitant, or they may leave no discernible sign at all. Nonetheless, quite a few invertebrates make obvious depressions, mounds, or holes with recognizable characteristics.

Effects of Earthworms on Soil

The burrow entrances of earthworms (Lumbricina) may be covered by distinctive castings or middens, which are described later in this chapter, but evidence of earthworm burrowing and feeding can go far beyond these discrete signs. Some species are *epigeic*, living and feeding in leaf litter and making no burrows. Others are *endogeic*, living and feeding in the soil and making networks of horizontal, branching burrows. Still others are *anecic*, feeding on litter but dwelling in vertical, unbranching burrows that may be up to 6.6 feet (2 m) deep. The combined actions of all of these translate into constant processing and mixing of the soil. Darwin (1883) devoted his last book to this subject and concluded: "When we behold a wide, turf-covered expanse, we should remember that its smoothness, on which so much of its beauty depends, is mainly due to all the inequalities having been slowly leveled by worms."

There are no native earthworms (except perhaps some riparian species) in the area of North America covered by the last glaciation, which includes New England, the Great Lakes region, parts of Montana and Washington, and most of Canada. Many European earthworm species have been introduced and spread through agriculture, fishing, and other human activities, with ecosystem-altering effects. An earthworm-free sugar maple forest typically has a lush and diverse understory, with low vegetation covering more than 75 percent of the forest floor. The forest floor is thick with leaf litter in various stages of decomposition. When earthworms are abundant, they quickly mix the leaf litter with the mineral soil to form a deep layer of dark topsoil. In extreme cases, there is nothing but a thin, or even incomplete, layer of the most recently fallen leaves lying on top of the rich, homogeneous soil. Most native forest plants, not to mention all the animals that live in litter and duff, are not well adapted to this altered environment, however nice it might be for plants in agricultural settings. As a result, the forest floor becomes either very sparsely vegetated or else dominated by a few plants that are well adapted to disturbed soil, such as certain ferns, sedges, and introduced Eurasian plants. Native earthworms in the rest of the continent tend to be restricted to wet areas, although native megascolecids are largely responsible for the soil structure in the forests of the Pacific Northwest.

Surface Scrapes and Digs

Some insects and crustaceans scrape the soil surface in characteristic ways when collecting nest material, feeding, or preparing to dig a burrow. Others make superficial burrows that do not quite amount to holes.

Wasps

Burrowing wasps often make "trial digs" before actually beginning a burrow. The wasp moves about the ground, digging in short bursts, apparently testing the soil to see if it is the right consistency—loose enough to dig, but

Mud daubers (Sphecidae: *Sceliphron caementarium*) made these 6- to 8-mm scrapes collecting mud balls to build their nests. (LA)

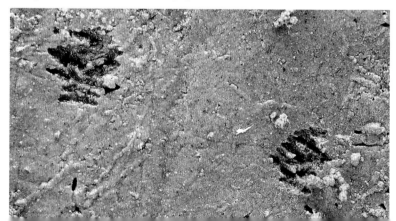

cohesive enough not to cave in. Wildlife tracker Mark Elbroch says he has seen a wasp making alternating scrapes that were a perfect match for the mysterious "elfin deer" tracks that Murie (1954) illustrated in his short chapter on invertebrate tracks and sign. (See chapter 18 for our own solution to this riddle.)

The black and yellow mud dauber (Sphecidae: *Sceliphron caementarium*) leaves conspicuous little digs at the edges of water bodies where it collects mud to use in its nests. In each trip to the collecting spot, it scrapes up a pea-size ball using its mandibles, holding it with its front feet. In coarser mud, this leaves an indistinct pockmark about 6 to 8 mm across, but in fine sediment, it shows up as a distinct cluster of paired mandible marks. Potter wasps presumably do something similar.

Fiddler and Ghost Crabs

Fiddler crabs (Ocypodidae: *Uca*) and ghost crabs (*Ocypode*) leave characteristic feeding traces when deposit feeding. They scrape surface sediment into small balls and roll them through their mouthparts to filter out organic debris. The balls (or short cylinders) are deposited in rows as the crabs stop to feed, walk a few steps, feed, walk a few more steps, and so on. These rows often radiate out from a burrow like spokes of a wheel. At each spot where a crab scrapes up sediment, it leaves a series of parallel lines that look as if made with short, gentle swipes of a hair comb.

Mole Crabs

Some distinctive but very ephemeral burrows are made by mole crabs (Hippidae: *Emerita*) in intertidal sand at the water's edge. The crabs scurry around feeding as a wave crashes on the shore, then rapidly bury themselves as it recedes. The retreating water rushing past a partly buried crab leaves V-shaped ripples of sand on either side of the exposed eyes and

These scrapes and 3-mm pellets are feeding sign of deposit-feeding crabs (Ocypodidae). (Costa Rica)

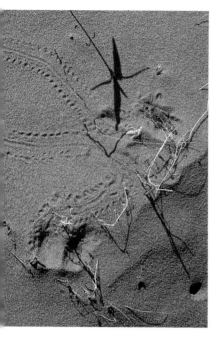

Resting digs of a toothed dune grasshopper (Acrididae: *Trimerotropis agrestis*), measuring 2 by 1 inch (5 by 2.5 cm) each. (UT)

antennae. Spotting this will give you just enough time before the next wave crashes ashore to scoop up one of these strange little creatures, along with a handful of sand, for a better look.

Resting Traces

Many animals rest for short periods in shallow digs. Grasshoppers in dunes often settle into the sand, presumably for thermoregulation. The resulting depressions are V-shaped in cross section, the length, width, and depth of the grasshopper's body, and often accompanied by nearby tracks. Ghost crabs are also known to leave body prints in the intertidal zone associated with hydration and respiration behaviors.

Funnel-shaped Pits

A funnel-shaped pit in sand is often an indication that an insect or other invertebrate is lurking beneath.

Antlions

Antlion larvae (Myrmeleontidae) in the genus *Myrmeleon* make distinctive pit traps in sand or dry soil, at the bottom of which they wait, buried, for an ant or other insect to stumble in. The larva creates the pit by digging

Pit traps of two antlion larvae (Myrmeleontidae: *Myrmeleon*). (FL)

backward in ever-tightening circles, tossing sand out with its head. The result is a regular, smooth-sided, inverted cone shape, which may be up to 1.2 inches (3 cm) deep and 3 inches (7.5 cm) across at its widest. Those of young larvae may be less than 1 cm across. When an insect stumbles in, the antlion flips sand at it, then seizes it when it tumbles within reach. These pits can be found in any sandy area, but in less arid regions, they tend to be concentrated under overhanging rocks and roofs.

Wormlions

Fly larvae known as wormlions (Vermileonidae: *Vermileo*) make pits that are similar to antlion traps in both form and function. The two North American species have very limited known ranges: *V. comstocki* is restricted to the Sierras of California, and *V. opacus* has been found at the head of King's Canyon in Nevada and near Alamogordo, New Mexico. Keep an eye out for them elsewhere, though—shortly before finishing this book, we received a letter from a man in Los Angeles County who had discovered some among the antlions along the side of his house. If you happen to be in one of the places where they exist, several features can help distinguish their pits from those of antlions. First, wormlions are found in fine dust or silt, whereas antlions can use much coarser sand. Second, according to Wheeler (1930) and more or less supported by our brief observations there, antlions at Yosemite tend to make their pits in the open, but wormlions make theirs close to rocks and cliffs or under other shelters. Third, a female wormlion lays all of her more than 50 eggs at once, resulting initially in very dense clusters of 2- to 3-mm-wide pits. Antlions lay eggs only one to a dozen at a time, so they are not found in such tight clus-

Pit traps (1.5 to 12 mm in diameter) of Sierra wormlion larvae (Vermileonidae: *Vermileo comstocki*). (CA)

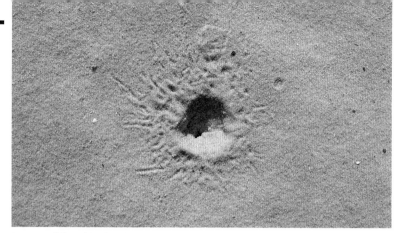

Burrow of the white beach spider (Lycosidae: *Arctosa sanctaerosae*), with tracks showing the extent of its nocturnal hunting forays. The burrow entrance is 2 cm across. (FL)

ters, and because antlion larvae form their traps by backing around in circles, the pits are never this small. Wormlion larvae, on the other hand, excavate by sitting in place and flicking out the dust with the front half of the body. This results in pits that are not only smaller, but also steeper-walled, narrower, more irregularly shaped, and often broad and rounded at the bottom. The largest wormlion pits are about 1.2 inches (3 cm) across and 2 cm deep.

Wolf Spiders

On an island off the Florida Panhandle, we came across a white beach spider (Lycosidae: *Arctosa sanctaerosae*) burrow that looked at first like an antlion trap. Closer inspection revealed that little dots and dashes made by spider feet surrounded the pit, distinguishing it from other, similar burrows. There was no obvious sign of silk, and the spider was at the bottom of the caved-in burrow, not more than 2 inches (5 cm) beneath the surface. Other members of this genus frequently burrow in loose dunes (see the section on unadorned holes), though we do not know how commonly they simply bury themselves in sand like this.

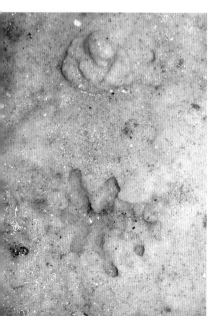

Wormlike Marine Invertebrates

On intertidal flats, funnel-shaped depressions may form many centimeters above the head of a buried lugworm (Arenicoli-

Burrow of a sea cucumber (Synaptidae: *Leptosynapta tenuis*), with characteristic star-shaped feeding trace and nearby mound of castings. The pit is about 1 inch (2.5 cm) wide. (FL)

dae: *Arenicola*), acorn worm (Hemichordata: Enteropneusta), or sea cucumber (Synaptidae: *Leptosynapta tenuis*). The funnel forms as the animal below sucks sediment into its burrow. Look for nearby castings extruded from the tail end of the burrow (see the section on castings of wormlike marine invertebrates on page 479). The burrow of a sea cucumber can be distinguished by the star-shaped depression that marks the head end, caused by the animal's radiating feeding appendages. The acorn worm *Saccoglossus kowalevskii* (Harrimaniidae) scrapes surface sediments toward its burrow, making a "feeding rosette" resembling spokes on a wheel.

Bivalves

If you look across a beach at low tide and see many different-size round holes around, you may be standing above a large variety of deeply buried bivalves. The surface trace of a bivalve is often no more than a slight depression above its hiding spot. Many bivalve burrows, such as those of jackknife clams, are permanently maintained by a mucous lining. A small hole with grooves radiating out like spokes on a wheel may mark the burrow of a *Macoma* clam (Tellinidae). Members of this genus bury themselves 8 inches (20 cm) or deeper and send up a long, skinny siphon to feed at the surface. The Atlantic jackknife (razor) clam (Pharidae: *Ensis directus*) produces a keyhole-shaped siphon hole.

Unadorned Holes

Various insects and spiders make simple holes in the ground without evident mounds of excavated earth, and these are often difficult to distinguish. Some go to considerable lengths to remove earth far from their burrows. A conspicuous mound may deter prey from venturing near the hole or may attract parasites, such as bee flies (Bombyliidae), that lay their eggs in burrow entrances. Most of the families that are discussed here will show up again in later sections, as they sometimes do produce turrets, mounds, or other distinctive features.

Tiger Beetle Larvae

Larvae of tiger beetles (Carabidae: Cicindelinae) make perfectly round, straight burrows, usually in bare soil. The edges of the burrow's mouth are characteristically smooth and rounded, and the immediately adjacent ground surface is always free of excavated earth. The diameter is about 2 to 5 mm, with each of the three instars making successively larger holes. When hunting, the larva plugs the entrance with its bizarre, disc-shaped head, springing like a jack-in-the-box to grab ants or other insects that come near. Burrows are usually vertical, but they may be nearly horizontal when in steep banks. They generally vary from a few inches to 1.5 feet (0.5 m) or so deep, but may be extended to a depth of 4 feet (1.2 m) for overwintering. The entrance may be plugged when the larva is molting or to prevent evaporation if the soil is too dry. Females of the different species

Three burrows of tiger beetle larvae (Carabidae: *Cicindela*). The entrance to the one at right is plugged by the larva's disc-shaped head. (VT)

are very particular about the type of soil in which they lay eggs, and therefore burrows of a given species may be found only in compacted soil, or beaches, or riverbanks, or dunes, and so on. The bee fly *Anthrax analis* (Bombyliidae) lays eggs at the openings of tiger beetle burrows. The larva lives as an ectoparasitoid on the beetle larva's underside, and bores into the beetle pupa in the spring before pupating itself. It then works its way to the surface and the adult emerges, leaving the pupal skin protruding from the ground.

Wolf Spiders

Some burrowing wolf spiders (Lycosidae: *Geolycosa*) make plain, round burrows that may be almost as perfectly circular as those of tiger beetle larvae. Although adult wolf spiders make substantially larger holes, those of younger ones can be exactly the same size. They tend to end abruptly at the ground surface rather than being smoothly rounded down like a tiger beetle burrow. Sometimes a tiger beetle larva or wolf spider can be coaxed out by sticking a blade of grass down the burrow. *Geolycosa* burrows can also be distinguished because, like most other spider burrows, they are lined with silk. See the section on plain silk-lined burrows for more examples of unadorned spider burrows.

Solitary Bees and Wasps

Burrows of some ground-nesting solitary bees and wasps have no excavated soil in evidence around the entrances. The openings may be approximately round, but they usually have a rough or irregular outline. They tend to enter the ground at an angle, and if they are vertical, they are some-

Burrow entrance of *Cerceris fumipennis*, a crabronid wasp. The hole is 6 mm wide. (MA)

what tortuous and uneven in width, not like the straight, perfect shaft of a tiger beetle larva. We once watched an *Oxybelus* (Crabronidae; a small wasp that provisions its nest with flies) digging a 4-mm-wide, angled burrow in the fine, hard-packed silt of a river terrace. It periodically backed up to the surface, spraying a cloud of dust behind it, which was well scattered and caused no visible accumulation. We also have seen species of *Cerceris* (related wasps that provision with beetles) and *Lasioglossum* sweat bees (Halictidae) peeking out of rough-edged burrows without piled soil. In some cases, the lack of visible excavated material may be a result of the burrow being on an open surface frequently disturbed by wind and foot traffic, but some wasps (e.g., Sphecidae: *Ammophila*) deliberately carry off material as they excavate it, and others disperse it after the fact by scraping the piled earth from side to side. Certain sweat bees and other bees and wasps nest in vertical banks, with the excavated earth falling away.

Sometimes solitary wasps leave dead or paralyzed prey just outside their burrows, and these are important clues to the wasp's identity. See page 482 for a list of wasp prey items.

Cicada Nymphs

Cicada nymphs spend their lives sucking on tree roots underground, and when mature, they emerge from distinct holes. Depending on the species and the size of the individual, the diameter can be anywhere from a few millimeters up to about 2 cm. These holes are often in hard-packed earth or woodlands, in microhabitats without an abundance of other insect burrows. The nymph tunnels upward by loosening the soil above it and packing it to the sides and below it. Therefore, there is not much excavated earth piled around the hole, although the nymph may deliberately construct a turret. Those without turrets are more or less round but have rough, irregular margins. The nymph's shed skin may be in evidence, clinging to some object above the ground in the vicinity of the hole. In the mass emergences of periodical cicadas (*Magicicada septendecim*), as many as

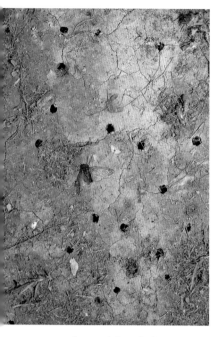

Emergence holes of periodical cicadas (*Magicicada septendecim*), along with several nymphal exuviae and an adult. The holes measure 5 to 11 mm in diameter, mostly about 10 mm. (PA)

eighty-four emergence holes, about a centimeter across, have been counted in a single square foot of ground, and up to forty thousand at the base of a single tree. The periodical species emerge earlier in the year than other cicadas, typically from late April in the South to late May in the North.

Scarab and Ground Beetles

When scarabs such as June bugs and May beetles (Scarabaeidae: Melolonthinae) emerge after pupation, they leave roughly round exit holes in the ground. In the Oregon Dunes, after a night when thousands of lined June beetles (*Polyphylla*) had been swarming around light posts, we found 1.5-cm-wide holes in the sand near some emerged adults. Many ground (Carabidae) and scarab beetle larvae maintain horizontal burrows just under the soil surface, some of which may be kept open.

Scorpions

Although many scorpions only create shallow scrapes under rocks, some make very definite burrows. The entrances are much wider than they are tall, with flattened bottoms. Entrance shapes range from rectangular to elliptical to a low, wide, obtuse isosceles triangle. Inside, the burrows slope gently (usually 20 to 40 degrees), sometimes spiraling down in a loose corkscrew. Giant hairy scorpions (Iuridae: *Hadrurus*) often dig down 2 to 3 feet (61 to 91 cm) in sandy areas and riverbanks. At least some toothed scorpions (Diplocentridae: *Diplocentrus*) are obligate burrowers.

Rectangular burrow of a toothed scorpion (Diplocentridae: *Diplocentrus whitei*), measuring 18 mm across. (TX)

Adult Tiger Beetles

Adult tiger beetles dig short, sloping burrows in loose sand, in which they hide in stormy or cold weather as well as at night and on hot days. Rather than being round and straight down, like those of the larvae, these burrows are semioval in cross sec-

An adult tiger beetle (Carabidae: *Cicindela lepida*) in its burrow. (MD) Photo by Rodger Gwiazdowski.

tion and enter the ground at an angle. Like the larvae, adults excavate deep tunnels for overwintering.

Ants

Entrances to some ant colonies have no excavated earth around them. They typically are highly irregular in shape, often slotlike, and usually begin with a "shelf" rather than going straight down. They may be much larger than the ants themselves, an unusual trait among animal burrows. Often there is a faint trail leading out, the same width as the hole. In large colonies of leafcutter ants (*Atta*), the low, rectangular entrances may be many centimeters wide.

Amphipods

In upper beaches and lower dunes, amphipod sandhoppers (Talitridae) often make shallow burrows in which to conceal themselves when they are resting. They burrow more or less straight down, spraying sand in all directions, until they are just deep enough to be out of sight. The holes have a characteristic oblong shape, about twice as long as wide, determined by the shape and size of the sandhopper. There may be a number of them in close proximity. Sandhoppers can cement the sandy walls of their burrows

Entrance (15 mm wide) to a busy harvester ant nest (Formicidae: *Pogonomyrmex*). (UT)

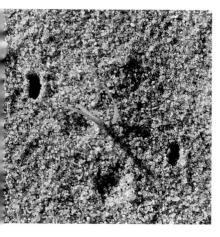

Typical oblong burrows (7 mm) of amphipod sand-hoppers (Talitridae) in drier sand. (MA)

in place with special secretions and sometimes close in the tops, leaving just their antennae sticking out.

Mantis and Mud Shrimp

Irregular holes in intertidal mud areas are often the burrows of mantis shrimp (Stomatopoda), mud shrimp (Thalassinidea), and snapping shrimp (Alpheidae). These holes may be a bit over 1 cm wide and 3.3 feet (1 m) deep, leading down to a network of interconnected burrows. Unlike mantis shrimp burrows, mud shrimp burrows tend to be much narrower right at the surface, growing wider deeper down.

Bivalves

Small, irregular cavities riddling hard muds, peats, and clay banks may be the deep burrows of bivalves such as the false angelwing (Petricolidae: *Petricolaria pholadiformis*) or Atlantic mud piddock (Pholadidae: *Barnea truncata*). The angelwing (Pholadidae: *Cyrtopleura costata*) tends to inhabit softer, stickier sediments, burrowing down to 6 inches (15 cm).

Crabs

Many crabs dig shallow, horizontal burrows in muddy intertidal areas. Mud and shore crabs (Grapsidae, Xanthidae, Panopeidae) excavate conspicuous burrows in banks of tidal ditches. Marsh and wharf crabs (Sesarmidae)

Five fiddler crab (Ocypodidae: *Uca*) burrows of varying sizes, from 4 to 14 mm, form an arc around the penny. (FL)

burrow under boards and driftwood at the edges of salt marshes. In the Florida Keys and down through the tropics, land crabs (Gecarcinidae) live a terrestrial life and dig squarish, horizontal burrows into muddy banks far from the shore.

Fiddler crab (Ocypodidae: *Uca*) burrows are found on coastal beaches and typically have tracks, excavated earth, or other distinctive features associated with them (see the other sections on pages 463 and 480). Rain or tides may obliterate the associated sign, however. On a small beach of hard-packed crushed shells in Florida's Everglades, we encountered a colony of fiddler crabs in which most of the holes were featureless. Under these conditions, the tide evidently removed any excavated material, but the substrate was hard enough that little or no reexcavation was necessary to reopen the burrows. The burrows were as small as 4 mm, occupied by very tiny, young crabs, ranging up to a little over 1 cm across. The entrances were all more or less smooth-edged and circular, but as with all fiddler crab burrows, they descended obliquely into the ground.

Plain Silk-lined Burrows

Most spider burrows have a fine silken lining. This is readily apparent if you dig up the upper portion of the burrow. A less destructive way of checking is to gently scrape the sides with a small twig and look to see if any strands catch on it.

Tarantulas

The largest and most conspicuous of silk-lined burrows, up to 1.2 inches (3 cm) or so across, are those made by tarantulas (Theraphosidae). They are usually in open areas but may be under large stones. Tarantulas start

Left: Webbed-over burrow entrance of a tarantula (Theraphosidae: *Aphonopelma*), measuring 17 mm across. (TX) *Right:* An open tarantula burrow with webbing around the edges, 1.2 inches (3 cm) across. (AZ)

their burrows as spiderlings and usually occupy them their whole lives, which may be eight to ten years. Some may inhabit natural cavities such as old rodent burrows rather than excavating their own. In either case, the upper portion is usually lined with silk. Tarantulas hunt at night, at most only a few yards from the burrow entrance. During the day, a screen of webbing usually covers the entrance, indicating that the spider is at home. In the winter, the entrance may be plugged with silk, leaves, and soil, and sometimes covered with a small mound. This may also be done during hot summer months in more arid areas.

Wolf Spiders

Many wolf spiders (Lycosidae) make silk-lined burrows in the ground with circular entrances. When excavating, they tie the soil together in little pellets, which they carry in their chelicerae and drop a short distance from the burrow entrance. *Geolycosa* species spend virtually their whole life in their burrows, which are found in sandy areas across North America. The burrows are up to 15 mm or so in diameter and usually 6 to 12 inches (15 to 30 cm) deep, but they may be extended up to 5.6 feet (1.7 m) deep for the winter. When the burrow is freshly dug, sand from different depths may form concentric rings of various colors around the opening. The burrow is vertical or nearly so, sometimes with an enlarged middle or bottom portion. The upper part is lined with silk. The entrance is closed with debris and silk for the winter. Often a turret of plant debris is built, but even if not, the entrance is not rounded downward as in a tiger beetle's burrow. Species that burrow in open sand, such as *G. wrighti* and *G. pikei*, ring the burrow entrance with an inconspicuous collar of coarse sand grains held together with silk. Some *Arctosa* species make burrows in the loose sand of dunes that may be 12 to 18 inches (30 to 45 cm) deep and 12

An excavated wolf spider burrow (Lycosidae: *Geolycosa*). This small, plain burrow looked much like a tiger beetle burrow, but when the sand was scooped up, the telltale sand-encrusted silk tube was revealed. (MI)

to 15 mm in diameter. These are often surrounded with tracks from short nocturnal hunting excursions. *A. littoralis* encircles the entrance with a collar of small stones. Some *Hogna* species are also burrowers. Their burrows are typically shallow, up to 8 inches (20 cm) deep; may be vertical or diagonal; and are often tortuous.

One wolf spider, *Pirata piraticus*, makes silk-lined vertical tubes through the sphagnum mats of bogs. The top of the tube is flush with the surface of the sphagnum and extends down 2.4 to 3.1 inches (6 to 8 cm). These tubes are made only by adult females, which sun their egg sacs at the openings; if disturbed, they can escape through the bottom and run away on the water surface.

Various other wolf spiders make shallow, silk-lined holes or depressions under rocks and logs, either when overwintering or when they have an egg sac. The shallow nest holes of some *Schizocosa* species may be in the open or under the edge of a stone or log. The nest holes of *Hogna helluo* females, under stones and logs, are often surrounded with a low wall of earth or of sticks and leaves. Some *Alopecosa* species make shallow, silk-lined burrows in soil or moss.

California Specialties

Calisoga species (Nemesiidae), found in northern and central California and adjacent Nevada, live in silk-lined burrows or crevices in the ground. Only the outer part of the burrow is lined, and scattered silk lines may be spun around the entrance. They are periodically reexcavated, and piles of small balls of soil wrapped in silk may be found near the entrance.

Lutica species (Zodariidae) are found only in the dunes of southern California's coast and islands. These 10- to 14-mm-long spiders make silk-lined tunnels in the sand, concentrated in vegetated parts of the dunes. The burrows have delicate, sand-covered, flaplike lids and thus are not usually visible, but they show up as dimples in the sand after strong winds. Most burrows descend into the sand at about a 45-degree angle, but some may have a horizontal portion just below the sand surface. Others may be vertical. The length is typically 1 to 6 inches (2.5 to 15 cm) but may be up to 12 inches (30 cm). The silk lining is usually very fragile and quickly falls apart if the sand is cleared around it. These tunnels are used much like the tubes of purseweb spiders; the prey is pulled through the wall, and the hole is quickly repaired.

Burrows with Trapdoors or Lids

Spiders in three mygalomorph families make burrows covered by hinged trapdoors. There are two basic types of lids: a thin "wafer" door, and a thick "cork" door made of layers of soil and silk. In either case, the door is generally camouflaged with debris and usually very hard to spot. The spider is active at night, waiting at the entrance with the door open a crack, and rushing out to grab prey that happen by. (Cork door types catch most of their prey without completely leaving the burrow; when disturbed, the spider holds the door shut, and it is very hard to pry open.) During the hottest part of the summer, the burrow opening may be closed tightly with earth and silk.

Ctenizidae

All ctenizids except for *Cyclocosmia* make a cork door, which is thick and beveled to fit the burrow entrance perfectly. These are often very cryptic. Their burrows are generally 5 to 8 inches (13 to 20 cm) deep, with a constant diameter. They are straight, unbranched, and typically lined with a thick layer of parchmentlike silk, which in some cases can be pulled out intact. The most common species is the California trapdoor spider (*Bothriocyrtum californicum*), found on sunny, grassy hillsides in the southern part of the state. *Hebestatis theveneti*, also found in California, makes very short, shallow burrows that often form small pockets on the sides of rocks and other structures. *Ummidia* species are found from Arizona to the East Coast. *U. audouini* typically makes its burrows in the sides of steep ravines in deciduous forests. These are distinctively shallow, usually less than 5 inches (13 cm) deep, and can be about 1 inch (2.5 cm) in diameter. The desert *Ummidia* species tend to be found in open spaces.

Among the Ctenizidae, only the two *Cyclocosmia* species (both in the Southeast) make a wafer-type door. This is a thin, flexible flap of silk, which does not fit as snugly as a cork type but still may be very well camouflaged. The burrows are typically vertical and are usually in or under leaf litter on steeply sloped banks of ravines. These spiders have a distinctive habit of resting head-down, with the flat, circular end of the abdomen plugging the burrow and giving it a false bottom. The entrance is up to about 2 cm across, and the burrow may be up to 8 inches (20 cm) deep. It is enlarged for two-thirds of the upper length, then narrows abruptly to the diameter of the spider's abdomen.

Antrodiaetidae

Aliatypus species (Antrodiaetidae) also make a wafer-type door. They are found on moderate to steep slopes in California and adjacent Nevada, plus one species in the mountains of Arizona. The burrows are in sheltered spots and usually approximately perpendicular to the surface, as is typical of the family in general. They are circular, unbranched, and lined with silk; the silk-lined entrance rim flares out to form a lip against which the door fits snugly. This lip may be elevated up to 4 mm above the surrounding substrate. The edge of the closed door extends slightly beyond the rim, so that it is not normally visible. The hinge is at the uphill side of the door, allowing it to close automatically. Most species have flexible to somewhat stiff doors 1 to 2 mm thick in the center; in two species, it is up to 2.5 mm thick and quite stiff. In one of these, *A. aquilonius*, this stiff door has slightly beveled edges and approaches the cork-type door. Adult burrows range from 1.2 to 20.1 inches (3 to 51 cm) long, with the entrance 6 to 23 mm across. Most doors are composed of silk and soil, and they are often camouflaged with bits of moss and debris from the surrounding ground surface. Sometimes one or two older, smaller doors are still attached above the current door at the hinge.

Cyrtaucheniidae

Wafer doors are the rule for the Cyrtaucheniidae, which are western except for *Myrmekiaphila*, found in the Southeast. The door is thin, soft, and pliable, almost entirely made of silk, without layers of earth, but it may be camouflaged on the outside with moss, earth, or debris. It lies on the burrow entrance, rather than fitting snugly, and is not heavy enough to fall over the opening if pushed back. These burrows typically have a relatively thin silk lining. *Aptostichus* and *Promyrmekiaphila* have an underground branch in the burrow; *Myrmekiaphila* goes a step farther and covers this second door with a thin trapdoor (others may do this too), which can close either the main burrow or the side branch. *Myrmekiaphila* burrows, most often on deciduous forest floors under several inches of leaf litter, may be 4 to 5 inches (10 to 13 cm) deep with a single spider or 18 inches (46 cm) deep with multiple branches and spiders. They are excavated diagonally with respect to the soil surface.

Left: Cryptic burrow of a trapdoor spider (probably Cyrtaucheniidae). (Costa Rica) *Right:* The same burrow with the door open. The hole measures 11 mm.

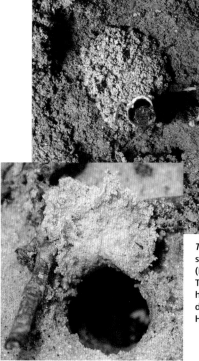

Top left: This coarse lid of sand held together with silk conceals the shallow burrow of a wolf spider (Lycosidae). The lid is 17 mm across. (TN) *Top right:* The lid has been removed to reveal the spider and her spiderlings. *Left:* Burrow of *Hogna lenta* (Lycosidae) with the lid propped open. (FL) Photo by Jeff Hollenbeck.

Wolf Spiders

Hogna lenta, a southeastern wolf spider that is most common in Florida, lives in sandy areas and covers its burrow with a thin lid. It is much like a wafer door, but even thinner than the flimsiest made by any of the mygalomorphs. The top is coated with a thin layer of sand. Rather than waiting inside the door as trapdoor spiders do, *H. lenta* hunts outside, but it darts under the cover of the door when disturbed. *H. aspersa* sometimes constructs a hinged lid on top of a turret, as described in the next section. On a steep riverbank in Tennessee, we lifted a thick, coarse lid of soil held together with silk to reveal an unidentified wolf spider resting in a shallow depression, her back covered with her recently hatched spiderlings.

Burrows with Turrets

Many invertebrates build turrets or "chimneys" surrounding their burrow entrances, such that the entrance holes are elevated above the ground level. These are thought to protect the occupants from predators and parasites, keep out surface water, provide an escape route from rising groundwater below, or in the case of spiders, assist in capturing prey.

Burrow of a burrowing wolf spider (Lycosidae: *Geolycosa*), complete with turret of plant debris. The entrance is 1 cm across. (FL)

Wolf Spiders

Burrowing wolf spiders (*Geolycosa*) often build a turret around the burrow entrance, using sand and whatever plant debris is available in the vicinity. This is sometimes very neatly constructed, with short twig pieces stacked around the hole like the walls of a log cabin. The twigs and other materials are held in place by threads of silk, and the turret is lined with a continuous sheet. The turret may be up to 1 inch (2.5 cm) high. At night, the spider can be seen perched on top waiting for a meal to pass by. The extra height evidently helps it survey its surroundings or gives it an advantage in ambushing prey. Prey remains accumulate at the bottom of the burrow.

Geolycosa species are the only wolf spiders that spend their whole lives in a burrow, but some *Hogna* species make burrows with similar turrets, sometimes in areas more vegetated than those normally inhabited by *Geolycosa*. *H. carolinensis* digs a burrow with the upper part always inclined, and the deeper part often tortuous. It occasionally makes a prominent turret of grass blades, twigs, or pebbles. *H. aspersa* digs vertical burrows in the rich soil of eastern woodlands. It makes a high turret of moss and debris, which may include a silk-reinforced canopy extending halfway across the opening. In some cases, this even becomes a complete, hinged lid, comparable to the wafer door of a trapdoor spider.

Folding-Door Spiders

The burrow of the folding-door spiders (Antrodiaetidae: *Antrodiaetus*) has a distinctive flexible collar, or sometimes a more rigid turret, around the entrance. This collar can be collapsed to close the burrow, and when this is done, it looks like two semicircular valves that meet in a straight line down the middle. The burrows may be 6 to 12 inches (15 to 30 cm) or more deep and often bend considerably. The turrets are generally left open all day but closed at night while the spider is foraging. The turret spider (*A. riversi*) is abundant along shaded streams in the San Francisco Bay area. Its burrow is very deep, usually inclined, and heavily lined with white silk right up to the top of the collar. The turret may be short, or it may be a long tube extending through thick moss or debris. The outside is adorned with bits of moss, lichen, twigs, leaves, and whatever else is available. The entrance is up to 1 cm or so across. Other species are found throughout much of North America. Their burrows are generally much less conspicuously decorated and located, and some turrets may be found projecting from the undersides of rotting logs. The two *Apomastus* species (Cyrtaucheniidae),

Left: Burrow of a folding-door spider (Antrodiaetidae: *Antrodiaetus*), with a 4-mm internal diameter. (TN) *Right:* This burrow of a turret spider (Antrodiaetidae: *Antrodiaetus riversi*) has a 5-mm entrance with 1-cm-high turret. (CA)

found only in southern California (primarily in oak woodlands), similarly make a short, flexible turret, sometimes with a small mound of soil at the burrow entrance.

Crayfish

The most prominent turrets are the "chimneys" built by certain crayfish (Cambaridae) along the edges of freshwater bodies. These turrets may not have a function beyond being safe, convenient places to deposit mud removed from the burrows. The burrow systems allow crayfish living in shallow, stagnant water to seek refuge in the cleaner, cooler water below. In floodplains and other places with high water tables, chimneys can be found far from the nearest stream. Crayfish construct their chimneys at night by bringing up balls of mud and depositing them around the opening, resulting in a lumpy appearance. Chimney shape depends in part on soil type, varying from a low, wide mud pile 8 inches (20 cm) or so across to a tall, skinny clay turret up to 18 inches (45 cm) high. A typical chimney is about 3 inches (8 cm) wide by 6 inches (15 cm) tall. The entrance is usually left open

A crayfish (Cambaridae) chimney. (TN)

The 1.6-inch (4-cm) chimney of a fiddler crab (Ocypodidae: *Uca*). (FL)

but may eventually be plugged with mud. Old burrows are used by hibernating or estivating amphibians, reptiles, and fish, and may be important refuges for other invertebrates when ponds dry up.

Crabs

On coastal beaches, several fiddler crab species (Ocypodidae: *Uca*) ornament their burrows with pillars (narrow piles), hoods (partial covering, concave on burrow side), or chimneys (encircle burrow). The key feature that distinguishes these from mere piles made during burrow excavation (see the section on page 480 on burrows with a mound of earth to one side of the entrance) is that the crabs collect material from outside the burrow and bring it back to improve the sculpture. There is certainly a significant gray area of overlap between these two activities.

Usually only a small percentage of the crabs in a group build structures above their burrows. Full chimneys may serve to guard burrows against being taken over by other crabs of the same species and are more often built by smaller individuals and females. In the southern tip of Florida, female mangrove (*U. thayeri*) and hairback (*U. vocator*) fiddlers construct chimneys. Those of hairback fiddlers are up to 2.4 inches (6 cm) high and 2 inches (5 cm) wide.

Males also construct hoods of various shapes that are used as mating signals. Larger hoods presumably indicate healthier males, and there is evidence that hoods may offer females protection from predation when they visit a male's burrow to mate. On the Atlantic and Gulf coasts, male Atlantic sand fiddlers (*U. pugilator*), marsh fiddlers (*U. pugnax*), and red-jointed fiddlers (*U. minax*) build low, half-dome–shaped piles on one side of the burrow. Male Gulf sand fiddlers (*U. panacea*) construct rims around the burrow openings. Marbled fiddlers (*U. leptodactyla*) are rare in the southern tip of Florida, where the males construct delicate, tall, wide vertical hoods. Along the Baja peninsula and northern Mexico in the Gulf of California, *U. musica* males build similar structures. From Baja to Peru, *U. latimanus* constructs narrow columns that are even taller.

The heavy marsh crab (Sesarmidae: *Sesarma reticulatum*; E) burrows under driftwood at marsh edges and reportedly also constructs a mud chimney above its hole.

Cicada Nymphs

Cicada nymphs may tunnel up to the ground surface several weeks before actually emerging to become adults. Those emerging in wet areas, or wet seasons, often construct round chimneys above their burrows, apparently

A cicada nymph (Cicadidae) emerging from its turreted hole. (TN)

as a retreat from high soil moisture. This is especially common in periodical cicadas, which emerge in the spring, substantially earlier than other cicadas do. The chimney may be a neat, round structure, up to 2 to 3 inches (5 to 7.6 cm) high, with the exit hole in the top and center. In coarser soil, it may be only a slight, lopsided encrustation at the edge of the burrow, or sometimes a little dome with a side entrance. Packard (1878) includes an illustration of a hollow mud tower, 6 inches (15 cm) tall, with a closed, bent tip in which a cicada nymph is perched and a side exit hole at ground level.

Bees

Various digger bees (Apidae: Apinae) construct turrets at the entrances of their nests. The female hibiscus bee (*Ptilothrix bombiformis*; E) builds a short, thick-walled turret, about 1 cm high and 2 cm across. She carries water from a nearby source and uses it to soften the soil, applying the mud with her hind legs, and then using her abdomen to pack and smooth the interior. *Anthophora abrupta* (E) nests in sunny, vertical clay banks, sometimes in dense colonies. It builds turrets as the hibiscus bee does, but they

Burrows of digger bees (Apidae: Apinae; probably *Diadasia*), with 4- to 6-mm hole diameters. (CA)

Burrows of *Diadasia australis* digger bees (Apidae) with horizontal turrets. The entrances are 4 to 5 mm. (CA) Photo by Hartmut Wisch.

are long and narrow, about 13 mm wide and up to 3 inches (8 cm) long. They tend to be bent downward and often have an open slot along the length of the upper (outer) side. *A. occidentalis* (W) and *A. bomboides* (widespread) make similar turrets, somewhat smaller. *Melitoma taurea* (E) also makes slotted tubes in clay banks, but its burrows are vertical. *Diadasia* species (W) nest in coarser soil and make complete, narrow turrets of varying lengths, which may be upright, curved, or in some cases lie horizontally on the ground. They do not carry water but may use nectar to soften compacted soil.

Wasps

Some vespid wasps also top their burrows with turrets. *Euparagia scutellaris* is a rare wasp inhabiting dry hillsides in California. It makes slender, curved chimneys atop shallow burrows in hard ground, which end in one or more cells provisioned with weevil larvae. The rest are all mason wasps (Eumeninae), which make mud partitions in their burrows as their relatives do in hollow stems, likewise provisioning them with caterpillars or leaf-feeding beetle larvae. *Euodynerus annulatus* makes a thick-walled tube that is about 1 inch (2.5 cm) long and is usually curved, usually within 100 feet (30 m) of water. Like *Anthophora* bees, females carry in water to soften soil as they excavate it and incorporate it into the tube. The wasps, however, break down their tubes and use the material to close the burrows after they are provisioned. They level the ground and leave little trace of the nests. *Odynerus dilectus* nests gregariously and builds turrets that are 0.5 to 1.2 inches (12 mm to 3 cm) high, sometimes curved, but straight 80 percent of the time. These two species are widespread. The western species *Stenodynerus microstictus*, *S. claremontensis*, and *S. papagorum* also make turrets, the last one nesting gregariously. Various other mason wasps excavate burrows, or use existing ones, without turrets.

Ants

A few fungus-growing ants (Formicidae: Myrmicinae: Attini), such as *Trachymyrmex turrifex* and young colonies of *Atta* species, construct earthen turrets. The material in these turrets reflects the well-sorted soil typical of ant mounds in general (see section on anthills on page 469).

Burrows Topped with Middens

The burrows of certain earthworms and ants are marked by conspicuous piles of leaf fragments and other plant material.

Earthworms

Walking through a dormant cornfield in upstate New York, we became curious about some piles of debris, a few inches across, that were conspicuous because they were surrounded by bare soil. Even though we saw an earthworm retreat into the ground when we scraped aside the first pile, we did not see how the worm could have been what made it. Each pile, however, had a hole at the center like the one into which the worm had retreated, with some leaves pulled into it. Sure enough, these "middens" are a charac-

Midden of a common nightcrawler (Lumbricidae: *Lumbricus terrestris*), concealing the entrance to its burrow. The surrounding leaf litter has been completely cleared away by this worm and its neighbors.

teristic sign of the common nightcrawler (Lumbricidae: *Lumbricus ter-restris*), and Darwin (1883) devoted an entire chapter to describing the phenomenon. The nightcrawler is an *anecic* species, which means that it burrows deep in the soil but feeds on surface litter. It is able to pick up smaller leaves by clamping its mouth onto an edge, and larger ones it holds on to by creating suction on the flat surface with its pharynx. It then drags whatever it has grabbed down the burrow. It is said that nightcrawlers alone can consume all the leaf litter produced in a forest each year.

Earthworm middens, however, are more than mere artifacts of food acquisition; they serve to regulate the burrow's temperature and humidity. Some of the leaves are used to line the upper part of the burrow. When leaves are abundant, many more are dragged into the pile than will be used. On a forest floor, these piles are less likely to be seen than in a bare area like the cornfield where we first noticed them, but they have a clumped, twisted look and become easy to spot with a little practice. When leaves are not available, the worms gather pebbles and whatever else is around to protect their burrows.

Ants

Leaf fragment middens are also created by leafcutter ants (Formicidae: *Atta*). Though most species occur in the tropics, a few make it well into North America, such as the Texas leafcutter ant (*A. texana*; TX, LA). These remarkable ants cut and carry fresh leaves to feed their underground fungus gardens, which may be 23 feet (7 m) below the surface. Leaves that do not make it into the farm, perhaps because they were deemed unsuitable

This pile of leaf fragments, 4 inches (10 cm) high, marks an entrance to a colony of Texas leafcutter ants (Formicidae: *Atta texana*). (TX)

for fungus growing by quality-controlling ants, are deposited on the ground around burrow entrances in large, volcano-shaped piles. Unlike in earthworm middens, the leaf fragments in leafcutter ant midden piles are very regularly cut into fairly uniform-size pieces. Often well-worn, meandering trails lead from these entrances to the plants whose leaves are being cut. You may see many of these piles spread across an area the size of a football field, all belonging to the same ant colony. Long underground tunnels connect each of these satellite entrances to the central burrow system where the high-quality leaves are ultimately taken.

Labidus coecus (SE), a legionary ant, is another species that piles leaf fragments, but in a very different way. Every few weeks, workers use bits of leaves to construct tunnels through which the colony moves to a new location. Various other ants make craters or mounds that may include organic debris in addition to excavated earth. Examples are given in the next section.

Burrows with an Earthen Mound Surrounding or Covering the Entrance

Anthills are probably the most familiar invertebrate-created mounds and craters, but somewhat similar piles of earth may mark the burrows of bees, beetles, crickets, or other invertebrates. Earthworm burrows are often capped with their castings, which are simply processed earth, and this is also the case with various marine invertebrates. Burrows in which soil is pushed up as in a mole tunnel, forming linear ridges or flat patches rather than mounds, are discussed in chapter 17.

A modest-size complex of Texas leafcutter ant (Formicidae: *Atta texana*) mounds, measuring 20 feet (6 m) across. (TX)

Anthills

The mounds of soil above ant nests are usually straightforward to recognize because of the unique way in which they are excavated. Unlike the work of one or two small animals digging or pushing clods of earth out of a burrow, ant excavation consists of many workers carrying out grains of sand one at a time. This results in a characteristically well-sorted, fine texture, without big clumps. The removed material is not compacted, such that there is often much air space between the grains. If you watch for long enough, you will probably see the ants themselves, though when it is cold, they may be less active. Poking the mound with a stick may release a wave of ants pouring out to defend their nest. Each species has its own style of mound, and within a region, it may be possible to learn to recognize the conspicuous species by their nests. (Many ant nests are under

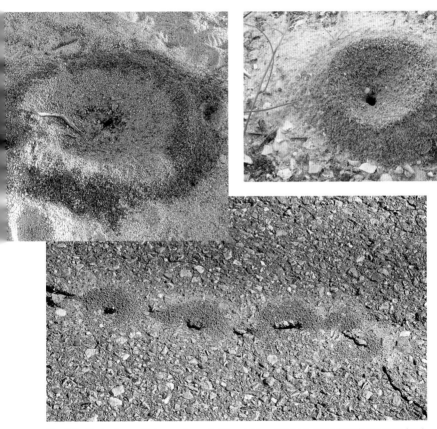

Top left: Nest of smooth harvester ants (Formicidae: *Messor*), edged with creosote bush seeds. The nest is 22 inches (55 cm) across and 2.4 inches (6 cm) high. (CA) *Top right:* Crater nest of pyramid ants (*Dorymyrmex bureni*), 3.5 inches (9 cm) across, 1.2 inches (3 cm) high. (FL) *Above:* These craters of excavated sand from *Lasius neoniger* ant burrows along a sidewalk crack measure 2.4 to 2.8 inches (6 to 7 cm) across. (VT)

stones, in rotting wood, or are otherwise hidden; some species nest in single acorns.) With several hundred North American species, only a few examples of different types can be mentioned here.

Large, wide mounds of earth appear above the central underground chambers of leafcutter ant (*Atta*) colonies. Initially, each mound has a central hole through which soil excavated from the chambers below is removed. Over time, these mounds run together, forming a solid miniature mountain range several meters across.

Many ants produce a crater-type nest, a ring-shaped hill with a depression in the middle where the nest entrance is. Workers come and go from the entrance, depositing their sand grains a certain radius from the center, building up the crater rim. Sometimes the hole is off to one side of the crater (a common arrangement in *Trachymyrmex* leafcutter ants), and the mound forms only half of a ring. The little brown *Lasius* ants (in particular *L. neoniger*) are very common in the Northeast in disturbed habitats

Top left: Fire ant (*Solenopsis*) mound in a lawn. (NM) *Top right:* A more substantial fire ant mound, 20 inches (50 cm) across and 9 inches (22 cm) high. (GA) *Above:* A 2-cm-wide linear mound made by red imported fire ants (*Solenopsis invicta*) on a riverbank. (LA)

Top left: This flat, bare area, measuring 24 inches (60 cm) wide, indicates the nest of ants in the *Formica fusca* group. The larger of the several irregular, 5- to 25-mm-wide burrow entrances are visible. (MA) *Top right:* A mound made by thatching ants (*Formica obscuripes*). (WA) Photo by Lynette Schimming. *Right:* Mounds of Allegheny mound ants (*Formica exsectoides*), with a moss-covered, abandoned one in the foreground, and an active one in the background. (NH)

such as lawns and sidewalks. Their craters have entrances as small as 2 mm wide and are typically flattened and 2.4 to 2.8 inches (6 to 7 cm) across, but when the soil is moist, they sometimes build narrow, little towers. Pyramid ants (*Dorymyrmex*) are common in the South, making a crater that often has a sharp, well-defined crest, about 3.5 to 4.7 inches (9 to 12 cm) across and 1.2 inches (3 cm) tall. *Messor* harvester ants (SW) often produce a crater ringed with chaff from seeds stored in their nest. Craters of honeypot ants (*Myrmecocystus*) are common in the arid Southwest; those of *M. mexicanus* are piles of pebbles with a large, circular entrance in the center. There are numerous other crater-making ant genera.

Other ants build large mounds without a central entrance, but with tunnels running throughout. In some cases, these are made entirely of excavated material; in others, foreign material is gathered to build them. These mounds allow the ants to avoid soil moisture. The mounds of imported fire ants (*Solenopsis*) are extremely abundant in some parts of the Southeast. Small, irregular mounds a few inches high may be seen in sidewalks and lawns; in less frequently disturbed open areas, they grow into smooth domes up to 3 feet (91 cm) high and 5 feet (1.5 m) wide. A few native fire ants make similar mounds. Occasionally fire ants construct a long, narrow ridge of excavated earth snaking across the ground. The examples we have seen were all on banks of rivers or creeks, but this may or may not be significant. *Lasius interjectus* and *L. latipes* are more widespread, making large earthen mounds in open woodlands and meadows; *L. minutus* (NE) builds such mounds in open wetlands.

Formica is a prolific genus of ants that build a variety of large and small mounds. Several species in this genus are referred to as "field ants" and

A circle more than 13 feet (4 m) wide cleared by western harvester ants (*Pogonomyrmex occidentalis*). Note the central mound. Taller mounds in the background are the work of prairie dogs. (ND)

are common in lawns, woods, and other habitats, especially in the East. Field ants construct low, wide, irregular mounds with many entrance holes. The width of these mounds may exceed 3.3 feet (1 m), but their height is usually less than a few centimeters. Sometimes these ants simply form a completely flat, bare patch in a field. Other *Formica* species, sometimes called "thatching ants," build substantial mounds out of twigs, blades of grass, and other debris. Allegheny mound ants (*F. exsectoides*) are responsible for some of the tallest ant mounds in North America. Their rounded hills may be more than 3.3 feet (1 m) tall and 6.6 feet (2 m) wide at the base. Several of these hills may occur in close proximity. Active mounds have the vegetation cleared around them, but old ones can become completely covered with a dense layer of low plants, and it might not be obvious that ants originally shaped the terrain.

Pogonomyrmex harvester ants are among the most conspicuous ants in the Southwest. A large circle cleared of debris centered on a single entrance hole is typical for this genus. Some species clear all live vegetation within the circle, at times with evident trails radiating out. Cleared trails leading from red harvester ant (*P. barbatus*) mounds may be more than 3.3 feet (1 m) wide and 200 feet (60 m) long. Right around the central hole, many species construct small, volcano-shaped mounds ranging from a few centimeters to 20 inches (50 cm) wide. Although harvester ants are mostly a southwestern phenomenon, the nests of *P. occidentalis* punctuate the prairie like crop circles as far northeast as North Dakota, and the comparable nests of *P. salinus* can be found into British Columbia and Saskatchewan.

Just west of El Paso, visible from I-10, are some very large mounds—more than 5 feet (1.5 m) tall by 25 feet (8 m) wide—inhabited by Maricopa harvester ants (*P. maricopa*). Close inspection of these mounds reveals that they are mostly composed of fine sand, with caps of coarser gravel on top (such a gravel cap is typical of many harvester ants). It seems to us that the

The darker color on this large mound is gravel placed there by the Maricopa harvester ants (*Pogonomyrmex maricopa*) that dwell within it. (TX)

ants have appropriated small, wind-driven dunes that were originally stabilized by plants, rather than having built these hills up from level ground. The tops of preexisting mounds would certainly be prime real estate, and the ants' main task would be to kill off the existing vegetation. The coarser pebbles placed by the ants presumably help stabilize the denuded mounds. An interesting successional cycle might be occurring here.

Solitary Bees

The burrow of a solitary bee (Andrenidae, Halictidae, or Colletidae) tends to be topped with a mound of excavated earth, up to about 1 inch (2.5 cm) high. The entrance hole is often near the center of the pile, but it may be near the edge. Only very rarely is it actually at the edge, which is the typical configuration for a wasp burrow. This is simply the way the material

Left: A colony of *Andrena* mining bees (Andrenidae). The mounds are about 2 inches (5 cm), and the entrances about 5 mm. (VT) *Right:* A cellophane bee (Colletidae: *Colletes inaequalis*) peeks out from its burrow. The mound is 2.4 inches (6 cm) wide, with a 7-mm entrance. (VT)

naturally falls as it is dug out of a more or less vertical shaft. These bees generally nest in compacted, sandy soil. Mounds are often about 2 inches (5 cm) wide at the base, but we have seen more flattened mounds of cellophane bees (Colletidae: *Colletes*) that were up to 4 inches (10 cm) across. The entrance tends to be rounder and proportionally larger than in a similar-size anthill, about 4 to 7 mm wide depending on the species. Bee burrows are typically 4 to 12 inches (10 to 30 cm) or so deep, up to more than 24 inches (60 cm) in some cellophane bees. The main shaft has several side branches that lead to oval brood cells, which are provisioned with balls of pollen and nectar. These bees are called "solitary" because they are not social in the sense that honeybees and yellowjackets are, but they often nest in dense colonies. In many *Halictus* sweat bees (Halictidae), daughters stay with their mothers, helping expand the nest, with one always stationed at the entrance as a sentinel.

Wasps

A small minority of wasps excavate nearly vertical burrows by backing out and pushing the soil behind them, rather than using the typical methods described in the next section. The result is a mound with the entrance near the middle, much like a bee's burrow. Examples include *Cerceris* species, which provision their nests with beetles, and some *Tachytes*, which provision with Orthoptera (both Crabronidae).

Cicadas

In the days leading up to its emergence, a cicada nymph may push up a small mound of soil that caps its hole until it finally crawls out.

Mounds covering the entrances to periodical cicada (Cicadidae: *Magicicada septendecim*) burrows that have not yet been abandoned. The mounds measure 1.2 to 1.6 inches (3 to 4 cm) across. (MA)

Crickets

The common short-tailed cricket (Gryllidae: *Anurogryllus arboreus*; SE) is unique among true crickets in constructing an elaborate, multichambered burrow. A freshly excavated burrow has a conspicuous mound on top, up to about 2 inches (5 cm) high and 3 inches (7 cm) wide, fluffy, and made of small "crumbs" rather than the "ropes" of earth-boring dung beetles. Under the mound is a short diagonal or vertical shaft, about 6 mm wide. Below this, the burrow initially consists of a shallow upper cavity 0.8 to 1.2 inches (2 to 3 cm) wide, containing leaves cut from nearby plants, with a vertical shaft descending from it into which the cricket can retreat. The burrow becomes more elaborate, with the bottom being enlarged into a second chamber and additional short chambers excavated for disposal of droppings and unused plant material. After a month or two, the cricket may add a second entrance, so that there are two mounds of unequal size close together. The whole burrow ranges from several to 20 inches (51 cm) deep.

The Japanese burrowing cricket (*Velarifictorus micado*) now occurs throughout the southeastern United States. It does not produce a mound but may construct a hood of soil particles over its burrow entrance.

Earth-boring Dung Beetles

Adult earth-boring dung beetles (Geotrupidae) dig usually perfectly vertical burrows, pushing up the excavated earth in a conspicuous mound. The beetles carry to the bottom a mass of leaf litter or other decomposing matter (occasionally dung), on which the female lays her eggs and the larvae feed. Because these beetles excavate by slowly pushing soil up the burrow, the mounds have a characteristically chunky look, sometimes with distinct "ropes" of sand that retain the form of the burrow. In very dry sand, this may not be evident. The beetles make clear, central exit holes when they leave, but otherwise the mounds have no visible openings. The burrows often occur in groups. A number of species have very limited ranges, and all of them spend most of their lives underground, so recognizing their burrows is the main way to detect their presence. Burrow depth can be an important clue to the species, and this can be measured without digging by attaching a fishing sinker to a line and dropping it to the bottom.

Entomologists David Almquist, Skip Choate, Phillip Harpootlian, and Paul Skelley have all shared their observations of burrow characteristics of various earth-boring dung beetle species, which are summarized here along with those of Manee (1908), Bryson (1939), and Young et al. (1955), approximately in descending order of size. Most are found only in sandy soil. The Florida deepdigger scarab (*Peltotrupes profundus*) and Ocala deepdigger scarab (*P. youngi*) both occur exclusively in Florida. Their burrows are 13 mm wide (or somewhat smaller in *P. youngi*) and often about 6 feet (1.8 m) deep, with the resulting mounds sometimes more than 6 inches (15 cm) across. They may start out at various angles before becoming vertical. The more widespread *Bradycinetulus ferrugineus* (SE) makes a burrow the same size, often 2 to 3 feet (61 to 91 cm) deep but sometimes only several inches deep, topped with a mound about 2 inches (5 cm) high

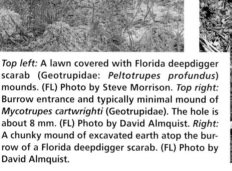

Top left: A lawn covered with Florida deepdigger scarab (Geotrupidae: *Peltotrupes profundus*) mounds. (FL) Photo by Steve Morrison. *Top right:* Burrow entrance and typically minimal mound of *Mycotrupes cartwrighti* (Geotrupidae). The hole is about 8 mm. (FL) Photo by David Almquist. *Right:* A chunky mound of excavated earth atop the burrow of a Florida deepdigger scarab. (FL) Photo by David Almquist.

and 4 inches (10 cm) wide. Manee noted that the top of the shaft is plugged with soil 1 inch (2.5 cm) thick when a pair is working together, but not when there is only one beetle, as if he or she is waiting for a mate. *Mycotrupes* burrows are about 8 mm in diameter, and the mounds are correspondingly smaller, 3 inches (8 cm) being a typical diameter. Those of *M. gaigei* (FL) and *M. retusus* (SC) are commonly 4 feet (1.2 m) deep, but rarely any deeper. *M. cartwrighti*, in Georgia and northern Florida, tends to burrow only about 14 to 18 inches (36 to 46 cm) deep, leaving little or no mound—there may be just a slight lip of pushed-up soil around a circular hole. *Geotrupes* species (E) make relatively shallow burrows that start out diagonal, with mounds that are very loose and relatively small. *Eucanthus* burrows are vertical, about 6 mm in diameter, and may be fairly deep or as shallow as several inches. The mounds are similar to those of *B. ferrugineus* but smaller. *Odonteus* species usually make shallow, diagonal burrows, with a "push-up" about 2 inches (5 cm) across. They sometimes burrow in very hard-packed clay soil. *Bolbocerosoma* species often make Y-shaped burrows, about 10 inches (25 cm) deep, with the openings 3 to 4 inches (8 to 10 cm) apart. They also use compact, claylike soil, and the small amount of pushed-up material stays stuck together.

True Dung Beetles

Some of the true dung beetles (Scarabaeidae: Scarabaeinae) may produce distinct mounds over their burrows. Generally their burrows are near, if not under, the dung they use to provision their nests, with the exception of the tumblebugs (*Canthon*), which make dung balls and roll them for a considerable distance before digging shallow (less than 2 inches [5 cm] deep), vertical tunnels in which to bury them. The female lays a single egg in the ball, and the larva completes its development inside it. Tumblebugs range in size from 4 to 21 mm, and their burrows vary correspondingly. *C. lecontei*, a species that rolls and buries rabbit pellets, digs a 5-mm-wide burrow with a mound the size of a garden pea.

Ground Beetles

Geopinus incrassatus (Carabidae), a nocturnal ground beetle of dry fields, burrows into the ground each morning to rest and escape the heat of the day. According to Bryson (1939), it burrows 3 to 4 inches (8 to 10 cm) at a 45-degree angle, producing a mound of about 2 tablespoons of soil. Manee (1908) found the same species at the bottoms of 8- to 10-inch (20- to 25-cm) vertical burrows beneath mounds essentially identical to those of short-tailed crickets. If the mound is brushed aside, the 8-mm-wide burrow is barely detectable, because the beetle firmly plugs it with the soil it pushes behind itself as it burrows.

Ground and Scarab Beetle Larvae

In sandy Florida soil, we came across 5-cm-wide, flat-topped, biscuit-shaped mounds that belonged to burrowing ox beetle larvae (Scarabaeidae: *Strategus*). These rhinoceros beetles are among the largest North American beetles; other beetle larvae presumably make similar but smaller burrows. The larva of the murky ground beetle (Carabidae: *Harpalus caliginosus*), for instance, makes small mounds in cultivated fields. The burrow beneath is J-shaped, about 6 mm wide and 6 inches (15 cm) long, and closed with soil except for the last third, where the larva is found.

Burying Beetles

The habits of burying beetles (Silphidae: *Nicrophorus*) were discussed in chapter 4. When they bury a carcass that they find lying on bare ground, they may produce an irregular patch of soil that is not substantially elevated above the surrounding ground surface but is noticeably churned and disturbed. Because they bury the animal by pushing the earth out from under it, they affect a surface area much larger than the animal itself.

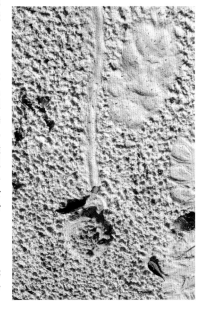

This burrow of an ox beetle larva (Scarabaeidae: *Strategus*), with the larva's trail leading up to it, measures 2.4 inches (6 cm) wide. (FL)

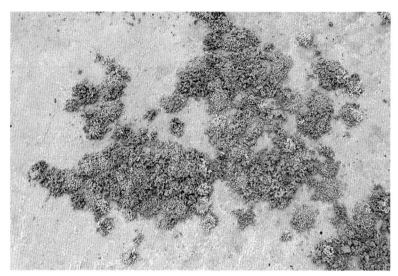

A cluster of many small mounds excavated by *Bledius* rove beetle adults and larvae (Staphylinidae). (TX)

Rove Beetles

Along a creek in Texas not far from the Gulf of Mexico, we found aggregations of what at first glance appeared to be worm castings, but they had a granular texture and were made of unprocessed excavated sand. Scraping them aside revealed openings of 2- to 3-mm-wide burrows that were tortuous and at least several centimeters deep. Eventually we determined the makers to be adult and larval rove beetles (Staphylinidae) in the genus *Bledius*.

Earthworm Castings

The castings of earthworms (Lumbricina) can be very conspicuous. In fine, moist soil, they are extruded in a string and collect in a lumpy heap.

In sandier soil, they form discrete, oblong pellets, which may form piles several centimeters across. Pellets are made of compacted processed soil and thus have a uniform, very fine-grained texture. The worm deposits its castings such that they conceal its burrow, and later castings are forced up through the previous ones. If you brush aside worm castings, the burrow entrance should be evident near the middle of the pile.

Earthworm (Lumbricidae) castings formed in fine river silt. (VT)

Earthworm castings in sandier soil. The pile measures about 1.6 inches (4 cm) across. (GA) Photo by Christopher G. Brown.

Castings of Wormlike Marine Invertebrates

Wormlike marine organisms also produce castings that are largely made of the substrate in which they burrow. On intertidal flats, acorn worms (Hemichordata: Enteropneusta) and lugworms (Arenicolidae: *Arenicola*) exude continuous soft, ropy piles of sand that coil atop their burrows as the sand comes out. Nearby, look for a depression in the sand indicating where the head of the animal far below is sucking out sediment. Sea cucumbers (Synaptidae: *Leptosynapta tenuis*) may also make similar fecal piles above their U-shaped burrows, but they tend to leave a distinctive star-shaped depression at the other end. The horseshoe worm *Phoronopsis harmeri* (Phoronida) secretes many thin, sandy casts that can look like a mess of fine, dark spaghetti on the beach.

Ghost Shrimp

Ghost shrimp (Callianassidae) make fairly distinctive burrows on intertidal flats, usually with at least two entrances. Carolinian ghost shrimp (*Callichirus major*) are the largest, with 5-mm holes. Each hole is at the center of a low, volcano-shaped pile of sand. The mud and mucus-lined burrows can sometimes form little chimneys at the center of the excavated sediment. Around the hole, there are often a number of dark, slightly flattened, cylindrical pellets, 1 mm in diameter. These well-formed, durable pellets have been seen popping out of a hole at a rate of forty per minute. Reaching as far as 16 feet (5 m) below ground, the burrow systems form

Ropy castings similar to these may mark the burrow of a lugworm (Arenicolidae: *Arenicola*), sea cucumber (Synaptidae: *Leptosynapta*), or acorn worm (Enteropneusta). (FL)

A plugged, amorphous crayfish (Cambaridae) chimney in a typical location. (TN)

complex mazes that may support a large number of individuals. Various other animals use ghost shrimp burrows, and several eat their fecal pellets.

Crayfish

As mentioned above, crayfish burrows sometimes look like amorphous mounds of mud rather than distinct chimneys formed of round pellets. When the entrance is plugged, these can be quite nondescript. Given the context, though—along a freshwater body or ditch—there is not much to confuse them with.

Burrows with a Mound of Earth to One Side of the Entrance

Burrows with the excavated earth piled to one side of the hole are characteristic of crabs and wasps. Other invertebrates occasionally make burrows with a similar setup, including tiger beetles, scorpions, and ants. All five of these groups should be easy to separate, for the most part.

Crabs

Crabs usually excavate diagonally sloping burrows that allow the crustaceans to remain largely upright while walking down into them. Because of this geometry, the sand naturally tends to be deposited asymmetrically

as it is carried out of the burrows during excavation. The most familiar crab burrows are made by the closely related ghost crabs (*Ocypode*) and fiddler crabs (*Uca*). Shafts of these burrows tend to be more vertical than in other crab burrows, but still somewhat slanted.

The ground outside fiddler crab burrow entrances is usually decorated with large balls of sand carried out of the tunnels one at a time during burrow excavation. These

Burrow of a fiddler crab (Ocypodidae: *Uca*), with the excavated sand rolled out one ball at a time. Note the much smaller sand balls from deposit feeding. (MA)

Burrows of Atlantic ghost crabs (Ocypodidae: *Ocypode quadrata*). The entrances are up to 3 inches (7 cm) across. (NC)

balls may be placed in a neat pile or well dispersed, but they are usually distributed within a 180-degree radius. As they dry out, the balls disintegrate into smooth piles of sand. Much smaller sand balls surrounding crab holes are the remnants of feeding activity (see the section on surface scrapes and digs above). Burrows of the different species of fiddler crabs can be distinguished, to some extent, based on which part of the beach they occur in. Some species prefer sandy areas in salt marshes (e.g., the sand fiddler, *U. pugilator*), whereas others prefer muddy areas (e.g., the marsh fiddler, *U. pugnax*).

Ghost crabs are much more terrestrial than other North American crabs, and their burrows can be found in sand hundreds of feet from the water. The burrow entrance of an Atlantic ghost crab (*O. quadrata*) is up to 3 inches (7 cm) wide and surrounded by an asymmetric mound of excavated sand up to 4 inches (10 cm) high and 28 inches (70 cm) wide. Larger fiddler crab burrows are only about 2 cm across.

To escape hot midday sun or rising tides, ghost crabs and some fiddler crabs, especially sand fiddlers, plug their burrows, unlike other burrowing crabs. Biologists disagree about whether the plug maintains a pocket of air in the burrow beneath the tidewaters.

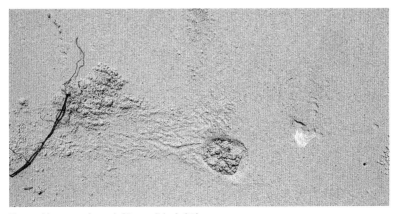

Plugged burrow of a crab (Ocypodidae). (FL)

Wasps

A large number of solitary wasps (Crabronidae; Sphecidae; Pompilidae) dig burrows in which their larvae will develop. Just as with wasps that build mud nests or use preexisting cavities, each species has a particular type of prey it hunts, paralyzes, and uses to provision its burrow. Multiple species often burrow fairly close together, as in general they have similar habitat requirements: an abundance of sand that is loose enough to dig but firm enough not to collapse on them as they burrow. Nevertheless, some *Bembix* sand wasps (Crabronidae), for instance, do nest in very loose sand of dunes.

Although there is a fair amount of diversity in internal burrow structure, the burrow entrances of most solitary wasps are of the same basic form. The tunnel is more or less round, generally 4 to 20 mm across, and descends into the ground at an angle. Most species dig by *raking* the soil with their mouthparts and front legs and ejecting it backward beneath their bodies, essentially the way a dog digs. As a result, the excavated earth is deposited in a low pile on one side of the entrance hole. Certain wasps instead *pull* the soil out in small loads by grabbing a lump between the head and front legs and backing out with it, more like what a fiddler crab does. This naturally results in a lumpier pile than is produced by spraying sand backward. A given species may use the first method with the dry surface sand and the second with the moister sand beneath.

Some wasps take steps to prevent parasitic bee flies, velvet ants, and others from finding their larvae. Various species conceal their burrows by plugging the hole with sand and scattering the mound after the burrow is complete. In some cases, there are several small holes nearby from which fill was dug. Species of *Bembix*, *Philanthus* (Crabronidae), and *Sphex*

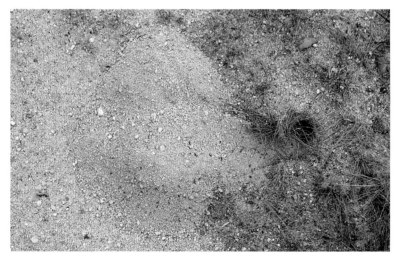

Burrow of an eastern cicada killer (Crabronidae: *Sphecius speciosus*). The hole is 2 cm, with an 8-inch (20-cm) sand pile. (MA)

(Sphecidae), among others, dig up to five decoy burrows, which are left open, around the plugged true nest burrow to deceive would-be predators.

Among the most impressive solitary wasps are the cicada killers (Crabronidae: *Sphecius*). Their burrows are 2 cm in diameter, often closer to 1.2 inches (3 cm) at the entrance, with mounds of excavated earth up to 16 inches (40 cm) long. If you sit and wait, you may catch the formidable sight of a giant wasp flying an even bigger cicada toward its hole. Sometimes these or other wasps will leave their prey abandoned by the hole, which can be a helpful clue in identifying the type of wasp responsible for the burrow:

- Many of the cicada killers' smaller relatives in the Bembicinae prey on the cicadas' smaller relatives: leafhoppers, planthoppers, treehoppers, and spittlebugs. Among the Pemphredoninae, the Psenini specialize in leafhoppers, and the Pemphredonini in aphids (with a species of *Pulverro* recorded as preying on thrips).

- *Anacrabro*, *Belomicrus*, and *Encopognathus* (Crabroninae) mostly prey on plant bugs; and *Bicyrtes* (Bembicinae) and the Astatinae on various true bug nymphs.

- Many of the ground-nesting sphecid wasps prey on Orthoptera: *Chlorion* hunts true crickets; *Prionyx* specializes in grasshoppers; and *Sphex* and *Palmodes* both hunt primarily katydids, the former often nesting gregariously and the latter almost always solitarily. *Stizus* species (Crabronidae: Bembicinae) also prey on grasshoppers and katydids, and a number of the Crabroninae take Orthoptera as well, though often using preexisting burrows.

- Most of the Philanthinae (Crabronidae) prey on other Hymenoptera. *Philanthus* species primarily use bees, as does *Trachypus mexicanus* (Mexico, S TX). *Clypeadon* and *Listropygia* prey on *Pogonomyrmex* harvester ants, and *Aphilanthops* specializes in winged *Formica* queens.

- The Cercerini (Crabronidae: Philanthinae) prey on beetles. *Bothynostethus* and *Entomognathus* (Crabroninae) hunt chrysomelid beetles in particular.

- A number of crabronids in the Bembicinae, Crabroninae, and Mellininae provision with flies, sometimes with distinct preferences (e.g., *Stictia* for horse flies; *Steniolia* for bee flies).

- The Pompilidae all prey on spiders, using one large spider per cell. *Miscophus* species (Crabronidae: Crabroninae) make shallow nests in loose, sandy soil, provisioning with small, usually immature spiders, two to thirty per cell.

- The Ammophilinae (Sphecidae) use caterpillars. *Stictiella* (Crabronidae: Bembicinae) provisions with adult moths.

- *Xerostictia longilabris* (Bembicinae; SW) perhaps has the most unusual tastes, using adult antlions as well as planthoppers.

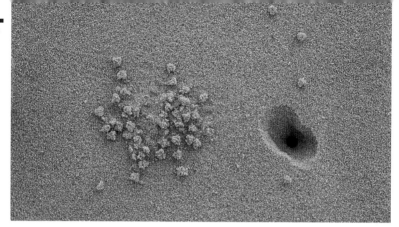

Burrow of a Coral Pink Sand Dunes tiger beetle (*Cicindela limbata albissima*), with 3-mm pellets flicked out by the larva. (UT)

All of the wasps listed here are (or include) ground nesters, but some may make burrows with no excavated earth apparent, whereas others make a pile to one side. To add a little uncertainty, note that several crabronid genera have less discriminating tastes. *Glenostictia* (Bembicinae) and *Lindenius* (Crabroninae) both include species that may prey on true bugs or adult flies or Hymenoptera. *Microbembex* species (Bembicinae) scavenge various dead arthropods. And there still are many wasp species that no one knows anything about yet.

Tiger Beetle Larvae

Burrows of tiger beetle larvae (Carabidae: Cicindelinae) sometimes have distinctive piles nearby. As a larva digs its burrow deeper, or cleans it after a heavy rain, it throws one coarse pellet of soil out of the hole at a time. Most of these pellets accumulate in a neat pile up to a few centimeters from the hole. If the soil were not discarded in a neat pile far from the burrow, the messy entrance might prevent prey from stumbling within reach of the beetle larva. Because the burrows are often quite deep, the color of the soil mounds may be markedly different from that of the surface soil.

Scorpions

Most scorpion burrows we have seen were simple holes in the ground, as described previously. In dunes of the Mojave Desert, however, we encountered giant sand scorpion (Vaejovidae: *Smeringurus mesaensis*) burrows that had mounds of excavated sand in front of the entrance. Presumably the unstable substrate requires them to reexcavate frequently.

Burrow and throw mound of a giant sand scorpion (Vaejovidae: *Smeringurus mesaensis*). The entrance is 1.2 inches (3 cm) wide by 1 cm tall. (CA)

A half-crater of excavated sand beside the entrance to a honeypot ant (Formicidae: *Myrmecocystus*) nest. The 18-inch (45-cm) mound has a 1.2-inch (3-cm) entrance. (AZ)

Ants

See the discussion of ant mounds in the previous section. Depending on the slope of the terrain and the species involved, some ant mounds may look like a semicircular crater with the hole on one side.

Underwater Burrows

In shallow puddles and standing backwaters, you can often find short tubes of sediment projecting from the bottom, 0.5 to 3 mm across. These are constructed by midge larvae (Chironomidae), whose burrows can extend up to 6 inches (15 cm) down, and usually have two entrances forming an irregular U. When the water level is low and in low-oxygen habitats, the tubes may lie on top of the soil, where they are easy to see. In marine habitats, some amphipods (e.g., Corophiidae) make similar tubes of mud or algae extending above U-shaped mucus-lined burrows in the sediment. See the section on stationary aquatic retreats and

Underwater burrows of midge larvae (Chironomidae). The holes are about 1 mm wide. (CA)

The interruption in the ripples marks the spot where a horseshoe crab (Limulidae: *Limulus polyphemus*) has buried itself. (MA)

tubes in chapter 8 for other examples of underwater burrows involving constructed tubes.

Burrowing mayfly naiads (Ephemeroidea) construct horizontal, U-shaped burrows in bottom sediment with two exposed exit holes next to each other, 1 to 5 mm in diameter. These holes can be abundant in the calm water of lakes and reservoirs. Mayflies are among the only non–tube-building aquatic invertebrates that make conspicuous burrows underwater. Other insects, such as dragonfly naiads, tend to disappear into the sediment without a trace. Larger paired, submerged holes likely belong to crayfish.

Horseshoe Crab Burrows

On protected Atlantic beaches in late spring, horseshoe crabs (Limulidae: *Limulus polyphemus*) come ashore to lay eggs. Looking out at low tide during the day, you may see slight mounds or flat spots, visible as breaks in the ripple pattern of the beach if ripples are present, marking buried crabs waiting for nighttime high tides to wash in.

Molelike Excavations and Simple Surface Trails

17

The types of sign covered in this chapter represent a transition between the burrows of chapter 16 and the trails of chapter 18. By molelike excavations, we mean disturbances created by animals moving along just under the soil surface, as opposed to material excavated from a burrow that descends into the ground. Many of these are linear features, and there is no good place to draw the line to separate such burrows from trails. Not only do some subsurface burrows look as if they could have been made by an animal moving along the surface, but a few in fact are made by animals with the top of the body exposed to the air but the bottom plowing along beneath the surface. The surface trails discussed here show no footprints, because the invertebrates that make them either lack legs or have legs that are too short to register. Trails with footprints of any kind are the subject of chapter 18.

Subsurface burrows in a cohesive substrate appear as a single raised ridge protruding above the ground, looking like a miniature mole tunnel. In some cases, this may collapse as it ages, and in certain substrates, such as saturated soils or dry sand, the tunnel may collapse as soon as the animal passes. The cross section of the resulting trail is a V-shaped central valley below the ground surface flanked by two ridges that rise above the ground surface. On slopes, the downhill ridge may be much more prominent. In contrast with subsurface burrows, the shape of a linear trail made on top of the ground surface often reflects the shape of the bottom of the animal, such as the round bottom of an earthworm or the flat foot of a snail.

Keeping the habitat context in mind is very important for distinguishing these signs. Many taxa may create similar burrows and trails, but the examples collected here are the ones most familiar to us. They are presented in a rough progression from the most clearly molelike tunnels to trails that are made entirely on the surface, with a slight deviation to group the underwater ones together.

The burrow of a mole cricket (Gryllotalpidae) alongside the much wider burrow of a mole (Talpidae) in the bank of a creek. The insect's burrow is 2 cm wide and the mammal's is 4.3 inches (11 cm). (LA)

Mole Crickets

Mole crickets (Gryllotalpidae) burrow in moist sand or mud, frequently near the edge of water. These bizarre-looking crickets have enlarged, flattened forelegs not unlike a mole's, and they are similarly used to push aside soil as they move along just beneath the surface, excavating branching horizontal tunnels that look very much like miniature mole burrows. The ones we have seen have been about 2 cm wide, but adults of the different species range from 1 to 2 inches (2.5 to 5 cm) long, and their burrow size varies accordingly. Some are insectivorous like moles, but others feed on plant roots. There may be an occasional hole where the cricket pops its head above the surface, and the burrow may go several inches underground to chambers where the female lays eggs and guards the nymphs when they hatch.

Chamberlain (1975) once watched a wasp make a burrow "almost identical to that made by mole crickets," 24 inches (60 cm) long, while it was collecting mud for a nest. The inside of this tunnel bore scrape marks typical of mud dauber mud collecting.

Pygmy Mole Crickets

Pygmy mole crickets (Tridactylidae) are in fact very small grasshoppers, not crickets. Like mole crickets, they live in moist sand or mud, usually near water. Their burrows typically are not more than a few centimeters below the surface and are often quite evident aboveground. In some cases, these insects actually construct tunnels on top of the surface by sticking

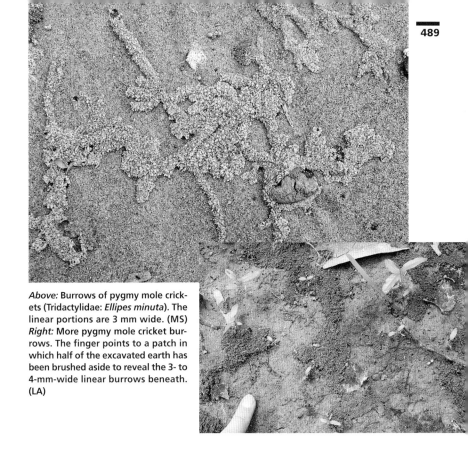

Above: Burrows of pygmy mole crickets (Tridactylidae: *Ellipes minuta*). The linear portions are 3 mm wide. (MS)
Right: More pygmy mole cricket burrows. The finger points to a patch in which half of the excavated earth has been brushed aside to reveal the 3- to 4-mm-wide linear burrows beneath. (LA)

balls of sand together and building a series of connected arches over themselves. The result is a pattern of branching, linear tunnels made of raised, processed soil that contrasts sharply with the surrounding ground texture. Surface tunnels are usually less than 4 inches (10 cm) long and vary in diameter from 3 mm to more than 1 cm. In places, they may merge into a broad patch of disturbed soil. Lightly scraping away the disturbed soil where the tunnels merge together will reveal discrete horizontal trails, 3 to 4 mm wide, etched in the ground surface.

Rove Beetles

We have found several different styles of burrows made by at least three different species of *Bledius* rove beetles (Staphylinidae), always adjacent to a water body. One, found in Texas, is illustrated in chapter 16 and involves little piles of excavated earth atop holes that descend into the ground. We discovered another type that covered large areas of wet sand on the Gulf coast of Florida. On the surface, the excavated earth was distributed similarly to the first type, but fluffier. When we brushed it aside, however, there were no holes leading underground; it was simply a surface disturbance, and the beetles could reliably be found inside the fluffed sand. A third type, and seemingly the most widespread, consists of linear, mole-

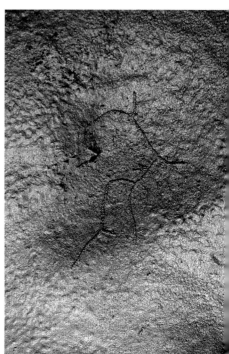

Left: Low piles of sand processed by *Bledius* rove beetles (Staphylinidae). (FL) *Right:* The 2-mm-wide larval burrows of another species of *Bledius* rove beetle in sand at the edge of a river. (WA)

like tunnels in riparian sand and mud, 1 to 5 mm wide, the smaller ones being made by larvae. These are sometimes quite long, tending to branch at nearly right angles. They may also form small, convoluted patches, reminiscent of those made by some pygmy mole crickets.

Variegated Mud-loving Beetles

On the muddy edges of fresh or brackish waters, adult variegated mud-loving beetles (Heteroceridae) dig small subsurface tunnels that branch at various angles. The tunnels curve more, are less uniform in diameter, and branch more frequently than rove beetle or mole cricket burrows. Within one tunnel system, several branches may bump into each other, and there are many dead ends. As with mole crickets and some burrows of pygmy mole crickets, the roofs of variegated mud-loving beetle burrows are said to be "hummocky," because the beetles tunnel by pushing upward, taking a few steps forward, then pushing up again.

Ground Beetle Larvae

Bryson (1939) described meandering subsurface burrows of ground beetle larvae (Carabidae) being abundant on rich organic soil in the morning or

Burrows of variegated mud-loving beetles (Heteroceridae), with 4- to 5-mm-wide tunnels. (VT)

after summer rains. These small, molelike trails are covered with granular excavated soil. They range in length from 2 to 10 inches (5 to 25 cm) and can be as dense as a hundred per square meter.

Stiletto Fly Larvae

Larvae of stiletto flies (Therevidae) burrow in dry soils such as sand dunes. Many of their subsurface burrows curve regularly back and forth on a very fine scale, forming a sinusoidal pattern with a wavelength of about 1 cm.

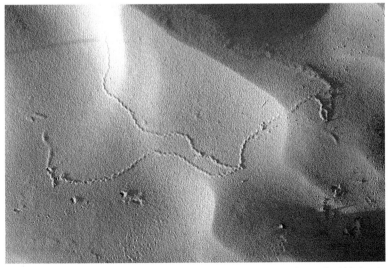

Sinusoidal trail of a stiletto fly larva (Therevidae) in a sand dune. The trail width (peak-to-peak amplitude) is 4 mm, with an 8-mm wavelength. (TX)

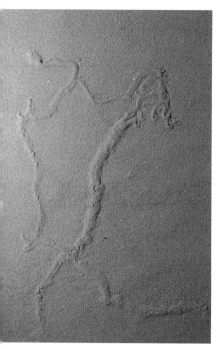

Burrow of a darkling beetle larva (Tenebrionidae) in a sand dune. (UT)

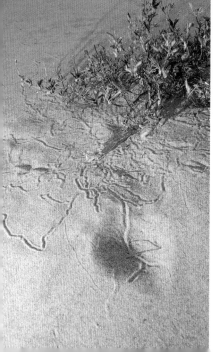

Darkling Beetle Larvae

Darkling beetles (Tenebrionidae) frequent dry, sandy areas such as dunes. The larvae of many species tunnel under the surface, forming irregularly wandering trails. We have found them to be responsible for the majority of the linear trails in western dunes, ranging from 2 to 10 mm wide. The trails may be fairly straight or erratically wiggly, but never regularly sinusoidal like those of stiletto fly larvae.

Adult Dune and Clown Beetles

Adult dune beetles (Tenebrionidae: *Coelus*) burrow just below the surface of dry sands of Pacific coastal dunes. These burrows tend to collapse immediately, producing grooves with a simple V-shaped profile. Around dune vegetation, you may see dense concentrations of dune beetle foraging trails meandering about the roots. On Cape Cod's dunes, we found similar burrows made by adult *Spilodiscus arcuatus* clown beetles (Histeridae). Trails of this particular clown beetle species, as well as the dune beetles we have encountered, measured about 12 mm wide.

Antlion Larvae

In loose, dry soils, especially in sheltered areas such as under eaves, bridges, and rock overhangs, the looping trails made by tunneling antlions (Myrmeleontidae) can often be found. These tend to have a simple V-shaped profile and are usually less than 15 mm wide. They frequently cover considerable ground only to end up fairly close to where they started. Usually the trail ends in a funnel trap, confirming its identity (see chapter 16).

Marine Isopods and Amphipods

In the high intertidal zones of beaches, several types of marine isopods tunnel under

Burrows (12 mm wide) of adult dune beetles (Tenebrionidae: *Coelus*). (OR)

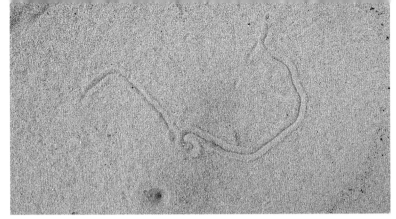

An antlion larva (Myrmeleontidae: *Myrmeleon*) trail, 2 cm wide. (FL)

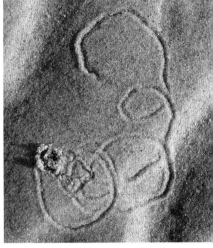

A 5-mm-wide subsurface burrow of a marine isopod in moist beach sand. (MA)

the surface of wet sand, leaving small, slightly flattened, linear subsurface burrows a few millimeters wide. The examples we have seen traced aimless, looping squiggles in the sand and had V-shaped profiles. Small amphipods also tunnel in these areas, and each species is thought to produce tunnels with distinct depths and patterns (for details, see Howard and Elders 1970).

Moon Snails

Moon snails (Naticidae) often leave trails on open, sandy intertidal flats. The moon snail cruises about with an oversize foot below the sand, searching for another mollusk to feed on, while the shell often pro-

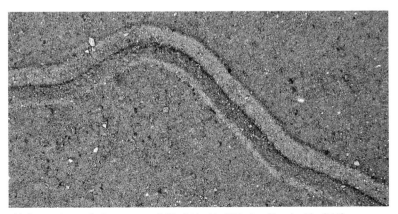

This burrowing trail of a moon snail (Naticidae) is 1.2 inches (3 cm) wide. (MA)

trudes somewhat above the surface. The trails are meandering and have a distinct V-shaped profile similar to those of antlions and other subsurface burrowers. When not hunting, moon snails sometimes glide along the surface like periwinkles. Their trails can exceed 2.4 inches (6 cm) wide.

Periwinkles

When a snail such as a periwinkle (Littorinidae: *Littorina*) crosses sandy flats in search of more solid, algae-covered substrates to graze on, it does not burrow under the sand as moon snails do. The snail's foot produces a wide, flat-bottomed trail as it glides along the surface. Under certain moisture and particle-size conditions, clumps of sand may stick to the snail's foot as it travels and be deposited in the trail. This series of irregular clumps forms a long, raised trail behind the snail, but overall it is still wide and flat.

Top: The broad, flat, 10-mm-wide trail of a periwinkle (Littorinidae: *Littorina*) on moist beach sand. (MA) *Above:* Trail of another periwinkle, with irregular clumps of sand being picked up and redeposited. (MA)

This trail of a Florida rock snail (Muricidae: *Stramonita haemastoma*) in intertidal sand is 2 inches (5 cm) wide. (FL)

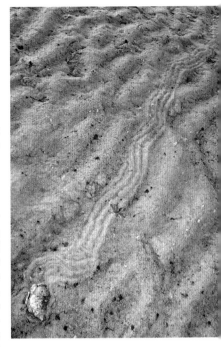

Other Marine Snails

Rock snails (Muricidae) and other gastropods with complicated shells may leave trails that consist of series of parallel drag lines. Some of these drag marks may be caused by other organisms, such as barnacles, attached to the outside of the shell.

Freshwater Mussels

Freshwater mussels (Unionoida) plow along the bottoms of the rivers and streams they inhabit. The mussel's foot and half of the shell are under the sediment, with the top of the shell sticking out. In more packed soils, a mussel's motion leaves a long groove. In loose, soft sediment, the otherwise indistinct trail may still be obvious if the mussel's mixing of the layers exposes underlying soil that is a different color than the surface.

Other Underwater Trails

In fine bottom sediments of a shallow, braided stream channel in Washington's Olympic Peninsula, we found irregularly meandering, 3-mm-wide, lumpy ridges made by subsurface tunneling of crane fly larvae (Tipulidae). Similar trails are known to be made by rat-tailed maggots (Syrphidae: *Eristalis*) in sediment under shallow, stagnant water. Soldier fly larvae (Stratiomyidae) also leave meandering trails on the surface of fine, muddy silt in shallow waters. Narrow (1-mm) subsurface burrows in underwater soil could also be made by larval midges (Chironomidae), whose burrows are punctuated by enlarged nodes where the larvae poke through the surface.

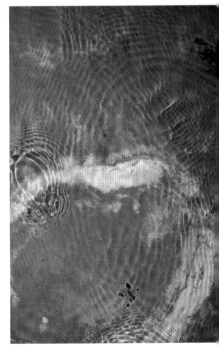

Trail of a pocketbook mussel (Unionidae: *Lampsilis*) in a river bottom, measuring 1.6 inches (4 cm) wide. (WI)

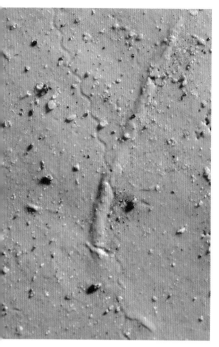

Tiny trails like this one (0.5-mm trail width, 1.3-mm wavelength) may belong to biting midge larvae (Ceratopogonidae) or roundworms (Nematoda). (ND)

Larval horseflies (Tabanidae) produce trails in sediments under a variety of aquatic habitats. Flatworms (Turbellaria) leave shallow, rounded furrows. Clam shrimp (Diplostraca) in vernal pools may make looping trails 3 mm wide that have a W-shaped cross section, with a central ridge lower than the edges.

Roundworms and Biting Midge Larvae

On the surface of wet mud, roundworms (Nematoda) and biting midge larvae (Ceratopogonidae, which have a wormlike body plan similar to that of roundworms) are known to make small but distinctive, regularly meandering sinusoidal trails that reflect their undulatory locomotion—similar to the much larger subsurface burrows of stiletto fly larvae in dry sand. Other wormlike animals and fly larvae may also be capable of producing these traces. We, and others, have found these trails on the shores of small water bodies where a thin film of water covers the mud. The wavelengths of these tiny trails are typically about 1 to 2 mm, with a peak-to-peak amplitude (trail width) of 0.5 to 1 mm, while the line itself is only about 0.2 mm wide. Examples of similar traces (known to geologists as *Cochlichnus*) in the fossil record have wavelengths up to 7 mm long and amplitudes of 4 mm.

Earthworms

At night and when it rains, earthworms (Lumbricina) come out and crawl across the ground surface, leaving trails in muddy areas. Their trails are fairly straight and

Trails of three earthworms (Lumbricidae) in a dried-up mud puddle. (VT)

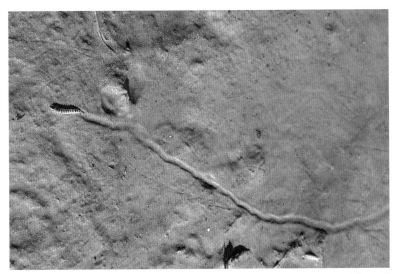

A woodland ground beetle larva (Carabidae: Pterostichini) making a wormlike trail through a mud puddle. (MA)

have relatively round bottoms. They are usually less than 5 mm wide. An earthworm that finds itself on dry sand or dust is unable to glide forward smoothly and leaves irregular broad marks as it struggles along.

Beetle Larvae

Beetle larvae moving on the ground surface can leave linear trails similar to those of earthworms, but whereas earthworms tend to leave fairly straight, uniform trails as they glide along, beetle larvae move less gracefully, and their trails tend to have an irregular wiggle to them. In Florida, we found 1-cm-wide trails where ox beetle larvae (Scarabaeidae: *Strategus*) crawled across the sand to find new places to burrow underground. Their fat, stubby bodies left wide, rounded-bottomed, uneven-width trails with transverse lines as they inched along. These are among the largest North American beetles, and various other beetle larvae may leave similar but smaller trails.

Ants

Ant colonies can create visible paths that traverse the landscape. Unlike mammal runs, these are not merely worn pathways but are made by the collective efforts of many ants actively clearing away debris and larger soil particles. Keeping their trails clear facilitates efficient movement of resources, like a well-maintained highway system. The result is often a faint path that appears as a different color than the rest of the ground. Harvester ants (*Pogonomyrmex*) often also clear living vegetation to make their trails. Looking closely, you can tell that ants are responsible because the soil parti-

Above left: Edge of a leafcutter ant (Formicidae: *Atta*) trail showing fine-scale sorting of particles. (Costa Rica) *Above right:* Galleries of red imported fire ants (Formicidae: *Solenopsis invicta*) found under a rock in a garden. (NC) Photo by Lynette Schimming. *Left:* A harvester ant (Formicidae: *Pogonomyrmex*) trail, 4 inches (10 cm) wide. (AZ)

cles are very well sorted, having been carefully relocated one at a time by diligent workers. Notice the sharp line between particle sizes at the edge of the leafcutter ant trail pictured. Leafcutter ants (*Atta*) provide extreme examples, with trails that can be 1 foot (30 cm) wide and over 650 feet (200 m) long. You may see the more modest-size trails of other ants, 1 cm or so wide, in northern woodlands. Linear, branching galleries of various species can also be found at the soil surface on the undersides of rocks and other objects on the ground.

Tracks and Trails

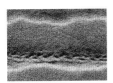

18

A pickup truck passed as we crouched in the adjoining road studying the patterns in the dust. We looked up as it stopped and backed toward us and the driver rolled down his window. This farmer was used to naturalists visiting his riverside cornfield to look for animal tracks—the bare, fine silt on the roads displays the most intricate details beautifully—but evidently he sensed that we were looking more closely than would normally be warranted. His curiosity was piqued.

"Are you guys looking at tracks or bugs?"

"Well . . . tracks of bugs, actually."

He nodded thoughtfully, then continued on his way without another word.

Learning to identify "bug tracks" may seem like a silly pursuit, but in certain habitats, they can be abundant and conspicuous enough to make even a relatively normal person stop and wonder what they are. Sand dunes are probably the most likely places for this to happen, but dusty roads and drying mud puddles often show tracks in equal or better detail, albeit in smaller doses. Tracks of larger invertebrates such as crustaceans can register clearly in firmer substrates such as riverbanks and beaches. Having six or more legs, invertebrates leave more complicated track patterns than those of two- or four-legged vertebrates, and the different patterns can be interesting puzzles to try to sort out.

In this chapter, we have divided the trails into a few groups based on the overall appearance as best we can. Generally we use *track* to refer to an individual mark of an appendage and *trail* for the whole pattern of tracks and drag marks left by the animal. The groups are as follows: alternating track groups with no central drag line; alternating track groups with a central drag line; "tire tread" trails, essentially a catchall category for more difficult to decipher trails, which may or may not have a central drag line and often evoke the image of tire treads because of their closely repeating patterns; and hopping trails. At the end is a brief discussion of underwater trails.

We do not presume to be able to tell every individual species apart by its tracks. Our aim is to provide the tools to identify trails to broader taxonomic groups. Trail sizes are often excluded from our descriptions, because the species within a single group can vary widely in size, and because many invertebrates begin life as miniature versions of adults, growing ever larger. Thus size is not normally much help in identification. The photographs in this chapter are of typical-size trails in our experience, and sizes are given in the captions in most cases. We focus on groups likely to encounter good substrates for leaving minute tracks that you might encounter in the field.

Linking trails even to broad taxonomic groups is not simple, especially given that most taxa with six legs have a roughly similar body plan that produces a similar trail pattern. Moreover, an individual invertebrate may make different types of trails depending on the circumstances. A beetle that is just slowly moseying along may leave more closely spaced tracks that are angled differently than when it is running fast. More problematic is the fact that many of these creatures are so small that individual sand grains may be larger than their feet. Because of this, invertebrate tracks vary widely with substrate. A beetle may leave nice, clean tracks in fine sand, but it might swim through fluffed silt, leaving a messy swath behind, and you might see no tracks at all when it walks over coarse sand. Furthermore, invertebrate tracks are often highly ephemeral, readily blown away by wind or wiped out by dew. Even when protected from weather, a barrage of other invertebrates may doom a set of tracks. Researchers experimenting with coastal substrates found the soils to be loaded with 0.5-mm ostracods, copepods, malacostracans, annelids, nematodes, and juvenile mollusks that completely wiped out hermit crab tracks protected inside a lab over the course of a few days. Despite all this, you can and will encounter clear invertebrate tracks if you look in the right places, and we hope that the images and descriptions collected here will help you make sense of what you find.

We invite you to experiment further, as our sample sizes are small in many cases. For maximal photo clarity, we occasionally run animals through prepared tracking boxes. For your own studies, we recommend using a wide, translucent plastic container with a tight-fitting lid, such as Tupperware, and fine, dry silt. You can get silt from riparian farm fields or filter it out of unsorted sands with a fine-mesh aquarium dip net or something similar. Light the box from the side to bring out the details, and have fun!

Alternating Track Groups with No Central Drag Line

The classic trail pattern of six-legged arthropods consists of alternating groups of three. It is produced when they walk in an alternating-tripod motion. Although many arthropods walk with this gait, only those with long legs relative to their body size leave trails with distinct individual footprints. In the photograph of the walking darkling beetle, the left front, right middle, and left rear feet are planted on the ground like a tripod, while the other three legs are moving forward together.

The positions of the tracks of individual legs vary among species and change somewhat with slope and substrate. Most of the time, the middle legs register on the outside of the trail relative to the front and hind legs. The hind *tarsus* (the leg segment that contacts the ground, plural *tarsi*) points outward behind the animal, creating a long dash with the backward part farthest from the center of the trail. The length of the dash may be extended by the foot dragging as it leaves the ground. The tarsus on the middle leg creates a similar dash, but it is angled much farther out to the side. The front footprint is often shorter and may consist of a forward-angled dash along with a perpendicular drag mark. It is sometimes obscured by the other tracks. When we indicate the direction a dash-shaped footprint is pointing or angled, we mean the trajectory followed by tracing the dash from the center to the outside of the trail. As just described, then, the tracks of an insect's front two feet typically point forward, in the direction of travel, and the tracks of the other four generally point backward, opposite from the direction of travel.

As of yet, we have not found a good way to determine speed based on trail patterns. In a walking gait, we initially hypothesized that at higher speeds, strides would be larger, and each group of three tracks would be more isolated from other groups; the middle track would land farther forward relative to the front track, so that at low speeds, the middle track would be in

Darkling beetle (Tenebrionidae: *Eleodes obscurus*) walking, trail 1.4 inches (3.5 cm) wide. (UT)

Darkling beetle (Tenebrionidae: *Eleodes hispilabris*) trail, 1.2 inches (3 cm) wide. (NM)

between the front and rear tracks, but at high speeds, both the front and rear would be behind the middle track; and the middle foot would be angled farther backward. Pilot experiments with crickets walking at varied speeds did not validate these hypotheses, however, except that tracks are spaced closer together in extremely slow searching gaits. Further study is warranted.

Darkling Beetles

Darkling beetles (Tenebrionidae) of the genus *Eleodes* are large, long-legged beetles whose tracks are readily found in sand dunes. Tracks left by the front, middle, and hind feet tend to differ from each other within a trail. Marks left by hind feet are long and straight, pointing mostly backward, and those made by the middle feet are similar but angled farther out to the side. The front feet tend to be the smallest and angle slightly forward. In general, tracks made by all of their tarsi are thin and simple, reflecting their slender, mostly bristle-free legs. *Eleodes* trails can be 1.6 inches (4 cm) wide.

Ground Beetles

Ground beetles (Carabidae) tend to have much shorter legs then *Eleodes*, and thus there is less space between track groups. The track of the middle leg is often noticeably smaller than the hind track. The hind and front tracks may join together to look like a continuous bent line. In deeper soil,

Ground beetle (Carabidae: *Harpalus*) trail, 15 mm wide, headed to left. Note how front and hind tracks join to form a single bent line. (MA)

Ground beetle (Carabidae) trails crisscrossing on a silty road. (MA)

or when moving uphill, the hind tracks stretch into unbroken drag lines down the trail, with the other legs registering outside these lines. Burying beetle (Silphidae: *Nicrophorus*) trails we have seen are similar.

Earwigs

Although earwig (Dermaptera) trails are similar to those of ground beetles, in our limited studies the tracks of the hind and front feet seem much straighter and more rigidly parallel than the slightly curved, angled hind tracks of beetles. Perhaps their low profile makes for less wobble in their hind tracks.

Earwig (Dermaptera) trail headed to right, 1 cm wide.

Erratic trail of a common shore tiger beetle (Carabidae: *Cicindela repanda*) headed to right, 15 mm to 2 cm wide. (MA)

Tiger Beetles

Tiger beetles (Carabidae: Cicindelinae) are medium-size, fast-moving, predaceous beetles frequently encountered in open, sandy areas and on dusty roads across North America. Their trails can be very similar to those of other ground beetles, although the strides tend to be longer, with more negative space between tracks. A typical tiger beetle trail is also more erratic than a typical ground beetle trail, with frequent direction changes and spots where the beetle flies up and lands not too far away. The much longer hind tarsi are often quite evident. If you can use weather conditions to age the trails, this may help you decide whether they were made by diurnal tiger beetles or nocturnal ground beetles.

Ants

Individual ant (Formicidae) trails may be very small, but they are basically similar to beetle trails. The innermost footprints tend to be made by the front feet, and the individual tracks are sometimes distinctly curved.

Ant (Formicidae) trail headed to right, 9 mm wide. (MA)

House cricket (Gryllidae: *Acheta domesticus*) trail headed to top of frame, 24 mm wide.

Field Crickets

In field cricket (Gryllidae: Gryllinae) trails, the hind footprints may be parallel, as in earwig trails, or angle out to the sides. The middle feet often register far from the trail center and point almost straight out to the side, in some cases making perfect right angles with the hind tracks. Perhaps these long side legs offer stability while jumping. Although this middle foot position is characteristic, it can also be rotated backward, leaving trails more like those of darkling beetles. Crickets have more bristles on their legs than darkling beetles, and you may sometimes find these registering in their tracks. Large individuals may drag their back feet, leaving continuous lines down the trail. The palps (mouth appendages), the plump abdomen of a mature female cricket, and the female ovipositor often make intermittent marks along the trail center.

"Sand Treader" Camel Crickets

Certain camel crickets (Rhaphidophoridae), known as "sand treaders," are specially adapted for living in sand dunes. Large sets of bristles on their hind legs help push them through loose sand. When a sand treader

Left: "Sand treader" camel cricket (Rhaphidophoridae: *Ammobaenetes*) trail, 2 cm wide. *Right:* Detail of the same sand treader's trail, showing marks of bristles used for maneuvering in loose sand. (UT)

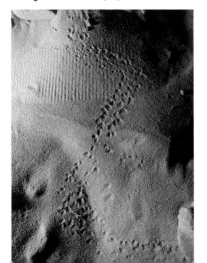

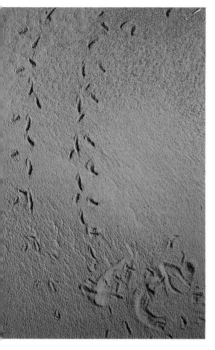

Vinegaroon (Thelyphonidae: *Mastigoproctus giganteus*) trail headed to the top of the photo, 2.6 inches (6.5 cm) wide.

walks in fine sand, the bristles may register separately; in other substrates, they may merge together to make it look as though the animal has overly fat feet.

Vinegaroons

You probably will not often encounter tracks of vinegaroons (Thelyphonidae: *Mastigoproctus giganteus*), because they tend to live under debris in microhabitats with subprime tracking conditions. Their trails are quite distinctive, however, and should be recognizable if encountered. Although they are arachnids, vinegaroons walk on only six legs. They have a very wide stance with a lot of negative space in the trail center; short strides with much overlap between track groups; and short, straight tarsal prints of similar lengths and at distinct angles from each other. Trail width is up to 2.6 inches (6.5 cm).

Scorpions

Although scorpions usually walk with eight legs, the prints of the front feet often do not register or are obscured by those of the other feet, producing trails that may be confused with darkling beetle trails. The tarsal segments are all very short, and as a result, the actual foot impression is a small, oval dot. When they do not drag their feet, scorpions' tracks are grouped in distinct, neat clusters of three or four dots. They often do drag their feet, however, making marks similar to those of long beetle tarsi. This may be more common at warmer temperatures when they are more active (see Brady 1947). In a scorpion trail, all of the footprints are very similar to each other and regularly spaced within each track cluster. The lines produced by foot drag are

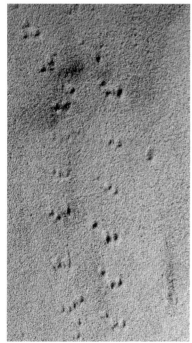

Trail of giant sand scorpion (Vaejovidae: *Smeringurus mesaensis*), 1.8 inches (4.5 cm) wide. (CA)

usually distinctly curved and nearly paral-lel to the direction of travel. In contrast to darkling beetles, scorpions also tend to have more negative space in the center of the trail, shorter strides, occasional "tail" (*metasoma*) drag, and occasionally oppo-site placement of track groups along the trail. Trails of adult bark scorpions (*Cen-truroides*) may be only 15 mm wide, but we have measured trails of both giant hairy scorpions (Iuridae: *Hadrurus*) and giant sand scorpions (Vaejovidae: *Smeringurus mesaensis*) at 1.8 inches (4.5 cm) wide.

Spiders

Spiders walk on eight legs, and sorting out the feet in a spider trail can be confusing. At first they may look like a scattered mess of dots and dashes, but enough staring usu-ally reveals some kind of pattern. Often repeating groups of four are readily appar-ent. Unlike those of scorpions, in spider tracks, the different feet within a group tend to have different shapes, angles, and positions that are maintained over many strides. Sometimes, as with funnel-web spi-der (Agelenidae) tracks, the front four feet register as small dots, while the other four register as longer, curved line segments.

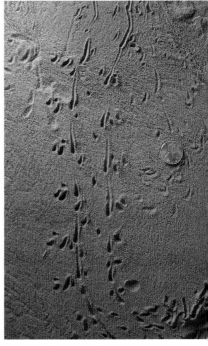

Tarantula (Theraphosidae: *Aphon-opelma chalcodes*) trail headed to top, 2.6 inches (6.7 cm) wide, with the pedipalps registering and the hind tarsi leaving drag marks.

In tarantula trails, all eight legs usually register as short, stubby line segments or simple dots. The hind tarsi may sometimes be dragged, leav-

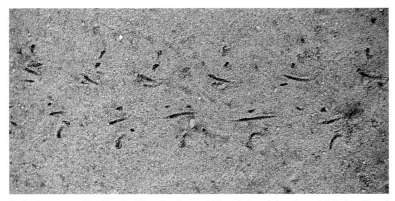

Trail of a grass spider (Agelenidae: *Agelenopsis*) headed to right, about 1.2 inches (3 cm) wide. (MA)

ing longer lines. The *pedipalps* (leglike appendages around the mouth) often register as two additional marks near the trail center. Tarantula trails can exceed 4 inches (10 cm) in width.

Alternating Track Groups with a Central Drag Line

Trails in this section may be similar to some of those described in the previous section, but they differ in having a more or less conspicuous drag line down the middle. The size and shape of this line varies considerably depending on what is being dragged, ranging from the pointed tip of a wasp's abdomen to the broad, rounded body of a Jerusalem cricket.

Rove Beetles

In large rove beetles (Staphylinidae), the tip of the abdomen drags and leaves three continuous lines down the trail center. These are also present in trails of smaller rove beetles we have seen, but they can appear to be one broad line, particularly in a coarser-grained substrate. The shape and pattern of tarsal tracks are similar to those of other beetles.

Blister Beetles

In blister beetle (Meloidae) trails, the bulbous abdomen leaves a continuous deep drag down the center. This central drag mark is fairly narrow compared with the trail width, leaving some negative space between the body drag and tarsal tracks. The hind and middle tarsal tracks are long, with the terminal portion curving gracefully outward and forward like thick eyelashes lined up along the trail. Strides may be short, leaving little space between sets of tracks.

Adult hairy rove beetle (Staphylinidae: *Creophilus maxillosus*) trail moving to right, 15 mm wide. (MA)

Blister beetle (Meloidae) trail headed to left, 2 cm wide. (MA)

Long-horned Beetles

In Zion National Park, a large long-horned beetle (Cerambycidae) crossed our path, leaving a trail similar to that of a darkling beetle, with large tarsi and short strides, but a wide, flat body drag in the center. The front legs registered farther forward and out to the side than in typical darkling beetle tracks.

Jerusalem Crickets

Jerusalem crickets (Stenopelmatidae) have the classic tarsal tracks reminiscent of *Eleodes* beetles, but with a wide, round body drag. The heavy, stout stature is reflected in their deep, short-strided tracks. Large tarsal bristles may register in the tracks and may produce drag marks.

Long-horned beetle (Cerambycidae: Prioninae: Macrotomini) trail headed to top, 1.8 inches (4.5 cm) wide. (UT)

Jerusalem cricket (Stenopelmatidae: *Stenopelmatus*) trail headed to top, 1.8 inches (4.5 cm) wide. (CA)

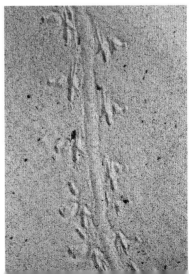

Yellowjacket (Vespidae: *Vespula*) trail headed to left. (MA)

Wasps

Trails of various wasps may be found near stream banks approaching water. Based on our limited observations, the wasp's downward-pointed abdomen produces a prominent, deep, narrow, V-shaped central line in the trail. In yellowjackets (Vespidae: *Vespula*), the front and hind feet register at the same distance from the trail center and may overlap to form one continuous curve. The middle feet register out to the side as very short line segments, and unlike those of most other insects, they point forward.

One might expect long-legged hunting wasps, which spend more time on the ground, not to drag their abdomens. When we watched a spider wasp (Pompilidae) leaving tracks in Michigan's Sleeping Bear Dunes, however, the central line was the most prominent feature of the trail. The hind and middle legs left long, outwardly curved, backward-pointing tracks that were fairly indistinct.

Scorpions

See the description of scorpion track patterns in the previous section. Because the "tail" (metasoma) drags so far behind the body when it registers, as a scorpion turns, the position of the tail drag relative to the track centerline may change. Murie and Elbroch (2005) suggest that a scorpion trail without a tail drag indicates that the animal was in a defensive posture. The vast majority of scorpion tracks we have encountered did not have a tail drag, however, including some that we followed for hundreds of feet. There are no doubt differences among the many species in this regard.

Sun Spiders

In our few encounters with sun spider (Solifugae) trails, they are reminiscent of a wide-straddled trail of a true spider, with a broad central drag that sometimes registers. Sun spiders seem very lightweight for their size, so their trails are fairly faint.

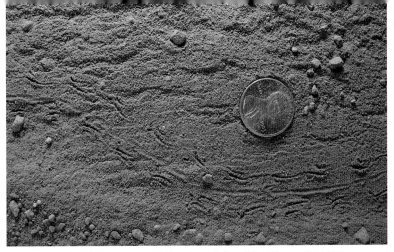

Bark scorpion (Buthidae: *Centruroides*) trail headed to right, 15 mm wide. (AZ)

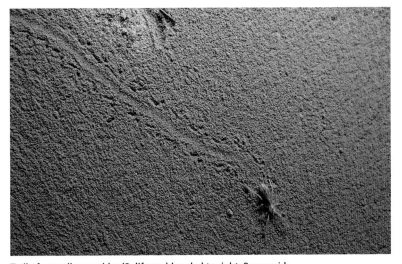

Trail of a small sun spider (Solifugae) headed to right, 8 mm wide.

Centipedes

Murie's (1954) illustration of a centipede (Chilopoda) trail closely resembles the millipede trails we have seen. In our experience with giant centipedes (Scolopendridae: *Scolopendra heros*) of the desert Southwest, these trails superficially resemble the alternating trails of lizards more than they do those of other invertebrates.

If you put your eye at ground level and watch a giant centipede moving by, you will see all of the legs on one side of the body touching down in the same place, then moving like a wave, one after the other, to the next place to touch down. Because the legs are so long, the stride length is fairly significant. Viewed from above, the centipede's body winds gently back and forth around the staggered footfalls.

Above left: Trail of a giant redheaded centipede (Scolopendridae: *Scolopendra heros*) moving quickly to the top, 1.8 inches (4.5 cm) wide. *Above right:* Resting place in the trail of a giant redheaded centipede (Scolopendridae: *Scolopendra heros*), 1.2 inches (3 cm) wide. (TX) *Left:* Trail of a giant redheaded centipede (Scolopendridae: *Scolopendra heros*) moving slowly to the right, 1.2 inches (3 cm) wide. (TX)

The alternate track groups in a centipede trail each consist of many tiny dots together in a short row. There is also usually a wide body drag in the center. In fine sediment, the body sections may sometimes leave transverse lines in the drag mark. When a centipede stops, all of its legs fan out and touch down, though they may continue to wave, and you will find a short section that more closely resembles the continuous trail of a millipede. Giant desert centipede trails can exceed 1.6 inches (4 cm) wide, with running strides of more than 2.2 inches (5.5 cm).

"Tire Tread" Trails: Intricate, Continuous Patterns

In these types of trails, the tracks and drag marks are spaced so closely together, or are so numerous, that the individual tracks may be difficult to distinguish. At first glance, these trails read like a continuous pattern, as if a miniature treaded tire rolled by.

A beach crisscrossed with fiddler crab (Ocypodidae: *Uca*) tracks. (MA)

Fiddler and Ghost Crabs

Walking along a sandy beach at low tide, you are likely to encounter tracks of fiddler and ghost crabs (Ocypodidae) running about, often to and from their burrows. These crabs walk sideways on eight legs, which register as a series of dots laid in a complicated repeating pattern with telltale asymmetry. Because they usually walk sideways, unlike in all the other trails we describe, the track pattern on the left side differs from the pattern on the right; the left and right are not simply forward-shifted mirror images of each other about the centerline as in darkling beetle trails. Sometimes the dots of the feet line up in parallel rows cutting across the trail at a sharp angle.

Hermit Crabs

The trail of a hermit crab (Paguroidea) usually has a broad drag mark in the middle left by the shell, although the nature of this drag mark depends in part on the type of shell the crab is wearing. Some crabs can walk without dragging the shell at all, but there is still a large negative space in the trail center. On each side of the trail is a row of footmarks, which may be placed either directly opposite each other or alternately. These are made by two pairs of relatively thick walking legs that curve back around the shell as the crab walks. The resulting individual tracks are short, wide, curved

Trail of a hermit crab (Paguroidea), 22 mm wide. (MA)

line segments with the pointier end aimed backward. The angle of these leg tracks can point either inward or outward. In the tracks of terrestrial hermit crabs observed in Costa Rica, the backward point consistently aimed inward. Tracks of more aquatic hermit crabs on Cape Cod, Massachusetts, seem to have the opposite pattern. Hermit crabs are capable of moving in any direction, sometimes turning around to climb hills, get past obstacles, or avoid threats. We watched one with an awkwardly shaped shell continuously spinning around while walking a straight path.

Horseshoe Crab

Horseshoe crabs (Limulidae: *Limulus polyphemus*) congregate in large numbers on Atlantic beaches, especially in protected bays, during the spring breeding season. Their trails can be as wide as car tires (8 inches [20 cm]) and consist of a central tail (*telson*) drag, shell (*carapace*) drag at the outer edges, and a complicated pattern of footfalls in between. The hatchlings leave tiny versions of the same trail, which may resemble those of dragonfly naiads but in the wrong habitat. Horseshoe crabs have one set of small front legs that they mostly use to feed, followed by four sets of larger walking legs, and finally a hind set of larger specialized pushing legs. All of their legs terminate in claws, but the last pair has extra projections that can fan out like snowshoes. They sometimes burrow a bit as they walk, pushing aside sediment, which is deposited as ridges on both sides of the trail. Some-

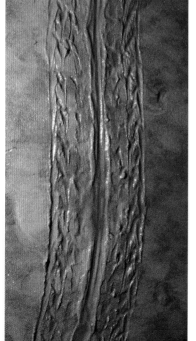

times the trail terminates in a mound of sand, beneath which a horseshoe crab waits for the tide to come in.

Mole Crabs

Mole crab (Hippidae) tracks are not commonly encountered, as these animals forage in the surf zone, burying themselves in the sand before the waves recede. Under just the right conditions, they may leave trails with alternating impressions of robust appendages. If you follow one of these trails, it should end very shortly in a burrow.

Sandhoppers

When they walk on sandy beaches of just the right firmness, amphipod sandhoppers (Talitridae) leave 2-cm-wide trails of alternating tracks with short strides. The slender tracks of their individual feet, which

Trail of a horseshoe crab (Limulidae: *Limulus polyphemus*). (NJ)

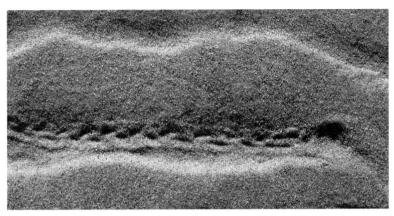

This appears to be the uncommon walking trail of a mole crab (Hippidae). (MA)

Sandhopper (Talitridae) walking trail headed to right, 2 cm wide. (MA)

stick far out to the sides, are aimed perpendicular to the direction of travel and curved backward.

Crayfish

The thin drag marks left by the outer edges of the tail projections (called *uropods*) are usually an obvious distinguishing feature of crayfish (Astacoidea) trails. Trails appear as two well-spaced parallel lines, with tracks from the legs registering outside these lines. Crayfish walk primarily on the four pairs of legs (*pereiopods* 2 through 5) behind their claws (pereiopod 1), the first two of which have two fingers at the ends that form small pincers. Tracks often register in groups of three or four, depending on whether the last pair of legs leaves distinguishable imprints. The arrangement is reminiscent of a scorpion's trail, not surprisingly, given the similarity in body plan. On good substrates, the pincers on each of the front two leg pairs register as two distinct dots.

Top: Trail of a crayfish (Cambaridae) with clear tail drag. (MA) *Above:* Crayfish trail in a fairly firm substrate, with only the pereiopod tips registering. Note the paired dots from the pincers. (MA)

Dragonfly Naiads

When dragonfly naiads are ready to emerge as adults, they crawl out of their natal water to find a good spot to affix their old exoskeletons before bursting out the back and eventually flying away. On the shore, the naiad often leaves behind a trail consisting of three parallel lines. The central line is the deepest, a V-shaped groove carved by the body dragging along. The outer two lines are made by the legs, which usually are all about the same distance from the trail center and may overlap considerably. In firmer substrates, individual footprints may be discernible; in wet mud, the feet can produce troughs as continuous as the center drag line.

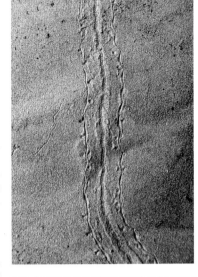

Trail of a dragonfly naiad (Anisoptera) crawling on shore, 15 mm wide. (MA)

There is considerable variation in the morphology of dragonfly naiads, and some likely leave broader central drag marks than we have witnessed. We have not seen trails of emerging stonefly naiads or dobsonfly larvae, but these and other insects with aquatic immature stages should be considered as suspects when you find trails emerging from water.

Millipedes

Millipedes (Diplopoda) have many legs, all of which register more or less in a row along each side of the trail. Their legs move in waves and form concentrations of dots, with the deepest part on the outside edge of the trail. There is a large amount of negative space in the center of the trail between the footprints. A feature peculiar to millipede trails is the presence of occasional places where the millipede changes direction abruptly or stops forward movement while searching with its head from

Right: Millipede (Xystodesmidae: *Pachydesmus crassicutis*) trail headed to the top of the photo, 15 mm wide. (MS) *Below:* Millipede (Xystodesmidae: *Harpaphe*) trail headed to right, 1 cm wide. Note where the animal swept its head from side to side. (CA)

Sowbug (*Porcellionidae*) trail headed to left, 6 mm wide. (CA)

side to side. At these locations, the front of the millipede starts in one direction but then sweeps over to a new direction, pivoting from a point in the middle of the body. This creates a fan-shaped pattern like the wing of a snow angel, and it tells you the direction of travel. Large millipede trails (e.g., Xystodesmidae: *Pachydesmus crassicutis*) are up to 15 mm wide.

Woodlice (Sowbugs, Pillbugs, Roly-Polies)

Woodlouse (Isopoda: Oniscidea) trails are similar to millipede trails, but with much less negative space in the center. In contrast to millipedes, individual tracks left by woodlouse feet are large relative to the trail width, blocky, and about as deep on the inner part of the trail as on the outer part. In some conditions, woodlice also leave a row of impressions down the trail center almost as if a third line of feet were marching underneath the animal.

Caterpillars

As a caterpillar inches along, the anal prolegs at the end of its body work in tandem to push the animal forward. With short strides, these final stubby appendages stomp out the tracks of the other legs. The result is a

Trail of a white-lined sphinx moth caterpillar (Sphingidae: *Hyles lineata*). (MA)

Trail of a fall webworm caterpillar (Arctiidae: *Hyphantria cunea*). (MA)

series of paired tracks, side by side, with very little negative space. Hairy caterpillars, such as the larvae of tiger moths (Arctiidae), leave a swath of fine, feathery drag marks on each side of the trail.

Grasshoppers

Walking grasshoppers (Acrididae) tend to leave a narrow abdomen drag line in the center of the trail and a row of relatively stubby tarsal tracks on each side of the trail, although there is great variation among species. The central drag may be continuous, intermittent, or absent. There is usually a lot of negative space between the center drag and the leg marks, and very little space between the individual tracks in each row of foot marks (in other words, the strides are very short relative to the straddle). Tracks of the middle legs tend to register farthest from the trail center and be the most conspicuous. If you squint, these tracks might appear as two continuous dotted lines bounding the trail. The center drag mark can stray noticeably from the center, meandering closer to one set of legs or the other. Presumably this is because the long legs allow great flexibility in their position relative to the body. Look for these trails to end in a jump or a resting burrow.

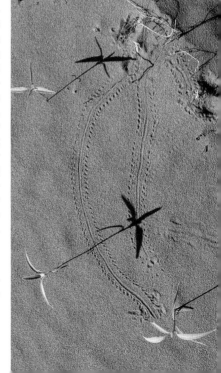

Walking trail of toothed dune grasshopper (Acrididae: *Trimerotropis agrestis*); moving clockwise, 1 inch (2.5 cm) wide. (UT)

Kissing bug (Reduviidae: *Triatoma*) trail headed to left, 2 cm wide.

Assassin Bugs

The few kissing bug (Reduviidae: *Triatoma*) trails we have seen each had a broad, shallow central body drag, with a continuous wavy line on each side from the front and hind legs. The middle feet registered as short, outward-pointing dashes outside these lines.

Dragging Trails with Short Strides

When insects that are not built for walking on loose substrates encounter fluffed fine soil, wet mud, or uphill sandy slopes, they often have difficulty walking with a normal gait, and instead their tracks look as if they were swimming through the soil. The body leaves a wide, continuous drag mark, flanked on both sides by numerous closely spaced, outward-pointing dashes left by their legs trying to inch the body forward. Scarab beetles, with their fat, bumbling bodies, are especially prone to making these trails. Most other beetles leave similar patterns under certain circumstances, and we have seen comparable trails made

Weevil (Curculionidae: *Apleurus saginatus*) trail headed to top, 15 mm wide. (NM)

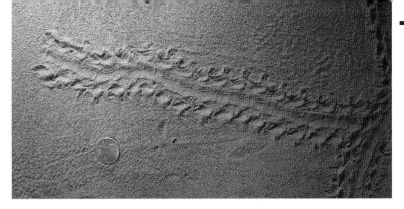

Top: Rhinoceros beetle (Scarabaeidae: *Xyloryctes jamaicensis*) trail headed to right, 1.7 inches (4.2 cm) wide. *Center:* June bug (Scarabaeidae: *Phyllophaga*) trail headed to left, 1.4 inches (3.5 cm) wide. (MA) *Bottom:* Trail of an emerging periodical cicada nymph (Cicadidae: *Magicicada*) headed to left, 1.2 inches (3 cm) wide. Although these tracks were created in a sandbox, and most periodical cicadas would never encounter good tracking substrates, relatives living in dune environments might be expected to make trails like this one.

Silverfish (Lepismatidae) trail headed to left, 6 mm wide. (MA)

by cicada nymphs, earwigs, silverfish, moths, various true bugs, and many more. Chamberlain (1975) described seeing an injured earwig in a mud puddle making tracks that looked like the complex grazing marks of a marine organism.

Hopping Trails

Hopping is an uncommon mode of locomotion among invertebrates that frequent good tracking substrates. Although we have facilitated some nice jumping spider tracks by placing a spider in a sandbox, we have encountered only two examples of hopping arthropod tracks in natural circumstances.

Sandhoppers

Amphipods in the family Talitridae are aptly called sandhoppers, among many other names. They are typically nocturnal and hide under debris during the day, but at dusk, they can be seen in large numbers springing like popcorn on coastal sand. Each time one lands, it leaves a small, round indentation, and these are erratically spaced, 4 to 8 inches (10 to 20 cm) apart, more or less.

Grasshoppers

A set of hopping grasshopper tracks is composed of two deep impressions left by the rear legs, with four lighter tracks radiating out like the four toes on a rodent's front foot. When a grasshopper moves with short hops, the long abdomen can make a continuous or intermittent drag line down the

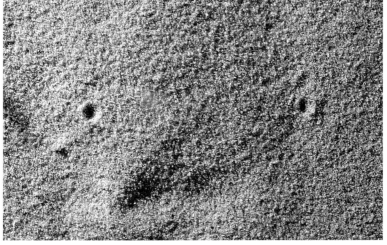

Sandhopper (Talitridae) tracks, 7 mm wide and spaced 3.7 inches (9.5 cm) apart. (MA)

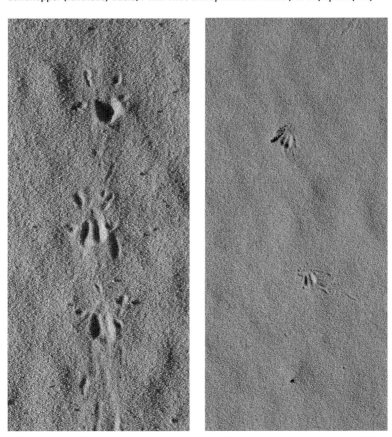

Left: Hopping trail of a toothed dune grasshopper (Acrididae: *Trimerotropis agrestis*) facing top, 1.2 inches (3 cm) wide. (UT) *Right:* Another hopping trail of a toothed dune grasshopper, facing top. Compare with the "mysterious tracks" in Murie (1954) and see what you think. (UT)

trail center. On harder substrates, only the rear legs may register. A trail of longer hops on a firm surface can look very much like the mysterious "elfin deer" tracks described and illustrated by Murie (1954).

Underwater Trails

In soft sediment at the bottom of freshwater bodies, you may see a variety of invertebrate trails, some of which are apparent from the shore. Many are simple lines, as discussed in chapter 17. In the right substrate, a caddisfly larva leaves a drag mark from its portable case, flanked by a row of dots on each side made by its legs. Writhing horsehair worms (Gordioidea) leave brush marks on the bottoms of shallow puddles. Amphipod legs scratching the substrate leave a series of small, crisscrossing slash marks when the animal is crawling upright, but an amphipod may also lie on its side and create a series of irregular marks as it plows through the sediment.

A recent study (Knecht et al. 2009) of the tadpole shrimp (Triopsidae: *Triops longicaudatus*) native to western North America showed that they make a variety of interesting traces. When they dig into the sediment, tadpole shrimp leave paired, angled depressions reminiscent of deer tracks. The continuous trails of tadpole shrimp crawling along the sediment surface resemble large (to 15 mm wide) millipede trails with added thin drag marks on the inside and occasionally farther out from the trail. The tail-like appendages (*thoracopods*) that produce the inner drag marks are sometimes all that registers as the tadpole shrimp swim near the bottom, leaving pairs of long, thin, slightly angled lines as if only the outer edges of a deer hoof registered, each pair about one and a half times as long as wide.

Traces deep underwater are prone to being preserved and even fossilized by constantly accumulating sediment, and they have thus attracted considerable attention from geologists. These are beyond the scope of this book, but for more information, take a look at Crimes and Harper (1970), Sarjeant (1983), Donovan (1994), Bromley (1996), Miller (2007), or the journal *Ichnos*.

APPENDIX A:
Plants Mentioned in this Book

Common Name	Latin Name	Family
Acacia	*Acacia*	Fabaceae
Agave	*Agave*	Agavaceae
Agrimony	*Agrimonia*	Rosaceae
Ailanthus	*Ailanthus altissima*	Simaroubaceae
Alder	*Alnus*	Betulaceae
Alfalfa	*Medicago*	Fabaceae
Alumroot, American	*Heuchera americana*	Saxifragaceae
Andromeda	*Pieris japonica*	Ericaceae
Apple	*Malus* (usually *pumila*)	Rosaceae
Apricot	*Prunus armeniaca*	Rosaceae
Arborvitae	*Thuja occidentalis*	Cupressaceae
Arrowgrass	*Triglochin*	Juncaginaceae
Arrowwood	*Viburnum dentatum*	Caprifoliaceae
Ash	*Fraxinus*	Oleaceae
Ash, White	*Fraxinus americana*	Oleaceae
Asparagus	*Asparagus officinalis*	Asparagaceae
Aspen, Bigtooth	*Populus grandidentata*	Salicaceae
Aspen, Quaking	*Populus tremuloides*	Salicaceae
Aster		Asteraceae
Aster, Flat-topped	*Doellingeria umbellata*	Asteraceae
Aster, Heart-leaved	*Symphyotrichum cordifolium*	Asteraceae
Avocado	*Persea americana*	Lauraceae
Azalea	*Rhododendron*	Ericaceae
Baccharis	*Baccharis*	Asteraceae
Basswood	*Tilia americana*	Tiliaceae
Bayberry	*Morella caroliniensis*	Myricaceae
Beaksedge, Shortbristle Horned	*Rhynchospora corniculata*	Cyperaceae
Bean, Lima	*Phaseolus lunatus*	Fabaceae
Bean, Nicker	*Entada gigas*	Fabaceae
Beebalm	*Monarda*	Lamiaceae
Beech	*Fagus*	Fagaceae
Beet (incl. Sugar Beet	*Beta vulgaris*	Chenopodiaceae
Bergamot, Wild	*Monarda fistulosa*	Lamiaceae
Bindweed, Hedge	*Calystegia sepium*	Convolvulaceae
Birch, Black	*Betula lenta*	Betulaceae
Birch, Gray	*Betula populifolia*	Betulaceae
Birch, Paper	*Betula papyrifera*	Betulaceae
Birch, River	*Betula nigra*	Betulaceae

Common Name	Latin Name	Family
Birch, Yellow	*Betula alleghaniensis*	Betulaceae
Bittersweet	*Celastrus*	Celastraceae
Blackberry	*Rubus*	Rosaceae
Bladdernut	*Staphylea trifolia*	Staphyleaceae
Blueberry	*Vaccinium*	Ericaceae
Bluegrass, Canada	*Poa compressa*	Poaceae
Boxelder	*Acer negundo*	Sapindaceae
Boxleaf, Oregon	*Pachystima myrsinites*	Celastraceae
Boxthorn	*Lycium*	Solanaceae
Boxwood	*Buxus*	Buxaceae
Bramble	*Rubus*	Rosaceae
Breeches, Dutchman's	*Dicentra cucullaria*	Fumariaceae
Bromegrass	*Bromus*	Poaceae
Buckbrush	*Ceanothus cuneatus*	Rhamnaceae
Buckthorn	*Frangula; Rhamnus*	Rhamnaceae
Buckthorn, California	*Frangula californica*	Rhamnaceae
Buckthorn, Lanceleaf	*Rhamnus lanceolata*	Rhamnaceae
Buckwheat family		Polygonaceae
Bugleweed	*Lycopus*	Lamiaceae
Bulrush	*Schoenoplectus; Scirpus*	Cyperaceae
Bulrush, River	*Schoenoplectus fluviatilis*	Cyperaceae
Bunchberry	*Cornus canadensis*	Cornaceae
Burdock	*Arctium*	Asteraceae
Bur-reed	*Sparganium*	Sparganiaceae
Butternut	*Juglans cinerea*	Juglandaceae
Cabbage	*Brassica oleracea*	Brassicaceae
Caper	*Capparis*	Capparaceae
Carrot (wild or otherwise)	*Daucus carota*	Apiaceae
Catalpa	*Catalpa*	Bignoniaceae
Cattail	*Typha*	Typhaceae
Ceanothus, Desert	*Ceanothus greggii*	Rhamnaceae
Ceanothus, Hairy	*Ceanothus oliganthus*	Rhamnaceae
Ceanothus, Hoaryleaf	*Ceanothus crassifolius*	Rhamnaceae
Cedar		Cupressaceae
Cedar, Incense	*Calocedrus decurrens*	Cupressaceae
Cherry, Black	*Prunus serotina*	Rosaceae
Cherry, Hollyleaf	*Prunus ilicifolia*	Rosaceae
Chestnut	*Castanea*	Fagaceae
Chokeberry	*Photinia*	Rosaceae
Chokecherry	*Prunus virginiana*	Rosaceae
Cholla	*Cylindropuntia*	Cactaceae
Chrysanthemum	*Chrysanthemum*	Asteraceae
Cinquefoil	*Potentilla*	Rosaceae
Citrus	*Citrus*	Rutaceae
Clearweed	*Pilea pumila*	Urticaceae
Clematis	*Clematis*	Ranunculaceae
Cleome	*Cleome*	Cleomaceae
Clover	*Trifolium*	Fabaceae
Clover, Alsike	*Trifolium hybridum*	Fabaceae
Clover, Bush	*Lespedeza*	Fabaceae
Clover, Red	*Trifolium pratense*	Fabaceae

Common Name	Latin Name	Family
Clover, White	*Trifolium repens*	Fabaceae
Cocklebur	*Xanthium*	Asteraceae
Coltsfoot, Arctic Sweet	*Petasites frigidus*	Asteraceae
Columbine	*Aquilegia*	Ranunculaceae
Columbine, Garden	*Aquilegia vulgaris*	Ranunculaceae
Coneflower	*Rudbeckia*	Asteraceae
Copperleaf	*Acalypha*	Euphorbiaceae
Cordgrass	*Spartina*	Poaceae
Corn	*Zea mays*	Poaceae
Cotton	*Gossypium*	Malvaceae
Cottonwood	*Populus*	Salicaceae
Cottonwood, Fremont	*Populus fremontii*	Salicaceae
Cowpea	*Vigna*	Fabaceae
Coyote Brush	*Baccharis pilularis*	Asteraceae
Cranberry	*Vaccinium*	Ericaceae
Creeper, Trumpet	*Campsis radicans*	Bignoniaceae
Creeper, Virginia	*Parthenocissus*	Vitaceae
Creosote Bush	*Larrea tridentata*	Zygophyllaceae
Croton	*Croton*	Euphorbiaceae
Currant	*Ribes*	Grossulariaceae
Currant, Wax	*Ribes cereum*	Grossulariaceae
Custard-apple	*Annona*	Annonaceae
Cypress	*Cupressus*	Cupressaceae
Cypress, Bald	*Taxodium distichum*	Cupressaceae
Cypress, Lawson's	*Chamaecyparis lawsoniana*	Cupressaceae
Dahlia	*Dahlia*	Asteraceae
Dandelion	*Taraxacum officinale*	Asteraceae
Dewberry, Northern	*Rubus flagellaris*	Rosaceae
Dewberry, Pacific	*Rubus vitifolius*	Rosaceae
Dock	*Rumex*	Polygonaceae
Dock, Bitter	*Rumex obtusifolius*	Polygonaceae
Dogbane	*Apocynum*	Apocynaceae
Dogwood	*Cornus*	Cornaceae
Douglas-fir	*Pseudotsuga*	Pinaceae
Eggplant	*Solanum melongena*	Solanaceae
Elderberry	*Sambucus*	Caprifoliaceae
Elm	*Ulmus*	Ulmaceae
Elm, American	*Ulmus americana*	Ulmaceae
Eucalyptus	*Eucalyptus*	Myrtaceae
Eucalyptus, Lemon Gum	*Corymbia citriodora*	Myrtaceae
Eucalyptus, Spotted Gum	*Corymbia maculata*	Myrtaceae
Eugenia	*Eugenia*	Myrtaceae
Euonymus	*Euonymus*	Celastraceae
Everlastings	*Anaphalis, Antennaria, Gnaphalium*	Asteraceae
Farkleberry	*Vaccinium arboreum*	Ericaceae
Fern, Bracken	*Pteridium aquilinum*	Dennstaedtiaceae
Fern, Christmas	*Polystichum acrostichoides*	Dryopteridaceae
Fern, Cinnamon	*Osmunda cinnamomea*	Osmundaceae
Fern, Interrupted	*Osmunda claytoniana*	Osmundaceae
Fern, Ostrich	*Matteuccia struthiopteris*	Dryopteridaceae

Common Name	Latin Name	Family
Fern, Royal	*Osmunda regalis*	Osmundaceae
Fern, Sensitive	*Onoclea sensibilis*	Dryopteridaceae
Fern, Virginia Chain	*Woodwardia virginica*	Blechnaceae
Fig	*Ficus*	Moraceae
Fir, Balsam	*Abies balsamea*	Pinaceae
Fir, Grand	*Abies grandis*	Pinaceae
Fir, Red	*Abies magnifica*	Pinaceae
Fir, White	*Abies concolor*	Pinaceae
Fireweed	*Erechtites*	Asteraceae
Fleabane	*Erigeron*	Asteraceae
Floatingheart	*Nymphoides*	Menyanthaceae
Foxglove, False	*Aureolaria pedicularia*	Scrophulariaceae
Garlic	*Allium sativum*	Alliaceae
Geranium, Spotted	*Geranium maculatum*	Geraniaceae
Goldenrod, Gray	*Solidago nemoralis*	Asteraceae
Gooseberry	*Ribes*	Grossulariaceae
Gourd	*Cucurbita*	Cucurbitaceae
Grape	*Vitis*	Vitaceae
Grass, Bottlebrush	*Elymus hystrix*	Poaceae
Grass, Deertongue	*Dichanthelium clandestinum*	Poaceae
Greasewood	*Sarcobatus*	Chenopodiaceae
Greenbrier	*Smilax*	Smilacaceae
Groundcherry	*Physalis*	Solanaceae
Ground Ivy	*Glechoma hederacea*	Lamiaceae
Guapira	*Guapira*	Nyctaginaceae
Hackberry	*Celtis*	Ulmaceae
Hawthorn	*Crataegus*	Rosaceae
Hazelnut	*Corylus*	Betulaceae
Helianthella, Five-nerve	*Helianthella quinquenervis*	Asteraceae
Hemlock, Eastern	*Tsuga canadensis*	Pinaceae
Hickory	*Carya*	Juglandaceae
Hickory, Bitternut	*Carya cordiformis*	Juglandaceae
Hickory, Shagbark	*Carya ovata*	Juglandaceae
Hog Peanut	*Amphicarpaea bracteata*	Fabaceae
Holly, American	*Ilex opaca*	Aquifoliaceae
Holly, English	*Ilex aquifolium*	Aquifoliaceae
Holly, Mountain	*Ilex mucronata*	Aquifoliaceae
Hollyhock	*Alcea*	Malvaceae
Honewort	*Cryptotaenia canadensis*	Apiaceae
Hophornbeam	*Ostrya virginiana*	Betulaceae
Hoptree	*Ptelea trifoliata*	Rutaceae
Huckleberry	*Gaylussacia*	Ericaceae
Hyacinth, Water	*Eichhornia*	Pontederiaceae
Hydrangea	*Hydrangea*	Hydrangeaceae
Indian paintbrush	*Castilleja*	Scrophulariaceae
Inkberry	*Ilex glabra*	Aquifoliaceae
Iris	*Iris*	Iridaceae
Ironweed	*Vernonia*	Asteraceae
Jewelweed	*Impatiens*	Balsaminaceae
Jimsonweed	*Datura*	Solanaceae
Joe-Pye weed	*Eupatorium*	Asteraceae

Common Name	Latin Name	Family
Juniper	*Juniperus*	Cupressaceae
Juniper, Utah	*Juniperus osteosperma*	Cupressaceae
Lambsquarters	*Chenopodium album*	Chenopodiaceae
Larch	*Larix*	Pinaceae
Larkspur	*Delphinium*	Ranunculaceae
Laurel, Great	*Rhododendron maximum*	Ericaceae
Laurel, Mountain	*Kalmia latifolia*	Ericaceae
Laurel, Sheep	*Kalmia angustifolia*	Ericaceae
Leadwood	*Krugiodendron ferreum*	Rhamnaceae
Leatherleaf	*Chamaedaphne calyculata*	Ericaceae
Leatherwood	*Dirca palustris*	Thymelaeaceae
Leek	*Allium ampeloprasum*	Alliaceae
Lemon	*Citrus limon*	Rutaceae
Lilac	*Syringa*	Oleaceae
Linden	*Tilia*	Tiliaceae
Lizard's Tail	*Saururus cernuus*	Saururaceae
Locust	*Gleditsia; Robinia*	Fabaceae
Locust, Black	*Robinia pseudoacacia*	Fabaceae
Loosestrife, Purple	*Lythrum salicaria*	Lythraceae
Lupine	*Lupinus*	Fabaceae
Madrone	*Arbutus*	Ericaceae
Magnolia	*Magnolia*	Magnoliaceae
Mahogany, Mountain	*Cercocarpus*	Rosaceae
Mallow		Malvaceae
Mallow, Globe	*Sphaeralcea*	Malvaceae
Manfreda	*Manfreda*	Agavaceae
Manroot	*Marah*	Cucurbitaceae
Manzanita	*Arctostaphylos*	Ericaceae
Maple, Norway	*Acer platanoides*	Sapindaceae
Maple, Red	*Acer rubrum*	Sapindaceae
Maple, Silver	*Acer saccharinum*	Sapindaceae
Maple, Sugar	*Acer saccharum*	Sapindaceae
Mastic, False	*Sideroxylon foetidissimum*	Sapotaceae
Meadowsweet	*Spiraea*	Rosaceae
Mercury, Three-seeded	*Acalypha*	Euphorbiaceae
Mesquite	*Prosopis*	Fabaceae
Mesquite, Screwbean	*Prosopis pubescens*	Fabaceae
Milkweed	*Asclepias*	Asclepiadaceae
Mimosa	*Mimosa*	Fabaceae
Mint	*Mentha*	Lamiaceae
Mint family		Lamiaceae
Monkshood	*Aconitum*	Ranunculaceae
Morning glory		Convolvulaceae
Mountain-ash	*Sorbus*	Rosaceae
Mouse's Eye	*Bernardia myricifolia*	Euphorbiaceae
Mullein, Common	*Verbascum thapsus*	Scrophulariaceae
Musclewood	*Carpinus caroliniana*	Betulaceae
Mustard family		Brassicaceae
Myrtle, Sand	*Leiophyllum buxifolium*	Ericaceae
Narcissus	*Narcissus*	Amaryllidaceae
Nasturtium	*Tropaeolum*	Tropaeolaceae

Common Name	Latin Name	Family
Nectarine	*Prunus persica*	Rosaceae
Nettle	*Urtica*	Urticaceae
Nettle, False	*Boehmeria cylindrica*	Urticaceae
Ninebark	*Physocarpus*	Rosaceae
Oak, Black	*Quercus velutina*	Fagaceae
Oak, Blue	*Quercus douglasii*	Fagaceae
Oak, Chestnut	*Quercus prinus*	Fagaceae
Oak, Oregon White	*Quercus garryana*	Fagaceae
Oak, Pin	*Quercus palustris*	Fagaceae
Oak, Post	*Quercus stellata*	Fagaceae
Oak, Red	*Quercus rubra*	Fagaceae
Oak, Red (group)	*Quercus with pointed lobes*	Fagaceae
Oak, Southern Red	*Quercus falcata*	Fagaceae
Oak, White	*Quercus alba*	Fagaceae
Oak, White (group)	*Quercus with rounded lobes*	Fagaceae
Oleander	*Nerium oleander*	Apocynaceae
Onion	*Allium cepa*	Alliaceae
Orache	*Atriplex*	Chenopodiaceae
Orange	*Citrus sinensis*	Rutaceae
Orange, Mock	*Philadelphus*	Hydrangeaceae
Palm		Arecaceae
Palmetto		Arecaceae
Paloverde	*Parkinsonia*	Fabaceae
Panicgrass, Cypress	*Dichanthelium dichotomum*	Poaceae
Parsley family		Apiaceae
Parsnip, Cow	*Heracleum maximum*	Apiaceae
Parsnip (wild or otherwise)	*Pastinaca sativa*	Apiaceae
Pea	*Pisum sativum*	Fabaceae
Pea, Beach	*Lathyrus japonicus*	Fabaceae
Pea, Veiny	*Lathyrus venosus*	Fabaceae
Peach	*Prunus persica*	Rosaceae
Pear	*Pyrus (*usually *communis)*	Rosaceae
Pear, Prickly	*Opuntia*	Cactaceae
Pecan	*Carya illinoinensis*	Juglandaceae
Penstemon, Palmer's	*Penstemon palmeri*	Scrophulariaceae
Persimmon	*Diospyros virginiana*	Ebenaceae
Phacelia	*Phacelia*	Hydrophyllaceae
Phlox	*Phlox*	Polemoniaceae
Pickerelweed	*Pontederia cordata*	Pontederiaceae
Pine, Bishop	*Pinus muricata*	Pinaceae
Pine family		Pinaceae
Pine, Jack	*Pinus banksiana*	Pinaceae
Pine, Jeffrey	*Pinus jeffreyi*	Pinaceae
Pine, Knobcone	*Pinus attenuata*	Pinaceae
Pine, Monterey	*Pinus radiata*	Pinaceae
Pine, Ponderosa	*Pinus ponderosa*	Pinaceae
Pine, Red	*Pinus resinosa*	Pinaceae
Pine, Virginia	*Pinus virginiana*	Pinaceae
Pine, White	*Pinus strobus*	Pinaceae
Pitcher Plant	*Sarracenia*	Sarraceniaceae
Plantain	*Plantago*	Plantaginaceae

Common Name	Latin Name	Family
Plantain, Common	*Plantago major*	Plantaginaceae
Plum	*Prunus*	Rosaceae
Poison Ivy	*Toxicodendron*	Anacardiaceae
Pond-lily, Yellow	*Nuphar lutea*	Nymphaeaceae
Poplar	*Populus*	Salicaceae
Potato	*Solanum tuberosum*	Solanaceae
Potato, Sweet	*Ipomoea batatas*	Convolvulaceae
Prickly-ash	*Zanthoxylum americanum*	Rutaceae
Privet	*Ligustrum*	Oleaceae
Purslane	*Portulaca oleracea*	Portulacaceae
Quince	*Cydonia oblonga*	Rosaceae
Radish	*Raphanus sativus*	Brassicaceae
Ragweed	*Ambrosia*	Asteraceae
Ragwort	*Packera; Senecio*	Asteraceae
Ragwort, Golden	*Packera aurea*	Asteraceae
Raspberry	*Rubus*	Rosaceae
Rattlebox	*Crotalaria*	Fabaceae
Redbud	*Cercis canadensis*	Fabaceae
Redcedar, Western	*Thuja plicata*	Cupressaceae
Redwood	*Sequoia sempervirens*	Cupressaceae
Reed, Common	*Phragmites australis*	Poaceae
Rhododendron	*Rhododendron*	Ericaceae
Rhubarb	*Rheum rhabarbarum*	Polygonaceae
Rocket, London	*Sisymbrium irio*	Brassicaceae
Rose	*Rosa*	Rosaceae
Rush	*Juncus*	Juncaceae
Sagebrush	*Artemisia*	Asteraceae
Saguaro	*Carnegiea gigantea*	Cactaceae
St. Johnswort		Clusiaceae
Sarsaparilla, Wild	*Aralia nudicaulis*	Araliaceae
Sassafras	*Sassafras albidum*	Lauraceae
Seablite, Mojave	*Suaeda moquinii*	Chenopodiaceae
Sebastiania	*Sebastiania*	Euphorbiaceae
Sedge		Cyperaceae
Shadbush	*Amelanchier*	Rosaceae
Skeletonweed, Rush	*Chondrilla juncea*	Asteraceae
Skullcap	*Scutellaria*	Lamiaceae
Skullcap, Heartleaf	*Scutellaria ovata*	Lamiaceae
Skullcap, Hoary	*Scutellaria incana*	Lamiaceae
Smartweed		Polygonaceae
Snakeroot, White	*Ageratina altissima*	Asteraceae
Snapdragon family		Scrophulariaceae
Snowberry	*Symphoricarpos*	Caprifoliaceae
Solomon's Seal, Starry False	*Maianthemum stellatum*	Liliaceae
Sorghum	*Sorghum*	Poaceae
Sowthistle	*Sonchus*	Asteraceae
Soybean	*Glycine max*	Fabaceae
Spicebush	*Lindera benzoin*	Lauraceae
Spinach	*Spinacia oleracea*	Chenopodiaceae
Spruce, Black	*Picea mariana*	Pinaceae

Common Name	Latin Name	Family
Spruce, Red	*Picea rubens*	Pinaceae
Spruce, White	*Picea glauca*	Pinaceae
Squash	*Cucurbita*	Cucurbitaceae
Strawberry	*Fragaria*	Rosaceae
Sumac	*Rhus*	Anacardiaceae
Sumac, Skunkbush	*Rhus trilobata*	Anacardiaceae
Sumac, Staghorn	*Rhus typhina*	Anacardiaceae
Sunflower	*Helianthus*	Asteraceae
Sunflower, False	*Heliopsis helianthoides*	Asteraceae
Sweetbay	*Magnolia virginiana*	Magnoliaceae
Sweetclover	*Melilotus*	Fabaceae
Sweetfern	*Comptonia peregrina*	Myricaceae
Sweetgale	*Myrica gale*	Myricaceae
Sweetgum	*Liquidambar styraciflua*	Hamamelidaceae
Sweetvetch	*Hedysarum*	Fabaceae
Sycamore	*Platanus*	Platanaceae
Tamarack	*Larix laricina*	Pinaceae
Tea, Labrador	*Ledum*	Ericaceae
Thermopsis, Prairie	*Thermopsis rhombifolia*	Fabaceae
Thistle	*Cirsium*	Asteraceae
Thistle, Russian	*Salsola*	Chenopodiaceae
Tobacco	*Nicotiana*	Solanaceae
Tomato	*Solanum lycopersicum*	Solanaceae
Toothwort	*Cardamine diphylla*	Brassicaceae
Touch-me-not, Pale	*Impatiens pallida*	Balsaminaceae
Trefoil	*Lotus*	Fabaceae
Trefoil, Tick	*Desmodium*	Fabaceae
Tulip	*Tulipa*	Liliaceae
Tuliptree	*Liriodendron tulipifera*	Magnoliaceae
Tupelo	*Nyssa sylvatica*	Cornaceae
Turnip	*Brassica rapa var. rapa*	Brassicaceae
Turtlehead	*Chelone*	Scrophulariaceae
Velvetleaf	*Abutilon theophrasti*	Malvaceae
Vervain, White	*Verbena urticifolia*	Verbenaceae
Vetch	*Vicia*	Fabaceae
Viburnum	*Viburnum*	Caprifoliaceae
Walkingstick, Devil's	*Aralia spinosa*	Araliaceae
Walnut	*Juglans*	Juglandaceae
Walnut, Black	*Juglans nigra*	Juglandaceae
Waterlily		Nymphaeaceae
Watermelon	*Citrullus lanatus*	Cucurbitaceae
Watershield	*Brasenia schreberi*	Cabombaceae
Wheat	*Triticum*	Poaceae
Willow	*Salix*	Salicaceae
Winterberry	*Ilex verticillata*	Aquifoliaceae
Witch hazel	*Hamamelis virginiana*	Hamamelidaceae
Wolfberry	*Lycium*	Solanaceae
Woodfern, Intermediate	*Dryopteris intermedia*	Dryopteridaceae
Wormwood	*Artemisia*	Asteraceae
Yew	*Taxus*	Taxaceae
Yucca	*Yucca*	Agavaceae

GLOSSARY

Annelida. The animal phylum including earthworms, leeches, and polychaete worms.

Arachnida. The arthropod class including spiders, scorpions, mites, and ticks.

Arthropoda. The animal phylum including chelicerates, crustaceans, hexapods, and myriapods.

Asteraceous. Belonging to the aster family (Asteraceae).

Auchenorrhyncha. The hemipteran suborder including leafhoppers, planthoppers, treehoppers, spittlebugs, and cicadas.

Bug, True. A member of the hemipteran suborder Heteroptera.

Carton. A paperlike material that certain wasps and ants manufacture from plant fibers.

Chelicerae. The "jaws" of an arachnid or horseshoe crab.

Chelicerata. The arthropod subphylum including arachnids and horseshoe crabs.

Chitin. The primary material in the tough exoskeletons of arthropods.

Chorion. The outer shell of an arthropod egg.

Chrysalis. The pupa of a butterfly.

Class. A subdivison of a phylum, containing a group of related orders.

Cocoon. A silken case that a larva spins around itself in which to pupate. In other literature, sometimes used to describe egg coverings of spiders, earthworms, and leeches.

Composites. Plants belonging to the aster family (Asteraceae).

Cribellate spider. A spider possessing a row of hairs on its leg, called the *calamistrum*, that combs out silk from a silk-producing organ, called the *cribellum*, to produce a microscopically woolly type of silk, without sticky droplets, known as *cribellate silk*.

Crustacea. The arthropod subphylum including true crabs, shrimp, crayfish, and woodlice.

Cucurbit. A plant in the gourd family (Cucurbitaceae); e.g. squash, melon, and cucumber.

Eclosion. Emergence from a pupal skin or hatching from an egg.

Ecribellate spider. A spider lacking a cribellum and calamistrum and therefore not producing cribellate silk.

Exarate pupa. A pupa with free appendages.

Exuviae. The shed skin of an arthropod.

Family. A subdivision of an order, containing a group of related genera. Family names of animals end in "-idae," and those of plants in "-aceae."

Frass. The byproducts of insect feeding, such as "sawdust" from wood-boring species. Often used to refer to pure excrement, though this is not technically correct.

Gall. An abnormal growth of plant tissue caused by another organism.

Genus (plural: Genera). A subdivision of a family, containing a group of related species. It is the first name in a binomial scientific name and is always capitalized and italicized.

Goosefoot. A plant in the family Chenopodiaceae (e.g., spinach, beet, and lambsquarters).

Hemiptera. The insect order including Auchenorrhyncha, Sternorrhyncha, and Heteroptera.

Heteroptera. The hemipteran suborder containing the true bugs.

Hexapoda. The arthropod subphylum including insects and three smaller groups of wingless six-legged animals, best known of which are the springtails.

Hymenoptera. The insect order including bees, wasps, ants, and sawflies.

Instar. The life stage of an arthropod between molts. The first instar begins upon hatching from the egg.

Introduced species. A species brought to a region by humans, either intentionally or accidentally.

Invertebrate. Any member of the animal kingdom that lacks vertebrae (see chart on inside cover).

Kingdom. One of several broad groups into which living things are divided, each of which is further divided into nested groups from phyla down to species.

Kleptoparasite. An animal that takes prey from another animal that caught or killed the prey.

Larva. The often wormlike immature form of an insect that undergoes complete metamorphosis, between the egg and pupal stages.

Leaf mining. A mode of foliage feeding in which a larva feeds inside a leaf, between the epidermal layers.

Legume (adjective: Leguminous). A plant belonging to the pea family (Fabaceae).

Lepidoptera. The insect order including moths and butterflies.

Megaloptera. The neuropterid order including dobsonflies, fishflies, and alderflies.

Metamorphosis. Change in form during development.

Micropyle. A tiny opening in the chorion of an insect egg, through which sperm enter.

Mollusk. A member of phylum Mollusca, which includes cephalopods (octopuses, squids), gastropods (snails, slugs), and bivalves (clams, mussels).

Mygalomorphae. The spider suborder including tarantulas and their relatives.

Myriapoda. The arthropod subphylum including centipedes and millipedes.

Naiad. An aquatic nymph.

Native (to North America). Occurring in North America prior to the arrival of Europeans.

Neuroptera. The neuropterid order including lacewings and their relatives.

Neuropterida. The insect superorder containing the Megaloptera, Neuroptera, and Raphidioptera (snakeflies).

Nightshade. A plant in the family Solanaceae (e.g., tomato, potato, and eggplant).

Nymph. The immature form of an insect that lacks a pupal stage; typically similar to the adult form but lacking wings.

Obtect pupa. A pupa in which the appendages are fused to the body, rather than free.

Ootheca. The egg case of a cockroach or mantis.

Order. A subdivision of a class, containing a group of related families. Names of insect orders often end in "-ptera."

Orthoptera. The insect order including grasshoppers, crickets, and katydids.

Ovipositor. A tubular structure with which females deposit eggs (oviposit).

Parasite. An organism that feeds and lives on or within another organism.

Parasitoid. An organism that at first lives as a parasite but ultimately kills its host, consuming most or all of its tissues.

Petiole. A leafstalk.

Pharate adult. An insect that has metamorphosed but is still inside its pupal skin.

Phylum. A subdivision of a kingdom, containing a group of related classes.

Prunus. The genus in the rose family that includes cherry, plum, peach, almond, apricot, and nectarine.

Pupa. The nonfeeding, resting stage of insects with complete metamorphosis, between the larval and adult stages.

Puparium. A pupal case formed by the hardening of the last larval skin.

Radula. A straplike organ in a mollusk's mouth, covered with small teeth.

Rosaceous. Belonging to the rose family (Rosaceae).

Sawfly. A member of one of several related families of hymenopterans with plant-feeding, caterpillarlike larvae.

Skeletonizing. A style of foliage feeding in which only the tissue between the veins is eaten, leaving the "skeleton" of the veins.

Species. The fundamental taxonomic unit of biological classification, theoretically comprising a group of similar organisms that can interbreed to produce fertile offspring, and that do not normally interbreed with other such groups. The scientific name of a species consists of a capitalized generic name followed by a lowercase specific epithet, both of which are italicized.

Stabilimentum. A silk decoration in the web of certain orb-weaving spiders.

Sternorrhyncha. The hemipteran suborder including aphids, whiteflies, mealybugs, and scale insects.

Subfamily. A group of related genera within a family, sometimes further divided into tribes. Subfamily names end in "-inae."

Superfamily. A group of related families within an order or suborder. Superfamily names end in "-oidea."

Taxon (plural: Taxa). A group of related organisms, such as a genus, family, or order.

Tribe. A group of related genera within a subfamily. Tribe names end in "-ini."

Woodlice. Members of the isopod suborder Oniscidea, sometimes known as sowbugs, pillbugs, and roly-polies.

REFERENCES

To aid you in finding literature relevant to your topic of interest, we have subdivided our references based on taxonomy, habitat, and academic discipline. Most of the information presented in this book can be found among the literature below, although often key tidbits we gleaned about a certain topic are hidden in a publication about another topic. The groups are organized from taxonomically broad accounts to specific accounts. If you don't find a specific reference you're looking for under the appropriate taxon, look in the groups of taxonomically broad literature.

General Nature Guides

Eastman, John, and Amelia Hansen. *The Book of Field and Roadside*. Mechanicsburg, PA: Stackpole Books, 2003.

———. *The Book of Forest and Thicket*. Mechanicsburg, PA: Stackpole Books, 1992.

———. *The Book of Swamp and Bog*. Mechanicsburg, PA: Stackpole Books, 1995.

Stokes, Donald W. *A Guide to Nature in Winter*. Boston: Little, Brown and Company, 1976.

Multitaxon Invertebrate Accounts

Askew, R. R. *Parasitic Insects*. New York: American Elsevier Publishing Company, 1971.

Barker, Will. *Familiar Insects of America*. New York: Harper & Brothers, 1960.

Borror, Donald J., and Richard E. White. *A Field Guide to Insects: America North of Mexico*. Boston: Houghton Mifflin, 1987.

Brusca, Richard C., and Gary J. Brusca. *Invertebrates*. Sunderland, MA: Sinauer Associates, 1990.

Bryson, Harry R., and K. A. E. Station. "The Identification of Soil Insects by Their Burrow Characteristics." *Transactions of the Kansas Academy of Science* 42 (1939): 245–53.

Burton, Robert. *Eggs: Nature's Perfect Package*. New York: Facts on File Publications, 1987.

Chamberlain, C. K. "Recent Lebensspuren in Nonmarine Aquatic Environments." In *The Study of Trace Fossils: A Synthesis of Principles, Problems, and Procedures in Ichnology*, edited by R. W. Frey, 431–58. New York: Springer-Verlag, 1975. Reprinted in Sarjeant 1983.

Chu, H. F. *How to Know the Immature Insects*. Dubuque, IA: Wm. C. Brown Company Publishers, 1949.

Comstock, John Henry. *Insect Life*. New York: D. Appleton and Company, 1903.

De Prins, Willy, and Jurate De Prins. *World Catalogue of Insects*. Vol. 6, *Gracillariidae (Lepidoptera)*. Stenstrup, Denmark: Apollo Books, 2005.

Dunn, C. W., A. Hejnol, D. Q. Matus, K. Pang, W. E. Browne, S. A. Smith, E. Seaver, G. W. Rouse, M. Obst, G. D. Edgecombe, M. V. Sørensen, S. G. D. Haddock, A. Schmidt-Rhaesa, A. Okusu, R M. Kristensen, W. C. Wheeler, M. Q. Martindale, and G. Giribet. "Broad Phylogenomic Sampling Improves Resolution of the Animal Tree of Life." *Nature* 452 (2008): 745–9.

Eaton, Eric R., and Kenn Kaufman. *Kaufman Field Guide to Insects of North America*. New York: Houghton Mifflin Company, 2007.

Eisner, Thomas. *For Love of Insects*. Cambridge, MA: Belknap Press of Harvard University Press, 2003.

Frost, S. W. *Insect Life and Insect Natural History*. New York: Dover Publications, 1959.

Hutchins, Ross E. *Insects*. Englewood Cliffs, NJ: Prentice-Hall, 1966.

Lutz, Frank E. *Field Book of Insects*. New York: G. P. Putnam's Sons, 1948.

Manee, Abram Herbert. "Some Observations at Southern Pines, N. Carolina: Three Mound Builders." *Entomological News* 19, no. 10 (1908): 459–62.

Milne, Lorus, and Margery Milne. *The Audubon Society Field Guide to North American Insects and Spiders*. New York: Alfred A. Knopf, 1980.

Needham, James G., Stuart W. Frost, and Beatrice H. Tothill. *Leaf-Mining Insects*. Baltimore: Williams & Wilkins Company, 1928.

Neva, Franklin A., and Harold W. Brown. *Basic Clinical Parasitology*. 6th ed. Norwalk, CT: Appleton & Lange, 1996.

Oldroyd, Harold. *Insects and Their World*. London: Trustees of the British Museum, 1966.

Packard, A. S., Jr. *Guide to the Study of Insects*. New York: Henry Holt and Company, 1878.

Resh, Vincent H., and Ring T. Cardé, eds. *Encyclopedia of Insects*. Boston: Academic Press, 2003.

Ross, Edward S. *Insects Close Up*. Berkeley: University of California Press, 1953.

Stokes, Donald W. *A Guide to Observing Insect Lives*. Boston: Little, Brown and Company, 1983.

Swan, Lester A., and Charles S. Papp. *The Common Insects of North America*. New York: Harper & Row, 1972.

Teale, Edwin Way. *Grassroot Jungles*. New York: Dodd, Mead & Company, 1945.

Triplehorn, Charles A., and Norman F. Johnson. *Borror and DeLong's Introduction to the Study of Insects*. 7th ed. Belmont, CA: Thomson Brooks / Cole, 2005.

Wheeler, William Morton. *Demons of the Dust*. New York: W. W. Norton & Company, 1930.

Wigglesworth, Sir Vincent B. *The Life of Insects*. New York: Universe Books, 1964.

General Animal Tracking

Brown, R. W., M. J. Lawrence, and J. Pope. *The Larousse Guide to Animal Tracks, Trails, and Signs*. New York: Larousse and Company, 1984.

Elbroch, Mark. *Mammal Tracks and Sign: A Guide to North American Species*. Mechanicsburg, PA: Stackpole Books, 2003.

Elbroch, Mark, and Eleanor Marks. *Bird Tracks and Sign: A Guide to North American Species*. Mechanicsburg, PA: Stackpole Books, 2001.

Murie, Olaus J. *A Field Guide to Animal Tracks*. Boston: Houghton Mifflin, 1954.

Murie, Olaus J., and Mark Elbroch. *A Field Guide to Animal Tracks*. Boston: Houghton Mifflin, 2005.

Paleoichnology and Geology

Bader, K. S. "Insect Trace Fossils on Dinosaur Bones from the Upper Jurassic Morrison Formation of Northeastern Wyoming." *Geological Society of America Abstracts with Programs* 39, no. 3 (2007): 18.

———. "Traces Produced by Insects on Bone." In *Abstracts of the 138th Annual Meeting of the Kansas Academy of Science, Wichita State University, April 7–8, 2006. Transactions of the Kansas Academy of Science* 109 (2006): 247–67.

Bromley, R. G. *Trace Fossils Biology, Taphonomy and Applications*. New York: Chapman & Hall, 1996.

Crimes, T. P., and J. C. Harper. *Trace Fossils: Proceedings of an International Conference Held at Liverpool University, 6, 7, 8 January 1970*. Liverpool, UK: Seel House Press, 1970.

Donovan, S. K., ed. *The Palaeobiology of Trace Fossils*. Baltimore: Johns Hopkins University Press, 1994.

Kim, J. Y., D. G. Keighley, R. K. Pickerill, W. Hwang, and K.-S. Kim. "Trace Fossils from Marginal Lacustrine Deposits of the Cretaceous Jinju Formation, Southern Coast of Korea." *Palaeogeography, Palaeoclimatology, Palaeoecology* 218 (2005): 105–24.

Metz, R. "Nematode Trails from the Late Triassic of Pennsylvania." *Ichnos* 5 (1998): 303–8.

Miller, W. *Trace Fossils Concepts, Problems, Prospects*. New York: Elsevier, 2007.

Ratcliffe, B. C., and J. A. Fagerstrom. "Invertebrate Lebensspuren of Holocene Floodplains: Their Morphology, Origin and Paleoecological Significance." *Journal of Paleontology* 54 (1980): 614–30.

Sarjeant, W. A. S., ed. *Terrestrial Trace Fossils*. Stroudsburg, PA: Hutchinson Ross Publishing Company, 1983.

Uchman, A., V. Kazakauskas, and A. Gaigalas. "Trace Fossils from Late Pleistocene Varved Lacustrine Sediments in Eastern Lithuania," *Palaeogeography, Palaeoclimatology, Palaeoecology* 272 (2009): 199–211.

Marine and Coastal

Abbott, R. Tucker. *Seashells of North America*. New York: Golden Press, 1968.

Barnes, R. D. "Tube-Building and Feeding in the Chaetopterid Polychaete, Spiochaetopterus Oculatus." *Biological Bulletin* 127 (1964): 397.

Barrows, A. L. *The Occurrence of a Rock-Boring Isopod along the Shore of San Francisco Bay, California*. Berkeley: University of California Press, 1919.

Boekschoten, G. J. "On Bryozoan Borings from the Danian at Fakse, Denmark." In *Trace Fossils, Geological Journal Special Issue 3*, edited by T. P. Crimes and J. C. Harper, 43–48. Liverpool, UK: Seel House Press, 1970.

Botter-Carvalho, M. L., P. J. P. Santos, and P. Carvalho. "Spatial Distribution of *Callichirus major* (Say 1818) (Decapoda, Callianassidae) on a Sandy Beach, Piedade, Pernambuco, Brazil." *Nauplius* 10, no. 2 (2002): 97–109.

Carriker, M. R., and E. L. Yochelson. *Recent Gastropod Boreholes and Ordovician Cylindrical Borings*. Washington, DC: U.S. Government Printing Office, 1968.

Christy, J. H. "Pillar Function in the Fiddler Crab *Uca beebei* (II): Competitive Courtship Signaling." *Ethology* 78 (1988): 113–28.

Christy, J. H., P. R. Y. Backwell, S. Goshima, and T. Kreuter. "Sexual Selection for Structure Building by Courting Male Fiddler Crabs: An Experimental Study of Behavioral Mechanisms." *Behavioral Ecology* 13 (2002): 366.

Crane, J. *Fiddler Crabs of the World. Ocypodidae: Genus* Uca. Princeton, NJ: Princeton University Press, 1975.

Cullen, D. J. "Bioturbation of Superficial Marine Sediments by Interstitial Meiobenthos." *Nature* 242 (1973): 323–24.

Goiubic, S. "Distribution, Taxonomy, and Boring Patterns of Marine Endolithic Algae." *Integrative and Comparative Biology* 9 (1969): 747–51.

Goodhart, C. B. "Notes on the Bionomics of the Tube-Building Amphipod, *Leptocheirus pilosus* Zaddach." *Journal of the Marine Biological Association of the United Kingdom* 23 (1939): 311–25.

Gosner, K. L. *A Field Guide to the Atlantic Seashore: Invertebrates and Seaweeds of the Atlantic Coast from the Bay of Fundy to Cape Hatteras.* Boston: Houghton Mifflin, 1979.

Howard, J. D., and C. A. Elders. "Burrowing Patterns of Haustoriid Amphipods from Sapelo Island, Georgia." *Trace Fossils, Geological Journal Special Issue 3*, edited by T. P. Crimes and J. C. Harper, 243–62. Liverpool, UK: Seel House Press, 1970.

Kim, T. W., J. H. Christy, and J. C. Choe. "A Preference for a Sexual Signal Keeps Females Safe." *PLoS ONE* 2, no. 5 (2007): e422. doi:10.1371/journal.pone.0000422.

Kozloff, E. *Seashore Life of the Northern Pacific Coast.* Seattle: University of Washington Press, 2003.

Kríž, J., and R. Mikuláš. "Bivalve Wood Borings of the Ichnogenus Teredolites Leymerie from the Bohemian Cretaceous Basin (Upper Cretaceous, Czech Republic)." *Ichnos* 13 (2006): 159–74.

Lippson, A. J., and R. L. Lippson. *Life in the Chesapeake Bay.* Baltimore: Johns Hopkins University Press, 2006.

Lopez-Anido, R., A. P. Michael, B. Goodell, and T. C. Sandford. "Assessment of Wood Pile Deterioration Due to Marine Organisms." *Journal of Waterway, Port, Coastal, and Ocean Engineering* 130, no. 2 (2004): 70–76.

Martin, A. "Resting Traces of *Ocypode quadrata* Associated with Hydration and Respiration: Sapelo Island, Georgia, USA." *Ichnos* 13 (2006): 57–67.

Massin, C. "Food and Feeding Mechanisms: Holothuroidea." In *Echinoderm Nutrition*, edited by Michel Jangoux and J. M. Lawrence, 43–56. Rotterdam, Netherlands: AA Balkema Publishers, 1982.

Old, M. C. "The Taxonomy and Distribution of the Boring Sponges (Clionidae) along the Atlantic Coast of North America." *Chesapeake Biological Laboratory Publication* 44 (1941): 1–30.

Pollock, Leland W. *A Practical Guide to the Marine Animals of Northeastern North America.* Piscataway, NJ: Rutgers University Press, 1997.

Powell, E. N. "Particle Size Selection and Sediment Reworking in a Funnel Feeder, *Leptosynapta tenuis* (Holothuroidea, Synaptidae)." *Internationale Revue der gesamten Hydrobiologie* 62 (1977): 385–408.

Rouse, G. W. F. Pleijel. *Polychaetes.* New York: Oxford University Press, 2001.

Ruppert, E. E., and R. S. Fox. *Seashore Animals of the Southeast: A Guide to Common Shallow-Water Invertebrates along the Southeastern Atlantic Coast.* Columbia: University of South Carolina Press, 1988.

Savrda, C. E., and M. W. Smith. "Behavioral Implications of Branching and Tube-Lining in Toredolites." *Ichnos* 4 (1996): 191–98.

Shuster, Carl N., Jr. "A Pictorial Review of the Natural History and Ecology of the Horseshoe Crab *Limulus polyphemus*, with Reference to Other Limulidae." In *Physiology and Biology of Horseshoe Crabs: Studies on Normal and Environmentally Stressed Animals*, edited by Joseph Bonaventura, Celia Bonaventura, and Shirley Tesh, 1–52. New York: Alan R. Liss, 1982.

———. "Tracks and Trails." In Limulus *in the Limelight: A Species 350 Million Years in the Making and in Peril?*, edited by John T. Tanacredi, 65–78. New York: Kluwer Academic / Plenum Publishers, 2001.

Skutch, A. F. "On the Habits and Ecology of the Tube-Building Amphipod *Amphithoe Rubricata* Montagu." *Ecology* 7 (1926): 481–502.

Wada, K., and I. Murata. "Chimney Building in the Fiddler Crab *Uca*." *Journal of Crustacean Biology* 20 (2000): 505–9.

Warburton, F. E. "The Manner in Which the Sponge *Cliona* Bores in Calcareous Objects." *Canadian Journal of Zoology* 36 (1958): 555–62.

Freshwater

Crocker, Denton W., and David W. Barr. *Handbook of the Crayfishes of Ontario*. Toronto, ON: University of Toronto Press, 1968.

Kenney, Leo P., and Matthew R. Burne. *A Field Guide to the Animals of Vernal Pools*. Westborough: Massachusetts Division of Fisheries & Wildlife Natural Heritage & Endangered Species Program, 2000.

Knecht, R. J., J. S. Benner, D. C. Rogers, and J. C. Ridge. "*Surculichnus bifurcauda* n. igen., n. isp., a Trace Fossil from Late Pleistocene Glaciolacustrine Varves of the Connecticut River Valley, USA, Attributed to Notostracan Crustaceans Based on Neoichnological Experimentation." *Palaeogeography, Palaeoclimatology, Palaeoecology* 272 (2009): 232–39.

Lehmkuhl, Dennis M. *How to Know the Aquatic Insects*. Dubuque, IA: Wm. C. Brown Company Publishers, 1979.

Nedeau, Ethan Jay. *Freshwater Mussels and the Connecticut River Watershed*. Greenfield, MA: Connecticut River Watershed Council, 2008.

Pettibone, Marian H. "Fresh-water Polychaetous Annelid, *Manayunkia speciosa* Leidy, from Lake Erie." *Biological Bulletin* 105, no. 1 (1953): 149–53.

Usinger, Robert L., ed. *Aquatic Insects of California*. Berkeley: University of California Press, 1971.

Voshell, J. Reese, Jr. *A Guide to Common Freshwater Invertebrates of North America*. Blacksburg, VA: McDonald & Woodward Publishing Company, 2002.

Wiggins, Glenn B. *Larvae of the North American Caddisfly Genera (Trichoptera)*. 2nd ed. Toronto, ON: University of Toronto Press, 1996.

General Plant Damage and Horticultural Pests

Balciunas, Joseph K., and Marc C. Minno. "Insects Damaging Hydrilla in the USA." *Journal of Aquatic Plant Management* 23 (1985): 77–83.

Chittenden, F. H. *Some Insects Injurious to the Violet, Rose, and Other Ornamental Plants*. USDA Bulletin No. 27. Washington, DC: U.S. Government Printing Office, 1901.

Cranshaw, Whitney. *Garden Insects of North America*. Princeton, NJ: Princeton University Press, 2004.

Fichter, George S. *Insect Pests*. New York: Golden Press, 1966.

Hickin, Norman E. *The Insect Factor in Wood Decay*. London: Hutchinson & Co., 1963.

Hodson, Alexander C., and Marion A. Brooks. "The Frass of Certain Defoliators of Forest Trees in the North Central United States and Canada." *Canadian Entomologist* 88, no. 2 (1956): 62–68.

Johnson, Warren T., and Howard H. Lyon. *Insects That Feed on Trees and Shrubs*. Ithaca, NY: Comstock Publishing Associates, 1988.

Kelly, Jack, and Mary Olsen. *Problems and Pests of Agave, Aloe, Cactus and Yucca*. Bulletin AZ1399. Tucson, AZ: University of Arizona Cooperative Extension, 2006.

Morris, R. F. "The Use of Frass in the Identification of Forest Insect Damage." *Canadian Entomologist* 74, no. 9 (1942): 164–67.

Solomon, J. D. "Frass Characteristics for Identifying Insect Borers (Lepidoptera: Cossidae and Sesiidae; Coleoptera: Cerambycidae) in Living Hardwoods." *Canadian Entomologist* 109, no. 2 (1977): 295–303.

———. *Guide to Insect Borers in North American Broadleaf Trees and Shrubs*. Agriculture Handbook AH-706. Washington, DC: United States Department of Agriculture, Forest Service, 1995.

Southey, J. F. *Plant Nematology*. London: Her Majesty's Stationery Office, 1965.

Weeden, Catherine R., Anthony M. Shelton, and Michael P. Hoffman. Biological Control: A Guide to Natural Enemies in North America. www.nysaes.cornell.edu/ent/biocontrol/ (accessed December 2008).

Pollination and Nectar Robbing

Free, John B. *Insect Pollination of Crops*. Boston: Academic Press, 1993.

Heinrich, Bernd. "The Foraging Specializations of Individual Bumblebees." *Ecological Monographs* 46, no. 1 (1976): 105–28.

Inouye, David W. "The Ecology of Nectar Robbing." In *The Biology of Nectaries*, edited by Barbara Bentley and Thomas Elias, 153–73. New York: Columbia University Press, 1983.

———. "The Terminology of Floral Larceny." *Ecology* 61, no. 5 (1980): 1251–53.

Maloof, Joan E., and David W. Inouye. "Are Nectar Robbers Cheaters or Mutualists?" *Ecology* 81, no. 10 (2000): 2651–61.

Roubik, David W. "The Ecological Impact of Nectar-Robbing Bees and Pollinating Hummingbirds on a Tropical Shrub." *Ecology* 63, no. 10 (1982): 354–60.

Rust, Richard W. "Pollination in *Impatiens capensis* and *Impatiens pallida* (Balsaminaceae)." *Bulletin of the Torrey Botanical Club* 104, no. 4 (1977): 361–67.

Galls

Felt, E. P. *Plant Galls and Gall Makers*. Ithaca, NY: Comstock Publishing Co., 1940.

Gagné, Raymond J. *The Plant-Feeding Gall Midges of North America*. Ithaca, NY: Cornell University Press, 1989.

Hutchins, Ross E. *Galls and Gall Insects*. New York: Dodd, Mead & Company, 1969.

Keifer, Hartford H., Edward W. Baker, Tokuwo Kono, Mercedes Delfinado, and William E. Styer. *An Illustrated Guide to Plant Abnormalities Caused by Eriophyid Mites in North America*. Agriculture Handbook no. 573. Washington, DC: United States Department of Agriculture, Agricultural Research Service, 1982.

Patch, Edith M. "Gall Aphids of the Elm." *Maine Agricultural Experiment Station Bulletin* 181 (1910): 191–240.

Pirozynski, A. "Galls, Flowers, Fruits, and Fungi." In *Symbiosis as a Source of Evolutionary Innovation: Speciation and Morphogenesis*, edited by L. Margulis and R. Fester, 364–80. Cambridge, MA: MIT Press, 1991.

Russo, Ron. *Field Guide to Plant Galls of California and Other Western States*. Berkeley: University of California Press, 2006.

Weld, Lewis H. *Cynipid Galls of the Eastern United States*. Ann Arbor, MI: privately published, 1959.

———. *Cynipid Galls of the Pacific Slope*. Ann Arbor, MI: privately published, 1957.

———. *Cynipid Galls of the Southwest*. Ann Arbor, MI: privately published, 1960.

Fungus-Insect Interactions

Arora, David. *Mushrooms Demystified*. Berkeley, CA: Ten Speed Press, 1986.

Butt, Tariq M., Chris Jackson, and Naresh Magan, eds. *Fungi as Biocontrol Agents*. Wallingford, UK: CABI Publishing, 2001.

Evans, H. C. "Mycopathogens of Insects of Epigeal and Aerial Habitats." In *Insect-Fungus Interactions*, edited by N. Wilding, N. M. Collins, P. M. Hammond, and J. F. Webber, 205–38. Boston: Academic Press, 1989.

Kendrick, Bryce. *The Fifth Kingdom*. Newburyport, MA: Focus Publishing, 2000.

Mains, E. B. "New Species of *Torrubiella*, *Hirsutella* and *Gibellula*." *Mycologia* 41, no. 3 (1949): 303–10.

Annelids

Coleman, J. and D. H. Shain. "Clitellate Cocoons and Their Secretion." In *Annelids in Modern Biology*, edited by D. H. Shain, 328–43. Hoboken, NJ: John Wiley & Sons, 2009.

Darwin, Charles. *The Formation of Vegetable Mould, through the Action of Worms with Observations on Their Habits*. London: John Murray, 1883.

Hale, Cindy. *Earthworms of the Great Lakes*. Duluth, MN: Kollath-Stensaas, 2007.

Hendrix, Paul F., ed. *Earthworm Ecology and Biogeography in North America*. Boca Raton, FL: Lewis Publishers, 1995.

Snails and Slugs

Burch, John B. *How to Know the Eastern Land Snails*. Dubuque, IA: Wm. C. Brown Company Publishers, 1962.

Runham, N. W., and P. J. Hunter. *Terrestrial Slugs*. London: Hutchinson University Library, 1970.

South, A. *Terrestrial Slugs: Biology, Ecology and Control*. New York: Chapman & Hall, 1992.

Spiders, Mites, Scorpions, and Kin

Baker, Edward W., and G. W. Wharton. *An Introduction to Acarology*. New York: Macmillan Company, 1952.

Banks, Nathan. "A Rock-Boring Mite." *Entomological News* 17, no. 6 (1906): 193–94.

Beatty, Joseph A. "Web Structure and Burrow Location of *Sphodros niger* (Hentz) (Araneae, Atypidae)." *Journal of Arachnology* 14, no. 1 (1986): 130–32.

Bennett, R. G. "The Natural History and Taxonomy of *Cicurina bryantae* Exline (Araneae, Agelenidae)." *Journal of Arachnology* 13 (1985): 87–96.

Brady, L. F. "Invertebrate Tracks from the Coconino Sandstone of Northern Arizona." *Journal of Paleontology* 21 (1947): 466–72.

Bristowe, W. S. *The World of Spiders*. London: Collins, 1958.

Brown, Christopher A. "Life Histories of Four Species of Scorpion in Three Families (Buthidae, Diplocentridae, Vaejovidae) from Arizona and New Mexico." *Journal of Arachnology* 32, no. 2 (2004): 193–207.

Bukowski, Todd C., and Terry E. Christenson. "Natural History and Copulatory Behavior of the Spiny Orbweaving Spider *Micrathena gracilis* (Araneae, Araneidae)." *Journal of Arachnology* 25, no. 3 (1997): 307–20.

Cloudsley-Thompson, J. L. *Spiders, Scorpions, Centipedes and Mites*. New York: Pergamon Press, 1958.

Cokendolpher, James C. "Pathogens and Parasites of Opiliones (Arthropoda: Arachnida)." *Journal of Arachnology* 21, no. 2 (1993): 120–46.

Comstock, John Henry. *The Spider Book*. Ithaca, NY: Comstock Publishing Associates, 1940.

Coyle, Frederick A., and Wendell R. Icenogle. "Natural History of the Californian Trapdoor Spider Genus *Aliatypus* (Araneae, Antrodiaetidae)." *Journal of Arachnology* 22, no. 3 (1994): 225–55.

Cushing, Paula E., and Richard G. Santangelo. "Notes on the Natural History and Hunting Behavior of an Ant Eating Zodariid Spider (Arachnida, Araneae) in Colorado." *Journal of Arachnology* 30, no. 3 (2002): 618–21.

Dondale, Charles D., and James H. Redner. *The Wolf Spiders, Nurseryweb Spiders, and Lynx Spiders of Canada and Alaska*. Ottawa, ON: Canadian Government Publishing Centre, 1990.

Edwards, Robert L., and Eric H. Edwards. "Observations on the Natural History of a New England Population of *Sphodros niger* (Araneae, Atypidae)." *Journal of Arachnology* 18, no. 1 (1990): 29–34.

Emerton, James H. *The Common Spiders of the United States*. Boston: Ginn & Company, 1902.

———. *The Structure and Habits of Spiders*. Boston: S. E. Cassino & Co., 1883.

Foelix, Rainer F. *Biology of Spiders*. New York: Oxford University Press, 1996.

Gertsch, Willis J. *American Spiders*. New York: Van Nostrand Reinhold Company, 1979.

———. "A Review of the Genus *Hypochilus* and a Description of a New Species from Colorado (Araneae, Hypochilidae)." *American Museum Novitates* 2203 (1964): 1–14.

Gregory, Ben M., Jr. "Field Observations of *Gasteracantha cancriformis* (Araneae, Araneidae) in a Florida Mangrove Stand." *Journal of Arachnology* 17, no. 1 (1989): 119–20.

Guarisco, Hank. "Description of the Egg Sac of *Mimetus notius* (Araneae, Mimetidae) and a Case of Egg Predation by *Phalacrotophora epeirae* (Diptera, Phoridae)." *Journal of Arachnology* 29, no. 2 (2001): 267–69.

Hardy, Laurence M. "Trees Used for Tube Support by *Sphodros rufipes* (Latreille 1829) (Araneae, Atypidae) in Northwestern Louisiana." *Journal of Arachnology* 31, no. 3 (2003): 437–40.

Heiss, John Stabe, and Michael L. Draney. "Revision of the Nearctic Spider Genus *Calymmaria* (Araneae, Hahniidae)." *Journal of Arachnology* 32 (2004): 457–525.

Howell, W. Mike, and Ronald L. Jenkins. *Spiders of the Eastern United States: A Photographic Guide*. Boston: Pearson Education, 2004.

Kaston, B. J. *How to Know the Spiders*. Dubuque, IA: Wm. C. Brown Company Publishers, 1978.

Levi, Herbert W., and Lorna R. Levi. *Spiders and Their Kin*. New York: St. Martin's Press, 1987.

Manuel, Raymond L. "The Egg Sac of *Pityohyphantes costatus* (Hentz) (Araneae, Linyphiidae) and Its Phorid Parasite." *Journal of Arachnology* 12, no. 3 (1984): 371–72.

McCook, H. C. "A Spider that Makes a Spherical Mud-Daub Cocoon." *Proceedings of the Academy of Natural Sciences of Philadelphia* 36 (1884): 151–53.

Nørgaard, Edwin. "On the Ecology of Two Lycosid Spiders (*Pirata piraticus* and *Lycosa pullata*) from a Danish Sphagnum Bog." *Oikos* 3, no. 1 (1951): 1–21.

Opell, Brent D. "A Simple Method for Measuring Desiccation Resistance of Spider Egg Sacs." *Journal of Arachnology* 12, no. 2 (1984): 245–47.

Pekár, Stano, and Jiří Král. "A Comparative Study of the Biology and Karyotypes of Two Central European Zodariid Spiders (Araneae, Zodariidae)." *Journal of Arachnology* 29, no. 3 (2001): 345–53.

Poinar, George O., Jr. "Mermithid (Nematoda) Parasites of Spiders and Harvestmen." *Journal of Arachnology* 13 (1985): 121–28.

Polis, G. A. *The Biology of Scorpions*. Stanford, CA: Stanford University Press, 1990.

Ramirez, Martin G. "Natural History of the Spider Genus *Lutica* (Araneae, Zodariidae)." *Journal of Arachnology* 23, no. 2 (1995): 111–17.

Sabath, L. E. "Color Change and Life History Observations of the Spider *Gea heptagon* (Araneae: Araneidae)." *Psyche* 76 (1969): 367–74.

Savory, Theodore H. *The Biology of Spiders*. London: Sidgwick & Jackson, 1928.

Sedey, Kris A., and Elizabeth M. Jakob. "A Description of an Unusual Dome Web Occupied by Egg-Carrying *Holocnemus pluchei* (Araneae, Pholcidae)." *Journal of Arachnology* 26, no. 3 (1998): 385–88.

Shmitt, Alain. "Conjectures on the Origins and Functions of a Bridal Veil Spun by the Males of *Cupiennius coccineus* (Araneae, Ctenidae)." *Journal of Arachnology* 20, no. 1 (1992): 67–68.

Smith, Deborah R. "Notes on the Reproductive Biology and Social Behavior of Two Sympatric Species of *Philoponella* (Araneae, Uloboridae)." *Journal of Arachnology* 25, no. 1 (1997): 11–19.

Thewke, Siegfried E., and Wilbur R. Enns. *The Spider-Mite Complex (Acarina: Tetranychoidea) in Missouri*. Museum Contributions, Monograph No. 1. Columbia: University of Missouri, 1969.

Tso, I-Min. "Stabilimentum-Decorated Webs Spun by *Cyclosa conica* (Araneae, Araneidae) Trapped More Insects Than Undecorated Webs." *Journal of Arachnology* 26, no. 1 (1998): 101–5.

Ubick, D., P. Paquin, P. E. Cushing, and V. Roth, eds. *Spiders of North America: An Identification Manual*. American Arachnological Society, 2005.

Wise, David H. "Egg Cocoon of the Filmy Dome Spider, *Linyphia marginata*, C. L. Koch (Araneae: Linyphiidae)." *Journal of Arachnology* 1, no. 2 (1973): 143–44.

Millipedes

Hopkin, Stephen P., and Helen J. Read. *The Biology of Millipedes*. New York: Oxford University Press, 1992.

O'Neill, Robert V. "Adaptive Responses to Desiccation in the Millipede, *Narceus americanus*." *American Midland Naturalist* 81, no. 2 (1969): 578–83.

Preston-Mafham, Ken. *Discovering Centipedes & Millipedes*. New York: Bookwright Press, 1990.

Shaw, George G. "New Observations on Reproductive Behavior in the Milliped *Narceus annularis*." *Ecology* 47, no. 2 (1966): 322–23.

Leafhoppers and Treehoppers

DeLong, Dwight M. "The Bionomics of Leafhoppers." *Annual Review of Entomology* 16 (1971): 179–210.

Marlatt, C. L. "Notes on the Oviposition of the Buffalo Tree-hopper." *Transactions of the Annual Meetings of the Kansas Academy of Science* 10 (1885–86): 84–85.

Ants, Bees, Wasps, and Sawflies

Balduf, W. V. "Bionomic Notes on Some Parasites of *Achatodes zeae* Harris (Noctuidae, Lep.) and *Phlyctaenia tertialis* (Guen.) (Pyralidae, Lep.)." *Ohio Journal of Science* 29, no. 5 (1929): 218–42.

Buck, Matthias, Stephen A. Marshall, and David K. B. Cheung. "Identification Atlas of the Vespidae (Hymenoptera, Aculeata) of the Northeastern Nearctic Region." *Canadian Journal of Arthropod Identification* 5 (2008). Available online at http://www.biology.ualberta.ca/bsc/ejournal/bmc_05/bmc_05.html.

Custer, Clarence P. "The Bee That Works in Stone; *Perdita opuntiae* Cockerell." *Psyche* 35, no. 2 (1928): 67–84.

Evans, H. E. *The Behavior Patterns of Solitary Wasps*. Annual Reviews in Entomology 11 (1966): 123–54.

Evans, Howard E., and Mary Jane West Eberhard. *The Wasps*. Ann Arbor: University of Michigan Press, 1970.

Gauld, Ian D. *An Introduction to the Ichneumonidae of Australia*. London: British Museum, 1984.

Gess, Sarah K. *The Pollen Wasps: Ecology and Natural History of the Masarinae*. Cambridge, MA: Harvard University Press, 1996.

Grosman, Amir H., Arne Janssen, Elaine F. de Brito, Eduardo G. Cordeiro, Felipe Colares, Juliana Oliveira Fonseca, Eraldo R. Lima, Angelo Pallini, and Maurice W. Sabelis. "Parasitoid Increases Survival of Its Pupae by Inducing Hosts to Fight Predators." *PLoS ONE* 3, no. 6 (2008). Available online at http://www.plosone.org/doi/pone.0002276.

Howard, J. J. "Costs of Trail Construction and Maintenance in the Leaf-Cutting Ant *Atta columbica*." *Behavioral Ecology and Sociobiology* 49 (2001): 348–56.

Johnson, Charles W. "Notes on the Nests of *Odynerus (Ancistrocerus) birenimaculatus* Saussure." *Psyche* 30 (1923): 226–27.

Krombein, Karl V., Paul D. Hurd Jr., David R. Smith, and B. D. Burks. *Catalog of Hymenoptera in America North of Mexico*. Washington, DC: Smithsonian Institution Press, 1979.

Michener, C. D. *The Bees of the World*. Baltimore: Johns Hopkins University Press, 2000.

O'Neill, Kevin M. *Solitary Wasps: Behavior and Natural History*. Ithaca, NY: Cornell University Press, 2001.

Packard, A. S. "Notes on the Nesting Habits of Certain Bees." *Psyche* 6 (1892): 340–41.

Pezzolesi, L. S. W., and B. J. Hager. "Ant Predation on Two Species of Birch Leaf-Mining Sawflies." *American Midland Naturalist* 131, no. 1 (1994): 156–68.

Quaintance, A. L., and C. T. Brues. *The Cotton Bollworm*. U.S. Department of Agriculture Bureau of Entomology Bulletin No. 50. Washington, DC: Government Printing Office, 1905. [Information on parasitoids.]

Rau, Phil. "The Biology and Behavior of Mining Bees, *Anthophora abrupta* and *Entechnia taurea*." *Psyche* 36, no. 3 (1929): 155–81.

Ross, K. G., and R. W. Matthews. *The Social Biology of Wasps*. Ithaca, NY: Cornell University Press, 1991.

Schmidt, J. O. "Hymenopteran Venoms: Striving toward the Ultimate Defense against Vertebrates." In *Insect Defenses: Adaptive Mechanisms and Strategies of Prey and Predators*, edited by D. L. Evans and J. O. Schmidt, 387–419. Albany: State University of New York Press, 1990.

Shaw, Scott R. Aleiodes *Wasps of Eastern Forests: A Guide to Parasitoids and Associated Mummified Caterpillars*. Morgantown, WV: Forest Health Technology Enterprise Team, 2006.

Sheldon, Joseph K. "The Nesting Behavior and Larval Morphology of *Pison koreense* (Radoszkowski) (Hymenoptera: Sphecidae)." *Psyche* 75, no. 2 (1968): 107–17.

Smith, Harry Scott. "The Habit of Leaf-Oviposition among the Parasitic Hymenoptera." *Psyche* 24, no. 3 (1917): 63–68.

Tschinkel, Walter R. "The Natural History of the Arboreal Ant, *Crematogaster ashmeadi*." *Journal of Insect Science* 2, no. 12 (2002). http://insectscience.org/2.12.

Weed, Clarence M. "Notes on Some Illinois Microgasters: With Descriptions of New Species." *Bulletin of the Illinois State Laboratory of Natural History* 3 (1896): 1–8.

Wenzel, John W. "A Generic Key to the Nests of Hornets, Yellowjackets, and Paper Wasps Worldwide (Vespidae: Vespinae, Polistinae)." *American Museum Novitates* 3224 (1998): 1–39.

Wesson, Laurence G., Jr., and Robert G. Wesson. "A Collection of Ants from Southcentral Ohio." *American Midland Naturalist* 24, no. 1 (1940): 89–103.

Wheeler, William Morton. "A New Paper-Making *Crematogaster* from the Southeastern United States." *Psyche* 26 (1919): 107–12.

Butterflies, Moths, and Skippers

Allen, Thomas J., Jim P. Brock, and Jeffrey Glassberg. *Caterpillars in the Field and Garden: A Field Guide to the Butterfly Caterpillars of North America*. Oxford, UK: Oxford University Press, 2005.

Braun, Annette F. "Nepticulidae of North America." *Transactions of the American Entomological Society* 43 (1917): 155–209.

———. "Revision of the North American Species of the Genus *Lithocolletis* Hübner." *Transactions of the American Entomological Society* 34 (1908): 269–357.

———. "Tischeriidae of America North of Mexico (Microlepidoptera)." *Memoirs of the American Entomological Society*, no. 28. Philadelphia: American Entomological Society, 1972.

Bucheli, Sibyl, Jean-François Landry, and John Wenzel. "Larval Case Architecture and Implications of Host-Plant Associations for North American *Coleophora* (Lepidoptera: Coleophoridae)." *Cladistics* 18 (2002): 71–93.

Clemens, Brackenridge. *The Tineina of North America*. London: John Van Voorst, 1872.

Common, I. F. B. *Moths of Australia*. Boston: BRILL, 1990.

Covell, Charles V., Jr. *Moths of Eastern North America*. Boston: Houghton Mifflin Company, 1984.

Davis, Donald R. *Bagworm Moths of the Western Hemisphere*. United States National Museum Bulletin 244. Washington, DC: Smithsonian Institution, 1964.

Farquhar, Donald W. "Notes on a Psychid New to North America (*Fumea casta* Pallas, Lepidoptera: Psychidae)." *Psyche* 41 (1934): 19–28.

Forbes, William T. M. *The Lepidoptera of New York and Neighboring States*. Cornell University Agricultural Experiment Station Memoir 68. Ithaca, NY: Cornell University Press, 1923.

Gambino, Parker. "*Dolichovespula* (Hymenoptera: Vespidae), Hosts of *Aphomia sociella* (L.) (Lepidoptera: Pyralidae)." *Journal of the New York Entomological Society* 103, no. 2 (1995): 165–69.

Guillén, Marta, Donald R. Davis, and John M. Heraty. "Systematics and Biology of a New, Polyphagous Species of *Marmara* (Lepidoptera: Gracillariidae) Infesting Grapefruit in the Southwestern United States." *Proceedings of the Entomological Society of Washington* 103, no. 3 (2001): 636–54.

Heath, John, ed. *The Moths and Butterflies of Great Britain and Ireland*. Vol. 1, *Micropterigidae–Heliozelidae*. Martins: Harley Books, 1983.

Herlong, David D. "Aquatic Pyralidae (Lepidoptera: Nymphulinae) in South Carolina." *Florida Entomologist* 62, no. 3 (1979): 188–93.

Kulman, H. M. "Biology of the Hard Maple Bud Miner, *Obrussa ochrefasciella*, and Notes on Its Damage (Lepidoptera: Nepticulidae)." *Annals of the Entomological Society of America* 60, no. 2 (1967): 387–91.

Landry, Jean-François. "Taxonomic Review of the Leek Moth Genus *Acrolepiopsis* (Lepidoptera: Acrolepiidae) in North America." *Canadian Entomologist* 139 (2007): 319–53.

Peigler, Richard S. "Catalog of Parasitoids of Saturniidae of the World." *Journal of Research on the Lepidoptera* 33 (1994): 1–121.

Pyle, Robert Michael. *The Audubon Society Field Guide to North American Butterflies*. New York: Alfred A. Knopf, 1981.

Solis, M. Alma, and M. A. Metz. "*Aphomia* Hübner and *Paralipsa* Butler Species (Lepidoptera: Pyralidae: Galleriinae) Known to Occur in the United States and Canada." *Proceedings of the Entomological Society of Washington* 110, no. 3 (2008): 592–601.

Tuskes, Paul M., James P. Tuttle, and Michael M. Collins. *The Wild Silk Moths of North America*. Ithaca, NY: Cornell University Press, 1996.

Wagner, David L. *Caterpillars of Eastern North America*. Princeton, NJ: Princeton University Press, 2005.

Wilkinson, Christopher, and M. J. Scoble. *The Nepticulidae (Lepidoptera) of Canada*. Memoirs of the Entomological Society of Canada no. 107. Ottawa, ON: Entomological Society of Canada, 1979.

Flies

Devetak, Dušan. "Substrate Particle Size-Preference of Wormlion *Vermileo vermileo* (Diptera: Vermileonidae) Larvae and Their Interaction with Antlions." *European Journal of Entomology* 105 (2008): 631–35.

Eberhard, William G. "The Natural History of the Fungus Gnats *Leptomorphus bifasciatus* (Say) and *L. subcaeruleus* (Coquillett) (Diptera: Mycetophilidae)." *Psyche* 77, no. 3 (1970): 361–83.

Knipling, E. F. "The Biology of *Sarcophaga cistudinis* Aldrich (Diptera), a Species of Sarcophagidae Parasitic on Turtles and Tortoises." *Proceedings of the Entomological Society of Washington* 39, no. 5 (1937): 91–101.

Mangano, M. G., L. A. Buatois, and G. L. Claps. "Grazing Trails Formed by Soldier Fly Larvae (Diptera: Stratiomyidae) and Their Paleoenvironmental and Paleoecological Implications for the Fossil Record." *Ichnos* 4 (1996): 163–68.

Marston, Norman. *Taxonomic Study of the Known Pupae of the Genus* Anthrax *(Diptera: Bombyliidae) in North and South America*. Washington, DC: Smithsonian Institution Press, 1971.

Metz, R. "Sinusoidal Trail Formed by a Recent Biting Midge (Family Ceratopogonidae): Trace Fossil Implications." *Journal of Paleontology* 61, no. 2 (1987): 312–14.

Oldroyd, Harold. *The Natural History of Flies*. London: Weidenfeld and Nicolson, 1964.

Riley, C. V. "Larval Stages and Habits of the Bee-Fly *Hirmoneura*." *Science* 1, no. 12 (1883): 332–34.

Short, Brent D., and J. Christopher Bergh. "Separation of Three Common Hover Fly Predators of Woolly Apple Aphid Based on the Exochorionic Sculpturing of Eggs." *Canadian Entomologist* 137 (2005): 67–70.

Spencer, Kenneth A. *Host Specialization in the World Agromyzidae (Diptera)*. Boston: Kluwer Academic Publishers, 1990.

Spencer, Kenneth A., and George C. Steyskal. *Manual of the Agromyzidae (Diptera) of the United States*. USDA Agricultural Research Service, Agriculture Handbook, no. 638, 1986.

Uchman, A. "Treptichnus-like Traces Made by Insect Larvae (Diptera: Chironomidae: Tipulidae). Pennsylvanian Footprints in the Black Warrior Basin of Alabama." *Alabama Paleontological Society Monograph* 1 (2005): 1–380.

Weems, Howard V., Jr. "Natural Enemies and Insecticides That Are Detrimental to Beneficial Syrphidae." *Ohio Journal of Science* 54 (1954): 45–54.

Beetles

Arnett, Ross H. *The Beetles of the United States*. Ann Arbor, MI: The American Entomological Institute, 1973.

Arnett, Ross H., and Michael Charles Thomas. *American Beetles: Polyphaga: Scarabaeoidea through Curculionoidea*. Boca Raton, FL: CRC Press, 2002.

Britt, B. B. "A Suite of Dermestid Beetle Traces on Dinosaur Bone from the Upper Jurassic Morrison Formation, Wyoming, USA." *Ichnos* 15 (2008): 59–71.

Clark, G. R., and B. C. Ratcliffe. "Observations on the Tunnel Morphology of *Heterocerus brunneus* Melsheimer (Coleoptera; Heteroceridae) and Its Paleoecological Significance." *Journal of Paleontology* 63 (1989): 228–32.

Frost, C. A. "Notes on *Attelabus rhois* and Parasite." *Psyche* 15, no. 2 (1908): 26–32.

Hespenheide, Henry A. "A Reconsideration of *Pachyschelus schwarzi* Kerremans and a Review of American *Pachyschelus* North of Mexico (Coleoptera: Buprestidae)." *Coleopterists Bulletin* 57, no. 4 (2003): 459–68.

MacRae, Ted C. "Notes on Host Associations of *Taphrocerus gracilis* (Say) (Coleoptera: Buprestidae) and Its Life History in Missouri." *Coleopterists Bulletin* 58, no. 3 (2004): 388–90.

White, Richard E. *A Field Guide to the Beetles of North America*. Boston: Houghton Mifflin Company, 1983.

Young, F. N., T. H. Hubbell, and D. W. Hayne. "Further Notes on the Habits of *Geotrupes* (Coleoptera: Geotrupidae)." *Psyche* 62 (1955): 53–54.

Neuropterans

Badgley, M. E., C. A. Fleschner, and J. C. Hall. "The Biology of *Spiloconis picticornis* Banks (Neuroptera: Coniopterygidae)." *Psyche* 62 (1955): 75–82.

Brown, Harley P. "The Life History of *Climacia areolaris* (Hagen), a Neuropterous 'Parasite' of Fresh Water Sponges." *American Midland Naturalist* 47, no. 1 (1952): 130–60.

Gurney, Ashley B. "Notes on Dilaridae and Berothidae, with Special Reference to the Immature Stages of the Nearctic Genera (Neuroptera)." *Psyche* 54, no. 3 (1947): 145–69.

Henry, Charles S. "Eggs and Rapagula [*sic*] of *Ululodes* and *Ascaloptynx* (Neuroptera: Ascalaphidae): A Comparative Study." *Psyche* 79, no. 1–2 (1972): 1–22.

McEwen, P., T. R. New, and A. E. Whittington. *Lacewings in the Crop Environment*. Cambridge, UK: Cambridge University Press, 2001.

Pupedis, Raymond J. "Generic Differences among the New World Spongilla-Fly Larvae and a Description of the Female of *Climacia striata* (Neuroptera: Sisyridae). *Psyche* 87 (1980): 305–14.

Grasshoppers, Crickets, and Kin

Capinera, John L., Ralph D. Scott, and Thomas J. Walker. *Field Guide to Grasshoppers, Katydids, and Crickets of the United States*. Ithaca, NY: Comstock Publishing Associates, 2004.

Caudell, A. N. "An Orthopterous Leaf-Roller." *Proceedings of the Entomological Society of Washington* 6, no. 1 (1904): 46–49.

Fulton, Bentley B. "The Tree Crickets of New York: Life History and Bionomics." *New York Agricultural Experiment Station Technical Bulletin* 42 (1915): 3–47.

———. "The Tree Crickets of Oregon." *Oregon Agricultural College Experiment Station Bulletin* 223 (1926): 1–20.

Hartley, J. C. "The Egg of *Tetrix* (Tetrigidae, Orthoptera), with a Discussion on the Probable Significance of the Anterior Horn." *Quarterly Journal of Microscopical Science* s3-103 (1962): 253–59.

Hutchins, Ross E. *Grasshoppers and Their Kin*. New York: Dodd, Mead & Company, 1972.

McAtee, W. L. "Notes on an Orthopterous Leaf Roller." *Entomological News* 19, no. 10 (1908): 488–91.

Weaver, Joseph E., and Robert A. Sommers. "Life History and Habits of the Short-Tailed Cricket, *Anurogryllus muticus*, in Central Louisiana." *Annals of the Entomological Society of America* 62, no. 2 (1969): 337–42.

Stick Insects

Arment, Chad. *Stick Insects of the Continental United States and Canada: Species and Early Studies*. Landisville, PA: Coachwhip Publications, 2006.

Sivinski, John. "Eggs and Oviposition of the Stick Insect *Parabacillus coloradus* (Phasmatodea: Heteronemiidae)." *Florida Entomologist* 61, no. 2 (1978): 99.

Cockroaches

Bell, William J., Louis M. Roth, and Christine A. Nalepa. *Cockroaches: Ecology, Behavior, and Natural History*. Baltimore: Johns Hopkins University Press, 2007.

ACKNOWLEDGMENTS

We owe our thanks to the animals, plants, soil, waters, sun, moon, stars, and all the mysterious things that conspired to lead us to the tiny wonders we found for this book. Though we set out simply to identify the curious byproducts of invertebrate existence, we found ourselves in awe of the clever diversity of adaptations these creatures have come up with over the eons. Discovering the intricacies of relationships among nonhuman life forms reminds us to look beyond human societies to gain understanding of our own existence.

—C. E. and N. C.

My renewed interest in the world of insects and other invertebrates can be traced to the moment several years ago when Rob Stevenson, having never met me, decided to give me my first digital camera. He had received an NSF grant to start an online field guide, and he happened to ask my friends Laurie Sanders and Fred Morrison if they knew anyone who spends a lot of time in the woods and would make good use of a Nikon Coolpix. They recommended me, and with this camera's macro capabilities, combined with the freedom to take unlimited photos without worrying about developing film, I soon found myself turning my attention to all the small creatures around me, as I had not done since I was myself a small creature. So to Rob, Laurie, and Fred, I owe deep gratitude for starting me on this journey.

As I accumulated images of mystery objects and other signs of invertebrate activity, I longed for a book that would help me sort them out. Eventually I realized that such a book would fit well with the series Mark Elbroch had started with *Bird Tracks and Sign* and *Mammal Tracks and Sign*. I asked Mark if he thought he would ever write a guide to invertebrate tracks and sign, and he said it was up to me. I was skeptical that I could pull it off, but he encouraged me to go for it and suggested that having a deadline would motivate me to learn what I needed to learn. I thank Mark for giving me the confidence boost I needed to pursue this project.

Great thanks are due to Mark Allison at Stackpole Books for seeing the potential in this book and agreeing to publish it. Knowing that what I found would be shared with the world, I indulged myself in a quest for knowledge that I never would have undertaken if I thought the information would be forever trapped in my head and my private journals.

Noah and I have studied tracking and nature together for a decade, and it was only natural that this book would turn out to be a collaboration. I thank Noah for his enthusiasm and dedication (e.g., scrutinizing each log of firewood for signs of life before burning it), his lax housekeeping, his ability to notice absurdly tiny things, his persistence in taking countless photos of the same subject after I had stopped at one or two, and his willingness to largely ignore his PhD candidacy while we drove around the continent for forty days. In the final weeks of writing, he was always available for middle-of-the-night consultations, and as I became increasingly bound to my desk, he made deliveries of what amounted to a wheelbarrow full of books and journals that he gathered for me via interlibrary loans. It's hard to imagine what this book would be without Noah's help.

Thanks to everyone who accompanied me on photo-gathering missions. My brother Ted, despite a slipped disc, helped me explore Florida and other parts of the Southeast. Others who joined me on shorter excursions include my sister Katy, Carrie Bernstein, Corrie Miller, Lisa Passerello, and Sarah Rosow, all of whom waited patiently during my frequent stops to take photos, as well as helped to find subjects. Kasey Rolih did as well, which was especially appreciated since I was supposed to be working. On our forty-day odyssey, Noah and I were joined in some of our explorations by Orion Berdick, Louis Levine, Paula Peng, Eva Hausam, Josh Lane, and Ben Ramage. Some of them also gave us places to stay or fed us, as did Sharon Charney, Kavarra Corr, the Museum of Jurassic Technology, and Jon Young. Jeff Boettner and Laurie Sanders brought us to Cape Cod at just the right time to experience the periodical cicadas in their full glory.

Other friends and family helped make this book possible, directly or indirectly. Thanks to my parents, Judith and Jeffrey Eiseman, for choosing to live at the end of a dead-end road in the middle of the woods, beside a pond that teems with life. Growing up in this setting, more than anything else, has made me who I am. My mother also volunteered to read through the entire manuscript to make sure it made sense. John Reid, Charlie Camp, and Joe Choiniere were important mentors at different stages in my life who inspired and encouraged me in my naturalist pursuits, and I thank all the members of the Woodsy Club for helping me get my priorities straight at a critical time. Walker Korby and Danielle Botelho listened as I rambled on about all the crazy things I was learning as I conducted my research; Danielle also lent me some red wiggler egg cases to photograph. Colby and Ryan Crehan, through music, helped ensure that this project did not completely consume me, and their house and yard yielded a number of the photographs you see here. Abby Hood sent me some cocoons, and Jesse Poutasse brought gifts from his bees.

I am deeply grateful to all who have conducted and published natural history studies, and all who have endeavored to compile and synthesize this information before me. A book like this would be utterly inconceivable starting from scratch. Each book cited in the bibliography represents many lifetimes of patient, careful observations, painstakingly recorded for other curious minds. Thanks also to those at Google and The Internet Archive who have digitized old and obscure writings, making them accessible in ways in which their authors likely never dreamed possible.

As I began the daunting task of researching for this book, I became aware of BugGuide.net, an online community of amateur and expert entomologists who help each other identify arthropods from photographs. One day I entered the word "cocoon" into a query there, and among the hundreds of thumbnail images that popped up, I was quickly drawn to an image of a beautiful and utterly unfamiliar object. It had been submitted by Charles Lewallen, a retired mailman in Oklahoma, several months earlier, and no one had a clue what it was (although it had been tentatively placed in the weevil section). It immediately became my mission to discover what this thing was, and the very next day, I came across a description of a spongillafly cocoon that perfectly matched what I had seen. I excitedly reported my discovery, Charles generously agreed to contribute his photo, and so I entered the BugGuide community. I am grateful to founder Troy Bartlett for creating this phenomenal resource, and to all who have contributed photos, identifications, and information. The following BugGuide contributors have directly helped me by commenting on images and questions I posted: John S. Ascher, John and Jane Balaban, Brad Barnd, Jay Barnes, Vassili Belov, Margarethe Brummermann, Boris Büche, Matthias Buck, Bob Carlson, Donald S. Chandler, Ben Coulter, Eric Eaton, David J. Ferguson, Steve Ferguson II, Jason Forbes, Lloyd Gonzales, Dave Gracer, Bobby Grizzard, Jeff Gruber, Andy Hamilton, Sam W. Heads, Kojun Kanda, Stephen Luk, Ted MacRae, Kari J. McWest, Ron Melder, Laura T. Miller, Ed Mockford, Beatriz Moisset, Jae Nanthranoha, Steve Nanz, Hannah Nendick-Mason, Harsi S. Parker, Gerard Pennards, J. D. Roberts, David Ruiter, Lynette Schimming, Tony Thomas, James C. Trager, Richard Vernier, George Waldren, and Rob Westerduijn. Some of them provided additional help outside of BugGuide: Vassili Belov shared his experience with fungus-feeding beetles, also soliciting and translating the input of Alexey Kovalev; Dave Ferguson identified some desert plants and shared his observations of grasshopper egg pods; Andy Hamilton answered all my questions about leafhoppers, treehoppers, and spittlebugs. Special thanks are due to Nancy Collins and John Maxwell for their unsolicited help in cluing me in to photos and phenomena that had escaped my notice. Nancy also sent me some twigs to photograph, and Max's skepticism of some identifications I made on BugGuide prompted me to do more thorough research.

Many other people I have never met, some of whom I found through BugGuide, helped me go beyond what I was able to learn from my literature review. Terry Harrison was extremely generous with his time and knowledge of leaf-mining Lepidoptera. Jean-François Landry identified all my images of coleophorid cases to the extent possible. Alan Chin-Lee and Keith Wolfe provided information about frass chains, Marius Aurelian added some details about moth cocoons, and David Wagner helped with various moth-related phenomena. Andy Bennett and Michael Sharkey assisted me in my quest for information about ichneumonoid cocoons, and Scott Shaw and Jim Whitfield identified many of the ones I had photographed. Terry Prouty pointed me toward descriptions of hornet nests, and Nick Fensler answered a question about spider wasp nests. Paul Beuk examined my *Scaptomyza* specimens. Sonja J. Scheffer set me straight on agromyzid flies. Herschel Raney, Patrick Coin, and Valerie Bugh helped me refine my description of robber fly egg masses, Elizabeth Beers pointed me to information about syrphid eggs, and Greg Courtney answered a question about Blepharicerid eggs. Yen Saw commented on my photos of mantid oothecae. John D. Oswald prompted me to investigate beaded lacewing eggs. Christopher G. Brown helped with cryptocephalines and sent a CD of photos to peruse. Thanks to all the other photo contributors, many of whom provided useful information related to their images. Dave Almquist, Bonnie Caruthers, Kris Light, and Judy Semroc were particularly helpful, offering many images beyond what I originally asked them for. Dave also enlisted the help of Skip Choate, Phillip Harpootlian, and Paul Skelley, who all shared their observations of earth-boring dung beetle burrows. Rowland Shelley identified a millipede. Darrell Ubick responded to my call for help with mystery spider egg sacs, and Deborah Smith confirmed my identification of *Philoponella oweni*. Barry O'Connor answered questions about mites. Sarah K. Berke, Jim Blake, Bryan L. Brown, Judith Fournier, Nancy Maciolek, Paulo Cesar de Paiva, Mary Petersen, Geoff Read, Dan Shain, and Sarah Ann Woodin responded to my posts on annelida.net. Steven Arthurs, Joseph E. Funderburk, and Lance S. Osborne gave feedback on a thrips-related mystery.

John Carlson volunteered to write a chapter on bites and stings before I even had a chance to ask him. I am grateful for his generosity in sharing his expertise, and his willingness to subject himself to bites and stings to better understand and describe them. Thanks also to Mark Fox, who helped John with the photography for this chapter.

Thanks to copyeditor Joyce Bond, editorial assistants Janelle Steen and Kathryn Fulton, and everyone else at Stackpole Books who has had a hand in shaping our words and pictures into the book you are now holding.

—C. E.

Many people pointed us to curious finds, offered neat ideas, and provided support on our adventure. I want to thank everyone that helped along the way, including:

Sydne Record for being my best friend and best support, and putting up with the jars of hatching eggs, molding pupae, rotting water, breeding flies, and mosquito larvae, and for being patient in the face of incessant photography. My dad, Jonathan I. Charney for inspiring me toward perfection and truth. My mom, Sharon, my sister, Tamar, and my brother, Adam, for always playing with me and nurturing the naturalist and artist in me. Annie for bringing us bot flies.

Louis Levine for naturalist mentoring from childhood to today and guiding us through his spectacular collections of objects, several of which are featured in this book. Jeff Boettner for help in identifications, letting us photograph the creatures in his lab, and being a knowledgeable ear to bounce ideas off throughout this process. Rodger Gwiazdowski and Jeremy Andersen for consulting on scale insects and their relatives. Fred Gagnon at Magic Wings for providing sign of butterflies and such. John Alcock and Bob Childs for photos and guidance. Charlie at Organ Pipe National Monument. The Sonoran Desert Museum staff. Marcia at Tanque Verde Guest Ranch. Kate Wellspring at the Amherst College Natural History Museum. Tracie Stice of The Night Tour. Whitey Hagadorn. Rich Merritt, Jeff Adams, Christopher Rogers, Steve Hamilton, and William Taft for helping on aquatic IDs. Our new friend Wil at Restaurante el Rincon del Viejo for translating, humoring us, and pointing us to the tarantulas. All the previous researchers whose work made ours possible, and the journal *Ichnos* for carrying the academic pursuit of tracking.

Kavarra Corr for opening her home to us and providing the casebearer moth cocoons. Josh Lane for leading us under the bridge and pointing us to the bees. Alona Bachi for putting me up in Tucson and providing insights on scorpion tracking. Neill Bovaird for bringing us the psyllids; Rob Lynch and Meghan Arquin at Riverland Farm for the insects that flourish on organic veggies; along with Walker, Meggie, Jesse, James, and all the Woodsy Club members for inspiration. George Leoniak for offering insights on insect movement. Jon Young, along with Mark Elbroch, Sue Morse, and Tom Brown for tracking mentoring. Victor Wooten, for starting me down the tracking path.

The National Science Foundation for supporting me throughout the time of this research. Paige Warren, my PhD advisor, for understanding when I said, "So, the day after tomorrow I'm getting in my car to drive around the country for six weeks."

The Canon G-9 that drowned in the water of a vernal pool. The other that was choked by the earth of the Kelso dunes. The lens that was shaken to bits by the wind smacking against a tiny Central American plane. The current Rebel that is bound to melt down in some fiery volcano.

Charley, for bringing me along on this adventure, for doing most of the real work, and for trying to keep me honest.

Finally, we both thank you, the readers, for giving us purpose and for appreciating, respecting, and striving to understand the natural world.

—N. C.

INDEX

Aaroniella, 25
Abedus, 2, 53–54
Abia inflate, 231
Acalitus vaccinii, 392
Acalymma vittatum, 324, 328
Acalyptris punctulatus, 336
Acanthepeira, 35, 40, 213
Acanthocephala, 52, 297
Acantholyda, 64, 185–86
Acanthoscelides obtectus, 319
Acanthosomatid shield bugs, 2
Acaridae *(Acarus)*, 330
Acaridia, 118
Aceria, 330, 380, 381, 384, 393
Acericecis ocellaris, 386
Achaearanea, 39, 190
Acharia stimulea, 133
Achroia grisella, 275
Acraspis, 391
Acrididae, 12, 65, 157–58, 519
Acrobasis, 169–70, 323, 325, 369
Acroceridae, 58–59, 117
Acrolepiidae *(Acrolepiopsis)*, 171, 221
Acrolophidae, 187
Acronicta, 156, 243, 424
Acrosternum hilare, 50–51
Acteonidae, 9
Actias luna, 225
Aculops rhois, 381, 383
Acyrthosiphon pisum, 66
Adelges, 403–4
Adelgids, 172, 314, 403–4
Adelidae *(Adela)*, 254, 321
Adelpha bredowii, 158

Adicrophleps hitchcocki, 263
Adula, 441
Aedes, 60
Aeolothripidae, 238
Aeshnidae, 5, 84, 146
Agaonidae (Agaoninae), 327
Agapema, 226
Agarodes, 258
Agave bug, giant, 297
Agelenidae, 31, 33, 41, 44, 194–96, 507
Agelenopsis, 31, 33, 43, 195
Aglais milberti, 185
Aglajidae, 10
Agonopterix, 365–66, 369–70
Agrilus, 18, 63, 311, 401, 417–18, 421–22, 430
Agromyza, 341, 342, 360
Agromyzidae, 4, 302–3, 337–39, 341–42, 360, 399, 400, 406, 413, 428
Agrotis, 327
Agrypnia, 262, 263
Aleiodes, 111, 112, 113
Aleocharinae, 238, 294
Aleurocanthus woglumi, 68, 90–91
Aleurodicus disperses and *dugesii*, 24, 173
Aleurothrixus floccosus, 173
Aleyrodidae, 23, 68, 90–91
Aliatypus, 26, 458–59
Allocyclosa bifurca, 42
Allomyia, 259
Alopecosa, 457
Alpheidae, 454
Alsophila pometaria, 70–71

Altica chalybea, 305
Alticini, 305
Alypia octomaculata, 243
Amaurobiidae, 36, 44, 192, 196
Amauromyza pleuralis, 342
Amblycerus robiniae, 319
Amblyomma americanum, 136–37
Amblypygi, 2
Ambush bugs, 13, 16, 107–8
American snout, 95
Americonuphis magna, 268
Ametastegia glabrata, 327
Amiocentrus aspilus, 256, 263
Ammophila, 451
Ammophilinae, 483
Ampeliscids, 271
Ampeloglypter, 418
Ampharetidae, 271
Amphibolips, 390
Amphicosmoecus, 262
Amphinectidae, 192
Amphipods, 2, 271–72, 437, 453–54, 492–93
Amphisbatidae, 219, 370
Amphitoe, 271–72
Amphizoidae, 64, 246
Ampullariidae, 74–75
Amyelois transitella, 323
Anabolia, 264
Anabrus simplex, 65
Anacampsis, 365, 368
Anacrabro, 483
Anaea andria, 95, 158
Anaphylaxis, 141–42
Anapidae, 207
Anapistula secreta, 207
Anarsia lineatella, 243–44, 419

Anasa, 52
Anastatus mantis, 14
Ancistrocerus, 283, 284–85
Ancylis, 366–67
Ancylostomatidae (Ancylostoma), 139
Andrenidae (Andrena), 151, 441–42, 473
Andricus furnessae, 396
Anec, 467
Aneflomorpha, 416–17, 421
Anelaphus, 417, 420–21
Angelwings, 438
Anisakidae (Anisakis), 141
Anisocentropus pyraloides, 262
Anisoptera, 5, 78–79
Anisota, 155
Annelidsa, 19, 268
Annulipalpia, 260
Anobiidae, 237, 294, 322, 330, 436
Anomala orientalis, 316
Anopheles, 60
Anoplophora glabripennis, 63, 311, 425
Antheraea polyphemus, 70, 225
Anthidiellum, 288
Anthidium, 288
Anthocharis midea, 73
Anthomyiidae, 327–28, 329
Anthomyiid flies, 13, 57–58, 148, 327–38, 329, 357, 358, 416
Anthonomus, 315, 318, 325–26
Anthophora, 464–65
Anthrax analis, 101, 450
Anthribidae, 294, 330
Antispila, 345
Antlions, 50, 107, 242–43, 446–47, 492
Antmimic spiders, 29
Antocha, 267
Antrodiaetidae (Antrodiaetus), 26, 458–59, 461
Antron, 391
Ants, 2, 48, 49, 67
  brown, 470–71
  burrows topped with middens, 467–68, 485
  burrows with turrets, 466
  carpenter, 434
  eggs of, 64
  Egyptian, 317

field, 471–72
fire, 131, 145–46, 279, 471
harvester, 471, 472–73, 497
hills, 469–73
holes made by, 453
honeypot, 471
leafcutter, 304, 453, 467–68, 470, 498
nests, 279–80
as predator, 106
pyramid, 471
sign made by, 129, 131, 317, 322
sign on wood, 434
trails and tracks, 497–98, 504
velvet, 290
Anurogryllus arboreus, 475
Anyphaenidae, 27, 218, 373
Aonidiella aurantii, 2
Aoridae, 271
Apatania, 259
Apataniidae, 257, 259, 261
Aphelenchoididae (Aphelenchoides), 300
Aphelinidae, 109, 113, 177
Aphelinus, 109, 113
Aphilanthops, 483
Apidae, 424, 432, 464
Aphidiinae, 113
Aphidius, 113
Aphidoletes, 59
Aphids, 1, 47, 48, 56, 59, 61
  balsam twig, 314
  currant, 299
  eggs of, 66–67
  exuviae, 88
  galls and, 377, 386–86, 395–96
  pea, 66
  petiole swellings, 391
  sign made by, 298–99, 314, 330
  wasps, 289–90
  white fluff, 173–74
  white pine, 67
  witch hazel gall, 298, 378, 386, 395
  woolly, 173, 174, 298
Aphis rubifolii, 298–99
Aphodius, 148
Aphomia sociella, 228, 275
Aphotaenius carolinus, 148

Apidae (Apinae), 152–53, 273–75, 289, 317
Apis mellifera, 273, 274
Apodemia palmeri, 371
Apomastus, 461–62
Apple red bug, 296
Aprostocetus hagenowii, 14
Apterona, 250
Aptostichus, 459
Arachnids
  eggs of, 75–76
  sign made by, 133–34
  silken retreats of, 217–18
  vinegaroons, 506
Arachnopteromalus dasys, 46
Araecerus fasciculatus, 330
Araneidae, 28, 34, 38–42, 180, 201–2, 205–6, 208–12, 218, 272, 373, 375
Araneus, 34, 211, 218
Araniella displicata, 34, 212
Archanara, 359
Archips, 12, 22, 184, 368, 371
Archipsocidae (Archipsocus nomas), 182
Arctiidae, 22, 68–69, 156, 183–84, 185, 320, 519
Arctopora, 264
Arctosa, 448, 456–57
Arenicolidae (Arenicola), 10, 448–49, 479
Argasidae, 75
Argidae (Arge), 231–32, 308
Argiope, 38, 208–9
Argonauta argo, 21
Argonautidae, 21
Argonauts, greater, 21
Argulidae (Argulus), 143
Argyresthia, 361–62
Argyrodes, 41
Argyrodinae, 26, 40–41, 213
Argyrotaenia, 325, 368, 370, 371
Ariadna bicolor, 193–94
Arilus, 11, 12
Ariolimax columbianus, 74
Arionid slugs, 74
Aristotelia, 354, 365
Armored scales, 176–77
Arrenuridae, 118
Arrenurus, 118
Arthropods, 2

Ascalaphidae, 49, 243
*Ascaloptynx appendicula-
    tus*, 49
Asilidae, 16, 59, 100, 101,
    107
Asilini, 59
Asopinae, 106–7
Asphondylia, 387, 394, 395
Assassin bugs, 10, 11, 51
    as predators, 106
    sign made by, 132
    spined, 11–12
    trails and tracks, 520
    wheel bugs, 11, 51
Astacoidea, 515
Astala, 249, 250–51
Astatinae, 483
Asterolecaniidae, 176
Asteromyia, 387
Astrotischeria, 351
*Asymmetrura gramini-
    vorella*, 360
Athericidae, 127
Atta, 453, 466, 467–68,
    470, 498
Attelabidae, 307, 315,
    363–64
Attelabinae, 363–64
Attelabus nigripes, 363
Atteva punctella, 98, 185
Attini, 466
Atypidae, 28, 187–88
Augochlora, 432
Auplopodini, 106
Auplopus, 284
Austrotinodes texensis, 266
Automeris, 69, 133, 225

Baccha, 56
Bacillus lentimorbus, 125
Bacillus popilliae, 125
Bacillus thuringiensis, 125
Backswimmers, 5, 54–55,
    107
Bacteria, 125–27
Bactericera cockerelli, 67
Baculoviruses, 126
Badumna longinqua, 192
Baetidae, 78
Baetis, 78
Bagworms, 248–51
    Abbot's, 248–49
    evergreen, 249
    snailcase, 250
Baliosus nervosus, 356
Ballooning, 180
Banchinae, 233
Banksiola, 264

Baridines, 328
Bark
    beetles, 63, 246, 294,
        322, 425, 426–28
    galleries under, 426–29
    galleries under, or in,
        wood, 429–32
    stripping, 405
Barnea truncate, 454
Barn funnel weavers, 41,
    195
Basicladus, 249–50
Basketsnails, three-lined,
    21
Bathyphantes, 198
Bathyplectes, 233
Batrachedridae, 186
Battus philenor, 68
Bed bugs, 137, 153
Bedelliidae *(Bedellia)*, 352
Bees, 62
    bumblebees, 273–74,
        317
    burrows with earthen
        mounds, 473–74
    burrows with turrets,
        464–65
    carpenter, 152–53, 289,
        317, 424, 432
    cellophane, 288, 474
    digger, 464–65
    eggs of, 64–65
    holes made by, 450–51
    honeybees, 129, 130,
        273, 274
    leafcutter, 287–88, 303
    mason, 284–85, 286
    mining, 441–42
    nests, 273–75
    parasites of, 290
    plasterer, 288
    resin, 287–88
    rock borings, 441–42
    sign made by, 129–31,
        303, 317
    sign on wood, 424, 432
    social, 273–75
    solitary, 450–51, 473–74
Beetles
    See also Leaf beetles;
        Weevils
    ambrosia, 433–34
    aquatic, 5, 9, 47, 64,
        237–38, 245–46
    argus tortoise, 62
    Asian lady, 141
    Asian long-horned, 63,
        311, 425

asparagus, 62, 150, 326
bark, 63, 246, 294, 322,
    425, 426–28
beaver parasite, 143
beech splendor, 13
bess, 2
blister, 12, 62, 63, 133,
    160, 290, 312, 508
bombardier, 245, 285
buprestids, 63, 146, 164–65
burrows with earthen
    mounds, 475–78
burrows with mound
    of earth to side of
    entrance, 484, 489
burying, 147, 477, 503
carrion, 63, 146, 148
case-bearing leaf, 61,
    165, 167, 254
cactus long-horned, 164
cedar, 121
checkered, 12, 63, 147,
    290
cigarette, 237, 330
clavate, 93
click, 63, 64, 328
clown, 492
cocoons, 221–22,
    237–38
crawling water, 5, 64
darkling, 63, 147, 148,
    328, 492, 502
death-watch, *322, 330*,
    436
dermestid, 14, 147, 290
droppings, 159–60
drugstore, 237, 330
dune, 492
dung, 147–48, 475–77
eggs of, 61–64
elm, 427
false clown, 148
fire-colored, 63
flea, 165, 305, 313, 328
fungus, 63, 294
glowworm, 106
golden tortoise, 62
grain, 330
ground, 63, 285, 452,
    477, 490–91, 502–3
ham, 237
hickory bark, 426–27
hickory spiral borers,
    63, 311
hister, 146, 148
holes made by, 449–50,
    452–53
hydrophilid, 25

ironclad, 328
Japanese, 306–7, 328
June, 160, 312, 327,
    328, 452
ladybugs, 23, 24, 47, 61
lizard, 412
long-horned, 63, 160,
    164, 311, 312, 314,
    315, 400, 412,
    416–17, 424, 425,
    430–31, 509
long-toed water, 64
metallic wood-boring,
    18, 63, 115, 400–401,
    417–18, 429–30
Mexican bean, 61, 307,
    318
minute brown scav-
    enger, 64
minute moss, 25, 246
minute tree-fungus, 294
net-winged, 63
oriental, 316
ox, 497
palmetto, 165, 167
pine, 427–27
pleasing fungus, 63, 294
potato, Colorado, 62
potato, three-lined,
    61–62, 167
powderpost, 436
predaceous diving, 5,
    64, 107, 145
red turpentine, 427–28
rove, 63, 146, 148, 238,
    294, 478, 489–90, 508
sap, 146, 147, 294, 319,
    326
scarab, 63, 312, 328,
    452, 475, 477, 520
scavenger, 2, 19, 64
seed, 319
short-winged flower, 319
sign made by, 294,
    306–8, 311–12, 315,
    317, 318–19, 322,
    324, 325–26, 328
sign on wood, 400–401,
    417–18, 424–25,
    426–31, 433–34, 436
skiff, 64
soldier, 63, 317
spider, 237, 330
spruce, 427
squash, 61, 306
stag, 63, 247
stem and twig swellings,
    400–401

striped cucumber, 62,
    324, 328
tiger, 106, 449–50,
    452–53, 484, 504
tortoise, 62, 93, 165,
    167, 305, 306
trails and tracks,
    489–90, 497, 502–4,
    508–9, 510, 520–22
trout stream, 64, 246
tumblebugs, 477
tunnels made by,
    489–91, 492
variegated mud-loving,
    490
water, 2, 5, 19, 64, 328
water penny, 9, 87
wedge-shaped, 63, 290
whirligig, 47, 64, 245
wood-boring, 400–401
Bellura, 22, 359
Belomicrus, 483
Belostoma, 2, 53–54
Belostomatidae, 53, 107,
    132, 145
Bembicinae, 483, 484
Bembix, 244–45, 482
Beothukus complicates,
    263
Bephratelloides cubensis,
    327
Beraeidae *(Beraea),* 257
Berothidae, 49
Berytidae, 106
Bethylid wasps, 121
Bibio albipennis, 59
Bibionidae, 59, 148, 329
Bicyrtes, 483
Billbugs, 308, 328
Biphyllidae, 294
Bird flukes, 139
Bittacidae *(Bittacus),*
    77, 166
Bivalves
    anchor holes, 440–41
    freshwater, 2
    holes made by, 454
    piddocks, 438, 441
    shipworms, 437–38
    sign made by, 449
Blaberidae, 1
Black zigzag, 156
Blaesodiplosis, 383
Blastobasis glandulella, 323
Blattaria, 13
Blattella germanica, 13
Blattellidae, 13
Bledius, 478, 489

Blephariceridae, 60, 86–87
Blepharipa pratensis, 59
Boisea trivittata, 53
Bolbocerosoma, 476
Bolitophaginae *(Boli-*
    totherus cornutus),
    294
Bolitophagine, 294
Bombus, 273–74, 317
Bombyliidae, 13, 59, 100,
    101, 450
Boreidae, 77
Borers
    beetles, 411–12, 416–18
    boxthorn, 417
    branch pruner, 422
    in broad-leaved woody
        plants, 416–19
    chestnut, 418
    clover stem, 412
    in conifer twigs and
        leaders, 414–15
    coyote brush, 419
    currant, 419
    currant tip, 417
    elderberry, 417
    European shot-hole,
        434
    flat-headed cone, 322
    flies, 412–13
    grain, 319
    in herbaceous stems,
        411–13
    hickory spiral, 63, 311,
        421–22
    lima bean pod, 320
    linden, 425
    maggots, 416
    metallic wood-boring
        beetles, 417–18
    moths and skippers,
        413, 415, 419
    oak stem, 416–17
    oak twig girdler, 417–18
    peach tree, 244
    peach twig, 243–44, 419
    petiole, 419
    pinhole, 434
    pitch mass, 425–26
    poplar and willow, 400,
        430, 431
    red-necked cane,
        400–401, 417
    red pine flat-headed,
        425
    rhododendron, 419
    ribbed pine, 246, 430
    rock and shell, 439–42

round-headed, 431
rose stem girdler, 417
round-headed apple,
    425
round-headed oak twig,
    417
sawflies, 413, 415, 418
soybean stem, 412
spotted apple tree, 431
squash vine, 163–64,
    243, 413
stalk, 413, 419
stem, 359, 412
sugar maple, 431
twig girdlers, 420
twig pruners, 420–21
weevils, 414–15, 418
wharf, 436
Bostrichidae, 319, 436
*Bothriocyrtum califor-
    nicum*, 458
Bothynostethus, 483
Bourletiellidae *(Bourlet-
    iella hortensis)*, 314
Boxelder bugs, eastern, 53
Brachinus, 245, 285
Brachycentridae *(Brachy-
    centrus)*, 256, 257,
    263
Brachygastra mellifica, 279
Brachys, 356
Braconidae, 362
Braconid caterpillars, 65
Braconid wasps, 23, 109,
    111–14, 233–35
Bradycinetulus ferrugineus,
    475
Branchiobdellid worms,
    121
Branch pruner, 422
Braulidae *(Braula coeca)*,
    118, 275
Brentidae, 400, 411
Brevipalpus lewisi, 324
Bristletails, 2, 83
Brochymena, 51
Bruchinae, 62, 319
Bruchophagus, 319–20
Bruchus, 62, 319
Bruised nassas, 21
Bryozoans
    freshwater, 9, 441
    marine, 10
Buccinidae, 20
Buccinum undatum, 20
Bucculatricidae *(Buccula-
    trix)*, 219, 229, 313,
    336–37, 343

Buds
    dense growth of, 393–95
    swollen, 392–93
Buenoa, 5
Bulimulinae, 74
Buprestidae, 18, 63, 311,
    322, 360, 400–401,
    417, 421, 425, 429–30
Buprestids, leaf-mining,
    63, 164–65, 253, 356,
    360
Burrows
    horsehoe crab, 486
    plain silk-lined, 455–57
    underwater, 485–86
    with earthen mounds,
        468–80
    with middens, 466–68
    with mounds of earth to
        one side of entrance,
        480–85
    with trapdoors or lids,
        457–60
    with turrets, 460–66
Busycon, 20
Busycotypus, 20
Butterflies, 47
    See also Caterpillars
    admirals, red, 156–57,
        185
    brush-footed, 72–73,
        94–97
    checkerspots, 72, 95–96,
        185
    chrysalises, 94–97
    commas, 73, 96
    droppings, 151
    eggs of, 68–74
    falcate orangetips, 73
    gossamer-winged, 74,
        96
    harvester, 174
    metalmarks, 74, 96–97
    milkweed, 95
    monarch, 72–73, 95,
        156, 157
    mourning cloaks, 72,
        96, 156
    parnassians, 74
    queen, 73
    question marks, 73, 96,
        156, 158
    soldier, 73
    sulphurs, 73
    swallowtails, 68, 96, 157
    whites, 73
Byturidae *(Byturus
    unicolor)*, 326

Cacti, sign on, 315
Cactoblastis cactorum, 71
Caddisflies, 6–8
    cases, 255–64
    eggs of, 46–47
    fingernet, 215–16
    long-horned, 260–61
    micro-, 19, 255–56
    net-spinning, 213–14,
        260
    pupae, 85
    retreats and tubes,
        265–66
    saddlecase maker,
        259–60
    snailcase, 259
    trumpetnet and
        tubemaker, 214–15
Calamoceratidae, 261, 262
Calamomyia spp., 101
California sisters, 158
Caliroa, 313
Caliroini, 312
Calisoga, 457
Callianassidae, 479
Callichirus major, 479
Calligrapha serpentina, 62
Callilepis, 30
Calliphoridae, 1, 12–13,
    117, 145, 148
Callirhytis, 396, 398, 403
Callisto denticulella, 366
Callobiu, 36, 192
Callosamia promethea, 69,
    224, 310
Caloptilia, 348, 366, 368,
    369, 399
Calosoma, 285
Calymmaria, 44, 203
Cambaridae, 292, 462–63
Cameraria, 344, 348
Camouflaged loopers, 247
Camponotus, 280, 434
Camptonotus, 65, 318, 375
Cankerworms
    fall, 70–71
    spring, 243
Cantharidae, 63, 317
Canthon, 477
Canthonini, 147
Capulidae, 440
Carabidae, 63, 93, 245,
    285, 449, 452, 477,
    484, 490–91, 502, 504
Carabus, 285
Carcelia, 116
Carmenta bassiformis, 329
Carpophilus lugubris, 319

Carposinidae *(Carposina)*, 325
Carrion, 146–47
Carton, 275
Caryomyia, 389
Case-bearing aquatic insects, 5, 9, 47, 64, 237–38, 245–46
Case-bearing leaf beetles, 61, 165, 167, 254
Cases
  annulate, 253
  for aquatic case-bearing insects, 255–64
  composite leaf, 253
  from leaf pieces, 253–54
  lobe, 253
  loose debris coverings, 247
  mineral, 257–60
  mixed materials, 260–61
  pistol, 252
  plant materials, 261–64
  spatulate leaf, 253
  for terrestrial case-bearing insects, 247–55
  tubular leaf, 252–53
  tubular silk, 252
Cassidinae, 93, 167, 305, 306, 356
Cassidini, 93
Castianeira, 29
Cataclinusa pachycondylae, 121
Catasega, 170–71
Catastega aceriella, 366
Caterpillars, 4
  See also Butterflies; Moths; Tent caterpillars
  admirals, 73–74, 96, 158, 185, 309–10, 374
  braconid, 65
  buck, 133
  cabbage white, 308
  cattail, 373
  clover head, 317
  droppings, 155–58
  exuviae, 82
  flannel moth, 133, 230
  giant silkmoth (silkworms), 47, 68–70, 133, 155, 223–26
  gray hairstreak, 316
  ichneumonid, 65
  leaf-feeding, 59
  leaf-rolling, 91, 367

promethea moth, 69, 224, 310
puss, 133
saddleback, 133
sign made by, 132–33, 309–10, 317, 327
silk lines, 180
skippers, 97, 367, 371, 413
slug, 100, 133, 230
staghorn cholla moth, 315
swallowtails, 68, 96, 157, 372–73
trails and tracks, 518–19
uglynest, 12, 184
viceroys, 73–74, 96, 158, 309–10, 373–74
Caulocampus acericaulis, 419
Caulotops, 297
Cavernocymbium, 200
Ceanothus, 320
Cecidomyiidae *(Cecidomyia)*, 59, 100, 117, 237, 293, 321, 326, 377, 397, 398, 415, 426
Cecidophyopsis psilapspis, 392
Cecropia moths, 69, 155, 223
Celatoria diabroticae, 115–16
Celticecis, 389
Centipedes
  eggs of, 77
  geophilomorph, 2
  as predator, 106
  scolopendromorph, 2
  sign made by, 133–34
  sperm webs, 181
  trails and tracks, 511–12
Centruroides, 134, 507
Cephalcia, 185–86
Cephalopoda, 440
Cephenemyia, 144
Cephidae *(Cephus)*, 413, 418
Ceraclea, 256, 258–59
Ceraeochrysa smithi, 48
Cerambycidae, 63, 160, 164, 246, 311–12, 314, 315, 400, 412, 416, 420, 422, 424, 430–31, 509
Ceratina, 289, 432
Ceratocampinae, 99

Ceratomia catalpae, 69
Ceratopogonidae, 8, 132, 496
Cercerini, 483
Cerceris, 451, 474
Cercopidae, 4, 154
Cercyon, 25
Ceresa, 410
Cernotina, 215
Ceropales, 284
Ceroplastes, 176
Cerura, 243
Cesonia bilineata, 30
Cestoda, 141
Ceutorhynchus rapae, 412
Chaetocnema confinis, 313, 328
Chaetopsis aenea, 329
Chaetopteridae *(Chaetopterus)*, 268–69
Chalcids, 14, 46, 50, 64–65, 109, 120–21, 395
  sign made by, 319–20, 322, 323, 326–27
Chalcodermus aeneus, 318
Chalepini, 356
Chalybion californicum, 285
Chamaepsila rosae, 329
Chaoboridae, 8
Chaoborus, 8
Charaxinae, 95
Charidotella sexpunctata, 62
Charops, 233
Chauliodinae, 50
Cheese skipper, 147
Cheiracanthium inclusum, 27, 218
Chelinidea, 52, 315
Cheluridae *(Chelura terebrans)*, 437
Chelymorpha cassidea, 62
Chiggers, 136, 143
Chilopoda, 511
Chionaspis pinifoliae, 176
Chironomidae, 7, 121, 148, 168, 266–67, 485, 495
Chlaenius, 285
Chlamisini, 165
Chloealtis conspersa, 12
Chlorion, 483
Chlorochroa ligata, 51
Chloropidae, 45, 148, 321, 413
Chlosyne, 95, 185
Choristoneura fumiferana, 186

Chromagrion conditum,
    4–5
Chrysalises, butterfly,
    94–97
Chrysaster ostensackenella,
    348
Chrysididae, 74, 290
Chrysobothris orono, 425
Chrysocharis, 362
Chrysochus auratus, 62, 311
Chrysoesthia, 337, 354
Chrysomel, 93
Chrysomela scripta, 62
Chrysomelidae, 9, 61, 93,
    150, 160, 165, 166–
    67, 222, 237–38, 254,
    305, 306, 319, 324,
    326, 328, 356, 412
Chrysophana placida, 322
Chrysopidae *(Chrysoperla
    harrisii),* 47, 222, 247
Chrysops, 57
Chyranda centralis, 262
Cicadas, 81–82, 87, 409
    burrows with earthen
        mounds, 474
    burrows with turrets,
        463–64
    holes made by, 451–52
Cicadellidae, 3, 17, 297–98,
    411
Cicadidae, 87
Cicindelinae, 449, 484, 504
Cicurina, 44, 200, 272
Ciidae, 294
Cimbicidae *(Cimbex),* 185,
    231
Cimex lectularius, 137
Cimicidae, 137, 153
Cinara strobi, 67
Cingilia catenaria, 221
Cirratulidae, 271
Cistudinomyia cistudinis,
    145
Cladochaeta, 154
Clams, 449
Clam shrimp, 496
Clavicipitales, 122
Cleridae, 12, 63, 147, 237,
    290
Climacia, 162
Clionaidae *(Cliona),* 441
Clostera inclusa, 371
Clostoeca disjuncta, 262
Clubionidae *(Clubiona),*
    27, 373
Clubtails, 84
Clymenella, 10, 270

Clypeadon, 483
Clytrini, 165, 254
Coccidae, 23
Coccinellidae, 23, 24, 61,
    92–93, 141, 175, 306,
    318
Coccoidea, 22, 66, 175–77,
    238
Coccophagus, 177, 236
Coccotorus scutellaris, 325
Cochineal insects, 171
Cochlichnus, 496
Cochliomyia hominivorax,
    145
Cockroaches, 13–14, 140
    droppings, 153, 161
    German, 13
    giant, 1
    wood, 13
Cocoons
    antlions and owlflies,
        242–43
    beetle, 237–38
    flies, 236–37, 244
    giant silkmoth, 223–26
    hairy moth, 227–28
    hymenopteran, 235–36
    lacy, 220–22
    moths, 227–30, 243–44
    neuropteran, 222–23
    round, flat, 219–20
    sawflies, 231–32, 244
    silk retreats of
        arachnids, 217–18
    silk retreats of moth
        larvae, 218–19
    wasps, 244
    wasps, braconid,
        233–35
    wasps, ichneumonid,
        232–33
Coelus, 492
Coenagrionidae, 4
Coleophoridae *(Cole-
    ophora),* 167–68,
    251–53, 321, 323,
    352–53, 360–61
Coleoptera, 61–64
Coleotechnites, 361–62
Coliadinae, 73
Collembola, 77
Colletes, 288, 474
Colletidae, 288, 473, 474
Colobognatha, 241
Colomerus vitis, 381
Colopha ulmicola, 384
Colpoclypeus florus, 91
Colydiinae, 294

Common tan wave, 98
Comperiella bifasciata, 177
Compsilura concinnata,
    115, 116
Conchs, 20
Conchuelas, 51
Conenose bugs, 132
Conifers
    borers in twigs and
        leaders, 414–15
    cones and seeds, sign
        on, 321–22
    needle mines, 360–62
    needles, sign on, 314
    pitch masses, 415–16,
        425–26
    sawflies, 231
    tied needles, 370–71
    webs on, 185–86
Conifer seed bugs,
    western, 52–53
Coniopterygidae, 50, 220
Conophthorus, 322
Conopidae, 116
Conotrachelus, 323, 325
Contarinia, 321–22, 326,
    380–81
Copepods, 2
Copris, 147–48
Coptodisca, 345–46
Coptotriche, 342–43,
    350–51
Corambidae, 10
Coras, 44, 196
Cordyceps, 122
Coreidae, 52, 151, 153,
    297, 315
Corioxenidae, 119
Corixidae, 55, 121
Corophiids, 271, 485
Corrinnidae, 29
Corydalidae *(Corydalus),*
    15, 50, 316
Corythucha, 295, 296
Cosmopterigidae *(Cos-
    mopterix),* 352, 359,
    370, 379–80, 415
Cossidae, 244, 431–32
Cotesia congregate, 234
Cotesia melanoscela, 235
Cowpea curculio, 318
Crabronidae, 244–45,
    281–82, 284, 288,
    289, 451, 474, 482–83
Crabroninae, 289, 483, 484
Crabs, 2
    burrows with mound of
        earth, 480–81

burrows with turrets, 463, 480
fiddler and ghost, 445, 446, 455, 463, 480–81, 513
hermit, 513–14
holes made by, 454–55
horseshoe, 76, 81, 486, 514
marsh, 463
mole, 445–46, 514
scrapes and digs, 445–46
trails and tracks, 513–14
Crambidae, 71–72, 184, 187, 216, 262, 343, 354, 365, 372
leaf rollers, 368
Craponius inaequalis, 308, 326
Crayfish, 2, 292, 462–63, 515
Cremaster, 94
Cremastobombycia, 348
Crematogaster, 279–80
Crevice weavers, 193
Crickets, 147
burrows with earthen mounds, 475
bush, 106, 409
camel, 505–6
Carolina leaf-rolling, 65, 318, 364, 375
eggs of, 65–66
exuviae, 88–89
field, 505
Japanese burrowing, 475
Jerusalem, 65–66, 509
mole, 2, 66, 488
Mormon, 65
oviposition scars, 407–9
pygmy mole, 488–89
short-tailed, 475
sign made by, 302, 304, 324
trails and tracks, 505–6, 509
tree, 320, 324, 407–9
true, 65
two-spotted, 304
Criocerinae, 166–67
Crioceris asparagi, 62, 150
Crioceris duodecimpunctata, 62, 326
Crossocerus, 289
Crovettia theliae, 114–15
Crustaceans, 2
eggs of, 76

gribbles, 436–37
tubes, 271–72
Cryptcerya genistae, 23
Cryptocephalinae, 165, 167, 254
Cryptochia, 264
Cryptococcus fagisuga, 174
Cryptolestes, 237
Cryptomyzus ribis, 299
Cryptophagidae, 294
Cryptorhynchus lapathi, 400
Cryptothelea, 250
Crytolaemus montrouzieri, 24, 175
Ctenizidae, 26, 458
Ctenocephalides felis, 137–38
Ctenucha, 227
C. virginica, 69
Cucujidae, 63, 246
Cucullia, 171, 243
Cuerna, 3, 17
Culex, 60
Culicidae, 60
Culicomorpha, 8, 85
Culiseta, 60
Curculio (*Curculio*), 322–23
apple, 325–26
cabbage, 412
grape, 326
plum, 325
rhubard, 412
rose, 315
Curculionidae, 4, 63, 141, 222, 238, 246, 307–8, 312, 314, 315, 318–19, 322, 325–26, 327, 328, 357–58, 400, 411, 414, 425, 426, 433–34
Curicata, 5
Cuterebra, 58, 102–3, 144
Cybaeidae (*Cybaeus*), 197
Cyclocosmia, 458
Cycloplasis panicifoliella, 254, 359
Cyclorrhapha, 100
Cyclosa, 42, 209
Cydia, 163, 243, 320, 322, 323, 325
Cylas formicarius, 411
Cylindrocopturus, 414
Cylindropuntia, 315
Cylindrotoma, 92, 312
Cylindrotominae, 312
Cymbaeremaeidae, 442

Cymbiodyta, 19
Cynipidae, 323, 377, 395, 396, 399, 403
Cyrnellus fraternus, 215
Cyrtaucheniidae, 459, 461–62
Cyrtopleura costata, 454
Cytoplasmic polyhedrosis viruses, 126

Dactylopiidae (*Dactylopius*), 171
Daggerwings, ruddy, 158
Dahlica, 250
Daktulosphaira vitifoliae, 385
Damsel bugs, 106
Damselflies
aurora, 4–5
naiad exuviae, 84
spreadwings, 5
Danainae, 95
Danaus eresimus, 73
Danaus gilippus, 73
Danaus plexippus, 72–73, 95, 156
Darners, 5, 84, 146
Dasineura, 59, 317, 321, 379, 380–81, 387–88, 389, 393
Dectes, 412
Deinopidae (*Deinopis spinosa*), 199–200
Delia, 58, 327–28, 329–29
Demodecidae (*Demodex*), 142
Dendroctonus, 425, 427–28
Depressaria, 185, 371
Dermanyssidae (*Dermanyssus gallinae*), 142–43
Dermaptera, 312, 503
Dermatobia hominis, 144
Dermestid beetles, 14, 147, 290
Deroceras reticulatum, 74
Derodontidae, 294
Desidae, 192, 218
Desmia funeralis, 365
Desmocerus, 417
Deuterophlebiidae, 87
Diabrotica, 62, 328
Diadasia, 465
Dialytes, 148
Dianthidium, 288
Diapheromeridae (*Diapheroma femorata*), 74, 158

Diaspididae, 2, 176–77
Diastrophus, 403
Dibolia borealis, 165, 340
Dichomeris nonstrigella,
    371
Dichotomius, 147–48
Dicrocoeliidae *(Dicro-*
    coelium dendriticum),
    110
Dictyna, 31
Dictynidae, 31, 44, 191–92,
    200, 272
Digitivalva clarkei, 221
Diglyphus, 362
Diguetidae *(Diguetia),* 28,
    196–97, 272
Dineutus, 245
Dinocampus coccinellae,
    113–14
Dionycha, 29
Diopatra, 268
Dioryctria, 415
Diplocentridae *(Diplocen-*
    trus), 452
Diplolepis, 396–97
Diplopoda, 139, 517
Diplostraca, 496
Diplothyra, 441
Diplura, 2
Dipluridae, 26, 196
Dipogon, 290
Diprionidae, 3, 157, 231
Dipseudopsidae, 266
Diptera, 55–61
Disholcaspis quercusglobu-
    lus, 396
Dismemberment, 106
Dixa, 8
Dolichopodidae, 237, 244,
    413
Dolichovespula, 276,
    277–78, 423
Dolomedes, 37, 145
Donacia, 9, 306
Donaciinae, 237–38, 328
Dorcasta, 412
Doridella steinbergae, 10
Dorymyrmex, 471
Draeculacephala mollipes,
    324
Dragonflies, 5, 8–9
    eggs of, 47, 78–79
    naiad exuviae, 84
    as predator, 106
    trails and tracks, 516–17
Drapetisca, 198
Drassodes neglectus, 27
Drassodes saccatus, 27

Drassyllus rufulus, 30, 43
Dreissena polymorpha, 2
Dreissenidae, 2
Drosophilidae, 59, 102,
    154, 326, 344, 412
Dryinid wasps, 119, 244
Dryopidae, 64
*Dryopidae, 64
Dusona, 233
Dustywings, 50, 220
Dysdera crocata, 27
Dysderidae, 27
Dyseriocrania auricyanea,
    4
Dytiscidae, 5, 64, 107, 145

Earthworms, 13, 18
    aquatic, 19
    burrows topped with
        middens, 466–67
    castings, 478
    effect of, on soil, 443–44
    sign made by, 496–97
Earwigs, 2, 153, 312, 503
Ecclisomyia, 261
Ecdytolopha insiticiana,
    401
Ecnomidae, 266
Ecribellate amaurobiids,
    196, 200
Ectemnius, 289
Ectoedemia, 321, 336, 341,
    353, 391, 401, 406
Ectoparasites, 105,
    117–21, 142–44
Eelworms, leaf and bud,
    300
Eggs
    excrement-covered,
        164–66
    freshwater cases, 19
    gelatinous coverings
        (fresh water), 6–9
    gelatinous coverings
        (marine), 9–10
    hair covering, 21–22
    inserted in aquatic
        vegetation, 4–5
    inserted in terrestrial
        vegetation, 3–4
    marine cases, 19–21
    niches, 424–25
    opaque, solid, or frothy
        coverings (terres-
        trial), 13–18
    predators and para-
        sitoids, 79–80
    resinlike substance
        coverings, 10–13

silk coverings, 24–25
    waxy coverings, 22–24
Egg treaders, 5
Eight-spotted forester, 243
Elachistidae, 184–85, 366,
    369–70, 371
Elateridae, 63, 328
Elenchidae, 119
Eleodes, 502, 509
Ellobiidae, 9–10
Embiidina, 2, 187
Emblyna, 31
Emerita, 445
Empididae, 86, 154, 237,
    244
Empoasca fabae, 298
Empria maculate, 308
Enchenopa, 17, 410
Encyrtidae, 177
Endaphis, 117
Endomychidae, 148, 294
Endoparasitoids, 105,
    109–17, 144–45
Endothenia hebesana, 320
Ensis directus, 449
Enterobius vermicularis,
    141
Enteropneusta, 449, 479
Entiminae, 328
Entomognathus, 483
Entomophagai, 123
Entomophagai, 123
Entomophthora, 123, 125
Entomophthorales, 122
Entylia carinata, 301
Eobrachycentrus gelidae,
    263
Epargyreus clarus, 371
Ephemeroidea, 486
Ephemeroptera, 78, 83–84
Ephestia kuehniella, 186
Ephydra bruesi, 61
Ephydra thermophila, 61
Ephydridae, 61, 86, 360,
    413
Epiblema scudderiana, 399
Epicypta, 166
Epilachna, 61, 306, 318
Epilachninae, 93
*Epimetopidae, 2, 19
Epimetopus, 19
Epinotia, 185–86, 344, 361,
    371
Epipyropidae, 120, 228
Epitrix, 305, 328
Erebidae, 309
Erigone, 30
Erigoninae, 30, 180, 199
Eriocampa juglandis, 175

Eriococcidae, 23, 174
Eriocraniidae, 4, 354
Eriophyes, 381, 383, 387, 393
Eriophyidae, 330, 377
Eriosoma, 173
Eristalis, 495
Ernobius, 322
Ero, 33
Erotylidae, 63, 294
Erynia rhizospora, 123
Etiella zinckenella, 320
Euagrus, 196
Eucalyptolyma maiden, 178
Eucanthus, 476
Euchaetes egle, 22
Eucharitid wasps, 65
Eucosma dorsisignatana, 330
Eucosmini, 415
Eudistylia vancouveri, 269
Euleia, 357
Eulophidae, 14, 91, 236, 362
Eulophus, 162
Eumeninae *(Eumenes)*, 282–83, 284, 286
Eumeninae *(Leptochilus)*, 289–90
Eumerus, 329
Euodynerus, 283, 465
Eupackardia calleta, 225
Euparagia scutellaris, 465
Eupatorium, 366
Eupelmidae, 14
Eupelmus neoccidis, 14
Eupeodes americanus, 56
Euphorine braconids, 113–14
Euphranta canadensis, 326
Euphydryas, 95, 185
Euplectrus, 120–21, 162, 236
Eupristocerus cogitans, 401
Euproctis chrysorrhoea, 21–22
Euptoieta claudia, 95
Eurosta solidaginis, 398
Eurytomidae *(Eurytoma)*, 319–20, 326–27
Euscirrhopterus cosyra, 315
Euscrobipalpa, 163
Euura, 392, 399
Evaniidae, 14
Exema, 167

Exoteleia, 361, 415
Exuviae
  clinging to terrestrial vegetation, 87–89
  naiad, 83–84
  use of term, 82–83
Eylaidae, 118
Eylais, 118

Fabria inornata, 264
Faiditus, 41
Farula, 257
Fasciolariidae, 20
Fascista cercerisella, 365
Fattigia pele, 258
Feltia, 327
Felt scales, 23, 174
Feniseca tarquinius, 174
Fenusa, 355
Fenusella, 355
Ferns, webs on, 186
Ferrissia, 8
Ficopomatus enigmaticus, 270–71
Fidia viticida, 306, 328
Filatima, 365, 370
Filistatidae, 28, 193
Filograna implexa, 270
Firebrat, 77
Fish parasites, 143–44
Flatmesh weavers, 199
Flea beetles
  eggplant, 305
  grape, 305
  plantain, 165, 340
  sign made by, 305
  sweet potato, 313, 328
Fleas, 74, 143, 161, 238
  cat, 137–38
Flies, 3
  See Leafminers;
    Mayflies; Midges;
    Sawflies; Whiteflies
  agromyzid, 4, 302–3, 337–39, 341–42, 357, 358, 360, 399, 400, 406, 413, 428
  alder, 49–50
  anthomyiid, 13, 57–58
  bee, 13, 59, 100, 101
  big-headed, 116
  black, 60, 68, 86, 90–91, 132, 216
  black onion, 329
  blood-feeding, 131–32
  blow, 1, 12–13, 145
  bot, 1, 58, 74, 102–3, 144–45

brine, 61, 86
bulb, 329
burrows, 491
caddis, 6–8, 19, 46–47, 213–16
carrot rust, 329
citrus black, 68, 90–91
cluster, 117
cocoons, 236–37, 244
crane, 92, 267, 293, 312, 327, 329, 495
damsel, 4–5
dance (balloon), 86, 154, 237, 244
deer, 56–57, 60, 100, 132
dobson, 13, 15–16, 25, 50, 316
dragon, 5, 89, 47, 516–17
feather-legged, 116
fire, 64, 106
fish, 50
flat-footed, 293
flesh, 1, 116–17, 145, 290
frit, 45, 321, 413
fruit, 4, 59, 102, 154, 321, 326, 329, 357, 395, 398, 412
Hessian, 59, 100
horse, 2, 56–57, 100, 132, 496
house, 59
hover, 56, 91–92
humpbacked, 116, 121
lance, 293
long-legged, 237, 244, 413
louse, 1, 143, 162
mantid, 46, 49, 89, 223
march, 59, 329
marsh, 117
may, 486
onion, 328, 329
owl, 49, 243
parasitism, 115–17
picture-winged, 329
pupae, 100–103
pyrgotid, 116
rabbit bot, 58
retreats and tubes, 266–67
robber, 13, 16–17, 59, 100, 101, 107, 154
rodent bot, 58
sand, 132
screw-worm, 145
scuttle, 102, 293

shore, 86, 360, 413
sign made by, 293, 321,
    323, 326, 328–29
sign on wood, 428
small-headed, 58–59,
    117
snake, 50
snipe, 127
soldier, 57, 100, 495
spongilla, 25, 162, 222
stable, 132
stiletto, 491
stone, 46–47, 78, 83, 312
syrphid, 107, 148, 151,
    290, 329
tachinid, 1, 4, 59, 102,
    115–16
tangle-veined, 117
thick-headed, 116
true, 47, 55–61
walnut husk, 323
winsome, 116
woodlouse, 117
Florinda coccinea, 201
Flower buds, sign on,
    315–16
Flowers, sign on, 316–17
Formica, 471–72, 483
Formicidae, 466, 467–68,
    504
Frankliniella tritici, 316
Franklinothrips, 238
Frass
    chains, 158
    droppings from holes in
        vegetation, 163–64
    droppings with definite
        form, 154–62
    excrement-covered
        eggs, 164–65
    frothy secretions, 154
    line, 333
    liquid deposits, 149–53
    meconium, 151, 162
    use of term, 149
Frechinia helianthiales, 354
Frenesia, 261
Frontinella communis, 200
Fruitflies, 4, 59, 102, 154,
    321, 326, 357, 395,
    398, 412
Fruits, sign on fleshy,
    324–27
Fruitworms, 324, 325
Frumenta nundinella, 371
Fulgoraecia exigua, 120,
    228
Fulgoroidea, 4, 175

Fungi
    apple rust, 396
    dense growth of buds
        and, 393
    pathogenic, 121–25
    sign on, 292–94
    webs on, 181
Fungus gnats, 92, 153,
    166, 180, 237, 244,
    293
Furia, 123, 125
Fusitriton oregonensis, 20

Galerita, 285
Galerucella nymphaeae, 62,
    93, 306
Galerucinae, 93
Galiomyza viiolivora, 358
Galleria mellonella,
    274–75
Gallmaker, grape cane,
    400, 418
Galls
    ash flower, 393
    blackberry, 403
    buds, dense growth of,
        393–95
    buds, swollen, 392–93
    causes, 377
    cinquefoil, 395
    complex integral twig,
        403–4
    creosote bush, 394
    detachable stem and
        twig, 395–97
    elm, 384
    goldenrods, 387, 395,
        398–99
    grape, 385, 387, 389,
        392
    ground ivy, 395
    hackberry, 385, 389
    hickory, 389, 392
    meadowsweet, 394
    mossy rose, 397
    oak, 390–91, 396, 402–3
    poplar, 425
    spruces, 403–4
    stem and twig swellings,
        woody, 399–403
    stem swellings, herba-
        ceous, 398–99
    sumac, 385
    twig swellings, terminal,
        397–98
    willows, 388, 392, 393,
        397, 399–400
    witch hazel, 395

Galls, leaf
    detachable, 389–91
    elongate vein swellings,
        387–88
    erineum patches and
        small pouches,
        381–83
    globular or conical,
        with slits, 385–86
    leaves distorted into
        folds or rolls, 378–81
    nondetachable, 388–89
    petiole swellings,
        391–92
    pronounced pouches,
        lobes, and fingerlike,
        383–85
    spot and blister, 386–87
Gargaphia, 295
Gasteracantha, 209–10
    G. cancriformis, 34–35,
        210
Gasterophilus, 144–45
Gasteruptiid wasps, 290
Gastropoda, 74
Gea heptagon, 41
Gecarcinidae, 455
Geina, 98, 365
Gelastocoridae, 2
Gelechiidae, 243–44, 321,
    325, 330, 337, 344,
    353–54, 361, 365,
    398, 402, 415, 419
    leaf rollers, 368
    leaf tiers, 370, 371
Gelis, 46
Geolycosa, 36, 450, 456,
    461
Geometridae, 70–71, 157,
    180, 221, 247, 371
Geometrid moths, 70–71,
    243
Geopinus incrassatus, 477
Geotrupidae *(Geotrupes),*
    475, 476
Gerridae, 54, 107
Gertschanapis shantzi, 207
Glenognatha foxi, 206
Glenostictia, 484
Glischrochilus, 326
Glomerida, 241
Glossiphoniidae, 139
Glossosomatidae, 259–60
Glycaspis brimblecombei,
    67, 178–79
Glycobius speciosus, 431
Glycyphagidae, 141
Glyptapanteles, 112, 234

Glyptotendipes meridion-alis, 7
Gnaphosa muscorum, 30
Gnaphosidae, 27, 30, 44–45
Gnathamitermes tubifor-mans, 240
Gnathostomatidae *(Gnath-ostoma),* 141
Gnorimoschema, 398, 399, 402
Goera, 259
Goereilla baumanni, 261
Goeridae, 257, 259
Goerita, 257
Gomphidae, 84
Gonaspis potentillae, 395
Goniodorididae, 10
Gordioidea, 9, 109, 524
Gracillariidae, 219–20, 230, 332–34, 343, 344, 345, 346–49, 399
  leaf folders, 366
  leaf rollers, 368–69
  subcuticular mines, 406
Grammotaulius, 7, 264
Granulosis viruses, 126
Grape leaf skeletonizer, 220
Grapholita, 163, 317, 325
Graphopsocus cruciatus, 24, 182
Grapsidae, 454
Grasshoppers, 10, 12–13
  eggs of, 66
  exuviae, 88–89
  pygmy, 66
  resting traces, 446
  secretions, 154
  short-horned, 12, 65, 157–58
  sign made by, 310
  sprinkled broad-winged, 12
  trails and tracks, 519, 522, 524
Gribbles, 436–37
Gryllacrididae, 65, 318, 375
Gryllidae, 65, 106, 147, 302, 304, 324, 407–9, 475, 505
Gryllinae, 505
Gryllotalpidae, 2, 66, 488
Gumaga, 258
Gymnetron tetrum, 318
Gymnosporangium juni-periviginianae, 396

Gyponana, 411
Gyrinidae *(Gyrinus),* 64, 245

Hadrurus, 452, 507
Hagenella canadensis, 263
Hahncappsia, 372
Hahniidae, 33, 44, 199
Hahniinae, 33
Halictidae *(Halictus),* 451, 473, 474
Halictophagidae, 119
Haliplidae, 5, 64
Haliplus, 5
Halticotoma, 297
Hamamelistes spinosus, 298, 395
Hamataliwa, 43
Hapithinae, 409
Hapithus agitator, 106
Haploa contigua, 156
Harmonia axyridis, 141
Harpalus caliginosus, 477
Harrimaniidae, 449
Harrisina Americana and *metallica,* 220, 313
Hartigia, 418
Harvestmen, 4, 75
Hebestatis theveneti, 458
Hebridae, 55
Helcystogramma hystricella, 368
Heleomyzids, 148, 293
Helicopsychidae *(Heli-copsyche),* 259
Helicoverpa zea, 321
Heliodinidae, 254, 359
Heliozela aesella, 387
Heliozelidae, 253–54, 344, 345–46, 387
Hellinsia, 419
Helochares, 2, 19
Helophilus, 56
Helophora insignis, 198
Hemadas nubilipennis, 395
Hemerobiidae, 50, 222
Hemichordata, 449, 479
Hemileuca, 69–70, 133
Hemipterans, 316
Hemisphaerota cyanea, 165, 167
Heptagenia, 78
Heptageniidae, 78
Heringia calcarata, 56
Herminiinae, 309
Herpetogramma, 368–69, 371
Herpyllus, 30, 44

Hersiliidae, 191
Hesperiidae, 97, 367, 371, 413
Hesperiinae, 367, 413
Heterarthrinae, 312
Heterarthrus nematoratus, 355
Heteroceridae, 490
Heteroconis picticornis, 220
Heteroplectron, 261, 262
Heteropoda venatoria, 26, 37
Heteroptera, 50–55
Heterotermes aureus, 241
Hexomyza, 400
Hexura, 195
Hexurella, 195
Hilara, 213
Hippidae, 445, 514
Hippoboscidae, 1, 143, 162
Hippopsis, 412
Hirmoneura, 117
Hirmoneurinae, 117
Hirudinea, 19, 139
Hirudinidae, 139
Histeridae, 146, 492
Hogna, 457, 460, 461
Holes
  anchor, 440–41
  feeding, 439–40
  rock borings, 441–42
  unadorned, 449–55
Holobus oviformis, 63
Holocnemus pluchei, 202
Homaledra heptathalama and *sabalella,* 168
Homalodisca, 17
Homophylax, 264
Honeydew, 150
Hoplitis product, 286
Hoplocampa, 64, 327
Hornets, 276–79, 405, 423
Horntails, 128, 244, 433
Hyalophora, 224
Hyalophora cecropia, 69, 155, 223
Hyaloscotes, 249
Hydatophylax, 264
Hydrachnidae, *(Hydra-chna),* 5, 9, 118
Hydraena, 25
Hydraenidae, 25, 246
Hydrellia, 360
Hydrobiosidae, 260
Hydrochara, 19
Hydroides, 270

Hydrometridae, 54
Hydrophilidae, 2, 19, 148
Hydrophilus, 19
Hydropsychidae, 213–14, 260
Hydroptila, 256
Hydroptilidae, 255–56
Hydroscaphidae, 64
Hylaeus, 288
Hylurgopinus rufipes, 427
Hymenoptera, 64–65, 129–31, 162, 235–36, 483, 484
Hypera, 222–23
Hyperaspis, 175
Hyperdiplosis tritici, 321
Hyphantria cunea, 22, 183–84
Hyphantrophaga virilis, 59
Hypochilidae *(Hypochilus)*, 41, 44, 202
Hypoderma, 144
Hyposoter, 233
Hyptiotes, 33, 204–5

Icerya purchasi, 23, 176
Ichneumonidae, 46
Idia *(Idia aemula)*, 309
Incurvariidae, 254, 304–5
Instars, 82
Ips, 425, 427
Iridoviruses, 127
Iris oratoria, 15
Isa textual, 100
Isodontia, 106, 287
Isopoda, 518
Isopods, 2, 437, 441, 492–93
Isoptera, 147
Istocheta aldrichi, 116
Iteomyia, 388
Iuridae, 452, 507
Ixodidae, 75, 136–37, 142

Janetiella Siskiyou, 322
Janus, 418
Japanagromyza viridula, 302, 341–42
Japygidae, 2
Julioformia, 241, 242

Kalotermitidae, 435
Kaltenbachiella ulmifusa, 384
Kaltenbachiola, 321
Kateredidae, 319
Katydids, 3, 65
   angle-wing, 66

bush, 157
   eggs of, 66
   fork-tailed bush, 324
   narrow-beaked, 3
   Scudder's bush, 3
   sign made by, 310
Keiferia lycopersicella, 325, 353–54
Kellymyia kellyi, 116–17
Kermesidae, 176
Keroplatidae, 181
Kinbergonuphis jenneri, 269
Kleptoparasitic cobweb spiders, 26, 40–41, 213
Knemidokoptidae *(Knemidokoptes mutans)*, 142
Kukulcania hibernalis, 28, 193

Labidomera clivicollis, 61
Labidus coecus, 468
Lace bugs, 53, 150
   Andromeda, 295–96
   azalea, 296
   basswood, 295
   chrysanthemum, 296
   hackberry, 295
   hawthorn, 295
   oak, 295
   rhododendron, 296
   sign made by, 295–96
   sycamore, 295
Lacewings, 46
   beaded, 49
   brown, 50, 89, 222
   green, 47–49, 65, 89, 222, 247
   as predators, 107
Lacosoma chiridota, 254, 309
Lacuna, 9
Ladybugs, 47
   eggs of, 61
   mealybug destroyers, 24, 175
   pupae, 92–93
   sign made by, 306
   vedalias, 23
Laemobothriidae, 143
Laemophloeidae, 237
Laetilia coccidivora, 171
Lamiinae, 412
Lamprosomatinae, 165, 167
Lampyridae, 64, 106

Lancet liver fluke, 110
Languriidae *(Languria)*, 412
Lanice conchilega, 269
Larinia directa, 206
Larinioides, 28, 213
Lasiocampidae, 11, 156, 183, 228–29
Lasioderma serricorne, 237, 330
Lasioglossum, 451
Lasioptera, 386, 398, 402–3
Lasius, 470–71
Latridiidae, 64
Latrodectus, 40, 43, 134, 190
Lauxaniids, 148
Leaf beetles, 9, 47, 164–65, 222
   case-bearing, 61, 165, 167
   cereal, 306
   cocoons, 222
   cottonwood, 62, 93
   dogbane, 62, 311
   droppings, 160
   eggs of, 61–62
   elm, 62, 306
   larval coverings, 166–67
   lily, 167
   mines, 340, 356
   potato, 62–63, 167
   sign made by, 305, 306, 313–14, 328
   swamp milkweed, 61
   virburnum, 306
   waterlily, 62, 93, 62, 93, 306
   willow, 93, 306
Leaf crumplers, 169–70, 369
Leafcutters
   ant, 304
   bee, 287–88, 303
   maple, 254, 304–5
   morning glory, 372
Leaf folders
   feeding inside, 365–67
   gracillariid moths, 366
   grasslike leaves with two folds, 373
   simple, 372–73
   skippers, 367
   tortricid moths, 366–67
Leaf-footed bugs, 47, 52–53, 151, 153, 315
Leaf galls. *See* Galls, leaf

Leafhoppers, 3, 13, 17–18, 88, 378–79
  oviposition scars, 411
  potato, 298
  sign made by, 297–98, 301, 324
Leafminers
  Agromyzidae, 4, 302–3, 337–39, 341–42, 357, 358, 360, 406
  American serpentine, 339
  Bedelliidae, 352
  beetles, 355–56
  boxwood, 386
  buprestids, 63, 164–65, 254
  Bucculatricidae, 219, 229, 313, 336–37, 343
  Buprestidae, 63, 164–65, 253, 356, 360
  cabbage, 339, 344
  Coleophoridae, 167–68, 251–53, 321, 323, 352–53
  corn blotch, 360
  Cosmopterigidae, 352, 359
  Crambidae, 71–72, 184, 187, 216, 262, 343, 354
  Eriocraniidae, 4, 354
  excrement-covered eggs, 164–65
  Gelechiidae, 243–44, 321, 325, 330, 337, 344, 353–54
  Gracillariidae, 219–20, 230, 332–34, 343, 344, 345, 346–49
  goldenrod, 165
  Heliodinidae, 254, 359
  Heliozelidae, 253–54, 344, 345–46
  holly-mining, 303
  locust, 165, 313–14
  Lyonetiidae, 344, 351–52
  morning glory, 352
  moths, 4, 324, 359–60
  Nepticulidae, 220, 321, 334–36, 340–41, 353
  oak shothole, 302, 341–42
  parasitoids, 362
  pea, 339
  sawflies, 354–55

sign made by, 302–3, 324
  spinach, 58
  Tephritidae, 4, 323, 326, 357
  Tischeriidae, 341, 342, 343, 349–51
  vegetable, 339
  weevils, 4, 356–57
  Xyloryctidae, 360
Leaf mines
  blotch, 331, 344–58
  digitate, 343–44
  in grass and sedge leaves, 359–60
  linear, 332–40
  linear-blotch, 340–42
  needle, 360–62
  transition to stem borers, 359
  trumpet, 342–43
  underside tentiform, 346–48
Leaf rollers
  Carolina cricket, 65, 318, 364, 375
  crambid moths, 368
  feeding inside, 367–69
  fruit tree, 12
  gelechiid moths, 368
  gracillariid moths, 368–69
  rose, 12
  tortricid moths, 367–68
  weevils, 307, 363–64
Leaf shelters
  without silk, 363–64
  with silk, 364–76
Leaftier, gold-striped, 219, 313
Leaf tiers, feeding inside, 369–71
Leafwings, 158
  goatweed, 95
Leaves
  edge feeders, 309–12
  holes in, 305–9
  round cuts in, 303–5
  surface skeletonizers, 312–14
Lebia, 93
Lecanodiaspididae (*Lecanodiaspis*), 176
Leeches, 19, 139, 143
Leiodidae, 143, 294
Lema, 306
Lema daturaphila, 62, 167
Lenarchus, 264

Lepania cascada, 257
Lepidoglyphus destructor, 141
Lepidoptera, 68–74
Lepidosaphes, 176–77
Lepidostomatidae (*Lepidostoma*), 257, 258, 262, 264
Lepismatidae, 77
Leptinotarsa decemlineata, 62
Leptoceridae, 256, 257–59, 264
Leptocerus americanus, 256
Leptocheirus pilosus, 271
Leptocheliids, 272
Leptochilus, 289–90
Leptoglossus occidentalis, 53
Leptomorphus, 92, 180, 181
Leptonetid spiders, 44
Leptosynapta tenuis, 449, 479
Lestica, 289
Lestidae, 5
Lethocerus, 53
Leucanthiza, 349
Leucauge venusta, 35, 206
Leucochrysa floridana, 48
Leucoma salicis, 16, 99
Leucoptera pachystimella, 352
Leucospids (*Leucospis*), 290
Leucotrichia, 256
Libellulidae, 78–79, 84
Libytheana carinenta, 95
Libytheinae, 95
Lice, 74
  bark, 24–25, 182
  bee, 118, 275
  fish, 143
  head and pubic, 138
  wood, 2, 327, 518
Lilioceris lilii, 167
Limacidae, 74
Limacid slugs, 74
Limacodidae, 100, 133, 230
Limenitis, 73–74, 157, 158, 310, 373–74
Limnebius, 25
Limnephilidae, 7, 261, 262, 264
Limnephilus, 260, 264

Limnoriidae *(Limnoria),* 436–37
Limpets, 7–8, 292, 441
Limulidae, 486, 514
Limulus polyphemus, 76, 486, 514
Lindenius, 484
Lineidae, 269
Linyphiidae, 30, 36, 180, 197, 200–201
Linyphiinae, 36
Liogma, 92, 312
Liometopum, 280
Liposthenes glechomae, 395
Liriomyza, 337, 339, 342, 358, 407
Listroderes, 327
Listronotus oregonensis, 328
Listropygia, 483
Lithophaga, 441
Lithophane antennata, 324
Lithosiinae, 227
Littorinidae *(Littorina),* 9, 21, 494
Lixus, 238, 412
Loewia foeda, 116
Loliginidae, 10
Loligo pealeii, 10
Lomamyia, 49
Lonchaeidae, 293
Longfin inshore squids, 10
Lophocampa argentata, 185
Loxosceles reclusa, 31, 134, 191
Lucanidae, 63
Lumbricidae *(Lumbricus terrestris),* 18, 467, 478, 496–97
Lutica, 457
Lutzomyia, 132
Lycaenidae, 74, 96, 174, 316
Lycidae, 63
Lycosidae, 26, 36, 134, 195, 448, 450, 456–57
Lygaeidae, 4, 53, 317–18
Lygidea mendax, 296
Lymantria dispar, 21, 98–99
Lymantriidae, 16, 21, 69, 71, 98–99, 155, 185, 227–28, 375
Lymnaeidae, 7
Lyonetia alniella, 352
Lyonetia speculella, 352
Lyonetiidae, 344, 351–52

Lype diversa, 265
Lysiphlebus, 113
Lyssomanes, 28

Machimia tentoriferella, 219
Macoma, 449
Macrocentrinae *(Macrocentrus),* 234
Macrodiplosis, 380, 388
Macronoctua onusta, 329
Macrostemum, 260
Macrotera opuntiae, 441–42
Maggots
  apple, 326
  blueberry, 326
  cabbage, 328–29
  pepper, 326
  raspberry cane, 416
  red-tailed, 495
  root, 58
  seed, 58
  seedcorn, 327–28
  sugarbeet root, 329
Magicicada, 409, 451–52
Malacosoma, 11, 156, 183, 228–29
Maldanidae, 10, 270
Male trumpet skeletonizer, 170–71
Mallophora leschenaulti, 17
Manayunkia speciosa, 267
Manduca, 155
Mangora gibberosa, 205–6, 212–13
Manophylax annulatus, 261
Mantises, 13
  Carolina, 15
  chalcid, 14
  Chinese, 15
  European, 15
  Mediterranean, 15
  narrow-winged, 15
  praying, 106, 146
  shrimp, 454
  torymid, 14
Mantispidae, 46, 49, 223
Mantis religiosa, 15, 146
Mantodea, 14
Mantura, 340
Margarodidae, 23, 176
Marilia, 258
Marine brozoans, 10
Marine wood, galleries in, 436–38
Marmara, 230, 324, 333–34, 406

Marpesia petreus, 158
Marpissa, 28
Martesia, 438
Masked hunter nymphs, 247
Massospora cicadina, 125
Mastigoproctus giganteus, 506
Mastophora, 39, 180
Matsucoccus acalyptus, 176
Mayatrichia, 256
Mayetiola destructor, 59, 100
Mayetiola thujae, 322
Mayflies, 147
  eggs of, 46–47, 78
  naiad exuviae, 83–84
  subimagos, 89
Maymena ambita, 207
Mealybug destroyers, 24
Mealybugs, 2, 22–24, 56
  apple, 24
  cocoons, 238
  grape, 24
  white fluff, 174
Mecas, 412
Mecicobothriidae, 195
Meconium, 151, 162
Mecoptera, 77
Mecynogea lemniscata, 42, 201–2
Megachilidae *(Megachile),* 284, 286, 287–88, 303
Megahexura fulva, 195
Megalepthyphantes nebulosus, 198
Megalopodidae, 356
Megaloptera, 47, 85
Megalopygidae *(Megalopyge),* 133, 230
Megaphorus minutus, 17
Megarhyssa, 128, 433
Megaselia aletiae, 116
Megaselia halterata, 293
Megastigmus, 322, 323, 327
Megathymini, 413
Melampus bidentatus, 9–10
Melanagromyza marellii, 399
Melandryidae, 294
Melanochlamys diomedea, 10
Melanophora roralis, 117
Melaphis rhois, 385
Melitara, 71
Melitidae, 271–72

Melitoma taurea, 465
Melittia, 163–64, 243, 329, 413
Mellininae, 483
Meloidae, 12, 62, 133, 160, 290, 312, 508
Melolonthinae, 160, 327, 452
Melongenidae, 20
Melophagus ovinus, 143
Membracidae, 2, 17, 301, 410
Membracini, 17
Menoponidae, 143
Merodon equestris, 329
Merynchites bicolor, 315
Meshweb weavers, 31, 191–92
Mesochaetopterus taylori, 268–69
Mesoveliidae, 5
Messor, 471
Metallus, 355
Metaltella simony, 192
Meta ovalis, 35, 206
Meteorinae *(Meteorus),* 111, 235
Metepeira, 28, 42, 211–12, 272
Metophthalmus, 64
Metzneria lappella, 321
Miagrammopes, 180
Micaria, 27, 44–45
Micrasema, 256, 257, 263
Micrathena, 209–10, 375
Microbembex, 484
Microcentrum, 66
Microcoryphia, 83
Microdipoena guttata, 208
Microgastrinae, 111, 233
Microhexura, 26, 196
Microlinyphia, 198
Microplitis, 234–35
Microrhopala, 165, 356
Micrura, 269
Micrurapteryx salicifoliella, 349
Midges, 117
    biting, 8, 132, 496
    bromegrass seed, 321
    chironomid, 7, 121, 148, 168, 266–67
    chokeberry, 326
    clover leaf, 381
    clover seed, 59, 317
    dense growth of buds, 393 –95
    dixid, 8

gall, 59, 100–101, 237, 293, 321–22, 379, 398
    galls and, 380–81, 386–88
    mountain, 87
    net-winged, 60, 86–87
    ocellate gall, 386
    pear, 326
    phantom, 8
    pitch and resin, 237, 415, 426
    pupae, 85, 86–87
    sign made by, 317, 321–22, 326
    snowberry gall, 380
    sorghum, 321
    swellings, 392, 398, 399–400, 402–3
    swollen buds, 392–93
    symbiocladius, 121
    watershield, 168
    wheat, 321
Milacid slugs, 74
Milkweed bugs, large, 53
Millipedes, 2, 139–40, 160
    desert, 242
    nests and molting chambers, 241–42
    pill, 166, 241
    sign made by, 327
    sperm webs, 181
    trails and tracks, 517–18
Miltogrammini, 290
Mimallonidae, 254, 309
Mimetidae, 26, 33, 108
Mimetus, 33
Mimumesa, 289
Minagenia osoria, 121
Mindarus abietinus, 314
Mines
    See also Leaf mines
    cambium, 428
    stem, 406–7
    subcuticular, 406–7
Miridae, 3, 150, 296
Miscophus, 483
Mishocyttarus, 276
Misumena, Misumenoides, Misumenops, 108
Mites, 1, 50
    alder beadgall, 381
    bulb scale, 330
    dense growth of buds, 393
    eggs of, 75–76
    false spider, 75–76, 300, 324
    finger galls, 383–84

flour, 330
    galls and, 377, 380, 381, 387
    maple bladdergall, 381
    onion, 330
    parasitism, 118, 142–43
    pear leaf blister, 387
    rock boring, 442
    sign made by, 136, 141, 142–43, 300, 324, 330
    snowberry, 380
    spider, 63, 75–76, 88, 181–82, 300
    swollen buds, 392–93
    water, 5, 9
Miturgidae, 27, 218
Mochlonyx cinctipes, 8
Molannidae *(Molanna),* 259, 261
Molelike excavations and surface trails
    antlions, 492
    ants, 497–98
    biting midges, 496
    darkling beetles, 492
    defined, 487
    dune and clown beetles, 492
    earthworms, 496–97
    ground beetles, 490–91
    marine isopods and amphipods, 492–93
    mole crickets, 488
    moon snails, 493–94
    mussels, freshwater, 495
    ox beetles, 497
    periwinkles, 494
    pygmy mole crickets, 488–89
    roundworms, 496
    rove beetles, 489–90
    stiletto flies, 491
    underwater, 495–96
    variegated mud-loving beetles, 490
Monarthropalpus flavus, 386
Monarthrum mali, 434
Moneilema, 164, 315
Monobia quadridens, 286
Monocesta coryli, 62
Monochamus, 424–25
Monophadnoides rubi, 308
Mooreonuphis nebulosa, 269
Mordellidae, 412

Moselyana comosa, 257
Mosquitoes, 60, 135–36
    pupae, 85
Moths, 46, 47
    See also Butterflies;
        Caterpillars;
        Leafminers; Tortricid
        moths; Tussock
        moths
    acorn, 323
    aquatic, 71–72, 216
    armyworms, 22
    bee, 228, 274–75
    borers, 329, 413, 415,
        419
    browntail, 21–22
    buck, 69–70, 133
    bumelia webworm,
        220–21
    burdock seed, 321
    cactus, 71
    calleta silkmoths, 225
    carpenter, 244, 431–32
    catalpa sphinx, 69
    cattail borer, 22
    cecropia, 69, 155, 223
    clearwing, 329, 419,
        425, 431–32
    clothes, 147, 186
    cocoons, 220–21,
        243–44
    codling, 163, 243, 323,
        325
    corn earworm, 321
    crowned slug, 100
    cynthia, 224
    cypress bark, 163
    dagger, 156, 243, 424
    diamondback, 221
    eggs of, 68–74
    ermine, 184, 185, 229
    eye-spotted bud, 171
    fairy, 321
    fall cankerworms,
        70–71
    fall webworms, 22
    filbertworm, 323
    flannel, 230
    flannel moth caterpil-
        lars, 133, 230
    floatingheart waterlily,
        343
    flour, 186
    fruitworm, 325
    galls and, 379–80, 387,
        388, 398–99
    geometrid, 70–71, 221,
        243
    giant silk-, 47, 68–70,
        133, 155, 223–26
    gooseberry barkminer,
        406
    gracillariids, 366
    grain, 186, 321
    grape berry, 372
    grape plume, 98, 365
    gypsy, 21, 98–99
    hickory shuckworm,
        323
    hornworms, tomato or
        tobacco, 99, 155
    Indianmeal, 186
    io, 69, 133, 225
    jumping bean, 320
    leaf crumpler, 169–70,
        369
    leaf folders, 365–67
    leaf-mining, 4, 324
    leafrollers, 12, 367–69
    lima bean pod borer,
        320
    litter, 309
    luna, 225
    maple leafcutter, 254,
        304–5
    meal, 186
    navel orangeworm, 323
    oriental fruit, 163, 325
    owlet, 22, 72, 99, 156,
        157, 171, 243
    pea, 320
    pecan nut casebearer,
        323
    petiole swellings, 391
    pine tube, 370
    pitch twig, 415, 426
    planthopper parasite,
        228
    plume, 98, 184
    polyphemus, 70, 225
    promethea, 69, 224,
        310, 375
    pupae, 97–100
    pyralid, 274–75
    pyraloid, 187
    rattlebox, 320
    ribbed cocoon-maker,
        219, 229, 313
    royal, 99
    satin, 16, 99
    sequoia pitch, 425–26
    sign made by, 313, 315,
        320–21, 322, 323,
        324–25, 329–30
    sign on wood, 424,
        425–26, 431–32
    silk retreats of larvae,
        218–19
    silver-spotted tiger, 185
    slug caterpillars, 100,
        133, 230
    sphinx, 69, 99
    stem and twig swellings,
        401–2
    sunflower bud, 163
    tapestry, 186
    tent caterpillar, 10, 11,
        228–29
    tiger, 22, 68–69, 156,
        185, 227, 519
    uglynest caterpillars, 12,
        184
    webs on dried plant
        and animal products,
        186
    yucca, 320
Mud daubers
    black and yellow,
        280–81, 445
    blue, 285
    organ pipe, 281–82
    scrapes and digs, 445
Muricidae, 21
Murgantia histrionica, 51
Muricidae, 439, 495
Musca domestica, 59
Muscidae, 59, 132, 148
Mussels
    freshwater, 143–44, 495
    mytilid, 441
    zebra, 2
Mutillidae, 290
Mycetophagidae, 294
Mycetophilidae, 92, 153,
    166, 180, 237, 244,
    293
Mycotrupes, 476
Mygalomorph spiders, 26,
    195–96
    burrowing, 26–28
Mymaridae, 79–80
Myriapods, 77
Myrmecocystus, 471
Myrmecolacidae, 119
Myrmekiaphila, 459
Myrmeleontidae *(Myrme-
    leon),* 50, 242, 446–47,
    492
Myrmicinae, 466
Myrsidea rustica, 143
Mysmenidae, 207–8
Mystacides, 260–61
Myxicola infundibulum,
    269

Nabidae, 106
Nacerdes melanura, 436
Naiads
  exuviae, 83–84
  use of term, 82
Naididae, 267
Namamyia plutonis, 258
Narceus, 166, 242
Narnia, 315
Nassariidae, 21
Nassarius, 20–21
Nassas, bruised, 21
Naticidae, 10, 439, 493
Naucoridae, 55, 132
Nealyda kinzelella, 354
Neaspilota, 321
Necrobia, 237
Nectar robbing insects,
  316–17
Nectopsyche, 257, 261
Nemapogon granella, 186
Nematocera, 100
Nematoda, 139, 140, 496
Nematodes, sign made by,
  300
Nematomorpha, 9, 109
Nematus ribesii, 64, 308
Nemertea, 268
Nemesiidae, 457
Nemestrinidae, 117
Nemotaulius hostilis, 262,
  264
Neoamphitrite robusta, 269
Neoantistea, 199
Neobellieria cooleyi, 116
Neochlamisus, 167, 254
Neocnemidocoptes laevis,
  142
Neogalerucella, 62
Neolasioptera, 101, 389,
  392, 399, 402
Neophasia menapia, 73
Neophylax, 259
Neoptilia malvacearum,
  308
Neosabellaria, 271
Neoscona, 211
Neospintharus, 41
Neotama Mexicana, 191
Neotelphusa querciella, 368
Neotephritis, 321
Neothremma, 257
Neotrichia, 256
Neoxabea bipundtata, 304,
  409
Nepa apiculata, 5
Nephelodes, 327
Nephila clavipes, 206–7

Nephrocerus, 116
Nepidae, 5, 107
Nepticulidae, 220, 321,
  334–36, 340–41, 353,
  401, 406, 419
Nereididae (Nereis), 271
Neriene clathrata, 198
Neriene radiata, 36, 201
Nerophilus californicus,
  258
Nesticidae, 26, 37, 190–92
Nesticus, 26
Neureclipsis, 215
Neurobathra strigifinitella,
  219–20, 334
Neuropterans, 25, 50,
  222–23
Neuropterida, 47–50, 89
Neurotoma, 64, 185
Nicrophorus, 147, 477, 503
Niduses, 363
Nitidulidae, 146, 294, 319,
  326
Noctuidae, 22, 72, 99, 156,
  157, 171, 243, 315,
  321, 329, 365, 373,
  413, 419, 424
Norvellina chenopodii, 298
Noteridae, 238, 328
Notodontidae, 155, 243,
  371
Notonecta, 54–55
Notonectidae, 5, 54–55,
  107
Nucella, 21
Nuclear polyhedrosis
  viruses (NPVs), 126
Nudibranchs, 440
Nuts, sign on, 322–23
Nyctiophylax, 215
Nymphalidae, 72–74,
  156–57, 310, 373–74
Nymphalinae, 72
Nymphalis antiopa, 96, 156
Nymphulinae, 216, 262

Oberea, 314, 416
Obrussa ochrefasciella, 419
Ochrotrichia, 256
Ochteridae, 55
Ochthebius, 25, 246
Octagonal casemaker,
  167–68
Octopuses, 21, 440
Ocypode, 445, 480, 481
Ocypodidae, 445, 455, 463,
  513
Odonata, 78–79

Odonteus, 476
Odontoceridae, 257, 258
Odontopus calceatus, 307,
  357
Odontota dorsalis, 165,
  314, 356
Odynerus dilectus, 465–66
Oebalus pugnax, 51
Oecanthinae, 304, 324,
  407–9
Oecanthus, 302, 408–9
Oecetis, 257–58, 261, 264
Oecobiidae (Oecobius),
  199
Oedemeridae, 436
Oedophrys hilleri, 311
Oestridae, 1, 58, 102–3
Oestrinae, 1
Oestrus ovis, 144
Ogcodes adaptatus, 59
Oiketicus, 248–49
Okenia sapelona, 10
Oleacinidae, 440
Olethreutes, 366, 369
Oligonychus bicolor, 182
Oligophlebodes, 257
Oligostomis, 263
Oligotricha lapponica, 263
Oligotrophus, 394
Olios, 37
Oncideres, 420
Oncometopia, 17
Oncopeltus fasciatus, 53
Oniscidea, 518
Oniscomorpha, 166
Onopidae, 27
Onops, 27
Onthophagus, 147–48
Onuphidae, 268, 269
Onuphis eremite, 269
Oomorphus floridanus,
  165
Ophiomyia, 337, 406–7
Ophraella, 222
Opiliones, 4, 75
Orangetips, falcate, 73
Orbweavers, 25, 28, 34, 40
  feather-legged, 205
  golden silk, 206–7
  hackled, 41–42
  lattice, 218
  leaf shelters, 373, 375
  lined, 205–6
  long-jawed, 35, 43, 206
  as predator, 105–6
  shamrock, 34
  six-spotted, 212

spinybacked, 34–35,
   209–10
starbellied, 35, 213
trashline, 42, 209
Orconectes immunis, 292
Orgyia, 16, 22, 71, 185,
   228, 375
Orphinus fulvipes, 14
Orthalcidae, 74
Orthoporus ornatus, 242
Orthoptera, 47, 65–66,
   88–89, 157, 474, 483
Orthorrhapha, 100
Orthotrichia, 255–56
Oryzaephilus, 330
Oscinisoma alienum, 45
Osmia, 284, 286, 432
Osmoderma, 247
Otodectes cynotis, 142
Oulema melanopus, 306
Oviposition scars
   cicadas, 409
   leafhoppers, 411
   tree crickets, 407–9
   treehoppers, 410
Oviposition wounds, in
   vegetation, 301–3
Oweniidae *(Owenia
   fusiformis),* 268
Oxybelus, 451
Oxyethira, 256
Oxyopes, 31, 38
Oxyopidae, 43, 181
Oxyporus, 294
Oxyuridae, 141
Oyster drills, 21, 439

Pachydesmus crassicutis,
   518
Pachypsylla, 385, 387, 392
Pachyrhinus, 4, 314
Pachyschelus, 356
Paguroidea, 513
Palaeagapetus, 256
Paleacrita vernata, 243
Palm leaf housemaker and
   skeletonizer, 168
Palmodes, 483
Pamphiliidae, 64, 157, 185
Pandora bullata, 125
Panopeidae, 454
Panorpidae, 77
Panthea acronyctoides,
   156
Pantographa limata, 368
Papaipema, 329, 413, 419
Papilio, 68, 157, 372–73

Papilionidae, 68, 74, 96,
   157, 372–73
Papilioninae, 68, 96
Parabacillus coloradus, 74
Paraclemensia acerifoliella,
   254, 304–5
Paracymus, 19
Paragus, 56
Paraleucoptera, 351–52
*Parallelodiplosis subtrun-
   cata,* 386
Paralobesia viteana, 325,
   372
Parancistrocerus vagus,
   283
Parapamea buffaloensis,
   329
Parapholas californica, 441
Parapoynx seminealis, 343
Paraprociphilus tessellates,
   173
Parasites of bee and wasp
   nests, 290
Parasitidae, 118
Parasitoids, 79–80
   ecto-, 105, 117–21,
      142–44
   endo-, 105, 109–17,
      144–45
   hyper-, 105
   of eggs, 79–80
   of leafminers, 362
   of scale insects, 177
Parasitoid wasps, 14,
   45–46, 50, 64–65
Parasteatoda tepidariorum,
   39, 146, 189–90
Paratheuma insulana, 218
Parazanomys, 200
Pardosa, 37
Parectopa, 334–44, 345,
   349
Parnassius, 74
Parornix, 348, 366, 368,
   372
Parthina, 257
Passalidae, 2
Passaloecus cuspidatus,
   288
Patellogastropoda, 441
Pectinariidae *(Pectinaria),*
   270
Pectinophora gossypiella,
   321
Pediculidae *(Pediculus
   humanus capitis),*
   138

Pedomoecus sierra, 257
Pegomya, 58, 357, 416
Peltodytes, 64
Peltotrupes, 475
Pemphigus, 391
Pemphredoninae, 288,
   289, 483
Pemphredonini, 483
Penitella penita, 441
Pennisetia marginata, 329
Pentatomidae, 50, 106–7,
   153
Perilampidae, 65
Perilampus, 65
Periploca nigra, 415
Petaloproctus socialis, 270
Petricolaria pholadiformis,
   454
Petricolidae, 441, 454
Petrophila, 71–72, 216
Peucetia viridans, 43, 181
Phanacis taraxaci, 399
Phanaeus, 147–48
Phanagenia bombycina,
   284
Phanocelia canadensis,
   264
Pharidae, 449
Phasmatodea, 74, 140
Phenacoccus aceris, 24
Phengodidae, 106
Phereoeca, 251
Philanthinae, 483
Philanthus, 482, 483
Philarctus quaeris, 258
Philodromidae, 31, 373
Philodromus minutes, 373
Philoponella, 42, 205
Philopotamidae, 215–16
Philopteridae, 143
Philotarsidae, 25
Phloeosinus, 414–15, 427
Phobetron pithecium, 230
Phobocampe, 233
Pholadidae, 438, 441, 454
Pholcidae *(Pholcus phalan-
   gioides),* 26, 191
Pholetesor ornigis, 362
Phoresy, 118
Phoridae, 102, 116, 121,
   293
Phoronida *(Phoronis),* 268,
   269, 441, 479
Phronia, 166
Phruotimpus, 29
Phryganea, 7, 263
Phryganeidae, 7, 258, 261,
   262, 263

Phthorimaea operculella, 330, 353
Phylactolaemata, 9
Phyllaphis fagi, 174
Phyllochaetopterus prolific, 269
Phyllocnistis, 324, 332–34
Phyllocolpa, 379
Phyllocoptes triacis, 380
Phylloicus, 262
Phyllonorycter, 346–47, 348
Phyllotreta, 340
Phylloxera, 380, 385–86, 392
Phylloxeridae, 380, 385
Phylocentropus, 266
Phymatinae, 16, 107–8
Physidae, 7
Phytobia, 428
Phytoliriomyza, 342, 407
Phytomyza, 303, 337–39, 341, 358, 407
Piddocks, 438, 441
Pieridae, 73, 96, 308
Pierinae, 73
Pieris rapae, 73, 308
Pimoidae *(Pimoa),* 197
Pineleaf, 176
Pine needles, 176
   sign on, 4, 246, 314
Pine sawyers, 424–25
Pineus, 403
Piophilidae *(Piophila casei),* 147
Pipiza, 56
Pipunculidae, 116
Pirata, 36, 457
Pisauridae *(Pisaurina),* 26, 37, 145, 192, 218, 376
Pison koreense, 284
Pisonopsis birkmanni, 285
Pissodes, 246, 414
Pista, 269
Pitch masses, 415–16, 425–26
Pitch tubes, 425
Pits, funnel-shaped, 446–49
Pityogenes bidentatus, 427
Pityohphyantes costatus, 36, 197–98
Placobdella, 139
Plagiodera versicolora, 306
Plagiometriona clavata, 93
Planorbidae, 8
Planorbids, 8
Plant bugs, 5
   four-lined, 3, 296

scentless, 53
Planthoppers, 4, 120, 175, 228
Platycentropus, 264
Platydesmid, 2, 241
Platygastridae, 79–80
Platygastrid wasps, 13, 46, 50
Platyhelminthes, 19, 139
Platynota stultana, 371
Platypezidae, 293
Platypodinae, 434
Platypsylla castoris, 143
Plecoptera, 78, 83, 312
Plectreurids, 194
Plemeliella, 321
Pleroneura, 314, 415
Pleuroprucha insulsaria, 98
Plodia interpunctella, 186
Plutellidae *(Plutella xylostella),* 221
Pococera robustella, 169, 185
Podagrion, 14
Podapion gallicola, 400
Podisus, 50
Poecilocapsus lineatus, 3, 296
Poecilochirus, 118
Pogonomyrmex, 472, 483, 497
Polistes, 152, 276, 423
Polistinae, 64, 275–76
Pollenia rudis, 117
Polycentropodidae *(Polycentropus),* 214–15
Polychaete worms, tubes of, 267, 268–71
Polydesmida *(Polydesmus angustus),* 241, 242
Polydora websteri, 271
Polygonia interrogationis, 73, 96, 156
Polymitarcyidae, 147
Polypedilum braseniae, 168
Polyphemus moths, 70, 225
Polyphylla, 452
Polyplectropus, 215
Polystepha, 386, 388, 390
Polyxenidae *(Polyxenus lagurus),* 77, 181
Polyzoniida, 241
Pomacea, 74–75
Pompilidae, 106, 121, 284, 482, 483, 510
Pontania, 388

Porphyrosela desmodiella, 348
Porrhomma cavernicola, 198
Povolnya quercinigrella, 368
Praon, 113
Prays atomocella, 221
Predation
   with chewing mouthparts, 105–6
   with piercing mouthparts, 106–9
Prionapteryx nebulifera, 187
Prionyx, 483
Pristiphora appendiculata, 231
Pristiphora erichsonii, 3
Procecidochares, 395
Prochalia pygmaea, 250
Prociphilus, 173–74
Proconiini, 17
Prodidomidae *(Prodidomus rufus),* 194
Prodiplosis morrisi, 379
Prodoxidae *(Prodoxus),* 320, 413
Profenusa, 355
Proleucoptera smilaciella, 351
Prominents, 155, 243
Promyrmekiaphila, 459
Prostephanus truncates, 319
Protocalliphora, 145
Protolithocolletis lathyri, 348
Psenini, 483
Psenocerus supernotatus, 417
Psephenidae, 9, 87
Pseudips mexicanus, 428
Pseudococcidae, 23–24, 174
Pseudococcus maritimus, 24
Pseudodynerus quadrisectus, 286
Pseudogaurax, 45
Pseudogoera singularis, 258
Pseudomasaris, 282
Pseudopostega quadristrigella, 406
Pseudotelphusa, 368
Psilidae, 329
Psilocorsis, 370
Psilotreta, 258

Psithyrus, 274
Psocoptera, 24
Psoroptidae *(Psoroptes
 ovis),* 142
Psyche casta, 249
Psychidae, 248–51
Psychodidae, 132, 148
Psychoglypha, 261
Psychmorpha epimenis,
 365
Psychomyiidae, 265–66
Psyllidae, 67
Psyllids *(Psylla),* 47
 eggs of, 67
 lerp, 67, 177–78
 potato, 67
 redgum lerp, 67, 177–78
 spotted gum lerp, 178
 white fluff, 172–73
 woody swellings, 392
Psyrassa unicolor, 422
Pterocolus ovatus, 363–64
Pteromalidae, 14, 46, 236,
 395
Pteromicra varia, 117
Pterophoridae, 98, 184,
 365, 419
Pterostichus, 285
Pthiridae *(Pthirus pubis),*
 138
Ptilostomis, 263
Ptilothrix bombiformis, 464
Ptininae *(Ptinus),* 237, 330
Publilia concave, 301
*Pucciniastrum goepper-
 tianum,* 393
Pulicidae, 137
Pulmonata, 74
Pulverro, 483
Pulvinaria, 23
Pupae
 aquatic, 85–87
 attached to vegetation,
  90–93
 cells without silk,
  244–47
 fly, 100–103
 moth, 97–100
 use of term, 82
Purpuricenus axillaris, 421
Pyemotes tritici and *herfsi,*
 136
Pyralidae, 71, 169–70, 184,
 185, 186, 228, 320,
 323, 325, 369
Pyralis farinalis, 186
Pyrgotid flies, 116
Pyrochroidae, 63

Pyrophorous, 64
Pyrrhalta viburni, 306

*Quadraspidiotus pernicio-
 sus,* 177

Rabdophaga, 393–94, 397,
 399–400
Ramphocorixa acuminate,
 121
Ranatra, 5
Ranellidae, 20, 440
Raphidioptera, 50
Recurvaria ceanothiella, 353
Reduviidae *(Reduvius),* 11,
 16, 51, 106, 107–8,
 132, 247, 520
Reo eutypus, 34
Resseliella, 321, 386, 388
Reticulitermes hesperus,
 241
Retinia, 415, 426
Rhabdopterus picipes, 306
Rhagionids, 148
Rhagium inquisitor, 246,
 430
Rhagoletis, 323, 326
Rhamnus, 367–68
Rhamphini, 308, 356–57
Rhaphidophoridae, 505–6
Rheumaptera, 371
Rhinophoridae, 117
Rhinotermitidae, 240–41,
 435
Rhipiceridae, 121
Rhipiphoridae, 63, 290
Rhizoglyphus, 330
Rhomphaea fictilium, 41
Rhopalidae, 53
Rhopalomyia, 397–98, 402
Rhopalosomatid wasps,
 121
Rhopobota, 163
Rhyacophilidae, 260
Rhyssomatuss, 312, 411
Rhyzopertha dominica, 319
Ricinidae, 143
Rickettsia, 125
Rictaxis punctocaelatus, 9
Riodinidae, 74, 96–97, 371
Rock borings, 441–42
Rodolia cardinalis, 23
Roederiodes, 86
Roots and other
 underground parts,
 sign on, 328–30
Rossiana montana, 257
Rossianidae, 257, 261

Rostanga pulchra, 10
Rostangidae, 10
Rothschildia, 225
Rupellaria typical, 441

Sabellidae, 267, 269, 441
Saccoglossus kowalevskii,
 449
Sacculina (Sacculinidae),
 121
Sack-bearers, 254, 309
Sackenomyia, 386, 388
Saldidae, 55
Salticidae, 28, 218, 373
Samia Cynthia, 224
Sandalus, 121
Sandhoppers, 514–15, 522
Saperda, 400, 425, 431
Sarcophagidae, 1, 116,
 145, 148, 290
Sarcoptidae, 138, 142
Saturniidae, 69, 99, 133,
 155, 223–26, 310
Sawflies, 3, 4, 47
 apple fruit, 327
 borers, 413, 415, 418
 cherry fruit, 64, 64, 185,
  327
 cocoons, 231–32, 244
 dock, 327
 droppings, 150, 157
 eggs of, 64
 galls and, 379, 388, 392
 gooseberry, 64
 hollyhock, 308
 honeysuckle, 231
 larch, 3
 leaf-mining, 354–55
 pear fruit, 327
 plum web-spinning, 64,
  185
 raspberry, 308
 raspberry horntail, 418
 rose shoot, 418
 rusty willow, 185
 sign made by, 301, 308,
  312–13, 314, 326–27
 slug, 312–13
 stem swellings, 399
 strawberry, 308
 web-spinning, 64, 157,
  185
Scabies, 138
Scale, 1, 6, 22–23, 56, 61,
 66
 armored, 176–77
 beech, 174
 California red scales, 2

cocoons, 238
cottony, 23, 175–76
felt scales, 23, 174
oystershell, 176–77
pit, 176
pineleaf, 176
pine needle, 176
pinyon needle, 176
San Jose, 177
secretions/coverings,
  175–77
sign of, 314
soft, 176
*Scapheremaeus petropha-
  gus*, 442
Scaptomyza, 344, 412
Scarabaeidae, 147–48,
  160, 316, 327, 452,
  476–77, 497
Scarabaeinae, 476–77
Scardia, 294
Scatopsids, 148
Scelio, 13
Sceliphron caementarium,
  280–81, 445
Schistosomatidae *(Schisto-
  soma)*, 139
Schizobranchia insignis,
  269
Schizocerella pilicornis,
  355
Schizocosa, 36
Schizomida, 2
Schizomyia, 393
Schreckensteiniidae
  (Schreckensteinia),
  221
Sciaridae, 180, 293
Sciaroidea, 180
Sciomyzidae, 117
Scoloderus, 212
Scolopendridae *(Scolopen-
  dra heros)*, 511
Scolytinae, 322, 425, 426,
  433–34
Scolytus, 426–27
Scorpionflies
  common, 77
  hangingfly, 77
  snow, 77
Scorpions, 1
  Arizona bark, 133
  bark, 507
  burrows with mound
    of earth to side of
    entrance, 484
  giant hairy, 452, 507
  giant sand, 484, 507

holes made by, 452
pseudo, 2, 218
short-tailed whip, 2
sign made by, 133
tailless whip, 2
toothed, 452
trails and tracks, 506–7,
  510
water, 5, 107
whip, 2
Scotophaeus blackwalli, 30
Scrobipalpa, 163, 353, 371
Scudderia, 3, 157, 324
Scymnus, 175
Scyphophorus, 411–12
Scytodidae *(Scytodes)*, 26,
  108, 200
Sea cucumber, 449, 479
Sea slugs. See Slugs, sea
Sea urchins, 441
Sebastiania, 320
Seed bugs, 4
  western conifer, 52–53
Seedlings, sign on, 327–28
Seeds and seedpods, sign
  on, 317–21
Segestriidae, 28, 193–94
Selonpid spiders, 31
Sepsids, 148
Sequoiomyia taxodii, 322
Sericostomatidae, 258
Sericostriata surdickae, 256
Serpulidae, 270–71, 441
Servaisia falciformis, 116,
  117
Sesarmidae, 454
Sesiidae, 163–64, 171, 243,
  244, 329, 413, 419,
  425, 431–32
Setodes, 257
Shells, sign on, 439–42
Shield bugs, acanthoso-
  matid, 2
Shipworms, 437–38
Shivaphis celti, 174
Shore bugs, velvety, 55
Shrimp, 2, 454, 479–80,
  524
Sialidae, 49
Sialis, 49
Sicariidae, 31, 134, 191,
  218
Siederia walshella, 250
Silk
  balls of, 213
  pupal cells without,
    244–47
  tubes, 186–88

underwater, 213–16
unstructured lines,
  179–80
Silphidae, 63, 146, 147,
  477, 503
Silvanidae, 330
Silverfish, 77
Simuliidae, 60, 86, 132,
  216
Simyra insularis, 373
Sinea, 11–12, 51
Siphonaptera, 137–38,
  143, 238
Siphonella oscinina, 45
Siphonophorida, 241
Sipuncula, 441
Siricidae, 128, 433
Siricoidea, 244
Sisyridae, 25, 222
Sitona hispidulus, 63
Sitophilus granaries, 141,
  318–19
Sitotroga cerealella, 321
Skeletonizers, 312–14
Skimmers, 78–79, 84
Slugs, 47, 74
  arionid, 74
  banana, 74, 161–62
  droppings, 153, 161–62
  gray field, 74
  limacid, 74
  milacid, 74
  monkey, 230
  Pacific banana, 74
  sign made by, 292, 293,
    305–6, 318, 324, 330
Slugs, sea
  albatross aglaja, 10
  nudibranch, 10
  rainbow, 10
  red sponge doris, 10
  sea whip, 10
Smeringurus mesaensis,
  484, 507
Snails, 47
  aquatic, 292
  bruised nassas, 21
  channeled apple, 75
  chink shell, 9
  dogwinkles, 21
  droppings, 153, 161–62
  feeding holes, 439–40
  Florida apple and tree,
    74–75
  freshwater, 7–8
  moon, 10, 439–40,
    493–94
  nassa mud, 20–21

oyster drills, 21, 439
periwinkles, 21, 494
rock, 21, 439–40, 495
salt marsh, 9–10
sign made by, 292,
305–6, 439–40
striped barrel, 9
three-lined basket, 21
Soldier bugs, spined, 50
Solenopsis, 131, 145–46,
279, 471
Solifugae, 510
Sorhagenia nimbosa,
379–80
Sosippus, 195
Sparassidae, 26, 37, 373
Spercheidae, 19
Spercheus, 19
Sperm webs, 181
Sphaeridiinae, 2
Sphaeridium, 25
Sphaeritidae, 148
Sphaerocerids, 148, 293
Sphaeromatidae *(Sphaer-
oma)*, 437, 441
Sphaerotheriida, 241
Sphagnophylax meiops,
264
Sphecidae, 106, 280–81,
285, 287, 445, 451,
482–83
Sphecius, 483
Sphenophorus callosus,
308
Sphex, 106, 482, 483
Sphindidae, 294
Sphingidae, 69, 99, 155
Sphodros, 188
Spider mites, 63, 88,
181–82
false, 75–76, 300, 324
sign made by, 300, 324
Spiders, 2, 6, 58
See also Orbweavers
antmimic, 29
banded garden, 38
barn funnel weavers,
41, 195
basilica, 42, 201–2
black widow, 40, 134,
190
bolas, 39, 180
bowl and doily, 200–201
brown recluse, 31, 134,
191
brown widow, 43
burrowing mygalo-
morph, 26–28

burrows, 455–57
burrows with trapdoors,
457–60
burrows with turrets,
461–62
California specialties,
457
cave, 26, 37, 190–92
cellar, 26, 28–29, 45, 191
cobweb, 26, 34, 39–41,
108, 189–90, 213, 373
crab, 29, 31, 37–38, 41,
108, 181, 373
crevice weavers, 193
desertshrub, 28, 196–97,
272
droppings, 151–52
dwarf, 30, 180, 199
dwarf sheet, 33
egg sacs, 25–45
eggs of, 75–76
exuviae, 81, 82
filmy dome, 36, 201
fishing, 26, 37, 145
folding-door, 26,
461–62
funnel-web, 26, 44,
194–96, 507
garden, 38, 208–9
ghost, 27, 218, 373
giant crab, 37
grass, 31, 33, 195
gray cross, 28
green lynx, 42, 43, 181
ground, 27, 29, 30,
44–45
hacklemesh weavers,
36, 192
hammock, 36, 197–98
hatching, 45
hobo, 44
house, 28, 39, 40,
151–52, 189–190, 193
huntsman, 26, 37
jumping, 28, 29, 218,
373
labyrinth, 28, 42,
211–12
lampshade weavers,
41, 202
leaf shelters, 373,
375–76
leptonetid, 44
lynx, 31, 38, 42, 43, 181
meshweb weavers, 31,
191–92
mygalomorph, 26–28,
195–96

nursery web, 26, 37, 38,
192, 218, 376
ogre-faced, 199–200
orchard, 35, 206
parson, 30
philodromid, 31
pirate, 26, 33–34, 38, 46,
108
plectreurids, 194
predators and
parasitoids, 45–46,
105–6, 108
purseweb, 28, 152,
187–88
ray, 39, 204
recluse, 31, 191, 218
red widow, 40
retreats, 217–18, 272–73
sac, 27–31, 33–46, 218,
373
selonpid, 31
sheetweb, 30, 36,
197–98, 200–201
sign made by, 134, 448,
450
silver garden, 38
spitting, 26, 29, 45, 108,
200
stick, 180
sun, 510
tarantulas, 26, 105,
455–56, 507–8
theridiid, 26
Thomisid crab, 37–38
trails and tracks, 507–8,
510
trapdoor, 26
triangle, 33, 204–5
triangulate cobweb, 34
tube web, 28, 193–94
unstructured silk lines,
179–80
webs, 181, 188–213
wolf, 26, 36–37, 45, 105,
134, 195, 448, 450,
456–57, 460, 461
woodlouse hunters, 27
zorids, 31
Spilodiscus arcuatus, 492
Spilonota ocellana, 171
Spiochaetopterus, 269
Spionidae, 271
Spirobolidae, 166, 241,
242
Spirorbidae *(Spirorbis)*,
271
Spirostreptidae, 241, 242
Spittlebugs, 4, 88, 154

Spodoptera, 22
Sponges, boring, 441
Springtails, 77, 314
Spruce budworms, 186
Spruce needleminers,
    185–86
Spudastica, 233
Squash bugs, 52–53
Squids, longfin inshore,
    10
Stabilimenta, 208
Stagmomantis carolina, 15
Staphylinidae, 63, 146,
    238, 294, 478, 489,
    508
Stathmopoda, 186
Steatoda, 34, 190
Stegobium paniceum, 237,
    330
Stegophylla, 173
Stem borers, 359
Stem galls, detachable,
    395–97
Steneotarsonemus laticeps,
    330
Steniolia, 483
Stenodynerus, 283, 466
Stenolechia bathrodyas,
    362
Stenopelmatidae, 66, 509
Stenopsocidae, 24, 182
Stephanitis, 295–96
Sternorrhyncha, 1–2,
    66–68, 377
Stick insects, 74, 140, 157
Stictia, 483
Stictiella, 483
Stigmella, 220, 335–56,
    340–41, 353
Stilbosis tesquella, 370
Stilt bugs, 106
Stink bugs, 50
    conchuelas, 51
    droppings, 153
    green, 50–51
    harlequin bugs, 51
    as predators, 106–7
    rice, 51
    spined soldier bugs, 50
    tree, 51
Stomatopoda, 454
Stomorhina lunata, 12–13
Stomoxys calcitrans, 132
Stoneflies
    eggs of, 46–47, 78
    naiad exuviae, 83
Stored plant matter, sign
    on, 330

Strategus, 477, 497
Stratiomyidae, 57, 100,
    148, 495
Strepsiptera, 1, 118–19,
    162
Strongwellsea castrans, 125
Strongylocentrotidae
    (*Strongylocentrotus*),
    441
Strymon melinus, 316
Stylopidae, 119
Styloxus fuller, 417
Subimagos, 89
Sucking mouthparts,
    damge from, 295–300
Suleima helianthana, 163
Sumitrosis rosea, 62
Surface scrapes and digs,
    444–46
Surface trails. *See* Molelike
    excavations and
    surface trails
Swallowtails, 96
    black, 68, 157
    eastern tiger, 68
    leaf shelters, 372–73
    pipevine, 68
Symphytognathidae, 207
Synanthedon, 171, 244,
    329, 419, 425–26
Synaptidae, 449, 479, 495
Synchlora, 247
Syrphidae, 47, 56, 57, 59
Syrphinae, 56, 91
Syrphus rectus, 56
Systasis, 236
Systellogaster ovivora, 14
Systole, 320

Tabanidae, 2, 56, 100, 496
Tachinid flies, 1, 4, 59, 65,
    102, 115–16
Tachytes, 474
Talitridae, 453, 514–15,
    522
Tanaids, 272
Taniva albolineana, 185,
    361
Taphrocerus, 356, 360
Tarsonemidae, 330
*Taxodiomyia cupres-
    siananassa,* 403
Tegenaria agrestis, 44
Tegenaria domestica, 41,
    195
Tegeticula, 320
Tellinidae, 449
Telphusa latifasciella, 368

Temnothorax, 322
Tenebrionidae, 63, 147,
    148, 294, 328, 330,
    492, 502
Tenodera, 15
Tent caterpillars
    cocoons, 228–29
    eastern, 156, 181
    forest, 10, 11, 125, 156,
    181
    webs, 183
Tenthredinidae, 3, 64,
    174–75, 231, 308,
    312, 327, 354–55,
    379, 388, 392, 419
Tenuipalpidae, 75–76, 300,
    324
Tephritidae, 4, 323, 326,
    357, 395, 398
Terebellidae, 268, 269
Teredinidae, 437–38
Termites, 2, 49, 147
    dampwood, 435–36
    desert, 240
    drywood, 435
    encrustations and
    tubes, 240–41
    sign made by, 435–36
    subterranean, 240–41,
    435
Termitidae, 240–241
Termopsidae, 435–36
Terrestrial true bugs,
    50–53
Terrestrial true flies,
    55–59
Tetanops myopaeformis,
    329
Tetragnathidae (*Tetrag-
    natha*), 35, 43, 206
Tetraleurodes mori, 91
Tetraneura ulmi, 384
Tetranychidae, 75, 182,
    300
Tetraopes, 311, 412
Tetratomidae, 294
Tetrigidae, 66
Tetrix, 66
Tettigoniidae, 3, 65, 66,
    157, 324
Thalassinidea, 454
Thaumaglossa, 14
Thelaziidae (*Thelazia
    californiensis*), 140
Thelepus crispus, 269
Theliopsyche, 257
Thelyphonidae, 506
Theraphosidae, 26, 455–56

Therevidae, 491
Theridiidae, 26, 34, 39–41, 108, 134, 146, 189–90, 373
Theridion frondeum, 34
Theridion pictum, 190
Theridiosomatidae *(Theridiosoma),* 39, 204
Thermobia domestica, 77
Thomisidae, 31, 108, 181, 373
Thripidae, 316
Thrips, 2, 4, 132, 150, 238
flower, 316
gladiolus, 316
sign made by, 299–300, 301, 316
Thyridopterix, 248–49
Thysanoptera, 4, 132, 238, 299–300
Ticks, 75, 142
seed, 136–37
Tidarren, 190
Timemas (Timematidae: *Timema*), 166
Tinea pellionella, 251
Tineidae, 147, 186, 251, 294
Tineoidea, 187
Tineola bisselliella, 186
Tingidae, 53, 150, 295–96
Tinodes, 265
Tiphia (Tiphiidae), 236
Tipulidae, 92, 267, 293, 312, 327, 495
Tipulinae, 327
Tischeriidae *(Tischeria),* 341, 342, 343, 349–51
Titanoecidae *(Titanoeca),* 192
Toad bugs, 2
Tomoplagia oblique, 321
Torrubiella pulvinata, 122
Tortricidae, 12, 22, 91, 170–71, 184, 185–86, 243, 317, 330, 344, 361, 365, 369, 370–71, 372, 399, 401, 415, 426
Tortricid moths, 10, 12, 22, 163, 170–71
leaf folders, 366–67
leaf rollers, 367–68
leaf shelters, 364–65
leaf tiers, 371
sign made by, 315, 320, 322, 323, 324–25

Tortricinae, 365
Torymidae *(Torymus),* 320, 322, 323, 327
Toxomerus, 56
Trachymyrmex, 304, 466, 470
Trachypus mexicanus, 483
Trachys, 356
Trails and tracks
See also Molelike excavations and surface trails
alternating with central drag line, 508–12
alternating with no central drag line, 501–8
dragging trails with short strides, 520, 522
tire tread patterns, 512–20
underwater, 524
Trechalea gertschi, 37
Trechaleidae, 37
Treehoppers, 2, 13, 17, 88
buffalo, 410
oviposition scars, 410
sign made by, 301
two-spotted, 410
Tremex Columba, 433
Triaenodes, 263
Trialeurodes vaporariorum, 68
Triatoma, 520
Trichobaris, 411
Trichodes nutalli, 63
Trichogramma semblidis, 49–50
Trichogrammatidae, 50, 79–80
Trichophaga tapetzella, 186
Trichopoda, 116
Trichopsideinae, 117
Trichoptera, 85
Trichuridae *(Trichuris trichiura),* 140–41
Tridactylidae, 488–89
Trifurcula saccharella, 336
Trigonalid wasps, 4, 59, 64
Triopsidae, 524
Triops longicaudatus, 524
Triozidae, 67
Triplax, 294
Trirhabda, 306
Tritonia wellsi, 10
Tritoniidae, 10
Tritons, 20, 440

Tritoxa flexa, 329
Trogid beetles, 147
Trogossitidae, 294
Trombiculidae *(Trombicula),* 136, 143
True bugs, 46
aquatic, 47, 53–55
sign made by, 132
terrestrial, 50–53
True flies, 47
aquatic, 59–61
terrestrial, 55–59
Tryphoninae, 233
Trypoxylon, 281–82, 285
Tubulanidae *(Tubulanus),* 269
Tumblebugs, 147
Turbellaria, 440, 496
Turpilia rostrata, 3
Tussock moths, 13, 16, 21
browntail, 21–22
cocoons, 227–28
Douglas-fir, 22, 185
gypsy, 21, 98–99
leaf shelters, 375
milkweed, 22
pupae, 98–99
rusty, 71
satin, 16, 99
secretions/droppings, 154, 155
silk lines, 180
western, 22
white-marked, 16
Twig galls, detachable, 395–97
Twig girdlers, 415, 417–18, 420
Twig pruners, 420–21
Twig swellings, terminal, 397–98

Uca, 445, 455, 463, 480–81
Uenoidae, 257, 259
Ulidiidae, 329
Uloboridae, 33, 41, 42, 46, 180, 204–5
Uloborus diversus, 41
Uloborus glomosus, 41–42, 205
Ululodes, 49
Ummidia, 458
Unionoida, 143–44, 495
Uranotaenia, 60
Urodidae *(Urodus parvula),* 220–21
Uropodid nymphs, 118

Uropygi, 2
Urosalpinx, 21
Utetheisa ornatrix, 320

Vaejovidae, 484, 507
Vaness, 156–57, 185
Variegated fritillary, 95
Vasates, 381, 383
Vegetation, sign on, 294–314
Velarifictorus micado, 475
Veliidae, 54
Vermilionidae, *(Vermileo)*, 162, 447–48
Vespa crabro, 278, 405
Vespidae, 4, 64, 110, 275–76, 282–83, 317, 405, 423, 510
Vespinae, 276–79
Vespula, 110, 276, 278–79, 317, 510
Vinegaroons, 506
Virginia ctenucha, 69
Viruses, 125–27
Vitacea polistiformis, 329
Volucella, 290

Wadotes, 196
Walkingsticks, 47
    Colorado short-horned, 74
    common, 158
    northern, 74
    sign made by, 310
Walshomyia, 394
Wasps, 3, 59
    See also Galls
    amisegine cuckoo, 74
    aphid, 289–90
    braconid, 109, 111–14, 233–35
    burrowing, 444–45
    burrows with earthen mounds, 474
    burrows with mound of earth to side of entrance, 482–84
    burrows with turrets, 465–66
    chalcid, 14, 46, 50, 64–65, 120–21, 319–20, 323, 395
    cicada killers, 483
    cocoons, 244
    cuckoo, 74, 290
    droppings, 152
    dryinid, 119, 244

eggs of, 64–65
ensign, 14
eucharitid, 65
eulophid, 91, 162
fig, 327
gall, 323, 377, 390, 395
gasteruptiid, 290
grass, 106, 287
holes made by, 450–51
ichneumon, 4, 46, 109, 110, 121, 128, 232–33
katydid, 106
keyhole, 285
leucospids, 290
mason, 465–66
Mexican honey, 279
mummy, 112–13
paper, 64, 130, 152, 275–76, 423
parasites of, 290
parasitoid, 14, 45–46, 50, 64–65, 79–80
platygastrid, 13, 46, 50
pollen, 282
potter, 282–83, 445
as predator, 106, 109, 110–15, 119–21
pupae, 91, 244–45
sand, 244–45
sapygid, 290
scoliid, 121
scrapes and digs, 444–45
sign made by, 129–31, 319–20, 323
sign on wood, 423–24
social, 2, 64
solitary, 64, 482–83
spider, 106, 121, 284, 290, 510
stem swellings, 399
trails and tracks, 510
trigonalid, 4, 59, 64
twig galls, detachable, 396–97
vespid, 4, 64, 275–79
wood, 244
yellowjackets, 110, 276–79, 317, 423
Water boatmen, 55, 121
Water bugs
    creeping, 55, 132
    giant, 2, 53–54, 107, 132, 145
    velvet, 55
Water measurers, 54

Water striders, 47, 107
    broad-shouldered, 54
    eggs of, 54
Webs
    curved sheet, 200–203
    in dried plant and animal products, 186
    flat sheet, 197–200
    on fungi, 181
    funnel, 194–97
    irregular, 189–92
    irregular, on vegetation, 181–86
    orb, 203–10
    silk, balls of, 213
    silk, underwater, 213–16
    silk tubes, 186–88
    sperm, 181
    spider, 181, 188–213
    tubular retreats, 193–94
    unstructured silk lines, 179–80
Webspinners, 2, 187
Webworms
    ailanthus, 98, 185
    fall, 22, 183–84
    parsnip, 184–85
    pine, 169, 185
    pine false, 64
    sod, 187
Weevils
    agave and yucca snout, 411–12
    apple, 325–26
    bean, 319
    boll, 318
    borings in conifer twigs and leaders, 414–15, 418
    borings in herbaceous stems, 411–12
    broad-nosed, 328
    carrot, 328
    clover, 63, 222
    cocoons, 238
    coffee bean, 330
    cranberry, 315
    fungus, 294
    granary, 141, 318–19
    leaf-mining, 4, 356–57
    leaf-rolling, 307, 363–64
    milkweed, 312, 411
    mullein, 318
    nut and acorn, 322–23

pea, 62, 319
pine needle, 4, 246, 314
plum gouger and
  curculio, 325
potato stalk, 411
rice, 318–19
root-feeding, 63
sign made by, 307–8,
  314, 315, 318–19,
  322–23, 325–26, 327
stem and twig swellings,
  400
strawberry, 315
sweet potato, 411
thief, 363–64
tobacco stalk, 411
vegetable, 327
yellow poplar, 307–8,
  357
Western conifer seed bugs,
  52–53
Whelks, 20
channeled, 20
horse conchs, 20
knobbed, 20
tulip conchs, 20
waved, 20
Whiteflies, 1, 23, 47, 66
eggs of, 68
giant, 24, 173
greenhouse, 68
mulberry, 91
pupae, 90–91
spiralling, 24
white fluff, 173
woolly, 173
Whites, 96
cabbage, 73
pine, 73
Wiedemannia, 86
Witches' brooms, 393
Wockia asperipunctella,
  221
Wohlfahrtia vigil, 145
Wood
galleries entirely in
  wood, 432–36
galleries in marine
  wood, 436–38
galleries under bark,
  426–29
galleries under bark or
  in, 429–32
pitch masses, 415–16,
  425–26
shallow pits, grooves,
  and scrapes, 423–25

Wormlions, 162, 447–48
Worms
acorn, 449, 479
army, 22
bamboo, 10, 270
canker, fall, 70–71
canker, spring, 243
carpenter, 431–32
cellophane tube, 269
clam, 271
currant, 308
cut, 72, 99, 327
earth, 13, 18, 19,
  443–44, 466–67,
  478, 496–97
eunicid, 441
feather duster, 269,
  441
flat, 19, 440, 496
fringed, 271
hook, 139
hornworms, tomato/
  tobacco, 99, 155
horsehair, 9, 109, 110,
  524
horseshoe, 268, 269,
  441, 479
inch, 157, 180
limy tube, 270, 441
lug, 10, 448–49, 479
meal, 330
mermithid round-
  worms, 109–10
mud, 271
oak, 155
oyster mud, 271
parasitism, 109–10,
  121
parchment, 268–69
peanut, 441
pin, 140, 141, 325,
  353–54
plumed, 268
polychaete, 10, 267,
  268–71
potato tuber, 330, 353
ribbon, 268, 269
root, 306, 328
round, 109–10, 140,
  141, 496
shingle tube, 268
sign made by, 324, 325,
  440, 448–49
sludge, 267
soda straw, 269
spaghetti, 269
tape, 141

trumpet (ice cream
  cone), 270
tubes, 267–71
web, 22
whip, 140–41
wire, 328
wooly, 174–75

Xanthidae, 454
Xanthogaleruca luteola,
  62, 306
Xerostictia longilabris,
  483
Xiphocentronidae *(Xipho-
  centron mexico)*, 266
Xyelidae, 314, 415
Xyleborus dispar, 434
Xylocopa, 152–53, 317,
  424, 432
Xyloryctidae, 360
Xysticus, 31, 181
Xystodesmidae, 518

Yellowjackets, 110, 276–79,
  317, 423, 510
Ylodes, 264
Yphria californica, 258, 261
Yponomeutidae, 98, 184,
  221, 229, 361
Yucca plant bugs, 297

Zamopsyche commentella,
  250
Zanomys, 200
Zelleria haimbachi, 361
Zelotes, 30, 43
Zelus, 11, 12
Zeugophora, 356
Zirfaea pilsbryi, 441
Zodariidae *(Zodarion
  rubidium)*, 272–73,
  457
Zonosemata, 326
Zooids, 9
Zopheridae, 294, 328
Zophodia grossulariella,
  325
Zora, 31
Zorapterans, 2
Zorids, 31
Zorocratidae *(Zorocrates)*,
  192
Zosis geniculata, 41
Zumatrichia, 256
Zygaenidae, 220
Zygiella, 211
Zygoptera, 4

ABOUT THE AUTHORS

Charley Eiseman conducts plant and wildlife surveys for various non-profits, state agencies, and academic institutions. His work has included searching for rare plants and salamanders in his native Massachusetts; banding songbirds in New York and Oregon; mapping habitat and travel corridors of bobcats near Burlington, Vermont; and classifying natural communities throughout New England. He holds an MS from the University of Vermont's Field Naturalist Program and a BS in Wildlife and Fisheries Conservation and Management from the University of Massachusetts. He is an extreme generalist with a passion for learning about all living things and their interconnections. Charley was the lead author for this book, although much of the credit belongs to the hundreds of naturalists whose work set the stage for this book, and to all the fascinating creatures whose lives are its subject.

Noah Charney, MS, has conducted field research on amphibians, mammals, birds, and a variety of conservation issues. He is an author of several wildlife conservation journal articles and is currently pursuing a PhD in salamander ecology as a National Science Foundation Graduate Research Fellow at the University of Massachusetts. Together, he and Charley have taught many workshops on animal tracking over the past decade. From his Tennessee roots to his time in California and Massachusetts, Noah has trained as a naturalist to understand and celebrate natural diversity. Noah led the writing and research effort for tracks, trails, and all things marine, and made major contributions to the introduction and chapters 4, 16, and 17. He is responsible for about a third of the uncredited photos.

John Carlson received his MD, and a PhD in parasitology, from Tulane University in New Orleans, Louisiana. His medical specialties are pediatrics and allergy/immunology, and he has a particular interest in the clinical manifestations of arthropod bites and stings. John is working at Tulane as a physician-scientist, studying the ecology of medically important invertebrates in the urban environment. John contributed the bulk of the section on bites, stings and other sign on humans.

To see what else Charley and Noah are up to, and for supplementary material related to this book, please visit www.CharleyEiseman.com, www.NoahCharney.org, and www.NorthernNaturalists.com.